Transdisciplinary Play-Based Assessment 2ND EDITION

Other products available in the  system include:

- ***Transdisciplinary Play-Based Intervention, Second Edition (TPBI2),*** by Toni Linder, Ed.D., with invited contributors

- ***Administration Guide for TPBA2 & TPBI2,*** by Toni Linder, Ed.D., with invited contributors

- ***TPBA2 & TPBI2 Forms,*** by Toni Linder, Ed.D. a shrink-wrapped package of 5 complete tablets, each including key forms for TPBA2 and TPBI2

- ***TPBA2 & TPBI2 Forms CD-ROM,*** by Toni Linder, Ed.D. a CD-ROM of printable forms for TPBA2 and TPBI2

- ***Observing Kassandra: A Transdisciplinary Play-Based Assessment of a Child with Severe Disabilities, Revised Edition,*** produced and written by Toni Linder, Ed.D. a 50-minute DVD with workbook and forms tablet

- ***Read, Play, and Learn!®: Storybook Activities for Young Children,*** by Toni Linder, Ed.D., with invited contributors the transdisciplinary play-based curriculum that includes a *Teacher's Guide* and individual manuals of lesson plans based on popular children's storybooks, packaged in modules of 8

  Visit www.readplaylearn.com for excerpts, sample materials, and more information about *Read, Play, and Learn!®*

To order, contact Paul H. Brookes Publishing Co.:
- by phone: 800-638-3775
             410-337-9580 (outside the U.S.A.)
- by fax: 410-337-8539
- by web: www.brookespublishing.com
- by mail: P.O. Box 10624 Baltimore, MD 21285-0624, U.S.A.

Transdisciplinary Play-Based Assessment 2ND EDITION

TPBA Play-Based TPBI
TPBC ™

Toni Linder, Ed.D.
Professor
Morgridge College of Education
University of Denver
Colorado

with invited contributors

·P A U L·H·
BROOKES
PUBLISHING Cº®

Baltimore • London • Sydney

Paul H. Brookes Publishing Co.
Post Office Box 10624
Baltimore, Maryland 21285-0624

www.brookespublishing.com

 is a trademark of Paul H. Brookes Publishing Co., Inc.

Typeset by Integrated Publishing Solutions, Grand Rapids, Michigan.
Manufactured in the United States of America by Sheridan Books, Inc., Chelsea, Michigan.

For companion products to *Transdisciplinary Play-Based Assessment, Second Edition (TPBA2)*, including *Transdisciplinary Play-Based Intervention, Second Edition (TPBI2)*; *Administration Guide for TPBA2 & TPBI2*; *Observing Kassandra* (DVD, workbook, and forms tablet); *TPBA2 & TPBI2 Forms* (tablets and CD-ROM); and *Read, Play, and Learn!*® (the *Transdisciplinary Play-Based Curriculum*), see p. ii. Visit www.brookes publishing.com and www.readplaylearn.com for more information.

Library of Congress Cataloging-in-Publication Data
Linder, Toni W., 1946–
    Transdisciplinary play-based assessment / by Toni Linder ; with invited contributors. – 2nd ed.
        p.   cm.
    Includes bibliographical references and index.
    ISBN-13: 978-1-55766-871-4 (spiral bound)
    ISBN-10: 1-55766-871-X
    1. Transdisciplinary Play-Based Assessment.   I. Title.
    RJ51.T73L56   2008
    618.92–dc22   2007032714

British Library Cataloguing in Publication data are available from the British Library.

2012   2011   2010   2009   2008

10   9   8   7   6   5   4   3   2   1

Contents

5 Communication Development Domain **189**
with Renee Charlifue-Smith and Cheryl Cole Rooke

**6 Hearing Screening and Visual Modification of TPBA
for Children Who Are Deaf or Hard of Hearing** **279**
*with Jan Christian Hafer, Renee Charlifue-Smith,
and Cheryl Cole Rooke*

7 Cognitive Development Domain **313**

8 Emerging Literacy **401**
with Forrest Hancock

About the Authors

Toni Linder, Ed.D., Professor, Child, Family, and School Psychology Program, Morgridge College of Education, University of Denver, University Park, Denver, Colorado 80208

Dr. Toni Linder has been a professor in the Child, Family, and School Psychology program in the Morgridge College of Education since 1976. Dr. Linder has been a leader in the development of authentic assessment for young children and is nationally and internationally known for her work on *Transdisciplinary Play-Based Assessment* and *Transdisciplinary Play-Based Intervention*. In addition, she developed *Read, Play, and Learn!*® *Storybook Activities for Young Children: The Transdisciplinary Play-Based Curriculum* (1999), an inclusive literature- and play-based curriculum for preschool and kindergarten learning and development. Dr. Linder also is the Director of the Play and Learning Assessment for the Young (PLAY) Clinic at the University of Denver, where professional and student teams conduct transdisciplinary play-based assessments for young children and their families. Dr. Linder consults widely on assessment, intervention, early childhood education, and family involvement issues. She has conducted research on a variety of topics, including transdisciplinary influences on development, parent–child interaction, curriculum outcomes, and the use of technology for professional development in rural areas.

Tanni L. Anthony, Ph.D., Supervisor and State Consultant on Visual Impairment; Director, Colorado Services for Children with Combined Vision and Hearing Loss Project, Colorado Department of Education, 201 East Colfax Avenue, Denver, Colorado 80203

Dr. Anthony serves as a state consultant in visual impairment for the Colorado Department of Education. She also serves as the Director of the Colorado Services for Children for Children with Combined Vision and Hearing Loss Project. She is a nationally recognized trainer and author on topics specific to young children with visual impairment or deafblindness. Dr. Anthony has consulted internationally on program design of early intervention services for children with visual impairment and their families. She has worked on federal projects to design training materials for both preservice and inservice courses for personnel working with young children with sensory loss. Dr. Anthony received her Ed.S. degree from the University of Northern Colorado and her doctorate from the University of Denver in Child and Family Studies and Interdisciplinary Leadership.

Anita C. Bundy, Sc.D., OTR, FAOTA, Professor, Occupational Therapy, Faculty of Health Sciences, University of Sydney, P.O. Box 170, Sydney, New South Wales, Australia 2041

Professor Bundy's professional training is as an occupational therapist. She has taught and practiced in pediatrics for more than 30 years. Her research emphasizes children's play including the use of play to promote physical activity, mental health, and parent–child interactions. She is the author of two assessments related to play, the *Test of Playfulness*, which examines children's approach to play, and the *Test of Environmental Supportiveness*, which examines the contributions of caregivers, playmates, space, and objects to play. She also is the primary editor for *Sensory Integration: Theory and Practice* (2nd ed.), published by F.A. Davis, and is the author of several chapters in that book.

Renee Charlifue-Smith, M.A., CCC-SLP, Senior Instructor, Speech-Language Pathologist, JFK Partners, Department of Pediatrics, University of Colorado School of Medicine, 4900 East 9th Avenue, Denver, Colorado 80262

Renee Charlifue-Smith is a faculty member in the Department of Pediatrics at the University of Colorado School of Medicine. She is Director of the Speech-Language Pathology Department and is the coordinator of the ENRICH Early Intervention Team at JFK Partners. She has been a speech-language pathology consultant on a variety of federally funded demonstration, research, and training projects. Her special interests include early intervention, autism spectrum disorders, and motor speech disorders.

Jan Christian Hafer, Ed.D., Professor, Department of Education, Galludet University, 800 Florida Avenue NW, Washington, DC 20002

Jan Christian Hafer specializes in family-centered early education in the Department of Education at Gallaudet University, Washington, DC. Her scholarly interests include play, assessment of young deaf and hard-of-hearing children, and signing with hearing populations.

Forrest Hancock, Ph.D., Early Childhood Consultant, 2305 Pebble Beach Drive, Austin, Texas 78747

Dr. Hancock is an early childhood consultant in the Central Texas area. She has been an educator in general and special education for 40 years, and her experience has spanned teaching students and practitioners from the elementary to university levels. Dr. Hancock earned her master's degree in language and learning disabilities at Texas State University and her doctorate in early childhood special education from The University of Texas at Austin where she later taught graduate courses in early language development. She develops and presents professional development trainings for preschool educators and administrators, early intervention service coordinators, and early intervention specialists, and she supports first-year special education teachers seeking certification.

Cheryl Cole Rooke, M.A., CCC-SLP, Senior Clinical Instructor, Speech-Language Pathology, JFK Partners, University of Colorado Denver Health Sciences Center, 4900 East 9th Avenue, Denver, Colorado 80220

Ms. Rooke is a faculty member at the University of Colorado Health Sciences Center and has been working as a pediatric speech-language pathologist since 1994. She has substantial experience in transdisciplinary early childhood interventions, parent training, pediatric diagnostics, and the treatment of language-based learning disabilities. Her interests include child language development, social communication, autism, motor speech development, dyslexia, and parent education. Ms. Rooke currently participates on the University's Autism and Developmental Disorders diagnostic teaching team, provides family-based transdisciplinary services to infants and toddlers through the ENRICH team, teaches parent training programs, and works with children with autism. She has also worked as a speech-language specialist in the Denver Public Schools and as a private therapist working with children with reading disabilities.

Preface

Transdisciplinary Play-Based Assessment, Second Edition (TPBA2) has been revised to include many procedural and content changes that are intended to make the assessment of young children more holistic, family-friendly, comprehensive, and useful. Based on current theories, research, policies, and philosophy in the field of pediatric assessment and intervention, TPBA2 is now a multidimensional assessment that integrates information from families, teachers, and child care providers with the professionals' observations. TPBA2 integrates information from numerous sources and contexts into an ecologically based, as well as play-based, model. The result is a more comprehensive, efficient, and effective process. The *Administration Guide for TPBA2 & TPBI2* describes the use of new forms that are included in TPBA2, and this volume addresses the observational component of TPBA2.

TPBA2 contains the in-depth content for each domain and subcategory of the TPBA process. Research on each of the developmental domains—sensorimotor, emotional and social, communication, and cognitive—led to restructuring the subcategories used in the original TPBA into new and revised observation areas. Each developmental domain now contains up to seven subcategories. Although the actual TPBA observation process has not changed substantially, the content of each domain has been altered to reflect current theory, research, and practice. The changes within each of the domains are described below. In addition, the TPBA2 Age Tables for each domain are presented in a format that is more detailed and allows for a quick visual scan of the child's developmental level across all subcategories. The TPBA2 Observation Guidelines are structured to enable the TPBA2 team to review assessment questions and note observations in such a way that strengths and areas of readiness are immediately visible. This makes the TPBA process more efficient, and all the steps needed for discussion and report writing are available on the TPBA2 Observation Guidelines. Chapter 1 of this volume reviews the TPBA2/TPBI2 system.

Changes to the Sensorimotor Development Domain

Chapter 2, Sensorimotor Development Domain, has undergone extensive revision with Dr. Anita C. Bundy, based on current research and practical considerations in the field. The new subcategory, Functions Underlying Movement, examines foundational processes that allow the child to maintain stability and be able to move efficiently. In the original TPBA, this area was considered in three separate areas. Reactivity to sensory input has been expanded and is now termed Modulation of Sensation and Its

Relationship to Emotion, Activity Level, and Attention. Stationary positions used for play and mobility in play in the original TPBA now are integrated into Gross Motor Activity. Prehension and manipulation has been expanded into a new subcategory of Arm and Hand Use. The subcategory of Motor Planning and Coordination has been revised and expanded. All of these subcategories have been updated based on research and practice in the field.

Dr. Tanni L. Anthony contributed an important new component to the TPBA2 sensorimotor development domain: Chapter 3 is a new chapter on vision development containing TPBA2 Observation Guidelines for vision development as well as a Visual Development Indicators chart that can be used as part of TPBA2. Many children with disabilities have secondary vision issues that may not have been identified, even through traditional acuity testing. These new TPBA2 Observation Guidelines for vision provide a mechanism for looking at whether vision may be having an effect on other areas of development. They will also provide an initial vision screening for many children who have not yet had their vision screened.

Changes to the Emotional and Social Development Domain

The first major revision to Chapter 4 (Chapter 7 in the first edition) is the name. The original domain name, social-emotional development, has been changed to *emotional and social development domain* in order to reflect the importance of emotions and emotional development to the social arena. The content of the domain also reflects an increased emphasis on emotions and emotional adaptations within the subcategories.

In the original TPBA, the first subcategory was Temperament. Recently, researchers have begun to look more closely at temperament and how various aspects of temperament are related to other areas of development, such as attention, problem solving, and sensory integration. As a consequence, some researchers are redefining the area of temperament and developing new constructs that allow us to look at the role of emotions in social, cognitive, and communication development. In TPBA2, all of the traditional temperament categories are addressed, but they are integrated into a framework that reflects current research on self-regulation, sensory integration, and executive function.

Emotional Expression is the first new subcategory. Emotions are basic to human existence, and expression of emotions and feelings through affect is fundamental to emotional and social development. Emotional Expression not only looks at the child's ability to express emotions, but also investigates the contexts across which the various emotions are exhibited. This subcategory also examines the child's more extended emotional states, or moods. Observations of the child in this subcategory lay the foundation for observations in the other emotional and social subcategories. For example, the new subcategory of Emotional Style/Adaptability relates to Emotional Expression by examining how changes to the child's routines, activities, or interactions have an impact on emotions.

The subcategory of Regulation of Emotions and Arousal States has been added to examine the child's ability to regulate his or her state of arousal and emotional reactions to both internal and external stimuli. Aspects previously included in research on temperament (such as approach/withdrawal, adaptability, threshold of responsivity, and reactivity) are now being integrated into this new area of study. Regulation of emotions and arousal states includes physiological regulation, such as maintaining a normal body homeostasis, moving in and out of different states of arousal (such as sleeping and crying), and being able to calm oneself. Self-regulation also includes being able to modulate emotions and reaction to sensory input. The ability to modulate reactions to sensory input is addressed in Chapter 2 (Sensorimotor Development Domain).

Several of the regulatory aspects are assessed on the Child and Family History Questionnaire (CFHQ), with observations in the emotional and social domain of TPBA2 focused more on modulation of attention and emotion.

Behavioral Regulation has been included separate from Regulation of Emotions and Arousal States in order to examine how these self-regulatory skills are influencing behaviors such as compliance, impulse control, recognition of right and wrong, use of social conventions, and control of mannerisms. Behavioral regulation is closely aligned with emotional regulation but focuses more on behavioral outcomes rather than emotional control. Many of the issues addressed in this subcategory were contained in the subcategory previously called Social Conventions and Sense of Humor.

A new subcategory, Sense of Self, examines the child's ability to differentiate "self" characteristics from those of others and to take the initiative to build on individual strengths to accomplish goals. The child's awareness of self and self as separate from others is foundational to the development of emotional understanding and responsiveness to others and is also crucial to the development of effective social relationships. This subcategory also examines the child's motivation to reach goals, level of self-confidence, independence and persistence, and need for external support to accomplish skills. The subcategory of Mastery Motivation in the original TPBA has been reorganized and expanded to include the broader range of issues included in this new subcategory, Sense of Self.

The three original subcategories of Social Interactions with Parents, Social Interactions with the Play Facilitator, and Social Interactions with Peers have been collapsed into a single category called Social Interactions. This subcategory looks at the child's interaction patterns with different people, including the child's engagement in a group, the child's social reasoning skills with others, and his or her social status in a group.

The final subcategory in the revised emotional and social domain, Emotional Themes in Play, was included in the original TPBA but has been expanded in TPBA2 to include the level and social complexity of play in addition to what the child's play reflects about inner emotional states or needs.

Changes to the Communication Development Domain

The communication development domain (Chapter 5) has been revised with Renee Charlifue-Smith and Cheryl Cole Rooke. In this chapter, the previous TPBA subcategories of Pragmatic Stages and Range of Meaning and Functions of Communication have been combined into a new area called Pragmatics. Pragmatic abilities are closely related to social skills in the emotional and social development domain and should be examined together. Information from several former subcategories has been reformulated into the Language Comprehension and Language Production subcategories. These subcategories address the concepts children understand and children's ability to express what they understand.

Three additional or modified categories include Articulation and Phonology, involving the child's sound production and articulation abilities; Voice and Fluency, the child's voice quality and ability to produce fluent speech and language sequences; and Oral Mechanisms.

A major modification is the addition of a separate chapter on hearing screening and modifications of TPBA2 for children who are deaf or hard of hearing (Chapter 6), contributed by Jan Christian Hafer, Cheryl Cole Rooke, and Renee Charlifue-Smith. Again, after input from the field over the years, it was determined that many children seen in assessments had not had their hearing screened recently or, in some cases, not at all. Auditory processing abilities, or the child's ability to understand and remember sounds and words, is also considered along with hearing.

Changes to the Cognitive Development Domain

Chapter 7 (Cognitive Development Domain) has been reorganized and expanded. Recent research has revealed the importance of attention, memory, and problem solving to executive function, which is important for overall thinking strategies. Attention Span and Problem Solving from the original TPBA have thus been expanded into three sections: Attention, Memory, and Problem Solving.

A new subcategory, Social Cognition, also has been added to address children's cognitive understanding about the thinking of others. This area, important to cognitive understanding, communication, and social and emotional competence, is particularly relevant in the identification of autism and other related disorders.

Complexity of Play includes the levels and types of play seen in the child's play repertoire and the complexity of actions revealed within each level. The way the child uses objects in play, his or her ability to spontaneously produce or imitate play behaviors, and his or her ability to pretend is part of the child's ability to represent his or her world. The previous version of TPBA included this information in several different subcategories, including Categories of Play, Early Object Use, Gestural Imitation, and Symbolic/Representational play.

Conceptual Knowledge and Literacy (subsuming previous subcategories of Discrimination/Classification, One-to-One Correspondence, and Drawing) have been added based on the current emphasis on preacademic skills. Both the Conceptual Knowledge subcategory and the Emerging Literacy chapter (Chapter 8) overlap with and are related to the Language Comprehension and Language Production subcategories in the communication development domain. All of these subcategories should be examined in combination. Emerging literacy is an area of increasing importance as a result of the No Child Left Behind Act of 2001 (PL 107-110); thus, Chapter 8, contributed by Forrest Hancock, is a separate exploration of emerging literacy in order to adequately address the birth-to-6 scope of development in this area.

New forms that accompany each domain (TPBA2 Observation Notes and Observation Summary Forms) make it possible to note specific qualitative and quantitative strengths and concerns. In addition, the in-depth changes to the TPBA2 Observation Guidelines and Age Tables for all domains make TPBA2 more comprehensive, easier to use, and relevant to families and educators.

Acknowledgments

This revised version of the Transdisciplinary Play-Based System has been years in the making and consequently has involved the contributions of literally hundreds of children, families, students, and professionals. I know I will never be able to adequately acknowledge everyone who has been involved in this creative process, but I will endeavor to cite a few of the key people who have made significant contributions.

First, this work builds on the foundation established by the original TPBA and TPBI. For this I thank the key contributors to these volumes, Susan Hall, Kim Dickson, Paula Hudson, Anita C. Bundy, Carol Lay, and Sandy Patrick. All of these professionals helped shape the format and content of TPBA/I. When these people worked on the first TPBA and TPBI, they worked not from encouragement from the field, but purely from a belief that play was the best approach for young children and their families. Their faith in this process was critical to the completion of the first editions and the subsequent success of the TPBA system.

Those who have contributed to *Transdisciplinary Play-Based Assessment, Second Edition* (TPBA2); *Transdisciplinary Play-Based Intervention, Second Edition* (TPBI2); and the *Administration Guide for TPBA2 & TPBI2* come to the task with more of a sense of justification and validation, because there has been much research in the field of early intervention and early childhood special education to support that what we are doing is based on best practices. These people, too, are committed to providing functional, meaningful assessment and intervention for young children and their families. I again thank Anita C. Bundy who, although she has moved to Australia, has continued to offer her expertise in sensorimotor development in both TPBA2 and TPBI2. Susan Dwinal also served as a member of the PLAY Clinic team and the TPBA rural training team, and I thank her for her work on the intervention chapter for arm and hand use. Renee Charlifue-Smith has taught me much about speech and language and has been an invaluable PLAY Clinic team member. Her expertise has helped expand and build the empirical foundation for our work. Renee not only wrote significant portions of several chapters, she reviewed and contributed to all of the communication and hearing assessment and intervention chapters. Renee has been a steadfast advocate and loyal friend, and I greatly appreciate her support. Cheryl Cole Rooke and Natasha Hall came in to support Renee and gave us needed energy and input on the communication chapters. Jan Christian Hafer, from Galludet, brought her expertise in deaf education to both TPBA2 and TPBI2, adding a much-needed new hearing component to assessment and intervention. In the same way, Tanni L. Anthony contributed the vision perspective, an area that is often overlooked by those who are not vision experts. Tanni's research on the vision component of TPBA2 showed that professionals from a variety of disciplines can reliably observe vision and make determinations for the need for further vision evaluation. Ann Petersen-Smith brought her nursing background and expertise to our doctoral program, then to the PLAY Clinic, and subsequently to her research on the Child and Family History Questionnaire (CFHQ). Her work has shown the importance of this piece to both TPBA2 and TPBI2. Karen Riley has both led a PLAY Clinic team and done research on TPBA with children with fragile X syndrome. Her leadership in the clinic, her skill in report writing, her enthusiasm for research, and her undying friendship have been invaluable. Thank you, Karen! Forrest Hancock first supported TPBA and TPBI by bringing training to Texas. She subsequently contributed the assessment and intervention sections for literacy. In addition, she has a great editorial eye! Forrest's collaboration, friendship, and support have helped carry me through more than one hard night.

Numerous people have contributed to the fieldwork and research on various aspects of TPBA2 and TPBI2. I would like to thank Eisa Al-Balhan, Tanni L. Anthony, Ann Petersen-Smith, and Kelly DeBruin for their dissertation research on different components of the process. Kelly DeBruin's work on the concurrent and social validity of TPBA2 provided an important perspective on the whole process. In addition, several teams in Texas conducted evaluation research to examine the effectiveness of TPBA and were subsequently awarded a Promising Practices Award by the Texas Department of Education. Texas teams from Plano, Conroy, Round Rock, and Katy all collected data to show the effectiveness of the process and the impact of various outcomes. For example, Kellie Johnson and her team in Round Rock demonstrated that, contrary to popular belief, use of TPBA does not result in identification of more children as needing special services. In fact, Round Rock was able to eliminate two special education preschool classes due to children performing better and consequently not being found eligible for services. Children were able to demonstrate higher level skills with the TPBA approach. To all of these Promising Practices teams, thank you for your dedication to implementing and sharing child- and family-friendly practices. In addition, I'm grateful to Forrest Hancock, Elaine Earls, Jan Andreas, Margie Larsen, Lynn Sullivan, Stacey Shackelford, and the other Independent School Districts and Texas Regional Service Centers. Thank you for your leadership, field testing, and feedback! AnneMarie deKort-Young, Corrine Garland, and Stella Fair have been supportive colleagues throughout.

Many people also reviewed manuscript segments. I'd like to thank Carrie Davenport, from the Ohio School for the Deaf, who gave important feedback on the hearing chapter. I also would like to thank John Neisworth, Phillippa Campbell, Sarah Landy, Marci Hanson, Angela Notari-Syverson, Kathleen Stremel, and Juliann Woods, in addition to Anita C. Bundy, Karen Riley, Renee Charlifue-Smith, and Tanni L. Anthony, for their participation in the cross-domain influences study that demonstrated the validity of the transdisciplinary construct. I believe this work will lead to interesting future research on intervention planning.

One incredibly gratifying aspect of the work on TPBA2 has been the opportunity to share TPBA and TPBI with people from various cultures around the world. Because of the flexible nature of both the assessment and intervention models, they are easily adapted to different situations. I would like to thank the people who have begun to use TPBA and TPBI (both the first and second edition materials) for their support and ongoing research and feedback, in particular, Jenny Hsing and Anne-Merete Kleppenes in Norway; Margaret Galvin, Kevin McGrattin, and Ruth Connolly in Ireland, Manuela Sanches Ferreira and Susana Martins in Portugal; and Chen Xuefeng in China. You all have been an inspiration to me for how you advocate for and create change for children and families. Thank you!

Of course, as every professor does, I have worked with my students in many ways. Although I cannot thank each one individually, I would like to extend global thanks for all their hard work throughout the years. I have learned from each one of you! In particular, I'd like to thank Keri Linas, Kim Stokka, and Jeanine Coleman for their collaborative efforts throughout their doctoral programs. Each of you has embraced play as an important part of your studies and each of you will contribute much to our field. Thank you for your positive, can-do attitude! Go for it!

To all of the people at Paul H. Brookes Publishing Co. (past and present), including Paul Brookes, Melissa Behm, Heather Shrestha, Tara Gebhardt, Jan Krejci, and Susannah Ray, I am grateful for your continued support, tolerance, patience, and hard work.

And finally, to my family and friends, who have been virtually abandoned during this seemingly overwhelming and endless task, I thank you for your unwavering love and support (even when *I* was wavering, you kept me going!). Your love sustains me and provides my emotional refueling! Thank you!

To all the children and families with whom I have worked over the years,
I am grateful for all you have taught me about development,
learning, patience, flexibility, determination, and love.

1

A Review of the Transdisciplinary Play-Based System

The first edition of Transdisciplinary Play-Based Assessment (1990) presented a comparison of assessment by a multidisciplinary team using traditional approaches and transdisciplinary play-based assessment (TPBA) using a team conducting a play assessment together. Over the years, many people have commented on how the vignette presented in the beginning of the book opened their eyes to what their assessments might be like for the children they assessed. The vignette is presented again in this revised edition to illustrate how different the assessment process can be for children and families. Chapter 1 in the *Administration Guide* discusses why theory, research, and legislation are now dictating that assessment of young children should be natural, functional, and responsive to child and family needs.

TRADITIONAL ASSESSMENT

Imagine yourself as a 3-year-old child who has been referred to a developmental center for assessment because of suspected developmental delays. Both your mother and father have come with you to a place called "the Center."

When you walk in the door, a woman meets you and takes you to her office. You sit on your mom's lap while the woman behind the desk asks your mom and dad questions about your birth and your first 3 years of life. Your mom and dad sound worried and your mom even cries when she talks about you. You feel sad and think that something about you must be making her cry.

After a while, another woman comes to take you to "play some games." Your mom and dad tell you to go with the "nice lady" and it will be fun. The nice lady takes your hand. You walk down the hall with her to a small room with a table and two wooden chairs and some pictures on the wall. You don't see any games anywhere. Then the lady pulls out a suitcase and starts to put things like blocks and puzzles in front of you. She then asks you to do certain things with them. At first this is fun, but after a while the lady asks you to do some things that are not so much fun. It's hard. You tell her this, but she just keeps putting things that are not fun in front of you. She also asks you questions that you can't answer. You want to go back to your mommy and daddy, but the lady keeps saying that you'll be finished soon. "Soon" is a long time. Finally, the lady says that you're all done playing games. You feel relieved! This lady doesn't know much about how to have fun!

After a necessary potty break and a few tears, the lady lets you see your mommy and daddy. But not for long. Here comes another lady to take you to another little room with another table and chairs and different pictures on the wall. This lady doesn't talk much. She just keeps putting pictures in front of you and asking you what they are. Many of the pictures are things that you have seen, but you just don't know what to call them. So you look down at the floor and up at the pictures on the wall. You pull on your shirt and wiggle a lot. You wish this lady would quit with the pictures. You've seen more than enough pictures. Then the lady gets out another suitcase, only it's a different color. She pulls out a couple of toys at a time and tells you what she wants you to do with them. Some of these are neat toys, and you'd really like to play with them. Every time you start to do something other than what the lady told you to do, however, she takes the toys away. This lady sure is stingy. You are getting tired, so you put your head down on the table. The lady makes you sit up. Finally, she is through. She takes you back to your mommy and daddy and tells them that you were "somewhat resistant."

Mom and Dad look worried, so when they ask, you tell them you had fun playing games with the ladies. That was a mistake. In the car they tell you that you are coming back tomorrow for some more games! When you tell them you don't want to go back, you didn't like the ladies, they say tomorrow you will play with another nice lady.

Wrong. The next day a man comes out to meet you. He says you are going to play some more fun games. You are not convinced. This time you go to a big room with many stairs and boards that wobble and boards that don't wobble and hanging nets and balls and all kinds of neat stuff. You think that maybe this will be fun! You run and jump and climb the stairs and are generally having a great time. Then the man puts you up on a big ball and tries to make you fall off. At least that is how it feels, though the man keeps saying he won't let you fall. You don't trust him. You want your mommy and daddy, so you cry. Then the man makes your arms and legs go different directions and bounces you around some. This doesn't seem fun any more. The man is nice enough. He just doesn't know when to stop! You cry louder, and finally the man says, "We've had enough for today." He's right about that.

You go back to your mommy and daddy who are still sitting with that worried look on their faces. They tell you that they will take you to get a hamburger for being so good. You don't tell them that you weren't really that good. They don't need to know everything.

TRANSDISCIPLINARY PLAY-BASED ASSESSMENT

You are still the same 3-year-old child who has been referred for evaluation due to suspected developmental delays. As you enter the Center, you are greeted by the same woman who came out to your house to talk to your mommy and play with you. This time, however, she takes you to a large room containing many different toys. A playhouse is in one corner, an area with blocks and cars is in another, a table with puzzles and little toys is in another, and a water table with toys is in another. Wow! All your favorite things!

Hey! This place is neat! Mommy is holding your hand, but you let go and run to the dollhouse area. It has a sink, refrigerator, and stove just like at home, only smaller. And it has dolls and beds and dishes and telephones. You look in the refrigerator. There's a birthday cake with candles! Suddenly you notice another lady next to you.

She says, "Oh, you found the birthday cake!" She doesn't even seem to mind when you take the cake out of the refrigerator and pull out all of the candles. "Maybe we should invite some babies to a party," she says. "Yeah!" You pick up a doll and give her a piece of cake. The lady does the same thing with her baby. She says her baby is hungry. You say your baby is hungry. too. Well, actually, you say "ungy," but she seems to understand. She pours more "milk" in your baby's cup. You and the lady play together in the house. Sometimes she does what you do, and sometimes you look at her and do what she does. You think she is a nice lady.

All of a sudden you remember your mommy and daddy. You look around and see them sitting there watching you. They are talking to the other lady. A man is also watching you and he has a video camera. You say "hi" to Mommy and Daddy. The lady hands you a telephone and tells you Mommy and Daddy are on the phone. You talk to Mommy and Daddy, who say, "Hi, are you having fun playing?" Then you talk to the lady who is playing with you. The two of you have lots of fun dressing the dolls for bed, brushing their teeth, combing their hair, and putting them to bed. Every once in a while you check to see if Mommy and Daddy are still there. They are.

A little boy comes into the playhouse. You don't know who invited him, but he wants to play with the toys, too. The play lady says he wants to play with you. As long as he doesn't take your doll, it's okay with you. He plays with the dishes and cooks. He pours juice and gives you some. You take it but go back to putting your doll to bed. The play lady gives the boy some dishes and he puts them on the table. He says that dinner is ready, so you go to the table with your baby. You feed your baby. The boy talks to you, but you don't answer. You just don't feel like talking to him. After a while he wanders off to play somewhere else. That's okay with you.

Then the play lady goes over to the water table with her doll and starts to wash her doll. That looks like fun, so you go, too. You wash the doll for a while, and then you play with the water wheel, boats, funnels, and other fun stuff. When you get tired of this, you go over to see what's in the block area. This is fun, too. You and the play lady build bridges, drive cars over a road, put gas in your cars, have a car crash, and get the cars fixed. This place sure has nice toys.

Your mommy and daddy tell you they are leaving to get a cup of coffee and they'll be right back. You watch them go and are a little worried, but you don't mind staying here with the play lady. After a few minutes Mommy and Daddy come back, and Daddy comes over to play with you. You show him the cars, and you both drive them and crash them off bridges and laugh. Then Mommy comes over to show you some things at the table. The two of you put puzzles together. Some of them are hard and Mommy helps you. Mommy is a good helper. Then you and Mommy draw pictures, count the lines you drew and read a book. It's fun to have Mommy and Daddy playing too.

When you're all done with your pictures and puzzles, the play lady takes all of you to another room with stairs, boards that wobble, boards that don't wobble, hanging nets, balls, and tricycles. You run and jump and climb up and down the stairs. The play lady throws the ball to you and your daddy and mommy. You get the play lady to follow you up and over and through things. This play lady sure is a good sport! When she looks all worn out, you give her a rest. You try to ride the tricycle, but it's too hard. The play lady and your daddy toss you around in the air. You play with a big ball, and you and Daddy take turns bouncing and rolling on it.

After everyone is all worn out, including you, all of you go back to the playroom. There is a snack of crackers and juice in the middle of the table and the little boy is there. The play lady lets you pour the juice and put yellow cheese on the crackers. You give some to the boy and take some for yourself. You try to give some to Mommy and Daddy, but they don't seem too interested. The play lady talks to you and the boy. You ask the boy if he wants more. He seems to be a pretty nice boy after all.

After you're all done eating and drinking, the play lady says it's time to go. You are tired, but you'd still like to play with those cars some more. The play lady says maybe another day. That sounds good to you. How about tomorrow?

ALMOST 20 YEARS LATER

Although much has changed since 1990, rigid testing procedures are still used, and even required, in some states. TPBA is the same in many ways, but it has evolved as well. Now TPBA may be done just as easily in the home, in a classroom, or in a community setting. Parents may be the primary play facilitators more frequently, and they will have more involvement before, during, and after the assessment. The process, however, remains much the same: a child- and family-friendly assessment resulting in practical, meaningful information.

Whereas the *Administration Guide for TPBA2 & TPBI2* describes the total TPBA process and administration, including discussion of how to obtain preliminary information, presentation of strategies for talking to families and facilitating play with children, and ways to summarize data and integrate them into a report, this volume, *Transdisciplinary Play-Based Assessment, Second Edition* (TPBA2), includes detailed chapters with research and literature describing significant aspects of each domain. These chapters are extensive, providing a review of the literature for each of the subcategories as well as guidelines for observation and interpretation of information obtained. Extensive Age Tables are also provided, noting age ranges for acquisition of skills and the outer ages by which time a skill should be demonstrated. These chapters provide the heart of the TPBA2 assessment process. They should be read carefully so that the rationale for the TPBA2 Observation Guidelines and the implications for services and intervention needs are fully understood. The third volume of this system, *Transdisciplinary Play-Based Intervention, Second Edition* (TPBI2), presents a process for planning, implementing, and evaluating intervention for children from birth to 6 years of age who need supports to enhance their development by providing a framework for conceptualizing intervention strategies and a means for monitoring and evaluating the effectiveness of the strategies selected.

2

Sensorimotor Development Domain

with Anita C. Bundy

Generally, children move because they have thought of something they want to do. In a way, this indicates that movement underlies thought. In fact, we so often solve problems by manipulating objects or scratching out notes that some contemporary philosophers (Clark, 1997; Rowlands, 1999) have suggested that action is *a part of* thought. Movement has many functions; it enables growth and expression across developmental domains (e.g., cognitive, emotional, social), supports relationships, and is a major source of joy. Thus, we examine whether children's motor skills enable them to do what they need and want to do every day.

The ability to move skillfully is supported by the maturity and integrity of the sensory-neurological and musculoskeletal systems. This is why the movements of a confident 12-year-old ice hockey player differ significantly from those of a 5-year-old who has donned skates and walked onto the ice for the first time. Similarly, the attempts of an infant with cerebral palsy to stand will look quite different from those of his typically developing twin.

Children's capacities aside, task demands and environmental conditions also play a major role in determining what actions look like and how difficult they are. Any child will find it easier to pick up a drinking glass when it is dry than when it is coated with soapy water. Similarly, it is easier to kick a ball in the context of friendly competition than in the midst of a championship soccer game.

The sensorimotor domain in Transdisciplinary Play-Based Assessment (TPBA2) examines the status of children's motor skills and some underlying functions that support movement (i.e., posture, muscle tone). Specifically, the sensorimotor domain examines the following subcategories: 1) functions underlying movement; 2) gross motor activity; 3) arm and hand use; 4) motor planning and coordination; 5) modulation of sensation and its relationship to emotion, activity level, and attention; and 6) sensorimotor contributions to daily life and self-care.

Knowledge of the definitions of the words used to describe motor skills is important. *Sensorimotor,* the general term used to describe the content of this domain, acknowledges the dependence of all movement on vision, hearing, and touch. For ex-

5

ample, the simple act of reaching requires vision to guide the hand to the object and the sense that arises from the muscles (proprioception) to orient the hand for grasping. *Motor planning,* or the process of organizing purposeful movements, is particularly reliant on sensation that tells us where the body is in space. The modulation of sensation, which leads to actions that are in proportion to the sensory experience, is also a form of sensorimotor competence.

Several subcategories divide the broad classification of sensorimotor. For example, we distinguish between gross and fine motor skills. *Gross motor* refers to large movements like running, throwing, and climbing, whereas *fine motor* includes small movements like grasping or pointing. Movements of the arms and hands may be classified as either gross (e.g., throwing) or fine (e.g., grasping) motor. Although the small movements of the lips, tongue, and eyes are fine motor, they are also even more specifically *oral motor* and *oculomotor.* The terms *visual motor* and *eye–hand coordination* also pertain to the eyes, specifically to the coordination of eye and hand movements. (See Chapter 3 for a discussion of the research, development, and observation of vision, and Chapter 6 for a discussion of hearing and guidelines for screening and modification of TPBA for children with hearing impairments.)

I. Functions Underlying Movement

While watching a child play, we observe skilled movements defined by the context in which they occur, as well as functions that underlie those movements. Two important and interrelated functions thought to set the stage for, or interfere with, movement are posture and muscle tone.

I. A. How well does posture support action?

Posture is fundamental to all movements because it provides a means of stabilizing the body so that the limbs can act in concert with one another and with the body (Sugden & Keogh, 1990). Postural control is composed of two components: *postural orientation* and *postural stability* (Shumway-Cook & Woollacott, 2001).

Postural orientation enables children to maintain an optimal relationship with the environment. Being upright works best for most tasks, especially those involving hand use. Postural orientation also enables children to maintain optimal relationships among body segments, particularly the head and trunk. Generally, that means the head and trunk are in line with one another, although neither is held rigid. Both are stable and, yet, can be moved freely.

Postural orientation requires the integration of sensation from several sources: muscles, joints, skin, the ears (including both hearing and the sense of movement), and the eyes. Each sense plays a role in adopting and maintaining postures. For example, when sitting on the floor, a child gets information through pressure on the skin covering the legs and buttocks to tell her that she is in contact with the floor. The absence of pressure over other body parts (e.g., belly) provides additional information. Cues from muscles and joints inform the child that her hips are bent to 90 degrees. Cues from the eyes and ears tell her that she is upright.

Postural stability, the second component of postural control, is synonymous with balance; it enables children to maintain the body position within specific boundaries (base of support; Weisz, 1938) known as *stability limits* (Shumway-Cook & Woollacott, 2001).

When children move outside their stability limits, they establish a new base of support and a new position by extending one or more limbs and then moving the body over the limbs into the new position. These movements may be intentional. For example, a child may chose to move from sitting on a chair to hands and knees by "falling" to one side, extending the arms, moving weight over the arms, and derotating the lower body so that the knees come into contact with the floor. Establishing a new base of support also may occur unintentionally as, for example, when reaching too far in the sitting position, losing balance, and extending a limb to keep from landing on one's face.

Explaining Postural Control

Physical and occupational therapists have traditionally adopted a neuromaturation model to explain postural control (Alexander, Boehme, & Cupps, 1993; Campbell, Vander Linden, & Palisano, 2000; Piper & Darrah, 1994). In the neuromaturation model, postural reactions appear in a well-defined sequence enabled almost entirely by development of the central nervous system. Therapists using the neuromaturation model describe three components of an automatic postural mechanism: righting (head and trunk movements that enable a child to remain upright and assume new body positions), protective extension (extension of a limb to prevent falling), and balance (compensatory reactions of the head and trunk that keep the center of gravity over the base of support) (Bobath, 1985; Shumway-Cook & Woollacott, 2001). Each of these responses is the responsibility of progressively "higher" centers within the nervous system.

Although both the neuromaturation model and systems-based models such as the one described by Shumway-Cook and Woollacott (2001) can be used to explain developing postural reactions, the latter have greater contemporary appeal. They incorporate multiple factors (not simply the developing central nervous system) into their explanation for the acquisition of skills. Systems theorists explicitly consider both the task and the environment as equal partners in determining what actions look like (Reed, 1989; Shumway-Cook & Woollacott, 2001; Thelen, 1995; Thelen & Smith, 1994).

Unlike the neuromaturation model, systems approaches (compatible with TPBA) also address the *anticipatory* or *proactive* components of posture rather than simply its *reactive* roles (e.g., regaining balance). When a child *prepares* to catch a ball, the same muscles are activated as in the *compensatory* movements that enable that child to remain upright *following* a backward push (Nashner & McCollum, 1985, cited in Reed, 1989). Anticipatory postural sets establish a supporting framework for many voluntary, goal-directed movements. The ability to anticipate is a critical feature of postural control (Reed, 1989; Shumway-Cook & Woollacott, 2001).

Several considerations are relevant to the question of how well posture supports task performance. First, it is easiest to manipulate objects in an upright position in which both hands are free. Second, whereas sitting and standing are easier poses to maintain than prone (on belly) in terms of resisting gravity, they require better balance.

Although it is difficult to play with toys while prone or on hands and knees, these positions tell us a lot about postural control. They require good extension to counteract gravity, and to attain good body alignment, flexion must balance extension. When children have difficulty maintaining these positions with good alignment, we question postural control.

The development of postural control occurs first in the head and neck and gradually develops through the trunk and limbs. Postural responses are influenced by vision, movement, touch, and sensation from the muscles (Shumway-Cook & Woollacott, 2001), as well as by what the child wants to do. Coordinated postural responses in the neck begin to appear at about 2 months of age. By 4–6 months, the infant is able to use information from vision and movement to extend the neck, back, and hips while lying on his or her belly (Piper & Darrah, 1994). In the neuromaturation model, this position is known as the *Landau* or *pivot prone*.

The postural control necessary for sitting will not occur until 6–7 months of age. At this point and onward, touch and resistance from the support surface play a major role in postural control (Shumway-Cook & Woollacott, 2001). This is another example of the marked influence of sensation on balance.

By 8–10 months, most children are standing while holding on. Children generally are not able to free both hands while standing until 11–14 months, the time at which they begin walking. Even at the onset of walking they will balance with their arms for some weeks to come (Piper & Darrah, 1994). Running and walking place new demands on posture as the child needs to anticipate faster and more often in order to avoid obstacles, change directions, and stop.

Changing positions requires alignment of the head, trunk, and limbs. When body segments are not well aligned, children get stuck and cannot move out of a position. Sometimes children "sink into" a supporting surface and lose body alignment. Without good alignment, they also will find it difficult to use the arms and hands to reach for a toy.

I. B. How well does muscle tone support posture?

Muscle tone is the force that muscles use to resist being lengthened; it is typically felt as stiffness. Tone often is tested by moving a limb passively and assessing the degree of resistance (Shumway-Cook & Woollacott, 2001). However, in TPBA we assess tone, as all other functions, primarily through observation.

A certain amount of muscle tone is necessary for all action. Tone provides the base for an anticipatory postural set as well as for compensatory reactions that occur from changing position or losing balance. Tone also enables all limb movements: reaching, walking, running, kicking, and so forth.

The precise contribution of *normal* tone to movement and posture can be difficult to observe. However, abnormal tone results in poor control of movement and clearly limits what some children can accomplish, so observing the effects of abnormal tone is relatively easy.

Abnormal tone varies widely in appearance. Tone can be too high, too low, or apparently "fluctuating" (i.e., in the presence of tremors or involuntary movements) (Sugden & Keogh, 1990). Abnormal muscle tone is a part of many neurologically based disabilities (e.g., cerebral palsy, Down syndrome, dyspraxia).

When muscle tone is too high, there is increased resistance to movement and movements look stereotyped and lack variability. The more difficult the task, the more tone is likely to increase; this will be true in all involved limbs, not just the limb in use. The most common patterns of high tone include limbs on one body side or all four limbs; when tone is increased on both body sides, it generally is higher in one side than the other, and when all four limbs are involved, the legs may be more involved than the arms.

Children with increased muscle tone have difficulty initiating, sustaining, and terminating movement (Stamer, 2000). Consequently, they move slowly and appear to get stuck in certain postures. Some children seem to have difficulty moving in any direction, whereas others have greater difficulty moving in one direction than the other. Generally, children find it easier to flex the arms than to extend them and to extend the legs rather than flex them.

Researchers have suggested that some children who look as though they have high muscle tone may actually be voluntarily "[using] increased stiffness as a compensatory strategy to control posture and prevent unwanted or uncontrolled movement in other areas of the body" (Nashner, Shumway-Cook, & Olin, 1983; Stamer, 2000, p. 66). For example, a child who has tremors may stiffen his trunk and arms in an attempt to reduce the tremors and make reaching more accurate. Another child may stiffen her legs and walk on her tiptoes to counteract the effect of instability in her hips. Children can use stiffness to help themselves become more functional.

Abnormally low muscle tone is characterized by increased range of movement and unusually flexible postures (Dubowitz, 1980, cited in Stamer, 2000; Sugden & Keogh, 1990). Consequently, the movements of children with low tone look unusual. For example, they may move into sitting from lying on the stomach by spreading the legs wide and pushing up with the head or hands (Sugden & Keogh, 1990). Children with low tone may have difficulty initiating and completing movements, and their movements may be poorly graded (e.g., too hard, too fast). They may sustain positions (e.g., head erect, sitting, standing) by sinking into the support surface, "stacking" one body part on another, or locking joints, as their bodies are poorly aligned. Stamer (2000) indicated that these unusual movements and postures are the result of difficulties with muscle contraction, balancing muscles on opposite sides of joints, and recruiting muscles to work together. Children with low tone in the limbs generally also have decreased tone in the trunk.

Some children with slightly low muscle tone will develop new symptoms after the first year of life. Ataxia, a type of cerebral palsy characterized by tremors and a wide base of support in sitting and standing, is one possibility. Children with ataxia often are fearful of moving and have poor balance. Thus, their wide base of support and tendency to remain close to the ground serve them well. Despite their fear, they often seem to move a lot and may be labeled as overly active. To move they depend on visual fixation, which means they cannot scan the environment and, thus, often trip over or bump into objects. Furthermore, their movements are very poorly coordinated and poorly organized; they have difficulty initiating movements but then overshoot the target. Their abilities seem very inconsistent from day to day and situation to situation. Many children with ataxia have tremors in their arms, head, and eyes (Stamer, 2000).

Fluctuating tone, another symptom that begins as low tone, is characterized by highly complex, purposeless, uncontrolled, and seemingly involuntary movement (Stamer, 2000; Sugden & Keogh, 1990). The term *fluctuating* probably came from observations of alternating contractions of muscles on either side of joints in the trunk or limbs. Children who have these writhing or rotary motions generally have a diagnosis of athetoid cerebral palsy. Their movements occur with unnecessary force and may be initiated in a direction opposite of that of the intended movement. Their posture usually is very asymmetrical and they have profound difficulty with weight bearing and head control.

To make matters more confusing, individual children may have more than one type of abnormal tone. For example, increased tone in one or more limbs is often seen in the company of decreased tone in the trunk. Furthermore, the type of abnormal tone may change as children develop. As noted earlier, children who will be diagnosed later with athetoid cerebral palsy and who appear to have fluctuating tone often have very low tone as infants. Finally, children's muscle tone, whether normal or abnormal, often differs when they are in different states or when they are moving. For example, the tone of a child at rest appears lower than that of a child who is excited (Stamer, 2000).

▰▰▰▰ USING THE OBSERVATION GUIDELINES TO ASSESS FUNCTIONS UNDERLYING MOVEMENT

▰▰▰▰ I. A. How well does posture support action?

During TPBA, examiners should watch how well posture supports gross and fine motor skills. Which developmental positions do children assume and how well do they maintain them while engaged in play? The team should also observe children's abilities to keep the head and trunk in line and to move freely. Can they prepare for the inevitable perturbations that occur when they reach for or get ready to catch a ball, and how do they react when something unexpected happens (e.g., gentle jostling)? The team members also need to gauge whether children are able to catch themselves when they fall.

I. B. How well does muscle tone support posture?

The team should observe for the effects of muscle tone on appearance and actions. Is there evidence of decreased muscle tone in the trunk or limbs? Children with low tone appear to have "mushy" muscles. Their posture is poor and they have difficulty resisting gravity. For example, a child may have difficulty controlling his head. When he rises to sitting from lying down, he may lead with his chin rather than his forehead, causing his head to drop back slightly. Often, children with low tone sit with a rounded back. They may spread their legs widely apart, reflecting their low tone but also providing a very wide base of support. They may get stuck in a position because they sink into the support surface and lose their alignment. They may "lock" joints when in weight-bearing positions to minimize the demand on their muscles. For example, a child may tend to lock her knees when standing and her elbows when on hands and knees.

Is there evidence of increased muscle tone? When muscle tone is too high, children appear stiff. They tend to hold their arms and hands in characteristic postures (i.e., arms bent, hands fisted) and move in stereotypical ways. If they are able to sit, their legs tend to remain drawn together providing a very narrow base, and they may tend to sit on the sacrum rather than squarely on the buttocks. They often stand on their toes. Because of the stiffness in their limbs, they have difficulty initiating movements. However, children who have increased tone in their arms and legs may have decreased tone in the trunk.

Is there evidence of tremors or other involuntary movement that interferes with using the hands and arms? Such movements are often described as "fluctuating tone"; it seems as though someone is rapidly flicking a light switch when controlling a muscle contraction. Children with involuntary movements often have decreased tone in the trunk; they also may have increased tone in some body parts.

Because muscle tone underlies posture, children who have abnormal tone often have poor postural responses. They may lack stability and have difficulty maintaining and moving between positions. They may lose their balance easily and fail to catch themselves when falling.

> Alejandra's family sought TPBA for their quiet, shy 6-year-old daughter because of general concerns with her development. Her 4-year-old sister was already able to run and climb better than "Ali" and was beginning to surpass her in other ways, too. Ali's evaluation occurred in a play area covered, in part, with thick mattresses. She found it hard to walk across that area without falling, and her supporting muscle tone was clearly low. She stood with locked knees and a pronounced curve of her lower back; her muscles looked mushy. Ali's difficulties increased markedly when she tried to drag a large heavy bag full of toys across the floor. Her force came from her arms; her trunk did not appear to provide a sturdy base from which to work. Ali's parents reported that she had similar difficulties whenever she walked on a soft or uneven soft surface, especially when carrying large or heavy objects.

Although it is relatively easy for team members to see evidence of Ali's low muscle tone, it is the effect of her tone on her posture and motor skills that is of concern. Ali's low tone is resulting in poor stability in her trunk and limbs. Consequently, she stands in ways that minimize the demand to her muscles; she locks her knees, and there is a pronounced curve in her back. Her poor stability also is a major reason why she has so much difficulty carrying or dragging heavy objects; it also contributes to her poor balance. Because low tone and poor posture underlie many of Ali's difficulties, they will be reflected in her plan. However, her goals will be to improve specific skills (e.g., dragging or pushing heavy objects effectively) rather than the more generic objective of improving balance or building muscle tone.

II. Gross Motor Activity ▬▬▬▬▬▬▬▬▬▬▬▬▬▬▬▬▬▬

Gross motor actions are those involving big movements and large muscles. They involve several body parts working together to move the body through space and receive or propel large objects (Burton & Miller, 1998). For example, running is a gross motor activity, as is throwing. The motions are large and employ both the trunk and extremities. The actual definition of *gross motor* is rarely made explicit, perhaps because it reflects the simple dictionary definition of *gross:* "big" (Random House, 2000). However, the definition is reflected in the items included in assessments of gross motor ability (e.g., Bruininks, 1978; Folio & Fewell, 1983).

A caution: Because fine motor movements are so often performed with the hands, gross and fine motor sometimes are linked expressly (and incorrectly) to arms and legs, respectively. That is, sometimes speakers refer to any skill done with the upper extremities as fine motor and any done with the lower extremities as gross motor. The fact that there is no clear distinction between "big" and "small" only adds to the confusion. Reaching provides a good example. Is it a gross motor skill or a fine motor skill? A child standing on tiptoes and straining to get a toy from the top shelf clearly is performing a gross motor task. What about the child seated at a table reaching for a French fry on the plate in front of him or her? Is he or she performing a gross or fine motor action? Thus, for simplicity, in TPBA we have separated all activities where the primary action involves the upper extremities, whether gross or fine motor in nature, into a section titled Arm and Hand Use (Section III); this section follows the gross motor section.

▬▬▬▬ II. A. In general, how do you describe the child's gross motor movements?
How much do gross motor problems interfere with function?

When assessing gross motor activity, we begin by looking *in general* at children's actions. Can they do what they want to do (i.e., are their actions effective)? How well (i.e., do the actions reflect efficiency and quality)? How easily (i.e., how much effort do they expend)? How much do they enjoy gross motor play?

Children may be able to accomplish tasks but the quality may not be good, and they may expend a lot of energy doing things that should be quite simple. Running is a good example. When typically developing children (over the age of 5) run, they lean forward and pump their arms rhythmically (Keogh & Sugden, 1985; Seefeldt & Haubenstricker, 1982; Williams, 1983). They can pretty much stop on a dime. They may arrive breathless but recover quickly. Children who have difficulty with running look awkward and move relatively slowly. They fatigue easily, and many of these children will find it difficult to stop without running into something.

In addition, it always is important to ask about the circumstances that affect gross motor skills—both negatively and positively. For example, a child may be able to ride his two-wheeler in the basement but be afraid to ride it on slanted surfaces like the driveway or the hill in front of his house.

We also observe how much children seem to enjoy gross motor play. Children who are fearful of moving or who have been teased because of poor coordination may avoid gross motor actions. Sometimes parents and others mistake a child's difficulties for personal preference (Cermak & Larkin, 2002; Lane, 2002; Reeves & Cermak, 2002).

However, most children, especially boys, favor sensorimotor motor play through at least the preschool years (Clifford & Bundy, 1989).

II. B. What positions does the child play in?

Most children have access to a range of developmental positions. However, they play in only a few. Most typically developing children are able to assume the common play positions by approximately 15 months (Aylward, 1995; Bly, 1994; Case-Smith, 2001; Folio & Fewell, 1983; Piper & Darrah, 1994). These commence with lying on the back with arms and hands free (about 4 months) and further include lying on the belly with forearm support (5 months), reaching while lying on the belly (7 months), sitting reliably with arms free (about 8 months), standing propped against a surface (10 months), standing alone (13 months), and, finally, squatting (15 months) (Piper & Darrah, 1994). Once children are able to sit, it is relatively unusual for them to play in positions that are not upright (Alexander et al., 1993).

In order to play in a particular position, children must maintain it even when disturbed slightly by reaching or turning to look or when someone else bumps into them. They also need at least one, and preferably both, hands free. Children who lack sufficient internal stability to play independently can be supported externally by a chair or other piece of equipment. However, even when a chair is well fitted, it does not replace internal stability. That is, it will not enable the child to shift weight or turn easily. Thus, both play and independence will be limited to a degree.

Children who lack proximal stability or have increased tone in their lower extremities often prefer sitting with their legs in a "W" shape. W sitting has certain advantages. It is easy to assume this position from hands and knees by simply moving backward through the legs without rotating the trunk at all. Furthermore, the position is very stable and both hands are completely free. However, W sitting has certain disadvantages. Most important, it strains the hip and knee joints and may contribute to deformity of the legs, particularly in children who keep their legs bent for prolonged periods of time.

Children's abilities to maintain developmental positions contribute to the development of stability. For example, Alexander and colleagues (1993) described that as the 7-month-old baby rocks on hands and knees, postural stability, strength, and coordination develop, which in turn improves shoulder, pelvic, and hip control.

A similar case can be made for developing control and stability in all developmental positions.

II. C. How independent is the child when moving between positions?

To be independent in play, children must be able to move in and out of positions. Otherwise their options in play are extremely limited. Most typically developing children move frequently from position to position. They move as the play evolves, toys move, or their comfort demands.

Transitions between developmental positions depend on postural alignment (Alexander et al., 1993). They develop as a natural outgrowth of shifting weight. In fact, early transitions (e.g., rolling from belly to back) may occur first because children are unable to grade weight shifts and accidentally "fall" into new positions when they shift too far (Alexander et al., 1993). Gradually, as they gain greater control and stability, transitions become voluntary.

Transitioning from one position to another develops over time. It begins with rolling at 7–9 months of age and includes moving from sitting to hands and knees (8–10 months), from sitting to belly (8–12 months), pulling to stand (8–10 months), cruising along a low surface (9–13 months), getting down from standing (9–11 months), and standing from squatting or hands and knees (12–15 months) (Piper & Darrah, 1994). No doubt transitioning both reflects and contributes to the development of postural control.

II. D. How does the child move through the environment? How independent is the child? How good is the quality?

There are many ways of moving through the environment, and the play of young children generally incorporates a number of them. For example, children may walk or crawl, they may skip or hop, or they may ride a tricycle or use a walker or a wheelchair. As with developmental positions, however, children use only those actions that make sense in the context of their play. For example, children who can walk rarely revert to crawling except when the play demands it (e.g., pretending to be an animal).

Typically developing children have acquired most locomotion skills by 15 months of age, although many skills (e.g., running and skipping) continue to be refined for months and even years (Burton & Miller, 1998; Folio & Fewell, 1983; Keogh & Sugden, 1985; Williams, 1983). Locomotion begins with pivoting while lying on the belly between 6 and 8 months of age and includes rolling, crawling on the belly (8–9 months), creeping on hands and knees (9–13 months), and walking (beginning about 12 months) (Piper & Darrah, 1994). More advanced locomotion skills develop somewhat later. Some, like running, begin at about a year and a half and are retained through much of life. Others, such as hopping and skipping, begin later (2½–3 years and 4½–5 years, respectively) (Keogh & Sugden, 1985; Seefeldt & Haubenstricker, 1982; Williams, 1983).

Of course, not all means of locomotion are possible or acceptable in all circumstances. For example, a child who can get around quite well riding a tricycle may not be allowed to use it at school or in church. Also, he or she may lack the skills to ride on hilly terrain or in the sand.

Children who have significant motor impairments may not be able to move through all environments independently or safely. Some expend a great deal of effort accomplishing what their peers find to be quite easy. When children have difficulty moving through the environment, we try to determine the cause. Any of a number of factors related to their motor capacity (e.g., postural control, muscle tone, bilateral coordination, motor planning) may contribute. However, the team should also examine the nature of the task and the conditions of the environment to find their role.

II. E. How well does the child use two body sides together? (Bilateral coordination)

The ability to use two sides of the body in a well-coordinated fashion is of major importance to children's sensorimotor functioning. The ability to use a lead hand and an assisting hand together to perform a skilled task in any spatial orientation with respect to the body is a major milestone in the long development of bilateral coordination (Keogh & Sugden, 1985; Williams, 1983). Many bilateral tasks involve the anticipation of future conditions (e.g., catching a ball with two hands). In addition to their bilateral demands, such tasks also are highly reliant on the ability to develop a postural set to support the action and on their motor planning abilities.

Several authors (Keogh & Sugden, 1985; Williams, 1983) have provided information about the development of bilateral limb usage; the following is a summary (Koomar & Bundy, 2002). However, because bilateral demands change so much as a result of body position, the specific task, and the circumstances surrounding the task, little can be said about the ages when children master various aspects of bilateral limb use.

- Bilateral movements develop earlier in the arms than in the legs.

- Bilateral coordination develops from discrete movements to progressively longer sequences.

- Symmetrical movements appear earlier than alternating movements.

While the assessment of bilateral coordination typically focuses on the limbs, especially the upper limbs, the concept actually refers to the entire body, including the trunk. To fully understand this concept, we might think of an imaginary line bisecting the body in the midsagittal plane where the right and left body sides meet. Because limb movements require postural support, one might think of trunk rotation that occurs with crossing the body midline in order to use a limb in contralateral space as reflecting, and contributing to, bilateral coordination.

Of course, if a child has significant differences between the left and right body sides, bilateral coordination will be affected negatively. Large differences between body sides generally reflect differences in muscle tone and postural control. In that case, a child is likely to use one hand for nearly everything and may fail to use the other hand, even to assist.

Another manifestation of poor bilateral coordination occurs in almost the opposite circumstance, when a child does not seem to have developed a clear preference for one hand over the other. That child may use the two hands interchangeably to do a particular task (i.e., eat with a utensil, throw a ball). Some children, especially those who are left handed, typically perform some tasks with the right hand and others with the left. This is *not* a reflection of poor bilateral coordination.

USING THE OBSERVATION GUIDELINES TO ASSESS GROSS MOTOR ACTIVITY

II. A. In general, how do you describe the child's gross motor movements? How much do gross motor problems interfere with function?

Before the team looks in detail at gross motor actions, they should observe them in general. Are children able to perform the actions expected at their chronological age? How good is the quality? How much effort do they expend? Do they enjoy gross motor play?

If gross motor actions seem to be a source of difficulty, the team should try to establish, in general, how great the concerns are. That is, are you looking at a problem that substantially interferes with play and other childhood occupations, or is it a problem that is present but interferes less than some other difficulties? Answering this question gives you a kind of mindset. Many children come for assessment with a number of difficulties. Some interfere with their functioning more than others. Some are more germane to what a particular child or family values. In making decisions about the relative emphases of intervention, the team will weigh each area of development carefully. For example, at some point in her development, the family of a child with relatively more involvement in her legs than her arms may decide to focus intervention on the things that she does best and most easily rather than on walking. Thus, her goals may emphasize arm and hand skill, play, or dressing.

II. B. What positions does the child play in?

When administering TPBA, we "handle" children minimally. We prefer instead to obtain as much information as possible by observing. We emphasize how the child's ability to assume or maintain a position is affected by the play and by the environment. What factors increase the child's abilities? Which decrease them? Can the child develop a postural set in anticipation of events that will affect his ability to remain in a position?

II. C. How independent is the child when moving between positions?

Of course, some children can play only in positions in which they are placed. They cannot move out of that position without help. Then, it is important to find out from caregivers about the positions in which the child usually plays, to place or help the child into those positions, and then observe. Among the things we will observe is how much assistance the child needs to remain in the position (including the assistance of furniture or adaptive equipment) and how well the child can play with toys.

"W" sitting is a common observation. The relative advantages of W sitting from a child's point of view and the disadvantages from caregivers' perspective often lead to battles. Teams must weigh the costs and benefits for each child. When a decision is made to minimize or eliminate W sitting, team members have to work very hard to help the child develop an acceptable alternative (i.e., easy to assume and where hands are free). Besides W sitting, children may assume other unusual positions for playing. Team members always must weigh the benefits and disadvantages to come up with the best solution.

II. D. How does the child move through the environment?
How independent is the child? How good is the quality?

The TPBA team need not assess each gross motor action that children might be capable of using for locomotion. Rather, the team should evaluate those that occur spontaneously as the child plays. Take note of which actions occur and how closely they match the child's chronological age. Assess their quality. Are the actions similar to those of typically developing peers? Do the actions appear unusual? How safe is the child? How much effort does the child expend? Again, be prepared to emphasize how the child's ability to perform actions is affected by the play and by the environment. What factors increase the child's abilities? Which decrease them?

Bunny hopping (moving hands and then knees together) is a means of locomoting that has many of the same advantages and disadvantages as W sitting. As with W sitting, team members will have to work very hard to help the child develop an acceptable alternative if they wish to eliminate bunny hopping or any other form of locomotion that is effective but possibly detrimental to joints.

II. E. How well does the child use two body sides together? (Bilateral coordination)

In assessing the quality of bilateral coordination, the team should observe for both symmetry and asymmetry. Do the two body sides appear similar in size? Can the child can use them together for tasks that demand both hands or feet (e.g., clapping, pedaling a bicycle)? Because performing gross motor tasks that require use of the hands together at midline can be particularly demanding, the team should try to observe activities that involve this skill. Playing catch with (or rolling) a tennis ball can be a particularly good activity for this; it also allows the team to observe other bilateral skills (e.g., crossing midline). Table-top activities are also good for observing play at midline.

Midline crossing generally occurs together with trunk rotation; they should happen spontaneously but not because the child is asked to do it. The problem is with a tendency not to cross rather than an inability. We see midline crossing and trunk rotation particularly well in ball games when the ball comes relatively near the midline. If the ball is near the extremes of reach, it will be far more natural to catch it with only one hand. Again, table-top activities also work well.

We expect most preschoolers to have developed a preferred hand and we will see that in the context of tasks such as throwing, batting, or sweeping, and also in reaching and skilled or fine motor tasks. Does the child always use the same hand to do the same task?

We also want to be sure that the child has a good assisting hand. That hand holds objects that the preferred hand is acting on. When the skills of the assisting hand are well developed, the child can use it to orient objects for action. This may be easiest to see in the context of activities demanding manipulation.

Sequences of bilateral actions are particularly difficult and we look for opportunities to see how children handle them. Can they maintain rhythmic sequences over multiple repetitions? Clapping and jumping games are particularly good for observing repetitive bilateral actions. Propelling a swing or Sit 'n Spin (Playskool/Hasbro) also serves the same purpose. Symmetrical sequences where the hands or feet are acting in concert are easier than reciprocal sequences (see also TPBA2 Observation Guidelines, p. 45, IV. Motor Planning and Coordination).

Finally, observe activities where the child uses arms and legs together. Running fast, pumping arms and legs, is a good example. The child's actions should appear smooth and easy.

When assessing bilateral coordination, concentrate on observing actions that occur spontaneously. If the team is curious about whether a child can perform a specific action, ask the play facilitator to create a situation in which that action may occur spontaneously. If unable to elicit a particular action, the team should ask the parents if the child is able to perform the action.

William is a charming 4-year-old with a diagnosis of spina bifida. He attends a local preschool with his typically developing peers. William will begin kindergarten in the coming school year. His parents are concerned about how he will get around the school building and grounds. So far, they have avoided getting him a wheelchair, as they are worried that he might lose his motivation for walking. His means of locomotion, as well as other concerns regarding his school placement, are the major impetus for his evaluation.

William is able to creep on hands and knees independently, and this is his primary means of locomotion at home and in preschool. He also uses an adapted tricycle powered with his arms. During TPBA, William went everywhere he wanted to go by creeping. Although he recently began working with his physical therapist on using a walker and standing structure, he cannot use them safely without assistance. The team observed William using his equipment when he arrived. Later, they let him choose the way he got around.

William's family and the team agreed that one important focus of his intervention should be on locomotion in preparation for going to school. They discussed several options. William could use the tricycle in the hallways and on the playground but not in the classroom. Although he could creep in the classroom, and no doubt would some of the time, they all felt that creeping should not be his only means of getting around. They settled on two goals. One goal pertained to an intensive course of physical therapy to gauge the rate of his progress using the equipment. The second goal involved being fitted for a wheelchair. The team agreed that there were times when William would need to get somewhere quickly and when neither the tricycle nor the walker would be practical (e.g., fire drills, class trips). As much as they had been reluctant initially, William's parents completely embraced the decision. William was getting too big for the stroller they used in the community and, besides, they felt neighbor children viewed him as babyish when he rode in it.

William's family found the opportunity to share their fears, thoughts, and common observations with the whole team to be very valuable. They had begun the assessment process adamantly opposed to a wheelchair, a solution that they ultimately embraced. The process changed them and their opinions. They felt supported as full team members and came to see how the chair would be a benefit at home as well as at school.

III. Arm and Hand Use

Together, our arms and hands are our primary means of interacting with objects and an important way of communicating socially; they can be practical, creative, or social. The arm allows the hand to extend into space and orient itself to act on any object. The hand, in turn, can be a platform, a hook, a vise, or a pointer (Henderson & Pehoski, 1995).

With our arms and hands, we act on objects directly: reaching, grasping, manipulating, poking, prodding, and exploring. We also operate tools that, in turn, give our manipulations greater precision or force. We can catch a football in mid air, use a hammer or pliers, thread a needle, or play a flute (Henderson & Pehoski, 1995).

We also gesture, speak, and express emotion with our arms and hands. We can use them to deliver a caress, a slap, or a playful punch. We can say, "I love you," "Come here," or "Go away" (Henderson & Pehoski, 1995).

The hand movements required for precise manipulation are among the most advanced of all motor skills, requiring both conscious control and significant sensory input and feedback. Their complexity is reflected in a long developmental period, continuing into early adolescence (Henderson & Pehoski, 1995). Many types of disabling conditions result in difficulties with arm and hand use.

Because many tasks requiring skilled arm and hand use also have accompanying visual demands (e.g., ball games, arts and crafts), we often simultaneously observe eye–hand (visual-motor) coordination. Children commonly have concomitant difficulty with eye–hand coordination and skilled hand use.

▪▪▪▪▪ **III. A. In general, how do you describe the child's arm and hand use?**
How much do problems with arm and hand use interfere with function?

The team should begin by examining children's overall arm and hand use. In the general assessment, ask a number of questions. Is the child able to perform desired actions (effectiveness)? How well (efficiency, quality)? How easily (how much effort)?

Children may be able to use their arms and hands to accomplish tasks, but the quality of their movements may not be good and they may expend a lot of energy performing tasks that should be quite simple. Cutting with scissors provides a good example. By age 7, typically developing children are fairly skilled with scissors (Exner, 2001). They automatically insert thumb and middle finger into the loops and cut quickly and rhythmically, opening the scissors in proportion to the thickness of the paper. The assisting hand deftly holds the paper, repositioning it with each snip. Children who have difficulty cutting with scissors often find each step to be a "drama," beginning with the decision of which fingers to insert in the loops. They may have difficulty stabilizing with the little finger side of the hand. The actual cutting motion may be arrhythmic, reflecting variations in the amount of opening of the scissors. The assisting hand presents another kind of problem. Children may be unable to prevent it from opening and closing with the scissors so the paper drops. They may be unable to maintain the timing and rhythm of moving the paper so that there is a lot of stop–start in the cutting.

Another important aspect to observe is how much children enjoy play requiring arm and hand skill. Children who find arm and hand use difficult often avoid toys and activities that require intricate hand and finger movements or skilled use of eyes and hands together. A preference for big motor actions with few skill demands (e.g., roughhousing) over activities requiring precise skill may simply represent choice, especially for boys. However, if it co-occurs with difficulty performing tasks the child needs to do (e.g., self-care, preacademic tasks) or wants to do (e.g., sports), then it may reflect dysfunction (Clifford & Bundy, 1989).

When arm and hand use are a source of difficulty, the team should first establish how great the concerns are. That is, are we looking at a problem that substantially interferes with function, or is it a problem that interferes, but perhaps less than some other difficulties? Or, conversely, is the problem so great that adaptations will be required if the child is to carry out required activities that have a significant arm or hand skill component? For example, does it seem likely that the computer will be the best means for a particular child to write? As in the previous discussion of gross motor actions, answering this question helps with prioritizing and developing intervention plans.

III. B. How well is the child able to reach?

Reaching gets the hand into position to grasp an object. Reach is dependent on vision as well as touch and proprioception (a sense derived from muscles); hence, the term *eye–hand coordination.* The initial reaching movement is accomplished quite quickly and under proprioceptive control; this motion gets the hand to the approximate place where it will contact an object. As the hand moves closer to the object, it slows down and vision becomes more important for shaping the hand and orienting it to the object. The smaller the object, the slower the final approach (Rösblad, 1995).

Timing often is an important part of reach. Timing is particularly significant when the object is moving or is very small. Unless reaching is timed very precisely, it will be unsuccessful (Keogh & Sugden, 1985). As the reach comes to an end, the hand should be in position to act on the object; this requires that it be oriented with respect to the object and the action that will follow. Reaching, orienting the hand, and preparing to act on the object occur simultaneously (Rösblad, 1995). Thus, we will use the term "reach" to refer to the combined functions that get the hand where it is going in order to act on an object.

Very young infants are not able to obtain toys by reaching. However, by about 6 months of age, reaching movements are developing well. That is, the trajectory of movement contains fewer instances of speeding up and slowing down to get the hand near the place where it will contact the object. By 9 months of age, infants can prepare for grasping by adjusting the opening of the hand to match the object size. By 13 months of age, the timing of the opening of the hand is similar to that of adults. Early reaches are bilateral but as children gain postural control and can sit, they are more able to perform unilateral reaches (Rösblad, 1995).

Although little is known about the reaching skills of children whose development is atypical, several factors are likely to affect them, particularly in children with neurological impairments. These include poor postural control, poor timing of movements, and lack of correspondence between vision and proprioception or between proprioception from one body side to another. These difficulties mean that reaching will take longer and be less accurate, especially when the object is not stationary (Erhardt, 1992; Rösblad, 1995).

III. C. How effective is the child's grasp?

Grasping an object is synonymous with capturing it. Following the capture, the object is manipulated, used, transported, or held. A grasp is efficient when any size object can be captured with an economy of movement and in such a way that it is available for the next action. That sort of efficiency typically will develop over the first 2 years (Case-Smith, 1995).

When infants are first learning to grasp voluntarily, around 20–24 weeks, they use the ulnar (little finger) side of the hand. The thumb has little involvement. Thus, "captured objects" must be relatively large. Following grasp, the object will be in place for holding or transporting but not manipulating (Case-Smith, 1995).

Over the next 18 months, several overlapping aspects of grasp and forearm use will develop to enable an efficient capture. Grasp will move gradually from the ulnar side of the hand to the radial (thumb) side. The thumb begins to be active at about 24 weeks of age. By 36 weeks of age, a "scissors" grasp (i.e., prehension of a small object between the thumb and the side of the first finger) is common. At 40 weeks, the child is able to oppose the thumb against the pads of the fingers in an inferior pincer grasp. Not until children reach their first birthdays are they able to grasp tiny objects deftly between the tips of the thumb and fingers (superior pincer) without the aid of external stability (Case-Smith, 1995).

The efficiency and effectiveness of grasping depends on being able to orient the forearms so that the fingers are facing toward the object. Initially, the child keeps the forearms pronated. At about 28 weeks, the child will be able to supinate the forearm sufficiently to bring objects held between the radial fingers and palm to the mouth (Case-Smith, 1995). With increasing skill, the child will be able to orient the hand and forearm to any position required for deft prehension, and this movement will occur concurrently with reaching.

Another herald of the increasing efficiency of grasp is a decreased need for external stability. At about 20 weeks, the child's only hope for capturing an object is pulling it along the support surface to meet the other hand and squeezing it into that hand. This is not a true grasp. Even at 40 weeks, the child will need to stabilize the forearm on the surface while grasping small objects between the thumb and forefinger (inferior pincer). External support is replaced with increased stability of the hand itself. One example of this is a child's ability to stabilize with the ulnar side of the hand while using the radial side for grasping, which also often occurs in conjunction with the superior pincer grasp at about 1 year of age. Once children no longer need to stabilize the hand externally, they can easily grasp objects in any orientation and from any surface (Case-Smith, 1995).

Grasp also improves as the arches and intrinsic muscles of the hand develop. Several important observations tell us arches are developing. Although not obviously related to grasp, developing arches are visible as children bear weight on their hands. Because of arches, the hand does not appear flat and the child can move over the hands in a weight-bearing position (e.g., when shifting weight or rocking) (Boehme, 1988). More clearly related to grasp, as arches develop, children can bring the fingertips and thumb into opposition and hold objects with relatively extended fingers. Thus, the superior pinch, described above and present by about 1 year, also reflects arch development. This refined grasp, enabled by the presence of arches in the hand, enables the child to grasp more effectively and efficiently (Case-Smith, 1995).

As the child becomes able to control isolated fingers and move the two sides of the hand independently, grasp also becomes more efficient. By 1 year, the child is able to isolate the index finger for poking and can hold two small objects in one hand. These abilities will continue to improve over the next 6 months. Increasingly efficient grasp also means that a child can adapt to the weight and shape of an object to be captured.

We expect 18-month-olds to be able to pick up and hold small, relatively fragile objects (e.g., cracker, paper cup) without crushing them. Two-year-olds are able to adjust their grip to a variety of weights. However, even 8-year-olds continue to have more variable ability than adults (Eliasson, 1995). Similarly, children must learn to adjust their force to match the size of an object; this ability does not begin to develop until age 3 and is not complete until at least 7 years of age (Eliasson, 1995).

▦▦▦ **III. D. How well does the child release objects?**

Captured objects invariably have to be released. Because release follows grasp functionally, it is perhaps not surprising that it also lags behind developmentally. The precursor to release occurs when a child pulls an object out of one hand and into the other or uses an external surface to assist in rolling the object out of the fingers (about 28 weeks of age). That same child has been practicing grasping for 4–8 weeks. Active release will not begin until 40–44 weeks and even then it might best be described as "flinging," as it often involves elbow and wrist finger movement as well as widely opened fingers (Case-Smith, 1995; Erhardt, 1994).

Only at 1 year, when children can deftly grasp tiny objects, are they beginning to release without fully opening the hand. This is known as "controlled release." However, for the next 6 months, children must stabilize the forearm against a support surface to release small objects accurately. Not until about age 2 will the child adjust the amount of opening of the fingers to accommodate for the object's precise size and shape (Case-Smith, 1995; Erhardt, 1994).

▦▦▦ **III. E. How well does the child isolate finger movements for pointing, poking, and tapping?**

By 1 year, children can use the index finger separately from the other fingers to poke at and turn small objects so that they can be captured easily. This skill appears at about the same time as children develop the ability to hold a small object between the thumb and tip of the index finger (Case-Smith, 1995). Both skills are related, as both reflect increased separation of the two sides of the hand and increased ability to skillfully use fingers on the radial (thumb) side of the hand.

Although children are capable of separating the index finger from the others by 1 year, they generally do not use one isolated finger on toys that require any degree of force (e.g., toy piano, cash register) until they are 15–18 months of age. Even then they may prefer to use more than one finger.

Isolated finger use will continue to develop for some time. The ability to use isolated movements of all fingers (e.g., on a keyboard or piano) will not develop until 10–12 years of age and will require exposure and training (Case-Smith & Weintraub, 2002).

Activities that require isolated finger movements generally involve vision; however, once they are learned, they depend more on input from the muscles (Case-Smith & Weintraub, 2002). Most activities that involve isolated movements of multiple fingers are done quickly and sequentially. They involve anticipation and, thus, will involve motor planning.

▦▦▦ **III. F. How effective is the child's in-hand manipulation?**

Although release is more difficult than grasp, the ability to adjust the placement of an object within that hand prior to use or release is more difficult yet; in fact, it is the most skilled of all hand actions. Fine tuning the position of an object without using external support is known as in-hand manipulation. In keeping with their level of difficulty, in-hand manipulations may not be fully developed until a child is nearly 7 years of age. Even when children are capable of performing certain in-hand manipulations, they may choose not to use them (Exner, 1992, 2001; Pehoski, 1995).

Unlike many other hand skills, in-hand manipulation does not depend much on vision. Rather, touch and proprioception are most important. To be successful at in-hand manipulation requires holding the object tightly enough not to drop it but loosely enough to be able to move it (Pehoski, 1995).

Three basic types of in-hand manipulations have been described (Exner, 1992, 2001; Pehoski, 1995). The first involves using the thumb to move an object from palm to fingertips or fingertips to palm. This is known as *translation.* Children use translations, for example, when moving coins or food into or out of "storage" in the palm (Exner, 1992, 2001; Pehoski, 1995).

The second type of in-hand manipulation involves rotating an object between the fingers and thumb. When the object is rotated just a little, it is called a *simple rotation.* Simple rotations occur, for example, when repositioning a crayon held initially with the sharpened end pointing to the little finger side. When an object is rotated more than 180 degrees, a complex rotation is used. A complex rotation can be seen, for example, when a child holding a crayon in the palm of the hand with the sharpened end on the thumb side turns it (within the hand) to the typical position for drawing (Exner, 1992, 2001; Pehoski, 1995).

Finally, when an object is moved a small distance linearly, the in-hand manipulation is known as a *shift.* Shifts occur, for example, when moving the fingers down a crayon toward the point or when fanning playing cards (Exner, 1992, 2001; Pehoski, 1995).

Each type of in-hand manipulation may be done with or without "stabilization" (i.e., simultaneously holding another object in the ring and little fingers). Clearly, in-hand manipulation with stabilization is more difficult than without, and it develops later (Exner, 1992, 2001; Pehoski, 1995).

Even among the three basic types of in-hand manipulation (i.e., translation, rotation, and shift), there is a hierarchy of difficulty associated with the timing of emergence. Finger to palm translations are the easiest, appearing in some instances as young as 12–15 months of age when the child repositions a cracker or toy. Palm to finger translations and simple rotations (e.g., opening a jar lid) emerge between 2 and 2½ years. Shifts and complex rotations are more difficult; most 4- or 5-year-olds are capable of doing them, but they may not be seen reliably until about 6½ years. Even once young children are capable of these difficult skills, they do not necessarily *choose* to use them unless asked specifically. Skill at in-hand manipulation continues to develop through 12 years of age (Case-Smith & Weintraub, 2002; Exner, 1992, 2001; Pehoski, 1995).

Not all objects are equal when it comes to in-hand manipulation. A child who is able to manipulate one object in a particular way may not be able to use the same manipulation on an object of a different size or shape. In general, small objects are easier to manipulate than either large or tiny objects. Tiny objects require precise control with the fingertips, and large objects require skilled use of several fingers (Exner, 1992, 2001; Pehoski, 1995).

III. G. How good are the child's constructional abilities?

Constructional play involves putting things together. Placing toys in a container, stacking blocks, putting pegs in a peg board, and doing puzzles are common examples. Constructional play makes use of all the hand skills we have described above; it also relies heavily on vision and visual perception, touch, proprioception, and cognition. Children begin stacking blocks at about 1 year of age. Toddlers can stack multiple blocks and do simple puzzles and pegboards. By age 3 or 4, children build elaborate three-dimensional structures and put together interlocking puzzles. Construction continues to develop for many years and is reflected in crafts and school projects (Case-Smith & Weintraub, 2002).

III. H. How effectively does the child use tools?

Children use all kinds of tools—from hammers to pencils and tweezers. The purpose of tools differs widely from banging and making noise to drawing and cutting. Thus, it is not surprising that the hand skills required to use tools also vary widely from the very gross movements used on a hammer to precise finger movements used for writing. In addition to hand skills, tool use depends heavily on vision. Because force is involved, proximal stability also is important.

Striking one object with another happens when batting, hitting, or hammering. In each of these cases, children use the striking implement as though it is an extension of the arm to impart force to another object. Hammering develops very early. By 1 year of age, children bang with a spoon on the table surface, and by 1½–2 years they can use sticks and toy hammers. The movements required for such play are gross and unrefined. Initially, banging occurs from movements at the shoulder (Case-Smith & Weintraub, 2002).

Striking with a bat or toy golf club is done with a sidearm movement (Williams, 1983). Guidelines exist with regard to ages and stages associated with striking, a skill that appears by age 2 and is relatively mature by age 5 (Williams, 1983) but continues to be refined until 8 or 9 (Seefeldt & Haubenstricker, 1982). The motor requirements for striking are quite similar to those of throwing. The child must move the limbs to contact the object and finish at the time they contact it. They also must generate sufficient postural control to support their limb movements (Keogh & Sugden, 1985).

Drawing, writing, and cutting with scissors also are important examples of tool use that begin very early and continue across the life span. They involve precise finger movements. The contributions of vision, touch, and proprioception will continue to be significant; cognition also is increasingly important.

Two-year-olds scribble with a marker or crayon (Ziviani, 1995). By age 3, they copy lines and circles and can copy a cross (Folio & Fewell, 1983). They may hold the marker between the thumb and first two fingers (as adults do) but their movements will not be from the fingers until they are 4 or older. They may also be able to snip with scissors (Case-Smith & Weintraub, 2002), but scissors skills will continue to develop through age 6.

Difficulties with handwriting often contribute to referrals to specialist teams. Handwriting is a very complex function because it is dependent on cognitive abilities, such as sensorimotor; this is well beyond the scope of this section. However, while grasping a pencil with the thumb and first two fingers and writing with finger movements (dynamic tripod) is the most desirable pencil grasp, numerous other grasps are acceptable. Poor pencil grip alone is not a reason for concern (Ziviani, 1995).

████ USING THE OBSERVATION GUIDELINES TO ASSESS ARM AND HAND USE

████ III. A. In general, how do you describe the child's arm and hand use?
How much do problems with arm and hand use interfere with function?

Before looking in detail at arm and hand skills, the team members should observe them in general. Are children able to perform the actions expected at their chronological age? How good is the quality? How much effort do they expend? Do they enjoy play involving arm and hand use?

If arm and hand skills seem to be a source of difficulty, the team should try to establish, in general, how great the concerns are. That is, are we looking at a problem that substantially interferes with play and other childhood occupations, or is it a problem that is present, but interferes less than some other difficulties? Is the problem so great that we need to consider adaptive equipment to minimize the motor demands associated with play and school?

III. B. How well is the child able to reach?

Reaching is easy to observe in the context of TPBA. Children reach virtually every time they attempt to acquire any object. The most relevant factors seem to be accuracy and directness of movements. Good postural support for reach also is critical. Can the child reach with both arms simultaneously? When only one arm is required, can he or she use either arm equally well? How accurate is he or she at getting the hands precisely to the place where the object is located? Is he or she apt to knock into the object? Is the reaching direct or characterized by extraneous movements? As the hand approaches the object, is the palm facing it? Does the child's posture support reaching?

III. C. How effective is the child's grasp?

Grasp also is easy to observe, as it occurs every time a child picks up an object. If children have access to objects of numerous sizes and shapes, then examiners should take the opportunity to observe the ways in which tasks affect grasp. Several factors are relevant. First, how is the forearm oriented? Are the fingers and palm pointing directly to the object? Where in the hand is the object captured? Is it held by the fingertips and thumb or by fingers against the palm? Which fingers are used: ring and little finger or index and middle finger? Is the thumb active? Does the hand appear flat or nicely arched? How does the size of object affect grasp? Can the child isolate the two sides of the hand? Can he or she hold more than one object in his or her hand at a time? Observe how much external stability is required. Can the child pick up objects without having to rest the hand on the table? How does the size of the object affect the need for external stability? Finally, observe the quality of grasp. Does it appear easy and efficient?

III. D. How well does the child release objects?

Every time a child places an object, throws it, or drops it into a container, the team can observe release. If the child has access to objects of varying sizes and shapes, and the circumstances of release vary, examiners will have the opportunity to observe how objects and tasks affect release. Probably the most important aspect of release is accuracy. That is, does the object land where it was intended to go? When release is well developed, the child will be able to release accurately and easily even as his arm moves (carry).

The size and shape of the target and whether it is moving or stationary also will have a marked effect on release. The child's ability to grade the opening of the hand so that it is in proportion with the size of the object also will affect accuracy. In very young or relatively unskilled children, the team should be particularly concerned with the degree to which release is voluntary. Can the child release without using one hand to pull the object out of the other? Without the need for an external surface (e.g., table top, mouth, body part)? Without flinging it?

III. E. How well does the child isolate finger movements for pointing, poking, and tapping?

Pointing and poking appear similar but have completely different purposes and therefore will be seen under very different circumstances. Children point when they want to show something to another person or request something. They poke for the purpose of positioning small objects so that they can be grasped easily or to explore small spaces. The team should observe whether children are able to separate the index finger from the others to poke and point. Are the remaining fingers folded out of the way? Do the actions appear easy and smooth?

The ability to isolate all of the fingers for tasks such as keyboarding develops only with instruction and practice. It is not apt to be developed until at least 10 years of age.

▦▦▦▦ **III. F. How effective is the child's in-hand manipulation?**

In-hand manipulations occur when children need to reposition objects that have been grasped so that they can be used. Pencils, crayons, and pegs are particularly good for eliciting certain in-hand manipulations spontaneously. Depositing coins into a bank or other small objects into containers with small openings also provides opportunities to see spontaneous in-hand manipulation. For very young children, a cookie or cracker placed in the palm may provide adequate reason to perform an in-hand manipulation. When children are successful with in-hand manipulation, they reposition the object by using the fingers and thumb of one hand without using an external surface (e.g., the other hand, the mouth, table top). During TPBA, team members should focus on which in-hand manipulations the child uses spontaneously. If a member wants to see one in-hand manipulation in particular, make sure that the play activity demands it. Try not to disrupt the play session unnecessarily by asking the child to perform these difficult actions without good reason. In-hand manipulations are difficult and children may choose not to perform them even when they are capable of doing so. Thus, verbal requests, and even demonstration, may be necessary in some cases.

▦▦▦▦ **III. G. How good are the child's constructional abilities?**

Activities that involve construction and tool use are favorites of many children and many children's toys promote them. Examiners are, of course, interested in the quality of the finished construction (e.g., is it well organized; if it is copied, how well does it match the model) as well as the arm and hand skills described above. However, in addition to sensory and motor skills, construction and tool use also depend on cognition. Thus, Observation Guidelines related to cognition also are relevant (see Chapter 7).

▦▦▦▦ **III. H. How effectively does the child use tools?**

When observing constructional abilities, the team members should be interested in how effectively and efficiently children are able to use the materials. How easy is construction, and does the child seem to find constructional tasks enjoyable? Because construction is the basis for many common play and school activities, ease and enjoyment are very important.

Devon is a bright, mischievous 6-year-old boy with a diagnosis of athetoid cerebral palsy. He is integrated into the first grade class in his home school where he uses a number of strategies for expressing what he has learned (e.g., pointing and an electronic communication device). He has several good friends in the class. Despite his limited verbal ability, Devon and his friends have devised a number of activities that they enjoy doing together. The impetus for Devon's TPBA was, in part, based on his family's concerns about Devon's arm and hand use. Whereas most children interact with objects and communicate by using their arms and hands, Devon's arm use is characterized by involuntary movements and very delayed skills for grasp and release. His family is beginning to wonder whether Devon will ever use his hands in a functional way. They do not want his creative abilities to be hindered unnecessarily by his poor upper extremity use. They are wondering whether they should begin to focus on use of the computer and other devices rather than on developing better arm use.

During TPBA, Devon chose to play with action figures. However, when he reached for them, his movements were erratic and characterized by involuntary rotary movements. He could not aim his hand directly at a figure. However, Devon was very determined to play with the figures and his motions became gradually more refined until his hand landed on the toy. Devon's parents reported that this reaching is typical of his approach to any toy with which he is highly motivated to play.

When Devon contacted the action figure, his hand was oriented thumb down. Although that meant that he could grasp the figure between his thumb and forefinger, his fingertips were not involved and he could not rotate his forearm so that he could see it. Thus, although he captured the figure, he could not really use it, nor could he control the force with which he grasped it. Again, Devon's parents reported that this was typical of his grasp of similar objects.

Following the assessment, the team thought carefully about intervention. They reasoned that Devon was unlikely to develop refined grasp, release, or in-hand manipulation and that his cognitive and creative abilities far outstripped his hand skills. Thus, they felt that intervention would more effectively work toward other means for expressing himself and "manipulating" objects (e.g., virtual reality). However, given the great pleasure Devon got from manipulating his action figures, they also agreed to continue work on reach and gross grasp to support his preferences for play.

IV. Motor Planning and Coordination

Accomplishing a task involves more than simply executing it. At the very least, it also requires an idea of what to do and a plan for carrying it out. The idea is a major determinant of what actions look like. Motor planning allows the actions to happen in a well-coordinated manner. Planning is especially important in tasks that a child has not mastered. Poor motor planning manifests as poor coordination and shows up in a number of different ways (Case-Smith & Weintraub, 2002; Rodger et al., 2003; Smits-Engelsman, Wilson, Westenberg, & Duysens, 2003). For example, children with poor motor planning frequently have difficulty using the two sides of the body together in a well-coordinated fashion, and they may also have postural difficulties (Geuze, 2003; Johnston, Burns, Brauer, & Richardson, 2002; Wann, Mon-Williams, & Rushton, 1998).

IV. A. Does the child have good ideas for using toys?

Children who have good ideas are easy to spot. They often lead the play, even at a very young age, turning clothes poles into swords and an old shoe into a Thanksgiving turkey. In creating the idea, children "size up" toys and situations and envision what they can *do*; thus, the tie with motor planning. The idea often comes from past experience in the same or a similar situation. Having an idea is dependent, in large part, on cognitive ability and memory. When children have difficulty formulating an idea, they may have difficulty learning how to use new toys or recognizing similarities among toys or objects (Cermak & Larkin, 2002; Keogh & Sugden, 1985; Reeves & Cermak, 2002; Sugden & Keogh, 1990; Williams, 1983).

IV. B. How well does the child initiate, terminate, and sequence actions?

Children with poor motor planning may have difficulty initiating actions, seen as false starts. Terminating actions may be equally problematic, as a child may knock over a milk carton or run into a classmate or the wall. Problems with changing direction when running or even writing letters on lined paper may be related.

Difficulty with sequencing actions is a major characteristic of planning difficulties (Cermak & Larkin, 2002; Reeves & Cermak, 2002). Some children have difficulty even with simple action sequences, such as moving around the corner of a jungle gym.

Performing smooth sequences of repetitive actions also can be particularly difficult for children with poor motor planning. For example, they may turn the wheel on the

Sit 'n Spin once or twice but lose the rhythm quickly. Similarly, they may hop a few times in a relatively coordinated fashion but be unable to continue all the way across the "pond" (floor). The more structure the task imposes, the harder it is. Hopping from one "lily pad" (Hula Hoop) to another may require numerous pauses to reorient the body, especially if the lily pads are not arranged in a straight line (Reeves & Cermak, 2002).

In addition to sequencing actions, children with motor planning difficulties also are likely to have difficulty sequencing tasks. For example, intending to take a toy outside, a child may fail to pick it up from its resting place beside the door hinge *before* opening the door, making the toy inaccessible.

▬▬▬ IV. C. How good are the child's spatial and temporal abilities?

Difficulty with meeting the spatial and temporal demands of motor tasks is another major characteristic of poor motor planning. Spatiotemporal demands are in direct proportion to the movement of the child, the size of the target, and the target's relative movement in the environment (Keogh & Sugden, 1985; Sugden & Keogh, 1990).

Demands are minimized when a relatively still child acts on a large, stable object. For example, the spatiotemporal demand for a child sitting on the floor and rolling a ball toward a wall is not very great. However, demands are increased when the child must catch a ball. They change only a little when the child catches a beach ball thrown directly at her but quite a bit more when she must run to intercept a softball thrown to right field (Keogh & Sugden, 1985; Sugden & Keogh, 1990).

Children who have poor motor planning often have difficulty catching or kicking a ball. They fail to move the hands or foot to the proper location in time to intercept it. Consequently, they may trap the ball against the body in order to "catch" it or stop it before kicking. From a spatiotemporal perspective, riding a bicycle is a reasonably difficult task. Whereas propelling the bike is easy, avoiding obstacles is much harder. The faster the child is riding, the greater the spatiotemporal demand. Environmental conditions like rain or wind gusts only add to the difficulty as they make the task less predictable (Ayres, 1985; Keogh & Sugden, 1985; Reeves & Cermak, 2002; Sugden & Keogh, 1990; Williams, 1983).

▬▬▬ IV. D. Does the child seem to have a good sense of the body? Of objects as an extension of the body?

Many children who have poor motor planning lack an innate understanding of the relationships among their body parts and the precise location of their bodies in space (i.e., body scheme). They may position themselves poorly on furniture or equipment, resulting in awkward or unsafe actions. They often appear to be "fighting," rather than working with, play objects and equipment. Furthermore, they may not adjust the size of the body effectively and efficiently when moving into small spaces, especially when carrying objects. Either they fail to arrange body parts so that they are "small enough" to fit or they "shrink" the body excessively, expending more energy than necessary (Reeves & Cermak, 2002).

▬▬▬ IV. E. How well does the child organize clothing and personal space?

Perhaps reflecting their poor body scheme, children with motor planning difficulties often appear disheveled and their clothing awry. Their apparent disorganization of self also may extend to the play space (Ayres, 1972, 1985; Cermak & Larkin, 2002; Reeves & Cermak, 2002).

IV. F. Does the child generate appropriate force?

Generating the proper amount of force needed for a task provides a barrier for many children with poor motor planning. Frequently, they generate too much force, performing actions too hard or too fast. Exaggerated force results in broken toys and implements; it also leads to fatigue. In contrast, some children with motor planning difficulties fail to generate enough force to perform tasks successfully. They appear weak; their drawings or writing may be illegible (Ayres, 1972, 1985; Reeves & Cermak, 2002).

IV. G. Does the child perform actions in response to verbal request or demonstration?

The ability to perform motor tasks in response to a verbal request or modeling also reflects planning. However, in addition to or instead of the problems described above, those children may have language- or vision-based difficulties (Cermak & Larkin, 2002; Reeves & Cermak, 2002).

USING THE OBSERVATION GUIDELINES TO ASSESS MOTOR PLANNING AND COORDINATION

Motor planning occurs in the context of skilled activity that children have not yet mastered; it occurs in many play situations. Motor planning has many facets and children can be relatively better at some than at others. As with all abilities represented in TPBA, the team should try to observe motor planning as unobtrusively as possible.

When motor planning is good, actions appear smooth and well coordinated; they easily meet the demands of the task. When such is not the case and there is no other obvious reason, motor planning may be a problem. Poor motor planning results in poor coordination and delayed skill development. However, motor planning difficulties can be subtle. Thus, their assessment may require a skilled observer, such as an occupational or physical therapist, who is knowledgeable about what motor skills children have at particular ages and how well they are expected to perform those skills. Children with poor motor planning often have low muscle tone and poor posture; those Observation Guidelines also may be useful, as are those pertaining to gross motor ability and arm and hand use.

Assessing planning is a special challenge with young children and children who have cognitive limitations. Even though children may be unable to make their bodies do what they want them to do, their motor planning is not abnormal unless their problems are greater than those that can be accounted for by age or cognitive limitation (e.g., cerebral palsy) (Cermak & Larkin, 2002).

IV. A. Does the child have good ideas for using toys?

Having an idea is one important aspect of planning. Like all facets of planning, we see ideation most clearly when children encounter unfamiliar objects. If the team members only observe a child playing with his or her favorite toys, they may be simply observing well-learned actions or a script, perhaps borrowed from television, video, or another person. The teams should find out whether children have good ideas for using novel toys and whether they capitalize on features of the environment.

Similarly, children's ideational abilities are best seen when *they* lead the play. When examiners always suggest the next task or determine exactly how tasks will be done, children have little opportunity to demonstrate their ideational abilities. Ideation draws heavily on cognition. Thus, Chapter 7 also provides related Observation Guidelines.

▨▨▨▨ IV. B. How well does the child initiate, terminate, and sequence actions?

Sequencing also is difficult for children with poor motor planning. We observe whether children perform actions in a logical sequence. Sequencing in this context refers to sequences *within* a movement (e.g., shifting weight *before* attempting to move around the corner on the jungle gym). It is closely related to timing, because the sequence of actions must be completed with precise time. For example, logical sequencing allows a child to get her hands to the place where she needs them to be when the ball arrives.

Children with poor motor planning often find it difficult to maintain a rhythm. Perhaps that is, in part, because of the sequential nature of rhythmic actions. Observe whether they can hop or clap repeatedly and rhythmically. Can they propel a scooter board or a Sit 'n Spin for several seconds? Can they keep time to music?

▨▨▨▨ IV. C. How good are the child's spatial and temporal abilities?

The team should be particularly interested in children's abilities to meet the spatial and temporal demands of a task. How precisely do they move hands, feet, and the whole body? Do they initiate and terminate actions easily? Does the hand or foot make contact optimally with objects, or does the child frequently knock things over or make contact awkwardly?

Children who have poor motor planning invariably have difficulty with timing especially in the context of anticipatory actions. For example, a very young child or a child with poor motor planning may begin to extend his arms to catch a ball when the ball is at the optimal point for catching. By the time his hands get to that point, the ball will have moved beyond it. Likely, the ball will hit him in the chest and he will trap it there.

The team should look at several varieties of anticipatory actions, including those that involve the child moving as well as the target moving. Tasks that involve both target and child moving are the most difficult; the faster either moves, the harder the task. Can children intercept stationary objects when moving (e.g., kick a ball)? Can they intercept a moving object when standing still? When walking or running? Many anticipatory tasks are performed with both hands or both feet. Thus, the Observation Guidelines for bilateral coordination found in the gross motor activity section (II. E) also are relevant here.

▨▨▨▨ IV. D. Does the child seem to have a good sense of the body? Does the child seem to have a sense of objects as an extension of the body?

Planning how to carry out an action seems to depend on a sense of where the body is in space (i.e., body scheme). *Body scheme* is an abstract idea and not directly observable. Rather, the team should observe behaviors that suggest how good it might be. Do children use objects with ease? That is, do they work with objects or does it appear as though they are fighting them? Do they position themselves in the middle of chairs or riding toys? Or do they always look precarious or awkward? Can they move easily into, out of, and around in small spaces (e.g., tunnel, climber)?

▨▨▨▨ IV. E. How well does the child organize clothing and personal space?

Although the relationship to motor planning is not clear, children who have poor planning often are surrounded by disorganization. Their clothes appear disheveled; buttons may not be aligned with the proper buttonholes and shirt tails may be chronically untucked. The space where they play is chaotic, as are their closets and desk space. Of course, there are many reasons beyond those associated with motor planning for disorganization; cognition and emotional-social factors certainly play a role.

▨▨▨▨ IV. F. Does the child generate appropriate force?

Likely related to poor body scheme, children with poor motor planning often have difficulty generating the proper force for an action. For example, they may stomp around the room, sounding more like an elephant than a child. They may break toys because they use too much force. Their knuckles may turn white from exertion when gripping a pencil. No wonder they tire easily! Conversely, they may use so little force that actions are ineffective. Their drawings and writing may be illegible because they are so faint. They may be unable to push a chair across the floor or pull on a turtleneck.

▆▆▆▆ IV. G. Does the child perform actions in response to verbal request or demonstration?

Movement in response to a command or a model also requires motor planning. Like ideation, such actions are dependent on cognition. Thus, the Observation Guidelines in Chapter 7, again, are relevant. We pay close attention to whether imitation or verbal commands are easier. Although games such as Simon Says or Red Light, Green Light may be a good way to observe motor planning, asking children to imitate an action or move in a particular way can be very disruptive to play.

Five-year-old Andrew came for TPBA just before starting school. His preschool teacher had been worried about him for some time, but his parents, Ralph and Jill, believed he was simply immature. Andrew's pediatrician concurred until he watched Andrew really struggle to undress for an examination. Following his observations and further discussion with Jill, the physician recommended evaluation in a local outpatient facility.

Andrew chose to ride a scooter board during his evaluation. He was positioned on his stomach, pretending to make his "magic carpet" fly. Andrew had some difficulty getting on the scooter independently. He tended to place his body more to the right of the scooter. However, he seemed unaware of the problem until the scooter tipped. Even then, he did not realize that his positioning had caused the problem, and his play partner had to reposition him. When Andrew propelled his scooter all the way across the room, his play partner asked him if he could turn the scooter around and go the other way. Andrew got off of the scooter, turned it around, and got back on facing the direction he had been going initially. Even when he approached the wall, he seemed confused by what had happened. He and his play partner joked that she had "tricked him."

When Andrew played at a table laid out with art materials, his fine motor difficulties became evident. He "white knuckled" the kindergarten pencil and erased so hard that he put a hole in the paper. He tried to cut out some squares of colored paper to make a collage but resorted to tearing the paper instead. He had trouble separating his index finger to spread the paste on the paper. After 10 minutes, paper and paste were everywhere but where they were supposed to be.

The team translated Andrew's difficulties as reflecting poor motor planning. In fact, when they discussed their observations, they noted that most areas in the sensorimotor domain had several items that reflected concern. In contrast, their observations in the emotional-social, cognitive, and language domains were primarily listed as strengths. Putting all the pieces together, Ralph and Jill suddenly had a whole new perspective on many of Andrew's behaviors. The team developed goals for helping prepare Andrew for school. They were able to develop strategies for meeting those goals that utilized Andrew's many strengths and addressed his limitations.

V. Modulation of Sensation and Its Relationship to Emotion, Activity Level, and Attention ▆▆▆▆▆▆▆▆

Sensory modulation refers to the ability to process and respond to sensation in a manner that is consistent with the level of the sensation present in the activity and the environment (Lane, 2002). Neural modulation of sensation is thought to be tied to emotion, arousal, and activity level. Although the links are primarily theoretical or statistical, new research is helping to identify the physiological (sympathetic nervous system) under-pinnings of sensory modulation deficits (Mangeot et al., 2001; McIntosh, Miller, & Hagerman, 1999; Schaaf, Miller, Seawell, & O'Keefe, 2003). When children have good abilities to modulate, their responses to sensations generated by caregivers, playmates, and within the play space (e.g., touch, noise) do not seem unusual or unexpected. Their easy interpretation of incoming sensation contributes to adaptive interactions with objects and people. Thus, sensory modulation is critical to children's engagement in play and other daily life activities (Lane, 2002).

V. A. How well can the child regulate responses to sensory experiences? What effect do sensory experiences have on the child's emotional responses?

Dunn (1999) described children who have difficulty with sensory modulation as having thresholds that are either higher or lower than those of most children. In Dunn's conceptualization, children who have a high threshold to sensation need a great deal of input before they will respond, whereas those with a low threshold need very little. However, children who have altered thresholds do not necessarily act in accordance with them. That is, children with high thresholds *may* underreact to sensation but they also may appear to *seek* it, as though acting counter to the natural tendency of their nervous systems, perhaps in an attempt to help the central nervous system to modulate. Many responses to poor sensory modulation take the form of emotional responses (Cohn, Miller, & Tickle-Degnen, 2000; Lane, 2002; Mangeot et al., 2001; McIntosh et al., 1999; Schaaf et al., 2003).

When children with high thresholds are in situations where little sensation is available, their behavior is likely to become more pronounced. That is, those who are acting as expected given their high thresholds will appear quieter and more with-drawn, whereas children acting counter to expectation will seek sensation more ac-tively. Conversely, situations with high levels of sensation are apt to be easier for any child with a high threshold. Children who usually appear quiet and withdrawn may appear to wake up, whereas those who typically seek sensation may appear calmer. (See the example of Peta, p. 33.)

Similarly, children with *low thresholds* may appear overly sensitive or, if they are acting counter to expectations, they may avoid sensation and become overly rigid in their behavior. Many children with attention-deficit/hyperactivity disorder fit the for-mer description, whereas the latter applies to many children with autism. When chil-dren with low thresholds are in situations with a lot of sensation, their behavior is apt to become more pronounced, with those acting as expected becoming increasingly sen-sitive, perhaps reacting with fight or flight, and those acting counter becoming more withdrawn and rigid acting. In contrast, situations with minimal sensation will be eas-ier for both groups with lowered thresholds. Children who typically act in accord with their thresholds are likely to appear calmer and those who generally act counter to their thresholds may become more accepting and less rigid (Dunn, 1999).

Put another way, Dunn (1999) described four groups of children; two who *appear* overly active and two who appear relatively inactive, but for very different reasons. One overly active group and one underactive group is behaving in the way that would be expected given their central nervous systems' reaction to sensory information; the other two groups are acting in unexpected ways.

One overly active group has a lower threshold to sensation; that is, children in that group are overly sensitive to sensation. Those children tend to run around, theoreti-cally because they have failed to modulate incoming sensation and their arousal levels are quite high. We would expect those children to respond very emotionally to certain types of sensation. The second group that *appears* overly active actually has a *high* threshold. They also have failed to modulate incoming sensation but their arousal levels would be quite low if they did *not* run around seeking sensation. We might expect them to act as though they are very excited (Dunn, 1999).

The explanation for the less active group is similar to that proposed above. Some of those children have a high threshold to sensation. They appear not to notice or register sensation. As expected, their arousal levels are likely to be low and they appear uninterested, withdrawn, and overly tired. Other children actually have low thresholds; they are avoiding sensation to keep themselves under control, and they may appear rigid and resistant to change (Dunn, 1999). Some physiological support exists for this latter group (McIntosh et al., 1999).

V. B. What effect do sensory experiences have on the child's activity level?

If the observations and speculations of Dunn (1999) and others (Cohn et al., 2000; DeGangi, 2000; Lane, 2002; Mangeot et al., 2001; McIntosh et al., 1999; Schaaf et al., 2003) are correct, then clearly there is a relationship between modulation and arousal. In turn, activity levels, attention, and emotional responses appear to be related to level of arousal. However, as we noted earlier, those relationships may be very complex.

Children who do not modulate well may have increased or decreased levels of arousal. Generally, thresholds for sensory reception are inversely related to arousal levels, but emotional reactions are congruent with arousal. That is, children with lowered sensory thresholds who overreact to sensation often also have increased arousal and are likely to respond very emotionally. Conversely, children with increased thresholds who require a lot of input before reacting are apt to have decreased arousal levels and to show little emotion (Dunn, 1999). However, both increased and decreased arousal levels may lead to either increased or decreased activity levels. These hypothesized relationships are shown graphically in Figure 2.1.

The relationships among modulation, arousal, and activity level are not purely linear. That is, arousal levels likely affect sensory thresholds and level of activity probably influences arousal. These hypothesized relationships also are shown graphically in Figure 2.1.

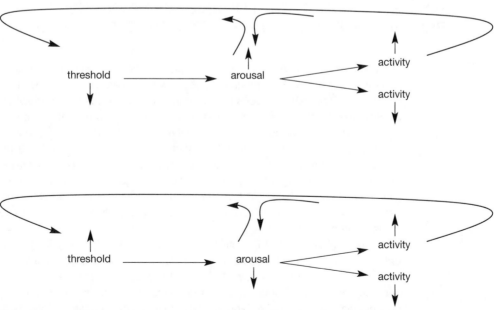

Figure 2.1. Hypothesized relationships among modulation (thresholds), arousal, and activity level.

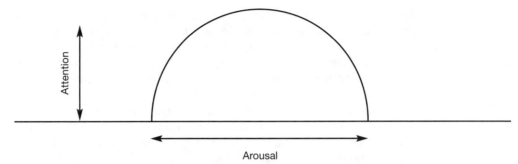

Figure 2.2. Hypothesized relationship of attention to arousal (*Source:* Hebb, 1949, 1955).

▨▨▨ V. C. What effect do sensory experiences have on the child's attention?

Children's abilities to attend also are related to modulation and arousal, although as mentioned previously, that relationship is neither simple nor linear. Hebb (1949, 1955) and later Kerr (1990) described relationships between performance and arousal, which seem applicable here because attention is a necessary component of performance and seems likely to covary with it. Hebb (1949, 1955) described this relationship as an inverted U. When this is applied to attention, we would say that a certain amount of arousal is necessary for optimal attention but that too much arousal leads to a decreased ability to attend. This relationship is shown in Figure 2.2.

More recently, Kerr (1990) proposed a slightly more complex relationship between arousal and performance, believing that each individual's interpretation of optimal level of arousal would be unique. Thus, we may hypothesize that children's abilities to attend will covary with level of arousal but that children will differ with respect to the amount of arousal necessary to support optimal attention.

▨▨▨ USING THE OBSERVATION GUIDELINES TO ASSESS MODULATION OF SENSATION AND ITS RELATIONSHIP TO EMOTION, ACTIVITY LEVEL, AND ATTENTION

The complexity of the relationships among modulation, arousal, and activity level make discrete observation of these phenomena difficult. However, in administering the sensorimotor section of TPBA, the team should focus on how sensory experiences and modulation seem to affect activity level, emotional reactions, and attention. We remember, however, that many factors can cause children to have abnormal emotional reactions, activity levels, and attention deficits; poor sensory modulation is only one of those factors. This same caution also applies to stereotypic or repetitive behaviors, which may be related to abnormal sensory processing but also may be a means for seeking attention, communicating, and attempting to avoid doing something (Durand & Crimmins, 1992). The Observation Guidelines associated with emotional and social development (see Chapter 4) also may provide particularly relevant information for interpreting these phenomena.

Sometimes during TPBA, children respond to sensation (e.g., light or unexpected touch; dirty hands; textures of food, clothing, or toys; movement, sounds, sights, tastes, or smells that would not bother others) in ways that are out of proportion to the experience (often too much) and nonproductive. (Although it is somewhat less common, some children's response may be unexpectedly little given the degree of activity in the environment.) Reactions that are out of proportion provide opportunities to experiment with types and quantities of sensation to try to help the child modulate. Watch carefully to see whether the reaction is in the expected direction. If a child had been overly active, emotionally reactive, or unable to focus attention, is she now a little more focused and less active or emotionally reactive and vice versa? If not, the child may be acting counter to her sensory thresholds or trying, unsuccessfully, to modulate for herself.

Team members are again reminded that discriminating between children who are acting in accord with, and those acting counter to, their sensory threshold levels can be a real challenge. Considering the possibility that a child's overt actions may be a mirror image of, rather than identical to, the child's sensory thresholds may shed light on the situation and open up possibilities for observation during TPBA assessment. Generally, it seems a good rule to begin with the assumption that children are acting in accord with threshold levels but to continually keep in mind that you may be wrong.

In general, slow repetitive movement (from rocking or gentle swinging), deep pressure (from being wrapped or lying underneath a heavy conforming surface), quiet sounds, and dim lights are calming, whereas their opposites are more stimulating (Koomar & Bundy, 2002). See Richter and Oetter (1990) for additional suggestions. Because sensation is very powerful, when altering it, teams should rely on a team member who is trained in sensory integration. Resistance to movement from jumping or moving heavy objects seems to be a particularly useful means for helping children to modulate. With resistance, children who are overly responsive and active will calm, but children who are underresponsive will perk up (Koomar & Bundy, 2002).

▰▰▰▰ V. A. How well can the child regulate responses to sensory experiences?
What effect do sensory experiences have on the child's emotional responses?

Poor modulation can be associated with either increased *or* decreased emotional reactivity. Overreaction seems more common and is certainly easier to see. Children who overreact easily become angry or upset in response to noise, touch, or other sensations that would not bother most people. In contrast, some children who are underreactive may appear inordinately "even-tempered."

▰▰▰▰ V. B. What effect do sensory experiences have on the child's activity level?

As with emotional reactivity, poor sensory modulation may be associated with either increased or decreased activity. Activity level often parallels emotional reactivity. Thus, a pattern of both increased activity and emotional reactivity is common. Although decreased activity levels and emotional reactivity also may be seen, they may be less common and likely are less disruptive at home and school.

▰▰▰▰ V. C. What effect do sensory experiences have on the child's attention?

Poor sensory modulation can contribute to difficulties maintaining an optimum level of arousal. In turn, less than optimal arousal may lead to difficulty with paying attention. Too little arousal tends to manifest as lethargy, whereas too much may result in anxiety. Both are accompanied by less than optimal attention. Thus, whether they over- or underreact to sensation, when children have difficulty modulating sensation, they are likely to have difficulty paying attention (Lane, 2002).

> *Eight-year-old Peta had a diagnosis of poor sensory modulation. Her story was typical. Her mother, Ruth, complained that Peta had only one outfit that she was willing to wear to school. Ruth found this behavior particularly troubling as she feared that Peta's teacher would think that her family could only afford one set of clothes. To keep Peta looking presentable, her mother washed Peta's clothes nightly. Although Peta's history*

suggested that she was defensive to touch (i.e., overreacting; seemingly lowered thresh-old), her play partner suspected that, in general, Peta's threshold for sensory experiences actually was very high (i.e., tendency to underreact), because Peta was unusually quiet and undemanding. She seemed to lack any enthusiasm for messy play with shaving cream or jumping into a big vat filled with small plastic balls, activities that brought her peers great joy.

Peta's play partner, a therapist with considerable training in sensory integration, devised some experiences to provide Peta with intense movement, including roughhous-ing and swinging rapidly. Peta immediately perked up and became more animated; she laughed and became much more engaged in the game and with her play partner. Although Peta's mother feared that Peta would become overstimulated, that never hap-pened. In fact, after the evaluation finished, Peta settled into a corner with the book she had brought, waiting contentedly for her parents.

Peta had originally come for TPBA because of her mother's concerns over Peta's re-actions to clothing and her parents' and teacher's complaints about her distractibility and inattentiveness. Reportedly, her father had many of the same issues and neither par-ent wanted Peta to experience what her father had gone through. Because Peta's play partner was very skilled at helping Peta to modulate sensation, the team, including her parents, saw a side of Peta that they would not have otherwise seen. This is particularly true because Peta's mother had grown up in a large and chaotic family. She valued calm and quiet and carefully monitored the activity levels of her two children. Suddenly Peta's distractibility took on new meaning and the team was able to devise successful strategies for helping her attend to, as well as for decreasing her negative reactions to, clothing. Prior to sitting down to do focused tasks, Peta engaged in active play (e.g., jumping, run-ning). She often chewed gum while reading or drawing. Peta's family also found CDs of peppy music that seemed to help her stay on task. She used headphones when the music might disturb others.

VI.   Sensorimotor Contributions to Daily Life and Self-Care

Every day, children use sensorimotor skills to perform a myriad of tasks and activities at home, in day care, at preschool, in school, at the park, at a friend's house, or wherever they find themselves. However, we are at risk for losing something very special if we dissect the tasks associated with play, or dressing, or any childhood occupation to the level of contributing skills. As usual, the sum is greater than the parts. Nonetheless, daily life activity *reflects* children's skills and it is in this spirit that TPBA has been cre-ated. There probably is no finer window on all aspects of childhood than play.

The sensorimotor domain of TPBA provides an in-depth look at one kind of skill that contributes to daily life activity. Because it is conducted primarily while children play, TPBA will not show us all the skills that children possess or all the activities they can accomplish. Rather, it provides a glimpse at the skills children *use* when they en-gage in the occupation they enjoy most—play. TPBA also involves a snack. Thus, it pro-vides an opportunity to see skills associated with some aspects of eating. There also may be opportunities to observe some dressing tasks as children often wear outdoor clothing that can be removed. Furthermore, some children like to play barefoot, and removing socks and shoes can be a natural part of the assessment.

In the Age Table (see p. 51) that accompanies this chapter, we have offered mile-stones associated with a selection of play and daily life activities. The list is not meant to be exhaustive because the purpose of TPBA is to observe skills in the context of play and a snack, not to see children perform every daily life task appropriate to their age. Thus, it is not necessary to seek information on all the milestones provided. Furthermore, when particular daily life tasks are of concern to children and families, it may be necessary to seek more in-depth information about those tasks than will be gained in the course of TPBA.

We also remember that, although daily life activities have been described under the sensorimotor domain, accomplishing these activities requires skills from all the domains. If a child cannot perform one or more of these tasks, then we examine contributing skills from across all the domains to see if we can uncover the reasons. We also must consider the contribution of the environment and the tasks, because these are equally important in determining children's success in meeting the challenges of daily life.

VI. A. How well does the child eat a simple snack?

Snack time presents opportunities to observe in three interrelated areas. These include oral motor, self-feeding, and behavior.

Oral-motor skills are the first of these to appear. Although many skills are not fully mature until age 2 (or older), a great deal happens in the first year. Two functions are particularly relevant: 1) coordination of sucking, swallowing, and breathing; and 2) biting and chewing (Case-Smith & Humphry, 2001; Klein & Morris, 1999; Morris & Klein, 1987).

Coordinating breathing with sucking and swallowing depends on the control of jaw, tongue, and lip movements. This control, in turn, depends on the type of food and the child's position (Case-Smith & Humphry, 2001).

Many typically developing children are first introduced to a cup with a spout at about 6 months of age. Over the next 6 months, they will gradually develop increased lip and jaw control and transition to exclusive use of the cup for meals. However, they will be about 2 years of age before they can efficiently drink from a cup by providing a seal with the lips, not the teeth, while their tongue tip is elevated when swallowing (Case-Smith & Humphry, 2001; Klein & Morris, 1999; Morris & Klein, 1987).

Biting and chewing begin at 4–5 months of age as an up–down movement of the teeth accompanied by rhythmical extension and retraction of the tongue; these work fairly well for pureed or soft food. Slowly, lateral movements of both jaw and tongue emerge. At 9 months, children can transfer food from the center of the tongue to either side for chewing. Increasing stability of the jaw and mobility of the tongue and lips mean that by 1 year of age children have a sustained and graded bite, can lick their lips, and can retrieve food from the lower lip by drawing it inward. By 2 years of age, children have circular rotary jaw movements and can eat most meats and raw vegetables (Case-Smith & Humphry, 2001; Klein & Morris, 1999; Morris & Klein, 1987).

For self-feeders, most snacks offered during TPBA will involve finger feeding and drinking from a cup. If utensil use is a particular concern, team members should incorporate a snack that requires a spoon (a fork and even a knife also may be relevant).

Children begin to develop the ability to drink independently from a cup and feed themselves finger food during the second half of the first year. By the time they are 1 year old, they can feed themselves part of a meal and drink from a spout cup (Haley, Coster, Ludlow, Haltiwanger, & Andrellos, 1992). By 1½ years they can drink well from an open cup, but they may drop the cup. Before 2, they can hold the cup well, lift, drink, and replace (Coley, 1978). By 3, the basic components of using a spoon are intact (Henderson, 1995). However, most children cannot eat soup with a spoon until they are between 4 and 6 years of age (Coley, 1978).

Drawing from old but apt sources (e.g., Gesell & Ilg, 1946; Hurlock, 1956), Henderson (1995) eloquently summarized the development of self-feeding behavior as a combination of acquiring skill and learning to conform to cultural standards.

Henderson indicated that children are 3 or 4 before they can eat and talk at the same time. They are almost 10 before they are entirely independent, using a knife and fork deftly and paying good attention to table manners!

▮▮▮▮ VI. B. How well does the child perform simple dressing tasks?

As with self-feeding, the development of dressing and undressing depends on hand skills as well as postural stability. Although a child can pull off socks easily with a fisted hand, putting them back on requires strength and bilateral coordination. Undressing is easier than dressing and most children can remove all but pullover garments, and possibly shoes, by the time they are 2 (Henderson, 1995).

Most children are able to dress completely (with the exception of fasteners) by the time they are 5½ (Key, 1936, cited in Henderson, 1995). The most rapid period of learning dressing skills seems to begin at about age 1½. Most dressing requires finger dexterity and planning sequences, and these skills are not all mastered until about 6½ years of age (Henderson, 1995). Separating zippers, back buttons, and shoelaces are the last of the common fasteners to be mastered.

In addition to motor skills, cognition and motivation play enormous roles in the development of dressing skills. Experience also plays an important part.

▮▮▮▮ USING THE OBSERVATION GUIDELINES TO ASSESS SENSORIMOTOR CONTRIBUTIONS TO DAILY LIFE AND SELF-CARE

Self-care represents a set of complex tasks that develops over time; it includes eating, dressing, toothbrushing, hair combing, blowing the nose, and many more tasks. As with play, self-care involves and requires much more than simply motor skills. Cognition, behavior, language, and emotions all come into play. Snack is a part of TPBA; thus, the team always has a chance to observe feeding and eating. Similarly, children commonly take off and put on at least one piece of clothing during the assessment (e.g., shoes and socks, jacket), providing opportunities to observe simple dressing skills. The team will need to learn about the child's performance on other self-care tasks through interview of the parents.

▮▮▮▮ VI. A. How well does the child eat a simple snack?

Snack time provides an opportunity to see sensorimotor, cognitive, and emotional-social skills in action. The team should observe oral-motor skills, self-feeding ability, food likes and dislikes, and table manners. If the child is unable to do what is expected, then the task is to determine what seems to be interfering.

Oral-motor skills are the most basic observations made during snack time. The team wants to know first if the child is safe and then if the child's skills are adequate for handling all types of food. Different types of food, ranging from semisolids to hard substances that fracture when a piece is bitten off to highly resistant substances, present different challenges to a child's oral-motor skills. Of course, it is not practical to serve all types of food at snack time. Thus, if team members question a child's ability, they may have to seek additional information from interview.

Having gotten the food into the mouth, the team is interested in how well the child chews and swallows and whether any food is lost. Watching the movement of the lower jaw provides some information about whether the child can use the tongue to move food side to side and chew in a rotary pattern or whether the movement is only up and down, which represents a less mature pattern.

If the child is a self-feeder, then the team will want to observe how well the child uses dishes and utensils to "capture" food and bring it to the mouth. Again, it may be impractical to include all utensils in snack time. The child's use of a glass or cup can be observed easily. If use of utensils is a particular question, then team members may want to arrange suitable snack food.

Regardless of whether the child is a self-feeder, the team will want to acquire information about how long it takes for the child to eat a meal, the child's food likes and dislikes, and table manners. Observation in all of these areas may need to be supplemented by interview. If the child has negative responses to foods, then the pattern of those responses may provide evidence for poor sensory modulation (e.g., a child who dislikes textures or resistive foods such as meat). If the child has an excessively narrow range of likes and dislikes or his or her table manners are poor, then the child may be difficult to include in family or school routines and celebrations.

▓▓▓▓ VI. B. How well does the child perform simple dressing tasks?

As with snack time, putting on or taking off clothing provides an opportunity to see sensorimotor, cognitive, and emotional-social skills in action. Is the child able and willing to perform the skills expected at that age? How much assistance is required? How much time is required? Does the child refuse to dress? Are the amount of time and assistance acceptable in the circumstances? Does the child tolerate a wide variety of clothing? Are his or her likes and dislikes acceptable in the situation? (Some children are particularly fussy about the arrangement of their socks or the tags in their clothing. If their negative responses fit a pattern, then they may provide evidence for poor sensory modulation.) It's a bit of a problem to provide an example as self-care and play are really the culmination of lots of skills—not simply sensorimotor. All of the above examples illustrate how particular motor skills affect play in particular.

Clearly, not all aspects of play or other activities of daily living (ADL) can be observed as a part of TPBA. Although a great deal of information regarding these areas can be gained through parent interview, they are what children do every day. When children cannot perform an age-appropriate ADL independently, someone else must do it for them, thus placing an additional burden on caregivers. When children cannot play, they miss out on an important source of joy and learning. Thus, play and ADL are particularly important to the welfare of children and their caregivers. Children for whom these areas are of particular concern may need further evaluation.

CONCLUSION

In the sensorimotor domain of TPBA, we have examined six subcategories related to action. These are

1. Functions underlying movement

2. Gross motor activity

3. Arm and hand use

4. Motor planning and coordination

5. Modulation of sensation and its relationship to emotion, activity level, and attention

6. Sensorimotor contributions to daily life and self-care

The seventh subcategory of the sensorimotor domain is vision. This will be addressed in Chapter 3.

Functions underlying movement provide examiners with a look at children's posture, balance, and muscle tone. Gross motor activity refers to whole-body actions. We have recommended making a general qualitative assessment of children's abilities and then focusing on several important areas: the developmental positions in which children play and how independent they are in moving between those positions, locomotion, and bilateral abilities.

Sensorimotor actions form the basis for many important daily life events. Some contemporary philosophers have even argued that action is a critical part of cognition (Clark, 1997; Rowlands, 1999). Thus, knowledge of sensorimotor abilities forms a crucial basis for intervention with many children.

In Chapter 3, Tanni L. Anthony expands the sensorimotor domain to incorporate vision, providing the Observation Guidelines for this subcategory. As most professionals have received little, if any, training in vision development, and vision specialists may not be included on assessment teams unless requested, it is important for all professionals to become more adept at observation of visual skills and visual-motor abilities.

REFERENCES

Alexander, R., Boehme, R., & Cupps, B. (1993). *Normal development of functional motor skills: The first year of life.* Tucson, AZ: Therapy Skill Builders.

Aylward, G.P. (1995). *Bayley Infant Neurodevelopmental Screener–Manual.* San Antonio: Harcourt Assessment.

Ayres, A.J. (1972). *Sensory integration and learning disorders.* Los Angeles: Western Psychological Services.

Ayres, A.J. (1985). *Developmental dyspraxia and adult onset apraxia.* Torrance, CA: Sensory Integration International.

Bly, L. (1994). *Motor skills acquisition in the first year.* Tucson, AZ: Therapy Skill Builders.

Bobath, B. (1985). *Abnormal postural reflex activity caused by brain lesions* (3rd ed.). London: Heinemann Physiotherapy.

Boehme, R. (1988). *Improving upper body control: An approach to assessment and treatment of tonal dysfunction.* Tucson, AZ: Therapy Skill Builders.

Bruininks, R.H. (1978). *Bruininks-Oseretsky test of motor proficiency: Examiner's manual.* Circle Pines, MN: American Guidance Service.

Burton, A.W., & Miller, D.E. (1998). *Movement skill assessment.* Champaign, IL: Human Kinetics.

Campbell, S.K., Vander Linden, D.W., & Palisano, R.J. (Eds.). (2000). *Physical therapy for children* (2nd ed.). Philadelphia: W.B. Saunders.

Caplan, F. (Ed.). (1973). *The first twelve months of life* (3rd ed.). New York: Perigee Books/Putnam.

Case-Smith, J. (1995). Grasp, release, and bimanual skills in the first two years of life. In A. Henderson & C. Pehoski (Eds.), *Hand function in the child: Foundations for remediation* (pp. 113–135). St. Louis: Mosby.

Case-Smith, J. (Ed.). (2001). *Occupational therapy for children* (4th ed.). St. Louis: Mosby.

Case-Smith, J., & Humphry, R. (2001). Feeding intervention. In J. Case-Smith (Ed.), *Occupational therapy for children* (4th ed., pp. 453–488). St. Louis: Mosby.

Case-Smith, J., & Weintraub, N. (2002). Hand function and developmental coordination disorder. In S.A. Cermak & D. Larkin (Eds.), *Developmental coordination disorder* (pp. 157–171). Albany, NY: Delmar.

Cermak, S.A., & Larkin, D. (2002). *Developmental coordination disorder.* Albany, NY: Delmar.

Clark, A. (1997). *Being there: Putting brain, body, and world together again.* Cambridge, MA: The MIT Press.

Clifford, J.M., & Bundy, A.C. (1989). Play preference and play performance in normal preschoolers and preschoolers with sensory integrative dysfunction. *Occupational Therapy Journal of Research, 9,* 202–217.

Cohn, E., Miller, L.J., & Tickle-Degnen, L. (2000). Parental hopes for therapy outcomes: Children with sensory modulation disorders. *American Journal of Occupational Therapy, 54,* 36–43.

Coley, I.L. (1978). *Pediatric assessment of self-care activities.* St. Louis: Mosby.

DeGangi, G. (2000). *Pediatric disorders of regulation in affect and behavior: A therapist's guide to assessment and treatment.* San Diego: Academic Press.

Dubowitz, V. (1980). The floppy infant (2nd ed.). *Clinics in Developmental Medicine Series: No. 76.* London: Mac Keith Press.

Dunn, W. (1999). *Sensory profile: User's manual.* San Antonio: Harcourt Assessment.

Durand, V.M., & Crimmins, D.B. (1992). *Motivation Assessment Scale.* Topeka, KS: Monaco & Associates.

Eliasson, A.-C. (1995). Sensorimotor integration of normal and impaired development of precision movement of the hand. In A. Henderson & C. Pehoski (Eds.), *Hand function in the child: Foundations for remediation* (pp. 40–54). St. Louis: Mosby.

Erhardt, R.P. (1992). Eye-hand coordination. In J. Case-Smith & C. Pehoski (Eds.), *Development of hand skills in the child* (pp. 13–27). Bethesda, MD: American Occupational Therapy Association.

Erhardt, R.P. (1994). *Developmental hand dysfunction: Theory, assessment, and treatment* (2nd ed.). Tucson, AZ: Therapy Skill Builders.

Exner, C.E. (1992). In-hand manipulation skills. In J. Case-Smith & C. Pehoski (Eds.), *Development of hand skills in the child* (pp. 35–46). Bethesda, MD: American Occupational Therapy Association.

Exner, C.E. (2001). Development of hand skills. In J. Case-Smith (Ed.), *Occupational therapy for children* (4th ed., pp. 289–328). St. Louis: Mosby.

Folio, M., & Fewell, R. (1983). *Peabody Development Motor Scales and Activity Cards.* Austin, TX: PRO-ED.

Geuze, R.H. (2003). Static balance and developmental coordination disorder. *Human Movement Science, 22,* 527–548.

Haley, S.M., Coster, W.L., Ludlow, L.H., Haltiwanger, J.T., & Andrellos, P.J. (1992). *Pediatric evaluation of disability inventory.* Boston: New England Medical Center Hospital, Inc. and PEDI Research Group.

Hebb, D.O. (1949). *The organization of behavior.* New York: John Wiley & Sons.

Hebb, D.O. (1955). Drives and the CNS (conceptual nervous system). *Psychological Review, 62,* 243–254.

Henderson, A. (1995). Self-care and hand skills. In A. Henderson & C. Pehoski (Eds.), *Hand function in the child: Foundations for remediation* (pp. 164–183). St. Louis: Mosby.

Henderson, A., & Pehoski, C. (Eds.). (1995). *Hand function in the child: Foundations for remediation.* St. Louis: Mosby.

Johnston, L.M., Burns, Y.R., Brauer, S.G., & Richardson, C.A. (2002). Differences in postural control and movement performance during goal directed reaching in children with developmental coordination disorder. *Human Movement Science, 21,* 583–601.

Keogh, J.F., & Sugden, D.A. (1985). *Movement skill development.* New York: Macmillan.

Kerr, J.H. (1990). Stress and sport: Reversal theory. In J.G. Jones & L. Hardy (Eds.), *Stress and performance in sport* (pp. 107–131). Chichester, England: Wiley.

Klein, M.D., & Morris, S.E. (1999). *Mealtime participation guide.* San Antonio: Therapy Skill Builders.

Koomar, J., & Bundy, A.C. (2002). Creating direct intervention from theory. In A.C. Bundy, S. Lane, & E. Murray (Eds.), *Sensory integration: Theory and practice* (pp. 261–309). Philadelphia: F.A. Davis.

Lane, S. (2002). Sensory modulation. In A.C. Bundy, S. Lane, & E. Murray (Eds.), *Sensory integration: Theory and practice* (pp. 101–122). Philadelphia: F.A. Davis.

Mangeot, S.D., Miller, L.J., McIntosh, D.N., McGrath-Clarke, J., Simon, J., & Hagerman, R.J. (2001). Sensory modulation dysfunction in children with attention-deficit-hyperactivity disorder. *Developmental Medicine and Child Neurology, 43,* 399–406.

McIntosh, D.N., Miller, L.J., & Hagerman, R.J. (1999). Sensory-modulation disruption, electrodermal responses, and functional behaviors. *Developmental Medicine and Child Neurology, 41,* 608–615.

Morris, S.E., & Klein, M.D. (1987). *Pre-feeding skills.* San Antonio: Therapy Skill Builders.

Nashner, L., Shumway-Cook, A., & Olin, O. (1983). Stance posture control in select groups of children with cerebral palsy: Deficits in sensory organization and muscular coordination. *Experimental Brain Research, 49,* 393–409.

Pehoski, C. (1995). Object manipulation in infants and children. In A. Henderson & C. Pehoski (Eds.), *Hand function in the child: Foundations for remediation* (pp. 136–153). St. Louis: Mosby.

Piper, M.C., & Darrah, J. (1994). *Motor assessment of the developing infant.* Philadelphia: W.B. Saunders.

Random House. (2000). Random House Webster's College Dictionary, 2nd revised and updated edition. New York: Author.

Reed, E.S. (1989). Changing theories of postural development. In M.H. Woollacott & A. Shumway-Cook (Eds.), *Development of posture and gait across the life span.* Columbia, SC: University of South Carolina Press.

Reeves, G.D., & Cermak, S.A. (2002). Disorders of praxis. In A. Bundy, S. Lane, & E. Murray (Eds.), *Sensory integration: Theory and practice* (2nd ed., pp. 71–100). Philadelphia: F.A. Davis.

Richter, E., & Oetter, P. (1990). Environmental matrices for sensory integrative treatment. In S. Merrill (Ed.), *Environment: Implications for occupational therapy practice, a sensory integrative perspective.* Rockville, MD: American Occupational Therapy Association.

Rodger, S., Ziviani, J., Watter, P., Ozanne, A., Woodyatt, G., & Springfield, E. (2003). Motor and functional skills of children with developmental coordination disorder: A pilot investigation of measurement issues. *Human Movement Science, 22,* 461–478.

Rösblad, B. (1995). Reaching and eye-hand coordination. In A. Henderson & C. Pehoski (Eds.), *Hand function in the child: Foundations for remediation* (pp. 81–92). St. Louis: Mosby.

Rowlands, M. (1999). *The body in mind: Understanding cognitive processes.* Cambridge, England: Cambridge University Press.

Schaaf, R.C., Miller, L.J., Seawell, D., & O'Keefe, S. (2003). Children with disturbances in sensory processing: A pilot study examining the role of the parasympathetic nervous system. *American Journal of Occupational Therapy, 57*(4), 442–449.

Seefeldt, V., & Haubenstricker, J. (1982). Patterns, phases, or stages: An analytical model for the study of developmental movement. In J.A.S. Kelso & J.E. Clark (Eds.), *The development of movement control and coordination* (pp. 309–318). Chichester, England: Wiley.

Shumway-Cook, A., & Woollacott, M.H. (2001). *Motor control: Theory and practical applications* (2nd ed.). Philadelphia: Lippincott Williams & Wilkins.

Smits-Engelsman, B.C.M., Wilson, P.H., Westenberg, Y., & Duysens, J. (2003). Fine motor deficiencies in children with developmental coordination disorder and learning disabilities: An underlying open-loop control deficit. *Human Movement Science, 22,* 495–513.

Stamer, M. (2000). *Posture and movement of the child with cerebral palsy.* San Antonio: Therapy Skill Builders.

Sugden, D.A., & Keogh, J.F. (1990). *Problems in movement skill development.* Columbia, SC: University of South Carolina Press.

Thelen, E. (1995). Motor development: A new synthesis. *American Psychologist, 50,* 79–95.

Thelen, E., & Smith, L.B. (1994). *A dynamic systems approach to the development of cognition and action.* Cambridge, MA: The MIT Press.

Wann, J.P., Mon-Williams, M., & Rushton, K. (1998). Postural control and coordination disorders: The swinging room revisited. *Human Movement Science, 17*(4–5), 491–514.

Weisz, S. (1938). Studies in equilibrium reaction. *Journal of Nervous and Mental Diseases, 88,* 150–162.

Williams, H.G. (1983). *Perceptual and motor development.* Englewood Cliffs, NJ: Prentice Hall.

Ziviani, J. (1995). The development of graphomotor skills. In A. Henderson & C. Pehoski (Eds.), *Hand function in the child: Foundations for remediation* (pp. 184–193). St. Louis: Mosby.

TPBA2 Observation Guidelines: Sensorimotor Development

Child's name: _____   Age: _____   Birth date: _____

Parent(s): _____   Assessment date: _____

Person(s) completing the form: _____

Directions: Record the child information (name, caregiver[s], birth date, age), assessment date, and person(s) completing this form. The Observation Guidelines listed provide common strengths, examples of behaviors of concern, and "ready for" next steps. As you observe the child, circle, highlight, or place a check mark next to the items under these three categories that correspond to the behavior(s) you observe. List any additional observations in the "Notes" column. Experienced TPBA users may opt to use only the TPBA2 Observation Notes as a method for collecting information during the assessment instead of the Observation Guidelines.

Questions	Strengths	Examples of behaviors of concern	"Ready for"	Notes
I. Functions underlying movement				
I. A. How well does posture support action?	Body oriented to task Head and trunk in line Sits independently Stands independently Can keep from falling When something expected happens (e.g., reaching) When something unexpected happens (e.g., jostled gently) Catches self with arm or leg when falling Can transport objects while crawling, walking All of the above	Holds head rigidly Head not in line with body Gets stuck when moving between positions Needs support to sit Needs support to stand Falls when reaching Cannot transport objects Apt to fall if something unexpected happens Not safe when falling	Increased stability of trunk/head More freedom when moving Less external support for sitting/standing/moving Decreased risk of falling Increased safety when falls occur	
I. B. How well does muscle tone support posture?	Lifts head easily Straight back Appropriate base of support Knees and elbows not locked when bearing weight Moves limbs easily and smoothly	Looks weak Muscles look "mushy" Difficulty holding head up Rounded back when sitting Spreads legs excessively wide when sitting or standing Locks knees or elbows	Minimized risk of deformity Decreased interference from tremor or involuntary movement Strategies to increase tone Proximally Distally	

Developed with Anita C. Bundy.

Transdisciplinary Play-Based System (TPBA2/TPBI2)
by Toni Linder.

(continued on next page)

(continued from previous page)

Observation Guidelines: Sensorimotor Development **TPBA 2**

Questions	Strengths	Examples of behaviors of concern	"Ready for"	Notes
I. Functions underlying movement (continued)				

I. B. How well does muscle tone support posture? (continued)	Moves body parts independently of one another
	All of the above
		Stands on toes
		Looks stiff
		Hands fisted
		Tremor or involuntary movement
			Strategies to decrease tone
			  Proximally
			  Distally
			External support to promote independence	

II. Gross motor activity				
II. A. In general, how do you describe the child's gross motor movements? How much do gross motor problems interfere with function?	Effective Efficient Enjoyable Easy	Ineffective Inefficient Difficult Fear inducing Not fun Avoids	New skills More fluidity More speed More ease Less fear More fun	
II. B. What positions does the child play in?	Plays in many positions Assumes positions where hands are free Easily maintains positions	Needs assistance to maintain Uses few play positions Positions stress joints unduly (e.g., "W" sitting) Hands are not free Expends too much effort	New play positions Increased play in positions where the hands are free Increased play in positions that are sound biomechanically Increased external support Decreased external support	
II. C. How independent is the child when moving between positions?	Completely independent Moves easily	Needs assistance from caregivers Expends too much effort Not safe	Assuming new positions Increased independence Decreased effort Increased safety	
II. D. How does the child move through the environment? How independent is the child? How good is the quality?	Age-appropriate skills Quality as expected for age Independent (with or without assistive devices) Moves easily Moves safely	Delayed Poorly coordinated Expends too much effort Looks unusual Stresses joints unduly Needs assistance from caregivers Not safe	New skills Improved coordination Increased independence Increased locomotion in ways that are sound biomechanically Assistive devices Increased safety Decreased effort	

(continued on next page)

Transdisciplinary Play-Based System (TPBA2/TPBI2) by Toni Linder.

Observation Guidelines: Sensorimotor Development **TPBA** 2

Questions	Strengths	Examples of behaviors of concern	"Ready for"	Notes
II. Gross motor activity *(continued)*				
II. E. How well does the child use two body sides together (bilateral coordination)?	Two body sides appear equal Uses two hands well at midline Reaches across the body Rotates the trunk Prefers one hand for skilled acts Uses assisting hand well Can do symmetrical activities (e.g., clapping, jumping) well Can do alternating activities (e.g., Sit 'n Spin, pedaling tricycle) well Can maintain bilateral sequences over multiple repetitions Coordinates arms with legs (e.g., running, jumping rope) well All of the above	One body side does not contribute well Does not use two hands well at midline Does not cross midline Little or no trunk rotation Hand preference not well established Does not use an assisting hand well Symmetrical activities difficult Alternating activities difficult Bilateral sequences difficult Uses too much effort	Increased use of one body side Increased coordination of body sides Increased crossing midline Increased trunk rotation Developing hand preference Better use of assisting hand Increased ability to do symmetrical activities Increased ability to do alternating activities	
III. Arm and hand use				
III. A. In general, how do you describe the child's arm and hand use? How much do problems with arm and hand use interfere with function?	Effective Efficient Enjoyable Easy	Ineffective Inefficient Difficult Not fun Avoids	New skills More fluidity More speed More ease More fun	
III. B. How well is the child able to reach?	Reaches to objects Without assistance Accurately With both arms equally well Orients palm to touch object All of the above	Requires assistance Overshoots or undershoots Extraneous movements Cannot orient palm to touch object	Decreased assistance Increased accuracy Increased ability to orient palm to objects	

(continued on next page)

Transdisciplinary Play-Based System (TPBA2/TPBI2)
by Toni Linder.

Observation Guidelines: Sensorimotor Development **TPBA 2**

III. Arm and hand use (continued)

Questions	Strengths	Examples of behaviors of concern	"Ready for"	Notes
III. C. How effective is the child's grasp?	Orients hands to objects Thumb and pads/tips of fingers touch Hand nicely arched No need for external stability Effective Efficient Easy All of the above	Ineffective Inefficient Primarily uses little/ring fingers when grasping Hand appears flat; arches not well developed Requires external stability to prehend object; can grasp in mid-air Thumb not actively involved Too much force Grasp is weak	Increased ability to orient hands to object Decreased need for external support of hand Improved use of thumb and index/middle fingers Increased ability to shape hands around objects Increased ability to modify grasp to fit object More appropriate force	
III. D. How well does the child release objects?	Transfers items easily from one hand to another and back Releases easily regardless of size Does not require assistance from external surface Opens hand in proportion to object size Released objects land precisely on target Releases one object while continuing to hold others in the same hand All of the above	Cannot transfer object from one hand to another Cannot release voluntarily Flings rather than releases Requires assistance from external surface Opens hand much wider than necessary Cannot release one object while retaining another Released object does not hit the target Cannot release large objects Cannot hit small targets	Voluntary opening of hand Decreased need for external support Better ratio of finger opening to object size Increased accuracy Increased ability to release one object while retaining another	
III. E. How well does the child isolate finger movements for pointing, poking, and tapping?	Effective Efficient Easy All of the above	Cannot isolate index finger Cannot move each finger in isolation Too much effort	More fluidity More speed More ease Better isolation	

(continued on next page)

Transdisciplinary Play-Based System (TPBA2/TPBI2) by Toni Linder.

Observation Guidelines: Sensorimotor Development **TPBA** 2

Questions	Strengths	Examples of behaviors of concern	"Ready for"	Notes
III. Arm and hand use (continued)				
III. F. How effective is the child's in-hand manipulation?	Repositions grasped objects with thumb and fingers of one hand (no external assistance)	In-hand manipulations are	Increased effectiveness	
		Ineffective	Increased efficiency	
	Can move objects	Inefficient	Greater ease	
	From fingers to palm	Too much effort/force		
	From palm to fingers	Cannot manipulate one object while holding another		
	Through rotations <180 degrees	Avoids performing in-hand manipulations		
	Through rotations >180 degrees			
	Can shift object slightly			
	Manipulates object with the fingers and thumb of one hand while retaining one or more objects in the palm			
	All of the above			
III. G. How good are the child's constructional abilities?	Effective	Avoids/not much fun	Increased skill	
	Efficient	Ineffective	More fun	
	Enjoyable	Inefficient	Greater ease	
	Easy	Too much effort	Devices or adaptations	
	All of the above			
III. H. How effectively does the child use tools?	Uses tools as though they are an extension of the arm	Ineffective	Increased effectiveness	
		Inefficient	Increased efficiency	
	Effective	Too much effort/force	Greater ease	
	Efficient	Too little strength	More appropriate force	
	Easy	Avoids	More fun	
	All of the above			
IV. Motor planning and coordination				
IV. A. Does the child have good ideas for using toys?	Takes advantage of properties of toys and environment	Frequently needs ideas	Using objects in new ways	
	Uses toys in many ways	Uses toys in limited ways		

(continued on next page)

Transdisciplinary Play-Based System (TPBA2/TPBI2) by Toni Linder.

Observation Guidelines: Sensorimotor Development **TPBA** 2

Questions	Strengths	Examples of behaviors of concern	"Ready for"	Notes
IV. Motor planning and coordination (continued)				
IV. B. How well does the child initiate, terminate, and sequence actions?	Initiates and terminates actions easily Sequences actions logically Sequences tasks logically	Difficulty beginning (false starts) or ending (runs into things) actions Sequences seem illogical Frequently knocks things over, bumps into things	Increased ability to initiate or terminate actions Improved sequencing	

IV. C. How good are the child's spatial and temporal abilities?	Keeps rhythm
	Intercepts stationary object when moving (e.g., to kick ball)
	Intercepts moving object
	  When standing still
	  When running or moving
		Poor rhythm
		Stops ball before kicking; traps ball rather than catching
		Can't catch/kick a ball while in motion
			Improved rhythm
			Improved timing/spatial ability for acting more effectively on objects	

IV. D. Does the child seem to have a good sense of the body? Does the child have a good sense of objects as an extension of the body?	Positions body in the middle of chairs and riding toys
	Easily moves in small spaces
	Uses objects with ease; works "with" rather than "against" them
		Looks unsafe on equipment
		Unaware of poor position
		Fails to make body small enough to fit or "shrinks" excessively
		Uses objects awkwardly
			Improved safety on equipment
			Improved body awareness for
			  Using objects
			  Moving fluidly	

IV. E. How well does the child organize clothing and personal space?	Clothes are neat (e.g., buttons in proper buttonholes, shirt tucked in) Play space is organized	Clothes are awry Play space poorly organized	Improved organization	
IV. F. Does the child generate appropriate force?	Uses proper force on objects	Too much or too little force	Generating more appropriate force	

IV. G. Does the child perform actions in response to verbal request or demonstration?	Performs novel actions easily in response to
	  Verbal request
	  Demonstration
		Difficulty with performing
		  Verbal requests
		  Demonstrated actions
			Increased ease in responding to
			  Verbal commands
			  Demonstration	

Transdisciplinary Play-Based System (TPBA2/TPBI2)
by Toni Linder.

(continued on next page)

Observation Guidelines: Sensorimotor Development **TPBA 2**

Questions	Strengths	Examples of behaviors of concern	"Ready for"	Notes
V. Modulation of sensation and its relationship to emotion, activity level, and attention				
V. A. How well can the child regulate responses to sensory experiences? What effect do sensory experiences have on the child's emotional responses?	Responses to sensory experiences from materials, space, playmates, and caregivers Are similar to those of other children Lead to adaptive and appropriate actions	Responses are in excess of those expected Hitting, anger Excessive activity Distractibility Pained expressions Nausea, dizziness Fear Response are delayed or significantly less than expected Seeks sensory experiences in unacceptable ways Constantly touching Self-injurious behavior Annoying sounds Repetitive movement of objects, self "Crashing" into things Pushing against others Falling Avoids sensory experiences Engages in stereotyped behavior to try to cut out sensation	Increase adaptive responses to sensation Utilize acceptable means for meeting sensory needs	
V. B. What effect do sensory experiences have on the child's activity level?	Maintains appropriate level of activity in the face of sensory demands (e.g., noise)	Activity level increases unacceptably Activity level decreases unacceptably	Decreased activity Increased activity	
V. C. What effect do sensory experiences have on the child's attention?	Maintains focus in the face of competing sensory demands	Competing sensory demands are very apt to draw the child's attention Child focuses on irrelevant sensory demands	Increased focus in the presence of minor competing sensory demands Increased awareness of relevant sensory demands	

Transdisciplinary Play-Based System (TPBA2/TPBI2)
by Toni Linder.

(continued on next page)

(continued from previous page)

Observation Guidelines: Sensorimotor Development **TPBA 2**

Questions	Strengths	Examples of behaviors of concern	"Ready for"	Notes
VI. Sensorimotor contributions to daily life and self-care				

VI. A. How well does the child eat a simple snack?	Eats snack safely
	Able to manage all foods
	  Liquids
	  Soft or pureed
	  Mashed with texture (e.g., applesauce)
	  Hard (e.g., raw vegetables)
	  Ground meat
	  Chewy (e.g., raisins)
	  Mixed texture (e.g., noodle soup)
	Likes food with a wide variety of textures, tastes, smells
	Eats independently
	  Finger feeding
	  Spoon/fork
	  Bottle/cup/glass
	Amount of time is reasonable
	Uses good table manners
		Cannot manage one or more textures of food
		Cannot manage one or more utensils
		Cannot manage cup or glass
		Requires assistance from caregiver
		Dislikes many foods
		Time is excessive
		Drools excessively
		Not safe
			New/improved oral motor skills
			New/improved skills for handling utensils
			Increased safety
			Increased independence
			Increased repertoire of foods
			Decreased time
			Decreased drooling
			Devices or adaptations	

VI. B. How well does the child perform simple dressing tasks?	Easily performs all tasks
	  Taking off socks
	  Putting on socks
	  Unbuttoning/buttoning
	  Zipping pants and coat
	  Tying shoes
	Amount of time is reasonable
		Requires assistance for one or more clothing items
		Requires assistance for fasteners
		Time/effort is excessive
		Refuses
			New skills
			Decreased time/effort
			Increased willingness
			Increased independence
			Devices or adaptations	

Transdisciplinary Play-Based System (TPBA2/TPBI2)
by Toni Linder.

TPBA2 Observation Notes:
Sensorimotor Development

Child's name: _____ Parent(s): _____

Birth date: _____ Assessment date: _____ Age: _____

Person(s) completing the form: _____

Directions: Record the child information (name, caregiver[s], birth date, age), assessment date, person(s) completing this form, and your observations about the child in the spaces below. You are encouraged to review the corresponding TPBA2 Observation Guidelines prior to recording your observations here, as the Guidelines list what to look for. Newer TPBA users may opt to use the TPBA2 Observation Guidelines as a method for collecting information during the assessment instead of the TPBA2 Observation Notes.

I. Functions underlying movement (posture, muscle tone)

II. Gross motor activity (level of skill, enjoyment, positions, independence, fluidity, bilateral coordination)

III. Arm and hand use (effectiveness, pleasure, reach, pushing, batting, grasp, release, in-hand manipulation, tool use)

(continued on next page)

IV. Motor planning and coordination (toy use, sequencing, spatial and temporal abilities, positioning and use of both sides of the body, organization, force, timing of movement, ease of movement)

V. Modulation of sensation and its relationship to emotion, activity level, and attention (regulation of sensation, sensation seeking, avoidance, timing of responses, activity level, attention)

VI. Sensorimotor contributions to daily life and self-care (eating, dressing, enjoyment, gross motor skills, fine motor skills, other self-care tasks)

TPBA2 Age Table: Sensorimotor Development

Child's name: _____   Age: _____   Birth date: _____

Parent(s): _____   Assessment date: _____

Person(s) completing the form: _____

Directions: Based on the observations recorded on the TPBA2 Observation Guidelines and/or TPBA2 Observation Notes, review the Age Table to determine the age level that most closely matches the child's performance. It may be helpful to circle items on the Age Table that the child can do. If items are circled across multiple age levels, find the child's age level by finding the mode (i.e., determine which age level has the most circled items). Age levels after 12 months/1 year represent ranges rather than individual months and are preceded by "By." If the most circled items appear in one of these age levels, consider the child's age level to be the month shown (e.g., if the most circled items appear in the "By 21 months" level, the child's age level for that subcategory is 21 months).

Note: This Age Table collapses Functions Underlying Movement and Gross Motor Activity subcategories into one column. Motor Planning and Coordination and Modulation of Sensation and Its Relationship to Emotion, Activity Level, and Attention subcategories have not been included in this Age Table. These subcategories help users observe qualitative performance but are not related to a child's age level.

Age level	Functions underlying movement and Gross motor activity	Arm and hand use	Sensorimotor contributions to daily life and self-care
1 month	Muscle tone: Unsupported head flops forward or backward. Posture and gross motor: Supine: Head to side; random arm and leg movements; hands open or closed. Prone: Weight on hands, forearms, and chest. Beginning to lift and turn head to clear nose. Sitting: Lifts and maintains head in line midline briefly when placed in sitting.	General: Keeps hands fisted or slightly open. Reach/bimanual skill: Asymmetrical arm movements. Grasp: Involuntary grasp in response to touch in palm. Release: No voluntary release. Hand opens if touched on top.	Eating: Oral reflexes (e.g., rooting) present. Tongue moves in and out (suckling). May lose liquid from sides of mouth. Rarely drools because of minimal saliva production. Sequences two or more sucks from the bottle/breast before pausing to swallow or breathe.
2 months	Muscle tone: Keeps head erect briefly in upright and rights when tipped forward or backward, but head still bobs. Posture and gross motor: Supine: Maintains head in midline. Cycles arms and legs smoothly. Prone: Lifts head asymmetrically to 45 degrees.	Grasp: Grasp becoming voluntary. Holds object for a few moments. Release: No voluntary release.	Eating: Drooling increases as jaw and tongue move in wider excursions.

(continued on next page)

Developed with Anita C. Bundy.

Transdisciplinary Play-Based System (TPBA2/TPBI2)
by Toni Linder.

(continued from previous page)

Age Table: Sensorimotor Development **TPBA** 2

Age level	Functions underlying movement and Gross motor activity	Arm and hand use	Sensorimotor contributions to daily life and self-care
3 months	Posture and gross motor: Supine: Head in mid-position and posture symmetrical. Brings hands to midline; kicks with both feet. Moves limbs reciprocally or arms together, legs together. Prone: Symmetrical head lifting 45–90 degrees. Shoulders slightly abducted. Sitting: When supported, helps maintain position; minimal head bobbing. Unsupported, maintains head in midline, supports weight on arms briefly in front. Standing: Held in standing, presses feet against surface and takes some weight briefly (0–3 months). May bend and straighten knees. When picked up, brings body up compactly; keeps head in line with body.	General: Hands held together on chest, usually without object. Pulls forearm toward body in response to stimulus on little finger side. Rotates forearm upward and spreads fingers in response to stimulus on thumb side. Reach/bimanual skill: Begins to swipe, but may be far off target (1–3 months). Reaches for object with arms, starting at sides and closing in front of body; often contacts object with closed fists. Grasp: Voluntary grasp emerges (e.g., actively holds rattle put in hand).	Eating: Sequences 20 or more sucks from breast/bottle. Uses a sucking or suckling pattern for pureed foods. Dressing: Body parts are easily manipulated by the adult for dressing. Child practices grasping by clutching and pulling at clothing.
4 months	Posture and gross motor: Supine: Turns head; tucks chin. May fall to side when lifting legs. Prone: Lifts and maintains head 90 degrees. Legs extended; may deliberately flex muscles from waist down, raising hips. Rolls from side to side. May have uncontrolled weight shifting. May roll from stomach or side to supine. Sitting: Sits supported 10–15 minutes, head erect and steady, back firm. Standing: Pulled to stand, extends legs and keeps body in same plane from shoulders to feet. Extends legs to catch self when lowered to ground.	General: Uses hands more agilely and with more variety. Reach/bimanual skill: Symmetric, midline movements. Objects held with both hands at midline. Grasp: Hands predominantly open. Grasps with ring and little fingers but cannot manipulate items. Release: Variety of hand movements used to avoid contact.	Eating: Opens mouth adaptively. Closes lips. Gums solid food. Ejects food with tongue.

(continued on next page)

Developed with Anita C. Bundy.

Transdisciplinary Play-Based System (TPBA2/TPBI2)
by Toni Linder.
Copyright © 2008 Paul H. Brookes Publishing Co., Inc. All rights reserved.

Age Table: Sensorimotor Development **TPBA 2**

Age level	Functions underlying movement and Gross motor activity	Arm and hand use	Sensorimotor contributions to daily life and self-care
5 months	Posture and gross motor: Head control and head righting have improved significantly. Supine: May roll to side accidentally (4–5 months). Pushes back into extension with legs. May lift head and shoulders. Prone: Lifts head with active chin tuck and elongated neck. Elbows in front of shoulders; hips abducted and externally rotated. May roll from stomach to back. May push on hands and draw up knees. Tipped in prone, trunk and limb reactions apparent. Rolls with trunk rotation. Sitting: Sits supported for long periods (30 minutes), back firm; holds head steady and erect continuously. When pulled to sit, chin is tucked and head in line or leading. May assist with arms and tummy muscles; head may lag slightly at first. Standing: Easily pulled to stand. Supported under arms, stands and moves body up and down, stamps one foot, then the other. Movement: On stomach, moves by rocking, rolling, or twisting; on back, moves by kicking against flat surface.	General: Gropes in response to tactile stimulus. Moves objects to mouth. Reach/bimanual skill: Fairly coordinated two-hand reach with one-hand grasp; object transfer hand to hand; bilateral holding and fingering. Grasp: Grasps objects tightly by pressing with flexed fingers against palm and all fingers. Can hold a small toy or rattle while shaking or banging it. Release: Two-stage transfer, taking hand grasps before releasing hand lets go.	Eating: May begin to regularly eat solids. Uses a primitive bite-and-release pattern on soft cookie, though may revert to sucking it. Dressing: Becomes more active and excited, tries to turn over.
6 months	Posture and gross motor: Supine: Contacts feet with hands (5–6 months). May bring feet to mouth and suck on toes. May roll from back to belly. Prone: Landau reaction complete when held in prone position. Head held vertically. Increased head, hip, and trunk control allows free movement; turns, twists in all directions. Bears weight on extended arms; may push backward. Movement of trunk, head, and limbs counteracts tipping.	General: Rotates wrist; turns, manipulates objects crudely. Reach/bimanual skill: Simultaneous, symmetric, bilateral approach with one- or two-hand grasp. Grasp: Grasps objects with whole palm and all fingers; adjusts hand to object using visual and tactile information. Can hold large ball with two hands. Release: Releases objects during mouthing or bimanual play.	Eating: Helps bring bottle to mouth. Takes one or two swallows from a cup. Rarely drools in supine, prone, or sitting unless babbling or attention is engaged elsewhere. Swallows some thicker pureed food (4–6 months). Dressing: Pulls off hat; lies still and cooperates with dressing.

(continued on next page)

Developed with Anita C. Bundy.

Transdisciplinary Play-Based System (TPBA2/TPBI2) by Toni Linder.

(continued from previous page)

Age Table: Sensorimotor Development **TPBA** 2

Age level	Functions underlying movement and Gross motor activity	Arm and hand use	Sensorimotor contributions to daily life and self-care
6 months *(continued)*	Sitting: Sits unsupported momentarily (5–6 months) with head in extension, arms lifted off surface and shoulder blades retracted; cannot maintain indefinitely or move in and out. May extend arms forward to catch self and prop. Can move head freely. Standing: When supported can take full weight on legs (5–6 months). Movement: Propels self on tummy with legs, steers with arms, goes backward or forward.		
7 months	Posture and gross motor: Head control is excellent. Most babies are very active against gravity—rolling, pivoting, assuming quadruped and bear-standing, trying to crawl, coming to sitting, and pulling to stand. Supine: When tilted on back, trunk, head, and limb reactions are well developed. Actions of trunk, head, and arms counteract falling to sides. May roll back to tummy. Prone: Controlled reaching with weight on one forearm. Rolls tummy to back. Sitting: Head leads when pulled to sit or stand. Hands free while sitting. Can catch self with hands when pushed forward; may catch self sideways.	General: Increased visual and hand control enables the baby to inspect toys. Reach/bimanual skill: Bilateral approach with unilateral prehension; bilateral object manipulation; associated bimanual movements. Grasp: Beginning to grasp with thumb side of hand; objects held against fingers with thumb; beginning differentiation of thumb and little finger sides of hand for holding objects. Release: Transfers object from one hand to the other, releases against a resisting surface.	Eating: Feeds self soft biscuit with one hand. Chewing is present.
8 months	Posture and gross motor: Prefers standing and being active. Does not like supine and moves to prone or onto side. Arms move freely away from body. Prone: Rocks (head and chest high off mattress), limbs extended and back arched. Uses arms and legs to pivot.	General: Little finger side stable. Reach/bimanual skill: Reaches for objects with fingers overextended. Must pay full attention. Grasp: Increased finger and thumb dexterity to pick up small objects, manipulate them, and so forth. Object held proximal to finger pads. Release: Releases above a surface with wrist flexion.	Eating: Takes ground or junior foods and mashed table foods. Can use upper lip to assist in removing food from spoon.

(continued on next page)

Developed with Anita C. Bundy.

Transdisciplinary Play-Based System (TPBA2/TPBI2) by Toni Linder.

Age Table: Sensorimotor Development **TPBA 2**

Age level	Functions underlying movement and Gross motor activity	Arm and hand use	Sensorimotor contributions to daily life and self-care
8 months *(continued)*	Sitting: Pushes up to sit with arms from side. Or in crawl position, flexes one leg to tummy, extends and pushes it against surface; other leg follows. Good balance; can be left alone in sitting. Standing: May pull to stand on support surface. Movement: Crawls, climbs; transitions through many positions.		
9 months	Posture and gross motor: Most babies are combining gross and fine motor activity. Prone: Rolls tummy to back with rotation. Can assume quadruped and rock. Lies propped on one side and reaches; rotation in trunk. Sitting: Uses arms behind body and head and trunk to counteract backward falls. Standing: Stands briefly with one hand held. Pulls to stand, shifts weight; may rotate; may remove one hand from support. Movement: Crawls on belly. May propel self forward by falling. May pull self from hands and knees to standing and cruise along furniture.	General: Combining hand skills with standing, sitting, and so forth. More interest in and control of small objects. Reach/bimanual skill: Dissociation of symmetric arm movements. Plays with two toys, one in each hand, banging together. Grasp: Grasps small objects between thumb and lateral border of index finger. Object rotation by transferring it hand to hand. Release: Voluntary (7–9 months). Finger movements: Index finger leads, points, tries to poke into holes, hooks and pulls.	Eating: Sitting in chair, no external support is needed; seat belt used for security not support. No longer loses liquid during sucking initiation or when breast/bottle is removed. Uses an up–down sucking pattern for semisolids. Feeds self spilled bits from tray. Dressing: Child anticipates adults' actions and starts to offer arm. Pulls off booties.
10 months	Posture and gross motor: Prone: Moves from hands-and-knees to sitting or half sitting. Reaches from hands-and-knees position. May assume a modified hands-and-knees position with one foot on ground and hands in use. Balance developing in hands and knees position. Sitting: Sits without support and can play with toys (5–10 months). Sits in both W and side sitting positions (8–10 months). Gets onto hands and knees, stomach from sitting. Standing: Stands with little support. Sits down from standing without falling. May assume stand by going through half kneel.	Grasp: Can grasp with thumb and first two fingers or occasional tip of thumb and forefinger; grasp accurate without stabilization. Can use spherical grasp. Release: Active release by flinging object; object released above surface.	Eating: Helps hold cup and spoon. Tips bottle to drink. Feeds self whole meals from bottle. Uses pincer grasp on finger food. Dressing: Pulls off socks.

(continued on next page)

Developed with Anita C. Bundy.

Transdisciplinary Play-Based System (TPBA2/TPBI2) by Toni Linder.

(continued from previous page)

Age Table: Sensorimotor Development **TPBA 2**

Age level	Functions underlying movement and Gross motor activity	Arm and hand use	Sensorimotor contributions to daily life and self-care
10 months **(continued)**	Movement: Very active (static sitting rare), exploring. Can crawl, and may begin to creep on all fours; climbs up and down from chairs. When tipped, trunk, head, and limb reactions are well developed.		
11 months	Posture and gross motor: Sitting: Variety of sitting and leg positions; moves in and out easily. Standing: May stand alone momentarily. Arm position varies. Movement: Creeps, stands, may walk (usually leaning on furniture or holding someone's hand), climbs.	General: Grasp is changing from three fingers to a neat pincer using thumb and first finger. Likes to carry objects during crawling and walking. Reach/bimanual skill: Cooperative bimanual movements. Release: Greater control of release. Finger movements: Uses a strong index finger approach for poking into small holes and labeling objects.	Eating: Grabs spoon in fist (10–11 months). Dressing: Holds foot out for shoe and arm out for sleeve.
12 months or 1 year	Posture and gross motor: Sitting: Uses rotation to attain a sitting posture. Reaches for distant objects, with one arm to lean on while the other reaches. Reaches above the head with both arms alternately and without losing trunk stability. Reaches behind the back with exaggerated twisting. Standing: May stand alone briefly (9–12 months). Actions: Rolls ball to adult. Movement: Active and independent. Walks with hand held or may take several steps independently; some children use walking as primary locomotion.	Reach/bimanual skill: Uses accurate reach for toy. Reaches across midline. Bimanual activities are performed as mirror movements. Increased capacity to associate objects. One hand stabilizes and one hand manipulates. Grasp: Tip of thumb and forefinger used in grasp. Complete thumb opposition. Begins to make appropriate wrist and hand adjustments for different weights. Release: Greater control of release. Able to release 1-inch cube into container and tiny objects into small holes. Objects still do not always land where intended. Finger movements: Points to toy and explores toy with index finger. In-hand manipulation: Moves small objects from finger to palm (translation). Tool: Imitates use of tools such as a comb.	Eating: Drooling is under control. Can take coarsely chopped table foods, including some easily chewed meats. Takes liquid primarily from a cup. Can hold and drink from bottle/spout cup with lid, hands pressed to sides. Often insists on self-feeding and can finger feed part of the meal. Takes bite-size pieces from plate with delicate grasp, appropriate force, and easy release. Dressing: Pushes off pants if soiled.

(continued on next page)

Developed with Anita C. Bundy.

Transdisciplinary Play-Based System (TPBA2/TPBI2)
by Toni Linder.

(continued from previous page)

Age Table: Sensorimotor Development **TPBA** 2

Age level	Functions underlying movement and Gross motor activity	Arm and hand use	Sensorimotor contributions to daily life and self-care

By 15 months	Posture and gross motor:
	  Standing: Stands, squats, and stoops.
	  Movement: Slower walking speed. Creeps up stairs.
		Reach/bimanual skill: Beginning of two-hand reach; one hand stabilizing and one manipulating.
		Grasp: Deft and precise grasp; a variety of grasps used. However, most grasps are stationary. Can hold two small objects simultaneously (dissociation of sides of hand).
		Release: Controlled release.
		In-hand manipulation: Objects transferred between hands rather than with in-hand manipulation.
			Eating: Sucking and swallowing from a cup well coordinated, with choking rarely occurring. Dips spoon in food and brings to mouth. Holds cup by handle but likely to tip. Fisted hand, pronated forearm, turns spoon to get contents into mouth.
			Dressing: Removes mittens (12–14 months). Can reach to toes while standing.
			Toileting: Will sit on toilet for 1 minute when placed and supervised.

By 18 months	Posture and gross motor:
	  Sitting: Sits in small chair. Climbs into adult chair.
	  Actions: Picks up toy from floor. Flings ball (9–18 months).
	  Movement: Walks well, pulling toys. Begins to run. Walks upstairs with one hand held.
		General: Increasing strength and dissociation of fingers and two sides of hands enable child to use tools and manipulate objects.
		Reach/bimanual skill: Improved use of lead and assist hands. Can perform sequences of alternating two-hand movements.
		Grasp: Static grasp on spoon.
		Release: Controlled release, but continued tendency to extend fingers all at one time limits precision of placement.
		Finger movements: Points to picture with index finger (12–18 months).
		Construction: Stacks 3 blocks.
		Tool use: Holds crayon and makes scribbles.
			Eating: Fills spoon, turns in mouth, spilling. Lifts cup to mouth, may drop.
			Dressing: Tries to put shoes on, usually getting half way. Pulls off hat, socks, mittens and helps with other clothing. Lifts foot for adult to put on shoe or pants.
			Toileting: Indicates by actions that he or she is wet. Will sit on toilet for 1 minute when placed and left alone.

By 21 months	Movement: Moves ride-on toy with no pedals. Climbs down from adult chair.	General: Begins to participate in multi-part tasks. In-hand manipulation: May begin to string beads.	Eating: Handles cup well. Unwraps food. Easy lip closure; no loss of food or liquid; eats variety of textures. Toileting: Indicates need to go to the toilet.

(continued on next page)

Developed with Anita C. Bundy.

Transdisciplinary Play-Based System (TPBA2/TPBI2)
by Toni Linder.

(continued from previous page)

Age Table: Sensorimotor Development

Age level Functions	underlying movement and Gross motor activity	Arm and hand use	Sensorimotor contributions to daily life and self-care
By 24 months or 2 years	Posture and gross motor: Standing: Balances when stationary. Can stand briefly on one foot. Actions: Flings ball forward at large target. Kicks ball forward (20–24 months). Movement: Walks with arm swing at elbow, heel–toe progression, and balanced gait. Jumps off floor (17–24 months). Walks upstairs holding on (12–23 months). Walks downstairs holding on (13–23 months).	Reach/bimanual skill: Uses hands consistently in a lead-assist fashion. Grasp: Precision tasks are performed with fingertip grasp and those requiring power with palmar grasp. Grasps crayon in palm and turns hand thumb up or grasps crayon with fingers. Release: Greater precision and control of release; adjustment of hand opening according to object's size and shape. In-hand manipulation: Can move one or two small objects from palm to fingers (translation). Can un-screw bottle cap (simple rotation). Can turn pages of book (18–24 months). Construction: Builds tower of 4 blocks (18–24 months). Completes 4–5-piece puzzle (18–24 months). Tool use: Begins to use simple tools (e.g., toy ham-mer; 18–24 months). Draws simple figure (18–24 months).	Eating: Lifts open cup to drink, some tipping. Can hold cup with one hand, free hand poised to help. Can suck and use straw. Point of spoon enters mouth first. Unwraps food. Uses spoon well with minimal spilling. Opens jars. Dressing: Can take off shoe if lace is untied (18–24 months). Helps to push down/pull up trousers (21–24 months). Is able to find large sleeve hole. Toileting: Rarely has accidents from lack of bowel control. Is bladder trained during the day and dry at night if taken up.
By 30 months	Movement: Walks upstairs with no support (18–30 months). Walks downstairs with no support (19–30 months). Jumps from bottom step (19–30 months). Begins to pedal tricycle. Climbs up and down furniture independently (24–30 months).	Construction: Lines up objects. Tool use: Begins to snip with scissors.	Eating: Eats the same food as the rest of the family; can grade mouth opening to the size of food. Holds fork in fist (28+ months). Spears and shov-els food with fork with little spilling. Can pour from small pitcher (24–30 months). Dressing: Can remove pull-down lower-body gar-ments with elastic waist (24–30 months). Tries to assist with fasteners and lacing. Buttons one large front button.

(continued on next page)

Developed with Anita C. Bundy.

Transdisciplinary Play-Based System (TPBA2/TPBI2) by Toni Linder.

(continued from previous page)

Age Table: Sensorimotor Development

Age level	Functions underlying movement and Gross motor activity	Arm and hand use	Sensorimotor contributions to daily life and self-care
By 36 months or 3 years	Actions: Catches 10-inch ball against chest (30–35 months). Movement: Walks with rotating trunk and reciprocal arm swing. Walks upstairs and downstairs alternating feet (23–36 months). Climbs nursery apparatus (30–36 months).	Grasp: Uses effective power grasp on tools. Uses palmar grasp on spoon. Release: Timing of release is such that can throw small ball at least 3 feet but not with high degree of accuracy. In-hand manipulation: Moves coin from palm to fingers. Shifts fingers to separate magazine pages or cards. Can use fingertips to roll clay into small ball (simple rotation). Construction: Can stack 9–10 small blocks (24–36 months).	Eating: Holds cup by handle with one hand. Sets table with help. Wipes up spills. Grasps spoon with fingers. Dressing: Can untie laces and take off shoes (24–36 months). Can put on shoe, but it may be on the wrong foot. Is independent with pull-down garments. Opens front and side buttons. Closes front snaps. Removes all clothing; can put on socks, shirt, coat. Toileting: Responds to routine times and usually does not have bowel movements at other times. Will seat self on toilet (33 months). Adjusts clothing to go to toilet with assistance. Attempts unsuccessfully to wipe self.
By 42 months	Actions: Throws ball 5–7 feet.	Tool use: Uses scissors, snipping with alternating full-finger extension and flexion.	Eating: Lifts open cup to drink with one hand. Obtains drink from tap. Chews with grinding movement (36–42 months). Dressing: Opens front zipper on pants or jacket (39+ months). Buttons series of three buttons. Undresses rapidly and well. Dresses self. Toileting: Is dry at night even if he or she does not wake up.
By 48 months or 4 years	Actions: Catches ball with elbows bent in front of body (36–48 months). Movement: Walks like an adult. Exhibits true running with trunk rotation and arm swing. Can steer tricycle around obstacles.	Grasp: Precision (static tripod) grasp emerges on pencil or crayon (36–48 months). In-hand manipulation: Can position marker or crayon using simple rotation. Tool use: Colors within the lines (36–48 months). Draws face (36–48 months).	Eating: Uses napkin. Holds spoon with fingers for solid foods. Dressing: Unbuckles belt or shoes (45+ months). Needs little assistance with removing T-shirt or sweater, or with putting on underpants, shorts, trousers, or socks and shoes (except laces). Distinguishes front and back of garment and turns clothing right-side out. Can put two hands together behind back. Toileting: Can manage clothes without difficulty.

Developed with Anita C. Bundy.

Transdisciplinary Play-Based System (TPBA2/TPBI2)
by Toni Linder.

(continued from previous page)

Age Table: Sensorimotor Development **TPBA** 2

Age level	Functions underlying movement and Gross motor activity	Arm and hand use	Sensorimotor contributions to daily life and self-care
By 54 months	Actions: Uses forward weight shift to throw ball further. Throws with some directional accuracy. Movement: 33% of 4-year-olds able to hop on one foot and 43% can gallop, but only 14% can skip (Clark & Whitall, 1989).	Reach/bimanual skill: Consistent hand preference emerges. Begins to stabilize paper when coloring, drawing. Grasp: Holds forearm in mid-position when gripping scissors. In-hand manipulation: Holds several small items in hand while moving individual items with radial fingers.	Eating: Eats with fork held in fingers rather than fist (51+ months). Chooses fork over spoon when appropriate. Pours from large pitcher or carton. Uses knife to cut soft foods. Dressing: Can insert belt in loops. Buttons/unbuttons most buttons (48–54 months). Closes front zipper and locks tab (48–54 months).
60 months or 5 years	Actions: Throws smoothly, releases on time and in line with target (36–60 months). When catching, adjusts body position in line with ball and has elbows at sides (54–59 months). When striking with a bat, the body is a good distance from object, contact is made with extended arms. Movement: Skips with coordination (alternate step-hop pattern, body suspended momentarily, reciprocal arm swing). Hops on one foot (36–60 months). Can stand on one foot for several seconds and walk along curb without falling. Jumps down from high step; jumps forward. Climbs ladder (48–60 months).	Grasp: Draws with dexterity, using a dynamic tripod grasp (movement comes from fingers rather than arm and hands). In-hand manipulation: Manipulates tiny objects in finger tips without dropping. Can shift fingers downward on marker or pencil to get it into position. Construction: Completes puzzles of 10 pieces (48–60 months). Tool use: Uses scissors to cut out shapes (48–60 months). Draws stick figures and copies name (48–60 months).	Eating: Fixes dry cereal; serves self; carries glass without spilling. Sets table without help. Dressing: Is able to dress with care. Can open back zipper (57+ months). Puts shoes on correct feet (54–60 months). Unties back sash on apron or dress. Toileting: Anticipates immediate toileting needs. Completely cares for self at toilet, including wiping. Flushes toilet after each use.
By 66 months	Movement: Mature running pattern develops (60–66 months); tests skills by racing.	Tool use: Draws shapes in proper spatial orientation.	Eating: Spreads with knife (60–66 months). Dressing: Opens back buttons. Closes back zipper. Puts shoes on correct feet.
By 72 months or 6 years	Actions: Kicks to a target. Movement: Skips effortlessly with elbows flexed, landing on balls of feet. Gallops with full coordination (60–72 months). Hops in straight line.	Grasp: Complex scissors grasp develops. Middle finger in lower hole, ulnar fingers flexed, index finger stabilizes lower part of scissors. In-hand manipulation: Rotates pencil to use eraser. Manipulates paper during scissors use.	Eating: Child is efficient at all aspects of eating. Use of knife and fork is being refined. Carries glass without spilling. Eats liquids, spoon held with fingers, few spills. Dressing: Can dress with care. Can tie a bowknot in apron or dress at front. Snaps back snaps. Toileting: Washes hands after toileting without reminder of technique.

Sources: Alexander, Boehme, & Cupps (1993); Caplan (1973); Case-Smith (2001); Coley (1978); Henderson & Pehoski (1995); Keogh & Sugden (1985); Klein & Morris (1999); Piper & Darrah (1994).

Developed with Anita C. Bundy.

Transdisciplinary Play-Based System (TPBA2/TPBI2) by Toni Linder.

TPBA2 Observation Summary Form: Sensorimotor Development

Child's name: _____ Age: _____ Birth date: _____

Parent(s): _____ Assessment date: _____

Person(s) completing the form: _____

Directions: For each of the subcategories below, shown in a 1–9-point Goal Attainment Scale, circle the number that indicates the child's developmental status, using findings from the TPBA2 Observation Guidelines or TPBA2 Observation Notes for this domain. Next, consider the child's performance in relation to same-age peers by comparing the child's performance with the TPBA2 Age Table. Use the Age Table to arrive at the child's age level for each subcategory (follow directions on the Age Table). Then, circle AA, T, W, or C by calculating percent delay:

If a child's age level < chronological age: 1 − (age level/CA) = _____ % delay

If child's age level > chronological age: (age level/CA) − 1 = _____ % above

To calculate CA, subtract the child's birth date from the assessment date and round up or down as appropriate. When subtracting days, take into consideration the number of days in the month (i.e., 28, 30, 31).

TPBA2 Subcategory	Level of the child's ability as observed in functional activities									Rating compared with other children of same age				
	1	**2**	**3**	**4**	**5**	**6**	**7**	**8**	**9**	Above average (AA)	Typical (T)	Watch (W)	Concern (C)	Age level (mode)
Functions underlying movement	Needs to have total body support in all positions.		Holds head steady and can sit with support.		Moves between variety of sitting and prone postures. May stand alone briefly.		Shows anticipatory postural adjustments. Stands independently and sits on chair.		Is able to assume and maintain functional positions and move smoothly and independently between them.	AA Comments:	T	W	C	_____
Gross motor activity	Remains wherever placed; no active movement out of a position.		Moves by rolling and commando crawl.		Moves around the environment on all fours, cruises, and takes a few steps.		Walks and runs easily.		Is able to do complex gross motor actions (e.g., hopping, skipping).	AA Comments:	T	W	C	_____

(continued on next page)

(continued from previous page)

Observation Summary Form: Sensorimotor Development TPBA 2

TPBA2 Subcategory	Level of the child's ability as observed in functional activities									Rating compared with other children of same age				
	1	2	3	4	5	6	7	8	9	Above average (AA)	Typical (T)	Watch (W)	Concern (C)	Age level (mode)
Arm and hand use	Tracks objects. No voluntary control of arms, hands, and fingers.		Reaches for objects and people; bats at objects without grasping.		Uses gross grasp to obtain objects; little active release.		Grasp matches size and shape of objects; gross release.		Can use arms, hands, and fingers efficiently and effectively to reach, grasp, manipulate in hand, and precisely release and place objects.	AA Comments:	T	W	C	___
Motor planning and coordination	Has volitional movements for simple, routine actions or events. Does not attempt novel or multistep actions independently.		Has difficulty understanding what to do with objects or things in the environment. Uses repetitive actions without a functional goal and has difficulty executing even simple, nonroutine action sequences.		Can conceive of a goal, but needs prompting, demonstration, conscious effort, and multiple opportunities for practice to organize and execute a multistep task. Actions may appear awkward and slow, and results may be inaccurate.		Can conceive of a goal, but needs prompting or demonstration and conscious effort to sequence and execute the necessary actions to achieve a multistep, complex task. With effort and practice, can achieve accuracy.		Can conceive of a goal, and with little conscious effort, can organize and sequence a complex sequence of actions effectively and efficiently to achieve the intended objective.	AA Comments:	T	W	C	___
Modulation of sensation and its relationship to emotion, activity level, and attention	Despite modification attempts, over- or underreactivity to sensory input has a markedly negative impact on engagement with objects, people, or events in the environment.		Requires major and/or frequent modifications of environment or interpersonal interactions to demonstrate appropriate responses to sensory input.		Demonstrates appropriate response to sensory input with moderate modification to the environment or interactions.		Demonstrates appropriate response to sensory input with minimal modification to the environment or interactions.		Is nearly always able to appropriately respond to all types of sensory input without environmental modifications.	AA Comments:	T	W	C	___

Transdisciplinary Play-Based System (TPBA2/TPBI2) by Toni Linder.

(continued on next page)

(continued from previous page)

Observation Summary Form: Sensorimotor Development **TPBA 2**

TPBA2 Subcategory	Level of the child's ability as observed in functional activities									Rating compared with other children of same age				
	1	2	3	4	5	6	7	8	9	Above average (AA)	Typical (T)	Watch (W)	Concern (C)	Age level (mode)
Sensorimotor contributions to daily life and self-care	Is dependent on adults for all aspects of self-care because of difficulty with motor skills.		Is able to minimally help adult with motor aspects of self-care activities.		Can participate in all forms of self-care with moderate assistance from adults for motor aspects.		Needs minimal help with self-care activities and routines.		Is able to use motor skills to independently conduct everyday self-care activities and routines, including use of fasteners and cutlery.	AA Comments:	T	W	C	____
Vision	Does not use vision functionally at all.		Has major functional vision loss even with glasses or adaptive equipment.		Has moderate functional vision loss with glasses or adaptive equipment.		Has minimal functional vision loss with glasses or adaptive equipment.		Is able to attend to, localize, and use vision functionally without adaptations.	AA Comments:	T	W	C	____
Overall needs:														

Transsdisciplinary Play-Based System (TPBA2/TPBI2)
by Toni Linder

3

Vision Development

with Tanni L. Anthony

Vision, often reported as the most valuable sense for interpreting one's world, and the most studied of all senses, is unique for its ability to organize other sensory information and to provide simultaneous information from near and distant locations (Teplin, 1995). Twenty percent of all waking hours of a child ages 8 months to 3 years are spent with the child staring at people and objects (White, 1975).

The integrity of a young child's visual system is paramount to the process of typical childhood development; it has been described as the major sensory modality for an infant's conceptual development (Teplin, 1982). During the first year of life, the sense of sight is considered the most effective avenue of communicating and learning, and it remains an important avenue in which these skills are learned throughout childhood and life (Hyvärinen, 1994). Vision makes a significant contribution to rate and pattern of typical development (Sonksen, 1982).

Changes that occur from birth through age 7 play a critical role in a child's visual development. Although the first year of life chronicles the most rapid phases of visual development, fine adjustments occur to the visual system up through 9–10 years of age (Hyvärinen, 1988). Interference of any kind with the developing visual system of a young child will have consequences on a child's visual outcome (Daw, 1995).

When vision is affected in the early years, the results can be detrimental to the developing child, because the visual sense has ties to every developmental domain. For example, poor depth perception may affect a child's motor skills, poor eye teaming may influence later reading abilities, and uncorrected visual acuity may result in missed or fragmented information tied to concept development. The greater the young child's vision problem, the greater the risk for delayed or altered development. This is especially true if the vision problem has an early onset and is accompanied by additional developmental challenges or disabilities (Allen & Fraser, 1983; Ferrell, 1998; Hatton, Bailey, Burchinal, & Ferrell, 1997).

Portions of this chapter are reprinted with permission from Anthony, T.L. (2002). The inclusion of vision-development guidelines in the Transdisciplinary Play-Based Assessment: A study of reliability and validity. *Dissertation Abstracts International, 63*(12), A4271, Pro Quest Information (No. 30-74361).

Screening of a young child's vision is vital, especially if the child may be predisposed to vision problems. This chapter reviews the purpose, content, and design of Transdisciplinary Play-Based Assessment (TPBA2) for vision development for children up to 5 years of age.

VISUAL PROBLEMS VERSUS VISUAL IMPAIRMENT

What exactly is a vision problem and when does such a problem become something to worry about with a young child? The spectrum of visual difficulties ranges from potentially correctable visual acuity problems and poor coordination of eye movements to permanent visual loss associated with damage to the eye and/or to the neurological structures of the visual pathways and/or visual cortex.

The term *visual problem* can be defined as a visual condition that interferes with day-to-day visual functioning and has the potential for medical correction, such as poor acuity that can be corrected with eyeglasses. At its best, a visual problem is short term in nature and has a limited impact on a child's development. At its worst, a visual problem can affect the young child's development and, if untreated, may become a permanent visual concern or impairment (American Academy of Ophthalmology, 1997). Even if the vision problem cannot be corrected medically, early detection is important for the child's referral to an appropriate early intervention program that can address developmental issues affected by a vision loss (Morse & Trief, 1985). Furthermore, when a vision problem is identified early, appropriate adaptations to the environment can assist learning in the early years (Calvello, 1989).

A significant proportion of the general population, including children, has a range of visual problems. Visual disorder accounts for the most prevalent disabling condition in childhood (Gerali, Flom, & Raab, 1990). One in 20 children has some level of significant visual defect that requires the attention of a medical specialist and/or a special educator (Schor, 1990). The vast majority of these difficulties likely fall into the visual problem category based on the known incidence of visual impairment. Actual visual impairment is a low-incidence disability. However, educational teams are likely to work with children who are visually impaired (have an uncorrectable vision loss that meets Individuals with Disabilities Education Improvement Act [IDEA] of 2004 [PL 108-446] eligibility guidelines for this disability label), including those children who have additional disabilities. Children at risk for visual problems or visual impairment include the following:

- Children who were born prematurely

- Children who were exposed to prenatal toxins

- Children who had a traumatic birth with complications of anoxia

- Children who have a syndrome

- Children who had postnatal infections such as meningitis

- Children who experience a traumatic head injury

Any child who enters an early intervention program with a disability has an increased risk for a visual problem or impairment.

COMMON VISION PROBLEMS WITH YOUNG CHILDREN

The three leading causes of significant visual problems in the general pediatric population include amblyopia, strabismus, and refractive errors (American Academy of Ophthalmology, 1997; Gerali et al., 1990). A fourth, less common, problem is color deficiency.

In layperson's terms, *amblyopia* is a "lazy eye." The two most common reasons for amblyopia are a difference in strength of vision in the two eyes and/or crossed eyes in the early years of life (American Academy of Ophthalmology, 1997). A leading contributor to amblyopia is *strabismus,* a misalignment of the eyes that is usually a result of problems with the eye muscles or ocular nerve (Miller & Menacker, 2007). In strabismus, the eyes can either turn in (esotropia), out (exotropia), up (hypertropia), or down (hypotropia) (American Academy of Ophthalmology, 1997; Daw, 1995). Early detection of strabismus is critical, as it may interfere with the proper development of the visual system (Schor, 1990). Infants showing signs of a strabismus as young as 6 months of age should be referred to an eye care specialist (Schor, 1990). The finding of strabismus may warrant medical treatment such as glasses, eye patching, and/or surgery.

The third primary vision problem found in young children is a *refractive error* or the need for corrective lenses, such as glasses. The three types of refractive errors include nearsightedness, farsightedness, and astigmatism. The result of a refractive error is blurred vision. *Farsightedness* is the most common refractive error in the early years of life (Miller & Menacker, 2007). Children who are farsighted will see better at far distances than at near distances. Children who are *nearsighted* have poor distance vision, and they can see objects best when they are up close. If a child is nearsighted at a very young age, the level of nearsightedness is likely to increase rapidly over the childhood years up until postadolescence (Daw, 1995). As with farsightedness, the vision of a child who is only nearsighted can be corrected to normal vision with glasses.

Astigmatism may occur independently of farsightedness or nearsightedness or in conjunction with either condition. Astigmatism occurs when the shape of the cornea is elliptical and not spherical. The altered shape of the corneas influences how the light rays enter the eye and are ultimately focused on the retina (Menacker & Batshaw, 1997). The result is a blurred image that may be compromised further if the person is also farsighted or nearsighted.

The fourth and a less common vision problem with young children is color deficiency or color blindness. Red-green color blindness occurs in 8% of white men and 0.5%–1% of white women (Goble, 1984). The incidence of color deficiency in African American and Asian American populations is about half of that in European Americans. Color vision problems range from a mild color deficiency problem to total color blindness. Color deficiencies will not affect visual performance except for those tasks that require an accurate color identification. Color perception problems may be a challenge to the developing child whose preschool and elementary program involves color identification, matching, sorting, and coding tasks. In cases of total *color blindness* (or complete achromatopsia), which is extremely rare, visual acuity will also be affected in the range of low vision to legal blindness.

Classically, occupational therapists (OTs) and certified teachers of students with visual impairments (TVIs) are the most trained to address a child's visual skills. Both disciplines have unique assessment roles with regard to a young child's visual skills. Typically, occupational therapists focus on eye–hand skills, as they relate to fine motor development, and visual-perception skills of children with motor difficulties (Menken, Cermak, & Fisher, 1987). Teachers certified in the area of visual impairment are trained to work with the educational needs of learners who are blind or have low vision. An exclusive role of a TVI is to complete a comprehensive functional vision assessment (FVA) on students who have a diagnosed or strongly suspected visual impairment (Anthony, 2002). A FVA addresses how the child uses his or her affected vision and what strategies, equipment, and environmental features assist the child in seeing better. The purpose of the embedded visual development screening in TPBA is not for all disciplines to learn how to do a FVA on children with visual impairment, but rather a cursory screening of the visual functioning of children referred for TPBA.

OBSERVATION GUIDELINES FOR VISION DEVELOPMENT

The development of vision, as with other senses, is "orderly, sequential, and predictable" (Fewell & Vadasy, 1983, p. 37). Unlike any other sensory system, the sense of sight cannot be used prior to birth (Slater, 1996). Despite this notion and the fact that the human visual system is not complete at birth, the infant is born with the ability to see (Daw, 1995). The first major steps of visual development occur within the first 18 months of life. Over the course of the next 7 years, the visual system evolves into full maturity. Physiological functions of visual attention, visual acuity, eye teaming, color sensitivity, and light-to-dark adaptation develop quickly within the first year of life, whereas development during the first 2 years is particularly influenced by the child's visual environment (Knoblauch, Bieber, & Werner, 1996).

The visual modality has been investigated with more frequency than any other human sensory system (Talay-Ongan, 1998). The following review of the literature on visual development will focus primarily on key areas that may be found in the Observation Guidelines for visual development. In the following discussion, visual development is reviewed as it relates to TPBA2 Observation Guidelines for visual development. The vision development skills included in TPBA do not require any specialized equipment other than objects that the child will be interested in and small food items that are typically used during the snack portion of the assessment.

I. Visual Ability

I. A. What visual concerns have been noted?

A preassessment conversation with the child's family, and the completion of the Child and Family History Questionnaire (CFHQ) and Family Assessment of Child Functioning (FACF), will present an ideal opportunity for the assessment team to learn whether people who know the child best have any concerns about his or her vision. Caregiver input is especially important to the assessment team in identifying areas of concern. Walker and Wiske (1981) credit parents as being the first and often best assessors of a child's functioning and problems. Glascoe, MacLean, and Stone (1991) confirmed this belief in their work with parents; their research found that parental concerns about a child's development and behavior were reliable indicators of real problems. This finding was also evident in a French study by Vital-Durand, Ayzac, and Pinsaru (1996) with 2,413 infants. The infants, ages 4–15 months, were evaluated for their visual status. When parents brought their child in because of a vision concern, such as crossed eyes, the assessment findings were frequently positive for visual problems. Langley (2004) referenced the criterion of parent concern as adequate reason to screen a child's vision by a qualified eye care specialist or pediatrician.

I. B. What is the appearance of the eyes and eyelids?

Detecting a vision concern in a young child is typically not a complex process. Visual disorders can often be observed by the appearance of the eye(s) and/or through behavioral indicators (Goble, 1984). In standard vision screening literature, the "ABC" format is used in which *appearance, behavior,* and *complaints* are analyzed for visual problems (Colorado Department of Public Health and Environment, 1991). The appearance of the eyes suggests their general health. A good rule of thumb is that if something does not look right, there is probably a problem that should be investigated by an eye care specialist (Anthony, 1993a). Any deviation in the size of the eyes, their symmetry, and alignment (or lack thereof), clarity of the cornea and pupil, shape of the pupil, and so on are important indicators of visual capacity (Hollins, 1989). If both eyes are abnormally small in size, the child may have a condition called microphthalmos, a disorder that equates with legal blindness (Levack, 1991). Misalignment (eyes are not equally straight) signals a problem with strabismus. Excessive eye mattering, especially found in children with Down syndrome, may indicate blepharitis (Shapiro & France, 1985). Although blepharitis may not affect visual performance initially, if it becomes chronic the results may be an eye that cannot open or is at risk of corneal scratches due to hardened crust on the lids. Corneal clouding is never normal and can be a serious symptom of visual impairment. A cloudy pupil may be indicative of a maturing cataract or the rare presence of retinoblastoma (cancer affecting the eye). An excessively red or tearing eye may be symptomatic of allergies, eye infection, eyestrain, or visual fatigue. Asymmetries of the pupils and/or obvious abnormalities in the shape of the pupils, such as coloboma, a cleft in of the pupil, are serious signs of visual concerns (Teplin, 1995). If one or both eyelids are drooping, the child may have a ptosis.

In addition to the size and shape of the eyes, attention should be paid to their general movement. The presence of nystagmus should always be noted as a sign of visual impairment (however, nystagmus brought on by fast movement which dissipates after the person is still for a while is normal). Sensory nystagmus describes the rhythmical oscillation (to and fro movement) of the eyes when there is an early-onset visual impairment involving both eyes in the first year of life.

I. C. What functional acuity is observed?

Researchers have found that newborn infants have an innate response to the human face. In fact, Glass (1993) and Morse (1991) suggested that the human face may be the most appropriate stimulus to promote visual development. By 6–8 weeks of age, an infant can make eye contact with other people and begin to smile back to a smiling face; by 2–3 months of age an infant can make intense eye contact (Hyvärinen, 1994). Prior to this time, the infant is visually attracted to the human face with focus on the external qualities such as the contrast change between the hairline and face, as opposed to the internal details such as the eyes, mouth, and nose (Bushnell, 1982). Bailey (1994) noted that the ability to detect incremental differences in contrast is important for the infant's ability to distinguish facial features. Between 4 and 6 months, infants are increasingly interested in other infants' faces and their own mirror image (Glass, 2002).

Slater (1996) explained that the newborn has rudimentary form perception and perceives wholes rather than separate elements or parts. Within hours after birth, the infant will show preference for his or her mother's face over that of a stranger (Bushnell, 1982; Slater, 1996). This is due to an immediate learning and experiential process that is tied to the visual system. Between 6 weeks and 4–5 months, infants begin to smile at a friendly face (Atkinson, 1996).

The visual acuity of a newborn has been found to be 10–30 times poorer than that of an adult (Slater, 1996). An infant's acuity moves from about 20/600 to 20/40 toward the end of the first year of life based on measurements taken from the Preferential Looking Acuity Cards (Teller, McDonald, Preston, Sebris, & Dobson, 1986). A functional example of visual acuity can be seen at 6–7 months, when infants first notice items as small as food crumbs (Hyvärinen, 1994). In addition, normally sighted infants of 8 months of age can fixate on a 1.25-mm cake decoration candy from a distance of 10 or more inches (Pike et al., 1994). By 6 months of age, a typical infant can extend his or her focus up to at least 5 feet away (Atkinson & Van Hof-van Duin, 1993). By 18 months of age, children can fixate on a 2.5-mm ball located 20 feet away (Pike et al., 1994).

███████ **I. D. What gross visual field is observed?**

Langley (2004) described a normal visual field, as "the entire area of physical space visible to the eye without shifting gaze" (p. 142). At an adult level, a normal visual field is about 65 degrees nasally, 95 degrees to either side (temporally), 50 degrees above (superiorly), and 70 degrees below (inferiorly) (Atkinson & Van Hof-van Duin, 1993). Although researchers cannot agree on the exact time frame for an infant's visual field development, most researchers agree that infants younger than 6 months of age do not have a fully developed visual field (Mohan & Dobson, 2000). The young infant's visual field is limited to 20–30 degrees (Groenendaal & Van Hof-van Duin, 1992). At 2 months, the visual fields are the same shape as those of adults but are significantly smaller in size (Schwartz, Dobson, Sandstrom, & Van Hof-van Duin, 1987). At 6–7 months of age, an infant's visual field is similar (93%) to an adult's (Mayer, Fulton, & Cummings, 1988). By 1 year, children appear to have the same extent of visual field as adults (Sireteanu, 1996).

███████ **I. E. How does the child demonstrate eye teaming?**

I. F. How does the child demonstrate depth perception?

These two questions are interrelated and are thus discussed jointly. Eye movement or oculomotor skills are present at birth and continue to refine over the course of the next several months. Nine minutes from birth, infants turn their heads and eyes to follow (track) a moving face pattern (Goren, Sarty, & Wu, 1975). At this point in time, the eyes do not have independent movement from the head.

Hainline and Riddell (1996) stated that in order to see well, an individual must have the physiological ability to see clearly (visual acuity) and control one's eye movements—"both adequate sensory systems and reasonable oculomotor control" (p. 222). A component of eye teaming is to establish eye alignment. The infants' eyes begin to align between 3 and 6 months of age (Catalano & Nelson, 1994). If an eye persists in turning *in* after 2–3 months of age or turning *out* after 6 months of age, a referral should be made to an eye care specialist (Catalano & Nelson, 1994; Teplin, 1995).

The infant's ability to track (visually follow) a moving target progresses quickly over the first months of life. Vertical tracking from midline (nose to upper gaze) can be elicited at 1 month of age; horizontal tracking at 2 months, from the nose out to the ears; and horizontal tracking across midline at 4 months (Bishop, 1988). Circular tracking is evident by 2–3 months (Hyvärinen, 1994). By roughly 6 months, the infant can follow the trajectory of a dropped object. Velocity and accuracy of eye movements have reached adult performance levels by about 5 months of age (Harris, Jacobs, Shawkat, & Taylor, 1993). The eye movements of a child should be well coordinated by 6 months. If they are not, it might indicate an immature visual system, a muscle imbalance, or some other type of visual problem (Bishop, 1988).

As the fovea (central macula part of the retina that has the highest spatial resolution) matures, the eyes are better able to fix on an object. Between 3 and 6 months of age, fixation improves and stereopsis (a form of depth perception involving the ability to detect the presence of more than one near-range object) becomes evident (Daw, 1995). At this time, convergence is noted and orthotropia is mature. Convergence is the ability to maintain one's visual focus on an oncoming object. The eyes converge (turn toward each other) in order to follow the object moving closer to one's face (Vaughan, Asbury, & Tabbara, 1989). Orthotropia is the ability of both eyes to look at an object with single vision (a fused image) (Daw, 1995).

Binocular vision depends on the teamwork of both eyes. A variety of components must be in place to achieve binocular function. The first component is vergence.

Vergence can be described as the "change in the alignment of the visual axes of the two eyes to look at objects at different distances" (Hainline & Riddell, 1996, p. 222). The eyes must be able to converge (holding fixation on an oncoming object) and diverge (holding fixation on a retreating object). Second, there must be good acuity in both eyes, and, third, there must be some level of depth perception (Daw, 1995). The three components of *eye teaming, binocularity,* and *stereopsis* appear at about 4–5 months of age (Birch, Shimojo, & Held, 1985; Yonas & Granrud, 1985). If there is a misalignment of the eyes, full stereopsis cannot develop (Hainline & Riddell, 1996).

Atkinson (2000) described the sequence of shift of gaze skills in the developing infant. Shift of gaze describes the ability to shift one's visual attention from one item to another. By 4 months of age, the infant can cross midline in order to shift his or her gaze from one item to another (Glass, 1993). Shift of gaze is accomplished first with items that are located in the same depth range or distance away from the child's eyes. By 6 months, the infant can shift his or her visual attention from one object in one depth plane (e.g., near range) to another in a different depth plane (e.g., far range). At the end of the first year, a child can follow an adult's pointing gesture to a visual reference of another object and, as such, shows the skill of a shift of gaze from another person's hand to an object in distant space.

▬▬▬ I. G. What compensatory visual behaviors are observed?

A variety of behaviors may suggest the presence of a vision concern. Simple observation of how a child views objects of different sizes, colors, and contrasts; reacts to changes in lighting; and positions his or her body in visual tasks will yield valuable information about a visual problem or impairment. This question should be addressed toward the end of the assessment after the team has observed the child's visual development skills for a sustained period of time. Specific behaviors will be reviewed for their possible explanation of a vision-related problem.

Close Viewing of Objects

Children with visual acuity difficulties may hold objects close to their eyes or bring their head to within inches of an object for visual inspection. By holding an object close to one's eyes, it is enlarged or magnified for better viewing. The action of close viewing also narrows the visual field. As the object moves closer to the eyes, it takes up more of the available visual field and reduces one's focus on other visual information. The latter might be seen in a child with cortical visual impairment who has difficulty screening extraneous visual information.

Unique Head Postures

Head turning and/or tilting behavior may be a clue to several different types of visual problems. Specific head postures can indicate a visual field loss (Good & Hoyt, 1989). For example, a child might tip his or her head back because of a reduced upper field or to the side due to a restricted side (peripheral) visual field. Another reason for a head turn or head tilt may be to compensate for poor eye alignment, such as in the case of strabismus (Langley, 1998b). Children who are light sensitive may bow their heads to avoid illumination that is too bright for them (Jan, Groenveld, & Anderson, 1993). Catalano and Nelson (1994) found that individuals with gaze palsies may also tilt their heads to accommodate for their limited eye movement abilities.

Children with cortical visual impairment have been observed to turn their heads to the side when reaching for an object. This behavior has been studied repeatedly and there are two main theories as to its purpose. One theory is that head turning causes the child to employ peripheral vision (Jan, Groenveld, Sykanda, & Hoyt, 1987). Another theory is that the head turn averts the eyes from the reaching hand, thus reducing the visual confusion of watching a moving target (the hand) while maintaining gaze on the stationary target (Jan & Groenveld, 1993).

Unique Eye Positions

The term *eccentric fixation* is used to describe a situation in which it may not be evident that a child is looking at a particular target because his or her eyes are not directed to that target (Shane Cote & Smith, 1997). A child may use eccentric fixation because of conditions that involve a central field loss, such as severe amblyopia (Langley, 1998a). A specific eye position (e.g., eyes too far right) may also accompany head turning/tilting to accommodate for sensory nystagmus, as discussed in the previous section (Good & Hoyt, 1989).

Eye Pressing or Rubbing

Certain behaviors such as eye pressing can indicate the source of the visual impairment. For example, children who eye press (using fingers/fist to create pressure against their closed eye lids) often have retinal disorders (Jan et al., 1983). Eye pressing may induce a "light sparking" response that is stimulating to the child.

Eye rubbing may also be the result of itchy eyes, due to allergies or an eye infection, visual fatigue, or eyestrain.

Eye Blinking/Eye Closing

Rapid blinking or closing one's eyes when there is a sudden increase in illumination may indicate light sensitivity or photophobia. There is an association of photophobia with cortical visual impairment (Good & Hoyt, 1989), dry corneas, and certain eye conditions such as albinism, congenital glaucoma, and aniridia, a condition affecting the iris of the eye (Jan et al., 1993).

Eye blinking can also be symptomatic of individuals with eye movement disorders (Good & Hoyt, 1989). Other symptoms of poor eye movement control may include head turning and head nodding. These behaviors may assist the person in establishing focus.

Visual fatigue may be characterized by a number of behaviors such as closing one's eyes, putting one's head down, and/or turning the eyes away from the visual task at hand. Visual fatigue can be noted with children with strabismus or nystagmus who work hard to sustain their attention on fixation and other eye movement tasks (Levack, 1991).

Sudden Decrease of Movement

With an eye condition such as retinitis pigmentosa (RP), an individual has difficulty adjusting to changes of lighting whether the illumination is increased or decreased (Levack, 1991). This is evidenced by a sudden decrease or complete cessation of movement until the eyes adjust to the new lighting situation. A behavioral example of a light-to-dark adaptation problem would be the transfer of a task from a visual means to a tactile means (visual reach for an object to a tactually guided reach). A young child might become clingy to his or her parents at dusk, not wanting to walk without contact with another person due to poor night vision (Hyvärinen, 1995).

Complaints of Vision-Related Problems

Very young children are not likely to vocalize their concerns about their visual performance, because they may not be aware that other people see differently than they do. Problems such as feeling dizzy, nauseated, or having a headache due to visual strain will undoubtedly manifest through physical behavior as opposed to verbal complaints.

In addition to recognizing the ABCs of visual problems, early intervention personnel should understand the normal sequence of visual development. Many practitioners may not be aware that there is a physiological sequence of visual developmental milestones. As these milestones are reviewed, their close ties to the motor and cognitive domains will be apparent.

I. H. What visual-motor/visual-cognitive skills are observed?

With improved fixation skills and the development of depth perception, an infant learns to reach for an object. Vision tutors fine motor development in the child with sight. Hand watching is evident by 3–4 months of age (Bayley, 1993; Hyvärinen, 1994). A coordinated visually directed reach is noted by 4–6 months of age in a healthy infant (Bishop, 1988; Hyvärinen, 1994). Sonksen (1993) described the developing infant's fourth through twelfth months as "the integrative phase." During this period, vision is integrated with motor functions related to speech, hand skills, and movement. An infant's initial discrimination of stereoscopic depth cues occurs at 4 months of age, the same time an infant demonstrates a more accurate reach to objects (Atkinson, 2000).

Rather than using a curved motion to reach for an object at midline, a child with monocular vision draws the hand in from the side to a midline position, then reaches straight ahead (Hyvärinen, 1994). As fine motor skill development progresses, the infant is able to pick up smaller and smaller objects. By 5 months of age, a child is able to pick up a pellet using a whole-hand grasp (Bayley, 1993). Following grasping and reaching comes more accurate eye–hand coordination skills such as putting different sized objects into different sized containers, stacking, and so forth.

Although color vision is not a cognitive skill, naming, matching, and sorting colors are. Color vision has been studied in young infants. Black and white forms attract an infant's attention during the first few weeks of life; colorful toys follow later (Hyvärinen, 1994). Most research on the color vision of infants has concluded that infants early in life show poorer color discrimination than do older infants (Atkinson, 2000). Specialized testing has verified that infants at 3 months of age can detect color contrasts (Brown & Teller, 1989).

The first true means to educationally evaluate the child's ability to demonstrate color discrimination is at a developmental age of 29–33 months, when matching of primary colors can be accomplished (Parks et al., 1994). Sorting colors is a developmental skill that occurs at 33–36 months of age (Parks et al., 1994).

Another purely visual-cognitive skill involves visual imitation. Vision is directly tied to a child's ability to imitate the actions of others. More than 20 researchers have reported that newborn infants imitated an adult's facial gestures including mouth opening, lip pursing, tongue protrusion, and happy or sad facial expressions (Slater, 1996). Two such researchers reported that a 6-week-old infant remembered a facial gesture that he had seen an adult produce after a 24-hour delay. When the adult returned 24 hours later and approached the infant with a static face, the infant imitated the facial gesture of that same adult from the day before (Meltzoff & Moore, 1994).

By 8–9 months, the infant can copy an adult's actions on objects (Bayley, 1993; Slater, 1996). An infant will engage in simple imitative play by 9–12 months (Parks et al., 1994). By 18 months, a child will imitate an adult's behavior using props such as clothing, dinnerware, and other familiar objects (Johnson-Martin, Attermeier, & Hacker, 2004). During the first and second years of life, children are in constant visual observation of their environment, watching and learning how other people behave (Hyvärinen, 1994). For more information about visual-cognitive skills, see Subcategory V. Complexity of Play in Chapter 7 (cognitive development domain).

Visual skills are tied to other cognitive skills including recognition of objects, people, pictures, and symbols. These skills are linked to visual acuity and figure–ground perception. Between 5 and 10 months, infants show an interest in pictures and recognize partially hidden objects (Bayley, 1993; Hyvärinen, 1994). The first signs of picture recognition skills occur at close to 1 year (Hyvärinen, 1994). From 17 to 19 months, a child can point to two pictures on request, and from 20 to 22 months, a child can name a picture (Bayley, 1993).

Once the sequence of visual development is understood, these skills can be assessed. Fewell and Vadasy (1983) stressed that our understanding of how a young child's vision development matures can provide important information on how to arrange the early learning environment to both support and enhance visual development: "Adult awareness of how vision matures can facilitate the child's acquisition of information through careful monitoring of visual development, arranging environments to enhance visual processing, and implementing strategies that promote visual learning" (p. 32).

PROCEDURES AND PURPOSE

As noted previously, the two most common experts in an educational setting for assessing the visual development domain are an occupational therapist and a teacher certified in the area of visual impairment. Unfortunately, many assessment teams will not have consistent access to these two experts. As such, other disciplines will play a key role in assessing a child's visual development during the TPBA process.

In the event that additional information is needed on the child's visual status, the child should be referred to a specialist. This holds true with all parts of TPBA for which the assessment team determines that more diagnostic or educational assessment is needed following the team assessment, whether it be vision, hearing, or another facet of the assessment.

The assessment capacity of the TPBA2 instrument is that it will offer the team information not only for a possible referral to a medical specialist (e.g., pediatrician, ophthalmologist), but it will provide information pertinent to educational programming for the child. For example, the team might note that a child with cerebral palsy performs best on visual tasks when his or her trunk and head are in a supported position, or that another child needs a healthy 30-second wait response before fixation occurs. The goal of the assessment team should be to continually observe how a child is using his or her vision; for example, whether small items are noticed, how far away an item of a certain size is noticed, and so forth.

▅▅▅▅▅ USING THE OBSERVATION GUIDELINES TO ASSESS VISION

▅▅▅▅ I. A. What visual concerns have been noted?

At the preassessment interview, the parents should be asked whether there are any specific concerns with the appearance of their child's eyes or vision. A simple, but important, question is, "Do you feel your child is seeing normally?" If there is a need for more elaboration, questions can be asked about whether the child recognizes a familiar person from across the room and/or notices small items. If concerns arise during the transdisciplinary play-based assessment about the child's vision, the parents should be consulted about these concerns. Sometimes a visual adaptation behavior, such as closing one eye while looking at something, is not noticeable to a parent until it is pointed out during an assessment.

The caregiver should be asked whether the child has ever seen an eye care specialist such as an optometrist or an ophthalmologist. If an eye care specialist has evaluated the child, it will be important to determine whether there was any diagnosis of vision concerns such as nearsightedness, farsightedness, and so forth. In addition, were glasses prescribed? This information should be recorded on the assessment protocol, and it should be noted further whether the child is wearing his or her glasses on the day of the assessment. Lastly, is the child currently on any prescribed medication(s)? Certain medications may affect visual performance; for example, certain anticonvulsant medications may cause light sensitivity (Langley, 1998b). The team should be aware of any unusual visual behaviors that may be attributed to the child's medication. This information will need to be discussed with the family's medical care professionals.

I. B. What is the appearance of the eyes and eyelids?

The simple rule of "if something does not look right" prevails when looking at a child's eyelids and eyes; however, care should be taken not to overscrutinize the child's eyelids and face. If there is a problem, it will most likely be readily noticeable. Are the eyes properly aligned throughout the duration of the assessment, as some misalignments will manifest with fatigue and be more obvious at the end of the assessment? Do the sizes of the eyes, irises, and pupils appear to be normal? Do the eyelids droop significantly? Is there any redness, tearing, cloudiness, crust, or involuntary movements of the eyes? Over time, teams will learn to discern things such as a pseudo-crossing, where an eye may look crossed when rather it is a situation of an extra eye fold in children of Asian descent or with certain syndromes.

I. C. What functional acuity is observed?

Because traditional measures of visual acuity require specialized testing equipment (e.g., acuity charts, preferential looking cards), an estimation of functional acuity is assessed in a transdisciplinary play-based model. The first item in this subcategory involves the child reciprocating eye contact with the caregiver or another person during the assessment. This behavior may occur at a variety of distances between the child and the reciprocating person. At a minimum, it should be assessed when a team member is within 10–12 inches from the child.

The remaining items in this subcategory involve different sized objects that are located at varying distances from the child. Observe the child's natural movements during a play session. Does the child notice a very small toy or piece of food that is in his or her environment? It may be necessary to ask, "Can you find the last Cheerio?" or to softly tap a finger near the object to draw the child's attention to it. If the latter clue is used, the finger should then be removed so the small item is the sole focus of the child's subsequent gaze.

If a child is younger than 6 months of age, he or she may not be visually responsive to objects as small as a piece of cereal. As such, this assessment indicator may not be appropriate to score. Snack time during the assessment provides a wonderful opportunity to evaluate the smallest item that a child visually notices—food is a great motivator for many people. The team should learn to pay attention to all objects in a child's environment, because it may not be the 1-inch toy that was brought into the session but the piece of lint on the carpet that provides information about visual attention to very small objects.

The term *visually regards* is used in this subcategory to describe a child's looking behavior toward an object. A child may simply stop what he or she is doing to look directly at a face or an object or may deliberately reach to touch the object while looking at it.

Some children will be more visually responsive to familiar objects. If the family has provided toys or favorite objects, these items can be incorporated into the assessment routine.

I. D. What gross visual field is observed?

When a child spontaneously notices things in a variety of places, visual field may be observed. Does the child turn his or her head in response to seeing someone walk by? Does the child casually reach over to the far left or right side to retrieve a puzzle piece while still looking at the puzzle in front of him or her? These are examples of peripheral vision or "side vision." Peripheral vision also can be used to describe noticing objects that are presented at the top of the head or at chin or chest level when the child is looking straight ahead. To deliberately test the child's visual field, a team member can move an object in the upper/lower/side fields of the child's vision to see whether he or she notices its presence.

Visual field assessment is an area in which team members will want to be very careful not to overreact to a child's seeming lack of response. It may be that the child is so engrossed with another object in front of him or her that he or she does not notice the newly introduced object. Certainly this alone does not indicate a visual deficiency.

I. E. How does the child demonstrate eye teaming?

When assessing eye-teaming skills, it is important to ensure that the child has good postural support. If a child is falling into gravity because he or she is too young to sit upright or has a physical challenge such as cerebral palsy that affects trunk stability, it may be necessary to provide positioning assistance.

Attention to the child's physical positioning may help to increase visual performance in general. Any time a child is in an unstable position, energy will be deflected from the visual concentration needed for the task at hand (Anthony, 2000). It may be too great a request for a child with a physical disability to provide both self-achieved motor stability *and* a visual response.

General guidelines for positioning are as follows: 1) the child should be visually symmetrical and should not be leaning off-center; 2) positioning support should be provided for the bony parts of the body for physical comfort; 3) support should be provided where it is necessary, but not at the expense of voluntary freedom of movement; and 4) the child should be positioned in a way that does not reinforce an abnormal muscle pattern (Yates, 1989). The consultation of an occupational and/or physical therapist may be helpful for children who have a physical disability.

Both eyes should work together during all eye-movement tasks and move in unison as they follow a moving object. The same is true for convergence—as the child watches an object coming closer to his or her face, both eyes should maintain their fixation on the object. Eye-teaming skills are usually readily observable as a child plays with toys, especially toys that have a built-in movement capacity such as Slinkies, cars or other wheel toys, and/or balls. Watching blown soap bubbles is a wonderful way to note eye-movement tasks. A bubble can be caught on the wand and brought closer to the child as a way to assess convergence. If needed, a team member can get the child's attention with a toy and then move the toy in deliberate directions to elicit tracking, convergence, and/or divergence.

Offering the child a choice of two items for snack or play can be done to assess shift of gaze skills. Would the child prefer cereal, as held up to the left, or crackers, as held up to the right? Shift of gaze may also be observed by the child's spontaneous behavior as he or she scopes out the playroom to see what items are in different locations or when the child visually checks in with a parent and then resumes gaze back to a play task at hand. The latter is an example of shift of gaze occurring at two very different distances.

I. F. How does the child demonstrate depth perception?

As a child reaches for objects during TPBA, it will be apparent as to whether he or she is consistently accurate with reach. Team members should notice whether the child can reach accurately for objects of different sizes. Care should be taken to notice if the child consistently over-

or underreaches for objects. Another aspect to notice is whether reaching skills are any more or any less accurate when an object is grounded on the floor instead of out in space (e.g., a toy in someone's offered hand). As the child moves, whether by crawling, rolling, or walking, the team can observe whether he or she is aware of changes in depth of the ground surface. If there are stairs to navigate to get in and out of the play area, team members should observe how the child visually responds to color changes in floor surfaces (does the child react as if there is a drop off?) and/or the presence of stairs or other surface changes. Signs that the child is aware of a change in depth will include slowing, stopping, and/or successfully navigating over the surface change. Some children may check the surface change out with their hands or feet before moving forward.

I. G. What compensatory visual behaviors are observed?

The items in this subcategory, which are all behavioral adaptations to visual problems, should be completed toward the end of the transdisciplinary play-based assessment. The idea is to observe the child throughout the session to determine whether the child shows characteristics of visual fatigue, as well as any behaviors that might indicate a red flag for visual development. These behaviors are clues to vision difficulties. They also are helpful strategies that the child has discovered to assist with seeing more clearly. It will be important to be prudent on items such as "squints excessively to bright light." This statement does not describe a child who squints slightly when coming into contact with bright sunlight. Rather, it describes a child who is *unusually* bothered by changes in lighting.

The same prudence is important for the compensatory behavior of bringing objects very close to the eyes for viewing. The assessment team will need to filter whether the child uses this behavior as a consistent strategy to see an object versus as an occasional tool to truly scrutinize an object. The size of the object will need to be taken into account—if the object has minuscule features, such as the tires on a small toy truck or the dots on the back of a small wind-up ladybug, it would not be surprising for the child to bring it very close to his or her eye or bend very close to the object.

I. H. What visual-motor/visual-cognitive skills are observed?

Items in this final category have been included to inform the assessment team further about the child's visual skills. The items were selected because, although not purely visual in nature, they give information as to how the child is using his or her vision for higher-level learning skills. Each item requires an interpretation of visual information. If a child's vision is compromised, it is likely that the indicators in this section will also be compromised. For example, if a child does not notice or cannot locate small details in a picture on request, it *might* indicate poor visual acuity. The child who has difficulty matching colored items *may* have a color deficiency. It is important to view each of these indicators with caution, however, as other factors such as eye–hand coordination and concept development may be the true reasons for a child's difficulty with a particular task. The performance of these indicators should be taken into consideration with other information gleaned from the visual development section *and* other developmental areas of TPBA2.

SCORING

The final outcome of the vision development screening will be an overall rating of *pass* or *fail*. It is not appropriate to give the child a developmental rating associated with an age level. If a 3-year-old child has poor visual acuity, for example, it would not be described as "the acuity of a much younger child." Furthermore, visual development cannot be described in percentages such as "the child has 75% of the visual development skills." There is not a way to quantify a child's visual status using this protocol, as it is not an appropriate way to report the results. TPBA2 is designed to raise the issue as to whether or not a child has vision concerns. As such, either the child will pass or will fail the TPBA2 Observation Guidelines for visual development.

Not every item will cause a child to fail the screening, as is typically the case in a standard vision screening instrument. "Knockout" items have been flagged with a diamond symbol (♦) in the Observation Guidelines for visual development. Such items will automatically cause a child to fail the TPBA2 Observation Guidelines for visual development, and the child should be automatically referred to an eye care specialist. For example, if the child were noted to have a crossed eye, this would result in an overall score of *fail*. There are no acceptable reasons why a child older than 6 months of age should have a crossed eye. This finding on its own will merit a discussion with the parents about the need for an eye care examination or, at a minimum, discussion with the family physician about a next step. As noted earlier, some visual problems can be corrected medically. If a visual problem cannot be corrected by an eye care specialist, the educational team will need to meet to determine appropriate accommodations. A child with a visual impairment should always be followed by a teacher certified in visual impairment who can recommend accommodations such as changes in lighting, provide needed equipment such as screen enlargement software, large-print books, and braille writers, and provide training on the use of prescribed low-vision devices.

Most items on the protocol are knockout items. Exceptions have been made with eye contact because this may not be the norm for some children. Furthermore, gross visual field and depth perception indicators have complicating factors. Gross visual field assessment may be difficult for some individuals to determine a passing or failing score based on the child's response to peripheral objects. At what point are there real concerns? The two visual field items have been retained in the protocol because visual field is so critical to a child's visual functioning, especially if the child uses sign language or other visual communication systems. The assessment team members should do their best to assess a child's gross visual field, but unless they are convinced that there is truly an abnormal response, these two indicators would not result in a global *fail* rating of the protocol.

The second area that has not been assigned as a knockout zone is the items pertaining to depth perception. The confounding factor with the items in this subcategory is the tie to motor skills. Children with cerebral palsy or other motor challenges may have poor eye–hand accuracy because of affected vision, poor motor control alone, and/or both factors combined. As such, the team will have to work to decipher whether a visual factor is involved. A child may still fail one or more items in the depth perception area. However, unless a contributing motor problem can be eliminated from the theory of why the child failed these items, it would not be a sole reason for a global rating of *fail*. It is likely, however, that if depth perception is truly affected, the child will show difficulty in passing other visual indicators.

Vision development screening items will be scored in the same format as the other domains in TPBA: further evaluation needed (✔), pass (P), fail (F), no opportunity (NO), or not developmentally appropriate (NA) (for I.H. only). Each score format will be described in further detail.

The score of (✔) should be reserved for a situation in which the assessor simply does not know how to score the item because more information is needed. Sometimes it may be difficult to judge whether a child does not make eye contact because this behavior is not within the acceptable cultural repertoire of the child or because lack of eye contact is a characteristic of another diagnosis such as an autism spectrum disorder (Peeters, 1997). In this situation, the team will need to calculate whether the child has demonstrated enough other visual skills to ascertain whether lack of eye contact is really something the child is not visually capable of, as opposed to something the child is not likely to do for other reasons. For example, the team may want to note whether the child noticed a piece of fuzz or lint on the floor or visually reacted to a toy from across the room. Both of these instances describe good visual acuity. In this scenario, if the eye contact indicator were the only one that has a score of (✔) or a fail (F), there would not be sufficient rationale for the child to fail the overall vision development screening.

Another example of when a (✔) might be used is with a child who has what appears to be a fleeting crossed eye. Sometimes the eye seems to be turned in, but more often it does not. When in doubt, a (✔) can be used. Again, this score should be reviewed with other indicator findings to see if there are visual concerns. In this situation, the questionable observation would still be a cause to refer the child to a medical specialist who can better assess the alignment status of the eyes.

At the completion of the assessment, a rating should be assigned to each subcategory of the Observation Guidelines for visual development. If the child has passed all knockout domains, the overall score of the protocol is *pass,* indicating that there are no concerns about the child's visual development. If a child has failed even one knockout item, the final score of the tool is *fail.*

A passing (P) score can be given when it is clear that there are no parental concerns about the child's vision, when there are no concerns with the child using compensatory visual behaviors, and when the child has demonstrated age-appropriate visual skills noted in the Observation Guidelines for visual development.

> *At age 3, Andrew came charging into the play-assessment room ready to go. He visually checked out all the people in the room, returned the smile of one person sitting a distance of over 10 feet away, found a piece of thread on the floor and handed it to the play facilitator, named small pictures on a book from a distance of 10 feet, tracked a moving ball and a series of falling soap bubbles, and so on. There were absolutely no concerns by his mom; in fact, she had taken him to an eye doctor just 3 months prior because of his diagnosis of Down syndrome just to check things out. Although the team found concerns with other areas of Andrew's development, the visual domain looked great.*

A failing score (F) occurs when there are concerns expressed by the caregiver about the child's vision, there is evidence of compensatory visual behaviors, and/or the child clearly cannot demonstrate the visual indicators on the vision development protocol. For example, if a child brings objects right up to his or her nose consistently for viewing, he or she would receive a (F) score on the compensatory vision behavior item of "moves very close to item being viewed."

> *Two-year-old Sara's grandfather came into the play-based assessment saying that he did not think Sara could see very far away. The team concurred; Sara squinted when a small ball rolled over 5 feet away from her and rubbed her eyes frequently during a book task that was toward the end of the assessment; there also was a question of an occasional eye crossing. These concerns, along with those mentioned by the family in the Child and Family History Questionnaire (CFHQ), warranted further evaluation by an eye care specialist. Three weeks later, the intervention team was greeted by a smiling Sara in a pair of stylish new glasses.*

A score of (NO) means there was no opportunity during the play-based assessment to observe the skill. Unless the child is very medically fragile or severely physically disabled, it is likely that most items will be observable as the child interacts with people and/or objects. With these young children, it will be important to ensure that the child is in a stable, secure position and given adequate time to respond to visual information. No child is "untestable"—there is always a way to assess basic visual responses. As such, it should be rare that the (NO) score is ever used. If a team does not have sufficient skills to assess a child with significant disabilities, further training should be pursued to acquire this needed expertise.

The play facilitator will need to check in with his or her teammates as the play assessment unfolds to see what skills may not have been observed. This will provide an opportunity to be deliberate with interactions that can entice a specific visual response.

Each subdomain will be reviewed for any unique scoring procedures:

A. *Caregiver Concerns:* If the caregivers do not have any concerns, the child should receive a passing (P) score. If there are noted concerns, a (F) score should be given and notes should be taken as to the exact nature of the concerns. If a caregiver cannot attend the assessment, information about possible visual concerns should be secured through the CFHQ.

B. *Appearance of Eyelids and Eyes:* The simple rule of "if something does not look right" prevails when inspecting the child's eyelids and eyes. If there are no concerns about the appearance of the eyelids and eyes, a passing (P) score should be given and the assessor can move to the next section of the protocol. If there are concerns, a failing (F) score should be given and the next section of the protocol should be completed listing any concern(s). The concerns should be detailed as to whether they are with the right, left, or both eyes.

The next sections, C. *Functional Acuity; D. Gross Visual Field; E. Eye Teaming; F. Depth Perception,* all have the scoring possibilities of (P), (F), (✔), or (NO). The same rules of scoring apply to these indicators.

G. *Compensatory Visual Behaviors:* This section should be completed toward the end of the assessment, after the child has been observed for a period of time. As the child fatigues, a particular behavior such as eye crossing or eye squinting may become more obvious. The global question of whether the child demonstrates any unusual visual behaviors should be addressed first. Pass (P) is the score if there are no such behaviors noted. If there is a noted compensatory visual behavior(s), a failing (F) score should be assigned and the next section should be completed to detail the type of observed behavior(s).

H. *Visual Motor/Cognitive Skills:* This section will be simply scored as (P), (F) or (NA). The (NA) rating may be appropriate due to the assigned age ranges of some items. These items will not be factored in to the overall *pass* or *fail* rating of the screening. They are designed to only provide additional information to the assessment team about the child's visual skills.

SHARING INFORMATION

If an overall rating of *fail* has been assigned to the child, it will be important to share this information with the family in a careful manner. The results do not stem from a clinical evaluation and so **there should be no reference to proposed diagnoses,** such as strabismus, amblyopia, refractive error, and so forth—only medical specialists can determine these eye conditions. Rather, the assessment team should describe the concerns raised as a result of the screening. For example, the play facilitator might describe how he or she noticed that the child brought items very close to his or her face for inspection and was not aware of medium-sized toys that were farther away than 5 feet.

The next step following a failed vision development screening will be to assist the family with obtaining more assessment/diagnostic information about the child's vision. The family may want to take a copy of the Observation Guidelines for visual development to their family physician or an eye care specialist. It might be helpful for the assessment team to prepare a packet of information to share with families when a child does not pass the TPBA2 Observation Guidelines for visual development. Information about the role of vision for the developing child, key warning signs of vision problems, and a list of questions to ask their family doctor would all be excellent handouts to share with the family.

If there is an educational specialist who can provide a more comprehensive visual assessment on the child, this individual should be consulted. For example, a child with a visual impairment should be referred to a teacher certified in this area for a comprehensive Functional Vision Assessment and a Learning Media Assessment. The latter is a tool that is used to determine the primary and secondary sensory modality(ies) used by a child with a visual impairment for information gathering and literacy purposes. This professional can offer the team further guidance on needed accommodations.

CONCLUSION

Children within the typical population, those at risk for developmental delay, and those with identified disabilities all have varying risk factors for visual problems or impairments. The earlier a visual concern is identified, the higher the probability for effective medical and educational intervention.

Visual development, as with other developmental domains, follows a sequence of milestone behaviors as the child evolves neurologically, motorically, and cognitively. Obstacles that interfere with a child's visual development may result in temporary or permanent deficits to visual development and other developmental domains. Fortunately, most visual problems are readily identifiable through simple observation of the child's appearance and behavior.

Developmental assessment during the first 5 years of life presents an optimal opportunity to screen young children for visual concerns. Such assessment should include evaluation of the typical domains of sensorimotor, emotional and social, communication, and cognitive, as well as the sensory abilities and limitations of the child. TPBA presents an ideal opportunity to infuse a visual development screening into its structure.

The vision development protocol has been designed to assess key vision development milestones of a young child through a play-based format. The protocol has been described in this chapter for its content, assessment considerations, and scoring procedures.

It is suggested that children who fail the TPBA2 Observation Guidelines for visual development be referred to a specialist (e.g., school nurse, pediatrician, ophthalmologist, and optometrist) for further evaluation. The decision of to whom to refer may be driven by the team's policy of referral. The process of referral should be discussed with the caregiver following the team assessment. The team may want to prepare appropriate handout materials for families about vision development and referral opportunities in their community prior to incorporating the Observation Guidelines for visual development into their TPBA2 protocol.

REFERENCES

Allen, J., & Fraser, K. (1983, Fall). Evaluation of visual capacity in visually impaired and multi-handicapped children. *Rehabilitative Optometry*, 5–8.

American Academy of Ophthalmology. (1997). *Preferred practice pattern: Pediatric eye evaluations.* San Francisco: Author.

Anthony, T.L. (1993a). Functional vision assessment for children who are young and/or multi-disabled. In L.B. Stainton & E.C. Lechelt (Eds.), *Proceedings of the Eighth International Conference on Blind and Visually Impaired Children* (pp. 73–94). Edmonton, Alberta, Canada: Canadian National Institute for the Blind.

Anthony, T.L. (2000). Performing a functional low vision assessment. In F.M. D'Andrea & C. Farrenkopf (Eds.), *Looking to learn: Promoting literacy for student with low vision* (pp. 32–83). New York: AFB Press.

Anthony, T.L. (2002). The inclusion of vision-development guidelines in the Transdisciplinary Play-Based Assessment: A study of reliability and validity. *Dissertation Abstracts International, 63*(12), A4271, Pro Quest Information (No. 30-74361).

Atkinson, J. (1996). Issues in infant vision screening and assessment. In F. Vital-Durand, J. Atkinson, & O.J. Braddick (Eds.), *Infant vision* (pp. 135–152). New York: Oxford Press.

Atkinson, J. (2000). *The developing visual brain.* New York: Oxford University Press.

Atkinson, J., & Van Hof-van Duin, J. (1993). Visual assessment during the first years of life. In A.R. Fielder, A.B. Best, & M.C.O. Bax (Eds.), *Clinics in developmental medicine series (No. 128): Management of visual impairment in childhood* (pp. 9–29). London: Mac Keith Press.

Bailey, I.L. (1994). Optometric care for the multi-handicapped child. *Practical Optometry, 5,* 158–166.

Bayley, N. (2005). *The Bayley Scales of Infant and Toddler Development* (3rd ed.). San Antonio, TX: Harcourt Assessment.

Birch, E.E., Shimojo, S., & Held, R. (1985). Preferential-looking assessment of fusion and stereopsis in infants aged 1–6 months. *Investigative Ophthalmology and Visual Science, 26,* 366–370.

Bishop, V.E. (1988). Making choices in functional vision evaluations: "Noodles, needles, and haystacks." *Journal of Visual Impairment & Blindness, 82*(3), 94–99.

Black, M.M., & Matula, K. (2000). Bayley Scales of Infant Development–II assessment. In A.S. Kaufman & N.L. Kaufman (Series Eds.), *Essentials of psychological assessment series: Essentials of Bayley Scales of Infant Development–II assessment* (pp. 1–145). New York: John Wiley & Sons.

Black, P.D. (1980). Ocular defects in children with cerebral palsy. *British Medical Journal, 281,* 487–488.

Brown, A.M., & Teller, D.Y. (1989). Chromatic opponency in 3-month old human infants. *Vision Research, 29,* 37–45.

Bushnell, I.W.R. (1982). Discrimination of faces by young infants. *Journal of Experimental Child Psychology, 33,* 211–229.

Calvello, G. (1989). Identifying vision impairments in infants. In D. Chen, C.T. Friedman, & G. Calvello (Eds.), *Parents and visually impaired infants* (pp. 5–7). Louisville, KY: American Printing House for the Blind.

Catalano, R.A., & Nelson, L.B. (1994). *Pediatric ophthalmology.* Englewood Cliffs, NJ: Appleton & Lange.

Colorado Department of Public Health and Environment. (1991). *Guidelines for school vision screening programs* (2nd ed.). Denver, CO: Author.

Daw, N.W. (1995). *Visual development.* New York: Plenum Press.

Ferrell, K.A. (1998). *Project PRISM: A longitudinal study of the developmental patterns of children who are visually impaired: Executive summary: CFDA 84.0203C: field-initiated research HO23C10188.* Greeley, CO: University of Northern Colorado.

Fewell, R.R., & Vadasy, P.F. (1983). *Learning through play: A resource manual for teachers and parents.* Allen, TX: DLM Teaching Resources.

Gerali, P.S., Flom, M.C., & Raab, E.L. (1990). *Report of children's vision screening task force.* Schaumburg, IL: National Society to Prevent Blindness.

Glascoe, F.P., MacLean, W.E., & Stone, W.L. (1991). The importance of parents' concerns about their child's behavior. *Clinical Pediatrics, 30,* 8–11.

Glass, P. (1993). Development of visual function in preterm infants: Implications for early intervention. *Infants and Young Children, 6,* 11–20.

Glass, P. (2002). Development of the visual system and implications for early intervention. *Infants and Young Children, 15*(1), 1–10.

Goble, J.L. (1984). *Visual disorders in the handicapped child.* New York: Marcel Dekker.

Good, W.V., & Hoyt, C.S. (1989). Behavioral correlates of poor vision in children. *International Ophthalmology Clinics, 29*(1), 57–60.

Goren, C.C., Sarty, M., & Wu, P.Y.K. (1975). Visual following and pattern discrimination of face-like stimuli by newborn infants. *Pediatrics, 56,* 544–549.

Groenendaal, F., & Van Hof-van Duin, J. (1992). Visual deficits and improvements in children after perinatal hypoxia. *Journal of Visual Impairment & Blindness, 86*(5), 215–218.

Hainline, L., & Riddell, P.M. (1996). Eye alignment and convergence in young children. In F. Vital-Durand, J. Atkinson, & O.J. Braddick (Eds.), *Infant vision* (pp. 221–247), New York: Oxford Press.

Harris, C.M., Jacobs, M., Shawkat, F., & Taylor, D. (1993). The development of saccadic accuracy in the first seven months. *Clinical Vision Science, 8,* 85–96.

Hatton, D.D., Bailey, D.B., Burchinal, M.R., & Ferrell, K.A. (1997). Developmental growth curves of preschool children with visual impairments. *Child Development, 68*(5), 788–806.

Hollins, M. (1989). *Understanding blindness: An integrative approach.* Hillsdale, NJ: Lawrence Erlbaum Associates.

Hyvärinen, L. (1988). *Vision in children: Normal and abnormal.* Meaford, Ontario, Canada: The Canadian Deaf-Blind & Rubella Association.

Hyvärinen, L. (1994). Assessment of visually impaired infants. *Low Vision and Vision Rehabilitation, 7*(2), 219–225.

Hyvärinen, L. (Ed.). (1995). Effect of impaired vision on general development. In *Vision Testing Manual 1995–1996* (pp. 1–7). Villa Park, IL: Precision Vision.

Individuals with Disabilities Education Improvement Act of 2004, PL 108-446, 20 U.S.C. §§ 1400 *et seq.*

Jan, J.E., Freeman, R.D., McCormick, A.Q., Scott, E.P., Roberson, W.D., & Newman, D.E. (1983). Eye pressing by visually impaired children. *Developmental Medicine and Child Neurology, 25,* 755–762.

Jan, J.E., & Groenveld, M. (1993). Visual behaviors and adaptations associated with cortical and ocular impairment in children. *Journal of Visual Impairment & Blindness, 87*(4), 101–105.

Jan, J.E., Groenveld, M., & Anderson, D.P. (1993). Photophobia and cortical visual impairment. *Developmental Medicine and Child Neurology, 35,* 473–477.

Jan, J.E., Groenveld, M., Sykanda, A.M., & Hoyt, C.S. (1987). Behavioral characteristics of children with permanent cortical visual impairment. *Developmental Medicine and Child Neurology, 29,* 571–576.

Johnson-Martin, N.M., Attermeier, S.M., & Hacker, B.J. (2004). *The Carolina Curriculum for Infants and Toddlers with Special Needs* (3rd ed.). Baltimore: Paul H. Brookes Publishing Co.

Knoblauch, K., Bieber, M., & Werner, J.S. (1996). Assessing dimensionality in infant colour vision. In F. Vital-Durand, J. Atkinson, & O.J. Braddick (Eds.), *Infant vision* (pp. 51–61). New York: Oxford Press.

Langley, M.B. (1998a). Alignment and ocular mobility. In M.B. Langley (Ed.), *Individualized systematic assessment of visual efficiency for the developmentally young and individuals with multihandicapping conditions* (Vol. 1, pp. 1–33). Louisville, KY: American Printing House for the Blind.

Langley, M.B. (1998b). Structural integrity. In M.B. Langley (Ed.), *Individualized systematic assessment of visual efficiency for the developmentally young and individuals with multihandicapping conditions* (Vol. 1, pp. 1–20). Louisville, KY: American Printing House for the Blind.

Langley, M.B. (2004). Screening and assessment of sensory function. In M. McLean, M. Wolery, & D.B. Bailey (Eds.), *Assessing infants and preschoolers with special needs* (3rd ed., pp. 123–157). Upper Saddle River, NJ: Pearson Education.

Leat, S.J., Shute, R.H., & Westall, C.A. (1999). *Assessing children's vision: A handbook.* Oxford, England: Butterworth-Heinemann.

Levack, N. (1991). *Low vision: A resource guide with adaptations for children with visual impairments.* Austin, TX: Texas School for the Blind and Visually Impaired.

Mayer, D.L., Fulton, A.B., & Cummings, M.F. (1988). Visual fields of infants assessed with a new perimetric technique. *Investigative Ophthalmology and Visual Science, 29,* 452–459.

Meltzoff, A.N., & Moore, M.K. (1994). Imitation, memory, and the representation of persons. *Infant Behavior and Development, 17,* 83–99.

Menken, C., Cermak, S., & Fisher, A. (1987). Evaluating the visual-perceptual skills of children with cerebral palsy. *American Journal of Occupational Therapy, 41*(10), 646–651.

Miller, M.M., & Menacker, S.J., (2007). Vision: Our windows to the world. In M.L. Batshaw, L. Pellegrino & N.J. Roizen (Eds.), *Children with disabilities* (6th ed., pp. 137–156). Baltimore: Paul H. Brookes Publishing Co.

Mohan, K.M., & Dobson, V. (2000). When does measured visual field extent become adult-like? It depends. *OSA Tops, 35,* 2–9.

Morse, A.R., & Trief, E. (1985). Diagnosis and evaluation of visual dysfunction in premature infants with low birth weight. *Journal of Visual Impairment & Blindness, 79,* 248–251.

Morse, M. (1991). Visual gaze behavior: Considerations in working with visual impaired multiply handicapped children. *Re:View, 23,* 5–15.

Parks, S., Furono, S., O'Reilly, T., Inatsuka, C.M., Hosaka, C.M., & Zeisloft-Falbey, B. (1994). *Hawaii Early Learning Profile (HELP): HELP (birth to three).* Palo Alto, CA: VORT Corporation.

Peeters, T. (1997). *Autism: From theoretical understanding to educational intervention.* London: Whurr Publishers.

Pike, M.G., Holstrom, G., DeVries, L.S., Pennock, J.M., Drew, K.J., Sonksen, P.M., & Dubowitz, L.M.S. (1994). Patterns of visual impairment associated with lesions of the preterm infant brain. *Developmental Medicine and Child Neurology, 36,* 849–862.

Sayeed, C., & Guerin, E. (2000). *Early years play.* London: David Fulton Publishers.

Schor, D.P. (1990). Visual impairment. In J.A. Blackman (Ed.), *Medical aspects of developmental disabilities in children birth to three* (2nd ed., pp. 269–274), Rockville, MD: Aspen Publications.

Schwartz, T.L., Dobson, V., Sandstrom, D.J., & Van Hof-van Duin, J. (1987). Kinetic perimetry assessment of binocular visual field shape and size in your infants. *Vision Research, 27,* 2163–2175.

Shane Cote, K., & Smith, A. (1997). Assessment of the multiply handicapped. In R. Jose (Ed.), *Understanding low vision.* New York: American Foundation for the Blind.

Shapiro, M.B., & France, T.D. (1985). The ocular features of Down syndrome. *American Journal of Ophthalmology, 99,* 659–663.

Sireteanu, R. (1996). Development of the visual field: Results from human and animal studies. In F. Vital-Durand, J. Atkinson, & O.J. Braddick (Eds.), *Infant vision* (pp. 17–31). New York: Oxford Press.

Slater, A.M. (1996). The organization of visual perception in early infancy. In F. Vital-Durand, J. Atkinson, & O.J. Braddick (Eds.), *Infant vision* (pp. 309–325). New York: Oxford Press.

Sonksen, P.M. (1982). The assessment of "vision for development" in severely visually handicapped babies. *Acta Ophthalmologica Supplement, 157,* 82–90.

Sonksen, P.M. (1993). Effect of severe visual impairment on development. In A.R. Fielder, A.B. Best, & M.C.O. Bax (Series Eds.), *Clinics in developmental medicine series (No. 128): Management of visual impairment in childhood* (pp. 78–90). London: Mac Keith Press.

Talay-Ongan, A. (1998). *Typical and atypical development in early childhood: The fundamentals.* St. Leonards, Australia: Allen & Unwin.

Teller, D.Y., McDonald, M.A., Preston, K., Sebris, S.L., & Dobson, V (1986). Assessment of visual acuity in infants and children: the acuity card procedure. *Developmental Medicine and Child Neurology, 28,* 779–789.

Teplin, S. (1982). Assessment of visual acuity in infancy and early childhood. *Acta Ophthalmologica Supplement, 157,* 18–26.

Teplin, S. (1995). Visual impairment in infants and young children. *Infants and Young Children, 8*(1), 18–51.

Vaughan, D., Asbury, T., & Tabbara, K.F. (1989). *General ophthalmology* (12th ed.). Norwalk, CT: Appleton & Lange.

Vital-Durand, F., Ayzac, L., & Pinsaru, G. (1996). Acuity cards and the search for risk factors in infant visual development. In F. Vital-Durand, J. Atkinson, & O.J. Braddick (Eds.), *Infant vision* (pp. 185–200). New York: Oxford Press.

Walker, D.K., & Wiske, M.S. (1981). *A guide to developmental assessments for young children* (2nd ed.). Boston: Massachusetts Department of Education, Early Childhood Project.

White, B. (1975). *The first years of life.* Englewood Cliffs, NJ: Prentice Hall.

Yates, C. (1989). *Positioning and handling. ADAPT-A-STRATEGY booklet series for parents and teachers*

of infants/young children with multiple disabilities. University of Southern Mississippi, Hatties-
burg.

Yonas, A., & Granrud, C.E. (1985). The development of sensitivity to kinetic, binocular and pictorial depth information in human infants. In D. Ingle, D. Lee, & R.N. Jeannerod (Eds.), *Brain
mechanisms and spatial vision* (pp. 113–146). The Hague: Nijhoff.

TPBA2 Observation Guidelines: Vision Development

Child's name: _____   Age: _____   Birth date: _____

Parent(s): _____   Assessment date: _____

Person(s) completing the form: _____

Directions: If a child has prescription glasses, they should be worn during the screening unless otherwise advised by an eye care specialist.
◆ = failure of this item results in an automatic referral to an eye care specialist.

Scoring legend:

P = child successfully demonstrates skill
F = child does not demonstrate skill
✓ = further assessment is needed to quantify the score
NO = no opportunity to observe this skill
NA = skill is not developmentally appropriate for child (for I. H., visual-motor/visual-cognitive skills only)

Questions	Strengths	Examples of concerns	Rating	Notes
I. Visual ability				
I. A. What visual concerns have been noted?	Caregivers report no concerns No prior vision evaluation concerns	Caregivers have a vision concern Previous evaluation identified vision concerns Medication effects on vision	P F ✓ NO ◆ Pass = there are no concerns with eye alignment or visual behavior Fail = there are concerns	

I. B. What is the appearance of the eyes and eyelids?	No concerns regarding appearance of eyelids and eyes	Deviation or asymmetry
		Size of eyes
		Alignment of eyes
		Shape and size of pupil and iris
		Concerns with
		  Unusual redness/crusting of eyelids
		  Significant droop of eyelid(s)
		  Unusual redness/irritation of eyes
		  Excessive mattering/tearing of eyes
		  Clarity of the cornea and pupil
		  Presence of involuntary shaking movements of eyes
			P F
			✓ NO
			◆
			
			Pass = there are no observable differences
			Fail = there are observable differences	

Guidelines developed with Tanni L. Anthony

Transdisciplinary Play-Based System (TPBA2/TPBI2)
by Toni Linder

Questions	Strengths	Examples of concerns	Rating	Notes
I. Visual ability (continued)				
I. C. What functional acuity is observed?	Reciprocates eye contact from at least 10 inches Fixates on 1–3-inch object located 10 inches away Fixates on 10-inch or smaller object from 5 feet away Visually recognizes a silent, familiar face from 7 feet or more	No reciprocal eye contact Does not see small objects (if >6 months of age) more than 10 inches away Does not visually notice a medium-sized object from 5 feet away Does not regard a silent, familiar face from 7 feet or more	P　　F 　✓　NO 　◆ Pass = behavior is observed Fail = behavior is not observed despite opportunities for it to occur	
I. D. What gross visual field is observed?	Notices objects in all visual fields	Does not visually notice a moving object presented in the following fields: Slightly above forehead Slightly below chin Left side (ear level) Right side (ear level)	P　　F 　✓　NO Pass = behavior is observed Fail = behavior is not observed despite opportunities for it to occur	
I. E. How does the child demonstrate eye teaming?	Eyes track, converge, diverge, and shift together	Has difficulty Maintaining fixation on objects or people of interest Following a horizontally moving object across midline from side to side Following an object moved in a circular pattern Shifting gaze from one near-range object to another near-range object Shifting gaze from a near object to a distant object Maintaining focus on an object slowly moving toward face (convergence) Maintains focus on an object slowly moving away from face (divergence)	P　　F 　✓　NO 　◆ Pass = behavior is observed Fail = behavior is not observed despite opportunities for it to occur	
I. F. How does the child demonstrate depth perception?	Accurate reach to objects, putting objects in narrow container, stacking items Visual awareness of surface changes (e.g., stops at step) Accurate stepping and climbing over surface changes	Concerns with Accuracy of reach, placement of objects Visual awareness of drop-offs or other depth changes in floor surfaces	P　　F 　✓　NO Pass = behavior is observed Fail = behavior is not observed despite opportunities for it to occur	

(continued on next page)

Guidelines developed with Tanni L. Anthony

Transdisciplinary Play-Based System (TPBA2/TPBI2)
by Toni Linder

Questions	Strengths	Examples of concerns	Rating	Notes
I. Visual ability (continued)				
I. G. What compensatory visual behaviors are observed?	No compensatory visual behaviors observed	Squints one eye when viewing Closes or blocks one eye when viewing Squints excessively to light Brings objects very close to eyes for viewing Uses an unusual eye or head position when viewing Rubs eyes excessively	P F ✓ NO ◆ Pass = no unusual viewing behaviors observed Fail = unusual behaviors observed	
I. H. What visual-motor/ visual-cognitive skills are observed?	Imitates movement Smiles when adult smiles (1–2 months), imitates movements or actions of another person on a toy (8–12 months); scribbling (10.5–16 months); crayon stroke (12–21 months); circle made by another person (30–42 months) Color identification Two items that are the same color (26–42 months); points to a requested color (30–42 months); sorts items by color (21–42 months) Visually aware of mirror image Responds to mirror image (4–6 months); recognizes self in mirror (15–16 months) Visually responds to pictures Looks at pictures in books (10–14 months); turns book right-side up (18–24 months); names one picture of a familiar item (18–22 months); matches object(s) with picture(s) of the object(s) (19–27 months); finds detail in picture book (24–27 months); matches pictures (26–30 months); names action happening in picture (24–36 months); identifies pictures of objects by their function (42 months); tells a story by looking at photos/pictures (42–48 months).	Concerns with Age-/developmentally appropriate visual imitation skills Age-/developmentally appropriate color discrimination Age-/developmentally appropriate responses to mirror image Age-/developmentally appropriate visual response to pictures Age-/developmentally appropriate symbolic understanding of pictures	P F NA ◆ Pass = skill present Fail = skill not present This information should contribute to the overall developmental scoring of the Cognitive section. NA = skill not developmentally appropriate for the child	

Guidelines developed with Tanni L. Anthony

Transdisciplinary Play-Based System (TPBA2/TPBI2)
by Toni Linder

Visual Development Indicators

This chart provides information on how the team can observe a particular visual behavior.

Category	Item	Age range	What is measured	How to assess
Caregiver concerns	Concerns about child's eye alignment and/or other visual behaviors	All age ranges	Appearance of eyes and general visual performance	Interview caregiver and ask if there are any concerns with the child's eyes and/or how the child is seeing. Ask about the alignment of the child's eyes—any history of eye crossing? What has the caregiver been told about the child's vision by other people such as doctors, teachers, and so forth?
Appearance of eyes and eyelids	Unusually red eyelid(s) or encrusted	All age ranges	General health of eyelids	Look to see if an eyelid might be unusually red or irritated looking. Look for an unusual amount of crust on the lid(s).
Appearance of eyes and eyelids	Eyelid(s) are drooping.	All age ranges	Status of eyelids	Check to see if both eyelids are symmetrical and appear to be level or drooping (significantly).
Appearance of eyes and eyelids	Eye(s) are usually red/irritated.	All age ranges	General health of eyes	Look at the white part of the child's eyes (sclera), Are the eyes unusually bloodshot/red? Child may rub eye(s) to relieve itching or burning.
Appearance of eyes and eyelids	Eye(s) tear excessively.	All age ranges	General health of eyes	Look to see if the child's eye(s) are unusually teary. Eye tearing may be due to an allergy.
Appearance of eyes and eyelids	Eye(s) appear cloudy.	All age ranges	General health of eyes	Look at the corneas (front transparent cover of eyes). Is the cornea clear? Is there any cloudiness of the cornea or the pupil (center black hole)?
Appearance of eyes and eyelids	Eye(s) are different shapes and/or sizes.	All age ranges	General health of eyes	Look to see if both eyes appear to be the same size and shape.
Appearance of eyes and eyelids	Pupils and irises are different sizes and/or shapes.	All age ranges	General health of eyes	Check to see if both pupils (center black hole of eye) and irises (colored circle around pupil) are equal in size and shape. A keyhole shaped pupil is atypical.
Appearance of eyes and eyelids	Eyes are not aligned (eye turned in, out, up, or down).	6 months	Alignment status of eyes	Check to see if both eyes are evenly aligned. Does one eye turn in (crossed eye) or turn out? Is one eye higher or lower than the other? A misalignment may be constant or occasional.
Appearance of eyes and eyelids	Shaky involuntary eye movements	All age ranges	General health of eyes	Look for shaky movements of both eyes (nystagmus). Nystagmus is most obvious when a child is fatigued or visually concentrating.
Functional acuity estimate	Makes eye contact from 1 foot distance.	2–3 months	Fixation, visual acuity	The child reciprocates eye contact with people from a distance of up to one foot and greater. Eye contact involves a mutual gaze in the eyes of another.

(continued on next page)

From Anthony, T.L. (2002). The inclusion of vision-development guidelines in the Transdisciplinary Play-Based Assessment: A study of reliability and validity. *Dissertation Abstract International,* 63(12), A4271, Pro Quest Information (No. 30-74361). Adapted by permission.

Transdisciplinary Play-Based System (TPBA2/TPBI2)
by Toni Linder

(continued from previous page)

Visual Development Indicators **TPBA** 2

Category	Item	Age range	What is measured	How to assess
Functional Acuity Estimate	Visual regard of a 1–3-inch object.	1–3 months	Visual acuity (near vision)	The child visually notices objects as small as 1–3 inches from a distance of 10 inches or greater. Child may stop and look directly at the object and/or make attempts to reach the item. What is scored is his or her visual attention on the object.
Functional Acuity Estimate	Visual regard of cereal piece, pellet, or other very small item.	4.5–7 months	Visual acuity (near vision)	During a task involving pieces of cereal, crumbs, or pellets, the child shows visual awareness of one such item that is separated from the group. Child may look directly at the item and/or attempt to reach it.
Functional Acuity Estimate	Sees 10-inch or larger object from 5 feet or greater.	5–6 months	Visual acuity (distance vision)	The child reacts to the presentation of toys or food from a distance of 5 feet by smiling, vocalizing, reaching, and so forth.
Functional Acuity Estimate	Recognizes face from 7 feet or greater distance.	6–8 months	Visual acuity (distance vision)	The child responds to a familiar (silent) face from a distance of 7 feet or more. Response shown by eye contact, smile, vocalization, reaching, and so forth. Does the child maintain eye contact with a person standing 7 or more feet away?
Gross visual field	Aware of objects in periphery (right and left sides of face)	6–12 months	Extent of visual field	The child visually notices a silent object held at 45 degrees (at eye level) of the side of his or her head when he or she is looking forward. The object may need to be "wiggled" to get the child's attention.
Gross visual field	Aware of objects in upper and lower visual fields	6–12 months	Extent of visual field	The child visually notices a silent object held at high forehead or upper chest level when he or she is looking forward. The object may need to be "wiggled" to get the child's attention.
Eye teaming	Maintains fixation on objects or people of interest.	Birth to 3 months	Visual acuity, eyes teaming	The child looks right at an object that is placed before him or her with both eyes on the object at the same time. Visual contact is made and held steady for several seconds.
Eye teaming	Follows object moving from side to side (180-degree arc).	2–4 months	Eye teaming, visual field	The child visually follows (both eyes on the object at the same time) a slowly moving object such as a person walking by, a wind up toy across a table, or an object deliberately moved horizontally from midline to one side, then back across midline to the other side.
Eye teaming	Follows object that is moving vertically.	2–4 months	Eye teaming, visual field	The child visually follows (both eyes on the object at the same time) an object that moves from chest level to high forehead level or vice versa.
Eye teaming	Follows object moving in a circle.	2–4 months	Visual field, eye teaming	The child visually follows an object that is moved slowly in a circular pattern in front of his or her face.
Eye teaming	Eyes shift from one object to another.	1–3.5 months	Visual field, eye teaming	The child looks from one object to another. Objects should be held at the same distance from the child, about 8–10 inches apart (objects should be held first in a horizontal and then a vertical position).

Transdisciplinary Play-Based System (TPBA2/TPBI2)
by Toni Linder

Category	Item	Age range	What is measured	How to assess
Eye teaming	Eyes shift from near object to one located farther away.	6–12 months	Eye teaming, visual field, the ability to fixate on a near and then distant object	The child moves his/her eyes from a near range object and then moves both eyes to look at something more than 5 feet away. The child may follow a pointing finger to a distance object (looks at person's hand and then to a distant object being pointed to by another person).
Eye teaming	Maintains focus on object moving slowly toward face (convergence).	2–4 months	Eye teaming while adjusting eye alignment as focal distance of the object changes	The child maintains fixation on an object as it is moved toward his or her face. The eyes will slowly move in toward the nose as the object approaches. Does one eye break away from the object first?
Eye teaming	Maintains focus on object moving slowly from face (divergence).	4 months	Eye teaming while adjusting to moderate distance	The child maintains his or her fixation on an object that is moving away from the child. This may occur naturally as in the situation of a ball rolling away from the child.
Depth perception	Reaches accurately for nearby objects.	5–9 months	Depth perception, eye–hand coordination	The child reaches accurately toward a silent toy held at midline from a distance of 8–10 inches from the eyes. Notice also whether there is consistent over or under reaching to objects located on a surface (e.g., table or floor).
Depth perception	Places small objects into narrow container.	13 months	Depth perception, eye–hand coordination, eye teaming	The child places small objects into a narrow container with a solid degree of accuracy. Notice whether there is consistent poor placement of the object in the opening of the container. An example might be putting 1-inch blocks into a can.
Depth perception	Accurately stacks 1–2-inch objects	12–19 months	Depth perception, eye–hand coordination, eye teaming	The child stacks one block/can/object onto another with good placement accuracy. Notice whether there is consistent inaccuracy in placing one item onto the next one.
Depth perception	Visually aware of steps, drop-offs, and so forth.	18–30 months	Depth perception	The child slows down, adjusts body movement, or stops when there is a step up or drop-off. The child may stop and feel the surface change with his or her foot and/or hand before continuing on his or her way.
Compensatory visual behaviors	Squints one eye when looking.	6 months	Refractive error, uneven vision in both eyes	Observe the eyes while child is looking intently at something. Note whether the squinting occurs during near and/or far viewing tasks.
Compensatory visual behaviors	Closes or covers one eye when looking.	6 months	Refractive error, uneven vision in both eyes	Observe eyes while child is looking intently at something. Note if the eye closing or covering behavior occurs during near and/or far viewing tasks.
Compensatory visual behaviors	Squints excessively to bright light.	All age ranges	Light sensitivity	Observe child's reaction to the presence of bright light coming from a window or when traveling outside. Does the child squint excessively or shield his or her eyes from the bright light such as sunlight?
Compensatory visual behaviors	Blinks more than usual.	All age ranges	Light sensitivity, refractive error	Observe whether the child blinks excessively when concentrating on a visual task (e.g., looking at a book, playing with toys).

(continued on next page)

Transdisciplinary Play-Based System (TPBA2/TPBI2)
by Toni Linder

Visual Development Indicators **TPBA 2**

Category	Item	Age range	What is measured	How to assess
Compensatory visual behaviors	Frequently rubs or pokes eyes.	All age ranges	Visual acuity, general health status of eyes	Note whether the child rubs or pokes his or her eyes on a regular basis. Does it occur with one or both eyes?
Compensatory visual behaviors	Moves *very close* to objects to look at them (e.g., 1–3 inches away).	All ages	Visual acuity, visual field	Note how close the child views a variety of objects—does the child bring eyes <u>unusually</u> close to object or does the child hold objects <u>unusually</u> close to his or her face when looking at them? Look for consistency of this behavior—not just one episode of viewing an object at an extremely close range.
Compensatory visual behaviors	Turns/tilts head when looking at objects.	All age ranges	Field of vision, equality of vision in both eyes	Observe the child's head position during visual tasks. Is there a consistent head turn/tilt when the child is looking at something? Is there a head turn or tilt when the object is in a certain area of the child's visual field (e.g., side, lower gaze)?
Visual motor/visual cognitive	Smiles in return to another's smile.	1–4 months	Visual imitation	The child returns the smile of a familiar or unfamiliar person. The other person should be no farther than 10 inches from the child.
Visual motor/visual cognitive	Imitates scribbling.	10.5–16 months	Visual imitation, eye–hand coordination	The child imitates scribbling after watching someone else scribble.
Visual motor/visual cognitive	Imitates a crayon stroke.	12–21 months	Visual imitation, eye–hand coordination	The child imitates making a mark on paper after watching another make a mark on paper.
Visual motor/visual cognitive	Copies a circle.	30–42 months	Visual imitation, eye–hand coordination	The child watches another person make a circle, then imitates circular motion with a marking tool on paper.
Visual motor/visual cognitive	Matches two or more colors.	26–42 months	Color matching	The child matches two or more primary colors (red, blue, green, yellow) when shown an example. "Can you show me one like this?"
Visual motor/visual cognitive	Completes colored pattern with blocks.	35–37 months	Color matching	The child duplicates a simple pattern of colored blocks from a model (three different blocks, three different colors).
Visual motor/visual cognitive	Points to a requested color.	30–42 months	Color identification	When asked, "show me," the child points to a requested color (red, blue, green, yellow).
Visual motor/visual cognitive	Sorts objects by color.	21–42 months	Color identification	Given same objects of different colors, the child sorts (without a model) the items by color.
Visual motor/visual cognitive	Responds to mirror image.	4–6 months	Visual response to self	The child smiles to, and/or vocalizes to and/or touches his or her mirror image.
Visual motor/visual cognitive	Recognizes self in mirror.	15–16 months	Visual recognition of self	The child smiles to the mirror and looks at others for their approval. Child touches self and watches movement in the mirror.
Visual motor/visual cognitive	Looks at pictures in books	10–14 months	Picture interest, picture recognition	The child is content to look at pictures in familiar or an unfamiliar book.

Transdisciplinary Play-Based System (TPBA2/TPBI2) by Toni Linder

Category	Item	Age range	What is measured	How to assess
Visual motor/cognitive	Turns book right-side-up.	18–24 months	Spatial orientation of pictures/books	The child rights familiar or unfamiliar book when it is handed to him or her upside down.
Visual motor/cognitive	Names one picture.	18–22 months	Picture recognition	The child says the name of the item in the picture.
Visual motor/cognitive	Matches object to picture.	19–27 months	Symbolic understanding of objects and pictures	The child matches an object to its picture (e.g., real shoe to a picture of a shoe); child locates an object shown in a picture (retrieves cup when shown a picture of a cup).
Visual motor/cognitive	Finds detail in familiar picture book.	24–27 months	Figure/ground discrimination, visual acuity, picture recognition	On request, the child locates small detail in familiar book such as a tiny flower, animal, or details of a face. The child may point to the item, speak its name, or intently look in the correct direction of the named item.
Visual motor/cognitive	Matches pictures.	26–30 months	Picture recognition, understanding of "same"	The child matches two identical pictures. Matching may occur verbally or physically.
Visual motor/cognitive	Names action happening in picture.	24–36 months	Picture recognition of actions	The child names an action(s) depicted in a picture or selects a picture when its action is named.
Visual motor/cognitive	Identifies pictures of objects by their function.	42 months	Picture recognition	The child names or points to picture of a particular object when asked, "Show me the one that is used for . . ."
Visual motor/cognitive	Tells a story by looking at photos and/or pictures.	42–48 months	Picture recognition, visual sequencing	The child recounts or makes up a story by looking at a series of pictures or photographs.

REFERENCES

Atkinson, J. (2000). *The developing visual brain.* New York: Oxford University Press.

Bayley, N. (1993). *The Bayley Scales of Infant Development* (2nd ed.). San Antonio, TX: Harcourt Assessment.

Brigance, A.H. (1991). *BRIGANCE Diagnostic Inventory of Early Development* (Rev. ed.). North Billerica, MA: Curriculum Associates.

Foundation for Knowledge in Development. (1988). *Miller assessment for preschoolers.* New York: Harcourt Assessment.

Frankenburg, W.K., & Dobbs, J.B. (1990). *Denver Developmental Screening Test II.* Denver, CO: University of Colorado Medical Center.

Glass, P. (1993). Development of visual function in preterm infants: Implications for early intervention. *Infants and Young Children, 6,* 11–20.

Good, W.V., & Hoyt, C.S. (1989). Behavioral correlates of poor vision in children. *International Ophthalmology Clinics, 29*(1), 57–60.

Hollins, M. (1989). *Understanding blindness: An integrative approach.* Hillsdale, NJ: Lawrence Erlbaum Associates.

Hyvärinen, L. (1994). Assessment of visually impaired infants. *Low Vision and Vision Rehabilitation, 7*(2), 219–225.

Hyvärinen, L. (1995). Effect of impaired vision on general development. In L. Hyvärinen (Ed.), *Vision testing manual 1995–1996* (pp. 1–7). Villa Park, IL: Precision Vision.

Johnson-Martin, N.M., Attermeier, S.M., & Hacker, B.J. (1990). *The Carolina curricula: The Carolina Curriculum for preschoolers with special needs.* Baltimore: Paul H. Brookes Publishing Co.

Johnson-Martin, N.M., Jens, K.G., Attermeier, S.M., & Hacker, B.J. (1991). *The Carolina Curriculum for infants and toddlers with special needs* (2nd ed.). Baltimore: Paul H. Brookes Publishing Co.

Parks, S., Furono, S., O'Reilly, T., Inatsuka, C.M., Hosaka, C.M., & Zeisloft-Falbey, B. (1994). *Hawaii Early Learning Profile (HELP): HELP (birth to three).* Palo Alto, CA: VORT Corporation.

Sireteanu, R. (1996). Development of the visual field: Results from human and animal studies. In F. Vital-Durand, J. Atkinson, & O.J. Braddick (Eds.), *Infant vision* (pp. 17–31). New York: Oxford Press.

Teplin, S. (1995). Visual impairment in infants and young children. *Infants and Young Children, 8*(1), 18–51.

Vital-Durand, F., Ayzac, L., & Pinsaru, G. (1996). Acuity cards and the search for risk factors in infant visual development. In F. Vital-Durand, J. Atkinson, & O.J. Braddick (Eds.), *Infant vision* (pp. 185–200). New York: Oxford Press.

Yonas, A., & Granrud, C.E. (1985). The development of sensitivity to kinetic, binocular and pictorial depth information in human infants. In D. Ingle, D. Lee, & R.N. Jeannerod (Eds.), *Brain mechanisms and spatial vision* (pp. 113–146). The Hague: Nijhoff.

4

Emotional and Social Development Domain

The emotional and social development domain often is given insufficient attention in a child's overall assessment. Assessments of abilities in cognitive, communication and language, and sensorimotor areas indicate *what* the child can do, but instruments often do not indicate *how* the child has acquired these proficiencies or *how* he or she uses them in interaction with others. The "how" of learning and development is based on emotional and social development, because much of learning is driven by emotional needs and responses and is dependent on social input. Emotions express the child's desire to initiate, maintain, repeat, avoid, or change interactions with people, objects, and events in the environment (Saarni, Mumme, & Campos, 1998). The ability to moderate one's own emotions and to read and respond to emotions in others greatly influences positive social interactions. Development thus focuses first on emotional development and then on the child's social relationships with parents, other caregivers, siblings, and peers.

Emotional development and social behaviors are critical to children's overall functioning (Cheah, Nelson & Rubin, 2001; Clark & Ladd, 2000; Gauthier, 2003; Sroufe, 1997), and delays or deficits of emotional functioning can have a negative impact on other areas of development (Brinton & Fujiki, 2002; Diamond, 2002). For example, a child who has difficulty reading others' emotional cues, extremely negative emotional reactions to certain types of sensory input, and a poor self-concept also may have difficulty with social interactions, difficulty attending to and remembering concepts, sensory integration issues, and inappropriate pragmatic skills in communication. Emotions can cause problems in other domains (e.g., extended crying can keep a child from attending to productive activities) and also can result from problems in other domains (e.g., dislike of intense tactile input may cause frustration or anger). Thus, developmental deficits should always be examined in relation to influences from and impact on other domains.

Emotional and social screening, assessment, and intervention have become increasingly important to developmental researchers as well as to early childhood service providers, who are examining the diagnosis, prevention, and treatment of emotional concerns in very young children. This new emphasis is seen in the emergence of the field of infant mental health into prominence in research and treatment. The following are areas in which key research is being done:

1. Self-regulation, behavioral regulation, affect, and behavior (Bronson, 2000; De-Gangi, 1991a, 1991b; Fox, 1994; Neisworth, Bagnato, & Salvia, 1995; Weatherston, Ribaudo, & Glovak, 2002; Williamson & Anzalone, 2001)

2. Achievement motivation and issues related to a child's sense of self (Erwin & Brown, 2003; Hauser-Cram, 1998; Morgan, Harmon, & Maslin-Cole, 1990; Roth-Hanania, Busch-Rossnagel, & Higgins-D'Alessandro, 2000; Wehmeyer & Palmer, 2000)

3. Attachment behaviors with parents as well as social interactions with other caregivers, siblings, and peers (Brown & Dunn, 1996; Clark & Ladd, 2000; Goldberg, 1990; Howes, Galinsky, & Kontos, 1998)

A diagnostic classification system for children from birth to age 3, *The Diagnostic Classification of Regulatory Disorders,* was developed by ZERO TO THREE: National Center for Infants, Toddlers, and Families (2005), and several assessment tools for addressing mental health in young children also have been developed. Assessment instruments that address emotional and social characteristics include the *Temperament and Atypical Behavior Scale* (Neisworth, Bagnato, Salvia, & Hunt, 1999); *Brief Infant Toddler Social Emotional Assessment* (BITSEA; Briggs-Gowan & Carter, 2005); *Infant Toddler Social Emotional Assessment* (ITSEA; Carter & Briggs-Gowan, 2005); *Infant-Toddler Symptom Checklist* (DeGangi, Poisson, Sickle, & Wiener, 1995); *Infant-Toddler Sensory Profile* (Dunn, 2002); *Sensorimotor History Questionnaire for Preschoolers* (DeGangi & Balzer-Martin, 1999); *Infant-Toddler Developmental Assessment* (Provence, Erikson, Vater, & Palmeri, 1995); *Ages & Stages Questionnaires®: Social-Emotional* (Squires, Bricker, & Twombly, 2002). Intervention resources also are more readily available (Bronson, 2000; DeGangi, 2000; Gomez, Baird, & Jung, 2004; Kranowitz, 1998, 2003; Weider & Greenspan, 2001; Williamson & Anzalone, 2001).

Areas previously seen as global constructs, such as "temperament," are being critically analyzed and broken into observable components that can be addressed in early intervention or through mental health treatment approaches (DeGangi, 2000; Neisworth et al., 1999; Williamson & Anzalone, 2001).

The development of social interactions and relationships also is being reexamined, and research addressing the importance of parent–child interaction, cultural influences, and other social contexts on the developing child's social skills gives us new directions for consideration in assessment and intervention (Gifford-Smith & Brownell, 2003; Goldberg, 1990; Shonkoff & Phillips, 2000; van IJzendoorn & Sagi, 1999). Scientists and practitioners are beginning to consider the contexts in which young children interact as well as the child's social skills.

Neurological research continues to reveal new information about which parts of the brain are responsible for various emotions and behavioral responses. Understanding the biochemistry of the brain is a burgeoning field, and drug therapies for a wide range of emotional disorders are currently available. However, the long-term effects of these treatments for children are unknown. The purpose of TPBA2 is to identify developmental functioning and not to associate neurological causes for problems that may have implications for drug therapy. For this reason, in all areas of development, but particularly in the emotional and social domain, further observations, discussions with parents to determine patterns of behavior, and referral for neurological or psychiatric evaluations may be needed.

This chapter provides Observation Guidelines for examining qualitative aspects of a child's emotional-social development, as well as an Age Table for determining the developmental level of the child's social skills. The TPBA2 Observation Guidelines and Age Tables are used together. Professionals refer to the Age Tables to see whether the child is demonstrating emotional and social skills applicable to his or her age level. The answers to questions asked by the Observation Guidelines provide information about the appropriateness of *how* the child expresses emotions and carries out social interactions. Areas addressed in the emotional and social domain include 1) emotional expression, 2) emotional style/adaptability, 3) regulation of emotions and arousal states, 4) behavioral regulation, 5) sense of self, 6) social interactions, and 7) emotional themes in play (see Table 4.1 for definitions of each subcategory). Modifications from the first edition of TPBA (see Chapter 1) were determined after reviewing current literature and assessment procedures in early childhood emotional and social development, pediatric mental health, play therapy, and early intervention research.

The first four subcategories in this domain address the child's "emotional dynamics" (Thompson, 1990) or parameters of emotional development. Although these aspects can be combined in one category called "self-regulation" or temperament (Bronson, 2000; DeGangi, 1991a, 1991b; Kopp, 1992; Neisworth et al., 1995; ZERO TO THREE, 2005), in TPBA2 these are subdivided into several areas that have direct implications for intervention. This chapter is built on the premise that *expression of emotions* is fundamental to development and includes physiological, cognitive, and behavioral components involving range, variability, intensity, and temporal factors dependent on biological and environmental characteristics. *Emotional style,* which relates to emotional flexibility and adaptability to various types of input, and to changes in routine, activities, or environment, is closely related to the next subcategory, *regulation of emotions and arousal states.* Children need to be able to move through arousal states and to monitor, evaluate, and modify their emotional reactions as well as the intensity and duration of their emotional reactions. *Behavioral regulation* is closely related to the above areas but addresses more of the child's responses to external, rather than internal, demands. The next two subcategories relate emotions to social development, building on the emotional influences identified in the first two subcategories. *Sense of self* builds on the pre-

Table 4.1. Emotional and social domain subcategories and definitions

Subcategory	Description
Emotional expression	Communication of reactions, feelings, or intentions to others through facial patterns, muscle tension, body posture and position of extremities, movements, gestures, and words. Includes overall disposition or mood
Emotional style/ adaptability	The child's typical affective response to different situations, including two elements of temperament—approach or withdrawal to new stimuli and adaptability to change
Regulation of emotions and arousal states	Ability to regulate physiological states of awareness (sleeping, crying, etc.) and control emotional reactions to both internal and external stimuli, including being able to self-calm and inhibit impulsive actions and emotions
Behavioral regulation	The ability to control impulses, monitor one's actions and interactions, and respond within the parameters of culturally accepted behavior, including compliance with adult requests, self-control over behaviors perceived as wrong, and use of social conventions
Sense of self	Understanding of self as a separate person capable of having an effect on his/ her environment, including desire to accomplish goals to be independent and competent
Emotional themes in play	Expression of inner feelings, including worries, fears, and traumas through the actions of play, especially through the dramatic representations of self or dolls
Social interactions	Ability to attend to social aspects of play, to read cues, to interpret and communicate social information, to get along with others and avoid negativity and conflict with others (including parents, strangers, siblings, and peers) within isolated, parallel, associative, cooperative or complementary roles in play interactions

vious emotional subcategories, emphasizing the child's differentiation of self from others, the expression of mastery motivation, and the desire for independence. The child's sense of self influences and is influenced by *social relationships* with parents, caregivers, other adults, siblings, and peers. Examination of interaction style and differentiation across people and contexts is incorporated into social relations, in addition to positive and negative social skills. The final subcategory, emotional *themes in play*, provides insight into how all of the categories influence the child's inner emotional world. Biological, psychological, social, and environmental influences come together to provide an internal emotional framework from which the child views the world. These influences may help the child approach experiences with trust and inquisitiveness or with distrust, anxiety, fear, or another emotionally and socially inhibiting mindset. These seven subcategories are interrelated (e.g., emotional regulation is related to emotional expression, emotional style, and emotional themes in play, and all of these may influence social relations and behavioral regulation). In combination, these subcategories encompass both qualitative emotional and social issues and quantitative skill and age-related expectations.

FORMAT OF THE CHAPTER

In the following sections, the emotional and social subcategories are addressed in detail. The questions that guide team members are found on the TPBA2 Observation Summary Form for the emotional and social domain (p. 186). Use of the Observation Summary Forms is described in Chapter 2 of the *Administration Guide* and in the directions on TPBA2 p. 168. Responses to these questions lead to identification of the child's best performance or behavior, areas of concern, and directions for program planning.

I. Emotional Expression

Although many times used interchangeably, the terms *emotion, feelings, mood,* and *affect* are distinct. Emotion, in the global sense, refers to a "complex feeling state, with psychic, somatic, and behavioral components" (Benham, 2000, p. 253) experienced by the child in response to internal or external stimuli. Characteristic facial expressions accompany most emotions, such as happiness, sadness, anger, and disgust. Feelings derive from emotions and involve autonomic nervous system changes that occur during an emotion. Feelings last longer than the emotion but typically not more than a few minutes (DeGangi, 2000). For example, the expression of anger may be brief, but the visceral feelings of anger may persist longer. Mood is a pervasive emotion experienced and observed by others over time (Benham, 2000). When a feeling lasts for a longer period of time, usually more than an hour, it becomes a mood (DeGangi, 2000). Extended periods of irritability, depression, or excitement are types of moods. Moods do not have a corresponding facial expression, although a person in an excited mood may have a smiling expression and feel predominately happy. Emotions provide social signals to others, and the term *affect* describes the expressions and behaviors that indicate what emotions the child is experiencing. As defined by Kaplan and Sadock (1988), "Affect refers to the expression of emotion as observed by others. Affect addresses qualitative aspects across different feeling states, including appropriateness, depth or flatness, intensity, and lability of affect" (cited in Benham, 2000, p. 256).

The range, clarity, intensity, duration, and frequency of expression of various emotions influence many aspects of development and learning. Emotions have an impact on motivation (Saarni et al., 1998), attention and cognitive processing (Lewis, 1999; Lewis, Sullivan, & Ramsay, 1992), social relations (Stein & Levine, 1999), communication (Sullivan & Lewis, 2003), and even physical health (Friedman, 2002).

Emotions and feelings play a major role in motivating actions and behaviors. Children tend to seek out activities that make them feel good and avoid activities that make them uncomfortable or angry. Because emotions infuse meaning into our lives, they provide a guidance function (Dodge & Garber, 1991). Emotions can prompt a child to action in order to accomplish a goal, they energize thinking and acting, and they can provide meaning for a situation (Campos, Mumme, Kermoian, & Campos, 1994; Saarni, 1999). Emotions related to various situations become a part of memory and thereby influence repetition of behaviors in the future (Charney, 1993; LeDoux, 1996; Sullivan & Lewis, 2003). For example, a child who gets a shot from the doctor may show fear of the doctor on the next visit. Emotions thus serve both as an outcome of mastery of a situation and as the foundation for the next learning experience. When a young infant sees a pop-up box, her first emotion may be interest; this emotion motivates her to push a button on the pop-up box. When a toy pops up, she may experience surprise, but as she assesses cognitively the action and the consequence, her emotion may turn to happiness. This feeling of pleasure provides an incentive to repeat the action in order to experience this emotion again. As the activity becomes repetitive and is no longer as pleasurable, the child is then driven to try new actions or activities that will lead to new feelings of pleasure.

Emotions help us see how children perceive themselves and others, how they interpret events in their environment, and how well they self-regulate when confronted with challenging situations (DeGangi, 2000). For example, a smile can indicate pride in being able to stack blocks without them falling over, a bashful frown may be read as discomfort with a new situation, and tears may indicate frustration at not being able to do what is desired. Emotions also serve as the foundation for reciprocity within social interactions, as the child both expresses emotions (which others respond to) and responds to the emotions of others (Sullivan & Lewis, 2003). In the following section, research on the development and significance of emotions and their importance to the establishment of self-identity and social relationships is presented under each of the Observation Guideline questions for the subcategories within the emotional and social domain.

▮▮▮ I. A. How does the child express emotions?

Emotional expression is the "communication of reactions, feelings, or intentions to others during social interactions" (DeGangi, 2000, p. 122). Children demonstrate wide variation in terms of how they experience, interpret, and respond to the events in their environment. Some children exhibit a broad range of emotions that are appropriate to the situation; some demonstrate a smaller range of emotions, with one type of emotion being predominant (e.g., primarily happy or sad); still other children may shift quickly into expression of extremely intense emotions (e.g., from smiling to angry screaming). The child's ability to express as well as to read and interpret a broad range of emotions in others is critical to successful social interaction.

The range, clarity, intensity, duration, and frequency of expression of various emotions as observed in the child's affect and mood influences many aspects of development and learning, such as attention to cognitive tasks and social interactions with others. The ability to demonstrate subtle ranges of emotion also is important, so that words or gestures, rather than tantrums, can communicate feelings. Children with disabilities often give expressive cues that are difficult to read because they are fleeting, subtle, or disorganized (Kasari & Sigman, 1996; Kasari, Sigman, Mundy, & Yirmiya, 1990; Sigman, Kasari, Kwon, & Yirmiya, 1992). Consequently, difficulties with emotional expression can influence the development of social skills (Sullivan & Lewis, 2003).

Expression of emotion is demonstrated through facial patterns, muscle tension, body posture and position of extremities, movements, gestures, and words. Such body language enables others to determine what the child is feeling and how the child is interpreting experiences (DeGangi, 2000; Ekman & Friesen, 1969). Emotional expressions are, thus, important for the child's social development, emotional regulation, early language development, and learning of cultural "emotional display rules" (Mundy & Willoughby, 1996).

In infancy, facial expression provides the best cues to the child's internal emotional state. The basic feeling states that can be inferred from facial muscle movements and expressions include happiness, surprise, fear, anger, sadness, and disgust. These are expressed much the same way worldwide (Izard, 1991; Izard et al., 1995), whereas facial expressions for interest, contempt, and shame are less universal. Signs of many emotions are present at birth, with more subtle emotions and those requiring cognitive understanding appearing later.

During infancy, internal state is identifiable through facial, vocal, gestural, and regulatory behaviors (Sullivan & Lewis, 2003; Weinberg & Tronick, 1994). Over time, the infant's emotions become adaptive, primarily through interchanges with the caregiver, as the child learns how his or her behaviors and emotions will be responded to over various circumstances. As the young infant's facial expressions change every 7–9 seconds, the caregiver has many opportunities to respond to and shape the child's emotional expression (Malatesta, Culver, Tesman, & Shapard, 1989). As a result of these interchanges and social interactions with others, the manner in which emotions are expressed are culturally influenced. When, where, and how an emotion is displayed is determined through "emotional display rules" unique to each culture. Parents have subcultural, familial, or personal goals and values for evaluating emotional events and displaying emotions in certain situations. Children learn through modeling and social transference the ways in which they should evaluate emotions in others and express emotions in different situations (Zahn-Waxler, Friedman, Cole, Mizuta, & Hiruma, 1996). Most cultures teach children to exhibit positive emotions and hide negative emotions in public arenas. For example, Asian children place greater importance on masking negative emotions when compared with American children (Cole & Tamang, 1998; Matsumoto, 1990). Gender differences also take into account emotional display rules, as young girls frequently are allowed to be more emotionally expressive than their male peers (Weinberg, Tronick, Cohn, & Olson, 1999). These emotional display rules are important, because culturally acceptable emotional expression enables children to be viewed more positively by adults and peers who hold these values (McDowell & Parke, 2000).

I. B. Does the child demonstrate a full range of emotions, including positive emotions, emotions of discomfort, and self-conscious emotions?

Positive Emotions

Positive emotions include interest and happiness. Surprise is included in this area, but it is actually a neutral emotion that can precede a happy, unhappy, or self-conscious emotion. Expression of positive emotions is particularly important, because it indicates awareness and understanding of pleasurable aspects of a situation on the part of the child. The developmental progression of interest and joy corresponds to the child's developing cognitive understanding. Lack of pleasurable feelings and expression of positive emotions can greatly hinder cognitive, communication, and social development.

Interest is a sign of positive approach and receptivity to the environment. Newborns demonstrate interest through alerting, quieting, and "wide-eyed" staring. "Knit brow" interest is seen in infants from 2 to 8 months and again regularly by 10–12 months (Malatesta & Haviland, 1982). This expression appears to demonstrate focused attention associated with increases in memory and problem solving (Sullivan & Lewis,

2003). Babies who show interest in their environment are easier for parents to engage, thus encouraging the foundations of social interactions. Lack of expression of interest holds diagnostic implications. Children with various types of disabilities may show interest in a restricted variety of things, may have a reduced amount of time in which they show interest (attention span), or may demonstrate limited or extreme intensity of interest.

Happiness, demonstrated through smiling, laughing, and general bodily excitement, engages adults and leads to increased interactions. From birth, babies smile when their tummies are full, during REM sleep, and occasionally in response to gentle touches. Between 6 and 8 weeks of age, babies smile in response to interesting visual, auditory, or tactile stimulation, and smiling to social interactions peaks between 12 and 14 weeks of age. Between 12 and 16 weeks, they also begin to smile at active stimuli and become more discriminating, as smiling occurs more with familiar people (Sullivan & Lewis, 2003). Feelings of happiness are first linked to physical states, such as feeling satisfied after a meal or being tickled, and later reflect psychological states, such as pleasure in game playing with the parent (Isley, O'Neil, Clatfelter, & Parke, 1999). The laughing or "play face" appears around 5 months of age (Sroufe & Waters, 1976) in response to intense visual, auditory, or tactile stimulation. The child's developing sense of humor also can be seen; by around 12 months of age, the child will laugh at incongruities, novelty, self-produced actions, and games like Peekaboo. Pleasure at mastery can be seen from 4 to 12 months of age and continues throughout life (Busch-Rossnagel, 1997; Lewis, Sullivan, & Alessandri, 1990).

Children with disabilities may demonstrate differences in emotional expression that will have an impact on development. Children with Down syndrome may show delayed positive expressions and may be less likely to initiate smiling, which can have an impact on social interactions (Carvajal & Iglesias, 2000; Kasari & Sigman, 1996); children with cerebral palsy may have an asymmetrical or "play face" smile; children who are blind or visually impaired may have lower rates and poorer quality of enjoyment in social interactions (Castanho & Otta, 1999); and children with autism spectrum disorders tend to show less pleasure in both social and toy play and exhibit conflicting emotions (Yirmiya, Kasari, Sigman, & Mundy, 1999).

The emotion of surprise usually occurs in response to an unexpected stimulus. Once the infant evaluates the meaning of the stimulus and determines how to respond, interest, smiling, or a negative expression usually follows (Bennett, Bendersky, & Lewis, 2002). Surprise is not exhibited by all children and seems to be seen in more emotionally reactive children. Research on the expression of surprise has not yet been shown to be as diagnostically relevant as other emotions.

For older infants and young children, the number and type of events that cause positive emotions expand rapidly. Social interactions grow in number and type, escalating language skills extend communication attempts, gross and fine motor skills increase opportunities for pleasurable exploration, and increasing conceptual and problem-solving abilities enable the child to experience feelings of mastery and success. All of these developing abilities provide opportunities for enjoyable learning and engagement. For many children with disabilities, delays or differences in emotional enjoyment have diagnostic and or intervention implications. It is important to examine pleasurable expressions for readability, frequency, and intensity and to analyze the situations that elicit positive emotions.

Emotions of Discomfort

Emotions of discomfort include disgust, anger, sadness, and fear. Expression of emotions of discomfort is natural and all such emotions develop during the first year of life. Lack of such expressions signifies a potential concern.

Disgust is an emotion of discomfort that is evident at birth. Babies react to bitter and sour tastes with expressions indicating dislike. They turn away, pucker up, or stick out their tongues. Although taste tests are not part of TPBA, parents may report such reactions. By 6 months of age, babies may begin to respond with aversion to visual or auditory stimulation that is unpleasant. Social elicitors of disgust develop later and are culturally and socially influenced by the reactions of others.

Although newborns respond with generalized distress to uncomfortable experiences, specific emotions of *anger* and *sadness* develop over the first months. Frequently, the negative facial expressions are blended into an "undifferentiated" distress state (Sullivan & Lewis, 2003). By 3–4 months of age, angry expressions are evident when a child is restrained or when access to a desired object is denied (Bennett et al., 2002; Braungart-Reiker & Stifter, 1996). As the infant acquires more ability to control his or her actions and a greater understanding of what causes events to occur, the child develops a target for angry feelings. He or she demonstrates anger through facial expressions, crying, and body language when a goal is not attained, or is thwarted, or when the caregiver responds in an undesired way. Although parents always prefer to see positive emotions, lack of expression of discomfort or unhappiness can indicate a lack of awareness and may be associated with a disability.

Although sadness, or the "pout face," is typically observed less frequently than anger in young infants, and it develops more during the second half of the first year, sad expressions are not associated with any specific stimulus or context (Sullivan & Lewis, 2003). Sadness can be a predominant emotion for infants experiencing extended loss of the familiar caregiver or who have a seriously depressed caregiver (Martins & Gaffan, 2000; Teti, Gelfand, Messinger, & Isabella, 1995). Knowledge of the family situation and parents' mental states, therefore, is important. By about 8 months of age, general distress shown by young infants has differentiated into anger, distress, disgust, and fear (Sroufe, 1997). Sad expressions are usually brief and because they are closely related to anger often turn into anger if not inhibited or influenced by a caregiver (Barr-Zisowitz, 2000). Observation of a predominance of sad expressions in an infant may have clinical implications, such as lack of attachment or depression on the part of the mother, and should be noted.

Fear develops during the second half of the first year. As children come to understand and recognize people and situations, and as they acquire the motor skills to explore their environment and encounter new situations, increased wariness develops. Fear of heights and stranger anxiety emerge from 6 to 9 months of age, although fear reactions are influenced by the expectations of the infant's culture (Saarni et al., 1998; Tronick, Morelli, & Ivey, 1992). Developing cognitive skills enable the infant to begin to differentiate threatening from nonthreatening situations from 7 to 12 months of age (Bronson, 2000). Learning and experience, as well as cultural modeling, appear to influence what may be experienced as fearful (Sullivan & Lewis, 2003).

From 2 years on, a child's developing imagination and difficulty separating fantasy from reality, combined with the child's increasing exploration, enable the child to encounter new mysteries and determine new threats, such as scary creatures. Children may develop fears of the dark or going to bed. As children become aware of death between 3 and 4 years of age, a concern about the parents' or their own death may be exhibited. Unique fears also may develop related to specific situations or experiences in the child's life that have felt threatening or intimidating to them.

Children with neurological deficits or emotional disturbance may lack fearful responses or respond with excessive fear to nonfrightening situations. In addition, some children may experience negative situations that can result in contingent fearful responses, for instance reactions to shots at the doctor's office. Discussion with parents about the child's fears in addition to observation of fearful responses can provide insight into the extent of the child's fearfulness.

Overall, Sullivan and Lewis (2003) note that expressions indicating pain, interest, and possibly anger and disgust remain fairly stable over the first 2 years. Instead, what shifts are the *contexts* that elicit these emotions. Major transitions appear to occur at 4 months of age, 7–9 months of age, and 18–20 months of age. Developmental status can be determined through observation of the child's responses to different contexts. In addition, parent report and observation can reveal the child's preferences, dislikes, and style of response.

Self-Conscious Emotions

As children develop they acquire new emotions that require more sophisticated cognitive understanding, including *shame, embarrassment, guilt, envy,* and *pride.* These emotions reflect how children feel about themselves and relate to children's developing sense of self (see p. 128). Self-conscious emotions begin to be demonstrated toward the end of the second year, although shyness and embarrassment may be seen earlier. Shame, pride, and embarrassment begin to be seen between 18 and 24 months of age, and envy and guilt are seen around the age of 3 years (Lewis, 2000; Lewis, Alessandri, & Sullivan, 1992). As these emotions develop, a child will demonstrate behaviors, such as gaze aversion, hiding her face behind her hands, turning away, or hanging her head to show shame, embarrassment, or guilt; taking toys or getting angry when envious of another child; or showing pride in accomplishments with broad smiles. These actions demonstrate that the child is becoming more aware of her own thoughts and actions, is comparing these actions and thoughts with those of others, and is understanding (although perhaps not following) the rules and expectations of those within her environment. Such behaviors lay the foundation for the evaluation of one's own behaviors and the development of conscience and self-concept. The conditions under which children experience self-conscious emotions differ with age. Very young children often feel guilty even if an act was an accident, because they are not yet able to differentiate consequences associated with accidents versus purposeful behavior (Graham, Doubleday, & Guarino, 1984). Preschoolers, on the other hand, often feel guilty only if an adult is present to witness the misdeeds (Harter & Whitesell, 1989). Adults play an important role in guiding children to understand standards of conduct.

Children who are unaware of others' thoughts and feelings, such as children with autism spectrum disorders, may not demonstrate self-conscious emotions. Children with emotional disorders or children who lack the cognitive understanding of right or wrong also may not demonstrate these emotions.

▨▨▨▨ I. C. What types of experiences make the child happy, unhappy, or self-conscious?

As noted previously, as children mature they express a broader range of emotions to an increasingly wider array of experiences (see I. A. and I. B.). The types of experiences that make a child happy or unhappy can have direct implications for assessment and intervention planning. Information about the child's favorite activities and disliked or avoided toys, materials, and experiences are determined prior to TPBA by asking family members and caregivers. Starting TPBA with favored activities, or activities that make the child happy, helps to establish an enjoyable play situation and a positive relationship with the play facilitator. Characteristics of these favored activities also are analyzed to determine developmental strengths. Toys and materials that are avoided or make the child unhappy may provide insight into areas of concern or need. For example, a child whose favorite type of play is caring for baby dolls is demonstrating interest in role play, understanding of representational thinking, and expression of positive emotions related to nurturance. Alternatively, a child who cries or covers his or her ears when a loud noise is heard may be demonstrating hypersensitivity to certain types or levels of auditory stimuli. Self-conscious emotions also are important to observe, because activities that elicit embarrassment, shame, or pride provide insight into the child's level of self-awareness and understanding of how his or her actions are perceived by others. Observational suggestions for what to look for during TPBA with regard to emotional expression are described in the following section.

▦▦▦ USING THE GUIDELINES TO ASSESS EMOTIONAL EXPRESSION

TPBA2 Observation Guidelines for the emotional and social domain ask several questions related to the type of input that seems to elicit various emotions, across people, objects, and events. Answers to these questions will assist in planning intervention to maximize pleasurable experiences for the child and assist the child in coping with uncomfortable situations. In the subcategory of Emotional Expression, the Observation Guidelines explore the child's emotional response to different types of input, including responses to different types of toys, materials, activities, and events that occur during TPBA. This information will be useful in planning intervention activities and making suggestions for family interactions in the home. The data from this subcategory of the emotional and social Observation Guidelines will be combined with data from other subcategories to look at the child's overall emotional development and social interactions.

It is important to recognize that some disabilities are associated with certain affective patterns or characteristics that influence the expression of emotion. For example, children with Angelman syndrome appear happy and smiling (Summers, Allison, Lynch, & Sandler, 1995). Children with autism spectrum disorders may exhibit a reduced range of emotion due to social limitations. Children with cerebral palsy may have motor challenges that inhibit the traditional behavioral expression of an emotion, even though the child may internally experience the emotion in the same way as a typically developing child. The team needs to attempt to examine the child's "experience" of an emotion as well as the expression of the emotion. This may require analyzing the child's behaviors, rather than facial expression, as indicators of emotional response. For example, repetition of an action may indicate pleasure in an activity, while withdrawal or pushing away from an activity may indicate displeasure or disgust. Children with disabilities may exhibit emotions in similar or different ways as their typical peers. The team may need to determine the child's emotional range through a combination of observation and interpretation of behavior in combination with discussion with the child's caregivers. Supporting the family in understanding the child's emotional expression is fundamental to reading and responding to the child's emotional cues.

▦▦▦ I. A. How does the child express emotions?

Regardless of the type of emotions the child is expressing, the team should watch the methods the child uses to communicate how he or she is feeling. The eyes, mouth, body posture, and movement of limbs and even fingers and toes provide cues, even if the cues are subtle, to indicate the child's feeling state. Unusual movements, such as flapping hands, grimacing, or repetition of actions, also may indicate an emotion. Some children may indicate emotions in idiosyncratic ways. Children with motor disabilities, such as cerebral palsy, may display atypical smiles or increased tone in limbs—behaviors that may appear to look like a negative response—when, in fact, they indicate enjoyment. The parent facilitator needs to discuss with the caregivers the specific behaviors or facial expressions that indicate to them that the child is happy or unhappy. Identification of the emotional meaning attached to sounds, gestures, and movements can help families and professionals respond more effectively to the child's needs.

I. B. Does the child demonstrate a full range of emotions, including positive emotions, emotions of discomfort, and self-conscious emotions?

During TPBA, the observers should determine what emotions a child exhibits and under what circumstances. Usually opportunities will arise during which the child may be shy or embarrassed (in front of unfamiliar people), interested (in new toys), excited (with fun activities), frustrated (when challenged), angry (when limits are set), or may show pride (when a skill is mastered) or guilt (if something is broken); some children may show fear (of strangers or scary situations). Most of these opportunities will happen naturally, but the facilitator can "arrange" for some of the events to occur in order to observe reactions. This is particularly important if the family has indicated concerns about certain emotions such as anger or fear. It is important that the team see emotions that are of concern. The team observes how long these feelings last and the intensity of the emotions. They also determine whether what is observed is similar to what is seen in other settings and how the caregivers interpret and respond to the child's emotions. Depending on the values and expectations of the family, the child's responses will have a different impact. For caregivers who find these "rougher" emotions trying or inappropriate, intervention supports may be necessary to help them modify the environment or their interactions in order to increase positive affect and pleasurable exchanges. Children who demonstrate extremes of negative affect also may exhibit difficulties with emotional regulation (see p. 111).

In addition to noting positive emotions and emotions of discomfort, the team also has an opportunity to observe the child's self-conscious emotions, such as pride in accomplishment as various tasks are tried. The child may show a parent his or her drawing or construction, smile, and say, "Daddy, look what I made!" Alternatively, the child may demonstrate accomplishments and show embarrassment when complimented. The team also can observe the child's response to accidents that occur, such as spilling bubbles or marking on the table when coloring. The child may avoid looking at the parent, hang his or her head, or try to cover up the error.

If the child oversteps a stated boundary or rule, how does the child respond to the adult's limit-setting or a caregiver's admonition? For example, one of the boundaries in the play room is that children are not allowed to break the toys or hurt people. If a toy is broken, does the child demonstrate expressions of embarrassment or shame? The rules and boundaries at home may be different for children, so it is important for the team to ascertain what the rules are at home and ask the parents how the child typically reacts when he or she has done something against the rules. The child's self-conscious emotional expressions need to be examined with regard to family expectations in addition to biological, developmental, and physiological considerations.

During a play session, the child may not have a reason to exhibit all of the possible emotions and the child's mood for that day may vary from his or her typical mood. When exploring the child's emotions, be sure to examine what emotions the family feels are important for the child to demonstrate and which ones they feel are inappropriate or should be limited to certain specific circumstances. Different cultures (or even individual families) have distinct expectations for which emotions are to be shown, to what extent, and under which circumstances (Chavira, Lopez, Blacher, & Shapiro, 2000). These should be explored because the child may be demonstrating emotional patterns characteristic of his or her culture or family, but these patterns may appear unusual in the main culture. For example, a child may be quiet and exhibit few emotions because the family has similar emotional patterns or because the child's culture expects children to be reserved and nonemotional. The opposite also may be true. A family that handles issues with explosive anger may have a child that mirrors those emotions. These patterns, which may resemble negative mood states, may, in fact, be familial or cultural expectations.

I. C. What types of experiences make the child happy, unhappy, or self-conscious?

Observers need to document the stimuli that elicit various emotional responses. The team should observe the child's play preferences, because these are usually activities that elicit positive emotions, as well as those activities that the child resists or avoids, which are typically not as pleasurable. Examination of play choices can assist the team in determining patterns of emotional expression.

Identifying interactions or environmental aspects that produce positive feelings for the child is important, because the characteristics of these stimuli can be integrated into early intervention programs. Positive emotions enhance attention, motivation, and learning (Goleman, 1995), and finding ways to increase positive emotions, affect, and mood is central to cognitive, emotional, social, communication, and sensorimotor development. It is important, therefore, to note the types of objects, activities, or interactions that spark interest, surprise, and happiness.

Observers also should watch for the situations that elicit signs of anger, sadness, disgust, and fear. Expression of these emotions should not be considered negative; rather, it reveals how the child is feeling. The team observes the situations that elicit these emotions, how long the feelings last, the intensity of the emotions, and whether what is observed is similar to what is seen in other settings.

As noted previously, it is important for the team to look at the child's entire range of emotions, but information on what elicits both positive and negative emotions is critical for intervention. Analysis of the situations eliciting these emotions can help interventionists and caregivers to adjust the environment and interactions to increase positive responses and thus provide motivation for engagement, or minimize negative feelings and thus reduce avoidance or resistance to engagement.

Nina is a 2-year-old who has been referred for TPBA as a result of suspected developmental delays. TPBA is conducted in her home with her mother, Tanya, and her father, Mike. Nina shows no interest in the new people coming into her home. She plays quietly with her soft, cuddly baby doll and only shows increased smiling and laughing when Mike tosses her around and tickles her. Nina takes books to her mother and crawls up into her mother's lap to look at the pictures. Nina avoids playing with the team members who have come to the home, withdrawing to her parents each time one of the team members offers her a toy. She shows interest in the bubbles that are produced, but only laughs when her dad blows the bubbles and makes big noises. Nina's parents report that she typically is extremely fearful with strangers, her affect is usually calm, and she displays little range in her emotions. Tanya states that although Nina smiles when she gets something she really wants, "it takes a lot" to get her to laugh, and "she's so quiet; it's easy to forget she's there." Mike agrees and says, "I think she's happy, but I wish she got excited more often. I'd even like to see her get mad once in a while!"

Looking solely at the area of emotional expression, the team and Nina's family agree that Nina shows a limited range of emotion. An "easy" and overall contented child, Nina only shows more intense emotions when she receives a great deal of tactile (tickling), vestibular (Dad throwing her in the air), or other physical input. She clearly wants to get that input from people who are familiar to her. Nina demonstrates interest in new toys and materials, especially those that provide a lot of tactile, visual, and auditory feedback for little effort. However, she demonstrates little excitement and, therefore, reduced motivation. Tanya and Mike would like to see Nina be able to demonstrate a broader range and a greater intensity of emotions. They also would like to see her begin to be less fearful of other children, because she will be going to a child care center soon.

Observations during TPBA will help the team (including the family) generate ideas to help Nina achieve the goals described above. They will use activities that elicit more positive emotions, such as sensory games to increase Nina's attention, and begin to combine these activities with activities that are not as motivating. For instance, a cause-and-effect toy that vibrates when pulled or put against her tummy may make her laugh. It also can be used to motivate her to explore cause-and-effect relationships.

II. Emotional Style/Adaptability ▬▬▬▬▬▬▬▬▬▬▬▬▬▬▬▬▬

Children commonly have a typical manner that characterizes their response to new situations or to changes from what is expected. For the purposes of TPBA, *how* a child typically approaches and responds to various stimuli, including new or modified experiences, is termed *emotional style*. Emotional style includes 1) reaction to novelty, or how easily the child accepts and engages *new* things, including people, objects, or events; 2) flexibility, or how easily the child handles *changes* or modifications of activities, routines, settings, or interaction patterns; and 3) emotional reactivity, or the child's *typical* level of positive or negative response to various types of stimuli. The above three aspects, as well as several factors examined in other subcategories (e.g., distractibility), are typically included under the concept of temperament.

There are nine areas of temperament: activity level, approach/withdrawal, distractibility, adaptability, persistence, mood, rhythmicity, sensitivity, and intensity of reactions (Thomas, Chess, & Birch, 1968; Thomas, Chess, Birch, Herzig, & Korn, 1963). From these, three different constellations of temperament traits that fit most children have been identified: the "easy" child, the "difficult child," and the "slow-to-warm-up" child (Thomas et al., 1963, 1968). "Goodness of fit," or match between the child's temperament and the demands of his or her environment, is critical to a child's successful adaptation (Chess & Thomas, 1996; Thomas & Chess, 1977). A similar relationship has been found to exist between a teacher and the temperament of a child with disabilities (Keogh, 2003; Martin, Olejnik, & Gaddis, 1994). Still other aspects such as parent personality and interaction style contribute to a child's temperament (Goldsmith & Campos, 1982; Kochanska, 1995).

Over the years, researchers have identified different aspects of temperament and defined temperament in slightly different ways (Buss & Plomin, 1975, 1984; Neisworth et al., 1999; Pelco & Reed-Victor, 2001, 2003; Pullis & Cadwell, 1985; Rothbart & Derryberry, 1981). Although the definition of temperament varies across studies, temperament has been shown to relate to children's behavior, social adjustment, and achievement (Carey, 1998; Goldsmith & Lemery, 2000; Keogh, Coots, & Bernheimer, 1995; McDevitt & Carey, 1996; Newman, Noel, Chen, & Matsopoulos, 1998; Pelco & Reed-Victor, 2001) and, therefore, has implications for social and cognitive development.

All aspects of temperament are addressed in some way in the TPBA2 Observation Guidelines, though not all are included in one subcategory. As a result, temperament is not considered a global construct in TPBA2. Several factors typically subsumed under the term *temperament* have been grouped under the subcategory of Emotional Style and are discussed in the next sections. These particular aspects are grouped together, because they frequently cluster in children with disabilities and, when looked at with patterns in other domains, can be diagnostically relevant (Benham, 2000; DeGangi, 2000; Neisworth et al., 1999).

▬▬▬ II. A. How does the child approach new
people, activities, or situations? (Consider age)

Emotional style refers to the ease with which the child adapts to new things in the environment. When faced with novel experiences, does the child respond with fear, anxiety, caution, interest, or eagerness? The manner in which the child indicates his or her interest or withdrawal also is informative. Interest may be evident if the child smiles, touches, verbalizes, or seeks proximity to people or objects. The child who is inhibited may move away from people or objects, resist eye contact, protest or cry, or seek proximity to more secure people (e.g., a parent) or objects (e.g., known toys or transition objects available during TPBA).

Inhibited or extremely shy children often react negatively to and withdraw from novel stimuli for extensive periods. Research has shown physiological differences in very shy children that resemble typical physiological responses of persons in highly threatening situations (Kagan, 1996, 1998; Kagan & Saudino, 2001; Kagan, Snidman, & Arcus, 1998). If early inhibition persists, it can lead to excessive social withdrawal and isolation (Caspi & Silva, 1995). These observations are important for determining how best to support children in exploring and learning in a way that is consistent with their personality style and needs (Carey & McDevitt, 1995).

II. B. How does the child adapt to transitions in activities and/or changes in routines?

Emotional style involves a child's flexibility or ability to adjust to changes or modifications from what is traditionally done or what is expected. Thomas and colleagues (1968) describe this as *adaptability*, or malleability to new or changed situations. Many children become very "set" in their routines and have difficulty changing expected patterns. Parents report that the child "hates to leave the house," "has to have things done the same way every day," or "gets upset if you ask him to stop doing one thing and do another." These children may show rigidity in their patterns of play and interaction as well. A child may have a difficult time shifting from one type of play activity to another, or even shifting to different actions in the same play activity. The child may expect a play partner to perform a specific role, such as following his or her lead, and become upset if this expectation is not met. The ability to adjust to changes within interactions and routines is important for the child's overall emotional and social adjustment (Neisworth et al., 1999) and requires investigation of patterns both in the home and in the play assessment.

II. C. How intensely does the child react to various types of stimuli?

A child's typical emotional intensity, both positive and negative, in reaction to stimulation is a third aspect of emotional style. This overlaps with flexibility but emphasizes the characteristic *level* of response to varying magnitudes of stimulation. Some children respond with a low level of emotional energy, whereas others display moderate emotions, and still others have powerful emotional responses. Children with low emotional energy may give cues that are more difficult to read. Such children also may be perceived to be less enjoyable by caregivers because they require a larger amount and longer duration of stimulation to evoke a positive response (Fox, Henderson, Rubin, Calkins, & Schmidt, 2000; Kagan et al., 1998; Landy, 2002). Children with high-intensity emotional responses also may be difficult, especially when the emotional response is negative. Information about intensity of reaction, when combined with other information about sensory integration and emotional regulation, will provide a basis for individualizing the type of input from which the child will benefit (DeGangi et al., 2000).

Teachers, therapists, and parents frequently must provide high levels of input to children with disabilities in order to obtain positive responses. For example, children with low tone or decreased tactile, visual, or auditory sensitivity may need more intense input in order to get a discernable or a positive response to engagement with toys or people. Some of these children who need more intense input also have a small "window" of response, or tolerance, resulting in overestimation of their ability to tolerate input. For example, in premature infants, a brief positive response to stimulation can suddenly shift to a cry of protest when the stimulation is too long or too intense (DeGangi, 2000; Field, 1983). Observations of the thresholds of responsiveness can help to gauge the level and amount of input the child needs and can tolerate (DeGangi, 1991a, 1991b, 2000). In other words, it is not enough to just look at what types of experiences cause the child to express various emotions. It also is necessary to look at the amount and intensity of different types of input that maintain optimal attention and interest. Keeping a child's engagement with people and objects at a pleasurable level will result in more effective intervention (Bronson, 2000; DiGangi, 1991b, 2000; Gowen & Nebrig, 2000; Landy, 2002).

▦▦▦ USING THE GUIDELINES TO ASSESS EMOTIONAL STYLE/ADAPTABILITY

The subcategory of Emotional Style examines a child's intensity of emotional response to various aspects in the environment, including novel stimuli or changes within or across environments. Observation of this subcategory begins at the very beginning of TPBA as new people, activities, or situations are encountered by the child. Most children interact and learn best when a moderate level of emotional response (rather than a low level or intense level) is experienced. Part of what is learned from observing the child is what approaches may be used to maximize the child's learning potential, such as modification of stimuli, implementation of transition strategies, or other interventions that may be helpful to assist the child to integrate and adapt to various environmental situations.

For some children with disabilities—for example, children with autism spectrum disorders, sensory integration dysfunction, or emotional disturbance—specific patterns of response in this subcategory may be seen (e.g., extremes of sensitivity or response). In combination with observations from other domains, the team may be able to integrate findings to make a meaningful diagnosis and treatment plan to respond to these characteristics.

▦▦▦ II. A. How does the child approach new people, activities, or situations? (Consider age)

Before conducting TPBA, the team should ask the child's parents to report how the child responds to the introduction of new foods, play materials, new caregivers, or new situations. This gives the team some insight about how the child will respond to the TPBA situation. For many children, the play assessment is a new experience with new toys and materials, unfamiliar people, and possibly an unknown setting. If conducted in a playroom, the team can note how the child reacts on entering the room and whether he or she appears anxious, cautious, eager, or interested in this new experience. Perhaps the child is cautious at first, but quickly settles in and becomes comfortable. The team should observe whether and how quickly the child relates to the unfamiliar adults in the room and whether he or she approaches the toys (caregivers will be able to point out which toys and materials are new to the child). If done in the home or community, the new people and materials (brought in by the team) will still be a factor. The child's selection of toys is relevant. Does the child select familiar or unfamiliar toys? Selection of new toys indicates a tolerance for, and perhaps even a preference for, novelty.

Observation of how the child copes with the new people, objects, and events, and how long the child takes to adjust, is important. The team should note the length of time it takes for the child to appear comfortable and the mechanisms that the child uses to make the adjustment. One child may hang back at first and then gradually move into or toward the new situation, person, or object. Another may vocalize to assure him- or herself, "that looks like a fun slide." Another child may use a parent as a base of security, entering an activity with the parent but remaining after the parent has withdrawn. Yet another child may need continual verbal assurance and reinforcement from a parent or other adult. Select children may not adapt at all and will continue to avoid the new or unfamiliar. It is important not to push the child, because this may cause further resistance or withdrawal. Respecting the child's warm-up time will ease the strain on the child, the parents, and the team. While the child is becoming comfortable, the team can talk to the family or let the family play with the child. It is important to ask the parents whether the behaviors the team is seeing are typical responses in a new situation. The team also needs to note the strategies that seem to help the child become comfortable. Information on how to help the child adjust to new people, objects, and/or situations will be beneficial to the family and to the intervention team.

II. B. How easily does the child adapt to transitions in activities and/or changes in routines?

During the play assessment, there will be many opportunities to observe the child's reactions to changes. Activities will be modified, parents may leave the room, and the level of stimulation will vary. In order to see the full range of the child's abilities, the child needs to be observed in a variety of different activities. Some children are motivated to explore and find out what play options are available. These children will move from toy to toy or area to area without much external support. Other children will stay with the same activity for the entire TPBA without assistance to transition. For this reason, the child who resists change may need assistance from the play facilitator to transition from one activity to another. The facilitator may try a variety of approaches. Transition strategies that may be tried include introducing a toy or activity gradually (first showing it, then listening to it, then demonstrating it), talking about what the possibilities are, having fun with an activity without involving the child, taking a preferred toy or activity to a new location, or combining a chosen activity with a less desired activity or toy. (See Chapter 7 in the *Administration Guide for TPBA2 & TPBI2* for a discussion of facilitation strategies.) The team should note the strategies that are most effective for application in future situations where transitions are difficult. The team also should note if the child needs certain preparations before a change is made. A child with visual impairment may need a touch and a verbal cue before new things are introduced. A child who is easily overwhelmed may need more time for a transition. A child who is rigidly fixated on a toy may need visual and/or auditory distracters to prepare him or her for change. TPBA provides a means for experimenting with a variety of methods of effectively helping the child to shift activities. Strategies that are successful can then be incorporated into intervention plans.

II. C. How intensely does the child react to various types of stimuli?

The level of affect and energy expressed by the child should be noted when the child engages in play with objects or people in varied situations. Many children with severe disabilities may enjoy a playful experience, such as a pop-up toy, but their reaction may be a grimace or a jerky body movement. The degree to which the child indicates pleasure, displeasure, anxiety, frustration, or other emotions is important, including how intense the reactions are and the mode in which they are exhibited. Highly intense reactions may interfere with the child's ability to focus, attend, and continue play sequences.

During TPBA, team members need to observe the type and amount of stimulation needed to obtain and maintain a response, be it positive or negative. For example, the speech-language pathologist can observe the type and amount of auditory input needed, the level of verbalization, the degree of intonation, and the volume required to elicit and maintain responses. Smiling, vocalization, and certain actions are indicators of a positive response. Observers also should note the level of input that causes the child to "shut down" or turn away. Looking away, crying, and cessation of verbalization or action may be cues to a negative response to input. The team should observe the amount and type of input that results in differing intensities of positive or negative reactions. Such observations can help determine whether environmental or interactional modifications could assist the child in responding at a more optimal level for learning.

Arsenio is a 3-year-old who was referred by his pediatrician for suspected developmental delays. Arsenio's parents are both architects. They report that they believe Arsenio is very bright because he knows all of the letters of the alphabet and is even beginning to read.

They are concerned about his unusual emotional responses, including resistance to any changes in routine, intense screaming when anything is out of place, a fascination with balls, and his difficulty adjusting to attending preschool. Arsenio walked into the playroom behind his mother, staying out of the vision of the team, until he spotted a basketball hoop across the room. He screeched loudly and ran to the basketball hoop, grabbing the ball to toss it in the hoop. After several tosses, the facilitator moved the hoop to give Arsenio more room to throw. This change resulted in unrelenting screaming, even when the hoop was placed back in its original spot. Arsenio then refused to look at the facilitator and would only interact with his father, lining up marbles he found in a bag. It took Arsenio 15 minutes to warm up to the facilitator again, and then he related only when the facilitator was imitating his actions with the marbles. When he did interact, he did not give her eye contact but talked to himself about what he was doing and remained emotionally detached.

This brief scenario demonstrates several interesting aspects of Arsenio's emotional style. First, he approached the situation with caution and then eagerly entered the new room when he recognized a familiar toy. Although he tolerated the facilitator's presence when his favorite toy, a ball, was involved, he had an extreme negative reaction and withdrew from her when she made a change to the environment that he did not like. Based on his parents' report, his difficulty adjusting to the new preschool, and observation in the play session, Arsenio is not very adaptable to change. He also is emotionally reactive, with both intense positive and negative reactions. It was interesting that he was not observed to have intense emotional responses to various types of input (e.g., auditory), but rather in reaction to his expectations of the play situation. This information is important for intervention because it seems that preparation for changes in expectations is critical for Arsenio.

The team discussed with Arsenio's parents the need to help him anticipate the changes, allow him some control over making them, and give him mechanisms for dealing with them. They also discussed how to help the preschool staff understand Arsenio's need for predictability and control, thus generating some ideas for a future meeting with the preschool teachers. Although emotional style was only one aspect of development discussed after TPBA, information on this area was critical to diagnosis and intervention planning for Arsenio.

III. Regulation of Emotions and Arousal States

DeGangi (2000) defines self-regulation as "the capacity to modulate mood, self-calm, delay gratification, and tolerate transitions in activities" (p. 10). Others look at self-regulation more broadly, as the child's ability to control sensorimotor, emotional, behavioral, and cognitive systems (Bronson, 2000). *Self-regulation* is a term gaining attention in the literature, and several recent texts have addressed the growing body of research in this area (Bronson, 2000; DeGangi, 2000; Gomez et al., 2004; Shonkoff & Phillips, 2000). Important for all areas of development, self-regulation enables the child to focus attention and maintain a level of organization and emotional stability to be able to function adequately.

For the purposes of TPBA2, the global construct of self-regulation has been broken down, with various aspects incorporated into different domains. Children need to learn to regulate their emotions, behaviors, and reactions to sensory input in order to function well socially. Emotional regulation, the ability to moderate the level of emotion that is expressed in response to various stimuli, is addressed within the current subcategory. Behavioral regulation, the child's ability to control his or her behavior to meet environmental expectations, is included in a separate emotional and social domain subcategory. Sensory regulation, the ability to modulate responses to various types and levels of sensory input, is included in the sensorimotor domain, and the related areas of attention and problem solving are addressed in the cognitive domain.

Children who have difficulty with emotional regulation often have difficulty with other types of regulation as well. They also may have sensory regulation or behavioral regulation challenges. Attention and problem solving may be compromised along with social relationships. Comparison of the TPBA2 findings in these subcategories can be instructive, both for diagnostic and treatment implications.

Although they are separated in the TPBA2 instrument, all of the areas related to regulation should be looked at together, because each influences the other. In discussion of observations, team members should integrate observations related to emotional expression, emotional style, and emotional regulation and determine whether other issues in sensorimotor and cognitive development may be related. For example, a child who has difficulty regulating sleep patterns, has frequent explosive outbursts, and has difficulty calming down also may demonstrate hypersensitivity to certain stimuli and may demonstrate a short attention span and difficulty with problem solving. Integrating the observations across domains can help the team develop a holistic, transdisciplinary plan that addresses all areas.

■■■■■ III. A. How easily is the child able to regulate physiological states of awareness (e.g., sleeping to waking)?

In early infancy, internal biological states and reflexive behaviors dictate behaviors, making infants greatly dependent on the adults in their lives to assist in regulating their sensory input, state of arousal, and emotional responses (Greenspan, 1997). Newborns move in and out of different states of arousal, including regular sleep, irregular sleep, drowsiness, quiet alertness, waking activity, and crying. As the infant's neurological system matures, the periods of time the infant spends in each of these states change, with arousal states becoming more expected and regular. By 2 years of age, the average child still sleeps 12–13 hours but in longer time intervals. The amount of wakefulness also is consolidated, with more time being spent in the quiet alert state, watching and engaging people and things in the environment, and learning. It is important to look at how much time the child spends in each of these states, because too much or too little time in any one state can be of concern to families and may have implications for learning and development. Cultural differences play a role in the development of these patterns. For example, in some families or child care centers, long naps may be expected or the parent may want the child to stay up late at night to be able to spend time with a parent who gets home late. However, the child may not be able to regulate his or her system to meet the needs of the family or child care center, causing stress for all concerned. Whether parents perceive a child's patterns as a problem or not also may be culturally related (Super et al., 1996). The implications of developmental findings relating to the child's need for regulation are, therefore, important and must be addressed within the context of family values and life style.

The actual regulatory patterns for each child, however, are extremely variable, and children who have difficulty getting to sleep and staying asleep are often irritable and have more behavior problems and more complicated interaction patterns with their parents and others. Sleep problems often co-occur with regulatory disorders and probably are related to biological, social, and attachment issues. Sleep concerns can be extremely stressful for families, so investigation of this area is warranted.

Studies have shown that sleep problems may be related to neurological (e.g., sleep apnea, sensory reactivity), physiological (e.g., ear infections, allergies, gastroesophageal reflux, pulmonary or other adverse medical problems), emotional (e.g., night terrors or fears), environmental (e.g., family stress or parental laxity), or a combination of these factors (Ghaem et al., 1998; Minde et al., 1993; Owens-Stively et al., 1977; Rosen, 1997).

Crying is the first means by which infants communicate with their caregivers, and as such serves a useful purpose in forming the bond between parent and child. Crying communicates hunger, distress (at temperature change, pain, a loud noise, or a physical problem), or, at a later age, anxiety, irritation, and anger. It also can indicate tiredness or a desire to be held and comforted. Adults have an immediate mental and physical reaction to hearing crying, which encourages them to respond (Crowe & Zeskind, 1992; Thompson & Leger, 1999). This protective reaction is beneficial for the child, but with a child who cries extensively or is difficult to calm, the result can be stressful.

Another important facet of emotional state regulation is the amount of time the child spends in the quiet alert state, which is critical for learning. As the infant matures, sleep becomes consolidated into longer blocks of time, and, consequently, awake times also are consolidated. The growing ability to self-calm allows the child to attend to the environment for longer periods. The maturing nervous system also provides the child with more visual, gross and fine motor, and communication skills. With increasing skills and increasing ability to maintain quiet attention, the child can learn through observation, manipulation, and interaction.

III. B. How easily is the child able to regulate (control and move in and out of) emotional states?

Emotional regulation involves being able to control and regulate the intensity of our emotions in such a way that we can experience a full range of feelings without them hindering our functioning. Emotional regulation is not just the suppression of intense emotions. Rather, it is being able to experience emotions in such a way that they enhance learning and social interactions (Eisenberg et al., 1995, 1998; Thompson, 1994). An ability to adequately regulate emotions contributes to a feeling of "emotional self-efficacy" (Saarni, 1999) and the ability to maintain standards of conduct (Zahn-Wexler, Radke-Yarrow, Wagner, & Chapman, 1992). Within the first few months of life, visual skills increase, and the child's neurological structures develop, particularly within the cerebral cortex and the limbic system, which enables tolerance of increasing stimuli and access to self-soothing (Bronson, 2000). Soothing routines and social interactions with family members also help the child to learn to calm.

Each culture has its rules for displaying emotions across all situations. Within each culture, children learn to seek comfort, to avoid emotionally arousing situations, to self-calm, and to camouflage emotions when necessary (Buss & Goldsmith, 1998; Grolnick, Bridges, & Connell, 1996; Harris, 1993; Thompson, 1990). Infants are dependent on adults to respond to their cues indicating the need for food, sleep, attention, and calming. During the first months of life, sleeping and eating become more organized and routines are established. Typically, infants begin to show an established routine by 3–7 months of age; however, children with immature neurological systems, chaotic environments, or hypersensitivities may demonstrate difficulties establishing eating and sleeping routines. These children may retain short sleep cycles, wake easily, exhibit fussy or crying behaviors for extended periods of time, and not engage in long periods of quiet, focused attention.

As infants gain a wider range of emotional expression, they also gain increasing control over their emotions, partially as a result of parent support (Sroufe, 1995). As the child gets older, parents talk to the child, explaining or reframing stressful events to reassure the child about the situation. These techniques eventually become internalized so that children can use them independently. Regulation moves from control by others to control by self (Schaffer, 1996; Sroufe, 1995). Developing motor skills also helps the child with emotional regulation, because the child is able to move toward objects or activities of interest and away from those that elicit negative responses (Boekaerts, Pintrich, & Ziedner, 2000). With increased exploration comes the need for increased impulse control and support from caregivers in demonstrating how to handle these impulses.

Self-reflection also becomes important as the child matures (Fonagy, Steele, Steele, Moran, & Higgitt, 1991; Gowen & Nebrig, 2002). Children become able to think about what they are feeling, differentiate various feelings, and associate these feelings with the causes of their emotions. After age 2, children can discuss their feelings and actively attempt to control their feelings through physical, verbal, or social means. They may avoid emotional situations, distract themselves, seek out comforting individuals, or talk themselves through the situation. They also become more aware of others' feelings and how others are managing their emotions, thus having the advantage of modeling other people's emotional regulation (or disadvantage, depending on how well others handle emotions). They become better able to read social cues, understand social situations, and evaluate how they should respond in diverse social contexts. Children who have difficulty with these aspects also may have difficulty with emotional regulation.

Caregivers play an important role in helping the child to analyze situations by reflecting on what the child is feeling and discussing with the child options for dealing with these emotions. Adult mediation often provides a bridge to the development of self-regulation (Boekaerts et al., 2000; Bronson, 2000; Butterfield, 1996; Shonkoff & Phillips, 2000).

III. C. Are there identifiable patterns or "triggers" when the child has difficulty modulating emotions?

Identification of specific stimuli that "set the child off" or lead to uncontrolled emotions is important, because early intervention to address modulation issues can help prevent later emotional, behavioral, and developmental issues (DeGangi, 2000; Teerikangas, Aronen, Martin, & Huttunen, 1998; Williamson & Anzalone, 2001). Stimuli that trigger intense emotions tend to vary by age as well by biologically related sensitivities. Hyper- or hyposensitivity to sensory stimuli, including auditory, tactile, visual, and vestibular stimulation, sleeping and eating issues, self-calming, ability to make transitions, and behavioral control can affect arousal levels and emotional reactions (DeGangi, 2000; DeGangi et al., 1995; Williamson & Anzalone, 2001). Triggers for withdrawal or emotional outburst may include an overstimulating environment; difficulty handling high levels of a specific stimuli such as loud noises, light, or visual stimulation; touch or tactile input; and discomfort with movement or postural changes (DeGangi, 2000; DeGangi & Breinbauer, 1997; Williamson & Anzalone, 2001). Children with hyposensitive systems may show regulatory issues by seeking out more intense sensory input in one or more of the sensory systems. *The Diagnostic Classification: 0–3* (Zero to Three, 2005), identifies three types of regulatory problems:

1. *The hypersensitive type,* which presents with either fearful or cautious responses to specific stimuli or situations or *the negative and defiant type,* which shows difficulty with change, is controlling, and is easily irritated and angered

2. The *underreactive type* who may be difficult to engage or be self-absorbed

3. *The motorically disorganized type,* who may show high activity level, impulsivity, aggression, and a craving for sensory input (Zero to Three, 2005). Careful observation is necessary to determine patterns of response.

The hypersensitive child may, for example, show a fearful or overly cautious response to certain types of tactile stimuli, movement, sounds, light, and so forth. An example of a child with the defiant-type regulatory concern is one who may scream or become angry when he or she must stop or change activities such as leaving the house to go to the store. An underreactive-type child may appear lethargic, have flat affect, and need extremely intense stimuli to elicit interest in engagement. The motorically disorganized child often appears hyperactive, rough, and inattentive. See Chapter 2 on the sensorimotor domain for more detailed descriptions.

▬▬▬ III. D. How easily is the child able to self-calm when emotions become intense?

Self-calming is an important aspect of emotional regulation. The ability to focus and relate is best done in a calm attentive state. At first, infants are very dependent on caregivers to help them calm down after being upset. As children gain greater control over their state of arousal, they also gain greater selectivity over their emotional expression. They can laugh or cry and then self-calm. A variety of methods are used for regulation of arousal and emotions as children become less dependent on a parent or adult for assistance. Redirecting attention is one method children use when they become overstimulated. Looking or turning away from the source of stimuli can give the child an opportunity to "regroup" and manage the intake of information (Thompson, 1994). Early emotional regulation is seen in very young infants as they turn away to "take a break" from stimulation.

Although the development of speech is supportive of emotional self-regulation, it is not a prerequisite. Children also may use *inner speech,* or silently talk to themselves about what they need to do to calm down. The ability to calm without needing adult support is an important emotional regulation accomplishment.

As the infant gets older, parents use redirection as a technique for calming. They may introduce new sights or sounds to the child to refocus attention. By the end of the first year, the infant can employ distraction and self-soothing. Between 12 and 18 months of age, children can move away from a source of distress and seek out adults for comfort. They may use a transition object and can identify the source of their distress (Kopp, 1992). By 2 years of age, children are able to redirect their actions in a purposeful way, playing with a new toy, for example, to reduce stress (Grolnick et al., 1996). Redirection of thoughts to those that are less stressful also is a strategy used by children as they get older.

▬▬▬ III. E. How well is the child able to inhibit impulsive actions and emotions (e.g., physical, vocal, or verbal outbursts) in order to attend to tasks?

The regulation of attention is dealt with in more depth in the cognitive domain but is important here because emotions are intricately intertwined with attention. Emotions can either help to sustain attention or disturb one's ability to attend. Positive emotions such as interest, pleasure, or even mild anxiety can help to maintain engagement in a social, mental, or physical task. Negative emotions, such as anger, fear, and extreme anxiety, on the other hand, have an adverse impact on attention and socialization (Calkins, 1994; DeGangi, 2000; Thompson, 1994). The child tends to *approach* and *engage* in activities that are *interesting* or *pleasurable.* He or she tends to *repeat* activities that are *interesting, pleasurable, or satisfying.* The child tends to *resist* or *avoid* activities that are *irritating,* make the child *anxious,* or cause *fear. Anger* is typically seen when attention to a desired goal is thwarted or the child is *overwhelmed.* By looking at the child's attention and reaction to specific activities an emotion can often be inferred, even if physical signs of the emotion are not obvious. This has important intervention implications for increasing attention and tolerance of various activities.

Attentional preferences do not always influence children who are highly distractible or who have attention-deficit/hyperactivity disorder. Children who are highly distractible are drawn from one activity to another. Everything looks interesting, but only briefly. These children may have difficulty finishing tasks, attending to and following directions, attending to details, and paying attention to speakers. Their attention is easily interrupted and derailed. Landy (2002) notes that "as a general rule 2-year-olds should be able to concentrate for at least 7 minutes, 4-year-olds for 12 minutes, and 5-year-olds for 15 minutes" (p. 495).

Controlling impulses is necessary for sustained attention and for regulation of emotions. Children need to be able to look at a situation, analyze what should or can be done, and follow through on their plan. Impulsive children do not plan an activity but tend to act without thinking. In fact, thinking about what is occurring and what is going to occur and monitoring responses require cognitive skills acquired in the second year of life (Rothbart & Bates, 1998). Children who have difficulty with impulse control may exhibit little frustration tolerance and consequently may be aggressive with other children (Gronau & Waas, 1997). Children with poor impulse control have difficulty with self-regulation and attention. They want to be in control and have difficulty delaying gratification. Furthermore, DeGangi (2000) describes a variety of behavior patterns seen in children who have difficulty with impulse inhibition: increased activity level, excessive talking and interrupting, inability to wait for a turn or event, need to touch things before thinking about subsequent actions, responding too quickly during tasks that require care, resisting transitions or transitioning without thinking about a logical consequence, high need for novelty, and frequent activity changes. Children who have difficulties with behavioral inhibition have problems organizing and sustaining play or activities but cannot integrate suggestions from others as to how to proceed.

▬▬▬ III. F. What is the child's predominant mood, and
how long do the child's feeling states or moods last?

In addition to looking at the child's ability to self-calm, the amount of time the child spends in various emotional states is a significant aspect of self-regulation. Children who experience extreme emotional feelings tend to maintain emotional states for longer periods of time. Intense feelings also may make it more difficult for the child to calm. As was indicated earlier, a feeling state that extends for a considerable time becomes a mood (DeGangi, 2000). Moods can be either positive or negative. Obviously, prolonged states of sadness, anger, or fear are not beneficial to the child and, in fact, interfere with cognitive and social processes. Determining how long the child's feeling states typically last, and the circumstances that contribute to initiation, maintenance, and termination of these states, is therefore important. In some cases, "flooding" occurs, in which almost any stimulus can trigger emotions and moods are difficult to moderate. When intense moods or flooding occurs, it is difficult for the child to function in everyday routines or learning experiences.

The developmental-structuralist approach described by Greenspan (1997) and Greenspan and Weider (1999) relates emotional regulation to the development levels of 1) engagement and attachment; 2) organization of affective, communicative, and cognitive experience; and 3) ability to represent thoughts and emotions symbolically.

Children with mood disorders need careful evaluation by professionals with expertise in this complex developmental approach.

USING THE GUIDELINES TO ASSESS REGULATION OF EMOTIONS AND AROUSAL STATES

During TPBA, as described in the previous sections, the team is observing the range, type, and amount of a child's emotional responses under various circumstances. In this subcategory, the team examines how easily the child can monitor, evaluate and control his or her emotional responses within specific situations. In other words, if the child is extremely excited or upset, can the child find a way to calm down? Within 1 hour the team may not have an opportunity to observe extremes of emotion; however, they can observe how the child moves in and out of emotional states. For example, if the child is bored, can he or she seek out a way to increase emotions by finding something pleasurable? The team also observes how the child deals with emotions such as anxiety, fear, or anger. Some children will seek out parents for support, others will handle such emotions independently, and still others seem to not know what to do to deal with their emotions. Observations in this area can help the team understand how external control strategies may be needed to support the child's development of internal control mechanisms.

III. A. How easily is the child able to regulate physiological states of awareness (e.g., sleeping to waking)?

Analysis of the child's states of arousal is done through the parent questionnaires and through discussion with the caregivers during TPBA. Questions on the Observation Guidelines relate to the child's ability to regulate arousal states. Can the child move easily from one state to another; for example, moving from sleep into drowsy and then into the quiet alert state? Does the child move from one state to another alone or does the child need adult support? For instance, can the child fall asleep when placed in the crib or does the parent need to rock the infant to sleep? Discuss with the family how much time the child spends in each arousal state and how much time they spend trying to calm the child or get the child to sleep. Problems with falling asleep and staying asleep are the most common sleep issues. Issues with fussiness and crying also are important to parents. Both issues are stressful to families and can have an impact on attachment and learning.

Occasionally, infants or young children will be sleeping at the beginning of the play session or will fall asleep during some part of the session (e.g., when given a bottle). The team can then observe the child's natural movement from one state of awareness to another.

III. B. How easily is the child able to regulate (control and move in and out of) emotional states?

During TPBA, the team has the opportunity to observe the child's ability to not only express various emotions, but also to see *how* the child moves from one emotional state to another. The play session presents both pleasurable and challenging situations for a child. The team can determine whether the child is able to transition from one emotional state to another either alone or with adult support. For example, when 4-year-old Lauren was putting together Marbleworks (Discovery Toys, Inc.), she smiled and talked about what was going to happen to the marbles as they went down the chutes. As she struggled to get one of the pieces in the right place, her face contorted and she said, "I hate it when it won't work!" She then stood up, threw the piece across the room and stood sulking, refusing to return to the game. Lauren demonstrated an ability to shift her emotions from happy to frustrated to angry, but her emotions tended to "flood" her, inhibiting her ability to attend and function.

The team also can examine what types of strategies the child uses or adults need to use to help the child move from an extreme emotional state to a more calm state (see III. E).

III. C. Are there identifiable patterns or "triggers" when the child has difficulty modulating emotions?

As described earlier, during the play session the child may occasionally display extreme emotion and have difficulty moving into another emotional state; for instance, squealing or laughing, crying, or screaming without being able to stop. Determination of what preceded the uncontrollable outburst is important. Examples of "triggers" include

1. A specific type of stimuli, such as fast movement or intense sensory stimulation

2. A verbal command or suggestion to do something or stop doing something

3. The sight of a specific person, object, or action that is particularly liked or disliked

The family facilitator should ask the caregivers if this type of response is generally seen in similar situations.

If the trigger can be identified, the team and family can then look for ways to help the child handle the situation in a more moderated way (see III. E). In some cases there may be no identifiable pattern of stimuli that prompt the reaction. In this case, the team may want more information or may need to try a series of strategies to determine what helps the child develop internal controls.

III. D. How easily is the child able to self-calm when emotions become intense?

The TPBA team should explore with the parents the child's ability to self-calm and determine what strategies the family has found helpful. During the play session, the team may or may not have an opportunity to see the child attempt to calm him- or herself after becoming upset. This is not an issue if the caregivers report that the child is able to self-calm in a variety of situations; for example, when going to sleep, after being frustrated when trying to solve a problem, or when a goal is thwarted. If the caregivers report, however, that self-calming is difficult for the child, it is recommended that the parents or play facilitator challenge the child with something the parents feel typically upsets the child (e.g., taking away a toy). The point is not to be "mean" but to be able to look at the strategies the child uses or that adults need to use to be able to help the child self-calm. This is often supportive to the caregivers, who are happy to explore options that will enable their child to be better able to calm him- or herself. Parents also are reassured that the team saw "the same child" they see at home, which is important for their acceptance of findings.

Once the behavior is elicited, the team can try various strategies to calm the child. Environmental modifications, verbal problem solving or reflection of feelings, physical prompts or sensory input, such as deep pressure, may be helpful. These strategies and other techniques may be tried during the play session to see if they are helpful, although more time may be needed for changes to be seen. If necessary, additional observations in other settings or another play session may be scheduled.

III. E. How well is the child able to inhibit impulsive actions and emotions (e.g., physical, vocal, or verbal outbursts) in order to attend to tasks?

Within the emotional and social domain, the team is looking at the role emotions play in maintaining the child's attention. Do emotions play a role in the child's attention, or is the child "driven" by other factors to move from one activity to another? Does the child maintain activities that are pleasurable? When frustrated or angry, can the child maintain attention to a task or activity?

During the play session, ability or inability to inhibit impulses will be evident. The play situation, whether in a clinic, a classroom, or at home, presents a variety of tantalizing opportunities for engagement with people and materials. Impulse control is needed for the child to be able to adequately explore and manipulate toys in an organized way. The team should watch the child's ability to stay with something in which he or she is interested, even though another toy catches his attention. What happens if the child becomes frustrated or cannot attain a goal? Are there particular types of actions or events that result in impulsive actions? For instance, some children will strike out or hit if someone gets too close to them or touches them. Other children will be impulsive when problems arise, acting without thinking. Both cognitive and social challenges (e.g., limit setting or conflicts) may cause a child to respond impulsively. Analysis of the types of events that result in impulsivity can lead to determination of delays or disorders and can promote development of more appropriate intervention plans.

The TPBA team needs to examine the relationship of impulse inhibition to overall self-regulation issues, social relations, sensory integration and sensorimotor abilities, and cognitive and communication abilities. For example, children with attention-deficit/hyperactivity disorder (ADHD) often display limitations with attention and impulse control, in addition to hyperactivity and cognitive processing concerns. Children with attention deficit disorder (ADD) may demonstrate many of the same characteristics, but without hyperactivity. Children with other emotional or behavioral disorders may demonstrate many of these characteristics as well. Careful analysis across all domains is needed to be able to differentiate what is occurring within a particular child.

III. F. What is the child's predominant mood, and how long do the child's feeling states or moods last?

TPBA typically lasts approximately 1 hour. During this time, the team observes the range of the child's emotions and the child's ability to move in and out of feeling states. The team can observe how long the child maintains each emotional state exhibited during the play session. However, the TPBA session does not provide enough time to ascertain how long the child's feeling states typically last. It is important to determine from the parents, by use of the questionnaires and interviews, how long both positive and negative feeling states last and the contexts relating to each. Moods are classified as feeling states that last longer than 1 hour. If the parents describe sad, fearful, or angry emotional states that last for long periods of time, further evaluation may be warranted. Asking the parents how they deal with prolonged feelings of sadness, anger, or fear also will give the team insights into what does and does not work for the child and family.

Children's moods may shift numerous times during the day. The number and duration of the moods children experience are important indicators of emotional status. Children who express sustained periods of fear, anxiety, sadness, or anger may have emotional disorders that negatively influence their social relationships and developmental progression. Clearly, a 1-hour observation is insufficient to determine the child's overall emotional status. Information from the family and other caregivers is essential. Review of the family questionnaires for family history of mental illness and concerns of parents around mood should always be done before the play session.

In addition, observation of the child over several sessions, and across different environments, may be warranted. The *Diagnostic Classification: 0–3* (Zero to Three, 2005) and the *Diagnostic and Statistical Manual of Mental Disorders of the American Psychiatric Association, Fourth Edition* (DSM-IV; American Psychiatric Association, 1994) should be reviewed by the team after the assessment for possible diagnostic profiles appropriate to the child. Certain affect or mood patterns should be examined carefully, along with other developmental indicators, when observed and/or identified by caregivers as being of concern. Disorders of affect can be seen as a characteristic of the child's overall functioning or can be specific to a situation or relationship. Assessment of the specific contexts under which the emotions are seen is important. Concerns include the following affective states or moods that persist for more than 2 weeks and interfere with the child's ability to relate, play, and/or participate in daily routines:

1. Excessive fear, anxiety, or panic

2. Withdrawal, lethargy, or a constricted range of affect over an extended period of time

3. Sad affect with diminished interest and pleasure

4. Excessive irritability, whining, crying or anger, not related to early infant colic (Zero to Three, 2005)

5. In children older than 3 years of age, patterns of extreme shifts in emotion

The concerns listed above may indicate mental health issues (e.g., bipolar disorder, depression) that may require a further evaluation by a qualified mental health professional, such as an infant mental health specialist, a psychologist, or a psychiatrist. These affective states may be seen concomitantly with self-regulation or various developmental concerns. As with all domains of development, team members need to examine the parameters of the concerns and interrelationships with other observations.

Joshua is a preschooler who was referred by his teacher because of concerns about his emotional outbursts in class. His teacher reports that Joshua is happy one minute and screaming the next. He screams whenever he doesn't get his way, when another child takes a toy, when frustrated by his inability to do something, or "just to hear himself scream." His teacher stated that Joshua is typically in an angry mood with his peers and tends to be impulsive in his actions within the class. He tends to "flitter," going from activity to activity within the classroom, and has frequently gotten in trouble for hitting and biting. Time out has not worked, because Joshua screams nonstop, disrupting the whole school. His teacher has resorted to letting him choose an activity away from the other children until he is calm enough to join the group again. Joshua's parents also struggle with him at home. They agree that time out does not work for Joshua, although they send him to his room, where he screams and cries until exhausted. His parents state that Joshua has always had difficulty controlling his emotions and that they "can't take him anywhere, for fear of how he'll act." During TPBA, Joshua first played with his teacher and then his parents. He was observed telling them what to do, ignoring their suggestions, and screaming or crying when things did not go as he expected. During the session, Joshua's expression was typically one of boredom, frustration, or anger. His only happy expression was seen when he jumped on bubbles his father blew. Joshua avoided any activity that required him to sit and focus, such as drawing or building something. He would make a face and say, "No, I don't want to."

After the play session, the team, teacher, and family discussed the findings. They determined that in the emotional and social domain Joshua needed assistance with emotional regulation, that his emotions were not assisting him to attend and, in fact, were inhibiting his ability to play well. Joshua needed to find ways to experience pleasure in his play and interactions, so that the predominantly negative emotions could be balanced with positive emotions. They discussed his need to develop the ability to inhibit impulsive outbursts. Social interaction, listening, and modeling are needed for learning. Joshua's need for control was limiting his ability to learn, and his impulsiveness resulted in unorganized and repetitive play. Joshua exhibited fine motor delays and some motor planning issues, which also were contributing to his lack of interest in more focused play. Language, however, was a strength when he chose to use it for communicating what he wanted or how he was feeling, instead of screaming or crying. The combination of cognitive, motor, and social issues, particularly related to planning, organizing, attending, and doing, were all overwhelming for Joshua. Because he was unable to adequately organize an appropriate response to others, he chose to try to be in control. This, however, was self-defeating, because he could only direct a brief, nonpleasurable interaction that resulted in frustration and anger. It was a vicious cycle that would only get worse as Joshua got older and demands became more complex.

In order to address the cognitive and sensorimotor issues influencing Joshua's development, the team felt it was important to simultaneously address emotional and social issues. In the meeting following TPBA, the family and team brainstormed ways to help Joshua share control of decision making and gain control of his emotions.

IV. Behavioral Regulation

Behavioral regulation is closely related to emotional regulation, cognitive understanding, social skills development, the development of conscience, and environmental influences such as cultural expectations. As a child develops an understanding of emotions and when and how to express them, the child also is acquiring the ability to remember previous consequences, anticipate reactions, and understand the social expectations for behavior. The ability to control impulses, monitor one's actions and interactions, and respond within the parameters of culturally accepted behavior develops concurrently with emotional regulation. Barkley (1997) states that in order to regulate behavior a child needs to be able to inhibit initial responses to an event, stop ongoing responses, and control interference with ongoing activities. As early as 5–12 months of age, infants show an ability to delay a response (Hofstader & Resnick, 1996). By 2–3 years of age, inhibitory control increases to enable children to be able to follow rules.

The subcategory of behavioral regulation examines the child's ability to understand and comply with the rules, values, and expected behaviors of both the family and the society in which the child lives. Self-regulation helps the child learn to comply with external and internalized standards of conduct (Zahn-Waxler & Radke-Yarrow, 1990; Zahn-Waxler et al., 1992). Four areas included in the subcategory of behavioral regulation are compliance, understanding right and wrong, use of social conventions, and unusual behaviors or mannerisms that are not culturally appropriate and are not typically under the control of the child.

IV. A. How does the child comply with adult requests?

Compliance involves learning how to obey "dos and "don'ts" requested first by parents and then by others. Landy (2002) says compliance is concerned with "a child's ability and willingness to modulate her behavior to meet the expectations and limitations expected by caregivers" (p. 369). It is dependent not only on a child's ability to control her reactions but also on her motivation to do so (Gowen & Nebrig, 2002). In order to be able to comply, the child needs to develop a sense of independence and an ability to make decisions about her behaviors.

During the first year of life, a child learns to read the parent's emotional cues and understand what the parent is feeling. Between 12 and 24 months of age, the child is not yet consistently following the adult's directions. During the second year of life, the child also is learning to walk, use words, and manipulate objects. The drive for independence is greater than the motivation to comply. By 12–18 months of age, the child becomes aware of the caregiver's wishes and can voluntarily comply with very simple requests and commands (Kaler & Kopp, 1990). However, at 14 months of age, infants follow "don't" requests only 45% of the time and "do" requests only 14% of the time (Kochanska, Coy, & Murray, 2001). With the development of language during this time, the child produces conscience-like "nos" and "don'ts" before doing something out of bounds (Kochanska, 1997), indicating that he knows that he is not supposed to be doing the act. For example, the child may reach for a plug in an electrical outlet while stating, "No, don't touch!" He knows the action is out of bounds but cannot resist the temptation! The increase in the child's ability to delay gratification between the ages of 18 and 30 months of age allows the child to develop more control and, therefore, more ability to wait for what he wants or to do something in order to get reinforcement (Vaughn, Kopp, & Krakow, 1984). Despite these abilities, this is a "no" phase for most children, and without the presence of the parent, boundaries disappear.

Beginning in the second year of life, children, with the support of parents, start to internalize rules. Children are observed checking a parent's facial expression before reaching for an off-limits object, reprimanding their dolls, and feeling bad when their actions make someone feel sad or mad (Hay, 1994; Landy, 2002). By 3 years of age, a child has the capacity for self-control and can make conscious decisions about behaviors. Between 3 and 4 years of age, compliance with "don't" requests increases to 85% but is only 30% for "do" requests (Kochanska et al., 2001). During this time, a child's self-conscious emotions of shame and guilt also are developing, which assist the child in establishing internal motivation for compliance. The development of language and cognitive skills enable a child to "argue" and negotiate regarding requirements and rules. As children reach the preschool years, they may "refuse" before they comply, try compromise, or assert themselves in other ways. This is consistent with a 3- to 4-year-old's growing sense of self and desire to feel in control.

Although frustrating for parents, "discussing" and arguing allow children to talk about and hear the reasons for the rules, which aids in later internalization of the rules (Hoffman, 2000). Discussion also enables children to learn to negotiate. Children learn strategies such as deferral ("I'll do it later"), compromise, justification for noncompliance, and acting as if no request had been made (pretending to not hear) (Kuczynski & Kochanska, 1990; Leonard, 1993). Children, however, may not tolerate the same type of negotiation from their caregivers. They may even tell the parent to "go to your room" when they perceive a rule has been broken or the parent has been "bad." By 5–6 years of age, children have internalized many standards for behavior. They then apply these standards to their siblings, peers, and parents and may become rigid about rules for behavior and what is allowed. It is difficult for them to understand how standards can be applied differently across children or settings.

Compliance, by definition, involves not only the child but also the parents or other caregivers who are setting the limits. Therefore, observation of the typical style of interaction between the parents and the child, and discussion regarding discipline techniques, is essential.

IV. B. How does the child control behaviors that are perceived as wrong?

The development of a conscience is a critical task in early childhood. Conscience, as defined by Landy (2002), is "the inner voice or the internal system of moral values that not only allows a person to judge whether certain acts are right or wrong, but makes him feel guilty or uncomfortable" (p. 369). Conscience develops as the child interacts with those around him or her, and experiences, observes, and listens to discussions about right and wrong. Parents and other close family members are highly influential because a child wants to please these people, and, as a result, children often internalize their family members' values and belief systems, including their ideas of right and wrong and morality and immorality (Hay, Castle, Stimson, & Davies, 1995).

Ability to understand rules and why something is considered wrong has an impact on social development as well. As noted previously, by 5 years of age a child has a good understanding of rules, and children who lack self-control and do not adhere to rules are often not popular with other children (or adults). Concern for the welfare of others is another key component of developing a conscience and an understanding of "right and wrong."

The development of compliance sets the foundation for the child to learn rules and the reasons why rules are important. Between 15 and 18 months of age, children begin to show signs of understanding right and wrong by beginning to "self-tattle" and seeking praise when complying. By 18–21 months of age, children can follow a one-step direction, demonstrating an understanding of what is expected of them. When children are reprimanded between 18 and 24 months of age, their feelings get hurt, thus demonstrating antecedents of shame and guilt. They also begin to feel guilt if another child is hurt by their actions. Between 21 and 24 months of age, a child shows active signs of guilt, shame, and embarrassment (e.g., hangs head, avoids eye contact) and use words such as "good" or "bad" to evaluate behavior (Eisenberg, 2000; Rose, 1999).

Moral understanding begins in the second year of life and extends into adulthood (Smetana & Braeges, 1990; Turiel, 1998). By age 2, children also recognize that their behaviors affect how another person feels, and they know that their actions can cause others to feel angry or sad. The development of a conscience and sense of right and wrong has its roots in the developing emotional system.

Concurrently, in the second year of life, children begin to establish a *sense of self* (see V. Sense of Self), and along with that, the idea of "mine" or ownership starts to become important. Conflicts with siblings and peers are usually centered around rights, possessions, and territory (Slomkowski & Dunn, 1992). "Right and wrong" is very personal. Even as early as 2 years of age, children understand the need to share, but the reasons for sharing have more to do with personal consequences than the idea of fairness. This personal perspective, when later combined with the ability to see the perspectives of others, also may contribute to the child's development of the concepts of *rights* and *freedom* (Nucci, 1996). Before 2 years of age, the idea of right and wrong is situation specific and adult guided. By 2 years of age, children begin to internalize rules, understanding what they should not do.

By age 3, children develop the concept of *harm* to another (Helwig, Zelazo, & Wilson, 2001). They understand that hurting another person is wrong in the eyes of adults. The self-conscious emotions of shame and guilt develop as a result of the child wanting to live up to the standards set by adults but recognizing that he or she has not done so. Neurological changes that accompany these emotions also lay the foundation for memory traces that will build a catalog of situations and associated feelings. This feeling "memory bank," when combined with developing cognitive skills, allows the child to begin to categorize not only what was punished, but also why it was wrong.

Children know a behavior is wrong between 36 and 42 months of age but may continue to misbehave anyway. By 42–48 months, however, children feel bad if they do something wrong and may try to help repair the situation. At the same time, children are becoming more sensitive to the feelings of others, and behavior is influenced by wanting to keep social relationships positive. By 54 months of age, children are aware that their behavior can hurt others or make them angry, so actions are moderated by a desire to make others happy (Brazelton & Sparrow, 2001).

As children develop a conscience, they become a stern judge of the behavior of others. Children from 4 to 5 years of age will tattle on others and recommend punishment, whereas 6- to 7-year-old children will understand when they have done something wrong and accept punishment. However, they may not understand all of the rules governing their behavior because they are still accumulating the experiences that will form overarching principles relating to right and wrong (Stillwell, Galvin, & Kopta, 1991).

This concern for the rights of others develops slowly. Between 2 and 5 years of age, children begin to develop the concept of *distributive justice,* or how to distribute materials fairly. By age 6, children understand the concept of equality, or equal distribution, as being a standard for "rightness" or fairness (Smetana & Braeges, 1990).

The development of the concept of right and wrong and the ability to act in concert with the standards of family and culture are perhaps two of the most important skills of early childhood. As noted previously, as early as the second year of life, children begin to display precursors of conscience, with a developing sense of rules and standards (Kagan, 1981). Certainly, children who do not develop this ability are a risk to themselves and others. For this reason, it is important to examine this budding capacity in young children along with the skills observed in the areas of compliance, social conventions, and sense of self and self-regulation. Together, these areas lay a foundation for social relations and societal contribution.

IV. C. Does the child recognize and use social conventions of the home and mainstream culture?

Social conventions can be differentiated from moral concerns, because they are "customs determined solely by consensus" (Landy, 2002). Such things as manners, dress styles, greetings, rituals, and so forth are determined informally by a culture or subculture. Violation of social conventions is not harmful to others but may elicit a reprimand or look of disfavor on the part of others. Social conventions are learned primarily through observation and direct teaching. Turiel (1998) found an interesting distinction between moral and social conventions. *Moral offenses* pertain to issues of harm, fairness, and rights, such as hitting or stealing (Helwig & Turiel, 2002). Peers react strongly to moral offenses, telling the child to stop and relating the consequences of the action. Adults also react more strongly to violations of right and wrong, lecturing on the rights and feelings of the victim. Alternatively, peers typically have a minimal or no response to infractions of social conventions, and adults typically demand compliance without explanation. It should be noted that in some cultures, conventions of dress, food, and behavior may imply moral offenses rather than social conventions (Shweder, Mahatra, & Miller, 1987). It is important for the team to determine what social conventions are expected for each family that is seen.

Social conventions typically have purposes related to acceptable social interaction (saying "please"), appropriate appearance ("Put your dress down"), or health and safety or organization ("Pick up your toys"). Again, these will vary across cultures, but American society as a whole tends to see these as valuable conventions. All cultures have social conventions but they differ greatly, and what might be a social convention in one may be a moral concern in another. It is important to understand the social conventions and moral imperatives of the cultures of the children and families who participate in TPBA. Social conventions may vary across families as well as across cultures. Some families may encourage boys to grow long hair, while other families may find this unacceptable. Wearing leather jackets with studs and piercing body parts may be fashionable in one family and dressing in designer apparel the custom in another. These individual differences are typically accepted in the larger culture, although they may serve as a disadvantage in certain situations.

Most parents actually put great emphasis on social conventions in the early years. Even before the first word is heard, parents start teaching "please" and "thank you," so that these are often among the child's first words. As the child gets older, parents teach a variety of social conventions so that the child is not considered rude by others. For example, cutting in front of someone who is waiting in line is considered rude.

Social conventions are of great importance to children with disabilities. Lack of understanding and use of social conventions can make children with disabilities stand out. For example, stuffing food in the mouth, talking with the mouth full, grabbing for more food, and interrupting while another person is talking are all behaviors that distance children with disabilities when eating out in public. Looking "typical" helps children with disabilities fit in. Although they may have to wear braces or hearing devices, they are more socially "acceptable" to their peers and the greater community when they adhere to the social conventions of appearance and action. For this reason, it is important to observe the child's adherence to social conventions during TPBA and to be aware of the social conventions that may be important in the child's culture.

The reasons some children do not adhere to certain social conventions may be related to their disability or disorder. For example, children who cannot keep their hands to themselves, cannot tolerate hair or teeth brushing, stuff their mouths, grab things, or cannot wait their turn may have regulatory disorders that contribute to these behaviors. It is important to see that these behaviors not only cause difficulties for the child's development but also affect how he or she is perceived in society.

No age tables are provided for this area because the age expectations for different social conventions vary by culture. Table 4.2 provides examples of three types of social conventions the team might observe or discuss with the family. Because many of these will differ by culture, discussion with parents about the acceptability of the observed behaviors in their family is crucial. Although some of these behaviors may appear in other subcategories (e.g., looking at people when talking to them is an important component of pragmatics of language), they also are included here because they indicate a level of social awareness.

▬▬ IV. D. Does the child demonstrate unusual behavioral
mannerisms that are not culturally meaningful and cannot be inhibited?

Children sometimes exhibit unusual, maladaptive, or even bizarre behaviors. Ritualized behaviors such as hand-flapping, eye-poking, constant jumping, and rocking are some of the behaviors sometimes seen in children with special needs. Many of these unusual behaviors may be associated with specific disabilities, such as autism spectrum disorders or blindness. Eccentric habits such as smelling things, picking at strings, and rubbing textures also are noteworthy and may relate to cognitive, sensory, or emotional disorders. Many unusual behaviors are typical for certain developmental phases.

Table 4.2. Social conventions

Social conventions of interaction	Social conventions of appearance	Functional social conventions
Greet people	Bathe regularly	Flush the toilet
Use "please" and "thank you"	Comb or brush your hair regularly	Wash hands before meals and after toileting
Look at people when talking to them (varies across cultures)	Wear clothing appropriate to the weather and the occasion	Sleep in your own bed (varies by culture and family)
Answer when someone talks to you	Do not talk with your mouth full	Look both ways before crossing the street
Wait your turn	Do not stuff your mouth	Pick up your toys
Respect others' things	Zip up your fly	Eat independently
Don't interrupt	Brush your teeth frequently	Shut the door
Talk within a normal range of loudness	Wear clean clothing (particularly underwear)	Be quiet during religious ceremonies (varies across cultures)
Keep your hands to yourself	Wear shoes in formal situations	Don't use others' eating or drinking utensils

For example, biting or hitting often is seen in young children. However, the age when the behavior is seen and the degree or extent of the behavior will dictate whether the behavior falls within the purview of developmental delay or disorder or whether it is perceived as a nondevelopmentally related mannerism or maladaptive behavior.

USING THE GUIDELINES TO ASSESS BEHAVIORAL REGULATION

Behavioral regulation can be observed in the play session but also needs to be discussed with caregivers. Children's behavior may be different with strangers, particularly if the play assessment is done in an unfamiliar setting. Information from the All About Me Questionnaire, described in the *Administration Guide for TPBA2 & TPBI2*, Chapter 5 (Obtaining Preliminary Information from Families), may provide some insights into the child's ability to control his or her behavior, and follow-up questions may provide more insight. Although the facilitator is following the child's lead and not challenging behaviors throughout most of the session, if caregivers report that the child's behavior is a problem, the specific situations that cause this behavior can be recreated at the end of the session. Often, the team can observe the child's response to requests, limit setting, or behaviors that are perceived as "wrong" when the parents are interacting with the child around common activities. In addition, the team should look for unusual behaviors that do not seem to be associated with cultural patterns of behavior. Situations that enable the team to see conventional mannerisms are part of the play session. The play session allows the team to observe patterns of greeting, eating, leaving, and interacting during the session. Dress and behavioral customs are seen during the session as well. A full range of behaviors and customs, however, cannot be seen in 1 hour.

IV. A. How well does the child comply with adult requests?

Compliance is observed during TPBA in a child's interactions with the play facilitator and parents. Information from the family on the child's compliance behaviors at home also is essential to obtain a complete picture. The child may demonstrate "best" behaviors in a play situation, particularly with unfamiliar team members present. The play facilitator seeks to establish rapport with the child and is, therefore, using strategies that are responsive to the child, such as following the child's lead and not directing the child or setting limits, particularly at the beginning of the play session. If the parents report that compliance is a major concern, the team will want to make sure to observe the child's ability to respond to "dos" and "don'ts" before the session is over. The team also will have opportunities to observe compliance during the play session when the child interacts with his or her parents. Typically, during this time, the parents give directions to the child to perform certain actions. Parents also frequently direct comments to the child during play (e.g., telling the child to not draw on the table, to pick up the blocks, to get a coat on to leave). The team should make sure that the child is challenged with limits before the session is over, so that they can observe the child's responses. Before setting limits, however, the parent facilitator should ascertain how the parents usually respond to the child's noncompliant behavior. The play session provides an opportunity to see how the parents handle noncompliance and to experiment with alternative strategies that might be helpful for the child and family.

If the play session is conducted in the home, the child and family are more likely to exhibit "typical" compliance issues. The setting is familiar and parents have access to the "time out" chair or other discipline approaches they may use routinely. The child also may be more likely to exhibit his or her usual compliance patterns in the home setting. Classroom observations also may be important when teachers report concerns about compliance.

IV. B. How well does the child control behaviors that are perceived as wrong?

During TPBA, the team will have an opportunity to observe a child's concern for rules and how the child responds if something is broken or misused. When peers or siblings are interacting, the team can look for the child's sense of equity, ability to share, and concern for others' rights. Much of what is learned in this area will come from the caregivers' reports of the child's actions and behaviors at home and in the community. Opportunities also can be inserted into the play session. For example, let a child divide and serve the snack. This will enable the team to look at the child's sense of equity. Having a toy that falls apart easily (e.g., a doll whose arm comes out easily) when a child plays with it allows the team to see how the child reacts when he or she thinks he or she "broke" it, and it also allows the team to observe any attempts to try to "correct" the perceived transgression. This presents an opportunity to talk with 4- and 5-year-olds about some things that are "wrong" to do and some things that are "right" to do. When a sibling or peer is included, having duplicates of some toys and only one of others enables the team to see how the children negotiate who should get the toy. As situations involving right and wrong occur, discuss with the parents how their child typically reacts to situations of right and wrong.

IV. C. How does the child recognize and use social conventions of the home and mainstream culture?

In TPBA, the team observes social conventions throughout the session. Children may greet the team members on entering, use manners during snack time, help pick up toys, and so forth. Much of the information related to this subcategory, however, must come from the parent report of what the child is doing at home and in the community. The team must then integrate information from the family with their observations in the play setting. The observations within this section are related not to moral evaluation, but to the child's compliance with behavioral expectations.

IV. D. Does the child demonstrate unusual behavioral mannerisms that are not culturally meaningful and cannot be inhibited?

The team will want to evaluate the pattern of these behaviors, as well as the environmental circumstances surrounding the behaviors, to determine possible causes and recommended intervention approaches. Observation of an unusual behavior one time during a play session is not necessarily indicative of a concern. The team should watch for, and confirm with caregivers, the existence of patterns of unusual behavior. Behavioral interventions for atypical behaviors are often effective but should not be assumed to be "the answer" without looking at all of the developmental or medical issues that could be related to the behavior as well. For example, children with Tourette's syndrome may demonstrate unusual verbal or physical behaviors, mannerisms, or tics, whereas children with autism spectrum disorders may demonstrate what appear to be "self-stimulating" behaviors. Team members need to be familiar with characteristics of various syndromes and medical conditions in order to understand when to make referrals for additional neurological or medical evaluations.

> *During TPBA with 5-year-old Jason, several instances occurred during which his compliance and understanding of right and wrong could be analyzed. While coloring, Jason pushed hard and broke a crayon. He did not look at either Mary, the play facilitator, or his parents for a response. He merely tossed the broken crayon aside and took out another one. When playing in the water table with toy zoo animals, Jason bit the rubber elephant's nose and said with a smile on his face, "I hurt him." When playing with a peer who was building a tower next to his, Jason intentionally knocked down the other*

child's tower and laughed. These instances reveal Jason's lack of concern for doing "right." The team noted not only that Jason did several things that could be considered "wrong," but also that he did not appear to understand that he could hurt another (even an inanimate object) and that this negative action even seemed to give him pleasure.

When interacting with his parents, Jason was asked several times to do a particular activity or to stop doing something. For example, his father stated, "Put the blocks back in their box so we can play with something else." His mother said firmly, "Please, don't throw those, Jason." In most instances, Jason ignored his parents and continued doing whatever he wanted. His parents commented, "Jason marches to his own drummer."

The team needed to ask several questions. Did Jason comprehend what was being asked of him and did he understand actions that are considered wrong? Did he understand why they are wrong? Did he understand how another person (or animal) could have felt? (This would be looked at in the subcategory of "emotional understanding and responsiveness"). In other words, the team needed to look at whether this was a cognitive issue of delayed understanding, a regulatory or behavioral issue, or an emotional issue that could develop into an emotional disturbance.

First, using all of the information from parents and TPBA observations, the team determined that delayed cognition was not the reason for Jason's actions. Although his play skills were slightly delayed, they were not at a level where he would not understand that breaking things, biting, and knocking down another's construction were wrong. Second, Jason did present with regulatory issues related to impulse control. However, his play overall was well organized and thoughtful. The impulsiveness seemed primarily to be associated with actions that were deemed "wrong." Behavioral issues with regard to compliance also demonstrated behaviors related to power and control. When looked at in combination, the compliance issues, Jason's lack of concern for others, and lack of awareness of right and wrong indicated a need for intervention to address these social and emotional issues.

V.   Sense of Self

As children learn that they are separate, independent beings, they also begin to identify their abilities, learn what they can do independently, and discover what type of effort is needed to get what they want. When they develop confidence in themselves, children also develop a desire to make choices and decisions for themselves. Between 18 and 30 months of age, children develop a *categorical self* and can classify themselves by age, gender, physical characteristics, "goodness" and "badness," and things they can do (Stipek, Gralinski, & Kopp, 1990). Young children also become aware of their individual desires. "Want" is often one of the first verbs a child learns. By preschool, children are constructing a self-concept consisting of concrete attributes about themselves, a sense of their abilities, their attitudes toward themselves, and a concrete ability to describe themselves and what they like and don't like. Self-concept is important to the child's overall functioning, and it derives from numerous developmental processes that occur during infancy, toddlerhood, and preschool years. TPBA addresses three aspects that contribute to the child's developing sense of self: autonomy, achievement motivation, and identity. These three elements were selected because of their long-term impact on the child's overall development and functioning (Shonkoff & Phillips, 2000; Yarrow, Morgan, Jennings, Harmon, & Gaiter, 1982). Autonomy and achievement motivation are particularly important for children with disabilities, because these elements contribute to overcoming difficulties associated with developmental concerns (Erwin & Brown, 2003). Children who work hard on their own to accomplish their goals are more likely to learn than those who are unmotivated or require constant support (Erwin & Brown,

2003). The level of independence and feeling of mastery also contribute to the child's overall self-concept, another important facet of development (Morgan et al., 1990).

V. A. How does the child demonstrate autonomy and a desire to make decisions consistent with the culture of family?

Autonomy is a child's desire and ability to make choices and decisions about what needs to be done (Erikson, 1950). Autonomy develops as the child develops a sense of self as separate from others during the first year of life. Many theorists have hypothesized stages through which infants proceed in acquiring a sense of autonomy. Most identify a first stage, during the first few months of life, at which the child does not *differentiate*, or recognize that she is a different person from others in her life. As a child begins to acquire abilities to make specific sounds, move body parts at will, and elicit reactions from adults, she begins to understand that she can make her body do things and cause something to occur. One of the first signs of beginning differentiation is the ability to share *joint attention*, or turn and look at what another person is looking at (Moore & Corkum, 1994). This typically occurs at about 6 months of age (Butterworth & Cochran, 1980). As infants become able to explore others' faces and examine their own hands and feet, they begin to discover their existence separate from others. When presented with two objects, a child can choose which one he or she wants. Individual interests begin to be expressed. Around 9 months of age, a child can crawl away from caregivers, look back and see them, and come and go as needed. Choices now expand beyond what is presented to the child and move to what the child can find in the environment. The expansion of the child's world and expression of will also coincides with the need for balance in control (see IV. Behavioral Regulation).

In some cases, a child may have difficulty achieving a balance between letting the parents make some choices and making all the choices him- or herself. Control issues are important for the developing sense of self, because having too much control over choices can be quite scary for a child. Children need to feel that they are competent to handle the consequences of the decisions they make. Often, children with emotional concerns will demand independence or control of choices, only to find that they are overwhelmed by the results.

The development of control is important across all developmental domains. As a child's motor skills are developing and enabling him to acquire independence, the child's cognitive skills also are expanding. The child recognizes familiar people, including himself. If given a mirror, the child will pat himself and smile in recognition. From about 12 to 18 months of age, the infant's ability to move away from the parents increases. As the child acquires the ability to walk, he practices moving away and coming back and explores what he can do within the environment without the caregiver. Self-representation is established from 18 to 24 months, as the child is able to represent his own and others' actions in pretend play, thus indicating an understanding of the various actions done by others. After 24 months of age, the child indicates his knowledge of self verbally, using his own name and referring to himself and his possessions as "me" or "mine" (Roth-Hanania et al., 2000). Beginning around age 3, the child recognizes that he has unique physical characteristics, and the view of self develops in relation to concrete attributes (Jacobs, Bleeker, & Constantino, 2003). (See section on Identity, p. 131.)

V. B. How does the child demonstrate achievement motivation?

Achievement motivation, an aspect of the child's sense of self, is related to self-concept and is critical to the overall development of the child, as each new developmental step requires mastery. According to Shonkoff and Phillips (2000), achievement motivation includes 1) *mastery motivation*, or the child's desire to explore, persist, and derive pleasure from accomplishing tasks (White, 1959); 2) *intrinsic motivation*, or the child's desire to perform activities without external demands or reinforcement (Deci & Ryan, 1985; Lepper, 1981); and 3) *cognitive aspects of motivation*, including whether the child expects to succeed, seeks challenge, and believes he or she is competent enough to succeed (Atkinson, 1964; Harmon, Morgan, & Glicken, 1984). Closely related to these is the emerging term *self-determination*, which has primarily been associated with older people with disabilities but is now being related to young children as motivation and determination to succeed are associated (Doll et al., 1996; Erwin & Brown, 2003; Wehmeyer & Palmer, 2000).

An important aspect of the child's sense of self concerns the child's efforts to accomplish desired goals. Achievement motivation is particularly important for children with disabilities who may have developmental issues that make accomplishing tasks more difficult. Achievement motivation is the emotional fuel or energy that encourages the child to keep trying in the face of challenging tasks.

Achievement motivation may be even more predictive of later success than standardized tests (Scarr, 1981; Yarrow et al., 1982). Although the majority of young children think they can do anything and are optimistic about their success (Stipek & Green, 2001), this positive judgment often drops with school entry. Achievement motivation is inextricably intertwined with cognitive development. A reciprocal relationship, therefore, appears to exist between persistence and competence (Morgan et al., 1990; Stipek & Kopp, 1990). The early work of White (1959), who developed a theory of *effectance motivation*, stated that mastery motivation begins with infants' early innate drives to master and control the environment. Jennings and colleagues (1979) found that children's motivation to explore and have an impact on their environment provides the basis for learning more competent skills. Children who show greater ability to sustain focused attention during free play complete more tasks successfully and persist longer on problem-solving tasks. An infant's quality of exploration, or cognitive maturity, is more important than the amount of exploration in which he engages. In particular, the infant's ability to produce effects with toys is related to mastery motivation. Infants as young as 6 months of age persist in goal-directed behaviors and seem to derive pleasure from attaining goals.

At 9 months of age, there is a shift from more general exploration to task-directed behavior (MacTurk & Morgan, 1995; Morgan & Harmon, 1984); children repeat successful cause-and-effect, combinatorial, or means–ends behaviors. By 15 months of age, children persistently work at multipart tasks, such as puzzles and form boards, or means–ends tasks, such as lock boards or cash registers. As children reach the preschool years, those with high levels of mastery motivation prefer challenging tasks to easy tasks. By 4 years of age, children self-initiate mastery activities and organize problem solving without asking for assistance.

As discussed in relation to self-concept, most preschoolers and kindergartners demonstrate optimism about their abilities (Stipek & Greene, 2001) and view themselves as much more competent than they were when they were younger (Frey & Ruble, 1990). For typical children, it is not until they reach school age, and for some children as young as 4 years of age, that they begin to react to failure. Some children are highly affected by failure experiences and develop *learned helplessness*, developing negative affect, avoidance of challenge, and low expectations for success (Cain & Dweck, 1995; Smiley & Dweck, 1994). Learned helplessness is particularly relevant for school-age children, but its initial signs seem to appear in the early years. For children with disabilities, lack of motivation may be seen even in the early months. Mastery behavior may be assessed by looking at the child's attention to and participation with the environment, appropriateness of behavior, elaboration of behavior, goal-directedness, and persistence (McWilliam & Bailey, 1992).

As students get older, several other factors affect their motivation to achieve. Schunk and Pajares (2002) discuss the factors that instigate, direct, and sustain efforts.

Self-efficacy, the belief about one's potential abilities to learn or perform a task, influences academic motivation, task choice, learning, and achievement (Pajares, 1996; Schunk, 1995). *Outcome expectancies,* children's beliefs about what the outcomes of their efforts will be, affects both effort and choice of tasks. Tasks that are *valued* also increase motivation. *Effectance motivation,* or the motivation to have an impact on and control aspects of the environment, influence learning as well. Self-competence includes comparisons of abilities to other children, as described previously. All of these factors are part of what is termed *mastery motivation* in infants and *achievement motivation* in school-age children.

▦ V. C. What developmentally relevant characteristics related to self can the child identify?

Identification of one's own feelings is an early indicator of sense of self. Within the first year of life, infants are beginning to discriminate themselves from others in a mirror (Bahrick, Moss, & Fadil, 1996). By the second year, children also identify themselves as "I" or "me" and know their body parts, what belongs to them, and their actions (Pipp, Easterbrooks, & Brown, 1993). Typically, acquisition of these words is viewed as an indicator of language development, rather than social development. This knowledge about self, however, lays the foundation for understanding how one is alike or different from others, and this is later viewed in terms of positive or negative attributes of self and others (Harter, 2003).

An increasing ability to remember events between 3 and 4 years of age enables the child to make comparison between self and others, typically with high regard for his or her own abilities (Harter, 2003). By age 5, children are comparing their performance with that of others, but they still maintain high self-beliefs and are optimistic that their skills will increase as they get older (Harter, 2003; Jacobs et al., 2003). Between 5 and 7 years old, children are compiling a view of themselves that is composed of different aspects and is based on a comparison of themselves with others. Multidimensional views of self-concept have explored a four-factor model, including social competence, physical/athletic competence, academic competence, and physical appearance (Marsh, 1990). More recently, family and affect were added as competency domains to make a six-domain model (Bracken, Bunch, Keith, & Keith, 2000). The importance of each of these areas is influenced by family and cultural values. A child's view of his or her competence is particularly relevant for children with compromised development. Helping children to understand and see their abilities and strengths is an important focus of intervention.

▦ USING THE GUIDELINES TO ASSESS SENSE OF SELF

In TPBA, the team can observe sense of self through observation of a child's level of autonomy, achievement motivation, and sense of identity during play and interactions with others. The play facilitator needs to make sure that the child has an opportunity to experiment, make decisions, and try to accomplish tasks independently. The facilitator needs to provide wait time to examine the child's goal orientation and persistence. In addition, opportunities for the child to talk about him- or herself also should be presented.

▦ V. A. How does the child demonstrate autonomy and a desire to make decisions consistent with the culture of family?

Through analysis of the TPBA2 Child and Family History Questionnaire (CFHQ), the TPBA2 Family Assessment of Child Functioning (FACF) Tools (Daily Routines Rating Form and All About Me Questionnaire), and the family facilitator's discussion with parents, it is important to determine what the family's expectations are for the child's independence. In Western societies, parents stress independence, separateness, and self-assertion. In many Eastern cultures, interdependence is emphasized (Lynch & Hanson, 2003). It is therefore important to discuss with caregivers the values they hold with regard to the child "doing things by him- or herself," "making his or her own choices," and "deciding for him- or herself."

In addition to looking at autonomy in making choices, the team also needs to look at the child's ability to carry out tasks independently. Again, cultural values are relevant and should be explored. For example, cultures differ in their expectations for independence with regard to such things as self-feeding, toilet training, dressing, and so forth. Actual accomplishment of such self-help skills is addressed in Chapter 2. This subcategory addresses the child's *desire* to function independently from the parents, not whether he or she has accomplished individual skills. If the child is not able to function independently, the team needs to examine which factors—cultural (e.g., family values), developmental (e.g., a physical disability), or environmental (e.g., lack of opportunity)—are affecting the child.

As noted previously, having too much control or autonomy can be a concern. This may be seen in a play session when a child demands to do certain play activities, or to do activities in a certain way, but then does not know how to expand the play without the adult's help. The child wants autonomy but does not have the skills or emotional capacity to deal with the choices that he or she made. The team, therefore, needs to examine the area of autonomy in relation to other areas, such as emotional regulation, behavioral regulation, and social relations.

▬▬▬▬ V. B. How does the child demonstrate achievement motivation?

TPBA provides an opportunity to examine a child's persistence on difficult tasks, internal versus external motivation, and what types of challenges the child seeks out. During the session, it is important to have age-appropriate toys that can provide a moderate challenge to the child. Toys are needed that allow the child to produce an auditory or visual effect using buttons, levers, or dials. Also, barriers can be erected that require the child to circumvent an obstacle to attain a goal. For older children, toys that require relational thinking or problem solving, such as pegboards, form boards, and shape sorters, are suitable for eliciting achievement motivation. Tasks for preschool-age children use higher-level, more complex toys or activities. Building a complex block structure with angular blocks or completing a challenging puzzle may interest a child. The TPBA process of following the child's lead offers the team an opportunity to observe the level of challenge involved in activities selected by the child. The facilitator may allow the child to choose from toys posing varying degrees of difficulty.

Team observations will include determining how children respond to challenging objects or situations. Some children may respond by examining, exploring, or using an object appropriately. Some children may exhibit persistent task-directed behaviors in only certain types of activities. How often a child repeats successfully completed, challenging activities, and the level of task difficulty that the child selects, also are observations that can be made by the team. In addition, the team can determine the amount of assistance the child requests in completing tasks and the degree to which the child prefers to figure out problems without adult assistance.

Achievement motivation is encouraged in an environment that allows the child freedom to initiate and follow through on activities. Having toys and materials available that are developmentally challenging is vital to the TPBA process. Minimizing the use of external reinforcement also is important. Many children with disabilities "perform" to please the adults rather than to derive pleasure from the activity. Eventually, children can lose intrinsic motivation and will strive to master a task only when they are reinforced (Brockman, Morgan, & Harmon, 1988). For this reason, teams need to be cognizant of the amount of reinforcement they are giving each child. Many children with disabilities are not strongly motivated internally and need support and encouragement to increase initiations, explorations, and problem solving. Minimal reinforcement should be offered at first and only increased as needed. The team should note the type of reinforcement that is most effective in getting the child to persist on tasks.

The TPBA team also can examine a child's emotional response to success and failure. Does the child demonstrate pride in accomplishment by smiling, clapping, and laughing, or is the child merely repeating the task? When a task is difficult to accomplish, what level of frustration is shown by the child? Does the child stop trying, throw the object, cry, or scream?

It also is essential to gain information from the parents about what the child's interests and efforts are like at home, what type of activities they expect the child to be able to do, and how much assistance and reinforcement they give the child. Priorities of the family also may become clear as they talk about their expectations and the child's efforts to accomplish valued activities. For children with a low persistence or frustration tolerance, intervention may focus on increasing mastery motivation. The intervention team should begin with the category of toys and materials that are of interest to the child and the types of reinforcement that are helpful in maintaining the child's efforts.

▊▊▊▊▊ V. C. What developmentally relevant
　　　　characteristics related to self can the child identify?

TPBA2 examines a child's understanding of his or her own identity. This occurs through both observation of the child's actions and listening to the child's remarks and comments about self and others. Toys and materials should be available that enable the child to show or talk about personal characteristics. For example, a mirror should be available so the child's response to seeing him- or herself in the mirror can be observed. In young infants, initial recognition of self can be observed, whereas with older children, their comments about their own appearance may be noted. As a child is able to use language, the facilitator can discuss with the child his or her emotions, likes and dislikes, and personal characteristics. For example, when engaging in dramatic play, the facilitator can let the child choose what he or she wants to be. "Look at all these dress-up clothes! What would you like to be?" Some children will be able to quickly select what they want to do, while others will hang back and wait for the facilitator to make a choice. When the child makes a choice, the facilitator can discuss the preference. "You want to be a doctor?" "Tell me about what kind of doctor you are." If needed, the facilitator could ask specific questions, such as "Are you a boy doctor or a girl doctor?" "Are you a mean doctor or a nice doctor?" This will enable the team to see whether the child is developing an understanding of his or her various attributes.

The child's view of his or her strengths also is important. In addition to listening for evaluative comments related to self-concept, such as "I'm good at that" or "I can do that one," the team also can ask the preschool-age child questions about what he or she is good at as they are playing. For example, "What do you really like to do? What are you good at?" or "What would you like to do better?" may lead to a conversation about how the child views his or her abilities.

Negative evaluative comments also are important to note. Comments such as "I can't" or "I don't know how" reflect the child's view of self and also are indicators of achievement motivation. Once identified, issues related to identity can be addressed in intervention as part of the overall developmental program.

Miles was a 13-month-old African American boy who had mild cerebral palsy. His parents preferred to have TPBA conducted in their home, so the occupational therapist and psychologist took toys and materials with them for the visit. Miles's parents had indicated on the family questionnaire that due to his motor difficulties, Miles did not play with many toys. He preferred to watch everyone else. Miles was not yet walking and did not use any words.

Mary, the occupational therapist who was the play facilitator, and Tamara, the psychologist, who videotaped the session, came into the living room and began to talk to Miles's parents. Miles, who was being held by his mother, looked on with interest as they set up the camera and pulled out a few toys. Mary invited Miles's mother, Robin, to play on the floor. Miles sat next to his mother and investigated the new toys. During the play session, Miles played with his mother, his father, Russell, and minimally with Mary. Miles moved quickly from object to object, picking them up, looking at them, and then throwing them. Whenever his mother or father demonstrated what the toy could do, Miles took the toy, made a brief swipe at it, screamed, and threw the toy. His parents would then comfort him and offer him a new toy, which would keep him engaged for a few seconds. Mary moved off to one side so that Miles would not be inhibited by her presence, but he made very few efforts to move. His hemiplegia made it somewhat difficult for him to move and manipulate objects, but his desire to explore seemed more limiting than his motor skills.

After observing Miles and his parents and interacting with him for an hour, it was clear that Miles had a very low level of mastery motivation and a low level of frustration tolerance. His attention seemed to be limited by his lack of effort rather than a lack of interest. In other words, if he had been more successful at using the toys meaningfully, he would have maintained attention for longer periods of time. His lack of persistence also resulted in "offering" and "comforting" being the main interactions between him and his parents. He was getting reinforced with a hug for throwing toys and crying. The team felt that it was important for Miles to get more feedback and pleasure from his toys in order for him to begin to pay more attention to the characteristics of objects and how to use them. They recommended introducing easily activated switch toys that produced a lot of action for little effort. Then, as Miles began to realize that he could have an impact on toys as well as on his parents, he could be introduced to toys that required a little more effort for a big result.

VI. Emotional Themes in Play

Play is a safe venue for children because it provides a vehicle for them to express themselves in a relaxed, nonthreatening setting. In play, children are in control of their world and can experiment with different emotions and express how they feel through the actions of dolls or their own dramatic representations. Such feelings as happiness, security, and nurturance may be demonstrated. Alternatively, worries, fears, and traumas also can be expressed (West, 2001). For children whose language is not yet fully developed, play is a mode that allows them to effectively communicate what they are thinking and feeling (Fall, 2001; Shen & Sink, 2002). We hope that the inner world of children is happy and that their play will demonstrate their carefree innocence and positive emotions. However, when that is not the case, children who have experienced trauma or have extreme anxiety may act out negative emotions or the events that caused the emotions.

Children develop at varying stages with regard to emotional-social development, but even very young children reveal inner feelings through their play. As discussed previously in the section on emotional expression, children begin to experience feelings of anxiousness, fear, and sadness in the first year of life (see I. Emotional Expression). Children who have experienced extreme deprivation or trauma will demonstrate their inner turmoil not only through facial expression but also through their play actions. Themes of concern to young children, such as separation, sibling relationships, discipline, or physical or sexual abuse, may be observed in animal or doll play by 2½–3 years of age (Benham, 2000). Caution, however, is needed when making judgments about children's behaviors, because many of the symptoms of emotional or psychiatric disorders are seen in typical children (Campbell, 1997). For example, it is not considered unusual for children to experience a period of time in which they are more fearful, anxious, or dependent on a caregiver. Similarly, children often desire power and control at some time during the early developmental years. Most children also have an active imagination and enjoy participating in fantasy play.

Emotions and behaviors that exceed the parameters necessary for adaptive functioning may be indicative of an emotional problem. When children are excessively withdrawn, lack delight and pleasure in play, or display seemingly unwarranted anger for an extended length of time in various settings, concern for the child's welfare may be warranted (Campbell, 1997).

Depending on the theoretical orientation of the psychologist, different approaches to play can be taken. Dodds (1987) notes that *ego-psychoanalytic theorists* examine children's play for evidence of psychosocial and psychosexual influences, feelings of guilt, and mechanisms that children may use to defend against their feelings. In contrast, he notes that the *phenomenological theorists* examine children's level of self-awareness and experiences that have contributed to this belief system. The *behavioral theorists* probably will not find the play assessment as helpful as observing "the child in real-life situations in order to discover the environmental stimuli and reinforcers of the target behavior" (p. 40). These and other perspectives influence the interaction style of the psychologist, as well as his or her interpretation of a child's behavior (Fall, 2001; Hall, Kaduson, & Schaefer, 2002).

The section that follows presents information on examining the structure and content of children's play and children's awareness of self and others, all elements that have been shown to be important to social and emotional development (Gitlin-Weiner, Sandgrund, & Schaefer, 2000). It is not meant to embrace any one theoretical perspective but to provide a more eclectic view of children's emotional life and view of self.

VI. A. How logical and flexible are the child's patterns of thought in play?

As children grow in their ability to carry out play sequences, they begin to be able to organize their play beyond the simple use of objects and incorporate time, space, context, and social roles. Cognitive, language, and social understanding merge in play to reveal logical thinking and social understanding. One of the characteristics that many children with emotional disturbance exhibit is illogical or disfluent thought processes. This can be reflected in dramatic play, wherein the sequence of ideas appears fragmented or disjointed. This behavior should be differentiated from developmentally lower levels of play, wherein the child's actions are not sequenced because of developmental limitations. Children with emotional problems usually are cognitively capable of more organized play, but emotional issues override the thought processes.

Depending on the age of the child, an understanding of the relationship of past, present, and future should be demonstrated. Children who have experienced trauma may confuse what happened in the past with what is happening in the present and what may happen in the future. They may, for example, repetitively dramatize a situation from their past that was emotionally infused.

Children with ADHD also may demonstrate disorganized play (Barkley, 1997; Westby, 2000). Their attention is easily diverted from one aspect or object in play to another. Although not an emotional problem, as such, this type of disorganization in thought processes will have an impact on social interactions in play.

VI. B. What awareness of others' emotional roles and actions is reflected in the child's dramatic play?

As noted in earlier discussions, even very young infants are aware of the actions of others and respond to others' emotions. Children who have emotional issues may be so involved in their own emotional worlds that they are unable to consider the feelings and actions of anyone else. Their own feelings are so intense that sensitivity to others is masked. Greenspan (1997) notes the importance of the child's ability to represent ideas, emotions, and relationships in play. These aspects reveal much about the child's emotional development. Westby (2000) also notes that the child's use of language may reflect what they understand about roles and emotions, but language in some types of disabilities (e.g., autism spectrum disorders or hydrocephalus) may be higher than social understanding. Therefore, it is important to look at all aspects of play to determine the developmental implications.

▆▆▆▆ VI. C. What emotional themes are expressed in the child's play?

The content of the child's play is another crucial element to examine. Again, depending on the psychologist's theoretical perspective, he or she will interpret this content differently. Themes that may appear in children's play include happiness, security, nurturance, dependency, loss, power or control issues, fear or anxiety in relation to specific concerns, and poor or inflated self-concept (Dodds, 1987). Fein (1989) identified five issues that children work through in their pretend play on a bipolar scale:

1. Connectedness (attachment versus separation)

2. Physical well-being (health versus bodily harm)

3. Empowerment (mastery versus helplessness)

4. Social regulation (support for social rules versus defiance)

5. Respect for or aggression against the material world

These are themes that emerge in children's play between 3 and 5 years of age and become more varied and elaborate, at least in Western societies, as children's communication and coordination of play increases (de Lorimer, Doyle, & Tessier, 1995; Goncu, Patt, & Kouba, 2002). However, in the play of children with emotional disabilities, an emphasis or predominant concern with one or more of these themes is observed. Their play will seem unbalanced and may lack spontaneity and exuberance commonly seen in the play of typical children. Their unhappiness, anger, or concern also may be reflected in the roles they choose to play and in their affect, language, and actions (Marvasti, 1997).

Mattingly (1997) suggests guidelines for interpretation, which can be helpful depending on the child's individual background and personality. She notes that when the child is telling or acting out a story, the use of specific props or characters may hold interpretive value. Various themes may be associated with repetitive play, including the following:

1. Witches and trolls may reflect fear

2. Wizards and fairies may indicate power

3. Giants, dinosaurs, and alligators may be used to show aggression

4. Trains, cars, and vehicles may show desire for escape

5. Forest, jungles, and darkness are often associated with emptiness

6. Rain, wind, and storms may show tumult

7. Sun, flowers, and birds are associated with contentment and hopefulness

All children may demonstrate these themes in their art or play at different times. The difference between children who are merely exploring these themes and feelings and children who are expressing worrisome levels of emotional expression is seen in the frequency, intensity, and affect associated with their play. Children who obsess about a particular theme, show intense emotions of discomfort with these themes, and consistently incorporate actions that symbolically represent concerns (e.g., being injured, lost, afraid) should be evaluated for potential emotional concerns.

In addition, children's ability to recognize and separate fantasy from reality is another important factor in their emotional play world. Play is fantasy and the means by which children make the world into anything they want. Problems arise when a child finds this fantasy so satisfying that he or she chooses not to enter the real world, or gets swallowed up into a fantasy world from which he or she cannot escape. Children of 4 and 5 years of age should understand that play is pretend, characters are acted out, and action figures or stuffed animals are not real. Absence of this awareness indicates a need for further evaluation.

VI. D. How does the child integrate and match thoughts, actions, and emotions in dramatic play?

As children's skills in handling and understanding objects develop, so does their understanding of what needs to be done with objects and people within various contexts and how these various contexts are related to specific emotions. As children move from expressing their own intentions to understanding the intentions of others, symbolic forms of play develop (Greenspan, 1997; Westby, 2000). Play reflects the integration of cognitive and affective development, as can be seen when the structure and content of play are matched to the emotions being mastered by the child (Russ, Niec, & Kaugars, 2000). For example, the child may show anger and "punish" the doll for misbehavior by putting it in the bed. The actions displayed by the child reflect his or her thoughts about what is correct behavior, and the emotions expressed depict what the child believes to be appropriate emotions to go with those actions. Children in play situations demonstrate creative problem solving with objects and social interactions. They attempt to master emotional conflicts by experimenting with various feelings and approaches. Children who have emotional disorders may not demonstrate a match between thoughts, actions, and feelings. For example, in the previous instance, the child who laughs while punishing the baby is showing emotions inconsistent with his or her actions. Contradictory thoughts and actions or emotions and actions should be examined to determine why such discrepancies are exhibited.

USING THE GUIDELINES TO ASSESS EMOTIONAL THEMES IN PLAY

Evaluation of the inner emotional world of children requires specialized expertise not possessed by all personnel who work with young children. As with other areas of TPBA2, should issues arise that are beyond the professional boundaries of the team members, the child and family should be referred to the appropriate experts for further evaluation. Although a qualified child psychologist or psychiatrist may be needed to fully assess social and emotional problems, themes that appear in the child's play can provide valuable information. The facilitator attempts to see the child's world from the child's point of view and attempts to identify the child's interpersonal needs, strengths, conflicts, heroes, and fears (Marvasti, 1994; Warren, Oppenheim, & Emde, 1996).

Observation and discussion with caregivers can provide information regarding the frequency, intensity, and duration of behaviors, as well as the developmental appropriateness of actions and feelings. Because a play session is usually a one-time occurrence, discussion with caregivers about the child's typical play materials and themes is important. Additional observations may be desired.

The team also must view behavior in context before determining the degree of concern. A child in crisis often responds in an atypical fashion to events in his or her life. Campbell (1997) advises, "isolated behaviors in and of themselves do not determine whether or not a disorder exists" (p. 4). Analysis of patterns of behavior that are seen in TPBA should, therefore, be compared with information from family members and other caregivers about the child's typical play patterns.

If a child is referred for TPBA because social and emotional problems are the primary concern, a psychologist would be the facilitator of choice. He or she may analyze the content of play from a different perspective than would an educator, assessing internal conflict as reflected by themes in the child's play. Cursory guidelines are offered to assist in observation of play in relation to emotional problems. If a psychologist is not a member of the transdisciplinary team, other team members may analyze the play to determine the need for a referral for further psychological evaluation. As with all areas of TPBA2, the evaluators should document and describe all behaviors carefully, without resorting to pathological labels.

VI. A. How logical and flexible are the child's patterns of thought in play?

As the play facilitator follows a child's lead, he or she can observe how the child organizes the play. If the child is cognitively at a level to be able to sequence thoughts and actions, the team will be able to see a beginning, a middle, and an end to a play sequence. Whether in construction, drawing, or dramatic play, the child should be able to organize actions to achieve his or her goals. Children with emotional problems may have difficulty with organization of thoughts, because their emotions and feelings overwhelm their thought processes. Their play ideas may wander without seeming logical. Before identifying emotional issues that may be having an impact on the child, the team needs to examine cognitive factors such as attention, memory, and problem solving to ensure that play patterns are not limited by cognitive deficit.

In addition to organizational abilities in their play, children need to be able to be flexible and shift a thought pattern to a new sequence as necessary. Children with emotional problems or a specific disability such as an autism spectrum disorder may be observed to adhere rigidly to the same play themes throughout their play. For example, a child with depression may draw dark, unhappy drawings, dramatize sad babies or sick animals, and choose books about getting lost. The child with autism may demand to play with the same type of toys or play in repetitive noncreative actions. The team should observe a child's choices and actions carefully, because they may reflect a prevailing emotional theme.

VI. B. What awareness of others' emotional roles and actions is reflected in the child's dramatic play?

How the child includes others in the play also is socially and emotionally relevant. Some children may demonstrate no awareness of others in the play setting, even the person who is attempting to interact in play. Other children are aware of the presence of others but allow them no role in the play. Still others are happy to have others engage them in play and will assign roles (e.g., "You build the bridge, and I'll drive the car") or assume a role in the play (e.g., the facilitator says, "I'd like a cup of coffee, please," and the child responds by getting her a cup). They are able to talk about "I," "me," "mine," "you," "yours," "his or hers," and "theirs." The child's ability to incorporate others into his or her play at the appropriate developmental level is an important indicator of both emotional awareness and social competence.

Awareness of and response to the emotions of others in play also is important (Charman et al., 2000) (see VII. A.). Another aspect to examine in the dramatic play arena is the roles the child chooses to assign to others and to him- or herself. Children typically choose to be the good guy or rescuer rather than the villain or victim. Analysis of the roles the child chooses and the consequent actions with other participants in the play can provide insight into the child's inner view of self.

VI. C. What emotional themes are expressed in the child's play?

As noted in the *Administration Guide for TPBA2 & TPBI2*, Chapter 7 (Play Facilitation), the right types of toys and materials are critical to an effective assessment. Determine ahead of time the type of toys the child prefers, have colors or markers available for drawing pictures, felt pieces or puppets for telling stories, and books relating to different themes for the child to look at and discuss. Emotional themes may be observed not only in the dramatic play area, but also in block play, drawings, and storytelling. Let the child choose the materials and topics of play, so as not to lead or direct the child's thoughts and actions. Commenting on what is happening and asking, "What's next?" will allow the child to determine the topic and sequence of play.

During TPBA, the team observes all of the child's actions and listens to the child's comments, looking for patterns. These patterns may be clues for the emotional themes that are influencing the child's thinking. A child may come back to certain toys repeatedly, may act on most toys in a particular way, or may reveal a predominance of certain emotions. For example, a child may choose to be aggressive with the toy dinosaurs, demonstrate aggressive shot-giving in doctor play, have a car crash and kill "pedestrians," or may show aggression toward the facilitator, peers, or parents, as well. Children who have been traumatized through accidents, abuse, or other traumatic experiences should be given materials and/or toys that allow them to illustrate or demonstrate their thoughts and feelings in a safe way. Puppets, art projects, dramatic play props, or action figures related to the trauma may elicit reenactments or feelings that are either overtly or covertly demonstrated through actions and/or words.

The patterns or themes of play observed should always be examined in relation to the child's overall development, in order to distinguish among cognitive, communicative, sensory, or emotional issues. This is particularly important because many psychologists or psychiatrists have not been trained in areas such as sensory integration or language processing, and issues in these areas often may look like emotional disturbance because of related behaviors. The input of the team regarding the child's overall development will be invaluable to others who may later perform additional psychological evaluations without the benefit of a transdisciplinary team.

VI. D. How does the child integrate and match thoughts, actions, and emotions in dramatic play?

Observation of the appropriate match of actions and feelings in play is another area for examination in TPBA. During the role play, is the child able to demonstrate emotions commensurate with the actions of the character or the feelings the character should be expressing? In other words, if the actions are angry, is the child's expression angry? A happy expression would show an inappropriate match of action and feelings. Is the child able to switch emotions in the play as needed? For example, if the child is pretending to be hurt and pretends to cry, is he or she able to shift emotions to a more appropriate emotional affect when "cured?" The ability to integrate thoughts and feelings is important for cognitive, communicative, and social development.

By age 6, Kelly had already lived in several foster homes. He was placed in foster care by court order due to incidents of child abuse by his parents. When observed playing with a toy soldier, he changed the identification of the doll with which he was playing several times. The soldier started out as "Kelly," became "mean monster," and then "my friend." When the doll was "Kelly" it was an evil person, attacking all the other dolls. As the "mean monster," it ate all the people. As "my friend," it had a fight and took away the other dolls' things. Even when putting the doll to sleep, Kelly demonstrated anger when giving orders, "Go to sleep right now! And don't get up!"

The sequence of Kelly's play also showed no continuity. The identity of the character shifted in the middle of an action without any announcement that the story had changed. The actions of the doll, which changed from a doll fighting, to a monster eat-

ing someone, to a doll being put to sleep, seemed inspired by whatever prop came into Kelly's view.

Also during the play session, Kelly confused time. He spoke of what he was going to do at his grandmother's that afternoon, when he had been to visit his grandmother in another state the week before. His focus on his grandmother also showed rigid thought patterns; regardless of the topic of discussion, Kelly shifted the subject to his grandmother. His grandmother was a stable, comforting person in his life, so her presence, even if just in thought, was important to him.

The psychologist stated that Kelly appeared to be a very angry child. His play demonstrated a desire for power and control that masked a deeper fear and anxiety about issues in his life. He also demonstrated being both a victim and a villain (both of which were accurate in his life history). Superimposed on this was a dependency on his grandmother, the one stable, loving person in his life.

Kelly also appeared to shift between his fantasy world and reality. Once he began to play in earnest with his toys, he became so engrossed that it was difficult to lure him back to the present reality, and the presence of the facilitator became irrelevant to him. He demonstrated a high degree of confusion concerning the boundaries between reality and fantasy. Kelly's play demonstrated significant indicators of emotional issues in need of further evaluation and treatment.

VII.   Social Interactions

Positive social relationships are critical to the healthy development of a child. Beginning with the child's first social relationship with his or her parents, interaction patterns are established. Inborn genetic characteristics (e.g., gender of the child) combined with environmental factors (e.g., parenting style) and cultural expectations together influence the development of a child's social competence. How the child functions in social situations influences the child's learning, because much of learning takes place through social interactions. The child's social competence also influences how she sees herself and how others view her.

Socially competent children are able to get along with others and avoid negativity and conflict (Dodge & Murphy, 1984). They are able to attend to social aspects of play, read cues, and interpret and communicate social information. Socially competent children also are able to regulate their emotions and employ good problem-solving skills. As a result, they can initiate and maintain relationships.

Errors in thinking and judgment may influence social skills. The way a child perceives and interprets social information influences his or her social actions. For example, a child may misread social cues, interpreting what another child says or does as being "mean." A child may have an inappropriate motivation—for instance, wanting to control or seek revenge rather than make friends (Welsh, Bierman, & Pope, 2000). A child also may have difficulty demonstrating appropriate reactions to another child's social initiations or responses. Impulsive reactions may prevent a child from processing all the relevant social information (Crick & Dodge, 1994). Analysis of social interactions and relationships requires integration of information about all of the previously discussed subcategories in the emotional and social domain.

▦▦▦ **VII. A. What emotions does the child respond to in others?**

Although it is not uncommon for professionals to observe a child's emotional reactions to various situations (see I. Emotional Expression), looking at the child's reactions to the emotions of *others* is more infrequent. Examination of both expressive and receptive emotional abilities is important because both are critical to the development of effective social relationships.

Children learn to understand their own emotions through observing, experiencing, and responding to emotions in others. They also learn to control their own emotions, behaviors, and social interactions through understanding how others control theirs. Emotional knowledge is helpful as children try to establish social relationships and friendships. In addition, much of higher-order thinking about responsiveness and responsibilities to others (including empathy and moral conduct) has its roots in the child's developing understanding about why people feel the way they do and how one should respond. Moral conduct is addressed in IV. Behavioral Regulation, discussed previously.

Empathy is awareness of another's emotions—the ability to detect different emotions, to take another's perspective, and to vicariously *feel with* that person the emotion he or she is experiencing (Zahn-Waxler & Radke-Yarrow, 1990). Empathy is considered a significant motivating factor and mediator for the development of social competence, prosocial behavior, and altruism (i.e., the ability to do something to benefit another without expectation of reward) (Denham, 1998; Roth-Hanania et al., 2000). However, empathy also can result in a distressed, self-focused, rather than other-focused, response on the part of children. Children can become "flooded" with the emotions they see and become upset themselves, rather than demonstrate sympathy for the person in need of caring (Eisenberg et al., 1998).

Relating to the positive emotions of joy and happiness also is an important emotional capacity. Recognizing what is making someone smile and reacting with corresponding emotion is a significant aspect of social turn-taking.

Babies first respond to others' emotions without understanding why. The "distress cry" in response to another infant's cry is involuntary and automatic. Sagi and Hoffman (1976) call this "empathetic distress" and view it as an innate reaction. During the first year of life, infants begin to be able to determine the meaning of others' emotional signals, but they cannot differentiate their own emotions from those of the other child.

As infants begin to be able to differentiate themselves from others, they show an increasing ability to express empathetic concern (DesRosiers & Busch-Rossnagel, 1997). They also are beginning to recognize that the facial expression they see is in response to an object or event in the environment. This recognition leads them to look for what caused the expression, and they will look at what the parent is looking at, using joint referencing. As joint referencing occurs, between 8 and 10 months of age, the infant then is able to attach emotional meaning to the object or event that is reflected on the face of the parent. This social referencing allows the child to use another person's emotional expression to judge what his or her own reaction should be. If the trusted adult (first the parent, then others) looks happy, fearful, or sad, the child will often respond accordingly. Children decode affective signals through their perceptions of the parents' cues (Prizant, Wetherby, & Roberts, 2000). Parents who give subtle cues or who have a flat affect may be difficult for their child to "read," and consequently, he or she may have difficulty using the parent as the emotional barometer for difficult situations. Also, children with sensory deficits may misperceive and/or misinterpret the parent's cues. Determining whether the child is able to accurately read the emotional cues provided by others is an important component of the assessment.

Between 12 and 18 months of age, a child will show concerned expressions when he or she views another in distress, imitate facial expressions of emotions, give comforting looks, and make prosocial offers of support (Roth-Hanania et al., 2000). By the middle of the second year of life, infants can use facial expression to judge others' preferences and realize that the feelings of another may be different from their own (Saarni et al., 1998). In response to the emotions of others, basic empathetic behaviors may be observed, including imitation of facial expression, concerned looks, and distressed crying (Roth-Hanania et al., 2000). By the second year of age, children can comment on the basic emotions they are feeling (e.g., happy, sad, mad). Also by 24 months of age, the child will actively intervene on behalf of a person in distress, and with increasing language from 24 months on, the child will verbally express caring.

By preschool, children can infer and explain the reasons for their own and others' emotions (Stein & Levine, 1999). They become better able to predict how someone will feel after an event and to predict behaviors that are likely to occur as a result of others' emotions (Russell, 1990). Prosocial behaviors, or active interventions on behalf of another person, become part of the child's repertoire during the preschool years.

Children who have difficulty with taking into account the perspective, feelings, or needs of others may have significant social and emotional disabilities. For example, lack of ability to read emotional cues, share joint attention, make empathetic responses, and understand why someone acts a certain way are all characteristics of children with autism spectrum disorders. Other identifiable disorders also may be associated with problems with cue-reading and expression of empathy. For example, children with severe cognitive delays also may demonstrate deficits of emotional understanding and responsiveness because cognitive understanding is necessary for social skills. Children with sensory integration disorders (see Chapter 2), who are either hypersensitive or hyposensitive to various types of stimulation, also may have difficulty reading and interpreting the sensory cues provided by others. A lack of ability to read and understand emotional cues is a significant factor and should be considered in relation to other subcategories and domains for both diagnostic purposes and intervention implications.

VII. B. How does the child demonstrate a sense of pleasure and trust in his or her parents?

The child's relationship with his or her primary caregivers, be they biological, adoptive, grandparents, or foster parents, plays an enormously significant role in the emotional and social life of the child. The impact of this relationship pervades almost every aspect of development and the effects are long-lasting (Benoit & Parker, 1994; Elliot & Reis, 2003; Peck, 2003). The caregiver–child relationship is a complex one, and parenting style, environmental factors, and child characteristics, including both inherited strengths and vulnerabilities, contribute to the resulting relationship (Collins, Maccoby, Steinberg, Hetherington, & Bornstein, 2000; Goldberg, 1990; Maccoby, 2000).

Parents help their children feel secure and confident by providing a mirror for how to deal with new situations and how to manage fear and stress, and by encouraging the child to explore and develop competence. The security of the attachment the child shares with the parents is of fundamental importance to the child's future development (Ainsworth, Blehar, Waters, & Wall, 1978; Carson & Parke, 1996; Denham, Mitchell-Copeland, Strandberg, Auerbach, & Blair, 1997; Lamb & Malkin, 1986; Tomasello, Kruger, & Ratner, 1993; Weinfeld, Sroufe, Egeland, & Carlson, 1999), particularly in relationship to social relationships, emotional regulation, behavior, and problem solving (Isabella, 1995; Lamb, Thompson, Gardner, & Charnov, 1985; Thompson, 1999). Because atypical attachment patterns are more common in parent–child interactions among children with disabilities, it is important to look at factors relating to attachment (Kelly & Barnard, 2000). Intervention can then focus on those aspects of the relationship that can strengthen pleasurable interactions.

Research on attachment traditionally examines the child's exploratory behaviors in the presence of the parent, response to separation, and the child's reaction to reunion. Securely attached infants play comfortably in the presence of the parents, exploring the environment and returning to check in as needed. They show pleasure when reunited with their parent after a separation. Insecurely attached infants, on the other hand, show resistance, avoidance, distress, or anger on reunion (Ainsworth et al., 1978).

Cultural differences are evident in parent–child relationships, although the secure attachment pattern is the most common in all societies studied (van IJzendoorn & Sagi, 1999). However, interaction patterns reflect the values of the parent's culture with respect to such things as cuddling, crying, and independence (Harwood, Miller & Irizarry, 1995; Takahashi, 1990). Parents from different cultures and even within the same culture have a wide range of beliefs about their roles with respect to their children, attachment, independence and dependence, sleeping patterns, and discipline (Greenfield & Suzuki, 1998; McCollum, Ree, & Chen, 2000; Rodrigo & Triana, 1996). Parents of children with disabilities may have perceptions of disability that are culturally influenced, and ascertaining the family's values and beliefs is an important role in the assessment process (McCollum & Chen, 2003). However, even across cultures, sensitive, responsive, and consistent parenting is important.

Literature on parent–child interaction emphasizes both the parent's and the child's role in dyadic interplay. The primary adults in the child's life need to provide nurturance and consistency, and they need an ability to read, interpret, and respond appropriately to the child's needs, communications, and actions. At the same time, they need an ability to provide limits, boundaries, supports, and resources to help shape the child's development. Many parents do not have all of these abilities. Some parents may experience emotional, economic, or familial problems that result in stress or behaviors that are not responsive to the child's emotional needs.

Parents' feelings of competence during interactions with their child partially depend on the child's readability, predictability, and responsiveness (Goldberg, 1977, 1990), all of which may be problematic in the child with a disability. Early research (Rheingold, 1977) proposed that several factors influence infants' social behaviors, including responsiveness to social stimuli, initiation of social contact, and modification of adult behavior. Infants with disabilities, however, often have difficulty with these social aspects. As Walker (1982) noted, the social interactions of the young child with disabilities are often characterized by

1. Reduced social interaction (i.e., interactions with adults being mainly of a caregiving or teaching nature)

2. Little spontaneous or child-initiated social contact

3. Noninteractive social engagement

4. Lack of awareness of the reciprocal nature of communication

5. One-sided activity, or extremes of activity and inactivity

Clearly, vital social components may be compromised in young children with disabilities, negatively influencing their interactions with caregivers.

Parent and child are equal contributors to interactions, and either party may lack appropriate behaviors or possess unusual response patterns (Cassidy & Berlin, 1999; Collins et al., 2000; Comfort, 1988; Goldberg, 1977). Characteristics of the child that may have a negative impact on interactions include level of affect displayed by the child, threshold of responsivity, muscle tone, irritable moods, poor emotional regulation, inability to interpret adult cues, and demanding behaviors (Barnett, Clements, Kaplan-Estrin, & Fialka, 2003; DeGangi, 2000; Emde, Katz, & Thorpe, 1978; Greenspan & Wieder, 1999; Watson, Baranek, & DiLavore, 2003; Wetherby & Prizant, 2003; Williamson & Anzalone, 2001). Thus, examination of these factors in relation to parent–child interactions is important.

Activity between the partners is another important aspect of social interaction. Investigators have found that the overall activity level of children with disabilities is lower than that of peers without disabilities (Hanzlik & Stevenson, 1986; Williamson & Anzalone, 2001). This is important for parent–child interactions, because the child who is inactive may engender passivity in the parent or, alternatively, may stimulate the parent to be overly active or controlling in the relationship. Children at high risk and those who have disabilities also initiate interactions with their parents less frequently than children who are not at risk or do not have disabilities (Hanson, 1996; Watson et al., 2003). Such children are placed in the role of responders rather than active transacters within their environments, and changing initiation patterns can be important for intervention.

Developmentally, it is possible to examine the progression of the caregiver–child relationship. Greenspan (1997) has detailed stages of emotional development of the child with respect to the parent–child relationship (see Table 4.3). Greenspan's model is useful in that it integrates the emotional and social components of parent–child interaction as they are influenced by cognitive, motor, and language development.

VII. C. How does the child differentiate among people?

Social differentiation is the ability to discriminate various characteristics or features of people in order to classify them into various categories (e.g., familiar or unfamiliar, boy or girl, young or old). Such differentiation helps the child to determine how he or she should relate to these people in social contexts. The ability to differentiate who is to be trusted and who is not to be trusted is an important one for young children. In early infancy a baby can differentiate his or her mother from others and can typically be comforted more easily by parents. However, it is not until the second half of the first year when the child develops the emotion of fear that the infant begins to be wary of strangers. The degree of stranger anxiety shown varies from child to child, depending on temperament, experiences, and culture (Saarni et al., 1998; Thompson & Limber, 1991).

Table 4.3. Greenspan's progression of caregiver–child relationship

Stage	Age of child	Relationship between parent and child during this stage
1	Birth to 2 months	• Child looks at parent, attends to faces, voices, and actions. • Parent is source of pleasurable interaction, comfort, and regulation.
2	2–4 months	• Child shows interest in interaction by smiling, reaching, touching. • Parent elicits and responds to child's movements, sounds, and expressions.
3	4–8 months	• Intentional two-way communication or turn-taking in "circles of communication" develop, with both child and parent initiating.
4	8–18 months	• Child combines facial, verbal, gestural and physical communication into 20–30 circles of communication. • Child is asserting independence. • Parent encourages exploration, gives labels to words and actions, and provides emotional cues about safety.
5	18–30 months	• Child learning to talk about emotions, balancing dependence and independence, becomes secure about return of absent parent. • Parent allows exploration within safe boundaries, explains reasons for actions, reactions, and emotions.
6	2½–5 years	• Child is able to relate thoughts and feelings; discuss time, space, and causality; and demonstrate complex pretend play. • Parent encourages problem solving, social interactions, and creativity through modeling, explaining, questioning, and reinforcing.

As children develop increasing cognitive abilities, they use discriminative abilities to construct categories of people and social information to determine how they should respond to individuals within these categories. Children learn that they need to respond uniquely to people of varying ages, gender, and abilities. However, for a variety of reasons, including lack of attachment, lack of cognitive understanding, or lack of social understanding, some children may not demonstrate appropriate social differentiation. For example, children who have suffered maltreatment, particularly sexual abuse, often show either extreme mistrust of adults or overly affectionate, indiscriminant behaviors.

Social differentiation is not only important for safety reasons, but also for cognitive and social reasons. As children begin to classify and distinguish characteristics of others, they begin to determine their own characteristics in relation to the characteristics of others. They begin to be able to tell old from young, girls from boys, one ethnic group from another, and so forth. As these skills develop, children also learn how roles and actions of others differ and begin to understand why people act differently. They also learn when, how, and why their own behaviors need to be varied with different people in distinct contexts. Although social differentiation is built on cognitive skills, it contributes to social appropriateness.

As indicated previously, children first differentiate their parents from others. As early as 7–12 months of age, children are beginning to differentiate people and their voices by gender and age (Bahrick, Netto, & Hernandez-Reif, 1998; Poulin-Dubois, Serbin, Kenyon, & Derbyshire, 1994). During the second year of age, children become more adept at distinguishing familiar and unfamiliar people. At about age 3, children can identify their own gender and that of others through hairstyle, clothing, and behavior. By age 3 or 4 years of age, children can modify their language and actions to fit the needs of a less advanced child (Howes & Farver, 1987). They also know to turn to older peers for information and play ideas. Preschool-age children also begin to differentiate characteristics of people, first concrete characteristics such as skill, hair, and eye color and later more abstract characteristics, such as who is nice and who is mean. Such categorization lays the foundation for children to understand such difficult concepts as "character" and "friendship."

▓▓▓▓ VII. D. What types of social play are demonstrated with siblings and/or peers?

Social competence with peers involves being able to engage in meaningful and rewarding interactions, being liked and accepted by other children, and being able to develop friendships. As stated previously, the ability to appropriately express and regulate emotions, read others' cues, show empathy and caring, take initiative, and relate to the unique characteristics of others are all important for the development of positive social relations with peers and siblings. Sociability with peers also is fostered by an early, warm, sensitive parent–child attachment.

As early as 3–4 months of age, babies will look at and touch each other. By 6 months of age, babies will smile and vocalize at other infants. By 12 months of age, the baby may offer a toy, making the first real gesture of sharing. They also may grin, gesture, and begin to imitate another infant's behavior (Vandell & Mueller, 1995). As the infant matures and develops more refined play skills, and the ability to walk and run, he or she may seek out and play near another infant. Especially after 18 months of age, peer play involving turns escalates. Coordinated interaction increases primarily through imitation of each other's actions, such as throwing a ball or running, and escalating verbal skills expand communication efforts (Eckerman & Didow, 1996). Contact around toys often involves tussles, as obtaining an object is more desirable than having pleasant social interactions. However, as noted previously, at this time the child is beginning to respond to the emotions of other children and is capable of using comforting gestures when another infant is unhappy.

A dramatic growth in the ability to play together occurs between 2 and 3 years of age. During this time, children learn how to use objects functionally and engage in *parallel play*, or play in which children play near each other with similar materials. *Associative play*, in which children engage in different activities but still interact and comment on each others' actions, is emerging along with early dramatic play. During this time, the child is developing the ability to use a variety of strategies for solving problems and can work with another child on a task such as building a structure.

Between the ages of 3 and 4, children are forming friendships. They are able to carry on conversations, engage in *cooperative play*, or play with a common goal in mind. From 4 to 6 years of age, children's social play becomes more cooperative and organized. Pretend play, with children assuming different roles in a script, or series of related action sequences, predominates. Throughout the preschool years, isolated, parallel, associative, and cooperative types of play are all still evident. Surprisingly, nonsocial activities comprise up to one third of the kindergartener's free time, with the other forms of play taking up approximately equal amounts of time (Howes & Matheson, 1992). The type of social interactions remain somewhat constant, but the content becomes more cognitively complex. This is important, because nonsocial play alone is not cause for alarm. However, the social play of children who do not play with other children because they are unaware, uninterested, or have immature or stereotypical play patterns should be examined in more depth. Also, children who avoid social interactions due to extreme fearfulness or anxiety may require support or intervention. These children also will probably demonstrate concerns in the subcategory of "Emotional Style."

In addition to the developmental level of social interactions outlined previously, several other dimensions of social interactions deserve attention. Gender preferences are important to socialization. Social activities among girls tend to be different from those for boys. Studies have shown that in addition to environmental influences, hormones may influence the play choices for boys and girls. Boys tend to prefer action-oriented play, including running, play-fighting, and building-up and knocking-down type activities. Girls tend to prefer calm, gentle play (Beneson, Apostoleris, & Parnass, 1997; Maccoby, 1998). These preferences may result in the gender segregation that occurs as children mature. As early as 2 years of age, girls may tend to withdraw from the roughhouse play of boys. Beginning in preschool, gender differences in peer play are evident, and both boys and girls tend to prefer same-sex interactions (Hartup, 1983). Girls will often play in small groups, engaging in dramatic play or artistic endeavors, whereas boys play in larger groups and play more active, competitive games (Eder & Hallinan, 1978).

▬▬ VII. E. How does the child deal with social conflict?

Conflicts between infants begin during the first year of life, as children's desires and goal orientation increase. Conflicts with siblings or peers often increase during the second year of life, when language may not be sufficient to express the child's needs and desires, with hitting and biting being used to express dissatisfaction. As associative play increases, conflicts with peers are frequent. The child knows he or she can seek assistance when necessary, and adult intervention is often required to resolve disputes. Between the ages of 3 and 4, children are more able to resolve conflicts through their own efforts. Specifically, yielding to the other child, disengagement, and negotiation are used to solve social conflicts (Cheah et al., 2001; Landy, 2002).

The amount and frequency of conflict and means of conflict resolution becomes particularly relevant during the preschool years. Aggressive acts such as pushing or hitting; verbal taunts; intrusive or impulsive behaviors; immature behavior such as whining or having a tantrum; solitary, withdrawn, or unoccupied behavior; or unusual behaviors are typically out of sync with the group (Bierman, Smoot, & Aumiller, 1993). Researchers have identified two different types of aggression in children and adults, specifically, relational and physical aggression (Crick, 1997; Crick, Casas, & Ku, 1999; Crick, Casas, & Mosher, 1997; McEvoy, Estrem, Rodriguez, & Olson, 2003). *Relational aggression* is defined as any verbal or nonverbal behavior that excludes others from play or encourages others to exclude a child or threatens to exclude or ignore. *Physical aggression* is defined as kicking, hitting, pushing, shoving, grabbing or throwing toys, destroying others' materials, or threatening to do these acts (cited in McEvoy et al., 2003, based on definitions by Crick et al., 1997) in order to obtain an item, to escape a task, to get someone's attention, or to provide sensory stimulation. Boys have been found to be more physically aggressive, whereas girls are more relationally aggressive, and boys, overall, demonstrate more of both types of aggression (McEvoy et al., 2003).

These are factors to be considered when distinguishing social problems. However, it also is essential to note the importance of culture influences and that cultures vary in their acceptance of aggression, affection, and reticence. Some families may value aggressive and assertive behavior in boys, whereas others may deem it more appropriate to be quiet and cooperative. It is important to understand the values and expectations of the child's family, because the child will be reinforced by family members for demonstrating the behaviors that they respect.

VII. F. How do other children react to the child in dyads or in group settings?

Another aspect that is important to social development is the social acceptability or likeability of the child. Research has demonstrated that children who are likable have more friends and more positive social relationships (Newcomb & Bagwell, 1995). Peer acceptance is a strong predictor of future psychological adjustment (Gest, Graham-Bermann, & Hartup, 2001). Children who are rejected by their peers, either because they are aggressive or because they are withdrawn, are more at risk for future social, emotional, and academic problems. For this reason, early identification of children in preschool classrooms who may be rejected from social interactions is important. Early intervention may help them to develop necessary social skills.

Children with disabilities often are not preferred play partners. Although this may be because typical peers lack a framework for interpreting and responding to the differences these children exhibit, reticence to play with children with disabilities also may be partially because of differences in play abilities. Children with disabilities may demonstrate difficulty entering a group, maintaining play, and problem solving around conflicts. Observation of the characteristics of the child can help the team to develop strategies for intervention related to social abilities with peers.

VII. G. How is the child's sense of humor demonstrated?

Humor is a broad and multifaceted construct (Klein, 2003; Martin, 2000) that involves the cognitive processes of creating, perceiving, understanding, and appreciating stimuli or events, and it results in amusement, smiling, or laughter. Although sense of humor is difficult to define, it is typically displayed through a pleasurable response to a physical, verbal, or cognitive element of surprise or the unexpected. Having a sense of humor is important for a variety of developmental reasons (Bergen, 1996; Klein, 2003; McGhee, 1991; Nevo, Aharonson, & Klingman, 1996), and it is important to both physical and mental health (Bizi, Keinan, & Beit-Hallahmi, 1988; Kuiper, Martin, & Olinger, 1993; McGhee, 1991; Nevo, Keinan, & Teshimovshy-Arditi, 1993; Zajdman, 1993; Ziv, 1983, 1988). Humor has been shown to help cope with anxiety, stress, and pain, strengthen the immune system, enhance positive emotions, increase learning and creative processes, reduce tension, increase attention, support memory retention, support relaxation, and encourage manipulations of language.

A child's sense of humor also can have an impact on social interactions. Although humor does not always involve social interactions (i.e., it is possible to laugh at something in isolation and laugh at events that do not involve people), humor often occurs in a social context, and a sense of humor influences social competence. For this reason, it is included in the subcategory of social relations. The cognitive aspects of humor also are addressed in the cognitive domain (see Chapter 7).

Aspects of humor may be either adaptive or maladaptive. Martin and his colleagues (2000) are finding that people who have a tendency to amuse others and engage in humor in a way that promotes social cohesiveness use "affiliative humor." Others use "self-enhancing humor" to help them cope or take a more positive perspective on situations. Both affiliative and self-enhancing types of humor are adaptive and positive. On the other hand, both "aggressive humor," which uses sarcasm or humor to ridicule and manipulate others, and "self-defeating humor," which is excessively self-disparaging, are viewed as maladaptive forms of humor (Martin, 2001). Although it is not possible to see all of these forms of humor in young children, by preschool it is possible to see the emerging sense of humor and whether humor is typically used for socially adaptive or maladaptive purposes (see Table 4.4).

Understanding others' humor demands cognitive understanding of any incongruities presented as well as social comprehension. Children need to recognize the expressions, inflections, and nuances that indicate when a person is intending to be funny. In that way, sense of humor requires awareness of emotion, perception of intention, and responsiveness that parallels that needed for empathy. The child's sense of humor also can tell us much about his or her level of cognitive development (Cicchetti & Sroufe, 1976; McGhee, 1977, 1979, 1991; Zillman & Bryant, 1993) (see Table 4.4 and Chapter 7).

Socially inappropriate expression of humor or lack of humor may be related to various mental disorders or neurological pathologies. People with autism spectrum disorders, schizophrenia, or depression may demonstrate unusual or absent humor. Pathological humor is defined by Duchowny (1983) as laughter that "superficially resembles natural laughter but differs by virtue of abnormalities of motor patterns, emotional experience, or appropriateness of social context" (p. 91). Pathological laughter may be seen in children with Angelman syndrome (Summers et al., 1995). Pathologi-

Table 4.4. Humor development

Age	Means of expression of sense of humor (additive from age to age)
Birth to 1 year	Social interactions, games (e.g., Peekaboo) Physical play (e.g., tickling, movement, sensory play)
1–2 years	"Chase me" Unexpected actions, sounds
2–3 years	Incongruous actions of people or animals Naming common objects "wrong" or making errors
3–4 years	Silly actions or use of sounds, words Playful turn-taking to make another laugh Negative humor may be seen (e.g., knocking down others' blocks and laughing)
4–5 years	Riddles and knock-knock jokes Bodily function words
5–6 years	Teasing or playing jokes on someone ("fooling") Sarcasm to hurt feelings or make fun of someone or something Self-deprecating humor first seen

cal laughter can be 1) excessive laughter, either when the situation is not funny or when laughter cannot be inhibited; 2) forced laughter, which is out of the child's control; or 3) gelastic epilepsy, in which laughter may be a convulsive symptom (Arroyo et al., 1993; Duchowny, 1983). Evidence of these forms of laughter should be incorporated into the overall assessment of the child, as such evidence may contribute to clarification of diagnosis.

USING THE GUIDELINES TO ASSESS SOCIAL INTERACTONS

As the TPBA team looks at the child's social interactions within a limited time frame and restricted context, it is important to gather social relationship information from more than one source. For this reason, in addition to observations of the child with parents, the facilitator, siblings, and/or a peer, the TPBA team asks parents and teachers or caregivers about the child's social functioning using the parent/caregiver questionnaires.

Within the subcategory of social interactions, observations are made relating to cue reading, parent–child interactions, response to strangers, interactions with siblings and peers, approach to social conflict, reactions of other children, type of social play, and use of humor for social purposes. Observations of social interactions with the facilitator, parents, and, whenever possible, peers and/or siblings are important. The team perceptions should be compared with information provided by parents and other caregivers or teachers regarding social interactions outside of the play assessment. The comparison of others' opinions of the child's social skills is relevant, not to determine who is "right" or "wrong" but in order to see how the child's social interactions may vary in different contexts.

VII. A. What emotions does the child respond to in others?

During TPBA2, the team has many opportunities to observe the child's reactions to the emotions of the caregivers, facilitator, peers, and/or siblings and other team members. The team should observe whether the child watches the faces of those around him. Regardless of whether the child is being observed in a play room or at home, the situation is a new one, which may elicit anxious emotions. Look for social referencing on the part of the child. Does he or she check in with the caregivers to see what emotions they are expressing? When someone smiles, does he or she smile in return? Watch how the child's expression or movements change in response to the parents' emotions. What happens if the parents indicate surprise or pleasure? Occasionally, parents will show anger toward the child during the play session. What is the child's facial, physical, or verbal response? Watch for the child's expression to change or reflect that of a parent or the facilitator. Also, look for joint referencing. If a parent or the facilitator looks at and talks about objects, does the child also look at these objects?

If the child is using both social referencing and joint referencing, is he or she able to associate the emotion seen on the adult's face with the cause of the emotion (e.g., the tower of blocks falls, the adult's face registers sadness, the child looks at the adult, looks at the blocks, and reacts)? With older children, dramatic play can be used to dramatize different emotional situations. The play facilitator can improvise situations that will elicit various emotions from the child and also allow the child to respond to the emotions of others involved in the play. For example, when the facilitator and child are playing doctor, does the child react with empathy to the facilitator's aches and pains? What does he or she do to make the facilitator feel better? During dramatic play, the team can examine the child's ability to role play various emotions in appropriate contexts and to carry out emotional dialogue that matches the emotions expressed (see I. Emotional Expression). Parents often are willing to be "co-conspirators" in play-acting different emotional situations. For instance, the parent may pretend to be sad about the child taking the toy with which she was playing. The facilitator can suggest this action either verbally or nonverbally to the parent. "Look, Mommy is sad you took her cookie." The team can then see the difference between the child's responses to the emotions of familiar versus unfamiliar people (see the TPBA2 Age Table, p. 178).

For children of preschool level abilities, the facilitators will want to listen to the language used by the child to determine what the child understands about emotions. When the child is discussing a trip to Disneyland, a recent fall, a time when he or she got in trouble, or other emotional episodes, the facilitator can take advantage of the opportunity to discuss how the child felt when the event occurred and what it was that made him or her feel this way. This will allow the team to ascertain the child's emotional memory and understanding of emotional causality. If something happens to make the child cry, the facilitator may see if the child can identify what might make him "feel better."

▥▥▥▥ VII. B. How does the child demonstrate a sense of pleasure and trust in his or her parents?

TPBA2 does not provide an assessment of attachment, but it does allow an opportunity to examine the child's relationship to the parent in what is known as secure base behavior, the child's ability to explore and enjoy the environment, while using the parent as a base to return to for comfort or encouragement. At some point during the session, when both the parents and the child are comfortable, each parent is asked to interact with the child in a nonstructured play situation and often in a more structured teaching task as well. Parents' interactions in informal play may look quite different than in a structured learning situation. The child's relationship to the parent also is observed when the parent is not directly interacting with the child but is in the room watching the play session. The team can observe how much the child needs the parent's support or attention, or conversely, how difficult it is for the parent to allow the child to play independently or with another person. The child's response to separation and reunion also can be observed, depending on the age of the child. The infant or young child should begin the session with a parent and remain with one or both parents as long as is necessary to ensure the child's optimal performance. In some cases, a parent may remain with the child throughout the entire session and, in fact, may be the play facilitator if the child chooses not to interact with team members.

Depending on the age of the child, a variety of behaviors may be seen that will indicate that the child is attached to the parents and has established a base of trust with them that allows him or her to reach out to explore the world. The team can watch for the child to initiate engagement with the parents and to seek out exchanges of affection, calming, or support and encouragement from the parents. In addition, the team can look for the child's responses to the parents' emotions and attempts at initiating and maintaining interaction with them.

The team also should be cognizant of behaviors that may indicate that the relationship is strained or may need some support. For example, the team may occasionally see a child who avoids interaction with a parent (even avoiding eye contact), has primarily negative interactions (anger or aggression), or may have fleeting or anxious interactions with one or both parents. These may be warning signs of stress in the parent–child relationship. However, the team needs to keep the developmental level of the child in mind as well. Older children may demonstrate a lack of interest in the parents and be more focused on the toys due to their high interest in the toys and materials.

Team members also can observe the types of responses the parent gives the child. In addition to comforting when the child is distressed, how does the parent respond to the child's accomplishments and positive affect? What does the parent say to the child, and are the comments positive, negative, educational, emotional? A parent who has been actively involved in the child's traditional therapy may begin to look more like a therapist than a parent, a position that can undermine the responsibility to be a responsive, supportive caregiver.

Interactions with both parents should be observed, because the child will probably relate differently to the mother and father. If other caregivers, such as grandparents or babysitters, are important in the child's daily life, their involvement in TPBA can be instructive to the team and beneficial to the child. In addition, it is important to look at how the child relates to the other team members, many of whom may be strangers, in comparison to how the child relates to his or her parents or people who are familiar. Children who have been abused or children with relationship disorders may not show appropriate differentiation of strangers. They may show inappropriate affection or fear or relate to both familiar and unfamiliar people in the same fashion. Depending on the age of the child, this inability to differentiate appropriate responses across people can be a clue that further investigation of this area is needed.

Occasionally, the team may observe characteristics or behaviors in the parent that negatively affect the child's emotional or social development. The team may observe that the parent appears depressed and/or noninteractive, demanding, overly controlling, and inconsistent or ambivalent in responses, or the parent may exhibit other behaviors that raise questions about the impact of the parenting style on the child's development. The purpose of TPBA is not to evaluate the parent, but to assess the child. The team has a responsibility, however, to support the child by helping the parents to develop interaction patterns that may be more successful in attaining their desired outcomes. Identifying the parents' goals or intentions and then talking about effective ways to achieve those goals is a positive approach.

If issues of concern arise relating to caregiver–child interaction, additional assessment or referral to a specialist may be needed. Again, the point is not to judge the parenting, but to examine how behaviors may be supporting or hindering the child's development. The team also should determine how the parents feel about what it is like to "parent" this child and whether they would like support for their efforts. Many parents will quickly admit their frustration and be willing to accept suggestions to make parenting more pleasurable. The team may then be able to assist the parents in identifying resources to support them in making the necessary personal or interaction modifications necessary to be more effective parents.

VII. C. How does the child differentiate among people?

During TPBA the team will observe the child's reaction to caregivers, strangers, and possibly siblings and/or peers. In addition, the team should look for the child's differentiation and preferences for play partners based on age, gender, or personal characteristics. During the play session the child may show a preference for or avoidance of interaction with different individuals. Some children may not indicate any preference and may, in fact, play equally with all people present with no indication of differential recognition. In addition, the team should listen for comments that indicate the child's awareness and understanding of different personal traits. For example, the child may comment on the facilitator's hair, dress, or personality (e.g., saying, "You're nice"). Based on the child's age and cultural expectation, the observations may provide information about the child's cognitive understanding as well as social awareness.

VII. D. What types of social play are demonstrated with siblings and/or peers?

The TPBA play session offers limited opportunities for observation of peer interactions, unless it is done in a classroom. For this reason, it is important to review the parent questionnaire (CFHQ) and the teacher or child care provider's feedback on the child's social interactions. On the Family Assessment of Child Functioning tools (see the *Administration Guide for TPBA2 & TPBI2*, Chapter 5), parents will be asked similar questions about the child's social interactions as those addressed by the team. During TPBA, the team will be able to observe interactions with siblings and/or peers, if they are available. Occasionally, no sibling or peer is available for team observation. In this case, information from parents and other caregivers is used for this section of TPBA2.

If TPBA is conducted in the home, the team members present should spend time interacting with the child and any siblings who are present at some point in the assessment. For children who are hesitant to engage with the play facilitator, play with the parents and siblings may make the child feel more comfortable. In this case, the sibling play may precede play with the facilitator. If the child is intrigued by the new person and toys, the sibling can be included later in the play session.

If TPBA is conducted in a play room and siblings are present, the same procedure can be followed. If siblings are not present, a peer can be included in one of several ways. First, the parents may bring one of the child's friends with them to the assessment (a familiar peer is preferable to an unfamiliar one). Alternatively, if the play assessment is conducted in a center where children attend programs, one of the children from a similar-age classroom may be included (with permission of the child's parents). A child who is of the same gender and is only slightly higher functioning is preferable.

During observations of interactions with siblings and/or peers, the team observes whether the child is aware of the presence of the other child and how the child responds to proximity with the other child. The level of play interaction, from various forms of nonsocial play to parallel, associative, or cooperative play, can be observed. In addition, the team observes how the child responds to the peer. Does the child withdraw, initiate an interaction, or respond to the other child's initiations?

▬▬▬ VII. E. How does the child deal with social conflict?

The team can observe whether a child is capable of turn-taking with another child or responds with impulsive or aggressive behaviors, such as taking toys, pushing, hitting, or biting. If the child is at a level of being able to engage in cooperative play (working together toward a goal), how does the child negotiate working together? Can the child see the common goal, negotiate roles, and share control of the actions? If conflicts arise, how does the child respond? Does the child "give in" and withdraw from the problem, use an adult as a mediator, negotiate a compromise, or revert to aggression? Observations of the child's responses will provide insight into the child's typical peer interactions.

▬▬▬ VII. F. How do other children react to the child in dyads or in group settings?

This particular component is not observable in the play session unless the child is observed in a group setting. If the child is of preschool age and attends a child care center or preschool program, the team also should endeavor to obtain input from the child's teacher or caregiver about the child's social acceptability or popularity with other children. Teachers are asked whether the child is popular with other children, accepted, or rejected and whether rejection is because of withdrawn behaviors or because of negative behaviors. As noted earlier, children who are rejected are at particular risk for later social and emotional problems, so this information is valuable to the TPBA team.

▬▬▬ VII. G. How is the child's sense of humor demonstrated?

In TPBA, humor is looked at both in the cognitive and in the emotional and social domain. In the cognitive area, sense of humor is analyzed for what it shows about the child's level of comprehension. In the emotional and social domain, sense of humor is examined with regard to how the child uses humor for social purposes and whether the social purpose is positive or negative. Negative humor is primarily relevant for preschool-age children who are capable of using humorous language, gestures, and actions for negative purposes, such as making fun of someone through imitation or making funny noises that are known to irritate someone. Comments from teachers are relevant here. Other aspects that can be observed in TPBA are whether the child can initiate humor and understand and respond to the humor of others. Does the child attempt to initiate games or use actions or words to try to get others to smile or laugh? If the child uses humorous acts, the next important question is whether the child uses these acts for affiliative, positive social purposes. Here the team can watch for actions, such as the child hiding under something and popping out to surprise someone, gestures such as the child putting a toy on his head to make someone laugh, or words, such as "You're a poo-poo head!" to elicit laughter from another child, who is equally enamored by bathroom humor. The child also may be observed using humor to hurt others. With preschool-age children, this may take the form of hitting another child with something and then laughing. In the above example, calling the child a "poo-poo head" would not be considered maladaptive because the other child appreciated the humor. However, the same term could be maladaptive if used to ridicule or tease someone.

Another area for the team to observe is the child's response to the humor of others. Can the child tell when someone is doing something funny (at his developmental level)? Can he or she read the facial expressions and vocal intonations or understand the humorous intent of an action? Children with disabilities may respond in unusual ways to actions meant to provoke laughter. Some children with sensory integration problems may find such actions such as tickling intrusive and not funny. Children with autism may totally miss the humor in actions and words, even when presented at their developmental level. The amount and control of laughter also is observed. Some children may find things funny that are not meant to be funny or laugh hysterically and uncontrollably once laughter begins. These types of observations should act as red flags that something unusual is taking place and should elicit team discussions to integrate observations from various areas to see patterns are emerging that might indicate that a delay or disorder may be present.

Because humor is most likely to be observed in "safe" or comfortable settings, the team may not observe the full range of the child's humor. Silly interactions that children feel comfortable doing with parents and siblings at home may feel inappropriate with strangers in an unfamiliar setting. For this reason, it is important to ask the parents and teachers about the types of things that elicit the child's laughter when at home or in the community (e.g., words, actions, books, events) and what the child says or does to make others laugh.

Diamond is a 3-year-old African American girl who is currently in foster care with George and Althea Brown. Diamond was removed from her single-parent home when she was 2 years old, due to her mother's use of drugs and consequent abuse and neglect. Since that time she has been with the Brown family, which has one other child, a boy who is 5 years old. If the court relinquishes custody of Diamond, the Browns want to adopt her. Diamond sees her biological mother once a week in supervised visits. The court-appointed supervisor has stated that the mother has made efforts at rehabilitation but that she has consistently relapsed. Althea remarked that Diamond is always "out of sorts" after a visit with her biological mother. The Browns feel that Diamond has made great gains since she has been with their family. They reported that she was not talking at all when they got her, that she was withdrawn, didn't move much, didn't play with toys, and acted frightened when anyone tried to pick her up. They stated that she is now cuddly, happy, and verbal, although, she is not "as far along" as her foster brother was at her age.

Two TPBA team members observed Diamond in her foster home. It was felt that this would be a more comfortable environment for her. Both of her foster parents and her foster brother were present. Diamond greeted the speech-language therapist and the psychologist at the door with a big smile. She had a cookie in her hand and said, "My cookie." Diamond and her foster brother, Benjamin, had been playing with plastic blocks when the TPBA team arrived, so the team observed as Benjamin tried to help Diamond put the pieces together to make a garage for his cars. Diamond observed Benjamin and imitated his actions. They then both laughed loudly as they took turns knocking the garage down. George picked Diamond up and put her on his lap. She said, "Blocks, Daddy. 'Benin' blocks."

George responded, "Yes, you and Benjamin made a garage for his cars." "Benin car," Diamond said, then jumped down and ran and got the cars.

When Althea played with her, Diamond got out the tea set and pretended to pour "coffee" for her foster mother. She looked at Althea frequently, offering her pretend cookies and pizza. Althea indicated that this was Diamond's favorite type of play and they did this every day, usually with real milk and cookies.

After observing the play of all the family members for about a half-hour, the facilitator joined in with Diamond and her foster father as they blew bubbles. Diamond was exuberant. She squealed with glee as she chased and jumped on each bubble. After several minutes, the facilitator asked the family to step out of the room for a few minutes. All three left to "go get us drinks" from the kitchen. Diamond watched them leave, then turned to the facilitator and said, "Blow more bubbles!" When the family returned Diamond looked up, smiled, and ran to get Benjamin. Althea commented that Diamond was extremely attached to Benjamin and that she waited every day for him to get home from kindergarten.

After the play session, the team reviewed the TPBA tape. Diamond's play behaviors and her language were delayed, but she was demonstrating a feeling of security and trust with her family. She looked to them for social cues, she sought them out for showing them her accomplishments and for affection, and she was obviously pleased to be reunited with them. She showed cooperative interactions with her foster brother and enjoyed a sense of humor about their actions. The gains she had made in 1 year showed increased exploration and cognitive skills, communication skills, social interaction, and emotional security.

CONCLUSION

The TPBA2 Observation Guidelines for emotional and social development provide a window into numerous factors that are critical to overall emotional and social development. Observation of *emotional expression* can determine a child's emotional range, which indicates if the child is easily able to communicate necessary feelings. *Emotional style* is examined to determine whether the child will need support to adjust to new situations, transitions, and changes and the amount and type of stimulation needed to obtain a positive emotional response. *Emotional and behavioral regulation* abilities are evalu-ated by looking at emotional and behavioral control during various activities. Information from these subcategories will assist in planning ways to help the child gain emotional stability. In addition, the guidelines look at the child's developing sense of self and whether intervention to encourage independence, motivation, and positive self-concept might positively influence learning and social interactions. The subcategory of *social interactions* with parents, peers, and others also is observed to ascertain what strengths exist and what needs should be addressed to enhance social relationships. Finally, the child's inner world is addressed through looking for the emotional themes that may be evident in the child's play. Identified internal conflicts that may be negatively affecting the child's emotional and social development can then be addressed as needed.

Results from the observations will be useful for developing intervention plans for children with wide ranges of emotional, behavioral, and social issues. In the case of a child who appears to have severe emotional problems, however, further evaluation will be recommended. Although these areas address many aspects of emotional and social development, the guidelines may not provide all of the information needed to enable a diagnosis of a specific emotional disturbance. A more in-depth evaluation could take into account the parent–child interaction, family dynamics, and other ecological factors, as well as the child's fantasy world, anxieties, and defense mechanisms. TPBA can provide initial information regarding some of these areas, but additional evaluation of specific concerns by a qualified professional may be necessary.

REFERENCES

Ainsworth, M.D.S., Blehar, M.C., Waters, E., & Wall, S. (1978). *Patterns of attachment.* Mahwah, NJ: Lawrence Erlbaum Associates.

American Psychiatric Association. (1994). *Diagnostic and statistical manual of mental disorders (DSM-IV), fourth edition.* Washington, DC: American Psychiatric Association.

Arroyo, S., Lesser, R.P., Gordon-Sumio Uematsu, B., Hart, J., Schwerdt, P., Andreasson, K., & Fisher, R.S. (1993). Mirth, laughter, and galastic seizures. *Brain, 116,* 757–780.

Atkinson, J.W. (1964). *An introduction to motivation.* Princeton, NJ: Van Nostrand.

Bahrick, L.E., Moss, L., & Fadil, C. (1996). Development of visual self-recognition in infancy. *Ecological Psychology, 8,* 189–208.

Bahrick, L.E., Netto, D., & Hernandez-Reif, M. (1998). Intermodal perception of adult and child faces and voices by infants. *Child Development, 69,* 1263–1275.

Barkley, R.A. (1997). Behavioral inhibition, sustained attention, and executive functions: Constructing a unifying theory of ADHD. *Psychological Bulletin, 121,* 65–94.

Barnett, D., Clements, M., Kaplan-Estrin, M., & Fialka, J. (2003). Building new dreams: Supporting parents' adaptation to their child with special needs. *Infants and Young Children, 16*(3), 184–200.

Barr-Zisowitz, C. (2000). "Sadness": Is there such a thing? In M. Lewis & J.M. Haviland-Jones (Eds.), *The handbook of emotions* (2nd ed., pp. 607–622). New York: Guilford Press.

Benenson, J.F., Apostoleris, N.H., & Parnass, J. (1997). Age and sex differences in dyadic and group interaction. *Developmental Psychology, 33,* 538–543.

Benham, A.L. (2000). The observation and assessment of young children, including the use of the Infant-Toddler Mental Health Status exam. In C.H. Zeanah, Jr. (Ed.), *Handbook of infant mental health* (pp. 249–265). New York: Guilford Press.

Bennett, D., Bendersky, M., & Lewis, M. (2002). Facial expressivity at 4 months: A context by expression analysis. *Infancy, 3,* 97–114.

Benoit, D., & Parker, K.C. (1994). Stability and transmission of attachment across three generations. *Child Development, 65,* 1444–1456.

Bergen, D. (1996). Development of the sense of humor. In W. Ruch (Ed.), *The sense of humor: Explorations of a personality characteristic* (pp. 329–358). New York: Mouton de Gruyter.

Bierman, K.L., Smoot, D.L., & Aumiller, K. (1993). Characteristics of aggressive-rejected, aggressive (nonrejected), and rejected (nonaggressive) boys. *Child Development, 64,* 139–151.

Bizi, S., Keinan, G., & Beit-Hallahmi, B. (1988). Humor and coping with stress: A test under real-life conditions. *Personality and Individual Differences, 9,* 951–956.

Boekaerts, M., Pintrich, P.R., & Zeidner, M. (2000). *Handbook of self-regulation.* San Diego: Academic Press.

Bracken, B.A., Bunch, S., Keith, T.Z., & Keith, P.B. (2000). Childhood and adolescent multidimensional self-concept: A five instrument factor analysis. *Psychology in the Schools, 37,* 483–493.

Braungart-Reiker, J.M., & Stifter, C.A. (1996). Infant responses to frustrating events: Continuity and change in reactivity and regulation. *Child Development, 67,* 1767–1779.

Brazelton, T.B., & Sparrow, J.D. (2001). *Touch points three to six: Your child's emotional and behavioral development.* Cambridge, MA: Perseus Publishing.

Briggs-Gowan, M., & Carter, A. (2005). *Brief Infant-Toddler Social Emotional Assessment (BITSEA).* San Antonio, TX: Harcourt Assessment.

Brinton, B., & Fujiki, M. (2002). Social development in children with specific language impairment and profound hearing loss. In P.K. Smith & C.H. Hart (Eds.), *Blackwell handbook of childhood social development* (pp. 588–603). Oxford, England: Blackwell.

Brockman, L.M., Morgan, G.A., & Harmon, R.J. (1988). Mastery motivation and developmental delay. In T. Wachs & R. Sheehan (Eds.), *Assessment of young developmentally disabled children.* New York: Kluwer Academic/Plenum.

Bronson, M.B. (2000). *Self-regulation in early childhood: Nature and nurture.* New York: Guilford Press.

Brown, J.R., & Dunn, J. (1996). Continuities in emotional understanding from 3 to 6 years. *Child Development, 67,* 789–802.

Busch-Rossnagel, N. (1997). Mastery motivation in toddlers. *Infants and Young Children, 9*(4), 1–11.

Buss, A.H., & Goldsmith, H.H. (1998). Fear and anger regulation in infancy: Effects on the temporal dynamics of affective expression. *Child Development, 69,* 359–374.

Buss A.H., & Plomin, R. (1975). *A temperament theory of personality development.* New York: John Wiley & Sons.

Buss, A.H., & Plomin, R. (1984). *Temperament: Early developmental traits.* Mahwah, NJ: Lawrence Erlbaum Associates.

Butterfield, P. (1996). The partners in parenting education program: A new option in parent education. *Zero to Three, 17*(1), 3–10.

Butterworth, G., & Cochran, E. (1980). Towards a mechanism of joint visual attention in human infancy. *International Journal of Behavioral Development, 3,* 253–272.

Cain, K.M., & Dweck, C.S. (1995). The relation between motivational patterns and achievement cognitions throughout the elementary school years. *Merrill-Palmer Quarterly, 41,* 25–52.

Calkins, S.D. (1994). Origins and outcomes of individual differences in emotional regulation. *Monographs of the Society for Research in Child Development, 59*(240, Pt. 2–3), 53–73.

Campbell, S.B. (1997). Behavior problems in preschool children: Developmental and family issues. *Advances in Clinical Child Psychology, 19,* 1–26.

Campos, J., Mumme, D.L., Kermoian, R., & Campos, R.G. (1994). A functionalist perspective on the nature of emotion. *Monographs of the Society for Research in Child Development, 59*(240, Pt. 2–3), 284–303.

Carey, W.B. (1998). Temperament and behavior problems in the classroom. *School Psychology Review, 27,* 522–533.

Carey W.B., & McDevitt, S.C. (1995). *Coping with children's temperament: A guide for professionals.* New York: Basic Books.

Carson, J., & Parke, R.D. (1996). Reciprocal negative affect in parent–child interactions and children's peer competency. *Child Development, 67,* 2217–2226.

Carter, A., & Briggs-Gowan, M. (2005). *Infant-Toddler Social Emotional Assessment (ITSEA).* San Antonio, TX: Harcourt Assessment.

Carvajal, F., & Iglesias, J. (2000). Looking behavior and smiling in Down syndrome infants. *Journal of Nonverbal Behavior, 24,* 225–236.

Caspi, A., & Silva, P.A. (1995). Temperamental qualities at age three predict personality traits in young adulthood: Longitudinal evidence from a birth cohort. *Child Development, 66,* 486–498.

Cassidy, J., & Berlin, L.J. (1999). The nature of the child's ties. In J. Cassidy & P.R. Shaver (Eds.), *Handbook of attachment: Theory, research, and clinical applications* (pp. 3–20). New York: Guilford Press.

Castanho, A.P., & Otta, E. (1999). Decoding spontaneous and posed smiles of children who are visually impaired and sighted. *Journal of Visual Impairment & Blindness, 93,* 659–665.

Charman, T., Swettenham, J., Baron-Cohen, S., Cox, A., Baird, G., & Drew, A. (2000). An experimental investigation of social-cognition abilities in infants with autism: Clinical implications. In D. Muir & A. Slater (Eds.), *Infant development: The essential readings in development psychology* (pp. 343–363). Malden, MA: Blackwell.

Charney, D. (1993). Psychobiologic mechanisms of posttraumatic stress disorder. *Archives of General Psychiatry, 50*(April), 294–305.

Chavira, V., Lopez, S.R., Blacher, J., & Shapiro, J. (2000). Latina mother's attributions, emotions, and reactions to problem behaviors of their children with developmental disabilities. *Journal of Child Psychology and Psychiatry, 41*(2), 245–252.

Cheah, C.S., Nelson, L.J., & Rubin, K.H. (2001). Nonsocial play as a risk factor in social and emotional development. In A. Goencue & E.L. Klein (Eds.), *Children in play, story, and school* (pp. 39–71). New York: Guilford Press.

Chess, S., & Thomas, A. (1996). *Temperament: Theory and practice.* New York: Brunner/Mazel.

Ciccetti, D., & Sroufe, L.A. (1976). The relationship between affective and cognitive development in Down syndrome infants. *Child Development, 47*(4), 920–929.

Clark, K.E., & Ladd, G.W. (2000). Connectedness and autonomy support in parent–child relationships: Links to children's socioemotional orientation and peer relationships. *Developmental Psychology, 36*(4), 485–498.

Cole, P.M., & Tamang, B.L. (1998). Nepali children's ideas about emotional displays in hypothetical challenges. *Developmental Psychology, 34,* 640–646.

Collins, W.A., Maccoby, E.E., Steinberg, L., Hetherington, E.M., & Bornstein, M.H. (2000). Contemporary research on parenting: The case for nature *and* nurture. *American Psychologist, 55*(2), 218.

Comfort, M. (1988). Assessing parent–child interaction. In D.B. Bailey, Jr., & R.J. Simeonsson (Eds.), *Family assessment in early intervention* (pp. 65–94). Columbus, OH: Charles E. Merrill.

Crick, N.R. (1997). Engagement in gender normative versus nonnormative forms of aggression: Links to social-psychological adjustment. *Developmental Psychology, 33*(4), 610–617.

Crick, N.R., Casas, J.F., & Ku, H. (1999). Relational and overt aggression in preschool. *Developmental Psychology, 33*(4), 579–588.

Crick, N.R., Casas, J.F., & Mosher, M. (1997). Physical and relational peer victimization in preschool. *Developmental Psychology, 35,* 376–385.

Crick, N.R., & Dodge, K.A. (1994). A review and reformulation of social information processing mechanisms in children's social development. *Psychological Bulletin, 115,* 74–101.

Crowe, H.P., & Zeskind, P.S. (1992). Psychophysiological and perceptual responses to infant cries varying in pitch: Comparison of adults with low and high scores on their child abuse potential inventory. *Child Abuse and Neglect, 16,* 19–29.

Deci, E., & Ryan, R. (1985). *Intrinsic motivation and self-determination in human behavior.* New York: Kluwer Academic/Plenum.

DeGangi, G. (1991a). Assessment of sensory, emotional, and attentional problems in regulatory disordered infants: Part 1. *Infants and Young Children, 3*(3), 1–8.

DeGangi, G. (1991b). Treatment of sensory, emotional, and attentional problems in regulatory disordered infants: Part 2. *Infants and Young Children, 3*(3), 9–19.

DeGangi, G. (2000). *Pediatric disorders of regulation in affect and behavior: A therapist's guide to assessment and treatment.* San Diego: Academic Press.

DeGangi, G.A., & Balzer-Martin, L. (1999). The sensorimotor history questionnaire for preschoolers. *Journal of Developmental and Learning Disorders, 3*(1), 59–83.

DeGangi, G.A., & Breinbauer, C. (1997). The symptomatology of infants and toddlers with regulatory disorders. *Journal of Developmental and Learning Disorders, 1*(1), 183–215.

DeGangi, G.A., Breinbauer, C., Roosevelt, J., Porges, S., & Greenspan, S. (2000). Prediction of childhood problems at 36 months in children experiencing symptoms of regulation during infancy. *Infant Mental Health Journal, 21*(3), 156–175.

DeGangi, G.A., Poisson, S., Sickel, R.Z., & Wiener, A.S. (1995). *Infant-Toddler Symptom Checklist.* Tucson, AZ: Therapy Skill Builders.

de Lorimer, S., Doyle, A., & Tessier, O. (1995). Social coordination during pretend play: Comparisons with nonpretend play and effects on expressive content. *Merrill-Palmer Quarterly, 41,* 497–516.

Denham, S.A. (1998). *Emotional development in young children.* New York: Guilford Press.

Denham, S.A., Mitchell-Copeland, J., Strandberg, K., Auerbach, S., & Blair, K. (1997). Parental contributions to preschoolers' emotional competence: Direct and indirect effects. *Motivation and Emotion, 27,* 65–86.

DesRosiers, F.S., & Busch-Rossnagel, N.A. (1997). Self-concept in toddlers. *Infants and Young Children, 10,* 15–26.

Diamond, K.E. (2002). The development of social competence in children with disabilities. In P.K. Smith & C.H. Hart (Eds.), *Blackwell handbook of childhood social development* (pp. 571–587). Oxford, England: Blackwell.

Dodds, J. (1987). *A child psychotherapy primer.* New York: Human Sciences Press.

Dodge, K.A., & Garber, J. (1991). Domains of emotional regulation. In J. Garber & K.A. Dodge (Eds.), *The development of emotion regulation and dysregulation* (pp. 3–14). New York: Cambridge University Press.

Dodge, K.A., & Murphy, R.R. (1984). The assessment of social competence in adolescents. *Advances in Child Behavior Analysis and Therapy, 3,* 61–96.

Doll, B., Sands, D.J., Wehmeyer, M.L., & Palmer, S. (1996). Promoting the development and acquisition of self-determined behavior. In D.J. Sands & M.L. Wehmeyer (Eds.), *Self-determination across the life span: Independence and choice for people with disabilities* (pp. 63–88). Baltimore: Paul H. Brookes Publishing Co.

Duchowny, M.S. (1983). Pathological disorders of laughter. In P.E. McGhee & J. Goldstein (Eds.), *Handbook of humor research* (pp. 89–108). New York: Springer-Verlag.

Dunn, W. (2002). *Infant-Toddler Sensory Profile.* San Antonio, TX: Harcourt Assessment.

Eckerman, C.O., & Didow, S.M. (1996). Nonverbal imitation and toddlers' mastery of verbal means of achieving coordinated interaction. *Developmental Psychology, 32,* 141–152.

Eder, D., & Hallinan, M.T. (1978). Sex differences in children's friendships. *American Sociological Review, 43,* 237–250.

Eisenberg, N. (2000). Emotion, regulation, and moral development. *Annual Review of Psychology, 51,* 665–697.

Eisenberg, N., Fabes, R.A., Shepard, S.A., Murphy, B.C., Jones, S., & Guthrie, I.K. (1998). Contemporaneous and longitudinal prediction of children's sympathy from dispositional regulation and emotionality. *Developmental Psychology, 34,* 910–924.

Eisenberg, N., Fabes, R.A., Shepard, S.A., Murphy, B.C., Maszk, P., Smith, M., & Karbon, M. (1995). The role of emotionality and regulation in children's social functioning: A longitudinal study. *Child Development, 66,* 1360–1384.

Ekman, P., & Friesen, W.V. (1969). The repertoire of nonverbal behavior: Categories, origins, usage, and coding. *Semiotica, 1,* 49–98.

Elliot, A.J., & Reis, H.T. (2003). Attachment and exploration in adulthood. *Journal of Personality and Social Psychology, 85*(2), 317–331.

Emde, R., Katz, E., & Thorpe, J. (1978). Emotional expression in infancy: II. Early deviations in Down syndrome. In M. Lewis & L. Rosenblum (Eds.), *The development of affect* (pp. 351–360). New York: Kluwer Academic/Plenum.

Erikson, E.H. (1950). *Childhood and society.* New York: Norton.

Erwin, E.J., & Brown, F. (2003). From theory to practice: A contextual framework for understanding self-determination in early childhood environments. *Infants and Young Children, 16*(1), 77–87.

Fall, M. (2001). An integrative play therapy approach to working with children. In Drewes, A.A., Carey, L.J., & Schaefer, C.F. (Eds.), *School-based play therapy* (pp. 315–328). New York: John Wiley & Sons.

Fein, G.G. (1989). Mind, meaning, and affect: Proposals for a theory of pretense. *Developmental Review, 9,* 345–363.

Field, T. (1983). High-risk infants "have less fun" during early interactions. *Topics in Early Childhood Special Education, 3,* 77–87.

Fonagy, P., Steele, M., Steele, H., Moran, G.S., & Higgitt, A.C. (1991). The capacity for understanding mental states: The reflective self in parent and child and its significance for security of attachment. *Infant Mental Health Journal, 12,* 201–218.

Fox, N.A. (1994). The development of emotional regulation: Biological and behavioral considerations. *Monographs of the Society for Research in Child Development, 59*(240, Pt. 2–3).

Fox, N.A., Henderson, H.A., Rubin, K.H., Calkins, S.D., & Schmidt, L.A. (2000). Continuity and discontinuity of behavioral inhibition and exuberance: Psychophysiological and behavioral influences across the first four years of life. *Child Development, 72,* 1–21.

Frey, K.S., & Ruble, D.N. (1990). Strategies for comparative evaluation: Maintaining a sense of competence across the lifespan. In R. Sternberg & J. Kolligan (Eds.), *Competence considered.* New Haven, CT: Yale University Press.

Friedman, H.S. (2002). *Health psychology.* Upper Saddle River, NJ: Prentice Hall.

Gauthier, Y. (2003). Infant mental health as we enter the third millennium: Can we prevent aggression? *Infant Mental Health Journal, 24*(3), 296–308.

Gest, S.D., Graham-Bermann, S.A., & Hartup, W.W. (2001). Peer experience: Common and unique features of number of friendships, social network centrality, and sociometric status. *Social Development, 10,* 23–40.

Ghaem, M., Armstrong, K.L., Trocki, O., Cleghorn, G.J., Patrick, M.K., & Shepherd, R.W. (1998). The sleep patterns of infants and young children with gastroesophageal reflux. *Journal of Paediatric Child Health, 34*(2), 160–163.

Gifford-Smith, M.E., & Brownell, C.A. (2003). Childhood peer relationships: Social acceptance, friendships, and peer networks. *Journal of School Psychology, 41*(4), 235–284.

Gitlin-Weiner, K., Sandgrund, A., & Schaefer, C. (2000). *Play diagnosis and assessment* (2nd ed.). New York: John Wiley & Sons.

Goldberg, S. (1977). Social competency in infancy: A model of parent–child interaction. *Merrill-Palmer Quarterly, 23,* 163–177.

Goldberg, S. (1990). Attachment in infants at risk: Theory, research, and practice. *Infants and Young Children, 2*(4), 11–20.

Goldsmith, H.H., & Campos, J.J. (1982). Toward a theory of temperament. In R.N. Emde & R.J. Harmon (Eds.), *The development of attachment and affiliative systems* (pp. 161–193). New York: Kluwer Academic/Plenum.

Goldsmith, H.H., & Lemery, K.S. (2000). Linking temperament, fearfulness, and anxiety symptoms: A behavioral-genetic perspective. *Biological Psychiatry, 48,* 1199–1209.

Goleman, D. (1995). *Emotional intelligence.* New York: Bantam Books.

Gomez, C.R., Baird, S., & Jung, L.A. (2004). Regulatory disorder identification, diagnosis, and intervention planning: Untapped resources for facilitating development. *Infants and Young Children, 17*(4), 327–339.

Goncu, A., Patt, M.B., & Kouba, E. (2002). Understanding young children's pretend play. In P.K. Smith & C.H. Hart (Eds.), *Blackwell handbook of child social development* (pp. 418–437). Oxford, England: Blackwell.

Gowen, J.W., & Nebrig, J.B. (2002). *Enhancing early emotional development: Guiding parents of young children.* Baltimore: Paul H. Brookes Publishing Co.

Graham, S., Doubleday, C., & Guarino, P.A. (1984). The development of relations between perceived controllability and the emotions of pity, anger, and guilt. *Child Development, 55,* 561–565.

Greenfield, P.M., & Suzuki, L.K. (1998). Culture and human development: Implications for parenting, education, pediatrics, and mental health. In W. Damon & R.M. Lerner (Eds.), *Handbook of child psychology, Vol. 4: Child psychology in practice* (5th ed., pp. 1059–1109). New York: John Wiley & Sons.

Greenspan, S.I. (1997). *Infancy and early childhood: The practice of clinical assessment and intervention with emotional and developmental challenges.* Madison, CT: International Universities Press.

Greenspan, S.I., & Wieder, S. (1999). *The child with special needs: Emotional and intellectual.* Boston: Butterworth-Heinemann.

Grolnick, W.S., Bridges, L.J., & Connell, J.P. (1996). Emotion regulation in two-year-olds; Strategies and emotional expression in four contexts. *Child Development, 67,* 928–941.

Gronau, R.C., & Waas, G.A. (1997). Delay of gratification and cue utilization: An examination of children's social information processing. *Merrill-Palmer Quarterly, 43,* 305–322.

Hall, T.M., Kaduson, H.G., & Schaefer, C.E. (2002). Fifteen effective play therapy techniques. *Professional Psychology: Research and Practice, 33,* 515–522.

Hanson, M. (1996a). Early interactions: The family context. In M. Hanson (Ed.), *Atypical infant development* (2nd ed., pp. 235–272). Austin, TX: PRO-ED.

Hanzlik, J., & Stevenson, M. (1986). Interaction of mothers who are mentally retarded, retarded with cerebral palsy, or nonretarded. *American Journal of Mental Deficiency, 90,* 513–520.

Harmon, R.J., Morgan, G.A., & Glicken, A.D. (1984). Continuities and discontinuities in affective and cognitive motivational development. *International Journal of Child Abuse and Neglect, 8,* 157–167.

Harris, P.L. (1993). Understanding emotion. In M. Lewis & J.M. Haviland (Eds.), *Handbook of emotion* (pp. 237–246). New York: Guilford Press.

Harter, S. (2003). The development of self-representation during childhood and adolescence. In M. Leary & J. Price Tangney (Eds.), *Handbook of self and identity* (pp. 610–633). New York: Guilford Press.

Harter, S., & Whitesell, N. (1989). Developmental changes in children's understanding of simple, multiple, and blended emotion concepts. In C. Saarni & P. Harris (Eds.), *Children's understanding of emotion* (pp. 81–116). New York: Cambridge University Press.

Hartup, W.W. (1983). The peer system. In E.M. Hetherington (Vol. Ed.), *Handbook of child psychology, Vol. 4: Socialization, personality, and social development* (4th ed., pp. 103–196). New York: John Wiley & Sons.

Harwood, R.L., Miller, J.G., & Irizarry, N.L. (1995). *Culture and attachment: Perception of the child in context.* New York: Guilford Press.

Hauser-Cram, P. (1998). I think I can, I think I can: Understanding and encouraging mastery motivation in young children. *Young Children, 53,* 67–71.

Hay, D.F. (1994). Prosocial development. *Journal of Child Psychology and Psychiatry and Allied Disciplines, 35,* 29–71.

Hay, D.F., Castle, J., Stimson, C.A., & Davies L. (1995). The social construction of character in toddlerhood. In M. Killen & D. Hart (Eds.), *Morality in everyday life: Developmental perspectives* (Cambridge Studies in Social and Emotional Development) (pp. 23–51). New York: Cambridge University Press.

Helwig, C.C., & Turiel, E. (2002). Children's social and moral reasoning. In P.K. Smith & C.H. Hart (Eds.), *Blackwell handbook of child social development* (pp. 475–490). Oxford, England: Blackwell.

Helwig, C.C., Zelazo, P., & Wilson, M. (2001). Children's judgment of psychological harm in normal and noncanonical situations. *Child Development, 72,* 66–81.

Hoffman, L.W. (2000). *Empathy and moral development.* New York: Cambridge University Press.

Hofstader, M., & Resnick, J.S. (1996). Response modality affects human infant delayed-response performance. *Child Development, 67,* 646–658.

Howes, C., & Farver, J. (1987). Social pretend play in 2-year-olds: Effects of age of partner. *Early Childhood Research Quarterly, 2,* 305–314.

Howes, C., Galinsky, E., & Kontos, S. (1998). Child care caregiver sensitivity and attachment. *Social Development, 7,* 25–36.

Howes, C., & Matheson, C.C. (1992). Sequences in the development of competent play with peers: Social and social pretend play. *Developmental Psychology, 28,* 961–974.

Isabella, R.A. (1995). The origins of infant–mother attachment: Maternal behavior and infant development. In R. Vasta (Ed.), *Annals of child development: Vol. 10* (pp. 57–82). London: Jessica Kingsley Publishers.

Isley, S.L., O'Neil, R., Clatfelter, D., & Parke, R.D. (1999). Parent and child expressed affect and children's social competence: Modeling direct and indirect pathways. *Developmental Psychology, 35,* 547–560.

Izard, C.E. (1979). *The maximally discriminative facial movement scoring system (MAX).* Newark, DE: University of Delaware, Instructional Resource Center.

Izard, C.E. (1991). *The psychology of emotions.* New York: Kluwer Academic/Plenum.

Izard, C.E., Fantauzzo, C.A., Castle, J.M., Haynes, O.M., Rayias, M.F., & Putnam, P.H. (1995). The ontogeny and significance of infants' facial expressions in the first 9 months of life. *Developmental Psychology, 31,* 997–1013.

Jacobs, J.E., Bleeker, M.M., & Constantino, M.J. (2003). The self-system during childhood and adolescence: Development, influences, and implications. *Journal of Psychotherapy Integration, 13,* 33–65.

Jennings, K.D., Harmon, R.J., Morgan, G.H., Gaiter, J.L., & Yarrow, L.J. (1979). Exploratory play as an index of mastery motivation: Relationships to persistence, cognitive functioning, and environmental measures. *Developmental Psychology, 15*(4), 386–394.

Kagan, J. (1981). *The second year: The emergence of self awareness.* Cambridge, MA: Harvard University Press.

Kagan, J. (1988). *Temperamental contributions to social behavior.* Presented as a distinguished scientific award address to the American Psychological Association, Atlanta, GA.

Kagan, J. (1996). The return of the ancients: On temperament and development. In S. Matthysse, D.I. Levy, J. Kagan, & F.M. Benes (Eds.), *Psychopathology: The evolving science of mental disorder* (pp. 285–297). New York: Cambridge University Press.

Kagan, J. (1998). Biology and the child. In N. Eisenberg (Ed.), *Handbook of child psychology, Vol. 3: Social, emotional, and personality development* (5th ed. pp. 177–236). New York: John Wiley & Sons.

Kagan, J., & Saudino, K.J. (2001). Behavioral inhibition and related temperaments. In R.N. Emde & J.K. Hewitt (Eds.), *Infancy to early childhood: Genetic and environmental influences on developmental change* (pp. 111–119). New York: Oxford University Press.

Kagan, J., Snidman, N., & Arcus, D. (1998). Childhood derivatives of high and low reactivity in infancy. *Child Development, 69,* 1483–1493.

Kaler, S.R., & Kopp, C.B. (1990). Compliance and comprehension in very young toddlers. *Child Development, 61,* 1997–2003.

Kaplan, H.I., & Sadock, B.J. (Eds.). (1988). *Synopsis of psychiatry: Behavioral sciences, clinical psychiatry* (6th ed.). Baltimore: Lippincott Williams & Wilkins.

Kasari, C., & Sigman, M. (1996). Expression and understanding of emotion in atypical development: Autism and Down syndrome. In M. Lewis & M.W. Sullivan (Eds.), *Emotional development in atypical children* (pp. 109–130). Mahwah, NJ: Lawrence Erlbaum Associates.

Kasari, C., Sigman, M., Mundy, P., & Yirmiya, N. (1990). Affective sharing in the context of joint attention interactions of normal, autistic, and mentally retarded children. *Journal of Autism and Developmental Disorders, 20,* 87–100.

Kelly, J.F., & Barnard, K.E. (2000). Assessment of parent–child interaction: Implications for early intervention. In J.P. Shonkoff & S.J. Meisels (Eds.), *Handbook of early childhood intervention* (pp. 258–289). Cambridge, England: Cambridge University Press.

Keogh, B.K. (2003). *Temperament in the classroom.* Baltimore: Paul H. Brookes Publishing Co.

Keogh, B.K., Coots, J.J., & Bernheimer, L.P. (1995). School placement of children with non-specific developmental delays. *Journal of Early Intervention, 20,* 65–97.

Klein, A.J. (2003). *Humor in children's lives: A guidebook for practitioners.* Westport, CT: Praeger.

Kochanska, G. (1995). Children's temperament, mothers' discipline, and security of attachment: Multiple pathways to emerging internalization. *Child Development, 66,* 597–615.

Kochanska, G. (1997). Multiple pathways to conscience for children with different temperaments: From toddlerhood to age 5. *Developmental Psychology, 33,* 228–240.

Kochanska, G., Coy, K.C., & Murray, K.T. (2001). The development of self-regulation in the first four years of life. *Child Development, 72,* 1091–1111.

Kopp, C.B. (1992). Emotional distress and control in young children. In N. Eisenberg & R.A. Fabes (Eds.), *Emotion and its regulation in early development: New directions for child and adolescent development.* San Francisco: Jossey-Bass.

Kranowitz, C.S. (1998). *The out-of-sync child: Recognizing and coping with sensory integration dysfunction.* New York: Berkley Publishing.

Kranowitz, C.S. (2003). *The out-of-sync child has fun.* New York: Berkley Publishing.

Kuczynski, L., & Kochanska, G. (1990). Development of children's noncompliance strategies from toddlerhood to age 5. *Developmental Psychology, 26,* 398–408.

Kuiper, N.A., Martin, R.A., & Olinger, L.J. (1993). Coping humour, stress, and cognitive appraisals. *Canadian Journal of Behavioural Science, 25*(1), 81–96.

Lamb, M.E., & Malkin, C.M. (1986). The development of social expectations in distress-relief sequences: A longitudinal study. *International Journal of Behavioral Development, 9,* 235–249.

Lamb, M.E., Thompson, R.A., Gardner, W., & Charnov, E.L. (1985). *Infant–mother attachment.* Mahwah, NJ: Lawrence Erlbaum Associates.

Landy, S. (2002). *Pathways to competence: Encouraging healthy social and emotional development in young children.* Baltimore: Paul H. Brookes Publishing Co.

LeDoux, J. (1996). *The emotional brain.* New York: Touchstone.

Leonard, R. (1993). Mother–child disputes as arenas for fostering negotiation skills. *Early Development and Parenting, 2,* 157–167.

Lepper, M. (1981). Intrinsic and extrinsic motivation in children: Detrimental effects of superfluous social controls. In A. Collins (Ed.), *Minnesota Symposia on child psychology: Aspects of the development of competence* (Vol. 14, pp. 155–214). Mahwah, NJ: Lawrence Erlbaum Associates.

Lewis, M. (1999). The role of self in cognition and emotion. In T. Dalgleish & M.J. Power (Eds.), *Handbook of cognition and emotion* (pp. 125–142). Chichester, England: Wiley.

Lewis, M. (2000). The self-conscious emotions: Embarrassment, shame, pride and guilt. In M. Lewis & J.M. Haviland-Jones (Eds.), *The handbook of emotions* (2nd ed., pp. 623–636). New York: Guilford Press.

Lewis, M., Alessandri, S., & Sullivan, M.W. (1992). Differences in shame and pride as a function of children's gender and task difficulty. *Child Development, 63,* 630–638.

Lewis, M., Sullivan, M.W., & Alessandri, S.M. (1990). Violation of expectancy and frustration in early infancy: The effect of loss of control. *Developmental Psychology, 26*(5), 744–753.

Lewis, M., Sullivan, M.W., & Ramsay, D.S. (1992). Individual differences in anger and sad expressions during extinction: Antecedents and consequences. *Infant Behavior and Development, 15,* 443–452.

Lynch, E.W., & Hanson, M.J. (2003). *Developing cross-cultural competence: A guide for working with young children and their families.* (3rd ed.). Baltimore: Paul H. Brookes Publishing Co.

Maccoby, E.E. (1998). *The two sexes: Growing up apart, coming together.* Cambridge, MA: Belknap/Harvard University Press.

Maccoby, E.E. (2000). Parenting and its effects on children: On reading and misreading behavior genetics. *Annual Review of Psychology, 51,* 1–27.

MacTurk, R., & Morgan, G. (Eds.). (1995). *Mastery motivation: Origins, conceptualizations, and applications. Advances in applied developmental psychology series, Vol. 12.* Norwood, NJ: Ablex.

Malatesta, C.Z., Culver, C., Tesman, J.R., & Shapard B. (1989). The development of emotion expression during the first two years of life. *Monographs of the Society for Research in Child Development, 54*(219, Pt. 1–2).

Malatesta, C.Z., & Haviland, J.M. (1982). Learning display rules: The socialization of affect expression in infancy. *Child Development, 53,* 991–1003.

Marsh, H.W. (1990). A multidimensional, hierarchical model of self-concept: Theoretical and empirical justification. *Educational Psychology Review, 2,* 77–172.

Martin, R. (2000). Humor. In A.E. Kazdin (Eds.), *Encyclopedia of psychology.* Washington, DC: American Psychological Association.

Martin, R. (2001). Humor, laughter, and physical health: Methodological issues and research findings. *Psychological Bulletin, 127*(4), 504–519.

Martin, R.P., Olejnik, S., & Gaddis, L. (1994). Is temperament an important contributor to schooling outcomes in elementary school? Modeling effects of temperament and scholastic ability on academic achievement. In W.B. Carey & S.C. McDevitt (Eds.), *Prevention and early intervention: Individual differences as risk factors for the mental health of children* (pp. 59–68). New York: Brunner/Mazel.

Martins, C., & Gaffan, E.A. (2000). Effects of maternal depression on patterns of infant–mother attachment: A meta-analytic investigation. *Journal of Child Psychology and Psychiatry, 41,* 737–746.

Marvasti, J.A. (1994). Play diagnosis and play therapy with child victims of incest. In C. Schaefer & K. O'Connor (Eds.), *Handbook of play therapy: Vol. 2* (pp. 319–348). New York: John Wiley & Sons.

Marvasti, J.A. (1997). Using metaphors, fairy tales, and storytelling in psychotherapy with children. In H. Kaduson & C. Schaefer (Eds.), *101 play therapy techniques* (pp. 35–39). Northvale, NJ: Jason Aronson Inc.

Matsumoto, D. (1990). Cultural similarities and differences in display rules. *Motivation and Emotion, 14,* 195–214.

Mattingly, L. (1997). Storytelling with felts. In H. Kaduson & C. Schaefer (Eds.), *101 play therapy techniques* (pp. 26–29). Northvale, NJ: Jason Aronson.

McCollum, J.A., & Chen, Y. (2003). Parent–child interaction when babies have Down syndrome: The perceptions of Taiwanese mothers. *Infants and Young Children, 16*(1), 22–32.

McCollum, J.A., Ree, Y., & Chen, Y. (2000). Interpreting parent–infant interactions: Cross-cultural lessons. *Infants and Young Children, 12,* 22–33.

McDevitt, S.C., & Carey, W.B. (1996). *Manual for the Behavioral Style Questionnaire.* Scottsdale, AZ: Behavioral Developmental Initiatives.

McDowell, D.J., & Parke, R.D. (2000). Differential knowledge of display rules for positive and negative emotions: Influences from parents, influences on peers. *Social Development, 9,* 415–432.

McEvoy, M.A., Estrem, T.L., Rodriguez, M.C., & Olson, M.L. (2003). Assessing relational peer victimization in preschool children: Intermethod agreement. *Topics in Early Childhood Special Education, 23*(20), 53–63.

McGhee, P.E. (1977). A model of the origins and early development of incongruity-based humour. In A.J. Chapman & H.C. Foot (Eds.), *It's a funny thing, humour* (pp. 27–36). Oxford, England: Pergamon.

McGhee, P.E. (1979). *Humor: Its origins and development.* San Francisco: W.H. Freeman.

McGhee, P.E. (1991). *The laughter remedy: Health, healing, and the amuse system.* Montclair, NJ: The Laughter Remedy.

McWilliam, R.A., & Bailey, D.B., Jr. (1992). Promoting engagement and mastery. In D.B. Bailey & M. Wolery (Eds.), *Teaching infants and preschoolers with disabilities* (pp. 229–253). New York: Macmillan.

Minde, K., Popiel, K., Leos, N., Falkner, S., Parker, K., & Handley-Derry, M. (1993). The evaluation and treatment of sleep disturbances in young children. *Journal of Child Psychology and Psychiatry, 34*(4), 521–533.

Moore, C., & Corkum, V. (1994). Social understanding at the end of the first year of life. *Developmental Review, 14,* 394–372.

Morgan, G., & Harmon, R.J. (1984). Developmental transformations in mastery motivation. In R.N. Emde & R.J. Harmon (Eds.), *Continuities and discontinuities in development* (pp. 263–291). New York: Kluwer Academic/Plenum.

Morgan, G.A., Harmon, R.J., & Maslin-Cole, C.A. (1990). Mastery motivation: Definition and measurement. *Early Education and Development, 1,* 319–339.

Mundy, P., & Willoughby, J. (1996). Nonverbal communication, joint attention and early socio-emotional development. In M. Lewis & M.W. Sullivan (Eds.), *Emotional development in atypical children* (pp. 65–88). Mahwah, NJ: Lawrence Erlbaum Associates.

Neisworth, J.T., Bagnato, S.J., & Salvia, J. (1995). Neurobehavioral markers for early regulatory disorders. *Infants and Young Children, 8*(1), 8–17.

Neisworth, J.T., Bagnato, S.J., Salvia, J., & Hunt, F.M. (1999). *TABS manual for the temperament and atypical behavior scale: Early indicators of developmental dysfunction.* Baltimore: Paul H. Brookes Publishing Co.

Nevo, O., Aharonson, H., & Klingman, A. (1996). The development and evaluation of a systematic program for improving sense of humor. In W. Ruch (Ed.), *The sense of humor: Explorations of a personality characteristic* (pp. 385–404). New York: Mouton de Gruyter.

Nevo, O., Keinan, G., & Teshimovshy-Arditi, M. (1993). Humor and pain tolerance. *Humor, 6,* 71–88.

Newcomb, A.F., & Bagwell, C. (1995). Children's friendship relations: A meta-analytic review. *Psychological Bulletin, 117,* 306–347.

Newman, J., Noel, A., Chen, R., & Matsopoulos, A.S. (1998). Temperament, selected moderating variables, and early reading achievement. *Journal of School Psychology, 36,* 215–232.

Nucci, L.P. (1996). Morality and the personal sphere of action. In E. Reed, E. Turiel, & T. Brown (Eds.), *Values and knowledge* (pp. 41–60). Mahwah, NJ: Lawrence Erlbaum Associates.

Owens-Stively, J., Frank, N., Smith, A., Hagino, O., Spirito, A., Arrigan, M., & Alario, A.J. (1997). Child temperament, parenting discipline style, and daytime behavior in childhood sleep disorders. *Journal of Developmental and Behavioral Pediatrics, 18*(5), 314–321.

Pajares, F. (1996). Self-efficacy beliefs in achievement settings. *Review of Educational Research, 66,* 543–578.

Peck, S.D. (2003). Measuring sensitivity moment-by-moment: A microanalytic look at transmission of attachment. *Attachment and Human Development, 5*(1), 38–63.

Pelco, L.E., & Reed-Victor, E. (2001). *Temperament and positive school outcomes: A two-year follow-up of at-risk children.* Paper presented at the meeting of the National Association of School Psychologists, Washington, DC.

Pelco, L.E., & Reed-Victor, E. (2003). Understanding and supporting differences in child temperament. *Young Exceptional Children, 6*(3), 2–11.

Pipp, S., Easterbrooks, M.A., & Brown, S.R. (1993). Attachment status and complexity of infant's self- and other-knowledge when tested with mother and father. *Social Development, 2,* 1–14.

Poulin-Dubois, D., Serbin, L.A., Kenyon, B., & Derbyshire, A. (1994). Infants' intermodal knowledge about gender. *Developmental Psychology, 30,* 436–442.

Prizant, B.M., Wetherby, A,M., & Roberts, J.E. (2000). Communication problems. In C.H. Zeanah, Jr. (Ed.), *Handbook of infant mental health* (2nd ed., pp. 282–297). New York: Guilford Press.

Provence, S., Erikson, J., Vater, S., & Palmeri, S. (1995). *Infant-Toddler Developmental Assessment: IDA.* Chicago: Riverside.

Pullis, M., & Cadwell, J. (1985). Temperament as a factor in the assessment of children educationally at risk. *Journal of Special Education, 19*(1), 91–102.

Rheingold, H.L. (1977). A comparative psychology of development. In H.W. Stevenson, E.H. Hess, & H.L. Rheingold (Eds.), *Early behavior: Comparative and developmental approaches* (pp. 279–293). New York: John Wiley & Sons.

Rodrigo, M.J., & Triana, B. (1996). Parental beliefs about child development and parental inferences about actions during child-rearing episodes. *European Journal of Psychology of Education, 11,* 55–78.

Rose, S.R. (1999). Towards the development of an internalized conscience: Theoretical perspectives on socialization. *Journal of Human Behavior in the Social Environment, 2,* 15–27.

Rosen, C.L. (1997). Sleep disorders in infancy, childhood, and adolescence. *Current Opinion in Pulmonary Medicine, 3*(6), 449–455.

Rothbart, M.K., & Bates, J.E. (1998). Temperament. In N. Eisenberg (Vol. Ed.), *Handbook of child psychology: Vol. 3. Social, emotional, and personality development* (5th ed., pp. 105–176). New York: John Wiley & Sons.

Rothbart, M.K., & Derryberry, D. (1981). Development of individual differences in temperament. In M.E. Lamb & A.L. Brown (Eds.), *Advances in developmental psychology, Vol. 1* (pp. 207–236). Mahwah, NJ: Lawrence Erlbaum Associates.

Roth-Hanania, R., Busch-Rossnagel, N., & Higgins-D'Alessandro, A. (2000). Development of self and empathy in early infancy: Implications for atypical development. *Infants and Young Children, 13*(1), 1–14.

Russ, S.W., Niec, L.N., & Kaugars, A.S. (2000). Play assessment of affect: The affect in play scale. In K. Gitlin-Weiner, A. Sandgrund, & C. Schaefer (Eds.), *Play diagnosis and assessment* (2nd ed., pp. 722–749). New York: John Wiley & Sons.

Russell, J.A. (1990). The preschooler's understanding of the causes and consequences of emotion. *Child Development, 61*, 1872–1881.

Saarni, C. (1999). *The development of emotional competence.* New York: Guilford Press.

Saarni, C., Mumme, D.L., & Campos, J.J. (1998). Emotional development: Action, communication, and understanding. In N. Eisenberg (Ed.), *Handbook of child psychology: Vol. 3. Social, emotional, and personality development* (5th ed., pp. 237–309). New York: John Wiley & Sons.

Sagi, A., & Hoffman, M.I. (1976). Empathic distress in the newborn. *Developmental Psychology, 12*(2), 175–176.

Scarr, S. (1981). Testing for children. *American Psychologist, 36*, 1159–1166.

Schaffer, H.R. (1996). *Social development.* Oxford, England: Blackwell.

Schunk, D.H. (1995). Self-efficacy and education and instruction. In J.E. Maddux (Ed.), *Self-efficacy, adaptation, and adjustment: Theory, research, and application* (pp. 281–303). New York: Kluwer Academic/Plenum.

Schunk, D.H., & Pajares, F. (2002). The development of academic self-efficacy. In A. Wigfield & J.S. Eccles (Eds.), *Development of achievement motivation* (pp. 15–31). San Diego: Academic Press.

Shen, Y., & Sink, C.A. (2002). Helping elementary-age children cope with disaster. *Professional School Counseling, 5*, 322–336.

Shonkoff, J.P., & Phillips, D.A. (Eds.). (2000). *From neurons to neighborhoods: The science of early childhood development.* Washington, DC: National Academies Press.

Shweder, R.A., Mahatra, M., & Miller, J.G. (1987). Culture and moral development. In J. Kagan & S. Lamb (Eds.), *The emergence of morality in young children* (pp. 1–83). Chicago: University of Chicago Press.

Sigman, M., Kasari, D., Kwon, J., & Yirmiya, N. (1992). Responses to the negative emotions of others by autistic, mentally-retarded, and normal children. *Child Development, 63*, 796–807.

Slomkowski, C.L., & Dunn, J. (1992). Arguments and relationships within the family: Differences in young children's disputes with mother and sibling. *Developmental Psychology, 28*, 919–924.

Smetana, J.G., & Braeges, J.L. (1990). The development of toddlers' moral and conventional judgments. *Merrill-Palmer Quarterly, 36*, 329–346.

Smiley, P.A., & Dweck, C.S. (1994). Individual differences in achievement goals among young children. *Child Development, 65*, 1723–1743.

Squires, J., Bricker, D., & Twombly, E. (2002). *Ages & Stages Questionnaires®: Social-emotional (ASQ:SE): A parent-completed, child-monitoring system for social-emotional behaviors.* Baltimore: Paul H. Brookes Publishing Co.

Sroufe, L.A. (1997). *Emotional development: The organization of emotional life in the early years.* Cambridge, England: Cambridge University Press.

Sroufe, L.A., & Waters, E. (1976). The ontogenesis of smiling and laugher: A perspective on the organization of development in infancy. *Psychological Review, 83*, 173–189.

Stein, N., & Levine, L.J. (1999). The early emergence of emotional understanding and appraisal: Implications for theories of development. In T. Dalgleish & M.J. Power (Eds.), *Handbook of cognition and emotion* (pp. 383–408). Chichester, England: John Wiley & Sons.

Stillwell, B.M., Galvin, M., & Kopta, S.M. (1991). Conceptualization of conscience in normal children and adolescents, ages 5 to 17. *Journal of the American Academy of Child & Adolescent Psychiatry, 30,* 16–21.

Stipek, D.J. (1993). *Motivation to learn: From theory to practice* (3rd ed.). Boston: Allyn & Bacon.

Stipek, D.J., Gralinski, J.H., & Kopp, C.B. (1990). Self-concept development in the toddler years. *Developmental Psychology, 26,* 972–977.

Stipek, D.J., & Greene, J. (2001). Achievement motivation in early childhood: Cause for concern or celebration? In S. Goldbeck (Ed.), *Psychological perspectives on early childhood education: Reforming dilemmas in research and practice.* Mahwah, NJ: Lawrence Erlbaum Associates.

Sullivan, M.W., & Lewis, M. (2003). Emotional expressions of young infants and children. *Infants and Young Children, 16*(2), 120–142.

Summers, J.A., Allison, D.B., Lynch, P.S., & Sandler, S.A.D. (1995). Behavior problems in Angelman syndrome. *Journal of Intellectual Disabilities Research, 39,* 97–106.

Super, C.M., Harkness S., van Tigen, N., van der Vlugt, E., Fintelman, J.M., & Dijkstra, J. (1996). The three R's of Dutch childrearing and the socialization of infant arousal. In S. Harkness & C.M. Super (Eds.), *Parents' cultural belief systems* (pp. 447–466). New York: Guilford Press.

Takahashi, K. (1990). Are the key assumptions of the "strange situation" procedure universal? A view from Japanese research. *Human Development, 33,* 23–30.

Teerikangas, O.M., Aronen, E.T., Martin, R.P., & Huttunen, M.O. (1998). Effects of infant temperament and early intervention on the psychiatric symptoms of adolescents. *Journal of the American Academy of Child & Adolescent Psychiatry, 37*(10), 1070–1076.

Teti, D.M., Gelfand, D.M., Messinger, D.S., & Isabella, R. (1995). Maternal depression and the quality of early attachment: An examination of infants, preschoolers, and their mothers. *Developmental Psychology, 31,* 364–376.

Thomas, A., & Chess, S. (1977). *Temperament and development.* New York: Brunner/Mazel.

Thomas, A., Chess, S., & Birch, H.G. (1968). *Temperament and behavior disorders in children.* New York: New York University Press.

Thomas, A., Chess, S., Birch, H.G., Herzig, M.E., & Korn, S. (1963). *Behavioral individuality in early childhood.* New York: New York University Press.

Thompson, R.A. (1990). Emotion and self-regulation. In R.A. Thompson (Ed.), *Socioemotional development: Nebraska symposium on motivation: Vol. 36* (pp. 383–483). Lincoln, NE: University of Nebraska Press.

Thompson, R.A. (1994). Emotion regulation: A theme in search of definition. *Monographs of the Society for Research in Child Development, 59*(240, Pt. 2–3), 25–52.

Thompson, R.A. (1999). Early attachment and later development. In J. Cassidy & P.R. Shaver (Eds.), *Handbook of attachment: Theory, research, and clinical applications* (pp. 265–286). New York: Guilford Press.

Thompson, R.A., & Leger, D.W. (1999). From squalls to calls: The cry as a developing socioemotional signal. In B. Lester, J. Newman, & F. Pedersen (Eds.), *Biological and social aspects of infant crying.* New York: Kluwer Academic/Plenum.

Thompson, R.A., & Limber, S. (1991). "Social anxiety" in infancy: Stranger wariness and separation distress. In H. Leitenberg (Ed.), *Handbook of social and evaluation anxiety* (pp. 85–137). New York: Kluwer Academic/Plenum.

Tomasello, M., Kruger, A.C., & Ratner, H.H. (1993). Cultural learning. *Behavioral and Brain Sciences, 16,* 495–511.

Tronick, E.Z., Morelli, G., & Ivey, P. (1992). The Efe forager infant and toddler's pattern of social relationships: Multiple and simultaneous. *Developmental Psychology, 28,* 568–577.

Turiel, E. (1998). The development of morality. In N. Eisenberg (Ed.), *Handbook of child psychology, Vol. 3: Social, emotional, and personality development* (5th ed., pp. 863–932). New York: John Wiley & Sons.

Vandell, D.L., & Mueller, E.C. (1995). Peer play and friendships during the first two years. In H.C. Foot, A.J. Chapman, & J.R. Smith (Eds.), *Friendship and social relations in children* (pp. 181–208). New Brunswick, NJ: Transaction.

van IJzendoorn, M.H., & Sagi, A. (1999). Cross-cultural patterns of attachment. In J. Cassidy & P.R. Shaver (Eds.), *Handbook of attachment: Theory, research, and clinical applications* (pp. 713–734). New York: Guilford Press.

Vaughn, B.E., Kopp, C.B., & Krakow, J.B. (1984). The emergence and consolidation of self control from eighteen to thirty months of age: Normative trends and individual differences. *Child Development, 55,* 990–1004.

Walker, J. (1982). Social interactions and handicapped infants. In D.D. Bricker (Ed.), *Intervention with at-risk and handicapped infants: From research to practice* (pp. 217–232). Baltimore: University Park Press.

Warren, S.L., Oppenheim, D., & Emde, R.N. (1996). Can emotions and themes in children's play predict behavior problems? *Journal of the American Academy of Child & Adolescent Psychiatry, 34,* 1331–1337.

Watson, L.R., Baranek, G.T., & DiLavore, P.C. (2003). Toddlers with autism: Developmental perspectives. *Infants and Young Children, 16*(3), 201–214.

Weatherston, D.J., Ribaudo, J., & Glovak, S. (2002). Becoming whole: Combining infant mental health and occupational therapy on behalf of a toddler with sensory integration difficulties and his family. *Infants and Young Children, 15*(1), 19–28.

Wehmeyer, M., & Palmer, S.B. (2000). Promoting the acquisition and development of self-determination in young children with disabilities. *Early Education and Development, 11,* 465–481.

Weinberg, M.K., & Tronick, E.Z. (1994). Beyond the face: An empirical study of infant affective configurations of facial, vocal, gestural, and regulatory behaviors. *Child Development, 65,* 1503–1515.

Weinberg, M.K., Tronick, E.Z., Cohn, J.F., & Olson, K.L. (1999). Gender differences in emotional expressivity and self-regulation during early infancy. *Developmental Psychology, 35,* 175–188.

Weinfeld, N.S., Sroufe, L.A., Egeland, B., & Carlson, E.A. (1999).The nature of individual differences in infant–caregiver attachment. In J. Cassidy & P.R. Shaver (Eds.), *Handbook of attachment: Theory, research, and clinical applications* (pp. 68–88). New York: Guilford Press.

Welsh, J.A., Bierman, K.L., & Pope, A.W. (2000). Play assessment of peer interaction in children. In K. Gitlin-Weiner, A. Sandgrund, & C. Schaefer (Eds.), *Play diagnosis and assessment* (2nd ed.). New York: John Wiley & Sons.

West, C. (2001). Play/therapy: A Vygotskian perspective. *Journal of Systemic Therapies, 20,* 60–67.

Westby, C. (2000). A scale for assessing development of children's play. In K. Gitlin-Weiner, A. Sandgrund, & C. Schaefer (Eds.), *Play diagnosis and assessment* (2nd ed.). New York: John Wiley & Sons.

Wetherby, A., & Prizant, B. (2003). *Communication and language issues in autism and pervasive developmental disabilities: A transactional developmental perspective.* Baltimore: Paul H. Brookes Publishing Co.

White, R. (1959). Motivation reconsidered: The concept of competence. *Psychological Review, 66,* 297–333.

Wieder, S., & Greenspan, S.I. (2001). The DIR (developmental, individual-difference, relationship-based) approach to assessment and intervention planning. *Bulletin of ZERO TO THREE, 21*(4), 11–19.

Williamson G.G., & Anzalone, M.E. (2001). *Sensory integration and self-regulation in infants and toddlers: Helping very young children interact with their environment.* Washington, DC: ZERO TO THREE: National Center for Infants, Toddlers, and Families.

Wolan, M., & Lewis, M. (2003). Emotional expressions of young infants and children: A practitioner's primer. *Infants and Young Children, 16*(2), 120–142.

Yarrow, L.J., Morgan, G., Jennings, K.D., Harmon, R.J., & Gaiter, J.L. (1982). Infants' persistence at tasks: Relationships to cognitive functioning and early experience. *Infant Behavior and Development, 5,* 131–141.

Yirmiya, N., Kasari, C., Sigman, M., & Mundy, P. (1989). Facial expressions of affect in autistic, mentally retarded, and normal children. *Journal of Child Psychology and Psychiatry, 30*(5), 725–735.

Zadjman, A. (1993). Humorous episodes in the classroom: The teacher's perspective. *Journal of Research and Development in Education, 26,* 106–116.

Zahn-Waxler, C., Friedman, R., Cole, P., Mizuta, I., & Hiruma, N. (1996). Japanese and United States preschool children's responses to conflict and distress. *Child Development, 67,* 2462–2477.

Zahn-Waxler, C., & Radke-Yarrow, M. (1990). The origins of empathic concern. *Motivation and Emotion, 14,* 107–130.

Zahn-Waxler, C., Radke-Yarrow, M., Wagner, E., & Chapman, M. (1992). Development of concern for others. *Developmental Psychology, 28,* 126–136.

ZERO TO THREE: National Center for Infants, Toddlers, and Families. (2005). *DC:0-3 R: Diagnostic classification of mental health and developmental disorders of Infancy and early childhood.* Washingon, DC: Author.

Zillman, D., & Bryant, J. (1993). Uses and effects of humor in education ventures. In P. McGhee & J.H. Goldstein (Eds.), *Handbook of humor research* (Vol. 2, pp. 1ZZ71–193). New York: Springer-Verlag.

Ziv, A. (1983). The influence of humorous atmosphere on divergent thinking. *Contemporary Educational Psychology, 8,* 68–75.

Ziv, A. (1988). Teaching and learning with humor: Experiment and replication. *Journal of Experimental Education, 57,* 5–15.

TPBA2 Observation Guidelines: Emotional and Social Development

Child's name: _____   Age: _____   Birth date: _____

Parent(s): _____   Assessment date: _____

Person(s) completing the form: _____

Directions: Record the child information (name, caregiver[s], birth date, age), assessment date, and person(s) completing this form. The Observation Guidelines provide common strengths, examples of behaviors of concern, and "ready for" next steps. As you observe the child, circle, highlight, or place a check mark next to the items listed under these three categories that correspond to the behavior(s) you observe. List any additional observations in the "Notes" column. Experienced TPBA users may opt to use only the TPBA2 Observation Notes as a method for collecting information during the assessment instead of the Observation Guidelines.

Questions	Strengths	Examples of behaviors of concern	"Ready for"	Notes
I. Emotional expression				
I. A. How does the child express emotions?	Facial Physical Vocal Verbal All of the above Idiosyncratic	Limited ways of expressing emotions Unusual ways of expressing emotions Hard to read emotions	Facial Physical Vocal Verbal Increase readability Increase modalities Increase intensity	
I. B. Does the child demonstrate a full range of emotions, including positive emotions, emotions of discomfort, and self-conscious emotions? (PR/TR)	Demonstrates full range of age-appropriate emotions	Limited range, mostly negative Limited range, not all emotions expressed Emotions do not match the situation	Happiness Anger, frustration Sadness Caution, fear Embarrassment Guilt Pride	

(continued on next page)

Observation Guidelines: Emotional and Social Development **TPBA 2**

Questions	Strengths	Examples of behaviors of concern	"Ready for"	Notes
II. Emotional style/adaptability				
I. C. What types of experiences make the child happy, unhappy, or self-conscious? (PR/TR)	A wide range of experiences give the child pleasure A wide range of experiences make the child unhappy A range of experiences make the child self-conscious	Emotions prompted by slight stimuli Emotions only prompted by intense situations Emotions triggered by limited number of stimuli Other:	Would benefit from increased pleasure from: Social interaction Sensory input Physical play Object play Dramatic play	
II. A. How does the child approach new people, activities, or situations? (Consider age) (PR/TR)	Easily adapts to new people, objects, events Shows caution in appropriate situations	Extreme caution or fear No caution or fear Unexpected emotions	Reduce: Anxiety Fear Withdrawal Anger Excessive friendliness Lack of caution	
II. B. How easily does the child adapt to transitions in activities and/or changes in routines? (PR/TR)	Transitions easily Adapts to changes in routines easily	Difficulty with transitions, change	Reduce: Difficulty with transitions Difficulty with change in routines	
II. C. How intensely does the child react to various types of stimuli? (PR/TR)	Average emotional expression to different types of input	Extreme emotions Minimal emotional intensity	Reduce amount of response to input Increase amount of response to input	
III. Regulation of emotions and arousal states				
III. A. How easily is the child able to regulate physiological states of awareness (e.g., sleeping to waking)? (PR)	No difficulty	Difficulty with state regulation	Increase ease of: Waking up Becoming drowsy Going to sleep Staying in quiet alert state Reducing fussiness/crying	

(continued on next page)

PR = see Parent Report on All About Me Questionnaire or in interview; TR = see Teacher Report on All About Me Questionnaire or in interview; M = mom; D = dad.

(continued from previous page)

Observation Guidelines: Emotional and Social Development **TPBA 2**

Questions	Strengths	Examples of behaviors of concern	"Ready for"	Notes
III. Regulation of emotions and arousal states *(continued)*				
III. B. How easily is the child able to regulate (control and move in and out of) emotional states? (PR/TR)	Can moderate emotions independently Can moderate emotions with a little support	Difficulty with emotional regulation	Provide verbal and/or physical assistance in transitioning from: Excitement Frustration Anger Sadness	
III. C. Are there identifiable patterns or "triggers" when the child has difficulty modulating emotions? (PR/TR)	No regulation issues	Sensitive to specific stimuli Difficulty tolerating limit setting Sensitive to change Sensitive to certain social interactions	Modification of: Social interactions Sensory input Specific materials Other:	
III. D. How easily is the child able to self-calm when emotions become intense? (PR/TR)	Ability to self-calm quickly	Difficulty with or unable to self-calm	Supports needed: Physical holding or movement Vocal or verbal soothing Removal of stimulation Environmental modifications Other:	
III. E. How well is the child able to inhibit impulsive actions and emotions (e.g., physical, vocal, or verbal outbursts) in order to attend to tasks?	Is able to inhibit impulses most of the time	Overly impulsive	Needs to inhibit when: Gets unwanted sensory input Interrupted in self-directed activity Adult attempts to direct Frustrated in problem-solving Frustrated in social situations Limits are set	

(continued on next page)

PR = see Parent Report on All About Me Questionnaire or in interview; TR = see Teacher Report on All About Me Questionnaire or in interview; M = mom; D = dad.

Observation Guidelines: Emotional and Social Development **TPBA 2**

Questions	Strengths	Examples of behaviors of concern	"Ready for"	Notes
III. Regulation of emotions and arousal states *(continued)*				
III. F. What is the child's predominant mood, and how long do the child's feeling states or moods last? (PR/TR)	Predominantly happy and contented	Wide mood swings Intense or extreme moods Concerning moods last a long time	Reduce: Flat affect Unhappy/sad moods Fussiness/irritability Anxiety/fear Unpredictable mood swings	
IV. Behavioral regulation				
IV. A. How well does the child comply with adult requests? (PR/TR)	Complies with adult requests most of the time Complies after negotiation or with support	Noncompliant Defiant/argumentative Does not respond intentionally Responds with fear or anxiety Responds with anger	Needs: Demonstration of behavior Assistance (visual, verbal cues) to comply Physical assistance Recognition of effort Other:	
IV. B. How well does the child control behaviors that are perceived as wrong? (PR/TR)	Controls behaviors independently Controls behaviors with adult reminders	No understanding of right and wrong Understands right and wrong, but does "wrong" anyway	Increase: Knowledge of acceptable behaviors Ability to monitor and control "right" and "wrong" behaviors	
IV. C. Does the child recognize and use social conventions of the home and mainstream culture? (PR/TR)	Use of: Social conventions Appearance conventions Functional conventions Of home Of mainstream culture	Unconventional behaviors or appearance at home Unconventional behaviors or appearance in the mainstream culture	Increase use of social conventions Increase use of appearance conventions Increase use of functional conventions Of home Of mainstream culture	

PR = see Parent Report on All About Me Questionnaire or in interview; TR = see Teacher Report on All About Me Questionnaire or in interview; M = mom; D = dad.

Transdisciplinary Play-Based System (TPBA2/TPBI2) by Toni Linder.

(continued on next page)

(continued from previous page)

Observation Guidelines: Emotional and Social Development **TPBA** 2

Questions	Strengths	Examples of behaviors of concern	"Ready for"	Notes
IV. Behavioral regulation *(continued)*				
IV. D. Does the child demonstrate unusual behavioral mannerisms that are not culturally meaningful and cannot be inhibited?	No unusual mannerisms	Stereotypical behaviors: Toward self Toward objects Unusual repetitive behaviors Unusual vocalizations Self-injurious behaviors Other:	Reduce: Facial movements Physical movements/ stereotypies Toward self Toward objects Vocalizations Self-injurious behaviors Other unusual behaviors	
V. Sense of self				
V. A. How does the child demonstrate autonomy and a desire to make decisions, consistent with the culture of family? (PR)	Can tolerate a balance between adult choices and his/her choices Can function as independently as expected by his/her family	Overly controlling Overly dependent	Reduce need to control all decisions Increase ability to make choices Reduce dependency on adult (as is culturally appropriate) for: Social interactions Play Self-help	
V. B. How does the child demonstrate achievement motivation?	Persists in trying to reach goals Shows pride in accomplishments	Too easily frustrated with challenging situations Limited mastery motivation	Decrease frustration with failure Increase mastery motivation for: Social interactions Play skills Self-help skills	
V. C. What developmentally relevant characteristics related to self can the child identify?	Emotions Possessions (my, mine, yours) Physical characteristics (boy, girl, big) Things he or she is good at	Limited understanding of self Negative understanding of self	Increase labeling of: Emotions Possessions Physical characteristics Increase awareness of positive attributes and abilities	

(continued on next page)

PR = see Parent Report on All About Me Questionnaire or in interview; TR = see Teacher Report on All About Me Questionnaire or in interview; M = mom; D = dad.

Transdisciplinary Play-Based System (TPBA2/TPBI2)
by Toni Linder.

Observation Guidelines: Emotional and Social Development **TPBA** 2

Questions	Strengths	Examples of behaviors of concern	"Ready for"	Notes
VI. Emotional themes in play				
VI. A. How logical and flexible are the child's patterns of thought in play?	Play has logical sequence Has ability to shift plans	Inflexible, repetitive themes in play	Increase sequential script play Reduce repetition of themes and sequences	
VI. B. What awareness of others' emotional roles and actions is reflected in the child's dramatic play?	Plays nurturer or "good guy" Range of actions, not all aggressive	Plays primarily negative roles (e.g., pessimistic, worried, depressed) Plays primarily aggressive roles	Replace roles of punisher or "bad guy" with more positive roles Replace excessive aggressive actions with more prosocial actions or problem solving	
VI. C. What emotional themes are expressed in the child's play?	Nurturance Security Happiness	Excessive expression of: Power/control Dependence/independence Loss Fear/anxiety Violence Trauma Lack of emotional expression	Further evaluation needed Express or expand range of emotional themes Support understanding of causes of emotions Support redirection of emotions to appropriate targets Support cognitive problem solving related to themes	
VI. D. How does the child integrate and match thoughts, actions, and emotions in dramatic play?	Shows consistent thoughts, action, and expression of feelings	Actions and thoughts don't match feelings expressed in play	Help child identify feelings and associate them with actions	
VII. Social interactions				
VII. A. What emotions does the child respond to in others? (PR/TR)	Reads and responds to the feelings of others: Pleasurable feelings Sad or fearful feelings Angry feelings	Does not respond appropriately to emotions of others	Increase responsiveness to feelings of others: Pleasurable feelings Sad or fearful feelings Angry feelings Appropriate expression of empathy	

(continued on next page)

PR = see Parent Report on All About Me Questionnaire or in interview; TR = see Teacher Report on All About Me Questionnaire or in interview; M = mom; D = dad.

Transdisciplinary Play-Based System (TPBA2/TPBI2)
by Toni Linder.

(continued from previous page)

Observation Guidelines: Emotional and Social Development **TPBA 2**

Questions	Strengths	Examples of behaviors of concern	"Ready for"	Notes
VII. Social interactions (continued)				
VII. B. How does the child demonstrate a sense of pleasure and trust in his or her parents? (PR/TR)	Looks for cues or reassurance (D/M) Shares affection (D/M) Seeks calming (D/M) Shares accomplishment (D/M) Plays turn-taking games (D/M) Responds to parent's emotions (D/M)	Angry, resistant, or avoidant interactions with mother Angry, resistant, or avoidant interactions with father	Increase the following: Looks for cues or reassurance (D/M) Shares affection (D/M) Seeks calming (D/M) Shares accomplishment (D/M) Plays turn-taking games (D/M) Responds to parent's emotions (D/M) Pleasurable interactions (D/M)	
VII. C. How does the child differentiate among people? (PR/TR)	Responds age appropriately to differences	Indiscriminant social interactions with people Overly selective interactions	Reduce anxiety or fear of unfamiliar people Reduce inappropriate affection and trust Increase ability to differentiate characteristics of people	
VII. D. What types of social play are demonstrated with siblings and/or peers? (PR/TR)	Observation of others' play Independent play Parallel play Associative play Cooperative play Reciprocal and complementary roles in play	Lack of social play Delayed or inappropriate social interactions with peers Delayed or inappropriate social interactions with siblings	Decrease: Solitary, repetitive, or non-purposeful play Increase: Observation of others' play Independent play Parallel play Associative play Cooperative play Reciprocal and complementary roles in play	

(continued on next page)

PR = see Parent Report on All About Me Questionnaire or in interview; TR = see Teacher Report on All About Me Questionnaire or in interview; M = mom; D = dad.

Transdisciplinary Play-Based System (TPBA2/TPBI2)
by Toni Linder.

(continued from previous page)

Observation Guidelines: Emotional and Social Development **TPBA** 2

Questions	Strengths	Examples of behaviors of concern	"Ready for"	Notes
VII. Social interactions *(continued)*				
VII. E. How does the child deal with social conflict? (PR/TR)	Occasionally gives in to others or shares Uses adult for support Negotiates/compromises	Cries/screams Excessive withdrawal Aggressive response directed toward toys or people	Increase: Use of adult for support Use of words, gestures, sign Compromise and problem solving Anticipation of problem situations	
VII. F. How do other children react to the child in dyads or in group settings? (TR)	Popular with other children Accepted by other children	Rejected or avoided by other children Bullied by other children	Increase social initiations to decrease neglect or rejection by peers Decrease negative behaviors causing rejection by peers	
VII. G. How is the child's sense of humor demonstrated? (PR/TR)	Laughs and uses humor appropriately to make others laugh	Uses mean or negative teasing or humor with others	Increase laughter in social situations Reduce inappropriate laughter Reduce use of teasing or cruel humor	

PR = see Parent Report on All About Me Questionnaire or in interview; TR = see Teacher Report on All About Me Questionnaire or in interview; M = mom; D = dad.

Transdisciplinary Play-Based System (TPBA2/TPBI2)
by Toni Linder.

TPBA2 Observation Notes:
Emotional and Social Development

Child's name: _____ Parent(s): _____

Birth date: _____ Assessment date: _____ Age: _____

Person(s) completing the form: _____

Directions: Record the child information (name, caregiver[s], birth date, age), assessment date, person(s) completing this form, and your observations about the child in the spaces below. You are encouraged to review the corresponding TPBA2 Observation Guidelines prior to recording your observations here, as the Guidelines list what to look for. Newer TPBA users may opt to use the TPBA2 Observation Guidelines as a method for collecting information during the assessment instead of the TPBA2 Observation Notes.

I. Emotional expression (means and range of expression, stimuli for happiness, sadness, anger)

II. Emotional style/adaptability (approach to novel situations, adaptability to change, emotional intensity)

III. Regulation of emotions and arousal states (regulation of physiological and emotional states, triggers for emotions, timing, self-calming, inhibition of impulsivity, mood)

(continued on next page)

IV. Behavioral regulation (compliance, inhibits wrong behavior, social conventions, mannerisms)

V. Sense of self (autonomy, desire for independence, mastery, motivation, understanding of self-characteristics)

VI. Emotional themes in play (logic, flexibility, awareness of others, roles, emotional themes, match of actions, and feelings)

VII. Social interactions (cue reading, empathy, attachment, differentiation, peers/siblings, conflict resolution, social play level, function of humor)

TPBA2 Age Table: Emotional and Social Development

Child's name: _____ Age: _____ Birth date: _____

Parent(s): _____ Assessment date: _____

Person(s) completing the form: _____

Directions: Based on the observations recorded on the TPBA2 Observation Guidelines and/or TPBA2 Observation Notes, review the Age Table to determine the age level that most closely matches the child's performance. It may be helpful to circle items on the Age Table that the child can do. If items are circled across multiple age levels, find the child's age level by finding the mode (i.e., determine which age level has the most circled items). Age levels after 12 months/1 year represent ranges rather than individual months and are preceded by "By." If the most circled items appear in one of these age levels, consider the child's age level to be the month shown (e.g., if the most circled items appear in the "By 21 months" level, the child's age level for that subcategory is 21 months).

Note: The Emotional Style/Adaptability subcategory is not included in this Age Table. This subcategory helps users observe qualitative performance, but is not related to a child's age level.

Note: There are no 10- and 11-month levels for the Emotional and Social Domain, because those months do not have specific associated milestones.

Age level	Emotional expression	Regulation of emotions and arousal states	Behavioral regulation	Sense of self	Emotional themes in play	Social interactions
1 month	Displays rage-anger, sadness-distress, pleasure-joy Wide-eyed staring Shows disgust with bitter or sour tastes	Can be comforted and calmed by touching and rocking Stares at faces and responds by quieting Alert about 1 out of every 10 hours	Expects feeding at certain intervals Cries for assistance	Studies environment Interested in faces of others	Play reflects interest, pleasure, distress (0–9 months) *See Emotional expression*	Focuses on faces and responds by quieting Responds to touch and vocalization Responds with synchrony to adults' mouth movements
2 months	Distinguishes between anger, surprise, and sadness in adults Infant's facial expression changes every 7–9 seconds Shows interest by staring Smiles at interesting sensory stimuli	Uses gaze aversion when over stimulated Quiets self with sucking Patterns of eating, sleeping, and alertness emerge	Responds positively to quiet voice of adult holding him/her Adjusts body to person holding him/her Anticipates movement of objects; reacts with body movement	Follows person's movement with eyes Coordinating senses (e.g., looking for sounds, sucking at sight of bottle) Begins to recognize family members	Play reflects interest, pleasure, distress (0–9 months) Responds with total-body excitement to familiar face *See Emotional expression*	Pays attention to parent's eyes (over mouth) Responds to people with excitement, leg waving, panting, or vocalizing Mouth and hand play

(continued on next page)

(continued from previous page)

Age Table: Emotional and Social Development **TPBA** 2

Age level	Emotional expression	Regulation of emotions and arousal states	Behavioral regulation	Sense of self	Emotional themes in play	Social interactions
3 months	Smiles at active stimuli Expresses all basic emotions (including surprise) Startles at loud noises, sudden movements	Sleeps regularly (16.5 hours/day, 3–4 hours continuously) Able to calm down or self-quiet for brief periods Uses sucking, looking, or other sensory modalities to calm self Cycles through various states with less crying and more alert times	Tracks slowly moving objects Stops sucking to listen May voluntarily hold and wave a toy Protests when left alone Has predictable eating schedule	Begins to recognize he or she can make things happen (0–3 months) Explores own face, eyes and mouth with hand Discriminates among voices, people, tastes, proximity, and object size	Play reflects all emotions Brightens up when provided appropriate visual, auditory, and/or tactile experiences Repeats pleasurable actions	Much of play is solitary (0–3 months) Enjoys responding to people and eye-to-eye contact Recognizes caregivers on sight True social smile Anticipates next step in familiar game Looks at one when talked to Enjoys caregiving from anyone (0–3 months) Smiles indiscriminantly (0–3 months)
4 months	Laughs while socializing Cries if play is disrupted Smiles more with familiar people Shows angry expression when desired object is denied (3–4 months)	Has ways to soothe self Sleeping and waking bouts become more regular May be responsive an hour or more at a time	Shows control over behaviors by self-soothing and self-stimulation	May smile at mirror image Begins showing pleasure at mastery	Play reflects extremes of emotion	Vocalizes to initiate socializing Responds differently to different people Shows interest by smiling, reaching, and touching Babies look at and touch each other (3–4 months)
5 months	Fear of loud or unexpected noises Laughing "play face" appears	Stops crying when people talk to him/her Can recover from distress with caregiver support within 15 minutes Alert almost 2 hours	May protest when adult tries to take toy Vocalizes to get attention Interrupts others' conversations by vocalizing	Discriminates between self and mother in mirror Knows parents, siblings, who is a stranger	Responds to social overtures with an emotional response Experiments with adult's responses to emotions expressed	Studies caregiver's face Shows anger or protest when frustrated Shows preference for familiar faces Responds differently to stranger (may withdraw)

(continued on next page)

Transdisciplinary Play-Based System (TPBA2/TPBI2) by Toni Linder.

Age Table: Emotional and Social Development **TPBA 2**

Age level	Emotional expression	Regulation of emotions and arousal states	Behavioral regulation	Sense of self	Emotional themes in play	Social interactions
6 months	Shows pleasure with gurgles and coos Growls and grunts to show displeasure Squeals, giggles, belly laughs with excitement	Sleeping and waking bouts begin to lengthen and consolidate (3–6 months) May have abrupt mood changes	Resists actions or objects he/she doesn't want Objects to toys being taken away (4–6 months)	Turns to own name Indicates need for help Explores body parts and how they move Smiles at own image in mirror	Responds to meaning of specific emotional expressions in others Imitates facial expressions and actions of others in play	Responds with enthusiasm to familiar social games and routines Calmed more easily by familiar caregiver Distinguishes a photo of mother from one of stranger Spontaneous greeting of mother
7 months	Distinguishes friendly and angry talking May show "pout face" or sadness Displays true anger (4–7 months)	Unexplained crying stops Has established routine (4–7 months)	Cries or shouts for attention Begins to learn behavioral implications of actions Learning meaning of "no" through tone of voice	May reach for and touch mirror image Derives pleasure in attaining goals May fear strangers Likes pictures of babies	Vocalizes attitudes and emotions of pleasure and displeasure in play Shows humor, begins to tease in play Repeats series of actions from past	Plays social games (4–7 months) Will "woo" caregiver with sounds, smiles, gestures Cries in response to another infant's cry
8 months	Anger, distrust, disgust expressed more intensely and can be differentiated Shows "knit brow" interest (2–8 months)	Regular naps several times a day	Responds to parent's facial expressions to help moderate emotions	Claps when does something he/she likes May try to kiss mirror image	Negative emotional response to play overtures from unfamiliar persons Resists pressure to play with something not of his/her choice	Explores own and caregiver's face and body parts (4–8 months) May cry if caregiver leaves or stranger is close by (3–8 months) Intentional two-way communication or turn taking (4–8 months)
9 months	Expresses fear Fears heights; aware of vertical space (4–9 months) High intensity elation in social game	Recovers within 10 minutes by being involved in social interactions Sleeps 14.25 hours/day; 84% sleep through the night (6–9 months)	Wants approval Looks to adult to see if he/she is in trouble Follows simple commands Beginning to respond to tone of voice with "no," but may not stop actions	Repeats actions if applauded Fights for possessions Moves away from adult and looks back to "check in" (showing understanding of separateness) Actions shift to task-directed outcomes with objects	Play reflects interest, pleasure, frustration (0–9 months) Understands that adult signals convey information and emotions (6–9 months) Understands his/her actions arouse emotions Repeats play that got laughter or applause May do nondesired action to test response	Initiates intentional interactions (e.g., reaches for nose, hair, mouth) Different responses to different people Wants to play near mother Tries to get attention of other babies Approaches peer Sensitive to other baby's cry

(continued on next page)

Transdisciplinary Play-Based System (TPBA2/TPBI2) by Toni Linder.

Age level	Emotional expression	Regulation of emotions and arousal states	Behavioral regulation	Sense of self	Emotional themes in play	Social interactions
By 12 months or 1 year	Surprise emerges (8–12 months) Shyness emerges (9–12 months) Demonstrates fear of strange people and places (7–12 months) Laughs at incongruities, novelty, self-produced actions "Knit brow" shows interest during problem-solving actions	Maintains security through social referencing (7–12 months) 90% of infants sleep through the night Self-soothes in own way May resist napping Has tantrums	Aware of own actions and implications Can obey requests Understands what "no" means Is not always cooperative May refuse new foods Can delay a response (5–12 months) Beginning to develop a conscience	Shows delight in making toy perform (7–12 months) May demand help from adult, even when not needed "Shows off" Pleasure at mastery seen (4–12 months) Differentiates others by voices, gender, age (7–12 months)	Communicates intentions and desires to listener (9–12 months) Differentiates threatening and nonthreatening situations in play Play reflects affection toward humans and favored objects Needs to be near parent in play	Enjoys exploring face and body of caregiver (8–12 months) Begins to imitate actions of caregiver or other child (8–12 months) Plays hide games (8–12 months) Isolated play and beginning parallel play (8–12 months) Can move away from parent but will maintain eye contact (7–12 months) Separation distress and anxiety (7–12 months) May offer a toy to another child Enjoys turn-taking games (e.g., Peekaboo, rolling ball) Begins organizing behavior and emotions Can initiate or respond to 3 sequential turns in communication Shows signs of empathy (10–12 months)
By 15 months	Shows guilt at wrong-doing Gives affection to toys and others	May throw temper tantrum to get his/her way Has appropriate emotional responses to various situations Sleeps 13.75 hours/day (12–15 months)	Understands simple "right" and "wrong" Resists adult control Follows "don't" requests 45% of time; "do" request only 14% Looks at adult before doing something out of bounds	Says "no," asserts independence Moves from showing signs of awareness of another's pain to doing something to help (12–15 months) Starts to enjoy moving away from adults Persists at accomplishing complex tasks	Shows affection and nurturing in role play with dolls Recreates common routines	Shares joint attention on an object (8–14 months) Imitates actions of another person (8–14 months) Capable of turn-taking (8–14 months) Likes to be around other children (8–14 months) Assists others in distress by patting, touching, offering objects

(continued on next page)

Transdisciplinary Play-Based System (TPBA2/TPBI2) by Toni Linder.

(continued from previous page)

Age Table: Emotional and Social Development **TPBA 2**

Age level	Emotional expression	Regulation of emotions and arousal states	Behavioral regulation	Sense of self	Emotional themes in play	Social interactions
By 18 months	Predominately happy (12–18 months) Pride and shame emerge Increase in anger and tantrums Increase in fears May show depression if loss experienced Jealousy, especially toward siblings or peers Frustration with inability to express wishes Whines and cries Shows rage (7–18 months)	Gets upset easily if routine is changed Naps once a day Beginning to move away from source of distress and seek out adult for comfort Beginning to gain self-control (15–18 months)	Shows anger; hits, bites, punches, yells, bangs, screams Shows awareness of caregiver's wishes and expectations Uses conscience-like verbalizations ("no" "don't") before doing something out of bounds Brings things when requested Seeks praise for good behavior	Wants praise for good performance Assertive and independent Pushes for autonomy and exploration but still needs to stay in touch with caregiver (12–18 months) Practices moving away and coming back (12–18 months) Persists with tasks of moderate difficulty (12–18 months) Is able to represent self and others in dramatic play (12–18 months) Awareness of failure	Possesses an understanding of self and others as communicators of emotion (12–18 months) Dramatic play may reflect worries Uses toys in pretend actions, relating them to one another, in reflection of daily actions	Parallel play (plays with same toys, but not with other child) (15–18 months) Pretends to feed dolls, mother Spontaneously shares food, toys Vocalizes to caregiver from a distance Sets limits on others (e.g., tells them to stop) Shows concern when someone is in distress, makes offer of support (12–18 months) Expresses caring for another vocally and physically Can engage in 20–30 circles of communication with verbal, gestural, and physical communication
By 21 months	Reacts to others' sadness and takes steps to comfort them (e.g., may offer an object) (18–21 months)	Uses objects to distract or calm self Uses cues that assistance is needed to calm (12–21 months) Intense crying when can't communicate needs with words	Follows single-step directions (18–21 months) Engages in self-tattling Sets a standard to evaluate success of actions Conscious of adult approval/disapproval Pulls hair, knocks other children down, hugs too tightly	Recognizes self in mirror (18–21 months) Refers to self by name Possessive of own things	Communicates needs, wishes, feelings with words and gestures Acts out things others do Play begins to symbolize thoughts and feelings	Is possessive of toys and has difficulty sharing (13–21 months) Engages in tug-of-war with other child over materials Constantly demands caregiver's attention Peer play involving turns escalates Imitation of peer is common Obtaining desired toy takes precedence over social interaction Beginning to respond to others' feelings

(continued on next page)

Transdisciplinary Play-Based System (TPBA2/TPBI2) by Toni Linder.

(continued from previous page)

Age Table: Emotional and Social Development **TPBA** 2

Age level	Emotional expression	Regulation of emotions and arousal states	Behavioral regulation	Sense of self	Emotional themes in play	Social interactions
By 24 months or 2 years	Shows self-conscious emotions of shame and embarrassment (15–24 months) Cries when angry or frustrated May have fear of the dark, thunder, trains, animal noises	Sleeps 12–13 hours at night, 1–2-hour nap Saying "no" is at its height (15–24 months) Frequent tantrums (15–24 months) Gets upset if he/she cannot meet standards (15–24 months) Masturbation may be self-calming (18–24 months) Connects actions and consequences (18–24 months) Attempts to control feelings through verbal, physical, or social means Redirects actions when upset	Displays some rudimentary self-control to stop self from wrong behavior Wants to control others and orders them around (15–24 months) Complies approximately 45% of the time (15–24 months) Shows feelings of shame, embarrassment, and guilt; uses words to evaluate behavior as good or bad (21–24 months) Can delay gratification May hit or bite others Knows own behavior can make others sad or mad	Interest in gender, body parts, functions "Me," "I," "mine" predominate (18–24 months) Self-description and self-evaluation (18–24 months) Sense of omnipotence and capability (19–24 months) Distinguishes and names self in pictures and mirror (19–24 months) Displays sense of pride in accomplishment (18–24 months) May cry at failure to accomplish goal (18–24 months) Works to do things by self ("me do") (18–24 months)	Onset of emotion language; begins to label emotions; plays emotion games; pretend play and object substitution emerge (18–24 months) Represents experiences and feelings through dramatic play, primarily nurturing and self-care Creates mental representations of feelings and ideas in dramatic play	Alternates between clinging and resistance to familiar adult Some pretend play directed toward others (13–24 months) Begins to enjoy parallel play, but still cannot cooperate (13–24 months) May offer toy and smile (13–24 months) Begins to use prosocial behaviors in interaction Girls may withdraw from the roughhouse play of boys
By 30 months	Shows empathy Conveys intense emotional expressions with whole body Fears spatial change (e.g., movement, change of location of objects) Produces complex facial expressions	Can delay gratification; wait for what he/she wants or for reward (18–30 months) Develops ability to adjust emotional responses to fit others' emotions Sleeps 13 hours/day May have whole-body tantrums	Shares toys, helps others, cooperates in games; shows empathic concern (24–30 months) Knows rules, standards, cultural values of family Shows remorse	May attack other children with intent to hurt May break toys May become aggressive in disputes with other children around possessions or interference with activities Has categorical knowledge of self (e.g., knows age, sex, physical characteristics, good or bad behavior, and competence) Names own and others' possessions	Role play in isolated play related to nurturing, care, control, and independence Can deal with more complex wishes and feelings (play may reflect closeness, separateness, exploration, assertiveness, anger, pride and showing off)	Able to be both leader and follower (25–30 months) Pretend play often reflects same theme as play of peer, not integrated (parallel play) (25–30 months) Shares feelings about own and others' emotions

(continued on next page)

Transdisciplinary Play-Based System (TPBA2/TPBI2) by Toni Linder.

Age Table: Emotional and Social Development **TPBA** 2

Age level	Emotional expression	Regulation of emotions and arousal states	Behavioral regulation	Sense of self	Emotional themes in play	Social interaction
By 36 months or 3 years	Experiences many visual fears (e.g., masks, the dark, animals) Full range of emotions evident, including envy and guilt (24–36 months) Refers to needs, emotions, and mental states Shows affection (18–36 months) Shows physical anger	Is able to talk about emotions and what elicits them (24–36 months) Is able to request adults' help to handle emotions (24–36 months) May begin to recover from tantrums by him/herself Has capacity for self-control Shows effort to control emotions	Begins to internalize rules and follow part of the time (24–36 months) Has difficulty transferring rules across time and settings (24–36 months) Needs adult support to control impulse (24–36 months) Begins to generalize about what can and can't be touched (24–36 months) Tries to "right" a "wrong" or "fix" a situation	Talks about all the things he/she can do (24–36 months) May show shame at not being able to do things (24–36 months) Offers concrete description of self Begins to understand harm to another and demonstrates understanding in play Prefers challenging tasks Identifies self by gender	Engages in doll play with attribution of emotion to dolls Uses pretend play to act out and talk about feelings (24–36 months) Pretends to be a variety of characters with a variety of feelings Play may be between "good" and "bad" characters Play may reflect separation, sibling relationships, discipline, or physical or sexual abuse (30–36 months)	Engages in associative play (playing together with same materials, but not same goals) Involves other children or adults in play sequences Needs adult to suggest alternative actions or sequences Sociodramatic play with cooperative, goal-oriented play evident Beginning to form friendships
By 48 months or 4 years	Exhibits jealousy Verbal anger Silliness Fear of night, loss of parent, extreme differences (e.g., old people, different nationalities) Development of more enhanced sense of guilt and shame motivate positive behavior	Occasional aggression with peers May demonstrate extremes of emotions Wants to feel in control, talks to self and others about feelings and how to feel better	Discriminates appropriate roles and behaviors Has internalized rules about "dos" and "don'ts" May do something even though knows it's wrong May argue with caregiver about what he/she is supposed to do Compliance about 85% of the time for "don't" requests; 30% for "do" requests	Describes causes and consequences of emotions Argumentative Proud of accomplishments (boasts) Knows what fears are (uses words "afraid," "scared") Can go on errands unattended Can self-initiate, plan, and organize problem solving without assistance Believes he/she can do anything	Enjoys pretending to be someone else Can reverse roles Dual representation; able to discuss hypothetical situations Often plays out aggression through "good" and "bad" characters Enjoys role playing, being afraid (chasing, scaring, laughing), and being in control May begin to use fantasy characters to represent own ideas or issues	Can usually distinguish between real and pretend 90% of pretend play is cooperative Preference for same-sex peers Little separation distress Formation of attachments to peers, making friends Silly, boisterous humor (silly names, rhyming, dancing) Attempts to solve conflicts independently (36–48 months)

(continued on next page)

Transdisciplinary Play-Based System (TPBA2/TPBI2) by Toni Linder.

Age Table: Emotional and Social Development **TPBA** 2

Age level	Emotional expression	Regulation of emotions and arousal states	Behavioral regulation	Sense of self	Emotional themes in play	Social interactions
By 60 months or 5 years	Easily has feelings "hurt" Fears being lost, sleeping alone	Able to think about emotions and use discussion to help child Self-talk helps child control emotions	Judges right and wrong by what gets punishment Knows what behavior is needed to make friends Has a good understanding of rules Tattles on others and recommends punishment	Judges own characteristics Eager to learn new things Can modify actions in different situations Begins to compare own performance to others, but still has high self-beliefs	Coordinates actions with other players; able to verbally reflect on emotions Elaborate fantasy play possible reflecting inner feelings, fears, nurturing Issues reflected in play may include connectedness, physical well-being, power, or control	Wants to please peers to keep them near by Starts enjoying jokes even when not understood Shares conversations and play related to wide variety of topics
By 72 months or 6 years	Resentment of correction Fears ghosts, witches, insects, thunder, fire, wind, storms, blood, injury, death	Can moderate emotions in different situations as appropriate (e.g., church, playground) Can think about emotions and make conscious changes to responses Aware of feeling more than one emotion at one time	Can play fairly Has values of what is right Justice and rules are unchangeable; may be rigid with rules for others' behavior Shows respect for others Can negotiate actions and consequences Understands and accepts punishment for doing wrong Understands concept of equality or equal distribution as standard for fairness	Desires acceptance of others, can modify actions so others will like him/her Attention-seeking behaviors Developing a sense of own abilities compared to others across many areas, including social, physical, academic skills, and appearance	Sexual curiosity can be expressed in doctor play (48–72 months) Increasingly plays out difficult emotional experiences (48–72 months) Plays themes of power, control, loss Able to identify causes of emotion in characters from stories (60–72 months) Fantasy play may be quite detailed and elaborate Plays exaggerated roles and actions	Plays joint games such as puppet shows (48–72 months) Play shows increasing awareness of others' thoughts and feelings Participates in group activities (48–72 months) Is capable of waiting for a turn Remembers and makes up jokes for others Plays with opposite-sex peers in discrete roles Can organize group play Playful conversations are typical

Transdisciplinary Play-Based System (TPBA2/TPBI2) by Toni Linder.

TPBA2 Observation Summary Form: Emotional and Social Development

TPBA Play-Based TPBI
TPBC ™

Child's name: _____   Age: _____   Birth date: _____

Parent(s): _____

Person(s) completing the form: _____   Assessment date: _____

Directions: For each of the subcategories below, shown in a 1–9-point Goal Attainment Scale, circle the number that indicates the child's developmental status, using findings from the TPBA2 Observation Guidelines or TPBA2 Observation Notes for this domain. Next, consider the child's performance in relation to same-age peers by comparing the child's performance with the TPBA2 Age Table. Use the Age Table to arrive at the child's age level for each subcategory (follow directions on the Age Table). Then, circle AA, T, W, or C by calculating percent delay:

If a child's age level < chronological age: 1 − (age level/CA) = _____ % delay

If child's age level > chronological age: (age level/CA) − 1 = _____ % above

To calculate CA, subtract the child's birth date from the assessment date and round up or down as appropriate. When subtracting days, take into consideration the number of days in the month (i.e., 28, 30, 31).

TPBA2 Subcategory	Level of the child's ability as observed in functional activities									Rating compared with other children of same age				
	1	2	3	4	5	6	7	8	9	Above average (AA)	Typical (T)	Watch (W)	Concern (C)	Age level (mode)
Emotional expression	Expresses emotions related to comfort and discomfort using sounds and physical movements.		Experiments with different types, levels, and forms of emotional expression to communicate needs.		Often expresses extremes of emotions to get needs met and to elicit a response from others.		Expresses full range of emotions, with the predominant emotions being positive.		Easily communicates full range of emotions in appropriate contexts, with an acceptable level of intensity.	AA	T	W	C	_____
										Comments:				
Emotional style/ adaptability	Does not adapt to new people, objects, events, or changes in routines without extreme, long-lasting emotional reactions.		Adapts to changes in people, objects, events, or routines with much verbal preparation and environmental support.		Adapts to changes in people, objects, events, or routines using motivating, logical connections to the transition situation.		Adapts to changes in people, objects, events, or routines with verbal preparation.		Adapts to new people, objects, events, or changes in routines, independently, with an appropriate amount of caution and emotional reaction.	AA	T	W	C	_____
										Comments:				

(continued on next page)

Transdisciplinary Play-Based System (TPBA2/TPBI2) by Toni Linder

(continued from previous page)

Observation Summary Form: Emotional and Social Development **TPBA 2**

TPBA2 Subcategory	Level of the child's ability as observed in functional activities									Rating compared with other children of same age				Age level (mode)
	1	2	3	4	5	6	7	8	9	Above average (AA)	Typical (T)	Watch (W)	Concern (C)	
Regulation of emotions and arousal states	Has a difficult time controlling arousal states and emotions; needs extensive environmental support and physical and verbal support from a caregiver. Regulation takes more than 1 hour.		Is able to control arousal states and emotions when receiving physical and verbal support from a caregiver. Regulation takes 30–60 minutes.		Is able to control arousal states and emotions in a soothing environment or when physical or emotional support is received from an adult. Regulation takes 15–30 minutes.		Is able to control arousal states and emotions with self-regulatory strategies (e.g., a blanket or special toy) or verbal suggestions from an adult. Regulation takes just a few minutes.		Is able to independently control arousal states and emotions in a way appropriate for the situation.	AA Comments:	T	W	C	____
Behavioral regulation	Does not understand or respond to adults' requests to stop actions.		Beginning to understand what not to do, but does it anyway. Resists adults' input and control.		Understands right and wrong with adult input, so sometimes chooses appropriate behavior. Is beginning to look to adults for input on what to do.		Independently understands right and wrong and chooses appropriate behavior most of the time, but needs adult assistance to choose and manage behavior.		Chooses appropriate behavior and responds to adults' requests most of the time; tolerates a balance of control.	AA Comments:	T	W	C	____
Sense of self	Is dependent on others to meet needs.		Tries to access toys and people, shows adults objects, and smiles when others respond to his or her actions. Does not request assistance when needed.		Focuses on specific goals related to movement, objects, or interactions with people. Often requests help or needs reinforcement to maintain effort.		Is motivated to independently reach multiple types of goals; is persistent, confident, and pleased with successful efforts. Knows when help is needed.		Is goal-oriented, persists in the face of challenges, feels confident of success and proud of accomplishments. Aware of own strengths and weaknesses.	AA Comments:	T	W	C	____

(continued on next page)

Transdisciplinary Play-Based System (TPBA2/TPBI2) by Toni Linder
Copyright © 2008 Paul H. Brookes Publishing Co., Inc. All rights reserved.

187

(continued from previous page)

Observation Summary Form: Emotional and Social Development TPBA 2

TPBA2 Subcategory	Level of the child's ability as observed in functional activities									Rating compared with other children of same age				
	1	2	3	4	5	6	7	8	9	Above average (AA)	Typical (T)	Watch (W)	Concern (C)	Age level (mode)
Emotional themes in play	Demonstrates limited range of emotions in play and/or lacks awareness of or concern for emotions of others in the play situation.		Demonstrates a range of emotions in play through verbal and nonverbal means, but emotions reflect reaction to play itself rather than the meaning of the play.		Recognizes and labels own and others' basic emotions in play situations. Has repetitive unresolved emotional themes in play.		Is able to attribute emotions to inanimate characters in dramatic play and uses play themes to experiment with resolving emotional conflicts.		Is able to appropriately represent own and others' emotions and can resolve emotional conflicts in interactions and themes within symbolic and sociodramatic play.	AA	T	W	C	____
										Comments:				
Social interactions	Watches caregivers and reacts to their initiations with vocal or physical responses.		Is responsive to affection and initiates positive interactions with others. May have difficulty with separation from key caregivers.		Takes turns in prolonged interaction with family members and familiar people. May be shy or anxious with unfamiliar people. Plays alongside peers but may have frequent social conflicts.		Primarily has positive reciprocal relationships with family members and peers in daily activities. Is able to initiate interaction and engage a peer for several minutes. Uses adults for conflict resolution.		Discriminates among familiar people and strangers, has close relationships with family, and maintains several friendships. Is able to initiate and maintain interactions in reciprocal, goal-oriented play and can negotiate conflict situations independently.	AA	T	W	C	____
										Comments:				
Overall needs:														

Transdisciplinary Play-Based System (TPBA2/TPBI2)
by Toni Linder

5

Communication Development Domain

with Renee Charlifue-Smith and Cheryl Cole Rooke

Communication is the process of transmitting ideas, information, and feelings, which may be accomplished through many modalities including eye contact; facial expressions; gestures; body posture; augmentative and alternative communication (AAC); and written, signed, or spoken language. Speech and language are encompassed within the broader meaning of communication. *Speech* refers to a verbal means of communication; *language* refers to a rule-governed system for representing concepts through symbols, which can be verbal or nonverbal. Communication is closely intertwined with, and provides much of the basis for, the continuing development of cognitive and social skills. Difficulties in the area of communication can affect a child's long-term ability to interact effectively and actively with other people and to learn.

The emphasis in Transdisciplinary Play-Based Assessment (TPBA2) is to analyze the child's *total* communication system, including content, method, attitudes and emotions, gestures, body posture and movement, and physical distance as well as quality, quantity, and effectiveness of communication. TPBA2 is a particularly suitable format for doing this, because communication can be performed in the context of play activities and daily routines such as snack time, washing hands and face, or getting dressed. The setup of the environment and the skills the facilitator elicits allow the assessment team to observe what modes of communication the child uses for self-expression, how the child responds to requests, and how the child interacts with a variety of play partners, such as familiar and unfamiliar adults and peers.

The communication domain of TPBA2 includes language comprehension, language production, pragmatics, articulation and phonology, voice and fluency, oral mechanism, and hearing (see Table 5.1 for definitions of each subcategory). Although each area is described separately, the development of the whole communication system is, in reality, the dynamic product of the interplay among all parts. Language is now separated into three different areas—language comprehension, language production, and pragmatics—emphasizing the importance of discretely assessing comprehension, expression, and use. Parents concerned about their child's communication often focus solely on expressive language. Assessment in all three language areas, however, will

Table 5.1. Communication domain subcategories and definitions

Subcategory	Description
Language comprehension	The child's ability to understand and respond to language including vocabulary, questions, grammatical structures, and requests
Language production	The child's ability to use language in any modality to express thoughts and feelings, relate events, and to ask and answer questions
Pragmatics	The child's ability to use intentional nonverbal and verbal communication for different purposes in different social contexts, including sharing joint attention, initiating and responding to language, using greetings, taking turns, maintaining a topic, exchanging and clarifying information, and telling stories
Articulation and phonology	The child's ability to produce the speech sounds (articulation) and represent the sound system (phonology) of his or her language to produce intelligible speech
Voice and fluency	The quality, pitch, loudness, and fluency of the child's speech
Oral mechanism	The structure and function of the articulators
Hearing	The child's ability to attend, to localize, and to process sounds and speech in his or her environment

help them understand how comprehension and language use (pragmatics) may be affecting expressive language development. Observations in each language area will have different implications for intervention. Special consideration is given to assessing the communication systems of children who are bilingual or multilingual, who are identified with autism spectrum disorders, or who may use—or be a candidate for—AAC. Hearing is discussed in a separate chapter; please refer to Chapter 6 for specific information on how hearing affects communication, learning, and social development. All children should have their hearing tested before TPBA so that the information gathered in TPBA is an accurate assessment of the child's abilities.

As mentioned in Chapter 5 of the *Administration Guide for TPBA2 & TPBI2*, it is important that the assessment team obtain a thorough history of the child's speech and language development and family history of speech and language delays. They also should note any incidences of regression and/or plateaus in development. Observations from parents and other caregivers (including teachers), the parents' estimation of the child's receptive and expressive language functioning (both strengths and weaknesses), and the parents' observations of the child interacting with familiar versus unfamiliar adults and peers are beneficial in obtaining a sample of the child's overall communication skills. By observing the parent–child interaction, the team can observe a parent's communication style with the child, exploring how the adult responds to the child's communication attempts, and how he or she facilitates the child's language. For example, how often does the child initiate the interaction versus the adult? The team also should be aware of the family's cultural expectations, dialect, and the behaviors of their community in order to assess and determine whether a child is truly exhibiting problems in the communication domain (Crais & Roberts, 2004).

Reviewing the videotape of the TPBA session is helpful for noting the contextual and linguistic information of the situation. A speech-language pathologist (SLP), if involved in TPBA, should record both the child's and adult's nonverbal and verbal productions used during the interaction. The data from these communication observations should be combined with assessment information from other domains to obtain the most complete picture of the child's abilities.

Format of the Chapter

In the chapter, discussion of each of the subcategories is presented, with first the research and developmental information related to the subcategory, then observational strategies, followed by an example of observation of the subcategory in the TPBA. The questions that provide direction for observation are found in the TPBA2 Observation Guidelines and Summary Form for communication at the end of this chapter. Use of the Observation Guidelines and Summary Form is described in Chapter 2 of the *Administration Guide*. An Age Table describing when specific processes and skills develop across all subcategories is presented at the end of this chapter (see p. 263).

LANGUAGE

Children around the world grow up in different cultures and learn different languages. The milestones they acquire within each language are universal, because the pattern of development is predictable. However, the rates at which children move through different language stages may vary. Many children with disabilities and those who use AAC also move through the same language stages and sequences as other children. There are times, however, when a child may exhibit delayed or disordered language development due to a variety of possible causes such as neurological disorders or environmental factors. Language development is considered *delayed* when a child is acquiring typical skills and is progressing through the milestones in sequential order, but at a slower rate when compared with same-age peers. Children whose language is delayed at age 2, but whose expressive language is near normal by age 3, are sometimes referred to as "late bloomers." Language development is considered *disordered* when a child is developing atypical skills and is not progressing through the milestones in a sequential order. For example, a child with autism who does not move through expected language milestones in the same ways as his or her peers is considered to have a language disorder. The child with autism demonstrates atypical skills in that he or she may have poor language comprehension skills such as not responding to his or her name or simple one-step requests (e.g., "give me" or "come here"), and demonstrates atypical production skills such as producing words or even sentences that are nonmeaningful (e.g., repeating lines from a movie or commercial).

In the assessment of infants, it is important to keep in mind that the purpose is to identify the child's strengths and needs (Sparks, 1989). Furthermore, with some young children or those who are medically fragile, the child's physiological organization may affect the child's ability to actively participate in the assessment process and to interact with others (Paul, 2001). Some behaviors the child might exhibit include changes in respiratory patterns, changes in body color of the skin, changes in body tone, and disorganized patterns of alertness (Browne, MacLeod, & Smith-Sharp, 1995).

I. Language Comprehension ▬▬▬▬▬▬▬▬▬▬▬▬▬▬▬▬▬▬▬▬▬▬

It is impossible to observe a child's actual moments of comprehension, because they occur within the seclusion of the mind. What may be observed during an assessment are acts that evidence this understanding, which Miller and Paul (1995) describe as the *products of comprehension*.

▬▬▬▬▬ **I. A. What early comprehension abilities does the child exhibit?**

Early in infancy, a child begins responding to voices, noise, and environmental sounds. During the first few months, for example, the child may startle to a loud sound, only to be soothed moments later by the soft sounds of the parent's calming voice. With increasing maturity and strength, the infant acquires the ability to move the head toward the sound source and develops increasingly refined localization skills (see Chapter 6 for more information). During the second half of the first year, the child begins to turn when his or her name is called, to identify family members by name, to recognize the names of familiar objects, and to respond to familiar words such as "up" or "bye-bye" with gestures.

Tomasello (2003) stated that "children begin to acquire language when they do because the learning process depends crucially on the more fundamental skills of joint attention, intention reading, and cultural learning, which emerge near the end of the first year of life" (p. 21). It is the development of these three areas that allows a child to understand words by determining what the adult is talking about, why they are talking about it, and how a word is used in a specific context. By the end of the first year, a child begins to discover the power of joint attention, using gaze shifts to get other people to look at an object or activity and also by following an adult's line of regard to discern the adult's focus of attention (Crais, Douglas, & Campbell, 2004; Delgado et al., 2002; Lock, 1978; Murphy & Messer, 1977; Tomasello, 2003).

In early childhood, comprehension is optimal when language occurs within familiar social and daily routines that are sequenced and predictable, such as naming body parts during diapering or getting dressed (Lund & Duchan, 1993). Language comprehension within many daily routines, such as dressing, is enhanced by the contextual support of the environment and by parent cues, such as pairing words with gestures or gaze. For example, the parent might say, "Time for bath," and the child responds based on the parent grabbing a towel, the bath water being turned on, and toys being placed in the tub. In this same time period, a child's participation in early social games, such as So Big and Peekaboo, also is instrumental to the development of language comprehension. Repetitive and highly structured communication routines and social games help children understand the meaning of words and nonverbal messages. Parents play an important role in scaffolding language learning and comprehension during these games. In the beginning, the parent initiates the game and shapes it to match the child's behaviors. In this stage, the child is inattentive; does not take true turns; and does not understand the content, gestures, or communicative value of the game. Over time, however, the child progresses through a hierarchy of understanding and eventually can initiate the game and participate using conventional responses that indicate comprehension of specific words (Platt & Coggins, 1990).

Between 12 and 18 months of age, the child's ability to understand words increases markedly, including identification of body parts and familiar objects, searching for objects in view, and understanding early action words. During this time the child often responds to a spoken word when it is coupled with a gesture to aid comprehension. As requests become familiar due to their frequent use in routines, the child's need for gestural and situational prompts decreases until the child can respond to the verbal instruction alone. However, it is often difficult to assess the child's comprehension of sentences within routines due to their predictable format and the many contextual cues and comprehension strategies that help the child understand the messages (Chapman, 1978; Haynes & Pindzola, 2004; Miller & Paul, 1995). The team should observe how much support the parent is providing to aid the child's comprehension. Examples of parent support include the following: saying, "Give me" paired with an open-hand gesture versus the parent saying, "Give me" without offering his or her hand; or the parent pointing to a book while directing the child to "Get the book" versus the parent giving the same direction when the book is out of sight or in another room. As the child's language comprehension improves, he or she will begin to rely less on context and more on linguistic knowledge and past experiences. For example, the child will search for a person or object when asked, "Where is __?" and respond to simple yes/no questions such as "Want juice?" without the object being present.

▦▦▦ I. B. What types of words and sentences are understood by the child?

Between 18 and 24 months, the child's understanding of decontextualized language increases dramatically. At this age, the child understands words when the object is not present in the immediate environment and can understand action words outside of the context of familiar routines. Between the ages of 2 and 3, the child's comprehension expands from an initial understanding of two-term relations between nouns and action words (e.g., *Kiss* the *baby*) to understanding three-term combinations (Paul, 2001). For example, a child playing farm with his father would understand the three-part statement, "Make the *horse bite* the *cow*" (Paul, 2001). During this same period, the child also is responding to two-step related commands such as "Get your napkin and put it in the trash." By the 34–46-month age range, the child is able to follow a much more difficult two-step unrelated command, such as "Go get your jacket and sit down."

Parents of children with autism are often concerned because their child is not talking; however, language comprehension for a child with autism also is an area of concern (Philofsky, Hepburn, Hayes, Hagerman, & Rogers, 2004). Sometimes parents have concerns about hearing because the child responds inconsistently to his or her name or to the parents' requests. However, the child's inconsistency in responding may be related to the many visual and contextual cues the parents are using when interacting with their child, such as showing of objects, gestures, and so forth (Lord & Richler, 2006).

Children with disabilities do not spend as much time engaged with peers, adults, and materials as children without disabilities (McWilliam & Bailey, 1995). Children who are not actively engaged may miss out on opportunities to communicate with others and opportunities for gaining new skills, such as exploring, in meaningful ways (Rosenberg & Robinson, 1990). In the early preschool years, a child relies on past experience and not strictly on the immediate context of the situation to help interpret what has been said, which is referred to as *world knowledge* (Coggins & Timler, 2000; Owens, 2004). In research by Carey and Bartlett (1978), a number of 3- and 4-year-old children understood a novel word used to name a novel object after being exposed to it only one time, and they retained this information 6 weeks later. From 42 to 60 months, a child begins to interpret language more consistently based on the word order and word relationships of the sentences (Tager-Flusberg, 1989) in addition to contextual cues (Owens, 2004).

Active voice statements, which contain a noun–verb–noun structure, such as "Terry ate the apple," are the most prevalent sentence type in English, and they are the most easily understood by a preschool child. Passive voice sentences, such as "The apple was eaten by Terry," are more difficult for a preschool child to comprehend (Lund & Duchan, 1993; McLaughlin, 1998) and usually are not understood until after a child is 5 years old (James, 1990). Compound sentences (i.e., clauses or simple sentences combined by conjunctions; e.g., *but, and, or*), such as "Terry ate the apple and drank her milk," and complex sentences containing dependent clauses, such as "Although Terry wasn't very hungry, she ate her apple," also are difficult for preschool children to understand.

A child's understanding of questions develops sequentially. The first "wh" questions that a child can answer are *what* and *where,* followed by *who,* and finally a later version of *what* questions, which are referred to as *what-doing* questions (e.g., "What is the girl doing?"). These early "wh" questions are followed by *when, why,* and *how* questions, which occur after a child develops some understanding of time, causality, and manner concepts (McLaughlin, 1998). The typical sequence of a child's question comprehension and approximate ages when they occur is presented in Table 5.2. Sometimes a child responds inappropriately because he or she is focusing on one word in a question. For example, the child might answer the query, "*When* are you going to eat?" by

Table 5.2. Comprehension of questions

Approximate age	Type of question	Example	Response
12–16 months	Where	"Where is ball?"	Searches for object and may vocalize.
18–30 months	Yes/no	"Do you want juice?"	Early form; shakes head "no" first and nods head "yes" at approximately 18 months.
		"Is he eating?"	Later form; responds with "yes" or "no."
18–24 months	What	"What's that?"	
30–36 months	Where	"Where is daddy?"	Responds with words.
30–36 months	What . . . doing	"What is the girl doing?"	
36–40 months	Who	"Who is that?"	
36–40 months	How many	"How many ducks?"	
36–40 months	Whose	"Whose coat is this?"	
36–40 months	Why	"Why did you do it?"	
42–48 months	How	"How do you do it?"	
52–58 months	When	"When do you sleep?"	
52–60 months	What happens if . . .	"What happens if you don't finish?"	

saying, "A banana," responding only to the verb in the question. Explaining *why* something happened may be problematic for most preschoolers, because the child has to think about what occurred before the event. Closely observing the child's responses to all types of questions will provide information about comprehension and help the team to determine whether or not further investigation is warranted.

A child's ability to identify objects and pictures and to follow oral directions of varying length and complexity often is affected by the child's understanding of basic concepts. Some of the ages at which concepts are understood are listed in Table 5.3. The development of basic concepts is addressed fully in Chapter 7, Cognitive Development Domain.

Table 5.3. Comprehension of concepts

Concept age	Approximate
Location	
in, out, on, off, under	33–36 months
in front of, behind	36–42 months
top, bottom, between, above, below	48–54 months
Quantity	
one, all, how many; up to 2	24–30 months
Descriptive	
big, little	27–30 months
hard, soft, rough, smooth	36–42 months
Time	
night, day, before, after	48 months
Primary colors	48 months
Basic shapes	48 months
Emotions	
happy, sad, mad	18–24 months

Summarized from the TPBA2 Age Tables for Cognitive Development (see Chapter 7).

▓▓▓ USING THE OBSERVATION GUIDELINES
TO ASSESS LANGUAGE COMPREHENSION

A preassessment review of the CFHQ, FACF, and other sources of information before the assessment will assist the team in determining the approximate developmental level of the child for planning purposes. The information will allow the play facilitator to match the child's vocabulary level and language complexity to ensure optimal situations for eliciting the child's language comprehension and language production.

The facilitator needs to be adept at creating an environment that allows the child maximal opportunities to demonstrate as many communication skills as possible. It is recommended that some of the child's favorite toys or activities be available in addition to the developmentally appropriate materials provided by the TPBA team. This is important because the presence of familiar objects may increase the child's interaction and communication during the assessment. Any one of the team members may be called on to be the facilitator. Each member must, therefore, be familiar with techniques for observing and eliciting communication. The following suggestions, adapted from Crais and Roberts (2004) and Lund and Duchan (1993), are useful when facilitating children's communication abilities during TPBA:

- Follow the child's lead, observing and responding to his or her interest in particular topics, objects, and activities.

- Be aware of the amount of talking you do. Pause often, and wait after making comments, requests, and questions to encourage the child to take a turn, to respond, or to initiate.

- Monitor your use of questions, asking authentic, open-ended instead of closed-ended questions such as yes/no questions which will stop the back and forth exchange of communication. Make comments about the materials. Describe what you are doing.

- Provide choices in objects and activities throughout the session.

- Toys that are broken or have parts that move elicit interest. Also think about having the parent bring a couple of the child's favorite toys.

- If there is another person who is interacting with the child, including the parent or a peer, have them model responses. The extra person takes some of the attention off the child to perform.

During the TPBA session, the "examiner" is an observer and facilitator and the goal is to follow the child's lead. Directing and questioning should be kept to a minimum to prevent the environment from seeming testlike. In some situations and with some particular children, the SLP on the team may be the best person for facilitating the assessment.

One goal of the communication portion of TPBA2 is to observe the interaction between the child and their parent(s). This provides the opportunity to observe the strategies the parents use to facilitate their child's communication. Observing interactions with the parent or the child's teacher may provide more information about the child's abilities because skills that are absent or that are limited in frequency during the interaction with facilitator may be exhibited or increase in frequency with familiar adults. Observations of daily routines or familiar activities also provide a good opportunity for gathering information. This can be accomplished by asking the parent to have a snack with the child or to help their child wash their hands following a messy sensory activity such as playing with shaving cream. During TPBA, parents often are anxious to show the team their child's abilities, which sometimes results in the parent being directive and asking too many questions. Instructing the parents about their role will be helpful in reducing these behaviors. Observing the child in an environment other than the TPBA assessment room, such as their home or classroom, also may provide a more representative sample of the child's skills. Observation of the child interacting with his or her peers also will elicit different information.

The MacArthur-Bates Communicative Development Inventories (Fenson et al., 2006), which are available in English and Spanish, include two norm-referenced parent checklists that were developed to obtain the information about a child's early communication skills. One checklist is used to obtain information about categories of words understood and used and gesture use for children 8–18 months of age; the second checklist is used to obtain information about words and sentences used by children 16–30 months of age. Used in combination with TPBA's spontaneous language sample, the checklist can provide additional information about the child's lexical comprehension and lexicon size and content.

The SLP or another team member will want to do an online transcription of the communication sample as it occurs during the TPBA session, making note of who was interacting with the child and their communication behaviors, the activity, and both the responses and the productions of the child to his or her communication partner. It is important to note imitated versus spontaneous behaviors and nonverbal behaviors observed. Review of the videotape will be helpful in supplementing the notes/transcription.

It then will be important to analyze the following aspects of the child's behaviors carefully: how the child communicates, the frequency of the child's communication (i.e., how often in a certain time period), the complexity of the child's communication, and why the child communicates with various communication partners and in different environments. This analysis will help the team determine the child's language comprehension and production abilities and identify whether a skill is emerging or mastered. Adequate information usually can be obtained in the TPBA session; however, a child will not exhibit all of the communication skills he or she knows. If warranted, the SLP may determine whether further assessment of the child's skills is necessary, especially for an older child.

All of the information obtained will be helpful for intervention planning and developing functional communication goals for the child, which should be integrated into the child's and the family's daily routines and activities.

Analysis of the child's ability to comprehend language is achieved through observation of the child's physical and verbal responses during the play session. Directing the child to respond to behaviors, manipulate objects, identify objects and pictures, or answer questions helps determine a child's cognitive skills and ability to understand language. Language comprehension should be assessed in both contextualized and decontextualized situations to determine whether the child can respond solely to the linguistic information as well as language embedded in routines and supported by cues implicit to an activity (Miller & Paul, 1995; Paul, 2001). The influence of the room setup and toy and activity selection will affect the extent to which contextual cues may be provided to the child and aid comprehension. Based on the information received before TPBA and the parent interview, the play facilitator will want to select carefully the level of vocabulary words and sentence complexity.

I. A. What early comprehension abilities does the child exhibit?

How does the child respond to environmental sounds and voices? How does the child respond to environmental sounds or speech, which are associated with meaning? In addition to localizing to sounds, does the child follow another person's eye gaze to share joint attention on an object or activity? For example, does the child look at the same object or activity as the father?

When assessing a young child, the team should look at the child's ability to anticipate events with routines. For example, does the child expect a snack when the mother says or signs, "You're hungry. Want to eat?" while getting the food ready. Do the parent's or facilitator's eye gaze, gestures, facial expressions, and tone of voice help the child understand what is being said? The team should determine to what extent the child relies on contextual cues to interpret language. For example, the child may be able to "get a cup" while playing in the kitchen area but not during activities in a different part of the room, such as the dress-up area. Can the child understand a variety of words (e.g., nouns and action words) in different contexts? It is okay to make nonsense requests of child, but be aware that some children will not respond because the request does not make sense. Repeating requests, using additional contextual information, and allowing a child extra time to process the language are a few strategies that may facilitate the child's success, in order to gather information that may be important during intervention planning.

I. B. What types of words and sentences are understood by the child?

Gathering information from the parent(s) about the child's ability to follow directions at home is beneficial. Ask the parent(s) to give examples of directions the child can follow and determine whether or not the directions are part of a daily routine. Observations also should be made about the child's ability to follow unfamiliar directions. Does the child experience difficulty or show inconsistency in following the direction? Does an older child complete only part of a multistep direction, "forgetting" to do either the first or last steps? If possible, assess the child's ability to follow directions in other familiar settings such as the preschool classroom or at child care. In some instances, the child may appear to understand classroom directions but is actually observing classmates and following their actions through the steps of an activity. However, when the child is asked individually to follow a unique direction, the child may not respond and may just look at the teacher or continue what he or she was doing. When a child does not appear to understand directions, further investigation of the situation is needed. The child's developmental status in other domains, such as cognitive, emotional and social, and sensorimotor, should be explored. The team also should determine whether external factors are adversely affecting the child's performance, such as the language complexity and the vocabulary level used by the teacher or the auditory and visual environment of the classroom. Other external factors may be facilitating the child's performance, such as transition songs, visual schedules (pictures of the day's events), or gestural cues. The team also should consider the consistency of the child's understanding of directions over time. Does the child respond to a direction on one day but not the next?

Question use during TPBA should be kept to a minimum to prevent "grilling" the child. The team often gathers information about the child's ability to respond to questions during the parent–child interaction; however, providing the parent with guidance about their role may be helpful in decreasing excessive questioning. The play facilitator can elicit the child's ability to identify objects and pictures, to understand action words, to follow directions containing a variety of basic concepts, such as color, shapes, descriptive (e.g., *big, little, dirty, wet, broken*), spatial (e.g., *on, off, in, out, under*), and quantity (e.g., *one, all, some*), and to comprehend word relations:

- Asking the child to put an object in a certain location: "Go put the book on the table."

- Asking the child to manipulate an object: "Cut the yellow paper."

- Requesting an object of the child by its color, shape, or description: "We need all the straight train tracks."

- Having the child identify a picture based on its color, shape, or description: "Where is the little car?"

- Asking a child to locate an object in a certain location: "The markers are in the box."

- Asking the child to comprehend people's names and possessions: "Where is the mommy's hat?"

II. Language Production

A child's language production is a unique window that offers glimpses of the child's understanding, knowledge, and experience of people and events in the world. It is through the child's production of language that others gain an idea about the child's understanding, knowledge, and experience about people and events in the child's world (Gerber & Prizant, 2000).

II. A. What modes of communication does the child use?

A child's communication first develops during early interactions with caregivers (Bruner, 1978), and it is widely believed that the first 2 years of life are the most important for developing language (Billeaud, 2003; Stoel-Gammon, 1998). Over time, infants display an impressive array of preverbal, nonvocal communication modes, which include: body movements, such as waving arms, kicking legs, or moving toward a desired object or person, which begin between 1 and 3 months; facial expressions, such as grimacing, frowning, or smiling, which begin at 2 months; eye-gaze shifts and looking at their caregiver's face, which begin at 2 months; babbling, which begins at 4 months and increases in complexity; physical manipulation of people and objects, such as pushing or pulling, which begins at 6 months; and gestures, such as reaching, pointing, and giving objects, and vocalizing (producing speech sounds) which begin at 7 months and develop over time (Prizant & Wetherby, 1993).

During the first month the child produces reflexive vocalizations or vegetative sounds (e.g., burping, sneezing), crying, and reflexive smiles (Stark, Bernstein, & Demorest, 1993; Stoel-Gammon, 1998). Cooing, which is a repetitive vocalization made with vowels and back consonants (e.g., k, g), occurs during the next few months. As the child's vision and motor control mature at around 3 months, the child begins to maintain eye contact and gaze at the parent's face (McLaughlin, 1998).

In these early months the child cries and vocalizes to express tiredness, hunger, or discomfort (Bates, 1976a, 1976b; Crais & Roberts, 2004). Although these early sounds the child makes are not goal directed, the parent begins to interpret the behaviors as meaningful and intentional.

At approximately 4 months the child enters the first of three phases of babbling: marginal babbling, reduplicated babbling, and nonreduplicated babbling (McLaughlin, 1998). The first step of babbling, referred to as *marginal babbling,* begins when the child produces vowel-like sounds coupled with occasional closures of the vocal tract. This results in the child approximating single vowel–consonant (VC) and consonant–vowel (CV) syllables (Oller, 1978). During the next couple of months, vocal play develops as the child begins to experiment with sounds, producing raspberries, squeals, and yells (Stoel-Gammon, 1998). By approximately 6 months, speechlike babbling occurs when the child begins to string together the same consonant–vowel syllable combinations, such as "ba-ba-ba," "ma-ma-ma," or "da-da." This is often referred to as *canonical* or *reduplicated* babbling. Oller and colleagues (1998) reported that an absence of canonical babbling at 10 months of age, predicts a delay in the production of words and phrases. Bilabial (lip) sounds (e.g., p, b, m) are the majority of the consonants produced (Owens, 1998). It also is during this time that the child is intentionally communicating with eye gaze, gestures, and vocalizations. At approximately 9 months of age, the child begins to use and combine idiosyncratic or conventional gestures and vocalizations to communicate with intent. He or she may pair the gesture with a vocalization. For example, the child may reach for his or her favorite ball and produce the vocalization "uh." He or she also produces *variegated* or *nonreduplicated* babbling, the third stage of babbling, varying the consonants and vowel syllable combinations in a string. Pointing to request an object or share attention about an object occurs at around 10 months (Tomasello, 2003). (For detailed information about the development of gestures and communicative functions, refer to the Pragmatics section of this chapter.) Jargon emerges at about 10–12 months, and is characterized by vocalizations combined with adultlike stress and intonation patterns.

A child's first true word occurs around the first birthday; although it might occur a little earlier for some children and later for others. These first word productions are often approximations consisting of simplified consonant (C) and vowel (V) syllable patterns (e.g., CV, *ba/ball*; CVCV, *dada*) containing speech sounds that were used in later babbling (Yoder & Warren, 1993). Words a child produces including word approximations are referred to as verbalizations. During this first word stage, a child uses "holophrases," which express complex, ideas with a single word. These single-word holophrases are comparable to sentences for the child. Over time, however, the child refines an understanding of the word's true meaning and specific use (Ninio, 1992; Tomasello, 2003).

By approximately 18 months, a child produces about 50 words. This also marks the beginning of the transition stage to two-word utterances, during which a child may begin to use or imitate two-word combinations, such as "More juice." Initially, a child may use apparent word combinations that are actually conceptualized as one giant word, such as "alldone" (McLaughlin, 1998). According to Bloom (1973), children go through another stage when they produce two words with a pause in between them as a precursor to combining words together. These utterances are referred to as successive single-word utterances. A child whose vocabulary contains only a few types of words may have a limited ability to combine two words. For example, if the child's lexicon consists primarily of labels and few action words, he or she may not be able to express ideas requiring location words, such as "Want up!" or "Go down!" (slide). Two-word combinations should be occurring consistently close to the child's second birthday. As the child's word production increases, the use of some gestures decreases.

A toddler's multiword utterances are often described as *telegraphic speech*. This is because the child may use mostly content words or key words (i.e., nouns, verbs, adjectives) and omit function words, such as conjunctions (e.g., *and*), articles (e.g., *the, a, an*), and helping verbs (e.g., *is, are*). Multiword combinations occur between approximately 2 and 3 years of age, becoming more complex as vocabulary knowledge and grammatical abilities increase.

As cognitive and motor skills develop during the first year, a child begins imitating and producing speech sounds others say, a typical and important strategy that also will be used for later language learning. One word that often is used to describe this verbal behavior in children with autism is *echolalia*. Echolalia can be described as either immediate or delayed (Prizant, Schuler, Wetherby, & Rydell, 1997). Immediate echolalia occurs when the child repeats words or phrases spoken by others immediately or shortly after they are said. Delayed echolalia occurs when the child repeats another person's phrase at a later time. Children with autism also may repeat lines from a favorite movie, book, or commercial. The child's echolalia may be an exact repetition of another person's statement, or it may be mitigated, meaning the child makes minor changes to it. Research (Prizant et al., 1997; Prizant & Rydell, 1993) indicates that for children with autism, echolalia may be a useful language-learning strategy, which is used for a variety of communicative functions. Excellent information on communication assessment and intervention strategies for young children with autism is available. Here are two examples:

Charman, T., & Stone, W. (Eds.) (2006). *Social and communication development in autism spectrum disorders: Early identification, diagnosis, and intervention.* New York: Guilford Press.

Wetherby, A.M., & Prizant, B.M. (Eds.) (2000). *Autism spectrum disorders: A transactional developmental perspective.* Baltimore: Paul H. Brookes Publishing Co.

Augmentative and Alternative Communication

Augmentative and alternative communication (AAC) may be used to improve, maintain, or increase the functional communication skills of children with expressive language delays and speech production difficulties. AAC encompasses low-tech and high-tech systems using a variety of nonverbal and verbal communication modalities. Manual signs (idiosyncratic and formal), objects, photographs, pictures, printed words, alphabet boards, and electronic communication devices are all included in the definition of AAC (ASHA, 2004b). Although sign language is considered a form of AAC, in-depth information about sign language is provided separately in Chapter 6. The milestones for American Sign Language (ASL) are included in the Communication Age Tables.

AAC may be the primary communication mode for some children. For others, it can provide a temporary method for enhancing communication or by augmenting and clarifying speech. It is critical to provide a way to communicate for the child who is nonverbal or has difficulty communicating effectively with others. AAC strategies sometimes are paired with prelinguistic communication skills to improve a child's productive language. For example, eye gaze can be coupled with an object or picture board, physical manipulation can be used to activate a voice output device, or a gesture can be shaped into a manual sign.

AAC provides opportunities for a child to request, make choices, comment, share emotions, and participate in group activities, such as songs or story time, or other daily routines and activities. Overall, AAC facilitates the child's speech, language, and social skills through increased interactions with family members, peers, and others, fostering the development and maintenance of friendships and other important relationships (Beukelman & Mirenda, 2005).

For more information about AAC, a variety of excellent books are available. Below are a couple:

Beukelman, D., & Mirenda, P. (2005). *Augmentative and alternative communication: Management of severe communication impairments* (3rd ed.). Baltimore: Paul H. Brookes Publishing Co.

Glennen, S.L., & Decoste, D.C. (1997). *Handbook of augmentative and alternative communication.* San Diego: Singular.

▨▨▨▨ II. B. What is the child's frequency of communication?

In addition to identifying the modes of communication, the child's frequency of communication should be assessed. Measurement of the *frequency* of communicative acts is accomplished by observing how many times the child communicates during the TPBA. When assessing an infant, the number of vocalizations should be divided by the total amount of minutes for the sample (Paul, 2001). The frequency is significant, because a prelinguistic child with developmental disabilities who communicates less than once every 4 minutes is less likely to produce functional speech 1 year later (Yoder, Warren, & McCathren, 1998). By the age of 18–24 months, however, a child is expected to communicate more frequently and for a greater variety of purposes. By 18 months, a child should use gestures, vocalizations, and words (or a combination of these) approximately two times per minute to communicate; a child who is 24 months old should intentionally communicate at a rate of five times per minute (Paul & Shiffer, 1991; Wetherby, Cain, Yonclas, & Walker, 1988). As a child's mean length of utterance (MLU) increases, the frequency of communication also increases (Wetherby et al., 1988). It is recommended that the team document and compare, perhaps by deriving a percentage, how often the child and the adults each initiate language (Bloom & Lahey, 1978; Wetherby et al., 1988).

Reduced frequency of communication may be an indicator of problems in different areas. The child with severe motor involvement may find it so difficult to speak that language production is minimal. Infrequent communication also may indicate social emotional concerns. A child who is highly withdrawn, for example, may choose not to communicate unless absolutely necessary. For example a child with selective mutism is able to communicate verbally but may speak with only a few select individuals and in select environments. These children have a fear of talking in some situations; therefore, the frequency of communicative interaction is reduced and their social relationships affected.

II. C. What are the child's semantic abilities?

Semantics refers to the rules for establishing the meaning of words, individually and in combination. This section of the chapter addresses the knowledge level expressed by words and the semantic relation exhibited in the child's language.

Word Meanings

Once referential understanding is acquired, a child will produce word approximations and then words. The early words a child produces include those that are important to the child and the family, which will vary from culture to culture. Gentner (1982) found that across many languages, children tend to learn nouns more than any other types of words. The most common early nouns are the names of familiar animals, foods, toys, and family members; however, a child's early vocabulary also contains words referred to as personal-social words (e.g., *hi, bye-bye, please, thank you, all gone*) (Mervis & Bertrand, 1993; Tomasello, 2003). Word learning accelerates from 1 to 5 years of age. Between 1 and 2 years of age, a child learns approximately one new word per week at the outset and approximately one new word per day toward the end of the year. Closer to 5 years of age, a child is learning up to one or two new words for each waking hour (Fenson et al., 1994). Fenson and colleagues (1994) found that at 18 months a child's average expressive vocabulary contains approximately 110 words, 312 words at 24 months, and 546 words at 30 months. By 3, a child's vocabulary is approximately 900–1000 words, and on entering kindergarten a child produces between 2,100 and 2,220 words. A child who has fewer than 50 words at 24 months is at risk for ongoing delays (Paul & Alforde, 1993; Rescorla, Roberts, & Dahlsgaard, 1997).

A child's vocabulary reflects his or her conceptualization of the world. Overextension occurs as the child uses a single word too broadly to symbolize a variety of items. For example, "Daddy" may mean all men, and "doggy" may mean all animals that are four legged (Bloom & Lahey, 1978; Clark, 1973). Overextension of concrete nouns occurs between 13 and 36 months (Dale, 1976), and according to Clark (1973), a selected perceptual property (i.e., shape, texture, movement, taste, sound) of the original object is the basis for extending the label to the new object. Underextension occurs when a child uses a word in a restricted manner. For example, a child may use "cup" for his or her personal cup, but not extend the label to all cups. As noted in the language comprehension section, the development of concepts (e.g., colors, spatial, descriptive, temporal, relational) is described in Chapter 7, Cognitive Development.

There are risk factors that may adversely affect the child's expressive vocabulary and language development. Hart and Risley (1995) found that the vocabulary of 1- and 2-year-old American children from diverse backgrounds varied significantly in the variety of words and word types according to the amount of interaction that occurred between parents and their children. The researchers concluded that the parents' educational level and the socioeconomic status (SES) of the family were significantly associated with the extent of communication in the home and, consequently, the size of a child's vocabulary. In addition to low SES, Olswang and colleagues (1998) identified other factors placing toddlers at risk for language difficulties, including a directive parent interaction style, a parent or sibling with a persistent learning and language problem, or long periods of untreated otitis media. Children within these risk groups displayed a 6-month delay in comprehension, fewer gestures, smaller expressive vocabularies including fewer verbs, more limited spontaneous imitations, fewer consonants, and more vowel errors in speech. These factors constitute important considerations when assessing a child and when providing recommendations to parents about facilitating language development at an early age.

Researchers have found that some language milestones parallel play milestones. For instance, as children produce single words they use single action play schemes, and when they combine words they use multiaction play schemes (McCune-Nicolich & Carroll, 1981; Shore, O'Connell, & Bates, 1984).

In addition to nouns, the child should have acquired action words (verbs) such as *drink* and other categories of words such as location words (prepositions), including *up* and *down*; possession words such as *mine*; agents such as *baby*; and words denoting recurrence, such as *more*. Children express the notions of existence (e.g., *this* ball); nonexistence (e.g., *all gone*); disappearance (e.g., *all gone*); recurrence (e.g., *more*); action (e.g., *drink*); location (e.g., *up*); possession (e.g., *my*); and characteristics of objects, people, or events (Bloom & Lahey, 1978; Brown, 1973; Tomasello, 2003). With progressive maturity, the child's language reflects a growing categorical understanding, or an ability to group concepts. A final stage of semantic development, which begins during preschool and continues, involves the ability to think more abstractly, as represented by the child's ability to talk about language, known as metalinguistic knowledge (Bloom & Lahey, 1978). Examples of this include a child's ability to rhyme words and segment the sounds in words (e.g., *c-a-t*). Table 5.4 summarizes the semantic knowledge areas and provides age ranges indicating when they begin.

Preschool children acquire vocabulary in two stages: fast mapping and extended mapping. During the fast mapping stage, the child acquires a cursory meaning of the word (Carey & Bartlett, 1978). During extended mapping, a longer stage, the child gradually clarifies the word's meaning based on more experiences with it (Carey, 1978). Understanding that words may have multiple meanings occurs as a child devel-

Table 5.4. Semantic knowledge levels reflected in words

Referential knowledge 9–15 months	A particular word represents a specific item (e.g., "bankie" refers to the child's blanket only).
Extended knowledge 15–18 months	A word represents various kinds of objects (e.g., "chair" can mean several types of chairs).
Relational knowledge 18+ months	A word is understood to relate to itself or something else. Categories of relational words include
	Reflexive relational (mark existence, nonexistence, disappearance and recurrence: "this" "all gone" "more")
	Action relational (movement implied: "up" "down" "bye-bye" "do")
	Location relational (direction or spatial relationship; where object is located)
	Possessional relational (object associated with a person: "mine")
Categorical knowledge 2 years +	The semantic category of words demonstrates the awareness of common aspects among objects (e.g., the word *toys*).
Metalinguistic knowledge 4–5 years	The ability is present to think about language and comment on it as well as produce and comprehend it (e.g., the child comments that "ball" begins with a "b")

Source: Bloom & Lahey, 1978.

ops increasingly specific word definitions as a result of different experiences with words. A preschool child may show examples of this emerging knowledge. For example, a little girl might ask, "Mom is your coffee *strong*?" When her mom replies "Yes," the girl shows her understanding of the word's different meanings. saying, "That means you're going to be really *strong*!" Sometimes preschool children invent words because they don't know a particular word or recall an associated word. These creative words are referred to as *idiomorphs* (Reich, 1986) and *invented words* (Pease & Berko Gleason, 1985). One area that also needs to be considered in the TPBA is the child's use of nonspecific words or empty words (e.g., *this, that, thing*) and word-finding difficulties that may be characterized by frequent pauses (e.g., *uh, um*), circumlocutions, and repetitions.

Semantic Relations

The relationship between the individual words in a sentence is referred to as *semantic relations*. At about 18 months, a child begins to combine newly acquired words into two-word combinations (Nelson, 1973) that express new semantic relations (18–36 months of age) (Paul, 2001). Semantic relational categories (e.g., agent–action, agent–action–object) expressed by children become more complex as multiword combinations are formed and the child's understanding of the various roles played by objects and people expands. See Table 5.5 for a comparison of the semantic relations expressed in prelinguistic, one-word, and multiword combinations.

▓▓▓▓ II. D. What grammatical morphemes does the child produce?

A *morpheme* is the smallest meaningful unit of language. Morphemes can be divided into two types: free morphemes and bound morphemes. A free morpheme can stand alone. A bound morpheme must be combined with a word and cannot stand alone. For example, adding the letter *s* to a word to make it plural changes its meaning. The word *dolls* consists of two morphemes: *doll* (noun) + *s* (denoting plural). Based on the child's language level, he or she may produce simple or more complex grammatical morphemes. Depending on what bound morphemes the free morpheme is connected to and how they function syntactically, a free morpheme can be separated into word classes: major word classes (nouns, verbs, adjectives, adverbs) and minor word classes (prepositions, conjunctions, pronouns) (Lund & Duchan, 1993).

Brown (1973) identified 14 grammatical morphemes that occur in young children's speech. The age of mastery of these morphemes ranges from 19 to 50 months. Brown's hierarchy of stages, occurring at 19 months, includes a child's earliest attempts at utterances, single words, which are mostly composed of nouns, verbs, and adjectives (see Table 5.6). As a child enters Brown's Stage II, at approximately 2 years 2 months of age, present progressive verbs (*verb* + *–ing*), prepositions (*in, on*), and regular plurals (*–s, –es*) word forms emerge. During Brown's Stage III, occurring between the ages of 2 and 3, a child begins to use irregular past tense verbs ("she *came*," "we *went*"). During Brown's Stages IV and V, occurring from ages 3 to 4, a child begins to use articles (*a, the*), regular past tense verbs (*verb* + *–ed*), third person regular verbs ("he *goes*," "she *eats*"), and the contractible copula use of *is* ("here*'s* the shoe"), In Brown's post-Stage V, occurring from ages 4 to 4½, a child begins to use contractible auxiliary verbs ("they*'re* playing"), the uncontractible copula ("Who's here? I *am*"), the uncontractible auxiliary ("Who was playing? I *was*"), and irregular third person singular verbs ("she *has*," "he *does*") (Bellugi & Brown, 1964; Brown, 1973; deVilliers & deVilliers, 1973; Miller, 1981).

Computing a child's MLU is a commonly accepted method of measuring the child's average number of morphemes per utterance. In addition, the MLU correlates chronological age to the stages of linguistic development, as described by Brown (1973). The child's MLU is derived by dividing the total number of morphemes in a

Table 5.5. Semantic relations expressed in prelinguistic, one-word, and multiword utterances

General relationship	Function/ meaning	Child behavior Prelinguistic	One word	Multiword
Agent	The individual performing the action	Throws ball to teacher and smiles proudly	Throws ball and says, "Me"	"Me throw"
Action	Requests action	Holds hands up to be picked up	"Up," to indicate *pick me up*	"Up Mommy"
Object	Comments on the object of action	Points to ball being pushed	"Ball," as ball is pushed	"Ball go"
Recurrence	Requests/comments on repetition of activity/object	Drinks milk and holds up empty bottle	"More," to indicate *more milk*	"Me more milk"
Disappearance	Comments on nonexistence/ disappearance of object or person	Points to missing wheel on car	"Wheel," while pointing to car	"No wheel"
Cessation	Comments on cessation of activity	Points to top that stopped spinning	"Stop," to indicate top is no longer spinning	"Top stop"
Rejection	Protests/ comments on undesired action or something forbidden	Turns head away from food	"No," in response to peas	"No peas"
Location	Comments on spatial location	Holds truck and points to box	"Box," while pointing to toy box	
"Put box"	Possession	Comments on possession of object	Reaches for own shoes among others' shoes and points	"Mine," while getting own shoes
"My shoes"	Agent–action*	Comments on agent and action		
"Boy hit"	Action–object*	Comments on action and object		
"Kick ball"	Agent–action– object*	Comments on agent, action, and object		
"Mommy throw ball"	Action–object– location*	Comments on agent, action, and location		

"Put ball chair"

*These are more commonly used examples of relational combinations; many possibilities exist.

From Roberts, J., & Crais, E. (2004). Assessing communication skills. In M. McLean, M. Wolery, & D.B. Bailey, Jr. (Eds.), *Assessing infants and preschoolers with special needs* (3rd ed., p. 349). Upper Saddle River, NJ: Pearson Prentice Hall.

language sample by the total number of utterances in the sample, which can be computed in the following way: Collect a language sample of consecutive and intelligible utterances; count the number of morphemes in each utterance and total the morphemes for the complete sample; and divide the number of morphemes by the total number of utterances. Owens (2004) and Lund and Duchan (1993) provide comprehensive examples of what constitute morphemes and which behaviors—for example,

Table 5.6. Brown's 14 morphemes

Age of mastery[a] (months)	Morpheme	Example
19–28	Present progressive –ing (no auxiliary verb)	"Mommy driving."
27–30	In	"Ball in cup."
27–30	On	"Doggie on sofa."
24–33	Regular plural –s	"Kitties eat my ice cream." Forms: /s/, /z/, and /ɪz/ Cats (/kæts/) Dogs (/dogz/) Classes (/klæslz/), wishes (/wɪʃlz/)
25–46	Irregular past	"Came," "fell," "broke," "sat," "went"
26–40	Possessives	"Mommy's balloon broke." Forms: /s/, /z/, and /ɪz/ as in regular plural
27–39	Uncontractible copula (verb to be as main verb)	"He is." (response to "Who's sick?")
28–46	Articles	"I see a kitty." "I throw the ball to Daddy."
26–48	Regular past –ed	"Mommy pulled the wagon." "Kathy hits." Forms: /d/, /t/, /ɪd/ Pulled (/puld/) Walked (/w_kt/) Glided (/gl al d l d/)
26–46	Regular third person –s	"Kathy hits." Forms: /s/, /z/, and /ɪz/ as in regular plural
28–50	Irregular third person	"Does," "has"
29–48	Uncontractible auxiliary	"He is." (response to "Who's wearing your hat?")
29–49	Contractible copula	"Man's big." "Man is big."
30–50	Contractible auxiliary	"Daddy's drinking juice." "Daddy is drinking juice."

[a]Used correctly 90% of the time in obligatory contexts.
Source: Brown, 1973; Miller, 1981; Owens, 1988.

unintelligible utterances, imitations, and rote utterances—should be excluded when computing the child's MLU (see Table 5.7).

II. E. What are the child's syntactic abilities?

Syntax refers to the rule system for combining words into meaningful phrases and sentences, including the parts of speech, word order, and sentence structure. This section of the chapter addresses the different type of sentences used by a child and the stages of syntactic development. Syntactic development can be analyzed once a child can combine words into two- and three-word utterances.

There are four basic sentence types: *declaratives,* which are statements (e.g., "She is eating"); *interrogatives,* which are questions, ranging from the earliest forms produced by pairing a statement with a rising intonation (e.g., "Go bye-bye?") to the later, more complex form (e.g., "Did daddy go bye-bye?"); *imperatives,* which are obligatory re-

Table 5.7. Predicting chronological age from mean length of utterance (MLU)

Brown's Stage	MLU	Predicted chronological age[a]	Predicted age ± 1 SD middle 68%
Early Stage I	1.01	19.1	16.4–21.8
	1.50	23.0	18.5–27.5
Late Stage I	1.60	23.8	19.3–28.3
	2.00	26.9	21.5–32.3
Stage II	2.10	27.7	22.3–33.1
	2.50	30.8	23.9–37.7
Stage III	2.60	31.6	24.7–38.5
	3.00	34.8	28.0–41.6
Early Stage IV	3.10	35.6	28.8–42.4
	3.50	38.7	30.8–46.6
Late Stage IV/	3.60	39.5	31.6–47.4
Early Stage V	4.00	42.6	36.7–48.5
Late Stage V	4.10	43.4	37.5–49.3
	4.50	46.6	40.3–52.9
Post Stage V	4.60	47.3	41.0–53.6
	5.10	51.3	46.9–59.7
	5.60	55.2	46.8–63.6
	6.00	58.3	49.9–66.7

[a]Age is predicted from the equation: Age (in months) = 11.199 + 7.857 (MLU). Computed from obtained standard deviations (SD).

From MCLEAN, MARY; BAILEY, DONALD B.; WOLERY, MARK, ASSESSING INFANTS AND PRESCHOOLERS WITH SPECIAL NEEDS, 2nd Edition, (c) 1996, Pg. 338. Reprinted by permission of Pearson Education, Inc., Upper Saddle River, NJ.

quests or commands (e.g., "Get the ball"); and *exclamatory* sentences, which are statements showing strong emotion or excitement (e.g., "I did it!").

Negatives, such as *no, not,* and *don't,* are sometimes identified as a type of sentence. Negative sentences are acquired when the child is between 12 and 48 months old. Initially, the child places the negative at the beginning of a sentence; for example, "No want more." By about 2½, the child will begin to place the negative between the subject and the predicate in the sentence; for example, "She don't have a cat." Later-emerging negative forms, such as *shouldn't, couldn't, isn't,* and *doesn't,* are used during the next few years. As a child nears 5 years of age, indefinite negatives, including *nothing, nobody,* and *no one,* may be observed (Owens, 1998).

A child's ability to produce different types of questions develops within a predictable hierarchy. Examples of different types of questions and the approximate ages at which they should emerge are listed in Table 5.8.

The length and complexity of a child's sentences increase predictably over time, moving through the following range of sentence structures:

- *Simple sentences* are made of one independent clause conveying a complete thought; for example, "Mommy cooks noodles."

- *Compound sentences* are made of two or more independent clauses or simple sentences that are combined by conjunctions such as *but, and, or*; for example, "I washed my hands and ate my cookie."

- *Complex sentences* are made by combining one independent clause and one or more dependent clauses that cannot stand alone; for example, "I took the candy *that was on the table.*"

- *Compound-complex sentences* are made by combining at least two independent clauses and one or more dependent clauses.

Table 5.8. Asking questions

Approximate age	Type of question	Example
24–28 months	Statement with rising intonation	"Daddy go bye-bye?
25–28 months	What	"What that?"
26–32 months	Where	"Where ball?"
33–36 months	Inverted yes/no	"Can I ride it?
36–40 months	Who	"Who's that?"
37–42 months	Is/do	"Is that mine?" "Do you have a
cookie?"		
42–48 months	When	"When can we go?"
42–48 months	Why	"Why can't I?"

Children begin to use compound sentences between 2 and 2½ years of age, and complex sentences appear between 2 and 3 years of age (Trantham & Pedersen, 1976). All basic and complex syntactic structures are used by the time a child turns 5, although complex sentences become increasingly sophisticated and refined into the school-age years (Crais & Roberts, 2004; Shipley & McAfee, 2004).

USING THE OBSERVATION GUIDELINES TO ASSESS LANGUAGE PRODUCTION

Observations based primarily on the child's language use can be deceptive. Historically, language comprehension has been believed to precede language production. Accordingly, it was thought that any statement used by the child also must be understood by the child; however, most children do use words and structures beyond their comprehension, often by recalling and repeating words and phrases heard within a specific context. Children with disabilities also may demonstrate this pattern. The team's observations should indicate specifically when and how the child used a language structure, word, or phrase across several different situations.

TPBA2 allows for the observation of spontaneous play and structured interactions to elicit language production behaviors. Following are some strategies to assess how and why the child communicates (Wetherby & Prizant, 1989; Wetherby & Prutting, 1984):

1. Activate an electronic toy that has an on/off switch or a nonelectronic toy that is difficult for the child to operate independently (e.g., a wind-up toy or jack-in-the box). If the toy has an on/off switch, do not let the child see you turn the switch to the off mode. Hand the toy to the child and wait to see if the child asks for help.

2. Give the child a toy in a clear zipper bag or tightly closed container. Wait for the child to ask for assistance in opening the bag/container.

3. During snack in any of the following ways, but *do not sabotage the whole snack time:* Pick one or two techniques that may best suit the child: give the child a food item that is unopened (i.e., a wrapped granola bar or a package of fruit chews); place a favorite food in a tightly closed container; "forget" to give the child a necessary item, such as a cup for the juice or spoon for the pudding; give the child a disliked food item; give the child a very small amount of a desired food item or drink; eat a desired food and do not offer any to the child.

4. Have the child complete an activity that has a missing piece; for example, a puzzle, or an activity that requires a tool for completion. For example, say, "Let's cut out a circle," but don't provide the scissors to the child.

5. Place a few favorite toys or items within sight but out of reach, or partially hide a few objects. If necessary, point to or comment on objects to encourage a comment or request by the child.

6. Allow/ask the child to choose between two items, but give the child the object he or she did not choose. Wait for a comment or protest.

7. Blow bubbles a few times, close the bubble jar tightly and hand it to the child. Wait to see how the child communicates that he or she wants to continue the activity.

8. Initiate a social game such as Peekaboo or a favorite song, or have a parent play a tickle game. Stop and wait for the child to request continuation of the game or song.

9. Blow up a balloon and let it deflate a few times. Before automatically blowing the balloon up again, hold it up to your mouth and wait to see how the child communicates that he or she wants the balloon blown up again. *Please be advised that latex balloons pose a serious risk to young children and should only be used with close supervision* (U.S. Consumer Product Safety Commission, 2003).

Tasks that will elicit complex, longer utterances will be more representative of the child's skills. Conversely, if the task is too structured or unnatural for the child, the child's language use may be limited, resulting in an unrepresentative sample. The interaction with the parent or the child's teacher may provide the most information about the child's skills.

II. A. What modes of communication does the child use?

Assessment of the various communication modes used by a child is important for successful intervention planning. The modes of communication used by a child vary, depending on his or her developmental level and the presence of any possible disability. During the play session, observers should note behaviors that occur both nonverbally and verbally and the frequency with which the child used either.

The child may primarily use one form or a combination of methods. A child with physical involvement, for example, may primarily use eye gaze, facial expressions, body movement, and vocalizations. Another child may produce words and gaze at objects, but avoid eye contact with people. A child with poor intelligibility may rely heavily on gestures in combination with speech attempts, whereas a child with autism may use physical manipulation by placing the adult's hand on top of a requested object that needs to be opened but not look at the adult or use a word. Overall, the team needs to assess the primary and supplemental communication modes that are used by the child, as well as those that are available but not being optimally used by the child. Does the child use more gestures than single words or phrases? Observation of the child's imitation abilities including motor, vocal (sounds), and verbal (words and structures) imitations should be included since this also will provide guidance for intervention planning.

The play facilitator should observe and respond to all communication modes used by the child, including eye gaze, facial expressions, body movement, physical manipulation, gestures, manual signs, sounds, and word approximations. Any of these should receive the same respect as verbalizations; for example, word approximations and words. Descriptions of specific gestures and vocalizations, as well as the context in which they were observed, allows the team to obtain a more comprehensive picture of how the child communicates. The facilitators must sometimes use personal judgment and consult with the parent(s) to determine the intent of the child's nonverbal communication. This is most often determined by analyzing the context of the communication. Alternative interpretations also can be discussed, particularly if the child has idiosyncratic movements, gestures, or sounds. Parents are particularly helpful in identifying the intent of idiosyncratic behaviors.

Children who continue to rely primarily on prelinguistic communication modes longer than would be expected may have limited oral language skills. A possible cause for some children may be severe motor involvement, which affects speech production and problems with the structures or function of the oral mechanism (refer to the Oral Mechanism section of this chapter). The use of alternative behaviors in the child's repertoire may be shaped into consistent and meaningful behavior that becomes intentional and functional. An example of this is a nonverbal child who can raise his or her hand to wave "hi" as an alternative to a verbal greeting (Rosenberg, Clark, Filer, Hupp, & Finkler, 1992). Discussion with the other team members and the parents about these behaviors and eliciting them during the assessment may provide ideas for intervention planning.

If a child is using a low- or high-tech AAC system in other environments, then the system should be used as part of the TPBA process. It is beneficial if the assessment team has some low-tech AAC systems available to assess and elicit communication skills in a child who is nonverbal or may have limited verbal skills. The child can use eye gaze or a point to touch the board to communicate. One low-tech AAC option is a communication board consisting of miniature objects, pictures, line drawings, letters, or words in which the child uses eye gaze or touches the board to communicate. In addition, communication devices, also known as *voice output devices,* allow for words or short phrases to be recorded into the device to help augment the child's speech; these can be single message, sequential message, or multiple message voice output devices. These types of AAC devices usually use digitized speech, which is the recorded voice of a caregiver or peer, preferably of the same gender, who records words, phrases, or sentences into the device. The child activates a button with a corresponding picture to activate his or her message. There are a variety of these types of devices that are commercially available for purchase. Similar devices also can be crafted from items purchased at local stores, such as a talking photograph frame that permits up to four different recorded messages to go with corresponding pictures.

High-tech AAC devices usually are very expensive and are more complex to use. They can be programmed to store hundred of words, phrases, or sentences and commonly use synthesized speech or computerized speech.

By having AAC options available during the assessment, the team may be able to make some suggestions for the use of AAC in intervention planning or deem that a more in-depth assessment by a team of professionals with assistive technology expertise would benefit the child and the family. Some preschool programs have assistive technology available as part of their program or may have access to loan banks or lending libraries in their community.

II. B. What is the child's frequency of communication?

Analysis of the range and frequency of the child's communicative acts also will yield relevant information. The team should confirm with the parents that the frequency of communication during the assessment was typical. The TPBA team also should note the situations in which and with whom the child demonstrated the greatest frequency of communication. What was the most frequent communication between the child and his or her caregivers, peers, or unfamiliar individuals? If the child was seen in an unfamiliar environment, did that affect his or her willingness to communicate more frequently? For example, a child seen at home, child care, or in a familiar preschool setting may be more willing to communicate more. However, an unfamiliar environment with new toys and activities may affect the child's willingness to communicate.

Reduced frequency of communication also may be an indicator of problems in other areas. The child with motor disabilities may find it so difficult to speak that language attempts are minimal. Infrequent communication also may be an indicator of emotional and social concerns. A child who is highly withdrawn, for example, may choose not to communicate unless absolutely necessary. The child may have speech and language capabilities that are typical, but the frequency of communicative interaction is reduced. Duration or length of communication also is important. Does the child communicate throughout an activity, or only when necessary?

The measurement of the quantity of communication acts is accomplished by observing the frequency of the child's attempts during the time of the sample. The team needs to observe how often the child attempts to communicate, using the previously discussed modes of communication, as well as the duration of those attempts.

*Alexis, nearly 3 years old, has not had a previous developmental evaluation. She came to the assessment with her father and mother. Observations included play with her parents and with the facilitator. During play Alexis followed two-step related directions containing spatial concepts (*on, off, in, out*) and responded to yes/no and simple* where *questions ("Where is ___?") by looking for requested objects. She primarily produced single words consisting of labels of objects and some two-word combinations (*more juice, go bye-bye, ball gone*) to request and comment. She responded to simple* what *questions ("What is that?") to label pictures when looking at a book. Her parents reported she will occasionally imitate phrases up to four words in length at home. It was noted that the frequency of the spontaneous words Alexis produced was good; however, the variety of vocabulary she produced was limited. She also produced nonspecific words (i.e.,* this, that, it, those*). According to her father, she produces rote phrases. He also stated that the productions observed during the TPBA were typical of Alexis. During the assessment, Alexis was cautious and observed before she was willing to interact with objects and with the play facilitator. When situations were set up for Alexis to request objects or assistance, she tended to easily give up and walk away or avoid the interaction. For example, the facilitator took Alexis to wash her hands after playing with shaving cream. The facilitator waited for Alexis to communicate assistance and even attempted to elicit a response (e.g., "What do we need to do?" "What do you need?"). Alexis did not look at the facilitator, gesture, vocalize, or verbalize her needs (i.e., to be picked up to reach the sink, to request a paper towel, to request help opening the door) but instead she stood there, attempted to do the tasks by herself, and then gave up. During the interaction with her parents, she would use gestures coupled with words to sometimes request objects and continue an activity, but she did not initiate the need for assistance. Her parents reported that her lack of initiation for requesting assistance was fairly typical and that most of the time she was independent in meeting her needs and would rarely initiate requests from them.*

II. C. What are the child's semantic abilities?

Through parent report and observation of the child playing, looking at books, and participating in daily routines, the team can assess the variety, amount, and types of words, semantic categories (e.g., animals, foods), and semantic relations the child uses. At the single-word stage, the team should catalogue the kinds of words the child uses and record why they were used. The team also should indicate whether words are underextensions, overextensions, or nonspecific as well as noting instances when gestures are substituted for specific words. In addition, obtaining information and analyzing the types of semantic relations (e.g., object + action, agent + object) and how the child uses them for different functions will be necessary.

Word knowledge is very context and experience bound. On one hand, a child will show the most highly developed semantic abilities when talking about his or her actual experiences in the world. On the other hand, a child may have limited word knowledge about things that are less familiar or absent from his or her life experiences. Accordingly, areas of needed exposure should be noted. For example, a child with limited mobility will probably not use many action words, or a child with limited sight might demonstrate limited use of visually descriptive words. Therefore, the focus in intervention would be to provide the child with the experiences necessary for gaining the knowledge pertaining to less well-developed word classes. For example, a child who demonstrates a fondness for movement activities will more readily recognize the effectiveness of action words when paired with a movement activity. Recording a semantic inventory across multiple settings will give the most representative sample.

II. D. What grammatical morphemes does the child produce?

During the play session, the child's production of grammatical morphemes and syntax may be documented informally; however, a sufficient language sample is essential for comprehensive analysis. According to Muma (1998), most language samples taken by SLPs are 50–100 utterances in length, but samples of up to 200–400 utterances are recommended to decrease the likelihood of error. The facilitator needs to provide opportunities for the child to demonstrate his or her spontaneous skills. The types of grammatical morphemes the child produces and the deletion of grammatical morphemes should be noted. Any articulation problems affecting the child's ability to produce grammatical structures must be noted. For example, a child who deletes final consonants will not be able to produce some morphemes, such as the final plural *s* in "ca<u>ts</u>," which would be said as "ca." Consequently, assessing the child's *comprehension* of omitted morphemes, such as in plurals and possessives, should be part of the process. The facilitator may model a certain grammatical morpheme to see whether the child will imitate it.

II. E. What are the child's syntactic abilities?

In assessing syntax, assess the sentence complexity and type of sentences produced. Are the sentences simple or complex? What types of sentences are used—questions, comments, requests, exclamations? Is the child using negative forms and, if so, what type?

The team should try to plan tasks that will encourage maximal production of spontaneous language and that will elicit examples of the child's most complex sentence structures. If the task is too structured or unnatural for the child, the team will probably not get a representative sample of the child's abilities. Playing with a familiar peer, sibling, or adult and doing favorite activities may increase the child's MLU.

> *While looking at a picture in a book of ducks getting out of the water, the mother said "The ducks are cold." Julianna asked, "They don't have towels, Mommy?" Her mother replied, "No, the ducks don't have towels." Julianna said, "They need to get towels like we got towels."*

III. Pragmatics

Three areas of pragmatics are examined in TPBA: *joint attention and communicative intent, communicative functions,* and *discourse skills.* Knowledge of these terms is necessary to obtain an understanding of how and why a child is communicating and to determine his or her overall communicative competence. A communicative intent is more complex than a simple, personal intent, such as the desire to return an overdue library book. Communicative intent requires an understanding that messages carry meanings and expectations that specifically affect the listener; for example, to fulfill a request, to pay attention to someone or something, or to be welcomed by a greeting (Tomasello, 2003; Wetherby & Prizant, 1993). Communicative functions cluster intentional messages into categories that frame the range of communicative purposes (Crais et al., 2004; Kaczmarek, 2002; Tomasello, 2003). Finally, discourse skills relate to specific aspects of contextualized language, including skills required to engage in communicative events such as conversations, narratives, stories, and humor (Kaczmarek, 2002; Yoshinaga-Itano, 1997).

Identifying and describing the child's pragmatic abilities with both familiar and unfamiliar partners during play allows the team to obtain a dynamic understanding of how and why the child communicates. Because pragmatic language skills are best assessed in meaningful interactions, TPBA may reduce the "context stripping problem" posed by formal pragmatic assessments (Duchan, 1988, as cited in Yoshinaga-Itano, 1997). Depending on the child's age, three broad areas should be assessed through behavior sampling, probes, and parent report or observation (Gerber & Prizant, 2000; Kaczmarek, 2002; Yoshinaga-Itano, 1997):

• An analysis of the rate and types of communicative functions the child uses

• An analysis of conversational skills, such as taking turns and maintaining a topic

- An analysis of oral discourse skills, such as retelling a personal event

- Observation of the how the child follows, establishes, and regulates joint attention.

The following three sections present information about a child's pragmatic development. Section III.A examines the general development of communicative intent with special consideration given to joint attention behaviors, gesture use, and a child's transition from nonverbal to verbal intentional communication. Section III.B discusses how specific communicative intents are expressed within a range of communicative functions. Finally, Section III. C moves beyond single intentional acts to describe aspects of discourse and extended communication, including conversational skills, storytelling and narration, cohesion, reciprocity, and the frequency and quality of social interaction.

III. A. Does the child understand and use joint attention (gestures, vocalizations, or words) to communicate intent?

Communicative intent is not present at birth but becomes evident long before a child produces the first word. This development follows a predictable progression from reflexive, unintentional nonverbal communication to intentional, verbal communication (Bates, Camaioni, & Volterra, 1975, as cited in Capone & McGregor, 2004). In addition, communicative intent may be expressed in many different forms, including words, gestures, vocalizations, and gaze shifts, all of which are intended to affect the listener's actions or focus of attention (Capone & McGregor, 2004; Crais et al., 2004; Wetherby & Prizant, 1993). As a child moves through the intricate process of acquiring intent, the communicative acts become more abstract, decontextualized, and symbolic over time, increasing in distance from objects, actions, and the communicative partner(s) (Werner & Kaplan, 1963, as cited in Crais et al., 2004). For example, a child first uses eye gaze or contact gestures, such as holding an object to show it to another person. Later, a child will draw an adult's attention to an object by pointing to it from across a room. Ultimately, a child may use words or signs to direct a person's attention.

Unintentional Communication

Between birth and 2 months, a baby's sounds and movements principally are reflexive or reactive, although these behaviors also are observed later. Reflexive sounds and movements are either vegetative, such as coughing, burping, sneezing, and yawning, or express distress, like crying, fussy sounds, grunts, sighs, flailing arms, and stiffening limbs (Stark et al., 1993). Reactive sounds emerge between 2 and 5 months. They include neutral sounds, which are made when the child gazes with a neutral face at an adult, the surroundings, or a specific object, and pleasure sounds and movements, which include laughter, excited limb movements, sustained vocalization, and a fixed gaze made in response to an adult who smiles, nods, or interacts playfully with the child (Crais et al., 2004; Stark et al., 1993). Between 6 and 9 months, vocalization increases, especially when a child is inspecting, mouthing, or playing with objects, bouncing, or clapping hands (Stark et al., 1993). The majority of these sounds do not convey true communicative intent.

Throughout this stage, the child's communication is primarily dyadic, occurring solely between the child and another person without shared attention to outside activities, to objects, or to other people (Tomasello, 2003). Nonetheless, during these early exchanges, the caregiver often responds to the baby's sounds and movements as though they carry specific meanings and intentions. For example, when the baby cries, the parent decides that the child is hungry or uncomfortable. The parent responds by saying, "You're hungry" or "Your diaper is wet" and feeds the child or changes the diaper. At first, the words are just noise to the baby. Toward the end of the first year, however, the child begins to understand that the words are related to something the adult intends to do for the child's benefit (Calandrella & Wilcox, 2000; Thal & Tobias, 1992b; Tomasello, 2003; Wetherby & Prizant, 1993). Soon, the child learns to repeat "showing off" behaviors that are successful in gaining adult attention (Capone & McGregor, 2004; Crais et al., 2004).

Prelinguistic Intentional Communication

Between 9 and 12 months, the child shows increased understanding of social interactions and intentional communication. Three important behavioral changes occur that usher in the onset of prelinguistic intentional communication (Tomasello, 2003): ability to establish joint attention, gesture use, and role reversal imitation.

Joint Attention

Joint attention moves a child from dyadic to triadic communication, which encompasses not only the child and the immediate communicative partner, but also an outside focus of attention, such as another person, an object, or a nearby event (Delgado et al., 2002; Markus, Mundy, Morales, Delgado, & Yale, 2000; Tomasello, 2003). Language learning appears to occur primarily within these established joint attention frames (Mundy & Sigman, 2006; Tomasello, 2003). Between 8 and 9 months, the child begins to use eye gaze to establish joint attention with an adult (Crais et al., 2004) and by 12 months, the child is consistently using gaze to alter others' behavior (Carpenter, Nagell, & Tomasello, 1998). This usually is accomplished with object–person–object gaze regulation (Crais et al., 2004; Tomasello, 2003). For example, to focus a parent's attention on a nearby cat, a 1-year-old first looks at the cat, then to her mother, and then back to the cat again, as though to say, "Look, Mom! A cat!"

Responding to bids for joint attention (e.g., visually following an adult's gaze or point) is an important aspect of understanding communicative intent (Delgado et al., 2002; Mundy & Sigman, 2006; Tomasello, 2003). Before the age of 12 months, a child begins to follow the direction of an adult's eye gaze within his or her immediate visual field, and by 15 months this skill is routine (Delgado et al., 2002). By approximately 15 months, a child can monitor the direction of an adult's gaze outside of his or her immediate visual field, which suggests development of object permanence and is predictive of positive expressive language development at 24 months of age (Markus et al., 2000). For example, if a father playing on the floor with his daughter looked at the television screen behind her to check the hockey score, she would follow his gaze and look at the television, too.

Gesture Use

Between 8 and 9 months, a child begins to use gestures, sometimes paired with vocalizations and gaze, to send intentional messages to others. Broadly speaking, gestures constitute purposeful communicative actions that are most often made with the fingers, hands, and arms, but also may include facial features (e.g., blowing a kiss) and body motions (Calandrella & Wilcox, 2000; Capone & McGregor, 2004; Crais et al., 2004). At first, gestures are imitative and context-bound, but over time they incorporate symbolic meaning and the power to reference, clarify, and add emphasis to communication (Capone & McGregor, 2004; Werner & Kaplan, 1963, as cited in Crais et al., 2004). It is very important to observe gestures in prelinguistic children because their use is tightly linked to vocabulary acquisition and the advancement of language (Brady, Marquis, Fleming, & McLean, 2004; Capone & McGregor, 2004; Crais et al.,

2004; Mundy, Kasari, Sigman, & Ruskin, 1995). In addition, gesture analysis can help differentiate late talkers from late bloomers and facilitate identification of children who are at risk for specific language impairment. Late talkers are children who have not advanced to two-word combinations by 18–24 months of age; late bloomers recover this delay by age 3 (Capone & McGregor, 2004). Gesture use of true late talkers is restricted, whereas late bloomers demonstrate typical, if not robust, gesture use. In fact, late bloomers are reported to use more gestures than their peers, especially to initiate and respond in communication (Thal & Tobias, 1992a). Children at risk for a specific language impairment will demonstrate immature gesture use, lagging behind age-matched peers (Capone & McGregor, 2004).

During the prelinguistic intentional stage, children commonly rely on two types of gestures: deictic and representational. Deictic gestures regulate behavior or frame joint attention (Capone & McGregor, 2004; Crais et al., 2004; Tomasello, 2003) and their developmental sequence reveals a gradual distancing from referenced objects or actions (Werner & Kaplan, 1963, as cited in Crais et al., 2004). At around 8 or 9 months, a child begins to use gestures to comment or request, primarily by showing or giving, open-handed reaching, and pushing to protest (Capone & McGregor, 2004; Crais et al., 2004). For example, a baby might ask for a sippy cup by reaching for it on the counter. Gestures are sometimes paired with vocalizations, although this happens in fewer than half of all communicative acts at this age.

Pointing, an important deictic gesture, emerges around 9 months but its early use may not always carry communicative intent. Pointing develops clearer purpose between 10 and 14 months as the child learns to use it intentionally, requesting actions, commenting on objects, and requesting information (Brady et al., 2004; Crais et al., 2004). Research has identified a relationship between pointing and language development. For example, pointing and object name recognition surface at nearly identical median ages, 10 months 21 days and 10 months 22 days, respectively (Harris, Barlow-Brown, & Chasin, 1995). Bates et al. (1975) and Folven and Bonwillian (1991, as cited in Capone & McGregor, 2004) reported that pointing with joint attention is a precursor to spoken and signed naming. In a longitudinal study of prelinguistic children, those who pointed had significantly better language comprehension abilities later than those who did not (Brady et al., 2004; Capone & McGregor, 2004). In addition, McLean, McLean, Brady, and Etter (1991, as cited in Brady et al., 2004) reported that children who point at an object from a distance (i.e., distal point) communicate more often, for more purposes, and more effectively repair their communication than children who do not.

Representational gestures usually emerge before the 25-word milestone (Capone & McGregor, 2004). They consist of either object-related, symbolic gestures, such as blowing to indicate "bubbles," or conventional gestures, which are culturally defined actions that have meaning, such as waving "bye." Most representational gestures first occur at about 12 months, are related to social interaction, and often develop within the context of social action games and routines. For example, children will make gestures while engaging in fingerplays or singing songs such as "The Itsy Bitsy Spider." Like deictic gestures, they become less context bound over time. The most commonly observed representational gestures include waving, clapping, showing the function of an object, hugging objects, smacking one's lips, blowing kisses, nodding "yes," and shrugging the shoulders (Crais et al., 2004).

The development of representational gestures anticipates and then parallels the emergence of early spoken words (Bates, Bretherton, & Snyder, 1988, as cited in Capone & McGregor, 2004). In fact, research indicates that children who use many open-handed, representational gestures are more likely to meet their first 10-word milestone earlier than children who use fewer gestures (Acredolo & Goodwyn, 1988).

Between 12 and 18 months, however, representative gestures and spoken vocabulary are generally mutually exclusive (Capone & McGregor, 2004), and by 28 months, the child typically prefers to use and hear communicated spoken words for objects and their categories.

Role Reversal Imitation

Role reversal imitation involves a child's ability to understand that intentional communication is socially shared and that there are no one-way signals (Tomasello, 2003). What an adult communicates to the child can be turned around and used by the child to elicit the same response or action from the adult. This requires the child to make a rudimentary perspective shift from communicative target to a communicator with intentional agency. For example, the adult might push the child's hand away from a hot-glue gun art project, and the child learns "push" (gesture) means "I don't want you to touch this" (communicator's intent). Later, in a role reversal imitation, the child can use this gesture with the same communicative intent and agency, such as pushing the adult's hand away from a favorite toy.

Intentional Verbal Communication

Near the age of 1 year, a child starts using words to communicate intentions previously expressed nonverbally. This shift is not abrupt, but occurs over time, with gestures gradually scaffolding word acquisition. By 15 months, representational gestures paired with vocalizations or words constitute the majority of a child's communicative acts (Capone & McGregor, 2004). As words begin to dominate communication, however, representational gesture use decreases and the use of deictic gestures, particularly pointing, paired with words increases. These combinations assume a variety of forms that are used to clarify different verbal communicative intents: equivalent information (pointing to a cup while saying, "cup"), complementary information (pointing to a cup while saying, "juice"), and supplementary information (pointing to a cup and saying, "hot"). Morford and Goldin-Meadow (1992) differentiated between these combinations, reporting that complementary word–gesture combinations at 16 months predicted more spoken words later than did equivalent combinations.

Between the ages of 2 and 3, a child begins to form two-word combinations and simple sentences. These combinations allow a child to refine early requesting and commenting acts by making them more precise. For example, the child can now request the recurrence of objects or actions (more juice) and differentiate reference to objects (big dog versus little dog). During this stage, pointing remains an integral part of the child's message as a means to support and clarify meaning. Words gradually become less context-bound through the preschool years as the child's symbol system becomes more abstract and less dependent on the presence of a referent object. By the child's third birthday, the variety of communicative intentions expands and is near adult-like (Paul, 2001), including requesting and clarifying information, fantasy, and humor. During the preschool years, beat gestures, which are devoid of any explicit symbolic content, appear (Capone & McGregor, 2004). Used only during speech, these rhythmic, staccato hand movements (e.g., a flick of the hand or fingers) stress key words and are believed to indicate increased awareness of word and sentence structure. By 42 months, gestures and speech are combined at approximately the same rate as for adults (Capone & McGregor, 2004). By the time a child is in school, communication with multiple partners is possible, permitting participation in group activities and discussion. In addition, as the ability to ask questions and exchange information with others develops, language becomes a tool for learning in addition to a vehicle for social interaction.

▰▰▰▰ **III. B. What functions does the child's communication fulfill?**

Communicative functions tell us why a child is communicating. There are many ways of describing functions and myriad taxonomies for categorizing them (Duchan, 2001; Goldstein, Kaczmarek, & English, 2002), but for purposes of the TPBA, communicative functions will be divided into three broad categories: regulatory, declarative-joint attention, and social interaction (Crais et al., 2004; Mundy & Sigman, 2006).

Most communicative functions develop during the first 2 years of life and follow unique, but predictable, developmental patterns. A child first engages in basic regulatory functions—requesting objects and actions or protesting (Crais et al., 2004). With increasing maturity, however, a child engages in a greater range of functions, which may all be expressed with gaze, vocalization, gesture, word, or sign, alone or in combination. When a child reaches the age of 3, communicative acts begin to serve a double function, such as using a point to direct an adult's attention to and request an unreachable toy from a shelf (Halle, Brady, & Drasgow, 2004). As perspective-taking abilities develop, 4- and 5-year-old children begin to show sensitivity to a communication partner's need for background knowledge when speaking about a topic, which is reflected in an expanding ability to request and provide information (Halle et al., 2004; Kaczmarek, 2002; Tomasello, 2003). For example, if two 5-year-olds decided to set up a lemonade stand on the street corner, one might explore the other's prior experience by asking "Ever had a lemonade stand?" The other might share her prior knowledge by saying, "I always like to fill the cups." Specific information about the forms and types of speech acts at different ages can be found in the communication Age Table (see p. 263).

Regulatory functions emerge first and include requesting objects, requesting actions, and protesting (Crais et al., 2004). Regulatory functions include initiations and responses to requests for objects, requests to make an action happen, refusal of an object, or communication to stop an action (Mundy & Sigman, 2006; Tomasello, 2003). The earliest regulatory behaviors are observed around the 6-month milestone and typically include requests for objects and actions or protests, which are accomplished with eye-gaze shift, vocalization, or gross physical action. At this age, a child may cry when a toy is taken away, or look away and grimace when offered food that is disliked. Over the next 6 months, a child begins to use more progressively refined movements—pushing away with the arm or hand, reaching, opening-closing the hand, and pointing—to request and protest. For example, a child might protest the offer of a toy by pushing it away. At about 1 year, a child begins to use object–person–object gaze shifts to request an object. For example, when the child wants an out-of-reach cookie, she or he would ask for it by looking first at the cookie, then at the caregiver, and then back at the cookie again, as if to say, "May I please have that cookie?" Finally, between 12 and 15 months of age, a child begins using word approximations and words to ask for objects or actions. During this same period, a child also begins to use more symbolic gestures to protest, such as shaking the head to say, "No!" (Crais et al., 2004).

Declarative-joint attention functions are used to monitor a partner's attention; to share attention on objects and actions; or to request, clarify, or provide information (Crais et al., 2004; Mundy & Sigman, 2006). These functions, which first emerge at about 9 months and continue developing to about 2 years, include initiations and responses to comments on objects, comments on actions, requesting information, providing information, and requesting clarification. Declarative-joint attention functions occur slightly later than regulatory functions, first emerging as comments made with vocalization and eye gaze at 7 months and later in commenting gestures—with or without accompanying vocalizations—between 9 and 10 months of age. Pointing, a powerful joint attention gesture, is used by children for different purposes at different ages. Pointing to comment or share attention emerges first in the tenth month.

Between 14 and 18 months, however, the child comes to understand that pointing—paired with vocalizations, word approximations, words, or a rising intonation pattern—can be used as a powerful tool to request information (Crais et al., 2004). For example, at this age children will often ask what something is by pointing at an object, looking at the caregiver, and saying "Dat?" with a rising question inflection.

Social interaction functions are used primarily to engage in social games or fantasy, to regulate face-to-face interactions, and to express social conventions (Capone & McGregor, 2004; Crais et al., 2004). They include responding, participating, and initiating social games such as Peekaboo; social conventions such as waving or saying, "Hi"; and representational gestures or play such as hugging objects, blowing kisses, shrugging the shoulders, and pretending to sleep or be a bird. A child's awareness of the social nature of games and play routines develops in stages between 9 and 15 months of age (Platt & Coggins, 1990). In the beginning, the child loosely attends to the adult's actions but quickly comes to understand the link between the movements and the game. By 15 months, the child becomes a full participant in the game, using conventional gestures to share turns. Representational gestures, which are more symbolic, mostly emerge during the second year. Basic pretend gestures, such as hugging objects, can be observed around the end of the first year; more abstract gestures, such as pretending to sleep and shoulder shrugs, can be observed as the child approaches the midpoint of the second year.

▓▓▓▓▓ III. C. What conversational or discourse skills does the child demonstrate?

An evaluation of discourse skills provides useful information about the child's desire and ability to participate in extended, reciprocal interactions. For the purpose of TPBA, discourse analysis will examine the elements of conversations and narratives.

Conversations

We all engage in conversations on a daily basis, talking with friends and family about what is going on in our lives, in the community, and in the world. On the surface, conversations look relatively simple, but a closer look at conversations reveals how dynamically complex they really are. Successful engagement in conversation demands the rapid-fire selection and deployment of a variety of discourse skills: topic management, including topic selection, introduction, maintenance, and change; cohesion, including relating all comments on a turn-by-turn and whole-conversation basis; knowledge of how to take turns; and how to repair the conversation if it stalls or breaks down. A child begins to learn these skills in back-and-forth exchanges in infancy (Capone & McGregor, 2004; McCathren, Yoder, & Warren, 1999; Stark et al., 1993; Tomasello, 2003), and true conversations occur by the time a child is 2 years old (Tomasello, 2003). Discourse skills, however, continue to develop into adolescence or beyond, when abstract topics are discussed in depth in lengthy conversations (Kaczmarek, 2002).

Topic Management

During the first year, a child begins to understand the concept of "topic" within joint attention frames and by 18 months begins to predict things about a share topic (e.g., nearby object or action) (Tomasello, 2003). At 2 years, a child can initiate a topic and expand it during a subsequent turn by commenting or adding new information (Tomasello, 2003). At this early conversational stage, however, a child introduces more topics more frequently than older children and largely depends on an adult to scaffold and structure the conversation (Kaczmarek, 2002). By about 3½ years of age, a child can maintain a variety of topics over several sequences (Bloom, Rocissano, & Hood, 1976).

This occurs as a result of the child's increased fund of knowledge and the acquisition of advanced linguistic structures. At this stage, the child's conversation skills resemble more closely those of an adult.

Cohesion

Cohesion refers to how the individual utterances in a conversation work together to make a logical and complete conversation. Each turn must build on the ones before it, known as *contingency,* and all turns must logically relate to the entire conversation (Haynes & Pindzola, 2004; Kaczmarek, 2002; Tomasello, 2003). These skills begin to develop in early childhood but are not mastered until adolescence or later. Cohesion requires sophisticated levels of perspective-taking, self-monitoring, semantics, and syntax. One of the most important skills for conversational cohesion is awareness of the need to provide the right amount of information to move the conversation forward without repeating what has already been said (Kaczmarek, 2002). Children with poor cohesion skills might demonstrate some of the following behaviors:

- *Information redundancy:* The child fixates on a fact or single aspect of the topic.

- *Insufficient information:* The child provides insufficient information in turns.

- *Inappropriateness:* The child produces an inappropriate or irrelevant comment or question.

Taking Turns

A conversation is a series of turns on a shared topic of interest. As with communicative functions, the types of turns a child initiates become more refined over time. At first, an infant engages in gaze exchanges, cries, or vocalizes; later, the child will yell, gesture, tug, and eventually use phrases like "Know what?" (Haynes & Pindzola, 2004). By the second birthday, a child takes one or two turns in conversations with adults, and they are executed with an appropriate give-and-take cadence (Kaczmarek, 2002; Tomasello, 2003). With increasing age and language development, the number of turns and the length and complexity of the conversation increase.

As a child's turn-taking skills develop, he or she must learn the rules for when and when not to take a turn, how to take a turn, and how long a turn should be. These rules are sophisticated nuances of conversation. TPBA observers should note whether the child takes roughly balanced turns during interactions, dominates the turns, takes very long turns, or fails to take turns at appropriate times during the interaction. The following turn-taking behaviors also should be observed: initiation; response; pause time (e.g., the amount of time that lapses between turns, usually no more than 2–3 seconds); interruption and overlap (e.g., how much partners talk over each other); and feedback to the listener, such as nodding to acknowledge continued participation (Prutting & Kirchner, 1987, as cited in Goldstein et al., 2002).

Breakdowns, Repairs, and Revisions

Sometimes conversations break down, resulting in awkward pauses, misunderstanding, or miscommunication. Young children experience conversational breakdowns for many different reasons, and describing them will provide useful information about a child's communicative competence. Yont and colleagues (2000) describe common reasons for children's conversational breakdowns:

- Low volume—the child speaks too softly to be consistently understood.

- Phonological errors—the child's speech errors interfere with understanding.

- Lexical errors—the child misuses words or word combinations.

- Pragmatic errors—the child violates language use rules, such as making abrupt and unmarked topic shifts or ambiguous statements.

- Nonverbal errors—the child uses idiosyncratic, unrecognizable, or misunderstood gestures.

- Incomplete utterance—the child starts a statement, but does not finish it.

In order to keep a conversation going, a child must first be aware that a breakdown occurred and then repair or revise what was said to get communication started again. It is the listener who usually signals a breakdown with a request for clarification—looking confused, specifically asking for more information ("You want me to do what?"), saying "Huh?" or "A what?" or repeating back what was said with a rising intonation ("We gotta go?"). At 18 months, children begin to respond to basic requests for clarification (e.g., "Huh?" "What?") typically by restating what they said (Tomasello, 2003). This ability expands between 3 and 5 years as a child becomes increasingly capable of responding to a broad range of requests for clarification (Tomasello, 2003). Children begin to initiate generic requests for clarification (e.g., "Huh?" "What?") toward the end of the second year. TPBA observers should note whether the child understands and responds to requests for clarification. In addition, observers should describe how the child asks for clarification or new information—verbally or nonverbally—and document absent or inappropriate use of these strategies (Halle et al., 2004; Yont et al., 2000).

Between 2 and 4 years of age, an emerging perspective-taking ability becomes evident as a child begins to assess the familiarity of the listener and what aspects of the communication are being misunderstood, and revise his or her language use accordingly. For example, a 2-year-old child differentiates between a parent and an unfamiliar adult when clarifying information. The child will repeat an utterance to a parent but will restate or rephrase an utterance for an unfamiliar adult (Tomasello, 2003). Presumably, the child understands an unfamiliar listener's need for more or different information. In addition, a 4-year-old child will use short, simple utterances when talking to a 2-year-old but will use longer, more complex utterances with an adult. TPBA observers should note any language adjustments related to perspective-taking, even though ability to monitor the self and the listener is not well developed in preschool-age children.

Narratives

Oral narratives are personal accounts of past events, such as talking about a trip to the zoo or explaining a movie plot to a friend. They are complex discourse activities that present a storyteller with considerable cognitive and communicative challenges. Among other things, a narrator must tell a story in a way that can be easily followed by the listener, adhere to the rules of a story grammar, and correctly sequence the story's events in time and space. The ability to tell oral narratives develops over decades and follows a predictable developmental path. Assessing narrative ability during the preschool and early school years is important, because these skills are predictive of academic success, particularly reading comprehension and writing (Haynes & Pindzola, 2004; McCabe & Rollins, 1994; Paul, Hernandez, Taylor, & Johnson, 1996). Some errors in storytelling should be expected in preschool children and do not necessarily indicate communication problems; other errors may signal communication problems.

Two-Year-Olds

First attempts at narratives may be seen just before a child turns 2 years old. These are not well-formed stories that begin with "Once upon a time" but are limited references to events that listening adults scaffold and structure for the child. The words *yesterday* and *last night* are used indiscriminately to denote when the events happened, reflecting an awareness of a need to anchor the story at some point in time; however, these references seldom indicate the actual time of the event (Tomasello, 2003). At this age, a child focuses mostly on negative events, such as injuries or a pet dying (McCabe & Rollins, 1994). For example, a 2-year-old might point to a bandage on her leg and say, "Owie, fall down!" The adult might ask where, and the child would add new information, saying, "On the slide . . . yesterday."

Three- and Four-Year-Olds

At age 3–4, children begin to tell longer, more complex narratives containing two different events, such as going to the zoo and having a picnic lunch there (McCabe & Rollins, 1994). Although the story may have a global sense of beginning, middle, and end, the events in the story often will be told out of sequence.

Five-Year-Olds

By the time a child is 5, stories evolve from chains of events to well-sequenced, hierarchical structures containing more characters and more events (Tomasello, 2003). Most stories, however, end prematurely, remaining focused on the most exciting, climatic event (McCabe & Rollins, 1994). Typically, there is no resolution or moral to the story.

Six-Year-Olds

A 6-year-old child can tell a well-formed story, containing sophisticated syntax structures and the following story grammar elements (Haynes & Pindzola, 2004; McCabe & Rollins, 1994):

- *Setting:* a description of the environment and characters

- *Initiating event:* a problem that sets the story in motion

- *Internal response:* a plan to solve the problem that reflects emotions, thoughts, and intents of the characters

- *Attempts:* efforts to attain a goal or solve the problem

- *Consequences:* the resolution of the problem or failure to do so

- *Reaction:* the character's response to the consequence; the moral of the story

Children with developmental disabilities and language impairments may show delayed narrative development and struggle with narrative production. For example, children with specific language impairment do not begin producing narratives until about age 3 (Kaderavek & Sulzby, 2000), and their narratives reveal organizational problems and qualitative differences. The narratives of children with language impairment may differ from those of typical children in the following ways (Kaderavek & Sulzby, 2000; McCabe & Rollins, 1994; Paul et al., 1996; Tomasello, 2003):

- Stories are very short and the vocabulary is limited.

- Expected story grammar components are missing.

- Events go backward and forward in time, making the sequence hard to follow.

- Stories include irrelevant events or omit important events.

- Conventional opening and closings are omitted.

- Too much or too little information is provided.

- Few cohesive ties are used (e.g., first, then, later, the next day).

- Stories do not accommodate the listener's need for background information.

▬▬ USING THE OBSERVATION GUIDELINES TO ASSESS PRAGMATICS

Please refer to Facilitating and Eliciting Communication Strategies, discussed in the earlier section, for guidelines for assessing language production and for suggested activities to encourage communication in a variety of play contexts. When identifying the level of joint attention, communicative intent, communicative functions, or discourse ability, descriptions of the child's behaviors and the context in which the behaviors were observed must be included. This description of specific gestures, vocalizations, verbalizations, and their contexts allows the team to obtain a more comprehensive picture of how the child uses his or her communication system. Alternative interpretations also can be discussed, particularly if the child has idiosyncratic movements, gestures, sounds, or words; parents are particularly helpful in interpreting the child's idiosyncratic behaviors.

▬▬ III. A. Does the child understand and use joint attention
(gestures, vocalizations, or words) to communicate intent?

Many aspects of pragmatics are culturally defined, such as physical proximity to the communication partner, gestures, facial expressions, eye gaze, and touch. Accordingly, observational criteria will differ within and among cultures. The team must determine what behaviors are consistent with interactions in the child's culture to perform the assessment. During the play session, observers should note behaviors that occur both verbally and nonverbally. When behaviors occur nonverbally, the professional must use personal judgment regarding the intent of the child, which is usually determined through analysis of the context of the situation. The level of intention—unintentional, prelinguistic, or linguistic—should be noted broadly, and the behaviors demonstrated within that level also should be noted. If the child does not yet use intentional communication, observe the child's use of eye contact and describe between the types of reflexive and reactive sounds or movements used.

> *Seven-month-old Mary's communication is both reflexive and reactive. She cries when she is hungry and fusses when she is getting tired, which are forms of reflexive communication. Mary enjoys interacting with her father at meal time and engages in many types of reactive communication. When her dad holds a spoonful of plums up for her, she looks at him, smacks her lips, and wriggles with excitement. When her father tries feeding her peas, which she doesn't like, she looks unhappy and turns her head away from her father.*

The team should observe carefully the nonverbal behaviors of a prelinguistic child during the assessment and in later videotape analysis to determine whether communication is intentional. The child's use of object–partner–object eye contact, showing gestures, and pointing should be examined to see if a child is establishing joint attention on objects or actions with the parent or facilitator. Gesture use in different play contexts should be inventoried, including showing or giving objects, open-handed reaching, pushing gestures, pointing, representational gestures, and social gestures (e.g., waving, blowing a kiss). Any coordinated eye contact and vocalizations used with these gestures also should be described. The team should pay particular attention to whether or not the child points or uses representational gestures, such as cupping an empty hand as though to drink. The absence of either of these types of gestures is seen in children with language impairment and autism spectrum disorders.

Four-year-old Anna, a child with severe disabilities, is nonverbal but demonstrates communicative intent in many ways. Her lack of breath control and difficulty with articulation interfere with speech and conversation. Nonetheless, when observed in pretend play with her mother, Anna used joint attention (object–person–object eye contact) to initiate play with a doll. Her mother then picked up the doll and asked, "Would you like to hold it, Anna?" Anna nodded and grunted. Her mother put the doll into her arms and Anna smiled. Her mother commented, "That's a nice doll, isn't it?" Anna nodded and looked at the baby bottle. "Should we feed her?" her mother asked. Anna nodded. Her mother held the bottle up to the doll's mouth and Anna said, "Mmm." Analysis reveals that Anna is a prelinguistic intentional communicator who used object–person–object joint attention to make requests, and used representational gestures combined with a vocalization (nodding paired with grunt) to answer questions and acknowledge comments, and representational vocalizations ("Mmm") when pretending to feed the doll. She communicates intentionally during interactions but does so with a limited range of gestures. Anna would benefit from intervention that emphasizes combining gestures, vocalizations, and eye contact as well as using a near and far point.

The team's observation of communicative intent in verbal children also should include comments about accompanying nonverbal behaviors and coordinated use of joint attention. The analysis of verbal communicative intent should describe how the child is combining words with gestures (e.g., equivalent word pairing, complementary word pairing, words paired with a point, emphasis of words in sentences) and whether the child is relying more on gestures or words to make his or her intent understood. In addition, the team should describe the level of verbal intention—one word, two-word combinations, sentences, and questions.

▓▓▓▓ III. B. What functions does the child's communication fulfill?

During the assessment, team members should note the following information about the child's communicative functions:

1. Which of the following types of functions does the child respond to and initiate?

   • Regulatory functions—requests for objects, requests for actions, protests

   • Declarative/joint attention functions—comments on objects, comments on actions, requests for information, requests for clarification, providing or adding information to clarify statements

   • Social interaction functions—showing interest, smiling, responding to social games, initiating social games, nodding head, social gestures (e.g., waving, blowing kisses, shrugs)

2. What modes are used to express each communicative function? Does the child use coordinated eye contact or gaze, vocalizations, deictic gestures, representational gestures, social gestures, words, two-word combinations, sentences, questions, or rising intonation patterns? The team should describe how any of these modes are used in combination. Does the child prefer one? Is the child's mode of expression appropriate to his or her age level?

3. How frequently does the child use each communicative function during the interaction? Does the child rely mostly on one or two functions and not use others? For example, does the child rely on asking questions or requesting objects? Or is a range of functions used appropriately throughout play?

4. In which contexts does the child use each communicative function? For example, in addition to requesting food or drinks at snack time, does the child also make comments, ask questions, show interest, and smile? Does the child communicate in some contexts but not in others during the assessment?

5. Is the child's use of communicative functions effective in achieving a goal? For example, does the child persist when requesting an action, such as blowing bubbles, or does he or she give up? Does the child give information or request clarification in a way that is understood by the listener?

Note: If the child is at the one-word stage, implied meanings are important to document.

These observations will help to determine the level of the child's functional communicative competence, profile the child's communicative strengths, and indicate areas in which interventions may be helpful. Some children with disabilities such as autism spectrum disorders develop idiosyncratic or socially inappropriate ways of expressing communicative functions. If a child uses idiosyncratic movements, gestures, or sounds, the parents will be particularly helpful in identifying and interpreting the child's communicative function and responses.

Sivan is a verbal 3-year-old girl who uses words and phrases in idiosyncratic ways. Sivan's parents say they are worried because she doesn't like to play with other children at her new preschool or to ask her teacher for help. Sometimes she just repeats what other people say (echolalia). When presented with a closed container of crackers during the snack portion of the assessment, Sivan reached for the box without looking at the facilitator. When she could not open it, she did not use a look, gesture, or word to ask the facilitator for help. In addition, Sivan did not direct the facilitator's attention to a cup of spilled juice by saying "Uh oh" or pointing. Although the majority of Sivan's communicative acts were requests or protests, she did not respond to requests made by others, such as "Give me the doll." Sivan's parents told the team that the same kinds of behaviors are seen at home and at school. Analysis of Sivan's interaction indicated a restricted range of communicative functions. Sivan uses immature gestures primarily to request objects, but she does not use eye contact, vocalizations, gestures, or words to make comments, establish joint attention, or engage in social interaction. Sivan's restricted functions suggest possible developmental disability or autism spectrum disorder, and further assessment was recommended.

III. C. What conversational or discourse skills does the child demonstrate?

Although children do not engage in true conversations until about age 2 and extended conversations until about age 4, prerequisite skills can be observed in younger children. For example, the ability to use eye contact to share joint attention on an object or action with another person is requisite to developing the concept of *topic*. As discussed previously, back-and-forth gaze exchanges during infancy establish a pattern and cadence for taking turns in conversation. During TPBA, the facilitator will have many opportunities to engage in back-and-forth exchanges with the child. Following the child's lead and observing and responding to his or her activities during play should encourage the child to demonstrate topics of interest. Once interactions get going, the team should observe discrete behaviors related to taking turns, topic management, recognizing and repairing conversational breakdowns, and the overall cohesion of interactions. The team should note contexts in which conversations come most easily and those that are more difficult for the child. Any behaviors used by the facilitators that may adversely affect communication, such as overuse of questions and inadequate wait time for the child's response, also should be described.

The following areas of conversational skills should be observed and described:

1. *Topic management:* Does the child establish a reference of joint attention while initiating a topic of conversation verbally (e.g., "Look!") or nonverbally (e.g., points at an object while looking at it)? Does the child verbally or nonverbally maintain his or her own topic of conversation over two or more turns? Can the child respond to the facilitator's topic and respond over two or more turns? The child's responses might include a verbal or gestural acknowledgment, such as a head nod or comment such as "Yeah," a repetition of what the speaker said, a statement that adds information about the topic, or a statement that extends the topic's scope. Does the child change topics during a conversation, and, if so, how does the child let the listener know a change is occurring? Finally, the team should observe how many different topics the child introduces throughout the assessment, noting whether the child's conversations are always focused on one or two restricted topics of interest.

Some children with disabilities may be unable to initiate, maintain, or change topics appropriately; others may demonstrate preoccupation with certain topics (Gerber & Prizant, 2000). For other children with disabilities, questioning in the absence of other topic management strategies becomes a means of continuing a conversation, even though excessive questioning can ultimately limit the exchange. An example of this is the child who asks one question after another but never follows up with comments. Sometimes, the use of the questioning technique may be a defense mechanism that enables a child to avoid sharing personal information. Finally, a child struggling with topic management may make inappropriate, off-topic comments and/or erratic topic changes. Observers should describe any types of behaviors that interfere with the child's ability to manage a topic of conversation.

Thomas, a 5-year-old boy, always talked about the cartoon character SpongeBob SquarePants. He could carry on long conversations about who SpongeBob is, what he looks like, where he lives, and who his friends are. If asked about a different topic, such as his kindergarten teacher, Thomas would tell the listener her name and then immediately change the topic back to SpongeBob SquarePants. Analysis reveals that Thomas can initiate, maintain, and expand a topic of conversation related to a specific interest; however, he shows difficulty maintaining a conversation on another person's topic. His preoccupation with a narrow interest constrains his topic management abilities in a variety of conversational contexts.

2. *Cohesion:* Team members should analyze all conversations during the assessment for their overall cohesive quality. In addition, they should note whether the child provides just the right amount of information needed or if he or she provides too much (like a monologue) or too little information. Any behaviors associated with poor cohesion should be described, such as fixation on a single fact or aspect of a topic or inserting inappropriate or irrelevant information into the conversation.

3. *Turn-taking:* Observation and videotape analysis will reveal much information about the child's abilities to take turns in conversations. Observers should note how many turns the child takes in relation to the partner (balanced, too many, too few), whether turns are very long or too short, and whether the child takes inappropriate turns, such as interrupting or speaking during the partner's turn. Does the child start turns in a conversation and, if so, how? Does the child respond to conversational bids with comments, questions, or acknowledgments? Because turns

can be either verbal or nonverbal, the communication mode also should be described in detail—gaze, vocalization, gesture, word, sign, or sentence.

4. *Breakdowns and revisions:* The team should describe any conversational breakdowns, their reasons, and the child's awareness of this occurrence. If a breakdown occurs because the child does not understand what the facilitator said, note whether the child can use requests for information or clarification or ask questions to keep the conversation going. If the child's turn caused the breakdown, the facilitator should probe whether the child can respond to simple requests for clarification, e.g., "What?" or questions. The type of clarification or revision the child gives should be noted, such as restating the utterance, rephrasing it, or adding new information.

5. *Narratives:* The facilitator should look for opportunities during play when the child may be encouraged to recall an event. Because young children like to recall incidents of personal injury, a pretend accident during a cooking activity or other pretend play may support narrative recounts. Try eliciting the story by saying something like, "Ow! I poked my finger" while pretending to chop with a knife. Then say, "Have you ever gotten poked?" Wait for the child to respond. Support additional turns with interest, but use neutral comments that won't guide the child's storytelling, such as "Then what happened?" or "Tell me more." Try eliciting two or three stories over the course of the assessment in order to get as representative a sample of narrative abilities as possible. Avoid eliciting stories on familiar themes, such as birthday parties or holidays, because they may represent an archetype experience rather than a specific event narration.

If possible, observers should transcribe narrative samples and describe the child's abilities in relation to the age expectations for performance noted in the Age Table and in the research section. Behaviors that might indicate possible language impairment or learning disability should be described in the context of the narrative samples, such as problems with organization and event sequencing, poor understanding of story grammar, lack of cohesion, and problems accommodating the listener's need for background information.

BILINGUALISM AND BICULTURALISM

Note: *A complete discussion of language development in children who are bilingual or multilingual or those who sign is beyond the scope of TPBA. Special considerations must be noted, however, because this group of children acquire language in a manner very different from their monolingual counterparts. Typical bilingual language behaviors are often misinterpreted as signs of language delay or disorder. Consequently, TPBA teams assessing children who are bilingual or multilingual or who sign must ensure that team members are properly trained and informed for this type of assessment. The term "bilingual" is used in this section, although the same kinds of considerations also would apply to children who are multilingual or who sign.*

Special considerations *must* be made when planning and executing TPBA2 with children who are bilingual. Current best practice for assessing children who are bilingual mandates the use of a facilitator fluent in the child's dominant language or an interpreter who is trained in the TPBA process. By definition, a SLP who is bilingual must be fluent in his or her primary language and also be capable of speaking or signing the child's language at near-native or native competency (ASHA, 2004a, 2004b). Because different cultures have unique caregiving practices and values, a cultural mediator who is familiar with the child's particular background is an essential team member (Moore & Perez-Mendez, 2003). Cultural considerations include the role of the child in the family; the role of extended family members; the family's perceptions of disabilities; an emphasis on different types of words in the child's environment, such as objects, people, food, or social words; the use of holistic medicine; and the role of religion. If a child's parents are from different cultures and speak two different languages, such as Bari and Arabic, the team must find mediators familiar with each language and the cultural group's customs and belief systems. In the course of TPBA, observations must be compared with the cultural expectations and norms for the family's culture using informed input from the cultural mediator and the interpreter (Kayser, 1998).

Team members also should assess language history and language use across the contexts of a child's daily life by asking the following questions:

When was the child exposed to both languages?

What were the child's speech and language milestones in each language?

What languages are spoken in the home, to what extent, and in what contexts?

What language(s) do the parents or other caregivers use to speak to each other?

What language(s) do the parents or other caregivers use to speak to the child or other children in the home?

What language(s) do the other children speak in the home?

What language do the other children speak to the child?

How consistent is the child's exposure to each language?

If the child is in preschool or school, what language is used? How many hours and days per week?

What languages are used in community places and activities?

What is the language of media in the home (e.g., television, radio, books, or newspaper)?

If the child is bilingual, are there speech and language concerns in both languages?

Is the child's language development similar to or very different from that of other siblings in the home?

Learning two or more languages is a unique process that follows different developmental patterns than single-language learning. Team observations must be adjusted to fit the norms not only for each language, but also for the child's specific type of bilingualism. There are two primary types of bilingualism, *simultaneous bilingualism* and *sequential bilingualism*. The developmental expectations and behaviors for each type are different.

Simultaneous Bilingualism

Simultaneous bilingualism occurs when a child is learning two different languages during the first 3 years of life. For example, one parent may speak Japanese and the other may speak English. Children who are simultaneously bilingual develop two separate language systems, and each will have different milestones (Genesee, Paradis, & Crago, 2004). Although many language-specific differences exist, four general aspects of language development are affected: vocabulary acquisition, cross-linguistic influences, code-mixing, and language dominance.

Sequential Bilingualism (Second-Language Learners)

Sequential bilingualism, sometimes called *second-language learning,* applies to a child who learns a second language after reaching the age of 3. This typically occurs when the child enters child care, preschool, or school (Hammer, Miccio, & Wagstaff, 2003; Romaine, 1997). Tabors (2008) defined the following four distinct stages of sequential bilingualism:

Home-language stage: Child only speaks the native language.

Nonverbal stage: Child may use a few words, but primarily communicates with gestures and facial expressions.

Telegraphic or formulaic stage: Child imitates sentences (sounding echolalic) or uses memorized phrases, such as "I don't know," often without understanding their meaning (Genessee et al., 2004; Wong Fillmore, 1979, as cited in Genessee et al., 2004).

Productive language stage: Child begins to use sentences that are partially or wholly original; relies on a carrier phrase such as "I want + ____," and ultimately constructs novel sentences; begins *interlanguage* use, a systematic and rule-governed hybrid language (Genessee et al., 2004; Selinker, 1972).

Bilingual children often are identified, mistakenly, as having a language disability, in part because frequently they make the same kinds of errors as children with language impairments. Differentiation can be difficult, and the team—particularly the parents, professionals trained in bilingualism, and cultural mediators—must consider carefully all cultural and bilingual aspects of the child's history and behaviors to reach consensus about whether a language problem truly exists.

> *Stefan, a 2-year-old boy, was born in an orphanage and remained there after his birth because his young mother could not care for him. He lived in the orphanage until 2 months ago, when he was adopted by his parents and brought to the United States. Little is known about his family, medical, prenatal, birth, or developmental histories. Only English has been spoken to him since he arrived in the United States. Stefan demonstrated good communication skills considering his short amount of time in the United States. He followed simple one-step commands in English with contextual cues (e.g., "Give me," "Go give to daddy," "Come here," "Stand up," "Sit down," "Let's go"). He identified some common objects and body parts (e.g., nose, tummy, feet), understood verbs in context (e.g., "Give ___ a hug/kiss"), and understood simple yes/no and where questions. Expressively, Stefan communicated through eye gaze, body movement, gestures coupled with vocalizations, and words. His mother says Stefan spontaneously produces 7–10 words in English to label, request, and greet. During the assessment, he consistently imitated words and then later produced some of the words spontaneously and appropriately. His sound productions were fairly accurate and were consistent with his language level.*

Many excellent books about bilingualism are available. Goldstein (2004) and Genessee and colleagues (2004) provide detailed information about all language aspects of typical and disordered language in children who are bilingual.

IV. Articulation and Phonology ▬▬▬▬▬▬▬▬▬▬▬▬▬▬▬▬▬▬▬▬

Speech is vocal communication, which requires coordinated respiration, phonation, resonation, and articulation to produce the speech sounds (phonemes) and sound system, or phonology, of a language. Articulation also requires one to use his or her motor and sensory (auditory, kinesthetic, proprioceptive, and auditory) systems to produce controlled movement in producing each sound and combining sounds to formulate words. Lastly, a child's overall cognitive-linguistic abilities, which encompasses language comprehension and production, contribute to the articulatory process (Hayden,

2004; Haynes & Pindzola, 2004). Acquiring intelligible speech is a long and complex process for children. It begins at birth with reflexive sounds and evolves through stages of increasingly complex preverbal vocalizations, until the child says his or her first words and eventually uses adult-like connected speech.

IV. A. What speech sounds does the child produce (e.g., vowel and consonant repertoire)?

Vocalizations in the first year of life are influenced strongly by simultaneous motor development (Morris & Klein, 2000). If a child has motor involvement, such as cerebral palsy in which there is poor respiratory control and limited movement of the oral-facial muscles, speech may be affected adversely (Beukelman & Mirenda, 2005). Furthermore, cognitive development is necessary for the child to acquire the caregiver's phonology, the language's sound rules (Creaghead & Newman, 1989).

The speechlike and non–speechlike sounds produced during the child's first year are precursors to future communication development (Bates, 1976a, 1976b; Oller, 1980; Stark, 1986). From birth to 3 months, the child produces vegetative noises (e.g., sneezes, burps) and preverbal sounds, such as a cry for hunger or discomfort and other sounds, such as cooing (Crais & Roberts, 2004; Oller, 1980; Stark, 1986; Stoel-Gammon, 1998). Children coo when they are in a comfortable state or when interacting with their parent. Cooing sounds are the vowel "oo" combined with a velar or uvular sound similar to the consonants, /k/ and /g/ (Stoel-Gammon, 1998). During the first year, the baby experiments with producing sounds that are universal to nearly all languages during vocal play (Oller et al., 1998). Between 4 and 6 months, the child expands vocal play by producing back-and-forth sounds with the caregiver. As imitation and reinforcement of culturally relevant sounds occur, however, the child's noises come to sound increasingly like those of the caregivers. Stages of babbling and jargoning allow for the practice of these sounds.

During the second half of the first year, preverbal vocalizations become more wordlike in form as the child progresses through stages of babbling and jargoning. In a literature review of variables that effectively predict early language development, McCathren, Warren, and Yoder (1996) determined that the extent of babbling and consonant use in vocalizations had strong predictive value. Reduplicated, or canonical, babbling occurs when the child begins to say the same consonant–vowel syllables in a series, such as "bababa," "mamama," or "dadada," which occurs at about 6 months. Nonreduplicated babbling, or variegated babbling, which occurs around 9 months, unfolds as the child is able to put together varied consonant–vowel combinations, such as "dabo," where the consonant, vowel, or both are changed (McCathren et al., 1996). Finally, babbling turns into jargoning. In this last stage of preverbal vocalization, a variety of intonation patterns and inflections overlays the consonant–vowel combinations, resulting in vocalizations that sound very similar to adult conversational speech. In fact, jargon may contain some true words at the later stages (Sachs, 1989; Stoel-Gammon, 1998).

IV. B. What are the articulation abilities of the child?

Spoken single words emerge in speech when a child is about 1 year of age. They are usually functional words that the child forms by combining early consonants made with the lip and tongue toward the front of the mouth, such as /b/, /d/, /m/, and a few vowel sounds, such as "ah," "eh," and "uh." Those consonants frequently produced in canonical babbling—nasals /m, n/, stops /p, b, t, d/, and glides /w, y/—typically are the ones that the child produces in early words (Lund & Duchan, 1993; Robb & Bleile, 1994; Stoel-Gammon, 1998). These words are simple, consisting of syllable structures:

consonant–vowel (CV), such as "bye"; or consonant–vowel–consonant–vowel (CVCV), such as "dada" or "mama." A child's first attempts to produce real words may be largely unintelligible and contain many errors. Children at this stage commonly omit final consonants in words, such as saying "bo" for *boat,* and omit some initial consonants in words, such as saying "at" for *hat.* In general, however, sounds at the beginning of a word tend to be learned more easily than sounds at the end (Dyson, 1988).

By the age of 18 months, a child produces approximately 50 words. Sounds are now combined to form consonant–vowel–consonant words, such as *pop,* although the final consonant may still be omitted. In addition, a child this age commonly deletes one consonant from words beginning with two consonants together, known as *blends.* For example, a child might say "bock" instead of "block."

Many factors can affect intelligibility (the degree to which a child's speech is understood), including articulation errors; phonological processes; idiosyncratic productions; dialectical variations; second-language phonology, if another language is spoken at home (see the Bilingualism section, p. 225); structural or functional anomalies of the articulators, such as cleft palate (see the Oral Mechanism section, p. 238); fatigue; anxiety; disfluencies and atypical pitch and prosody (see the Voice and Fluency section, p. 233). It is important to note, however, that the use of typical pitch and prosody patterns actually may help the observers interpret the meaning of unintelligible utterances. For example, vocal pitch is usually raised at the end of a question. Poor speech intelligibility must be considered when assessing language, because morphemes, such as plural *–s* and past tense *–ed,* may not be produced clearly by the child or discerned by the observers (Hodson, Scherz, & Strattman, 2002).

▬▬▬ IV. C. How intelligible is the child's speech?

With practice and improved proficiency, the child's speech becomes approximately 50% intelligible by the end of the second year and between 50% and 70% intelligible by age 2½. An analysis of syllable structure and consonant production at about age 2 can assist team members in differentiating between "late bloomers" and children with true language disorders. Haynes and Pindzola (2004) report that children with language disorders typically have fewer mature syllable structures and produce fewer consonants than late bloomers by age 2. It is normal for a child this age to substitute a consonant made at the front of the mouth for one made in the back of the mouth within a word, such as saying "tat" instead of "cat." Occasionally, the child will repeat syllables in some words, such as saying "wawa" instead of "water."

By age 3, all vowels are produced and a child's consonant inventory includes /p/, /b/, /m/, /n/, /w/, /h/, /t/, and /d/ (Sander, 1972). Although speech intelligibility is now at about 70%, some consonant substitutions and distortions are commonly observed. For example, a 3-year-old might say "pish" instead of "fish." Structurally complex words still may be too difficult for a 3-year-old to produce, and difficult words may be simplified. By age 3½, nearly all children will be easily understood by an unfamiliar listener (Creaghead, 1989).

A child's conversational speech becomes very intelligible by age 4 as an array of consonants is mastered, including /k/, /g/, /f/, and /y/. By five, many consonant sounds are used consistently and accurately, although they may not be mastered in all word contexts. The majority of errors occur on more difficult consonants and consonant blends. It is during the next couple of years that children continue to refine their production of sounds and multisyllabic words (Crais & Roberts, 2004). Between 5 and 6, three challenging consonants are mastered: *-ng, r* and post-vocalic *r (er, ar, or),* and /l/. In the following year, the child's consonant inventory should be complete, with the acquisition and mastery of *th* (voiced and voiceless), *sh, ch, j,* and *v,* and few errors should occur (Creaghead & Newman, 1989; Sander, 1972).

Difficulty pronouncing one or two discrete sounds is often referred to as an *articulation disorder.* Patterns of articulation errors are organized into the following categories: omissions, substitutions, additions, or distortions. It also must be noted whether these errors occur in the initial, medial, or final position of words.

- *Omissions* are noted when the child omits a sound(s) from a word. These errors have the most adverse impact on intelligibility.

- *Substitutions* are noted when the child substitutes one sound for another in a word.

- *Additions* are noted when the child adds a sound(s) in a word.

- *Distortions* are noted when the child substitutes a distorted sound for a standard sound.

The articulatory approach to treatment entails teaching the correct production of targeted speech errors one sound at a time.

Phonology

Phonology deals with the rules governing the sound system of a language. By the time a child can say approximately 25 words, a phonological system—an understanding of how the sounds of their language are combined—emerges (Hodson & Paden, 1991). Invariably, however, as the child begins to put words together, phonological errors occur, meaning that the child substitutes known sound patterns for ones not yet mastered, or complex sounds are omitted or altered. In effect, simpler sounds and patterns are substituted for more complex sounds and patterns. The child simplifies the adult language model, which is known as a *phonological process* (Compton, 1970; Hodson & Paden, 1991; Oller, 1973).

Shriberg and colleagues estimated that approximately 40%–60% of children with phonological difficulties also experience language problems (Paul & Shriberg, 1982; Shriberg & Austin, 1998; Shriberg & Kwiatkowski, 1994; Shriberg, Kwiatkowski, Best, Hengst, & Terselic-Weber, 1986). The phonological assessment proves especially useful when a child's speech is highly unintelligible, because it permits identification of immature speech patterns rather than just isolated misarticulations. As noted previously, a preschool-age child spends several years puzzling out the phonological rules that govern sound distribution and sequencing, mastery of which eventually results in mature, adultlike speech production. This process requires the child to determine which sounds can be put together, where sounds can appear in a word, and sound stress patterns (Ingram, 1976; Oller, 1974). Until these nuanced rules of mature speech are unscrambled, however, the child's productions may contain *phonological processes,* or sound replacement patterns that simplify speech acts and make them achievable by the child. Research suggests that most phonological processes are prevalent in children younger than 2 years of age and disappear between 3 and 4 years of age (Dyson & Paden, 1983; Grunwell, 1987). A young child, however, may use immature phonological processes far longer than other children, which can substantially affect intelligibility. Table 5.9 shows an example, but not inclusive listing, of frequently occurring phonological processes. The phonological approach entails decreasing the use of the processes by identifying those processes that are affecting the correct production of age-appropriate sounds (Dyson & Robinson, 1987).

Coarticulation occurs when the articulatory movements of one speech sound affects the production or perception of the previous or following sound. In other words, one phoneme is affected during production by the surrounding phonemes in the same

Table 5.9. Frequently occurring phonological processes

Assimilation	Duplicating a sound from the front of the word at the middle or back of the word (e.g., "wa<u>a</u>" for "<u>wa</u>ter"); or, duplicating a sound from the back of the word at the front of the word (e.g., "<u>sh</u>i<u>sh</u>" for "fi<u>sh</u>")
Backing	Producing a sound made in the back of the mouth for a sound made in the front of the mouth (e.g., "<u>c</u>op" for "<u>t</u>op")
Consonant cluster reduction	Deleting one or more sounds from consonant cluster (e.g., "_poon" for "<u>sp</u>oon")
Devoicing	Producing a voiceless sound for a voiced sound (e.g., "<u>t</u>o" for "<u>d</u>o")
Final consonant deletion	Deleting the final consonant of a word (e.g., "po_" for "po<u>p</u>")
Fronting	Producing a sound made in the front of the mouth for a sound made in the back of the mouth (e.g., "<u>t</u>a" for "<u>c</u>ar" or "<u>d</u>o" for "<u>g</u>o")
Gliding of liquids	Producing a glide sound (w, y) for a liquid sound (l, r) (e.g., "<u>w</u>abbit" for "<u>r</u>abbit")
Initial consonant deletion	Deleting the initial consonant of a word (e.g., "_at" for "<u>c</u>at")
Stopping	Producing a sound made with stopped airflow for a sound made with continuous airflow (e.g., "<u>d</u>is" for "<u>th</u>is" or "<u>t</u>u" for "<u>sh</u>oe")
Voicing	Producing a voiced sound for an unvoiced sound (e.g., "<u>b</u>ig" for "<u>p</u>ig")
Vowelization	Producing a vowel sound for a liquid sound (e.g., "ba<u>u</u>" for "ba<u>ll</u>")
Weak syllable deletion	Deleting an unstressed syllable from a word (e.g., "__nana" for "<u>ba</u>nana")

word or surrounding words. Consequently, assessment of individual speech sounds in the different positions of single words is not a sufficient assessment of speech. The child's spontaneous, connected speech also must be assessed in conversation ensuring an assessment of the child's overall intelligibility, phonological complexity, and speech variations during production. The results of this broader speech assessment will help the team to effectively select appropriate treatment targets.

▰▰▰ USING THE OBSERVATION GUIDELINES TO ASSESS ARTICULATION AND PHONOLOGY

▰▰▰ IV. A. What speech sounds does the child produce (e.g., vowel and consonant repertoire)?

Throughout the play session, observers should document all of the child's vocalizations (e.g., babbling and unintelligible productions) and verbalizations as part of the analysis (Stoel-Gammon, 2001). Many children with disabilities rely on vocalizations as their primary means of communication, and the information conveyed by them varies considerably. The size and variety of the sound repertoire does not always reflect the child's communication expertise; however, the larger the repertoire, the greater the opportunity for fostering consistent communication patterns. Analyzing vocalizations provides information about the child's prelanguage skills during the first year of life and also about an older nonverbal child's communicative strategies and functions. For the minimally verbal child, understanding the range and complexity of the vocalizations and their communicative function will inform the assessment and provide insight for intervention programming.

Knowledge of the typical developmental sequence of sounds is instrumental in determining whether the child is producing age-appropriate speech sounds as well as for providing activities to assess and elicit the production of developmentally appropriate sounds. The child, for instance, who produces only the consonants /b/ and /d/ is ready to work on other early sounds made in the front of the mouth and within the same plane of movement, such as /m/ and /p/.

▨▨▨▨ **IV. B. What are the articulation abilities of the child?**

A profile of the child's phonology and speech intelligibility is established by documenting the child's speech attempts during the session and through analysis of the videotape afterward. During TPBA, assistance from the parents may be necessary to interpret words that are unintelligible, idiosyncratic to the child, or influenced by cultural or dialectical variations (Stoel-Gammon, 2001). If the family speaks languages other than English, a history of the child's early language exposure should be taken, and the phonology of the other language(s) must be considered when determining whether the child's speech errors constitute a language difference or disorder.

Throughout the play session and during subsequent videotape analysis, notation should be made of the child's sound repertoire by transcribing all sounds, word approximations, words, and phrases produced. It is especially important to capture the vowel and consonant sounds of a child with limited speech production; this will help the team to determine whether the child is producing meaningful speech (Stoel-Gammon, 2001). In addition, any vowel distortions should be described, because these significantly affect speech intelligibility. If the child is using phrases and sentences, these also should be transcribed. Some children can make a sound correctly at the single-word level but make errors on the same sound at the phrase, sentence, or conversation level. The breakdown often is due to the complexity of executing the coarticulated speech movements required for multiword production. More errors may be present in connected speech than at the single-word level, and this should be noted. If appropriate, the facilitator should attempt to elicit correct imitations of words containing sound errors. Sometimes a child may produce a word in imitation that cannot be said spontaneously, and this should be noted.

During play, the facilitator may have the opportunity to use auditory and visual cues to determine whether the child can make a correct or improved production of a misarticulated sound or, perhaps, even a sound not in the child's repertoire. Can the child imitate the sound correctly? Is the child's imitation of a sound, word, or syllable better than when it is said spontaneously? During TPBA, the facilitator should focus on eliciting sounds the articulations of which are highly visible and easily modeled for the child. For example, the facilitator might try to get the child to imitate /h/ while playing in the kitchen, saying the food is "hot" and having the child feel the air on his or her hand. Eliciting imitations of less visible sounds, however, may involve the use of cues that are too intrusive or structured for TPBA. For example, trying to have the child say /k/, as in "cold" food, while playing in the kitchen might require touching the child's mouth or neck area or looking in a mirror to help the child understand how the sound is made. Assessing stimulability provides valuable prognostic information and helps delineate appropriate interventions for the child. Powell and colleagues reported, for example, that stimulable sounds not present in the child's speech inventory are likely to develop without intervention (Powell, Elbert, & Dinnsen, 1991; Powell & Miccio, 1996). Conversely, nonstimulable sounds may be the most likely to require intervention (Miccio, Elbert, & Forrest, 1999).

Young children may not be aware of their speech mistakes, especially if they are easily understood by their parents or other caregivers. As the child becomes more verbal and puts more words together, his or her speech may become harder to understand, and signs of frustration may surface. Some children may exhibit behavior problems; others may hesitate to talk if they think they will not be understood. At first, a child may be willing to repeat mispronounced words or phrases, but if repeated attempts are unsuccessful the child may act out by hitting or kicking, crying, or abandoning the interaction altogether. Early identification and intervention are important so that the child's behaviors, interest in communication, social relationships, and academic achievement are not affected adversely.

▨▨▨▨ **IV. C. How intelligible is the child's speech?**

If the primary referral concern is the child's speech intelligibility, then it will be useful for the team's SLP to be an observer rather than the facilitator. This allows him or her to observe the child's mouth closely and transcribe the child's speech using the International Phonetic Alphabet (IPA) symbols to obtain a detailed phonetic transcription. Firsthand observations of articulations often are easier to make and are more accurate than audio- or videotape transcriptions. Once transcribed, the SLP will analyze notations and transcriptions for patterns of errors at the sound, syllable, word, phrase, and conversational levels, providing a foundation for intervention planning. The SLP then will be able to determine whether the speech production errors are developmental in nature or if there is a concern based on typical phonological development of the child's language. Another consideration that needs to be explored is any dialectal variations based on the child's ethnicity or place of residence.

If the child's speech is highly unintelligible, it will be important for the facilitator, SLP, observers, and parents to tease out contributing factors and the extent to which intelligibility is influenced by the communicative context. Documentation should be made of utterances understood solely by the parents. Several questions may be asked to facilitate a representative description of the child's intelligibility:

1. Do individuals familiar with the child understand his or her speech and how well?

2. Do individuals unfamiliar with the child understand his or her speech and how well?

3. What is the degree of intelligibility when the context of the child's production is known versus unknown? For example, if the child is speaking about a toy in the tub at bathtime, it may be easy to infer the meaning of his or her unintelligible word. By comparison, if the child is talking about a toy not in the immediate environment, it may be difficult to understand or interpret what the child is saying.

Ultimately, the team will determine the percentage of utterances intelligible to the facilitator, observers, and parents and whether knowledge of context or actions, such as gestures, improved the intelligibility. An overall rating can be expressed specifically as a calculated percent of intelligible utterances, or generally with a descriptor word such as *poor*, *fair*, or *good.*

V. Voice and Fluency

Voice is produced by respiration (breathing), phonation (vibration of the vocal folds that produces a sound), and resonation (vibration of the airflow in the mouth and nose that amplifies and modulates the tone produced from the vocal folds). Breath flow plays a vital role in the production and duration of the voice, vocalizations, and speech. A variety of factors may contribute to poor breath support or maladaptive breathing behaviors and affect the child's ability to produce speech. For example, poor postural stability and limited muscle control may interfere with speech production for a child with cerebral palsy. Voice also serves both primitive and advanced communication functions, expressing emotional and biological states, such as comfort and pain, throughout one's lifespan. Voice behaviors also add meaning to verbal communication. For example, prosody and intonation, or variations in voice pitch and rate, can change the meaning of a simple statement. The rising intonation at the end of a phrase alerts the listener that a question is being asked; for example, "Daddy gone?" Conversely, a falling intonation at the end of the same statement signals a statement of fact: "Daddy gone." Interestingly, until 6 months of age all babies babble with a universal prosody; thereafter, the infant uses the prosody or melody of his or her primary language (Boone & McFarlane, 2000).

Fluency is the smooth, uninterrupted production of speech. Many children between 2 and 5 years of age exhibit speech disfluencies as their vocabulary and expressive language expand markedly and the child is producing phrases (Stuttering Foundation of America, 2002). In addition, the demands for coordinated respiration, phonation, and articulation reach a more complex level, which also can result in interrupted speech

(Bloodstein, 1995; Van Riper, 1982). Various research studies have concluded that young children who exhibit disfluency, but are not stutterers, average approximately 6–8 disfluencies per 100 words and as few as 3 disfluencies per 100 words for preschool children (Yairi, 1997). Occasionally, however, children show speech behaviors that indicate stuttering (Stuttering Foundation of America, 2002). TPBA team members must analyze the child's speech patterns to differentiate between typical disfluent behaviors and stuttering.

V. A. How are the pitch, quality, and loudness of the child's voice?

The identification of voice disorders is significant to a child's social-emotional status, educational development, and physical health (Lee, Stemple, Glaze, & Kelchner, 2004). A child's voice should be assessed for pitch, quality, and loudness compared with peers of the same gender, age, geographic location, and cultural background (Aronson, 1980; Boone & McFarlane, 2000; Green, 1972; Stemple, Glaze, & Klaben, 2000). There are three general etiologies of voice disorders: vocal abuse, medically related causes, and personality-related issues (Lee, Stemple, & Glaze, 2004), which can be classified into acquired (not present at birth) or congenital causes that affect laryngeal functioning (Gray, Smith, & Schneider, 1996). Breath flow plays a vital role in the production and duration of the voice, vocalizations, and speech. A variety of factors may contribute to poor breath support or maladaptive breathing behaviors and affect the child's ability to produce speech. The child's support for breathing also must be assessed because head control and diaphragm control affect the breath available for speech.

Many voice disorders are related to vocal abuse or misuse such as excessive voice use and poor vocal hygiene, which affect the mucosa of the vocal folds and their ability to function at their best (Sapienza, Ruddy, & Baker, 2004). Hoarseness often is caused by vocal abuses such as screaming, loud talking, crying, and making noises such as growls, grunts, or vehicle sounds (Boone & McFarlane, 2000; Hicks, 1998). Other signs of vocal strain could include voice breaks, breathiness, and varying pitch or monotone. Another sign of vocal strain is intermittent aphonia, a temporary loss of voice that the parents may report as occurring in the morning, evening, or after certain activities such as a sporting event (Hufnagle, 1982; Sapienza & Stathopoulos, 1994). A child with a severe respiratory illness such as asthma may have a medically related voice disorder due to increased throat clearing and coughing which may damage the vocal folds. These behaviors may result in irritation of the vocal folds and ultimately may result in the development of vocal fold polyps, nodules, or contact ulcers. With a combination of a vocal hygiene program and elimination of the behaviors, the condition can be reversed (Sapienza et al., 2004). Primary voice disorder etiologies can include cerebral palsy, hearing impairment, cleft palate, and velopharyngeal insufficiency (VPI). VPI is the improper function of the soft palate in partitioning the oral and nasal cavities during some speech acts, resulting in atypical resonance and nasal emission. A child with a cleft palate or VPI displays *hypernasality*; the opposite is *hyponasality*, in which the quality sounds similar to a child who has a cold. A child with cerebral palsy may have a limited pitch range and problems with loudness control. A child with a severe-to-profound hearing loss may have speech that is characterized by unregulated pitch and volume, slow rate, and little variation in prosody. The range and severity of voice symptoms in a child with hearing loss depends on whether the child ever had normal hearing. Other groups of children who may have a voice disorder may include those with a history of surgical trauma, disease, and head and neck injuries that may result in unilateral vocal fold paralysis. These children present with noisy breathing and often show reduced ability to increase volume or to speak during physical exertion (Sapienza et al., 2004). One particular population in this category may include children born prematurely who have had multiple medical procedures. Lastly, a child's emotional status also can affect his or her voice quality; it is important to identify with the family any stressful situations in the child's life.

Concerns about the child's voice will need to be referred for further and more in-depth evaluation by appropriate professionals, including an otolaryngologist (ear, nose, and throat physician, or ENT) to explore a possible organic pathology and an SLP who specializes in voice. Further information-gathering and assessment procedures are too structured and too intrusive for TPBA.

V. B. How fluent is the child's speech?

A child who occasionally repeats whole words and phrases and does not show signs of tension when speaking is most likely experiencing *normal disfluency*. Conversely, a child who prolongs individual speech sounds for 1 second or more; repeats monosyllabic words, parts of words, or single sounds; or who noticeably struggles to say certain sounds may be exhibiting true stuttering. Other behaviors also may occur in conjunction with the child's stuttering. These can include decreased or avoidance of talking, decreased eye contact, tension in the mouth area or jaw, facial grimacing, eye blinks, and extraneous body movement (Guitar, 1998). The child also may produce a *schwa* (i.e., "uh") or "um" frequently; use revisions (produce a different word or provide a description in place of the target word); or exhibit changes in his or her voice by producing a louder volume, change in pitch, forceful quality, or fast rate (Nelson, 2002). Another kind of fluency disorder is called *cluttering*. Cluttering is characterized by speech that is hard to understand because the rate is too fast and/or irregular. In addition, the speech may be slurred; sounds and syllables may be left out of words (e.g., consonant cluster reduction or syllable deletion); or words produced are not completed, resulting in unintelligible speech. Sentences also may be disorganized due to word-finding problems, use of nonspecific words, and poor syntax. These children often do not display struggle behaviors because they may be unaware that their speech is difficult to follow (St. Louis & Myers, 1997).

When assessing a child who stutters, it is important to explore the following: time of onset; possible family history of stuttering; how the family is responding to the disfluency; and the communication behaviors of the parents (e.g., their rate of speech, use of questions with their child, responsivity to their child, complexity of language that they use with their child, and possible pressures that they put on their child). Additional factors that may trigger or increase the occurrence of stuttering may be new or specific situations, people, activities, or environments. Stressful life events occurring in the family or elsewhere in the child's life also may affect fluency (Williams, 2002).

USING THE OBSERVATION GUIDELINES TO ASSESS VOICE AND FLUENCY

V. A. How are the pitch, quality, and loudness of the child's voice?

The initial step is assessing the child's respiration. Does the child have enough breath support to produce sustained sound production for speech? Is the breathing shallow? Is the breathing effortful? Does the voice sound fatigued or soft? What type of breathing does the child use? For example, does the child primarily exhibit *clavicular breathing*, in which most of the movement during inhalation and exhalation is in the shoulders and clavicle (collarbone) area? This type of shallow breathing may affect the quality of the child's voice. Or does the child exhibit *diaphragmatic* or *abdominal breathing*, in which the movement during inhalation and exhalation occurs in the abdominal area? This type of breathing does not require as frequent inhalation. Does the child exhibit an open-mouth posture and breathe excessively through his or her mouth when not speaking? Habitual open-mouth breathing may adversely affect articulation because the open posture also can affect tongue movement and position. In addition, chronic open-mouth breathing may be an indication of possible obstruction or deviation in the nasal or oral cavities, such as hypertrophied adenoids. It also may signal chronic congestion or respiratory illness such as asthma (Dworkin, 1978). If the child is open-mouth breathing and may or may not be congested, the parents should be asked if the child has a cold, allergies, or asthma. Children who are habitual open-mouth breathers exhibit an open-mouth posture throughout the assessment and only close the mouth momentarily. When asked, the parents often report that the child breathes with an open mouth during sleep. There may be a family history of allergies and/or asthma.

The types of disorders of the voice—pitch, quality, and loudness—can occur separately or in combination:

Pitch

- Tremulous, quavering speech that may be due to a neurological disorder such as muscular dystrophy or cerebral palsy

- Too low or too high

- Pitch breaks: pitch shifts during speech

- Monotone: little or no fluctuation

Quality

- Breathiness: audible airflow

- Harshness: raspy and rough voice

- Hoarseness: combination of breathiness and harshness

- Disorders of resonance

  Hypernasality: excessive nasal resonance or emission that occurs during production of non-nasal sounds

  Hyponasality or denasality: a lack of nasal resonance during production of nasal sounds /m/, /n/; produces a quality similar to a person who has a head cold

Loudness

- Loudness: too loud or too soft

- Aphonia or dysphonia: loss of voice, whisper

Two other areas to address while assessing the voice are the following:

- Rate: too fast or too slow

- Rhythm: too choppy

David is a 3-year-old boy who was referred for TPBA by his preschool teacher because he is easily frustrated. His parents would like to know how they can further his development in speech. Generally, David had typical development except that his speech and language development was slower compared to his twin brother and friends. David does not talk frequently but when he does talk, he usually is intelligible to his parents; however they reported that others often do not understand him. According to his parents, David is not as social as other children his age. He does not like big crowds or noisy environments and "he seems to need more attention." He gets cranky easily, loses his temper quickly, and can be very hard to calm down.

During TPBA, David's speech was characterized by sound substitutions that were developmental in nature. However, David often was unintelligible during the assessment due to whispering and the lack of pitch variation or the monotone quality of his voice. Attempts by the facilitator to elicit from David a typical volume, a voice to tell his parents something across the room, and a yelling voice (in the playground with his brother) and different inflections during play were unsuccessful in changing David's volume or vocal quality. At one time during the assessment, David spontaneously used a high pitch while talking; this behavior lasted for a few minutes. His teacher reported these vocal behaviors as typical in the classroom.

V. B. How fluent is the child's speech?

The team will need to gather information throughout TPBA including talking with the child's parents to gather information, distinguishing between typical childhood disfluency and true stuttering, as well as observing the parents and child interacting together. The information in Table 5.10 can be used to help team members identify stuttering behaviors.

Finally, the team should determine the child's awareness of the disfluencies. Some children have little or no awareness and are not bothered by their stuttering; others may be more self-conscious and adversely affected. Because stuttering can affect speech, language, pragmatics, and emotional and social development, early identification and intervention are imperative. If the team observes abnormal disfluencies, the child should be referred to an SLP with expertise in fluency disorders. The goal of early intervention is to increase the child's speech fluency by decreasing the duration and the frequency of the disfluencies. Therapy for young children who stutter has been found to be effective when it is identified and addressed early.

Allison is a 4-year-old girl who lives at home with her parents, older brother (age 8 years), and infant sister (age 6 months). The family moved a few months ago; Allison has since shared a room with her sister. Her parents stated that she started repeating the first sounds in words approximately at the time the family moved. They are concerned that she is stuttering. She is not aware of the disfluent behavior, but her older brother has been teasing her about it. During the assessment, Allison exhibited struggling behaviors and often repeated the consonants /m/, /b/, and /p/ in words.

Table 5.10. Stuttering behaviors

Criterion	Normally disfluent	Incipient stutterer
Incipient stutterer	Nine or fewer disfluencies per 100 words	Ten or more disfluencies per 100 words
Predominant type	Whole-word and phrase repetitions, interjections, and revisions	Part-word repetitions, audible and silent prolongations, and broken words
Unit repetitions	No more than 2 unit repetitions ("b-b-ball")	At least 3 repetitions ("b-b-b-ball")
Voicing and airflow	Little or no difficulty starting or sustaining voicing or airflow; continuous phonation during part-word repetitions	Frequent difficulty in starting or sustaining voicing or airflow; heard in association with part-word repetitions, prolongations, and broken words; more effortful disfluencies
Intrusion of the schwa buh-	Schwa not perceived ("ba-ba-baby")	Schwa often perceived ("buh-buh-baby")

From Haynes, W.O., & Pindzola, R. (2003). *Diagnosis and evaluation in speech pathology* (6th ed.). Boston: Allyn & Bacon. Copyright © by Pearson Education. Reprinted by permission of the publisher.

VI. Oral Mechanism ▬▬▬▬▬▬▬▬▬▬▬▬▬▬▬▬▬▬▬▬▬▬▬▬▬▬▬▬▬

Oral motor development, structure, and function provide the physiological foundation for production of speech sounds. During the first 6 months of life, children develop trunk stability and gain control of their neck, head, jaw, lips, tongue and the ability to swallow, all of which contribute to the development of speech-related oral motor skills (Morris & Klein, 2000). An examination of the oral mechanism, of both the structure and function, may provide information on the etiology, diagnosis, and prognosis, thus leading to appropriate intervention planning (Haynes & Pindzola, 2004). Concerns with a child's muscle tone, posture, breath support, and ability to execute the movement of the oral structures (jaw, lips, palate, tongue) must be investigated, because they can affect the child's ability to produce single sounds and sound sequences and can even preclude normal patterns of language development, depending on the degree of involvement. For example, children with severe motor involvement may have such severe oral motor problems that some form of augmentative and alternative communication (AAC) might be beneficial.

▨▨▨▨ VI. A. How are the structures and function of the articulators?

During TPBA, a cursory examination of the articulators (lips, teeth, tongue, lower jaw, and palate) and their function will provide information about any issues that affect speech production. The muscle tone in the jaw, lips, cheeks, and tongue needs to be observed to determine whether it is normal, weak (low), or tight (high). Does the child possess the muscle strength and tone, speed, range of movement, coordination, and sensory information (tactile and proprioceptive) of the jaw, lips, palate, and tongue to produce intelligible speech for his or her developmental age? In addition, the child's overall body tone and resulting postures directly influence movements of the articulators. If a child exhibits too little tone (hypotonicity) or too much tone (hypertonicity), for example, it can affect the child's balance in different positions, compromise breath support, and interfere with the refined and graded movement of the muscles and articulators required to produce intelligible speech (Hayden, 2004).

Difficulty with fluid movement of the oral structures may signify a motor speech disorder such as dysarthria or childhood apraxia of speech. *Dysarthria* is characterized by muscle weakness, paresis, or paralysis resulting in uncoordinated movement and reduced speed of the articulators. The speech of a child with dysarthria contains distortions, substitutions, omissions, and consistent speech errors. In addition, the speech rate is slow and labored, and overall intelligibility decreases as the length and complexity of utterances increases, taxing the weakened muscles (Crary, 1993). *Childhood apraxia of speech* (CAS), also referred to as *developmental apraxia of speech* (DAS), may occur in isolation or in conjunction with a language disorder. Children with apraxia have problems planning, executing, and sequencing volitional speech movements and often exhibit the following characteristics (Crary, 1993; Duffy, 2003):

- A history of limited babbling

- A limited sound repertoire, including vowels

- Omissions, distortions, and substitutions of vowels and consonants

- Receptive language skills that may be superior to expressive language skills

- A monotone voice quality and slow speech rate

- Difficulty imitating sounds and words on command

- Inconsistent imitation and spontaneous sound productions

- Increasing speech errors as length and complexity increase

- Groping speech movements

TPBA is an optimal situation for assessing children who have motor planning difficulties, because the team also may include an occupational therapist and physical therapist who can provide additional observations about the child's muscle tone and motor planning abilities. If TPBA observers note concerns about the appearance, structure, and function of the oral cavity as a result of this cursory examination, then a more in-depth oral examination by the SLP on the team is warranted.

USING THE OBSERVATION GUIDELINES TO ASSESS THE ORAL MECHANISM

▨▨▨ VI. A. How are the structures and function of the articulators?

The first step is to assess the overall posture and muscle tone of the child, which may affect breath support and the refined and graded movement necessary for speech production. TPBA observers should make the following observations:

- Is the child's head aligned with the body?

- Is the child's head in midline?

- Is the child's head extended or retracted?

- Does the child's posture allow adequate lung capacity for sustained sound production?

Please refer to Chapter 2 for detailed information about body tone and its affect on the child's performance.

The next step is to observe the overall presentation of the child's face, assessing the oral structures and their function at rest and during speech. Observations of the articulators (lips, teeth, tongue, lower jaw, and palate) are easily made during play with the child. Many activities during TPBA support observation of speech movement of the oral structures. Look for excessive or abnormal movement of the face or oral structures. Any asymmetries or atypical movements of the lips, tongue, or jaw should be noted as well as the overall appearance of the teeth. Following are guidelines for assessing the oral structures (Haynes & Pindzola, 2004; Shipley & McAfee, 2004).

Lips

Examine the overall appearance, symmetry, and mobility at rest and while moving. For example, comments would be made about the appearance of a repaired cleft lip and the resultant scarring. Lip rounding can easily be explored during speech activities such as saying "shhh" as the baby is sleeping or pushing the train while saying "choo-choo." Lip retraction, drawing back the corners of the mouth, can be assessed while the child says sounds such as "s-s-s" for a snake or "eat" when feeding the baby or at snack time. Some children may exhibit inappropriate retraction at rest and during speech, demonstrating difficulty rounding their lips for sounds in words such as in "uh-oh" or "moo." Inappropriate lip retraction may occur with either the upper or lower lip or both. This behavior affects the clarity or the correct production of sounds, resulting in distorted speech and, possibly, poor volume. Lip separation can be observed in speech activities that require the child to open and close his or her mouth while producing bilabial sounds in words such as "mom" or saying "pop" while popping bubbles.

Teeth

Missing and poorly aligned teeth, bite, and occlusion can affect a child's speech production and overall intelligibility. Poor oral hygiene, such as cavities or severe decay, should be noted. The daily activity of tooth brushing should be further assessed in the Activities of Daily Living section and in the parent interview.

Tongue

Observe the overall appearance, symmetry, tone, and mobility of the tongue at rest and during movement. First, examine the size, tone, and surface of the tongue. Also assess tongue elevation, a skill required to produce certain sounds such as /t/, /d/, /n/, or /l/. This can be done in play activities such as singing "la, la, la, la, la" or saying "ta-da!" at the end of a fun game. Some children make these dental sounds but achieve elevation using their jaw to lift the tongue. This suggests possible weakness or difficulty separating tongue and jaw movements and should be noted. Determine whether the child can retract and elevate the posterior tongue by eliciting /k/ (e.g., "car") or /g/ (e.g., "go") sounds. Some children show inappropriate tongue protrusion or a possible tongue thrust at rest, when producing specific speech sounds, or when swallowing; this should be noted; also note if the tongue is lax or tense when protruding. Occasionally, a child's tongue will pull to the right or to the left during speech or make inappropriate movements such as tremors when at rest. These behaviors are important to note because they suggest possible muscle weakness or neurological impairment.

Jaw

Assess the jaw's appearance and symmetry at rest and mobility while talking. What is the alignment of the upper and lower teeth and their occlusion, the points and surfaces of contact? The upper jaw (maxilla) is larger than the lower jaw (mandible). If the dental arches and teeth are misaligned and do not have a normal occlusion, then there will be a poor bite relationship between the upper and lower jaw, such as an overbite, underbite, open bite, or closed bite. Malocclusions can interfere with tongue and lower lip movement or placement, affecting the production of sounds such as /f/, /z/, /d/ and sounds made with both lips, such as /m/, /p/, and /b/. Some children have poor control of their jaw and have inappropriate or excessive movement such as thrusting forward or sideward movements during speech. All asymmetrical or atypical movements should be noted.

Palate

A cursory examination of the hard palate and soft palate can sometimes be done in TPBA. What is the shape of the hard palate—height and width? Is there any visible scarring or variation in color? Much further assessment of the hard and soft palate may be too structured or intrusive for the TPBA. If concerns arise, the palate should be investigated separately.

Drooling may be present in a child with motor involvement. Morris and Klein (2000) reported that the degree of motor integration achieved by the child, the activity, the child's position, and the child's oral motor control all affect drooling. Additionally, they provide the following developmental stages (see Table 5.11) by which drooling may be judged. Drooling is likely to occur when a child is completing a difficult motor

Table 5.11. Developmental stages of drooling behaviors

Age of child	Amount of saliva
0–3 months	Little saliva is present.
6 months	Control of saliva shown in all positions unless feeding, actively playing with objects, or teething.
9 months	Same as above, with less drooling occurring during mealtime.
15 months tasks.	Drooling may occur during teething and some fine motor
24 months	Drooling should not be present.

task or if the child is unable to close his or her lips. If the child is drooling in other situations, the observers should consider the following questions (Morris & Klein, 2000):

1. How much movement and control of the jaw is there at rest and during speech?

2. Is the child an open-mouth breather?

3. What is the position of the lips at rest, during speech, while eating, and during motor tasks? During what activities does the child drool?

4. What is the child's awareness of drooling?

Gene, an almost 3-year-old boy, presented with a consistent open-mouth posture and with a retracted upper lip. During production of the bilabial sounds /p/ and /b/, he brought his upper teeth to his lower lip to produce the sounds; he was successful in producing the /m/ sound by bringing his lips together. Raspberry sounds were modeled for him, but he did not attempt to produce the sound and instead looked at the facilitator. During production of speech sounds that required rounding of the lips (e.g., "o," "oo") his lips stayed in a retracted position with little rounding of the lips occurring. At times, this adversely affected his intelligibility. While kissing his mom and the baby doll, his mouth stayed open with no closure or rounding of the lips. His parents reported that he also sleeps with his mouth open. He has not been identified as having allergies or asthma.

CONCLUSION

Language, articulation and phonology, and voice and fluency intertwine intricately to support a child's communication development, whereas internal and external factors, such as the function of the oral mechanism and exposure to specific language cultures, exert proscribing influences. Exploration of these components as well as developing an understanding of the interplay of cognitive, emotional, sensorimotor, and social development is critical to obtaining a comprehensive profile of a child's communication abilities and potential.

As reported in this chapter, research on bilingual language learning over the past decade has provided rich information that should inform our assessments and allow differentiation between typical and disordered language development in children learning more than one language. Research in the area of pragmatic language has expanded our knowledge of milestones for the verbal and nonverbal development of joint attention, intentional communication, and a child's ability to participate in conversations. All aspects of communication development can be observed readily during play activities with a child and supplemented by interviews with the caregivers. Based on the information that is obtained during TPBA, intervention planning and intervention should reflect the developmental progression with which a child can be an active and effective communicator.

RESOURCES

American Academy of Audiology
11730 Plaza America Drive
Suite 300
Reston, Virginia 20190
www.audiology.org

American Cleft Palate Foundation
104 South Estes Drive, Suite 204
Chapel Hill, North Carolina 27514
www.cleftline.org

Autism Society of America
7910 Woodmont Avenue
Suite 650
Bethesda, Maryland 29814
www.autism-society.org

American Speech-Language-Hearing
   Association
10801 Rockville Pike
Rockville, Maryland 20852-3279
www.asha.org

Brain Injury Association of America
8201 Greensboro Drive
Suite 611
McLean, Virginia 22102
www.biausa.org

Childhood Apraxia of Speech Association
123 Eisele Road
Cheswick, Pennsylvania 15024
www.apraxia.org
www.apraxia-kids.org

National Institute on Deafness and Other
   Communication Disorders
National Institutes of Health
31 Center Drive, MSC 2320
Bethesda, Maryland 20892-2320
www.nidcd.nih.gov

National Stuttering Association
119 W. 40th Street
14th Floor
New York, New York 10018
www.nsastutter.org

RESNA (Rehabilatation Engineering and
   Assistive Technology Society of North
   America)
1700 N. Moore Street
Suite 1540
Arlington, VA 22209-1903
http://www.resna.org/

Stuttering Foundation of America
3100 Walnut Grove Road, Suite 603
Post Office Box 11749
Memphis, Tennessee 38111-0749
www.stutteringhelp.org

REFERENCES

Acredolo, L., & Goodwyn, S. (1988). Symbolic gesturing in normal infants. *Child Development, 59*, 450–466.

American Speech-Language-Hearing Association. (2004a). Knowledge and skills needed by speech-language pathologists and audiologist to provide culturally and linguistically appropriate services. Available from www.asha.org/policy

American Speech-Language-Hearing Association. (2004b). Roles and responsibilities of speech-language pathologists with respect to augmentative and alternative communication: Technical report. Available from www.asha.org/policy

Aronson, A. (1980). *Clinical voice disorders: An interdisciplinary approach.* New York: Brian C. Decker.

Bates, E. (1976a). *Language and context: The acquisition of pragmatics.* New York: Academic Press.

Bates, E. (1976b). Pragmatics and sociolinguistics in child language. In M. Morehead & A.E. Morehead (Eds.), *Language deficiency in children: Selected readings* (pp. 411–463). Baltimore: University Park Press.

Bellugi, U., & Brown, R. (1964). The acquisition of language. *Monographs of the Society for Research in Child Development, 29*(92), 1–192.

Beukelman, D.R., & Mirenda, P. (Eds.). (2005). Educational inclusion of students who use AAC. In *Augmentative and alternative communication: Supporting children and adults with complex communication needs* (pp. 391–431). Baltimore: Paul H. Brookes Publishing Co.

Billeaud, F.P. (2003). *Communication disorders in infants and toddlers: Assessment and intervention* (3rd ed.). St. Louis: Butterworth Heinemann.

Bloodstein, O. (1995). *A handbook on stuttering* (5th ed.). San Diego: Singular Publishing Group.

Bloom, L. (1973). *One word at a time: The use of single-word utterances before syntax.* The Hague: Mouton.

Bloom, L., & Lahey, M. (1978). *Language development and language disorders.* New York: John Wiley & Sons.

Bloom, L., Rocissano, L., & Hood, L. (1976). Adult–child discourse: Developmental action between information processing and linguistic knowledge. *Cognitive Psychology, 8,* 521–551.

Boone, D.R., & McFarlane, S.C. (2000). *The voice and voice therapy* (6th ed.). Boston: Allyn & Bacon.

Brady, N., Marquis, J., Fleming, K., & McLean, L. (2004). Prelinguistic predictors of language growth in children with developmental disabilities. *Journal of Speech, Language, and Hearing Research, 47,* 663–677.

Brown, R. (1973). *A first language: The early stages.* Cambridge, MA: Harvard University Press.

Browne, J., MacLeod, A.M., & Smith-Sharp, S. (1995). *Family–infant relationship support training (FIRST).* Manual, national workshop for community professionals. Denver: The Children's Hospital.

Bruner, J.S. (1978). Berlyn memorial lecture: Acquiring the use of languages. *Canadian Journal of Psychology, 32*(4), 204–218.

Calandrella, A., & Wilcox, M.J. (2000). Predicting language outcomes for young prelinguistic children with developmental delay. *Journal of Speech, Language, and Hearing Research, 43,* 1061–1071.

Capone, N., & McGregor, K. (2004). Gesture development: A review for clinical and research practices. *Journal of Speech, Language, and Hearing Research, 47,* 173–186.

Carey, S. (1978). The child as word learner. In M. Halle, J. Bresnan, & G. Miller (Eds.), *Linguistic theory and psychological reality* (pp. 264–293). Cambridge, MA: The MIT Press.

Carey, S., & Bartlett, E. (1978). Acquiring a single new word. *Papers and Reports on Child Language Development, 15,* 17–29.

Carpenter, M., Nagell, K., & Tomasello, M. (1998). Social cognition, joint attention, and communicative competence from 9 to 15 months of age. *Monographs of the Society for Research in Child Development, 63*(4, Serial No. 255).

Chapman, R. (1978). Comprehension strategies in children. In J. Kavanagh & W. Strange (Eds.), *Speech and language in the laboratory, school and clinic* (pp. 308–327). Cambridge, MA: The MIT Press.

Charman, T., & Stone, W. (Eds.). (2006). *Social and communication development in autism spectrum disorders: Early identification, diagnosis, and intervention.* New York: Guilford Press.

Clark, E.V. (1973). What's in a word? On the child's acquisition of semantics in his first language. In T. Moore (Ed.), *Cognitive development and the acquisition of language.* New York: Academic Press.

Coggins, T.E., & Timler, G. (2000). Assessing language and communicative development: The role of the speech-language pathologist. In M. Guralnick (Ed.), *Interdisciplinary clinical assessment of young children with developmental disabilities* (pp. 43–65). Baltimore: Paul H. Brookes Publishing Co.

Compton, A.J. (1970). Generative studies of children's phonological disorders. *Journal of Speech and Hearing Disorders, 35,* 315–339.

Crais, E., Douglas, D.D., & Campbell, C.C. (2004). The intersection of the development of gestures and intentionality. *Journal of Speech, Language, and Hearing Research, 47,* 678–694.

Crais, E.R., & Roberts, J.E. (2004). Assessing communication skills. In M. McLean, M. Wolery, & D.B. Bailey, Jr. (Eds.), *Assessing infants and preschoolers with special needs* (3rd ed.; pp. 345–411). Upper Saddle River, NJ: Pearson Prentice Hall.

Crary, M.A. (1993). *Developmental motor speech disorders: Neurogenic communication disorders series.* San Diego: Singular Publishing Group.

Creaghead, N.A., & Newman, P.W. (1989). Articulatory phonetics and phonology. In N.A. Creaghead, P.W. Newman, & W.A. Secord (Eds.), *Assessment and remediation of articulatory and phonological disorders* (2nd ed.). Columbus, OH: Charles E. Merrill.

Dale, P.S. (1976). *Language development: Structure and function* (2nd ed.). New York: Holt, Rinehart and Winston.

Delgado, C.E.F., Mundy, P., Crowson, M., Markus, J., Yale, M., & Schwartz, H. (2002). Responding to joint attention: A comparison of target locations. *Journal of Speech, Language, and Hearing Research, 45,* 715–719.

deVilliers, J., & deVilliers, P. (1973). Development of the use of word order in comprehension. *Journal of Psycholinguistic Research, 2,* 331–341.

Duchan, J. (2001). Impairment and social views of speech-language pathology: Clinical practices re-examined. *Advances in Speech-Language Pathology, 3*(1), 37–45.

Duffy, J.R. (2003). Apraxia of speech: Historical overview and clinical manifestations of the acquired and developmental forms. In L.D. Shriberg & T.F. Campbell (Eds.), *Proceedings of the 2002 childhood apraxia of speech research symposium* (pp. 3–12). Carlsbad, CA: Hendrix Foundation.

Dworkin, J.P. (1978). II. Differential diagnosis of motor speech disorders: The clinical examination of the speech mechanism. *Journal of the National Student Speech Hearing Association, 6,* 37–62.

Dyson, A. (1988). Phonetic inventories of two- and three-year-old children. *Journal of Speech and Hearing Disorders, 53,* 89–93.

Dyson, A., & Paden, E.P. (1983). Some phonological acquisition strategies used by two-year-olds. *Journal of Child Communication Disorders, 7,* 6–18.

Dyson, A.T., & Robinson, T.W. (1987). The effect of phonological analysis procedure on the selection of potential remediation target. *Language, Speech, and Hearing Services in the Schools, 18,* 364–377.

Fenson, L., Dale, P., Reznick, J.S., Bates, E., Thal, D., & Pethick, S. (1994). Variability in early communicative development. *Monographs of the Society for Research in Child Development 59*(5), v–173.

Fenson, L., Marchman, V.A., Thal, D.J., Dale, P.S., Reznick, J.S., & Bates, E. (2006). *MacArthur-Bates Communicative Development Inventories (CDIs), Second Edition.* Baltimore: Paul H. Brookes Publishing Co.

Genessee, F., Paradis, J., & Crago, M.B. (2004). *Dual language development and disorders.* Baltimore: Paul H. Brookes Publishing Co.

Gentner, D. (1982). Why nouns are learned before verbs: Linguistic relativity versus natural partitioning. In S. Kuczaj (Ed.), *Language development* (Vol. 2). Hillsdale, NJ: Lawrence Erlbaum Associates.

Gerber, S., & Prizant, B. (2000). Speech, language, and communication assessment and intervention for children. In *Clinical practice guidelines* (pp. 85–122). Bethesda: The Interdisciplinary Council on Developmental and Learning Disorders Press.

Glennen, S.L., & DeCoste, D.C. (1997). *Handbook of augmentative and alternative communication.* San Diego: Singular Publishing Group.

Goldstein, B.A. (Ed.). (2004). *Bilingual language development and disorders in Spanish-English speakers.* Baltimore: Paul H. Brookes Publishing Co.

Goldstein, H., Kaczmarek, L.A., & English, K.M. (Vol. Eds.). (2002). In S.F. Warren & M.E. Fey (Series Eds.), *Communication and language intervention series: Vol. 10. Promoting social communication: Children with developmental disabilities from birth to adolescence.* Baltimore: Paul H. Brookes Publishing Co.

Gray, S.D., Smith, M.E., & Schneider, H. (1996). Voice disorders in children. *Pediatric Clinics of North America, 43*(6), 1357–1384.

Greene, M. (1972). *The voice and its disorders* (3rd ed.). Philadelphia: J.B. Lippincott.

Grunwell, P. (1987). *Clinical phonology* (2nd ed.) Baltimore: Lippincott Williams & Wilkins.

Guitar, B. (1998). *Stuttering: An integrated approach to its nature and treatment* (2nd ed.). Baltimore: Lippincott Williams & Wilkins.

Halle, J., Brady, N.C., & Drasgow, E. (2004). Enhancing socially adaptive communication repairs of beginning communicators with disabilities. *American Journal of Speech-Language Pathology, 13,* 43–54.

Hammer, C.S., Miccio, A.W., & Wagstaff, D.A. (2003). Home literacy experiences and their relationship to bilingual preschoolers' developing English literacy abilities: An initial investigation. *Language, Speech, and Hearing Services in Schools, 34,* 20–30.

Harris, M., Barlow-Brown, F., & Chasin, J. (1995). The emergence of referential understanding: Pointing and the comprehension of object names. *First Language, 15,* 19–34.

Hart, B., & Risley, T.R. (1995). *Meaningful differences in the everyday experience of young American children.* Baltimore: Paul H. Brookes Publishing Co.

Hayden, D. (2004). PROMPT: A tactually-grounded treatment approach to speech production disorders. In I. Stockman (Ed.), *Movement and action in learning and development: Clinical implications for pervasive developmental disorders* (pp. 255–298). New York: Elsevier.

Haynes, W.O., & Pindzola, R. (2004). *Diagnosis and evaluation in speech pathology* (6th ed.). Boston: Allyn & Bacon.

Hicks, D.M. (1998). Voice disorders. In G.H. Shames, W.A. Secord, & E.H. Wiig (Eds.), *Human communication disorders: An introduction* (5th ed., pp. 349–393). Boston: Allyn & Bacon.

Hodson, B.W., & Paden, E. (1991). *Targeting intelligible speech: A phonological approach to remediation* (2nd ed.). Austin, TX: PRO-ED.

Hodson, B.W., Scherz, J.A., & Strattman, K.H., (2002). Evaluating communicative abilities of a highly unintelligible preschooler. *American Journal of Speech-Language Pathology, 11,* 236–242.

Hufnagle, J. (1982). Acoustic analysis of fundamental frequencies of voices of children with and without vocal nodules. *Perceptual Motor Skills, 55*(2), 427–432.

Ingram, D. (1976). *Phonological disability in children.* London: Arnold.

James, S.L. (1990). *Normal language acquisition.* Austin, TX: PRO-ED.

Kaczmarek, L. (2002). Assessment of social-communicative competence: An interdisciplinary model. S.F. Warren & M.E. Fey (Series Eds.) & H. Goldstein, L.A. Kaczmarek, & K.M. English (Vol. Eds.), *Communication and language intervention series: Vol. 10. Promoting social communication: Children with developmental disabilities from birth to adolescence* (pp. 55–115). Baltimore: Paul H. Brookes Publishing Co.

Kaderavek, J.N., & Sulzby, E. (2000). Narrative production by children with and without specific language impairment: Oral narratives and emergent readings. *Journal of Speech, Language, and Hearing Research, 43,* 34–49.

Kayser, H. (1998). *Assessment and intervention resource for Hispanic children.* San Diego: Singular Publishing Group.

Lee, L., Stemple, J.C., & Glaze, L. (2006). *Quick Screen for Voice.* Gainesville, FL: Communicare Publishing.

Lee, L., Stemple, J.C., Glaze, L., & Kelchner, L.N. (2004). Quick Screen for Voice and supplementary documents for identifying pediatric voice disorders. *Language, Speech, and Hearing Services in Schools, 35,* 308–319.

Lock, A. (1978). The emergence of language. In A. Lock (Ed.), *Action, gesture, and symbol: The emergence of language* (pp. 3–18). New York: Academic Press.

Lord, C., & Richler, J. (2006). Early diagnosis of children with autism spectrum disorders. In T. Charman & W. Stone (Eds.), *Social and communication development in autism spectrum disorders: Early identification, diagnosis, and intervention* (pp. 35–59). New York: Guilford Press.

Lund, N.J., & Duchan, J.F. (1993). *Assessing children's language in naturalistic contexts* (3rd ed.). Englewood Cliffs, NJ: Prentice Hall.

Markus, J., Mundy, P., Morales, M., Delgado, C.E.F., & Yale, M. (2000). Individual differences in infant skill as predictors of child–caregiver joint attention and language. *Social Development, 9,* 302–315.

McCabe, A., & Rollins, P. (1994, January). Assessment of preschool narrative skills. *American Journal of Speech-Language Pathology, 3,* 45–56.

McCathren, R.B., Warren, S.F., & Yoder, P.J. (1996). Prelinguistic predictors of later language development. In S.F. Warren & J. Reichle (Series Eds.) & K.N. Cole, P.S. Dale, & D.J. Thal (Vol. Eds.), *Communication and language intervention series: Vol. 6. Assessment of communication and language* (pp. 57–76). Baltimore: Paul H. Brookes Publishing Co.

McCathren, R., Yoder, P., & Warren, S. (1999). The relationship between prelinguistic vocalization and later expressive vocabulary in young children with developmental delay. *Journal of Speech, Language and Hearing Research, 42,* 915–924.

McCune-Nicolich, L., & Carroll, S. (1981). Development of symbolic play: Implications for the language specialist. *Topics in Language Disorders, 2*(1), 1–15.

McLaughlin, S. (1998). *Introduction to language development.* San Diego: Singular Publishing Group.

McWilliam, R.A., & Bailey, D.B. (1995). Effects of classroom social structure and disability on engagement. *Topics in Early Childhood Special Education, 15,* 123–147.

Mervis, C.B., & Bertrand, J. (1993). Acquisition of early object labels: The roles of operating principles and input. In A.P. Kaiser & D.B. Gray (Eds.), *Enhancing children's communication: Research foundations for intervention* (pp. 287–316). Baltimore: Paul H. Brookes Publishing Co.

Miccio, A.W., Elbert, M., & Forrest, K. (1999). The relationship between stimulability and phonological acquisition in children with normally developing and disordered phonologies. *American Journal of Speech-Language Pathology, 8,* 347–363.

Miller, J.F. (1981). *Assessing language production in children: Experimental procedures.* Boston: Allyn & Bacon.

Miller, J.F., & Paul, R. (1995). *The clinical assessment of language comprehension.* Baltimore: Paul H. Brookes Publishing Co.

Moore, S.M., & Perez-Mendez, C. (2003). *Cultural contexts for early intervention: Working with families.* Rockville, MD: American Speech-Language-Hearing Association.

Morford, M., & Goldin-Meadow, S. (1992). Comprehension and production of gesture in combination with speech in one-word speakers. *Journal of Child Language, 19,* 559–580.

Morris, S.E. & Klein, M.D. (2000). *Pre-feeding skills* (2nd ed.). San Antonio, TX: Therapy Skill Builders.

Muma, J. (1998). *Effective speech-language pathology: A cognitive socialization approach.* Mahwah, NJ: Lawrence Erlbaum Associates.

Mundy, P., Kasari, C., Sigman, M., & Ruskin, E. (1995). Nonverbal communication and early language acquisition in children with Down syndrome and in normally developing children. *Journal of Speech and Hearing Research, 38,* 157–167.

Mundy, P., & Sigman, M. (2006). Joint attention, social competence, and developmental psychopathology. In D. Cicchetti & D.J. Cohen (Eds.), *Developmental psychopathology* (2nd ed.). Hoboken, NJ: John Wiley & Sons.

Murphy, C.M., & Messer, D.J. (1977). Mothers, infants, and pointing: A study of gesture. In H. Schaffer (Ed.), *Studies in mother–infant interaction* (pp. 325–354). New York: Academic Press.

Nelson, K. (1973). Structure and strategy in learning to talk. *Monographs of the Society for Research in Child Development, 38,* 11–56.

Nelson, L.A. (2002). Language formulation related to disfluency and stuttering. In *Stuttering therapy: Prevention and intervention with children* (Publication no. 20). Memphis, TN: Stuttering Foundation of America.

Ninio, A. (1992). The relation of children's single word utterances to single word utterances in the input. *Journal of Child Language, 19,* 87–110.

Oller, D. (1973). The effect of position in utterance on segment duration in English. *Journal of the Acoustical Society of America, 14,* 1235–1247.

Oller, D. (1974). Simplification as the goal of phonological processes in child speech. *Language Learning, 24,* 299–303.

Oller, D.K. (1978). Infant vocalization and the development of speech. *Allied Health and Behavioral Sciences Journal, 1*(4).

Oller, D.K. (1980). The emergence of sounds of speech in infancy. In G. Yeni-Komshian, J. Kavanaugh, & C. Ferguson (Eds.), *Child phonology* (Vol. 1, pp. 93–112). New York: Academic Press.

Oller, D.K., Levine, S., Cobo-Lewis, A., Eilers, R., & Pearson, B. (1998). Vocal precursors to linguistic communication: How babbling is connected to meaningful speech. In S.F. Warren & J. Reichle (Series Eds.) & R. Paul (Vol. Ed.), *Communication and language intervention series: Vol. 8. Exploring the speech-language connection* (pp. 1–23). Baltimore: Paul H. Brookes Publishing Co.

Olswang, L.B., Rodriguez, B., & Timler, G. (1998). Recommending interventions for toddlers with specific language learning difficulties: We may not have all the answers but we know a lot. *American Journal of Speech-Language Pathology, 7*(1), 23–32.

Owens, R.E. (1998). Development of communication, language, and speech. In G.H. Shames, E. Wiig, & W.A. Secord (Eds.), *Human communication disorders: An introduction* (5th ed., pp. 27–68). Boston: Allyn & Bacon.

Owens, R.E. (2004). *Language disorders: A functional approach to assessment and intervention* (4th ed.). Boston: Allyn & Bacon.

Paul, R. (2001). *Language disorders from infancy through adolescence: Assessment and intervention* (2nd ed.). St. Louis: Mosby.

Paul, R., & Alforde, S. (1993). Grammatical morpheme acquisition in 4-year-olds with normal, impaired, and late developing language. *Journal of Speech and Hearing Research, 36,* 1271–1275.

Paul, R., Hernandez, R., Taylor, L., & Johnson, K. (1996). Narrative development in late talkers: Early school age. *Journal of Speech and Hearing Research, 39,* 1295–1303.

Paul, R., & Shiffer, M. (1991). Communicative initiations in normal and late-talking toddlers. *Applied Psycholinguistics, 12,* 419–431.

Paul, R., & Shriberg, L. (1982). Associations between phonology and syntax in speech-delayed children. *Journal of Speech and Hearing Research, 25,* 536–547.

Pease, D., & Berko Gleason, J. (1985). Gaining meanings: Semantic development. In J. Berko Gleason (Ed.), *The development of language.* Columbus, OH: Merrill.

Philofsky, A., Hepburn, S.L., Hayes, A., Hagerman, R., & Rogers, S. (2004). Linguistic and cognitive functioning and autism symptoms in young children with fragile X syndrome. *American Journal of Mental Retardation, 109*(3), 208–218.

Platt, J., & Coggins, T. (1990). Comprehension of social-action games in prelinguistic children: Levels of participation and effect of adult structure. *Journal of Speech and Hearing Disorders, 55,* 315–326.

Powell, T.W., Elbert, M., & Dinnsen, D.A. (1991). Stimulability as a factor in the phonological generalization of misarticulating preschool children. *Journal of Speech and Hearing Research, 34,* 1318–1328.

Powell, T.W., & Miccio, A.W. (1996). Stimulability: A useful clinical tool. *Journal of Communication Disorders, 29,* 237–254.

Prizant, B.M., & Rydell, P.J. (1993). Assessment and intervention considerations for unconventional verbal behavior. In S.F. Warren & J. Reichle (Series Eds.) & J. Reichle & D.P. Wacker (Vol. Eds.), *Communication and language intervention series: Vol. 4. Communicative alternatives to challenging behavior: Integrating functional assessment and intervention strategies* (pp. 263–297). Baltimore: Paul H. Brookes Publishing Co.

Prizant, B.M., Schuler, A.L., Wetherby, A.M., & Rydell, P.J. (1997). Enhancing language and communication: Language approaches. In D. Cohen & F. Volkmar (Eds.), *Handbook of autism and pervasive developmental disorders* (2nd ed., pp. 572–605). New York: John Wiley & Sons.

Prizant, B., & Wetherby, A. (1993). Communication and language assessment for young children. *Infants and Young Children, 5*(4), 20–34.

Prutting, C.A., & Kirchner, D.M. (1987). A clinical appraisal of the pragmatic aspects of language. *Journal of Speech and Hearing Disorders, 52,* 105–119.

Reich, P.A. (1986). *Language development.* Englewood Cliffs, NJ: Prentice Hall.

Rescorla, L., Roberts, J., & Dahlsgaard, K. (1997). Late talkers at 2: Outcomes at age 3. *Journal of Speech and Hearing Research, 40,* 556–566.

Robb, M.P., & Bleile, K.M. (1994). Consonant inventories of young children from 8 to 25 months. *Clinical Linguistics and Phonetics, 8,* 295–320.

Romaine, S. (1997). *Bilingualism* (2nd ed.). Malden, MA: Blackwell.

Rosenberg, S., Clark, M., Filer, J., Hupp, S., & Finkler, D. (1992). Facilitating active learner participation. *Journal of Early Intervention, 16*(3), 262–274.

Rosenberg, S., & Robinson, C. (1990). Assessment of the infant with multiple handicaps. In E. Gibbs & D. Teti (Eds.), *Interdisciplinary assessment of infants: A guide for early intervention professionals.* Paul H. Brookes Publishing Co.

Sachs, J. (1989). Communication development in infancy. In J. Gleason (Ed.), *The development of language* (pp. 35–57). Columbus, OH: Charles E. Merrill.

Sander, E. (1972). When are speech sounds learned? *Journal of Speech and Hearing Disorders, 37,* 55–63.

Sapienza, C.M., Ruddy, B.H., & Baker, S. (2004). Laryngeal structure and function in the pediatric larynx: Clinical applications. *Language, Speech, and Hearing Services in Schools, 35,* 299–307.

Sapienza, C.M., & Stathopoulos, E.T. (1994). Respiratory and laryngeal measures of children and women with vocal nodules. *Journal of Speech and Hearing Research, 37,* 1229–1243.

Selinker, L. (1972, August). Interlanguage. *International Review of Applied Linguistics in Language Teaching, 10,*(3), 209–231.

Shipley, K.G., & McAfee, J.G. (2004). *Assessment in speech-language pathology: A resource manual* (3rd ed.). Clifton Park, NY: Delmar Learning.

Shore, C., O'Connell, B., & Bates, E. (1984). First sentences in language and symbolic play. *Developmental Psychology, 20,* 872–880.

Shriberg, L., & Austin, D. (1998). Comorbidity of speech-language disorder: Implications for a phenotype marker for speech delay. In S.F. Warren & J. Reichle (Series Eds.) & R. Paul (Vol. Ed.), *Communication and language intervention series: Vol. 8. Exploring the speech-language connection.* Baltimore: Paul H. Brookes Publishing Co.

Shriberg, L., & Kwiatkowski, J. (1994). Developmental phonological disorders I: A clinical profile. *Journal of Speech and Hearing Research, 37,* 1100–1126.

Shriberg, L., Kwiatkowski, J., Best, S., Hengst, J., & Terselic-Weber, B. (1986). Characteristics of children with phonologic disorders of unknown origin. *Journal of Speech and Hearing Disorders, 51,* 140–161.

Sparks, S. (1989). Assessment and intervention with at-risk infants and toddlers: Guidelines for the speech-language pathologist. *Topics in Language Disorders, 10*(1), 43–56.

Stark, R.E. (1986). Prespeech segmental feature development. In P. Fletcher & M. Garman (Eds.), *Language acquisition: Studies in first language development* (2nd ed.). New York: Cambridge University Press.

Stark, R., Bernstein, L., & Demorest, M. (1993). Vocal communication in the first 18 months of life. *Journal of Speech and Hearing Research, 36,* 548–558.

Stemple, J.C., Glaze, L.E., & Klaben, B.G. (2000). *Clinical voice pathology: Theory and management.* San Diego: Singular Publishing Group.

St. Louis, K.O., & Myers, F.L. (1997). Management of cluttering and related fluency disorders. In R.F. Curlee & G.M. Siegel (Eds.), *Nature and treatment of stuttering: New directions* (2nd ed., pp. 313–332). Boston: Allyn & Bacon.

Stoel-Gammon, C. (1998). Role of babbling and phonology in early linguistic development. In S.F. Warren & J. Reichle (Series Eds.) & A.M. Wetherby, S.F. Warren, & J. Reichle (Vol. Eds.), *Communication and language intervention series: Vol. 7. Transitions in prelinguistic communication* (pp. 87–110). Baltimore: Paul H. Brookes Publishing Co.

Stoel-Gammon, C. (2001). Collecting and transcribing speech samples: Enhancing phonological analysis. *Topics in Language Disorders, 21*(4).

Stuttering Foundation of America. (2002). *Stuttering therapy: Prevention and intervention with children.* Memphis, TN: Author.

Tabors, P.O. (2008). *One child, two languages: A guide for early childhood educators of children learning English as a second language* (2nd ed.). Baltimore: Paul H. Brookes Publishing Co.

Tager-Flusberg, H. (1989). Putting words together: Morphology and syntax in the preschool years. In J. Gleason (Ed.), *Language development* (pp. 139–171). Columbus, OH: Macmillan.

Thal, D.J., & Tobias, S. (1992a). Communication gestures in children with delayed onset of oral expressive vocabulary. *Journal of Speech, Language, and Hearing Research, 35,* 1281–1289.

Thal, D.J., & Tobias, S. (1992b). Relationships between language and gesture in normally developing and late-talking toddlers. *Journal of Speech and Hearing Research, 37,* 147–170.

Tomasello, M. (2003). *Constructing a language* (pp. 19–31). Cambridge, MA: Harvard University Press.

Trantham, C.R., & Pedersen, J. (1976). *Normal language development.* Baltimore: Lippincott Williams & Wilkins.

U.S. Consumer Product Safety Commission. (2003). *CPSC warns consumers of suffocation danger associated with children's balloons.* Retrieved December 1, 2003 at http://www.cpsc.gov/CPSCPUB/PUBS/5087.html

Van Riper, C. (1982). *The nature of stuttering* (2nd ed.). Englewood Cliffs, NJ: Prentice Hall.

Wetherby, A.M., Allen, L., Cleary, J., Kublin, K., & Goldstein, H. (2002). Validity and reliability of the Communication and Symbolic Behavior Scales Developmental Profile™ with very young children. *Journal of Speech, Language, and Hearing Research, 45,* 1202–1218.

Wetherby, A., Cain, D., Yonclas, D., & Walker, V. (1988). Analysis of intentional communication of normal children from the prelinguistic to the multiword stage. *Journal of Speech and Hearing Research, 31,* 240–252.

Wetherby, A.M., & Prizant, B.M. (1989). The expression of communicative intent: Assessment guidelines. *Seminars in Speech and Language, 10,* 77–91.

Wetherby, A.M., & Prizant, B.M. (1993). *CSBS™ Manual: Communication and Symbolic Behavior Scales™, Normed Edition.* Baltimore: Paul H. Brookes Publishing Co.

Wetherby, A.M., & Prizant, B.M. (Eds.) (2000). In S.F. Warren & J. Reichle (Series Eds.) & A.M. Wetherby & B.M. Prizant (Vol. Eds.), *Communication and language intervention series: Vol. 9. Autism spectrum disorders: A transactional developmental perspective.* Baltimore: Paul H. Brookes Publishing Co.

Wetherby, A.M., & Prutting, C. (1984). Profiles of communicative and cognitive social abilities in autistic children. *Journal of Speech and Hearing Research, 27,* 364–377.

Williams, D.E. (2002). Emotional and environmental problems in stuttering. In *Stuttering therapy: Prevention and intervention with children* (Publication no. 20). Memphis, TN: Stuttering Foundation of America.

Yairi, E. (1997). Speech characteristics of early childhood stuttering. In R.F. Curlee & G.M. Siegle (Eds.), *Nature and treatment of stuttering: New directions* (2nd ed.). Boston: Allyn & Bacon.

Yoder, P.J., & Warren, S.F. (1993). Can developmentally delayed children's language development be enhanced through prelinguistic intervention? In A.P. Kaiser & D.B. Gray (Eds.), *Enhancing children's communication: Research foundations for intervention* (pp. 35–61). Baltimore: Paul H. Brookes Publishing Co.

Yoder, P.J., Warren, S.F., & McCathren, R. (1998). Determining spoken language prognosis in children with developmental disabilities. *American Journal of Speech-Language Pathology, 7,* 77–87.

Yont, K.M., Hewitt, L.E., & Miccio, A.W. (2000). A coding system for describing conversational breakdowns in preschool children. *American Journal of Speech-Language Pathology, 9,* 300–309.

Yoshinaga-Itano, C. (1997). The challenge of assessing language in children with hearing loss. *Language, Speech, and Hearing Services in Schools, 28,* 362–373.

TPBA2 Observation Guidelines: Communication Development

Child's name: _____ Age: _____ Birth date: _____

Parent(s): _____ Assessment date: _____

Person(s) completing the form: _____

Directions: Record the child information (name, caregiver[s], birth date, age), assessment date, and person(s) completing this form. The Observation Guidelines provide common strengths, examples of behaviors of concern, and "ready for" next steps. As you observe the child, circle, highlight, or place a check mark next to the items listed under these three categories that correspond to the behavior(s) you observe. List any additional observations in the "Notes" column. Experienced TPBA users may opt to use only the TPBA2 Observation Notes as a method for collecting information during the assessment instead of the Observation Guidelines.

Questions	Strengths	Examples of behaviors of concern	"Ready for"	Notes
I. Language comprehension				

I. A. What early comprehension abilities does the child exhibit?	Responds to or recognizes sounds
	
	Recognizes and responds to nonverbal cues (e.g., facial expressions, gestures)
	
	Associates sounds with meanings
	
	Responds to or anticipates the steps in common routines or sequences
	  With contextual cues
	  Without verbal cues
		Difficulty responding to or recognizing sounds
		
		Does not interpret or respond to nonverbal cues
		
		Does not respond to or anticipate familiar routines
		  With contextual cues
		  Without verbal cues
			Increase association of sounds with objects
			
			Increase understanding of nonverbal cues
			
			Increase association of actions with consequences	

I. B. What types of words and sentences are understood by the child?	Understands the meaning of
	  Concrete words (e.g., nouns, verbs, basic concepts)
	  Abstract words (e.g., feelings or ideas)
	  Multiple-meaning words
	  Phrases or expressions
		Limited understanding of words
		
		Limited understanding of sentences
		
		Limited or inconsistent following of directions (relies heavily on gestural and situational prompts)
			Increase understanding of
			  Variety of vocabulary words
			  Abstract words
			  Multimeaning words
			  Phrases or expressions
			  Sentences/statements	

(continued on next page)

Developed with Renee Charlifue-Smith and Cheryl Cole Rooke.

Transdisciplinary Play-Based System (TPBA2/TPBI2) by Toni Linder.

(continued from previous page)

Observation Guidelines: Communication Development **TPBA** 2

Questions	Strengths	Examples of behaviors of concern	"Ready for"	Notes
I. Language comprehension *(continued)*				
I. B. *(continued)*	Sentence types (e.g., simple, compound, containing phrases) Follows directions Rote direction One-step direction Two-step direction (related and unrelated) Multistep, complex directions All of the above Understands the following types of questions: Yes/no Simple "wh": what, where, who, what/doing Complex "wh": which, when, why, how, whose	Responds inappropriately to questions	Improve ability to follow directions of increasing length and complexity Increase understanding of different types of questions	
II. Language production				
II. A. What modes of communication does the child use?	Uses the following modes to communicate: Eye gaze Facial expressions Body movement Physical manipulation Gestures Vocalizations: vowels, consonants, babbling Verbalizations: words, including word approximations, phrases, sentences	Primary mode of communication is not at expected level Mode of communication is limited to Eye gaze Facial expressions Body movement Physical manipulation Gestures Vocalizations: vowels, consonants, babbling	Increase use of Eye gaze Facial expressions Body movement Physical manipulation Gestures Vocalizations: vowels, consonants, babbling Verbalizations: words, including word approximations, phrases, sentences	

(continued on next page)

Developed with Renee Charlifue-Smith and Cheryl Cole Rooke.

Transdisciplinary Play-Based System (TPBA2/TPBI2)
by Toni Linder.

251

(continued from previous page)

Observation Guidelines: Communication Development **TPBA** 2

Questions	Strengths	Examples of behaviors of concern	"Ready for"	Notes
II. Language production (continued)				
II. A. (continued)	Vocalizations or verbalizations paired with gestures Sign language Idiosyncratic Formal Augmentative and alternative communication (AAC) Low-tech High-tech	Verbalizations: words, including word approximations, phrases, sentences Sign language Idiosyncratic Formal AAC Low-tech High-tech	Sign language Idiosyncratic Formal AAC Low-tech High-tech	
II. B. What is the child's frequency of communication?	Communicates as frequently as other children of same developmental age in all settings and with a variety of communication partners	Reduced frequency and variety of communication with Familiar people Unfamiliar people Peers Adults	Increase frequency and variety of communication with Familiar people Unfamiliar people Peers Adults	
II. C. What are the child's semantic abilities?	Semantic knowledge levels reflected in words: Referential knowledge (9–15 months) Extended knowledge (15–18 months) Categorical knowledge (24+ months) Metalinguistic knowledge (48–60 months) Expresses the following semantic relations: Agent (e.g., baby) Action (e.g., drink) Object (e.g., cup) Recurrence (e.g., more)	Limited expression of semantic knowledge and semantic relations	Improve use and complexity of the following semantic relations: Agent (e.g., baby) Action (e.g., drink) Object (e.g., cup) Recurrence (e.g., more) Existence (e.g., this ball) Nonexistence (e.g., all gone) Cessation (e.g., stop) Rejection (e.g., no) Location (e.g., up) Possession (e.g., mine) Agent–action (e.g., baby drink)	

(continued on next page)

Developed with Renee Charlifue-Smith and Cheryl Cole Rooke.

Transdisciplinary Play-Based System (TPBA2/TPBI2) by Toni Linder.

(continued from previous page)

Observation Guidelines: Communication Development **TPBA 2**

Questions	Strengths	Examples of behaviors of concern	"Ready for"	Notes
II. Language production (continued)				
II. C. (continued)	Existence (e.g., this ball)		Action–object (e.g., drink juice)	
	Nonexistence (e.g., all gone)		Agent–action–object (e.g., baby drink juice)	
	Cessation (e.g., stop)		Action–object–location (e.g., throw ball up)	
	Rejection (e.g., no)		All of the above	
	Location (e.g., up)			
	Possession (e.g., mine)			
	Agent–action (e.g., baby drink)			
	Action–object (e.g., drink juice)			
	Agent–action–object (e.g., baby drink juice)			
	Action–object–location (throw ball up)			
	All of the above			
II. D. What grammatical morphemes does the child produce?	Uses the following:	Misuses or omits	Increase use of the following:	
	Present progressive (–ing)	Present progressive (–ing)	Present progressive (–ing)	
	Prepositions (in, on)	Prepositions (in, on)	Prepositions (in, on)	
	Regular and irregular past tense (–ed, came)	Regular and irregular past tense (–ed, came)	Regular and irregular past tense (–ed, came)	
	Possessives ('s)	Possessives ('s)	Possessives ('s)	
	Contractible and uncontractible copula ("dog's little"; "He is" in response to question, "Who is happy?")	Contractible and uncontractible copula ("dog's little"; "He is" in response to question, "Who is happy?")	Contractible and uncontractible copula ("dog's little"; "He is" in response to question, "Who is happy?")	
	Regular and irregular third person (jumps, does)	Regular and irregular third person (jumps, does)	Regular and irregular third person (jumps, does)	

(continued on next page)

Developed with Renee Charlifue-Smith and Cheryl Cole Rooke.

Transdisciplinary Play-Based System (TPBA2/TPBI2) by Toni Linder.

(continued from previous page)

Observation Guidelines: Communication Development **TPBA** 2

Questions	Strengths	Examples of behaviors of concern	"Ready for"	Notes
II. Language production *(continued)*				
II. D. *(continued)*	Regular and irregular third person (jumps, does) Contractible and uncontractible auxiliary ("Mommy's drinking"; "He is" in response to question, "Who is combing his hair?") Mean length of utterance (MLU) is at predicted age level All of the above	Regular and irregular third person (jumps, does) Contractible and uncontractible auxiliary ("Mommy's drinking"; "He is" in response to question, "Who is combing his hair?") MLU is below predicted age level All of the above	Regular and irregular third person (jumps, does) Contractible and uncontractible auxiliary ("Mommy's drinking"; "He is" in response to question, "Who is combing his hair?") Increase MLU All of the above	
II. E. What are the child's syntactic abilities?	Produces sentence structures Simple Compound Complex Compound-complex Produces different sentence types Declarative (i.e., statement) Interrogative (i.e., questions: yes/no) Simple "wh": what, where Complex "wh": which, why, how, when, whose Imperative (i.e., request) Exclamatory (i.e., strong emotion) Negatives (e.g., no, not, don't)	Makes syntactical errors	Increase appropriate production and complexity of syntax	

Developed with Renee Charlifue-Smith and Cheryl Cole Rooke.

Transdisciplinary Play-Based System (TPBA2/TPBI2) by Toni Linder.

(continued on next page)

(continued from previous page)

Observation Guidelines: Communication Development **TPBA** 2

Questions	Strengths	Examples of behaviors of concern	"Ready for"	Notes
III. Pragmatics				
III. A. Does the child understand and use joint attention (gestures, vocalizations, or words) to communicate intent?	Communicates unintentionally Makes eye contact Reflexive sounds and movements Follows and regulates joint attention Uses gaze to regulate joint attention Follows others' joint attention in visual field Follows others' joint attention outside of visual field Uses intentional deictic gestures Shows or gives objects Open-handed reaching for objects Pushes to protest Pushes to request Points to comment Pairs vocalizations and gestures Uses representational gestures Uses social gestures (e.g., blow kiss, bye-bye) Initiates social games (e.g., Peekaboo) Uses rising intonation to request information Uses words and gestures to express intent Equivalent word/gesture pairs	Does not communicate intentionally Does not establish joint attention Does not follow joint attention Does not gesture with intent Does not use words and gestures intentionally	Increase ability to Make eye contact Respond with reactive sounds Establish joint attention Follow others' bids for joint attention Use deictic gestures Use representational gestures Pair vocalizations and gestures Pair words with gestures Initiate social games Express intent with words Use beat gestures All of the above	

Developed with Renee Charlifue-Smith and Cheryl Cole Rooke.

Transdisciplinary Play-Based System (TPBA2/TPBI2)
by Toni Linder.

(continued on next page)

Observation Guidelines: Communication Development **TPBA**2

Questions	Strengths	Examples of behaviors of concern	"Ready for"	Notes
III. Pragmatics (continued)				
III. A. (continued)	Complementary word/ gesture pairs Pairs word with point Uses beat gestures to empha- size words			
III. B. What functions does the child's communication fulfill?	Child communicates for a variety of purposes (note mode of communication: eye gaze, sound, body movement, vocalization, gesture, word): Regulatory functions Requests objects Requests actions Protests Declarative-joint attention functions Comments on objects Comments on actions Requests information Provides information Requests clarification Clarifies meaning Social interaction Shows interest Smiles Responds to social games (e.g., Peekaboo) Initiates social games Nods head Social gestures: waves, blows kiss, shrugs Enjoys jokes	Limited range of functions Only requests Only comments Does not clarify Does not use social func- tions Rate of use is limited Less than one communica- tive act per minute Form of function is limited for age	Increase range of communica- tion functions Regulatory (i.e., request, protests) Declarative (i.e., comments, requests for information, clarification) Social (i.e., interest, smile, social games, gestures, jokes) All of the above	

(continued on next page)

Developed with Renee Charlifue-Smith and Cheryl Cole Rooke.

Transdisciplinary Play-Based System (TPBA2/TPBI2)
by Toni Linder.

Observation Guidelines: Communication Development **TPBA 2**

Questions	Strengths	Examples of behaviors of concern	"Ready for"	Notes
III. Pragmatics (continued)				
III. C. What conversational or discourse skills does the child demonstrate?	Uses the following conversational strategies: Attends/responds (nonverbally/verbally) to speaker Makes and maintains eye contact Initiates (gestural and vocal/verbal) Takes balanced turns Maintains topic Changes topic appropriately Acknowledges others Responds to requests for clarification Shares information, thoughts, and ideas Questions Terminates conversation All of the above	Demonstrates difficulty initiating a conversation Limited skills in joining a conversation Frequent revisions (e.g., starts talking, stops, and starts at beginning) Over reliance on clarification or repetition Fixates on a fact or topic and cannot shift Makes off-topic comments or rapid topic changes Does not seek clarification Asks repetitive, rote questions Does not supply enough information	Increase ability to use the following conversational strategies: Attending to speaker Initiating conversation Taking appropriate turns Maintaining a topic Changing topic appropriately Acknowledging other's speech Responding to requests for clarification Sharing information, thoughts, and ideas Questioning Terminating conversation	
Bilingualism and Biculturalism Is the child bilingual (simultaneous, sequential)?	*Speech and language developmental milestones are often different for bilingual or multilingual children, regardless of their form of bilingualism. Evaluators must consult with a cultural mediator or a competent bilingual speech-language pathologist to determine appropriate milestones for each of the child's developing language systems. Evaluators are also cautioned against attributing normal delays related to bilingualism to a language disorder.*			

Developed with Renee Charlifue-Smith and Cheryl Cole Rooke.

Transdisciplinary Play-Based System (TPBA2/TPBI2) by Toni Linder.

(continued on next page)

(continued from previous page)

Observation Guidelines: Communication Development **TPBA** 2

Questions	Strengths	Examples of behaviors of concern	"Ready for"	Notes
IV. Articulation and phonology				
IV. A. What speech sounds does the child produce (i.e., vowel and consonant repertoire)?	Appropriate sound repertoire	Sound repertoire is not appropriate	Increase sound repertoire and production of target sounds	
IV. B. What are the articulation abilities of the child?	Child consistently demonstrates age-appropriate articulation skills in increasingly complex contexts: Words Phrases Sentences Conversation	Inconsistently demonstrates age-appropriate articulation skills Demonstrates age-appropriate articulation skills in imitation Child's intelligibility is not age appropriate due to errors at the Word level Phrase level Sentence level Conversation level Child exhibits Articulation errors Phonological processes Inconsistent productions	Decrease articulation errors Decrease phonological processes Increase intelligibility	
IV. C. How intelligible is the child's speech?	Child is intelligible To family members To familiar people To unfamiliar people In known context In unknown context	Child is unintelligible To family members To familiar people To unfamiliar people In known context In unknown context	Increase intelligibility	

Developed with Renee Charlifue-Smith and Cheryl Cole Rooke.

Transdisciplinary Play-Based System (TPBA2/TPBI2)
by Toni Linder.

(continued on next page)

(continued from previous page)

Observation Guidelines: Communication Development **TPBA** 2

Questions	Strengths	Examples of behaviors of concern	"Ready for"	Notes
V. Voice and fluency				

V. A. How are the pitch, quality, and loudness of the child's voice?	Child has adequate breath support for speech production
	
	Appropriate for the child's age, size, and gender:
	Pitch
	Quality
	Resonance
	Rate
	Volume
		Child does not have adequate breath support for speech production
		
		Voice is not appropriate for the child's age, size, and gender:
		Pitch
		  Tremulous
		  Too high or too low
		  Pitch breaks
		  Monotone
		Quality
		  Breathy
		  Raspy
		  Hoarse
		  Hypernasal
		  Denasal
		Rate
		  Too fast or too slow
		Volume
		  Too soft or loud
		Rhythm
		  Choppy
			Improve quality:
			Pitch
			Intonation
			Resonance
			Rate
			Volume
			Refer for medical evaluation	

V. B. How fluent is the child's speech?	Child exhibits fluent speech Child exhibits typical disfluencies: Whole-word repetitions Phrase repetitions	Child exhibits disfluent behaviors: Primary: prolonged sounds, sound repetitions, part-word repetitions Secondary: facial grimaces, eye blinks	Increase fluency with different communication partners and in different settings Refer to speech-language pathologist	

Developed with Renee Charlifue-Smith and Cheryl Cole Rooke.

Transdisciplinary Play-Based System (TPBA2/TPBI2) by Toni Linder.

(continued on next page)

(continued from previous page)

Observation Guidelines: Communication Development **TPBA** 2

Questions	Strengths	Examples of behaviors of concern	"Ready for"	Notes
VI. Oral mechanism				
VI. A. How are the structures and function of the articulators?	Child's posture and muscle tone are appropriate for breath support and speech production	Head is not held at midline, is extended or retracted	Refer for further evaluation	
	Appearance of the articulators is symmetrical	Muscle tone affects speech production: too little tone (hypotonicity) or too much tone (hypertonicity)	Medical evaluation	
	Articulator movements are symmetrical	Posture is not adequate for breath support	Dental evaluation	
	Full range of tongue movements: elevation, retraction, protrusion	Appearance and movement of the articulators is asymmetrical	Speech-language pathologist	
	Full range of lip movements: rounding, retraction, separation	Limited tongue movement	Increase control of the articulators for speech production	
	Jaw movement: good control and no excessive movement	Limited lip movement: rounding, retraction, separation		
	Articulators are functional for speech production	Jaw movement: poor control or excessive movement		
	Child is able to produce rapid and alternating movements	Poor oral hygiene affecting teeth		
	Produces sound sequences accurately	Evidence of cleft lip and/or palate repair		
		Tongue protrudes at rest or tremors		
		Underbite, overbite, open bite		
		Chronic mouth breathing		
		Difficulty with fluid movement: Groping speech movements		
		Slow rate of speech		
		Inconsistent speech errors		
		Error increase with greater length and complexity		
		Limited sound repertoire		
		Drooling inappropriate for age: Awareness?		
		During which activities?		

Developed with Renee Charlifue-Smith and Cheryl Cole Rooke.

Transdisciplinary Play-Based System (TPBA2/TPBI2)
by Toni Linder.

TPBA2 Observation Notes:
Communication Development

Child's name: _____ Parent(s): _____

Birth date: _____ Assessment date: _____ Age: _____

Person(s) completing the form: _____

Directions: Record the child information (name, caregiver[s], birth date, age), assessment date, person(s) completing this form, and your observations about the child in the spaces below. You are encouraged to review the corresponding TPBA2 Observation Guidelines prior to recording your observations here, as the Guidelines list what to look for. Newer TPBA users may opt to use the TPBA2 Observation Guidelines as a method for collecting information during the assessment instead of the TPBA2 Observation Notes.

Note: Hearing is included on this Observation Summary Form but not on the Corresponding Observation Guidelines or Observations Notes forms, because hearing is not really being assessed by TPBA, but TPBA can result in a referral for hearing screening.

I. Language comprehension (understands and responds to language)	**II. Language production** (uses language in any modality)

Transcribed Play-Based System (TPBA2/TPBI2)
by Toni Linder.
Copyright © 2008 Paul H. Brookes Publishing Co., Inc. All rights reserved.

(continued on next page)

(continued from previous page)

III. Pragmatics (uses intentional nonverbal and verbal communication for different purposes in different social contexts)

IV. Articulation and phonology (produces the sounds [articulation] and represents the sound system of his/her language)

V. Voice and fluency (quality, pitch, loudness, fluency)

VI. Oral mechanism (structure and function of the oral articulators)

TPBA2 Age Table: Communication Development (including ASL skills)

Child's name: _____ Age: _____ Birth date: _____

Parent(s): _____ Assessment date: _____

Person(s) completing the form: _____

Directions: Based on the observations recorded on the TPBA2 Observation Guidelines and/or TPBA2 Observation Notes, review the Age Table to determine the age level that most closely matches the child's performance. It may be helpful to circle items on the Age Table that the child can do. If items are circled across multiple age levels, find the child's age level by finding the mode (i.e., determine which age level has the most circled items). Age levels after 12 months/1 year represent ranges rather than individual months and are preceded by "By." If the most circled items appear in one of these age levels, consider the child's age levels, consider the child's age level to be the month shown (e.g., if the most circled items appear in the "By 21 months" level, the child's age level for that subcategory is 21 months).

Note: The Communication Development Age Table also includes American Sign Language milestones.

Note: This Age Table collapses the Articulation and Phonology and the Oral Mechanism subcategories into one column.

Note: The Voice and Fluency subcategory is not included in this Age Table. Qualitative factors reflected in the Communication Observation Guidelines are more appropriate for voice and fluency than age-related changes.

Age level	Language comprehension	Language production	American Sign Language (ASL)	Pragmatics	Articulation and phonology and Oral mechanism
1 month	Differentiates between familiar and unfamiliar voices Can distinguish sound segments and intonation, prosody, and stress of his or her native language from another language Responds by quieting Can be comforted and calmed by touching and rocking Stares at faces	Cries to express hunger, discomfort, pain, or distress Uses body movements coupled with sounds		Smiles in response to high-pitched voices Gazes at caregiver's face Cries are undifferentiated May produce other sounds: burps, hiccups, sneezes, or coughs	Produces vegetative sounds (e.g., burps, sneezes) Cries Imitates tongue and mouth movements

(continued on next page)

Developed by Renee Charlifue-Smith and Cheryl Cole Rooke. American Sign Language milestones developed by Jan Christian Hafer.

Transdisciplinary Play-Based System (TPBA2/TPBI2)
by Toni Linder.

(continued from previous page)

Age Table: Communication Development **TPBA** 2

Age level	Language comprehension	Language production	ASL	Pragmatics	Articulation and phonology and Oral mechanism
2 months	Distinguishes among anger, surprise, and sadness in adult Discriminates between parents' voices and sounds Distinguishes native language from a foreign language Responds positively to quiet voice Startles at loud noises Smiles at mother's voice	Coos (i.e., throaty sounds with vowels) Cries and uses body movement and facial expressions to express needs Anticipates movement of objects by reacting with body movement Grunts in relation to movement; sighs; has a reflexive sound that is making peaks Smiles at speaker		Smiles back to familiar face Makes eye contact	Coos (i.e., sounds made in the back of mouth with vowels) Deferred imitation of facial movements
3 months	Discriminates between familiar and unfamiliar voices Stops sucking to listen Anticipates next step in familiar game Searches for sound source	Crying becomes differentiated Quiets when picked up Gurgles, laughs, and smiles Expresses all basic emotions (i.e., happiness, anger, sadness, distress, surprise) Vocalizes in response to familiar voices Moves body while vocalizing	Birth to 3 months: Fixes gaze on signer and/or scans face of signer Makes eye contact	Enjoys responding to people and eye-to-eye contact Produces true social smile Fixes gaze toward other Nods, smiles, and interacts with adults	Brings hand to mouth Sucks on hand and fingers Presents with little saliva Coos, squeals, and giggles
4 months	Turns head to sound source Differentiates and responds to different sounds and voices	Produces vocalization in response to other's sounds Cries if play is disrupted		Vocalizes to initiate socializing Responds differently to different people Laughs when socializing	Attempts imitation of sounds Cries vary in volume, pitch, and length Produces vowel "ah" Laughs
5 months	Fears loud or unexpected noises Remembers patterns of sounds (e.g., song, story)	Stops crying when talked to Babbles randomly Possibly cries when toy is taken away or if left alone Imitates sounds Fusses to demand attention Produces neutral and pleasure sounds toward objects (2–5 months)		Shows anger or protest when frustrated Shows preference for familiar faces (e.g., smiles) Responds differently to stranger (may withdraw or frown)	Babbles by producing consonant–vowel (CV) syllables Plays with sounds and patterns of sound Makes consonant sounds (e.g., p, b, n, k, g)

(continued on next page)

Developed by Renee Charlifue-Smith and Cheryl Cole Rooke. American Sign Language milestones developed by Jan Christian Hafer.

Transdisciplinary Play-Based System (TPBA2/TPBI2)
by Toni Linder.

Age Table: Communication Development **TPBA** 2

Age level	Language comprehension	Language production	ASL	Pragmatics	Articulation and phonology and Oral mechanism
6 months	Focuses on others' mouths Moves head to the side to search for sounds/voices with his or her eyes (3–6 months)	Shows pleasure with gurgles and coos Shows displeasure with growls and grunts Squeals, giggles, and belly laughs with delight Responds with enthusiasm to familiar game and routines such as Peekaboo Talks to self in mirror Vocalizes to objects held in hand (6–9 months)	3-6 months: Kicks, waves hands, and smiles when excited Ceases movement in response to signing "Mabbles" (i.e., manually babbles)	Resists actions or objects he/she does not want Objects to someone taking toy away	Often puts objects in mouth Makes different vowel sounds (e.g., *ah, eh, ee, oo*) and early consonant sounds (e.g., *p, b, t, d, m, n*) Makes raspberries Controls saliva in all positions unless feeding, actively playing with objects, or teething Imitates playful sounds
7 months	Is learning meaning of "no" through tone of voice Distinguishes friendly and angry talking Enjoys listening to own voice Likes complex sound stimulation	Anticipates actions and begins to get excited or upset before action occurs Cries or shouts for attention Reaches to be picked up and held Cries in response to another infant's cry Uses open-handed reach to request objects		Responds to playing games such as Peekaboo and Pat-a-cake (4–7 months) Shows desire to be included in social interactions Reacts to emotional display of others	Produces syllable chains (e.g., "babababababa"; reduplicated babbling) Babbles rhythmically Imitates speech sounds
8 months	Listens selectively to sounds and words Responds to own name with head turn, eye contact, or smile Anticipates familiar events Bilingual child differentiates L1 and L2 words spoken in a speech stream	Cries if caregiver leaves or stranger is nearby Protests Produces gestures and vocalizations that get interpreted by the parent as communicative intent (birth to 8 months)		Follows what someone points to Points to objects to show others Follows the visual gaze of others looking at objects within the child's visual field Uses eye gaze to affect the actions of others Points to objects when alone and shows communicative intent to protest Uses intentional two-way communication or turn taking (4–8 months)	Increases imitation of speech sounds Produces syllables repetitively

(continued on next page)

Developed by Renee Charlifue-Smith and Cheryl Cole Rooke. American Sign Language milestones developed by Jan Christian Hafer.

Transdisciplinary Play-Based System (TPBA2/TPBI2) by Toni Linder.

(continued from previous page)

Age Table: Communication Development **TPBA 2**

Age level	Language comprehension	Language production	ASL	Pragmatics	Articulation and phonology and Oral mechanism
9 months	Follows some simple requests paired with gestures Understands some words Dances to music	Repeats another's sounds back and forth Bilingual child: code-switches babble for speakers of each language Says nonspecific "mama" or "dada"	6–9 months: Responds to simple requests with gestures (e.g., bye-bye, up) Looks at family members when namesign is used Begins to associate signs with objects Visually attends to signer Follows eye gaze of signer	Initiates intentional interactions (e.g., reaches for nose, hair, mouth) Uses gestures paired with vocalization in 50% or less of communicative acts and uses contact gestures with object or caregiver (e.g., showing, giving, pushing away) Uses declarative giving (i.e., hands object to other to make a comment; precedes joint attention) Communicative intents: requests actions, requests objects, and comments on actions Uses eye gaze to establish joint attention on objects within the child's visual field Uses a nonintentional point when alone or when others are present	Produces nonreduplicated or variegated babbling: varied syllable and sound structures (e.g., "badebu") Bilingual child uses the phonetic features of each language in babbling Presents with less drooling during mealtime
10 months	Understands some object names Listens with interest to familiar words Understands more commands paired with gestures (e.g., "give me") Moves head horizontally and downward to sound source (6–10 months)	Babbles with intonation of language (i.e., jargon) Uses a near or contact point to request and comment on objects May repeat a word incessantly, making it a response to every question		Points to request objects Points to comment on objects Initiates social games Shows function of objects with representational gestures	Produces jargon (adult-like intonation)

(continued on next page)

Developed by Renee Charlifue-Smith and Cheryl Cole Rooke. American Sign Language milestones developed by Jan Christian Hafer.

Transdisciplinary Play-Based System (TPBA2/TPBI2) by Toni Linder.

(continued from previous page)

Age Table: Communication Development **TPBA**2

Age level	Language comprehension	Language production	ASL	Pragmatics	Articulation and phonology and Oral mechanism
11 months	Recognizes words and symbols for objects (e.g., airplane [points to sky], doggie [growls]) Responds to "no"	Plays games Pushes and pulls to communicate Produces sounds to gain other's attention		Uses distal gestures such as points to faraway objects, waves Uses single words to comment Uses single words to seek attention Gives others objects to request actions.	Speech primarily gibberish with a few intelligible sounds Imitates inflections, speech rhythms, and facial attitudes more than speech sounds
12 months or 1 year	Identifies common objects when named Shows intense attention to speech over prolonged time Uses gestures in response to words (e.g., up, bye) Associates properties with objects (e.g., sounds of animals, location of objects) Responds to "Where is _____?" by searching for object or family member (12–16 months) Understands up to 50 words	May ask for help from adult Produces first word around 1 year Begins to label objects "Talks" with others	9–12 months: Uses true words/signs to satisfy needs and wants Sign formation differs from that of adult (e.g., index finger for Mom/Dad instead of thumb)	Enjoys turn-taking games Vocalizes in response to others Monitors others' direction of gaze to establish joint attention	Produces first word Articulation may be understood by familiar listener Produces a variety of consonant and vowel approximations during babbling Imitates other's coughs, laughs, lip smacking
15 months	Moves head directly to sound source (15–18 months) Sustains interest for 2 minutes or more looking at pictures named Searches for objects named but not present Follows simple directions with cues (e.g., "Give me the ball," "Get the shoes," "Show me") Identifies an object from a group of objects	Uses exclamations (e.g., "uh-oh") Uses "dada" or "mama" meaningfully May produce 4–6 different words, including names of objects, family members, activities Says "hi" and "bye" Says a version of "thank you" May use "there." Imitates words		Shares joint attention on an object with another (8–14 months) Imitates actions of others (8–14 months) Consistently uses a far point to request actions and information Uses rising intonation to request information Uses single words to request actions	Produces early consonants: *b, m, n, t, d, w* Produces word approximations (e.g., "muh" for *milk*) Drools on occasion during teething and some fine motor tasks

(continued on next page)

Developed by Renee Charlifue-Smith and Cheryl Cole Rooke. American Sign Language milestones developed by Jan Christian Hafer.

Transdisciplinary Play-Based System (TPBA2/TPBI2) by Toni Linder.

(continued from previous page)

Age Table: Communication Development **TPBA** 2

Age level	Language comprehension	Language production	ASL	Pragmatics	Articulation and phonology and Oral mechanism
15 months *(continued)*	Moves head horizontally and downward to sound source (10–15 months)	Uses gestures coupled with vocalizations		Gestures paired with vocalizations constitute the majority of communication acts Follows visual gaze of another outside of immediate visual field Responds to a yes/no question (shakes head *no*) Follows direction to "look." Points to request information (12–16 months) Uses representational gestures (12–13 months)	
18 months	Recognizes and identifies objects and pictures by pointing Points to up to 3 body parts Follows single-step directions Understands the intent of questions Responds to yes/no questions with head shake and nod	Imitates animal sounds and other environmental sounds Produces jargon Imitates single words frequently Produces 5–20 words (mostly nouns) Acknowledges questions (e.g., "yes," "uh huh") Requests desired object with a word Attempts to sing Likes to use "all gone" or "more." Produces "no" Produces "my/mine" Produces present progressive *-ing*	12–16 months: Understands new signs weekly Begins to "listen" to simple signed stories Uses 1-word signs coupled with nonlinguistic pointing	Shows ability to control own emotions and behaviors Shows awareness of caregiver's wishes and expectations Shows frustration Sets limits on others' behaviors (e.g., "stop") Uses a point accompanied by a representational word more than any other gesture Responds to simple requests for clarification (e.g., "Huh?" "What?") (16–18 months) Makes verbal protests (10–18 months) Points to request action (11–18 months)	Imitates sounds and words Omits most final consonants in words; words have CV shape Omits some initial consonants in words Produces sentence-like intonation (jargon) Hums to songs Produces simpler version of the adult word (e.g., "baba" for *bottle*)

(continued on next page)

Developed by Renee Charlifue-Smith and Cheryl Cole Rooke. American Sign Language milestones developed by Jan Christian Hafer.

Transdisciplinary Play-Based System (TPBA2/TPBI2)
by Toni Linder.

(continued from previous page)

Age Table: Communication Development **TPBA** 2

Age level	Language comprehension	Language production	ASL	Pragmatics	Articulation and phonology and Oral mechanism
21 months	Identifies 5 body parts Listens to short rhymes with interesting sounds, especially with actions or pictures Understands some emotion words (e.g., happy, sad, mad) Understands some pronouns (e.g., my/mine, you, me) Responds to what questions	Attempts to tell about experience using words and jargon Asks, "What's that?" Names objects Imitates and produces 2-word combinations mostly consisting of nouns and verbs Produces more than 50 different single words spontaneously Names pictures Makes onomatopoetic sounds related to an activity or object (e.g., animal or car noises) Refers to self by name	Recognizes namesigns of others (16–20 months) Responds to headshakes or signs indicating negation (16–20 months) Recognizes signs for common objects in the environment (16–20 months)	Begins to request clarification (e.g., "huh?") 33% of time Uses gesture to clarify a word (e.g., representational gesture/cup to hand)	Produces speech that is less than 50% intelligible to unfamiliar listeners Inconsistently deletes final consonants in words
24 months or 2 years	Moves head all around to locate sound source Recognizes and points to most common objects Understands action words Identifies and points to extended family members Understands more than 300 words Listens to and enjoys simple stories	Produces more words than gestures Communicates needs, wishes, and feelings with gestures and words Uses early pronouns (e.g., me, my, I, you) Names body parts Uses gestures paired with nonverbal vocalizations less frequently Produces 2-word combinations (e.g., agent-action, action-object, agent-object, action-location, possessor-possession) Names almost anything he or she has daily contact with at home, outside, and in child care	Uses simple 2–3-word sentences (12–24 months) Linguistic pointing to people appears (12–24 months) Makes no morphological distinction between nouns and verbs (e.g., "chair," "sit") (12–24 months) Recognizes namesigns of others (20–24 months) Responds to headshakes or signs indicating negation (20–24 months) Recognizes signs for common objects in the environment (20–24 months)	Initiates topic with 1 word with shared attention (18–24 months) Begins to narrate past events with adult help Responds differently to a request for clarification by an unfamiliar adult Takes 1–2 turns in conversation Initiates a topic and responds with new information	Approximately 50% intelligible Produces consonant-vowel-consonant (CVC) structures (e.g., "mo mik"/more milk) using early consonant sounds: p, b, m, n, t, d, h, w Echoes adult's words and inflections Drooling should not be present

(continued on next page)

Developed by Renee Charlifue-Smith and Cheryl Cole Rooke. American Sign Language milestones developed by Jan Christian Hafer.

Transdisciplinary Play-Based System (TPBA2/TPBI2) by Toni Linder.

(continued from previous page)

Age Table: Communication Development **TPBA** 2

Age level	Language comprehension	Language production	ASL	Pragmatics	Articulation and phonology and Oral mechanism
30 months	Identifies actions in pictures Identifies objects by their function Knows difference between *big* and *little* Points to smaller body parts Follows two-step related directions Understands *one* versus *all*	Communicates previous experiences with prompting from adult Names at least one color Produces 2–3-word combinations Produces prepositions "in" and "on" Present progressive –*ing* (e.g., "baby eating") (19–28 months). Asks questions using rising intonation (25–28 months) Asks *what* questions (25–28 months)	Begins to use classifiers to show objects (e.g., "3" hand-shape sideways for "car") Negation demonstrated with headshake and NO sign Makes *yes/no* questions with raised eyebrows plus sign Makes *wh-* questions with eyebrows and sign Uses dietic pointing to refer to absent person Uses referencing to indicate timeline Uses directionality in verbs Uses topicalization (topic–comment word order) Uses role shift to indicate two or more characters in dialogue	Cooperates in games (24–30 months) Answers 33% of questions asked by adults	Produces speech that is 50%–70% intelligible to familiar listeners Deletes one consonant from a consonant blend (e.g., "_top"/*stop*) Repeats syllables in words (e.g., "wawa"/*water*)
36 months or 3 years	Understands descriptive words Identifies gender Identifies basic colors Understands *why* questions Understands spatial concepts (e.g., *in, out, on, off, under*) (33–36 months) Answers *where* and *what...doing* questions Understands categories	Requests adults' help to handle emotions (24–36 months) Gives first and last name Names smaller body parts Verbalizes toileting needs Uses pronoun "I" Produces spatial, comparative, contrastive, and temporal concepts Starts to produce "is" Produces rhymes Asks *where* questions (26–32 months) Produces regular plural –*s* (e.g., "dogs") (24–33 months) Produces overextension of concrete nouns (e.g., all four-legged animals are "dogs") (13–36 months)	Classifiers often involve unmarked or incorrect handshapes (24–36 months) Can follow discourse that contains more than one idea (24–36 months) Expands "listening" time to 20 minutes (24–36 months) More complex signs attempted but usually substitutes simpler handshapes (e.g., "water" with "5" handshape) (30–36 months)	Some generalization of rules across time and settings occurs (24–36 months) Regularly requests clarification (e.g., "Huh?" "What?")	Simplifies words that are multisyllabic Produces substitutions and distortions of consonants Produces speech that is 75% intelligible Produces sounds made in the back of the mouth (e.g., *c, car; g, go; –ing,* eating)

(continued on next page)

Developed by Renee Charlifue-Smith and Cheryl Cole Rooke. American Sign Language milestones developed by Jan Christian Hafer.

(continued from previous page)

Age Table: Communication Development **TPBA 2**

Age level	Language comprehension	Language production	ASL	Pragmatics	Articulation and phonology and Oral mechanism
42 months	Follows 2-3-step unrelated instructions Identifies most common objects and their pictures Understands what others say Understands terms for family relationships Understands words for basic shapes and sizes Understands descriptive concepts (e.g., *hard, soft, rough, smooth*) Understands *in front of, behind, top, bottom, between* Understands *how many, who,* and *whose* questions (36–40 months)	Asks *who* questions (36–40 months) Asks "Is…?" and "Do…?" questions (37–42 months) Produces hundreds of words Produces 3- to 4-word combinations Counts to 3 Produces pronouns appropriately States gender and age when asked Uses *and, but,* and *because* to combine sentences Uses possessives (26–40 months) Bilingual child's vocabulary often appears to be less well developed in one or both languages by observation or on standard measures because learning is contextualized and exposure is differential. Evaluators should be very careful not to assume a semantic deficit Verbs, grammar develop at about the same rate for each language, but timing may be different for each different language (e.g., Italian verbs may emerge at different ages than English verbs)		Combines two events in a narrative Gestures and speech are paired similar to adult level	Produces speech that is intelligible to unfamiliar listeners Produces the consonants *l, f, s,* and *y* in some positions of words Uses some phonological processes: cluster reduction, fronting, stopping, and vowelization

(continued on next page)

Developed by Renee Charlifue-Smith and Cheryl Cole Rooke. American Sign Language milestones developed by Jan Christian Hafer.

Transdisciplinary Play-Based System (TPBA2/TPBI2) by Toni Linder.

(continued from previous page)

Age Table: Communication Development **TPBA 2**

Age level	Language comprehension	Language production	ASL	Pragmatics	Articulation and phonology and Oral mechanism
42 months *(continued)*		*Note:* Bilingual child passes through the same stages at the same ages that are appropriate to each language being learned			
48 months or 4 years	Knows opposites (e.g., *long/short, hot/cold*) Shows understanding of time concepts (e.g., *before/after, yesterday/today*) Understands spatial concepts (e.g., *behind, in front, next to*) Identifies primary colors and shapes Answers *how* questions Answers *when* questions (42–48 months)	Produces 4- to 5-word sentences Asks *when, why,* and *how* questions (42–48 months) Produces irregular past tense (e.g., *fell, broke*) (25–46 months) Produces articles (e.g., *the, a*) (28–46 months) Produces regular past tense *–ed* (26–48 months) Bilingual child's dominant language will have higher MLU, more advanced grammatical structures, a greater variety of word types (especially verbs), fewer pauses and hesitations, and greater volume		Discriminates appropriate roles and behaviors Combines 3 sequences to describe an event Takes 4 turns in a true conversation Responds to request for clarification about 85% of the time (24–48 months)	Speech is approximately 80% intelligible Produces faster speech Produces a few consonant substitutions and omissions Produces more consonant blends but still may not be completely present with all consonants Produces more consonants: *z, v, sh, ch, j*
54 months	Differentiates between *night* and *day*	Retells the sequence of a story Produces songs/nursery rhymes Describes how to do something Gives descriptions of past events with support Creates rhyming words		Asks questions about how another person feels	

(continued on next page)

Developed by Renee Charlifue-Smith and Cheryl Cole Rooke. American Sign Language milestones developed by Jan Christian Hafer.

Transdisciplinary Play-Based System (TPBA2/TPBI2) by Toni Linder.

(continued from previous page)

Age Table: Communication Development **TPBA2**

Age level	Language comprehension	Language production	ASL	Pragmatics	Articulation and phonology and Oral mechanism
60 months or 5 years	Identifies coins Understands approximately 13,000 words Understands *some, more, less* Understands *above* and *below* Answers "What happens if…?" questions	Exhibits metalinguistic knowledge (i.e., ability to think about and comment about language) (48–60 months). Recites verses, short stories, and songs Names colors Answers questions about a story told Requests definitions of words Relays experiences with detail, without adult prompting Produces sentences 6–8 words in length Produces sentences that are grammatically correct Uses past tense verbs Uses conjunctions: if, *because, when, so* Likes to argue and reason Uses words such as *because* Repeats story narratives Uses relational words (e.g., *forward, then, first, next, behind, backward, in front of)*		Begins to understand humor (enjoys jokes even when not understood) Begins perspective shift/understanding others' points of view Sequences multievent story without a moral or meaningful outcome	Produces most consonants accurately in all positions; may still exhibit errors with the following sounds: *l, s, r, th* Speech is intelligible to unfamiliar listeners

(continued on next page)

Developed by Renee Charlifue-Smith and Cheryl Cole Rooke. American Sign Language milestones developed by Jan Christian Hafer.

(continued from previous page)

Age Table: Communication Development **TPBA** 2

Age level	Language comprehension	Language production	ASL	Pragmatics	Articulation and phonology and Oral mechanism
By 72 months or 6 years	Knows *right* versus *left* Responds appropriately to group instructions Enjoys wordplay and rhymes States differences and similarities among objects Understands passive sentences	Produces past tense and future tense verbs appropriately Produces irregular nouns and verbs Names the days of the week in the correct order Tells opposites Produces approximately 2,000 words States address Produces all sentence types Bilingual child: At age 6, 50% of total vocabulary composed of "singlet" words (i.e., no crossover mapping) in L1 or L2 The child will have "singlet" words well into college		Communicates actively in group activities Asks questions and exchanges information with others Tells a well-informed story with a climax	Produces all sounds in all positions by age 7 Exhibits difficulty with producing complex words

Developed by Renee Charlifue-Smith and Cheryl Cole Rooke. American Sign Language milestones developed by Jan Christian Hafer.

Transdisciplinary Play-Based System (TPBA2/TPBI2) by Toni Linder.

TPBA2 Observation Summary Form: Communication Development

Child's name: _____ Age: _____ Birth date: _____

Parent(s): _____ Assessment date: _____

Person(s) completing the form: _____

Directions: For each of the subcategories below, shown in a 1–9-point Goal Attainment Scale, circle the number that indicates the child's developmental status, using findings from the TPBA2 Observation Guidelines or TPBA2 Observation Notes for this domain. Next, consider the child's performance in relation to same-age peers by comparing the child's performance with the TPBA2 Age Table. Use the Age Table to arrive at the child's age level for each subcategory (follow directions on the Age Table). Then, circle AA, T, W, or C by calculating percent delay:

If a child's age level < chronological age: 1 − (age level/CA) = _____ % delay

If child's age level > chronological age: (age level/CA) − 1 = _____ % above

To calculate CA, subtract the child's birth date from the assessment date and round up or down as appropriate. When subtracting days, take into consideration the number of days in the month (i.e., 28, 30, 31).

Note: Hearing is included on this Observation Summary Form but not on the corresponding Observation Guidelines or Observations Notes forms, because hearing is not really being assessed by TPBA, but TPBA can result in a referral for hearing screening.

TPBA2 Subcategory	Level of the child's ability as observed in functional activities									Rating compared with other children of same age				
	1	2	3	4	5	6	7	8	9	Above average (AA)	Typical (T)	Watch (W)	Concern (C)	Age level (mode)
Language comprehension	Focuses on speaker's face and reacts to sounds and voices.		Attends to or responds to own name and familiar gestures, signs, or words.		Understands gestures, signs and/or single words, simple one-step requests, and early question forms: *yes/no, what, where.*		Understands familiar and novel two-step directions, *who* and *when* questions, and comments that are signed or spoken.		Understands age-appropriate basic concepts and vocabulary, *why* and *how* questions, grammatical structures, and multistep requests that are signed or spoken.	AA	T	W	C	___
										Comments:				

(continued on next page)

Observation Summary Form: Communication Development **TPBA 2**

TPBA2 Subcategory	Level of the child's ability as observed in functional activities									Rating compared with other children of same age				
	1	2	3	4	5	6	7	8	9	Above average (AA)	Typical (T)	Watch (W)	Concern (C)	Age level (mode)
Language production	Expresses needs reflexively (e.g., crying, grimacing, body movement).		Uses eye gaze, facial expressions, body movement, gestures, and vocalizations to communicate.		Uses gestures, vocalizations, verbalizations, signs (words, word combinations, or phrases), and/or AAC to communicate.		Uses gestures, words, phrases, signs, and/or AAC to produce sentences (not grammatically correct) and to ask and answer questions.		Consistently uses well-formed sentences and answers a variety of questions.	AA Comments:	T	W	C	____
Pragmatics	Does not understand or give "readable" physical, vocal, or verbal cues to communicate needs.		Uses and responds to eye gaze to share attention on an object/activity with the caregiver. Uses eye gaze, gestures, and vocalizations to send an intentional message to others.		Takes 1 or 2 turns on a topic of conversation and uses eye gaze, gestures, signs, and/or words to request, comment, protest, greet, and regulate the behaviors of others.		Initiates, responds, and expands on topics in a conversation by taking extended turns, asking for information or clarification, and talking about things that have happened in the past with caregiver support.		Uses and responds to verbal and nonverbal communication for a variety of purposes, in a variety of contexts.	AA Comments:	T	W	C	____
Articulation and phonology	Coos, squeals, laughs, and engages in vocal play.		Produces strings of vowel and consonant sounds that are nonmeaningful.		Produces word approximations, words, or phrases that may not be completely intelligible.		Speech often is intelligible to familiar and unfamiliar listeners in conversation and in a variety of activities.		Accurately and intelligibly produces the sounds of his/her language in conversation and in a variety of activities.	AA Comments:	T	W	C	____

(continued on next page)

Transdisciplinary Play-Based System (TPBA2/TPBI2) by Toni Linder.

(continued from previous page)

Observation Summary Form: Communication Development **TPBA** 2

TPBA2 Subcategory	Level of the child's ability as observed in functional activities									Rating compared with other children of same age				
	1	2	3	4	5	6	7	8	9	Above average (AA)	Typical (T)	Watch (W)	Concern (C)	Age level (mode)
Voice and fluency	Breath support is adequate for crying, grunting, cooing, or laughing, but not for voice production (phonation).		Breath support and voice production are adequate for sound, but the child does not yet babble or make single-word approximations.		Breath support is adequate for voice production, but any of the following behaviors are chronic, noticeable, and interfere with the child's communication: *Pitch:* very high, very low, or monotone *Quality:* very breathy, harsh, hoarse, nasal, or stuffy *Loudness:* inadequate or very loud *Fluency:* very choppy rhythm, and/or frequently occurring disfluencies (sound or syllable repetitions, e.g., "c-c-c-cat", prolonged sounds, e.g., "sssssat"; or silent blocks) *Speech rate:* very slow or very fast		Breath support is adequate for voice production. Any of the following behaviors are noticeable but do not markedly interfere with the child's communication: *Pitch:* slightly high, slightly low, or monotone *Quality:* slightly breathy, harsh, hoarse, nasal, or stuffy *Loudness:* slightly soft or slightly loud *Fluency:* slightly choppy rhythm, and/or occasional occurring disfluencies (sound or syllable repetitions, e.g., "c-c-c-cat"; prolonged sounds, e.g., "sssssat"; or silent blocks) *Speech rate:* slightly slow or slightly fast		Pitch, quality, and loudness of the voice and speech fluency and rate are appropriate for the child's age, size, gender, and culture.	AA	T	W	C	____
										Comments:				

(continued on next page)

Transdisciplinary Play-Based System (TPBA2/TPBI2) by Toni Linder.

277

(continued from previous page)

Observation Summary Form: Communication Development **TPBA** 2

TPBA2 Subcategory	Level of the child's ability as observed in functional activities									Rating compared with other children of same age				Age level (mode)
	1	2	3	4	5	6	7	8	9	Above average (AA)	Typical (T)	Watch (W)	Concern (C)	
Oral mechanism	The structure and/or symmetry of the palate, lips, jaw, tongue, or bite interfere with functional speech.		Structures are adequate, but speech is made primarily with gross jaw and lip movements. The range of movement may be excessive or limited.		Structures are adequate for speech. The child can round and retract the lips with good contact; move the tongue up, down, and front to back; and use finely graded jaw movements to produce sounds and simple words.		Structures are adequate for speech. The child moves the lips, tongue, jaw, and palate independently but has some difficulty integrating movements to say complex words (e.g., potato, buttercup) or phrases.		Structure and function of the oral mechanism are adequate for age-appropriate speech.	AA Comments:	T	W	C	_____
Hearing	Not aware or only minimally aware of sounds in the environment.		Distinguishes that one sound is different from another with or without adaptive support.		Differentiates environmental and some speech sounds with or without adaptive support.		Inconsistently responds to sounds and spoken language with or without adaptive supports.		Attends to and localizes to sounds and speech and uses hearing functionally in conversation with or without adaptive support.	AA Comments:	T	W	C	_____

6

Hearing Screening and Modification of TPBA for Children Who Are Deaf or Hard of Hearing

with Jan Christian Hafer, Cheryl Cole Rooke, and Renee Charlifue-Smith

Hearing allows an individual to attend, localize, and respond to voices and sounds in his or her environment. Hearing plays a pivotal role in the development of speech-language, social-emotional, and overall learning. The foundation for successful engagement with objects, people, and events in the environment is early access to communication and language, which is heavily influenced by hearing the sounds of language (see Chapter 5). This chapter is meant to fulfill two purposes. First, it provides information about the hearing domain and guidelines for hearing screening to be included as part of Transdisciplinary Play-Based Assessment (TPBA2). Use of these TPBA2 Observation Guidelines is appropriate for all children seen in TPBA and should be considered along with the TPBA2 Observation Guidelines for communication in Chapter 5 (see p. 250).

The second purpose of the chapter is to look at the adaptations that are needed for conducting TPBA with children who are deaf or hard of hearing. This includes considerations for families seeking assessment of their child, modifications that are needed for the environment and facilitation, and additional guidelines that should be considered for children who are using or may need to begin to use sign language or some alternative communication. The communication Age Table in Chapter 5 has been expanded to include the milestones of ASL for use with children who are using sign language to communicate.

HEARING SCREENING

Early identification of hearing loss in infants is crucial for optimal development (Yoshinaga-Itano, Sedey, Coulter, & Mehl, 1998). Research has found that if early intervention for children with hearing loss begins by 6 months of age, and includes active parent involvement, the language of a child with hearing loss can be comparable with that of a child of the same age with normal hearing by 3–8 years of age (Joint

---

Note: In this section, "deaf" with small "d" is used to refer to an audiological status, whereas "Deaf" with a capital "D" is used in reference to the linguistic minority that makes up the Deaf community, shares Deaf culture, and is composed of individuals who identify themselves as Deaf people (Marschark & Spencer, 2003).

Committee on Infant Hearing, 2000; Moeller, 2000; Yoshinaga-Itano et al., 1998). Without such early intervention, language delays and social, learning, and emotional difficulties will occur (Yoshinaga-Itano & Sedey, 2000). This is why early identification of hearing loss is critical. For example, if a child is born with a hearing loss, he or she cannot develop typical, age-appropriate communication skills without adaptations such as amplification and/or sign language and family education as to the impact of hearing loss on development. This is true for approximately 90% of children born with hearing loss to hearing parents. The remaining 10% are born to Deaf parents who already have an awareness of the adaptations necessary and who can communicate effectively with their deaf child from birth using sign language (Meadow, 1967).

Universal newborn hearing screening (UNHS) is now required in most states, so nearly all infants born in the United States will receive a hearing screening at the time of discharge from the hospital after birth. The purpose of the newborn screening is to identify children with hearing loss at the earliest age possible so that appropriate early intervention can begin; this is important because in 1–4 per 1000 births a hearing loss is present (Centers for Disease Control and Prevention, 2005; Culpepper, 2003). Although the advent of UNHS has enabled the medical profession to detect a possible hearing loss by 1 month of age, more than half of the newborns who did not pass the screening had no follow-up (Culpepper, 2003).

With the initiation of UNHS, many believe that most children with hearing loss will be identified immediately. Unfortunately, this is not the case. The infant screening examines hearing at a moment in time, and infants and children can acquire a hearing loss after they have passed an initial screening (Widen, Bull, & Folsom, 2003). Genetic disorders, traumatic injuries, infections, and other causes may contribute to hearing loss before or after birth. Also, 10%–20% of children will have three or more episodes of otitis media—inflammation of the middle ear—with each of the episodes lasting on average 1 month. It is important that episodes of otitis media be monitored closely due to the impact they may have on language development. During the first few years of a child's life, they are hearing and responding to the sounds and the speech of others. During an ear infection, the fluid in the middle ear may cause sounds and speech to be muffled. When there is fluid in the space instead of air, the middle ear bones may not vibrate properly, which in turn may result in a mild and temporary hearing loss. Acute otitis media (AOM) occurs when there is an infection of the middle ear with a build-up of mucus and fluid. Otitis media with effusion (OME) frequently occurs after an episode of AOM when fluid remains in the middle ear. Otitis media can happen in one ear or in both. If a child has a history of otitis media, hearing should be assessed periodically, especially if there are concerns with speech and language development.

The challenge today is to link screening programs with intervention services. Culpepper reports that both Hawaii and Rhode Island have established systems that link screening with intervention services, thereby increasing the possibilities for these children to develop communication skills equivalent to their hearing peers. The average age of identification and intervention services for children in these programs is now younger than 6 months (Culpepper, 2003).

Traditional Screening Procedures

Depending on the age of the child, two types of approaches are used for hearing screening: Physiological measures of auditory function are typically used with newborns or for those children who cannot provide a clear behavioral response to sound, and behavioral approaches are used for children older than 6 months of age. As described earlier, hearing loss can occur at all ages, so testing should be recurrent as the child gets older. Typically, infants that are identified as at risk for hearing loss (or have an identified loss) should be retested every 6 months. Children are screened on entry to kindergarten and afterward if behavioral indications are present.

Two commonly used physiological approaches for screening auditory function are conducted when the infant is sleeping. Otoacoustic emissions (OAEs) are sounds produced by the outer hair cells of the inner ear when stimulated by sound. A sensitive microphone picks up these sounds when generated. Alternatively, auditory brain-stem responses (ABRs) pick up the response from the auditory nerve through electrodes attached to the scalp and connected to a computer for interpretation (Widen et al., 2003).

Behavioral screening typically is done by conditioning the child to look at a stimulus, raise a hand, or in some other way indicate that he or she hears a sound administered through earphones.

Both the physiological and behavioral screening approaches are meant to be quick and inexpensive ways of identifying children who need further assessment. Children who fail to respond either to the physiological measures or to the behavioral screening are referred for a rescreening or further diagnostic hearing testing. Once a hearing loss is confirmed, a plan for intervention can be formulated by the parents and consulting professionals. This plan goes beyond simply the prescription of hearing aids and includes communication strategies, understanding the impact of hearing loss on language development, cultural considerations (including learning about Deaf culture), and educational program options. Most likely this plan will include a discussion of the efficacy of cochlear implantation soon after the diagnosis of hearing loss is made.

WHAT IS HEARING LOSS?

When parents suspect a hearing loss, they often will consult their pediatrician, thinking that there may be a medical problem (Gatty, 2003). The pediatrician then refers them to an otologist or an audiologist who conducts the diagnostic hearing testing (audiological testing) described previously to determine the amount of loss, the type of loss, and the hearing threshold levels for each ear (Widen et al., 2003). Once this information is documented, individualized appropriate intervention is planned.

The timeline from parents' suspicion to the audiologist's diagnosis is often 6 months or more (Mertens, Sass-Lehrer, & Scott-Olson, 2000). Frequently this process of determining a hearing loss will take several sessions because, as explained previously, infants and very young children do not yet have the cognitive and motor skills to respond voluntarily to hearing tests (Culpepper, 2003).

Definition of Hearing Loss

The diagnosis or audiological evaluation process will determine the degree, type, and configuration of the hearing loss. *Degree* refers to whether the loss is mild (15–30 decibels [dB]), moderate (31–60 dB), severe (61–90 dB), or profound (>90 dB) (Gatty, 2003). Any degree of hearing loss will put a child at risk for fully developing spoken language and listening skills; however, with increasing severity of hearing loss, the risk for delayed spoken communication skills is usually greater. *Configuration* refers to the slope or shape of the hearing loss, which will consider the degree (loudness) as well as the frequency (low to high) of sounds that are perceived by the child. (See Figure 6.1 to see the effect of a moderate hearing loss on the ability to hear a wide range of sounds.) The *type* of hearing loss refers to where in the hearing mechanism the hearing loss occurs. A *sensorineural* loss is located in the inner ear, where hair cells are not adequately functioning in the transmission of auditory stimuli to the brain. This is a permanent condition that may be the result of environmental factors such as medications, noise, fever, injury, genetics, or congenital factors. A *conductive* loss occurs in the outer or middle ear and often is the result of infection, accumulation of wax, or malformation. This type of hearing loss may be temporary if medical intervention is provided. Finally, a *mixed loss* combines both sensorineural and conductive components (Martin & Clark, 2000).

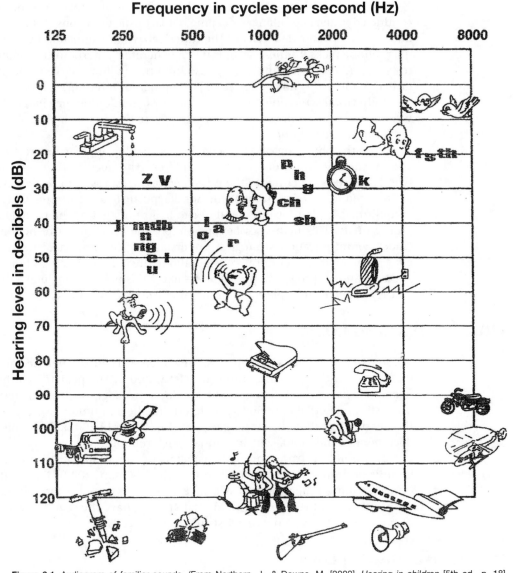

Figure 6.1. Audiogram of familiar sounds. (From Northern, J., & Downs, M. [2002]. *Hearing in children* [5th ed., p. 18]. Baltimore: Lippincott Williams & Wilkins. Reprinted by permission.)

Children should have received a formal audiological assessment prior to TPBA. Formal audiological examination using specialized instruments will examine the following:

1. *Threshold:* The loudness level (decibels) at which the sound is just perceptible. The threshold needs to be determined in order to provide the intensity of sounds needed by the child in order to hear. Although audiometers and other instruments are formally used to determine thresholds in each ear, general observation in TPBA should provide clues as to whether and what the child hears.

2. *Attention:* Children need to attend to auditory stimuli in order to process information. Some children may need assistance in order to prioritize and know what

sounds they should attend to. For example, adults may need to help the child pay attention to certain sounds in the world. Children may be encouraged to attend by modeling and creating high interest in attending through the use of games. Visual aspects can also be coordinated with sounds to help direct the child's attention (e.g., using toys with lights that accompany sounds).

3. *Quality of sound received:* Children who have a hearing loss do not have the same quality of sound through amplification as that of someone with a fully functioning ear. The use of a hearing aid analyzer will help parents detect distortion in an aid. Quality of sound perceived either with or without an aid also can be partially determined through observation of the child's imitation abilities.

4. *Auditory perceptual skills:* To benefit fully from amplification, a child must have the ability to select, synthesize, discriminate, remember, and sequence what is heard. The child's ability to use sounds in a meaningful way for auditory processing is dependent on neurological integrity (Gatty, 2003). Accuracy and timing of auditory processing can be partially determined by observing the precision and timing of the child's communicative responses and actions.

Schuyler and Rushmer (1987) identified behaviors that are indications of a child's use of hearing. These have been adapted for the Observation Guidelines for TPBA2. Regardless of whether the child is deaf or hard of hearing or has no previous indicators of hearing problems, it is necessary to examine the child's auditory skills. If a child has already been identified with a hearing loss and hearing aids have been prescribed, be sure that the child is wearing the aids during the TPBA session.

I. Hearing

The TPBA2 Observation Guidelines for auditory skills examine the child's responses to sounds and speech in the environment. What sounds are heard, as indicated by behavioral responses; what effort is made to identify the source of the sound; and what behaviors show understanding of the meaning of sounds and speech are all important aspects of hearing. The child's differential response to varying types and levels of sounds and the speed and accuracy of response to different types of auditory input have implications for language development and information processing, in addition to hearing.

I. A. What behaviors indicate that the child hears voices and sounds?

An infant's ability to localize to sound improves considerably in the first 6 months and continues to improve more gradually until approximately 7 years of age (Eliot, 1999). Children who hear a sound will typically respond by showing a behavioral response of some sort (Northern & Downs, 2002). They may stop moving or vocalizing and smile or turn their head. If startled by a sound, crying may result. A change in behavior is a possible indicator that the child heard a sound (Northern & Downs, 2002). Babies younger than 36 months will exhibit a startle response (Moro's reflex) to a sudden, loud sound (65 dB sound pressure level [SPL] or greater). Eye blinks, eye widening, and a rudimentary head turn also are indicators that the child hears an auditory signal.

I. B. Does the child look for or turn to the source of sound?

Looking for the source of a sound, not only indicates hearing, but also the understanding that something caused the sound to occur (Flexer, 1999; Schuyler & Rushmer,

1987). As children learn to engage their environment, they need not only to understand that a sound occurred, but also to recognize the source of that sound so that their interactions can be directed correctly. This is particularly relevant to human communication, because the child needs to know to whom to address responses (Northern & Downs, 2002).

I. C. Does the child respond meaningfully to sounds or words?

Once the child hears a sound or word, he or she needs to know what the sound or word means so that an appropriate response can be made. The ability to assign meaning to a sound or word requires not only that the brain register that auditory information, but also that the information be mentally associated with its source, that it be interpreted for meaning, and that an appropriate response be formulated (Flexer, 1999; Gatty, 2003; Schuyler & Rushmer, 1987). For example, when the child hears the sound of a door banging, he or she hears the sound, associates that sound with previous experiences of the sounds of doors, turns to look, and says, "Da-da" in anticipation of Daddy coming into the room. The child's response indicates what the sound means to her (Schuyler & Rushmer, 1987). When a funny joke is told, the brain has to identify the words, provide their meaning, remember associations with those words, identify the incongruity presented in the words, and then send a message to respond with a laugh (Schuyler & Rushmer, 1987). The laugh in response to the words presented tells observers that the words were heard and understood. Children need to make sense of the auditory information they take in. Absence of or difficulty with this ability indicates the need for further evaluation to determine the extent and influence of the comprehension issues on learning (Flexer, 1999).

I. D. How quickly does the child act in response to sounds or words?

The amount of time it takes for the child to hear, make sense of, and respond to sounds and language is considered "processing time." Normally, processing time should take only milliseconds. For some children, however, the processing of auditory information takes more time. The presence of processing difficulties has implications for intervention, because children will need more "wait time" and may benefit from multisensory input to help them make sense of auditory information (Cacace & McFarland, 1998; Hafer, 1984). Visual, tactile, or kinesthetic cues may assist a child to interpret or respond to information. Delayed response, however, can be an indicator of difficulty with hearing, because the child is taking time to make sense of what he or she can hear (Jones & Jones, 2003; Schuyler & Rushmer, 1987).

I. E. Does the child accurately imitate sounds?

Imitation is a means of determining that a child is hearing sounds accurately (Schuyler & Rushmer, 1987). If a child is able to produce a precise imitation of a model, it indicates that the child hears the sound correctly, remembers the sound, and has the ability to move the articulators precisely in order to reproduce the sound. Imitation is critical to speech production. A child with a moderate hearing loss may be able to produce the vowel sounds in a spoken word but not the consonants. For example, the child may repeat the word "cat" as "at."

▰▰▰ USING THE OBSERVATION GUIDELINES TO SCREEN HEARING

All children should have received a complete audiological assessment before TPBA, with results of the assessment forwarded to the TPBA team. Because permanent or transient hearing loss may result in language delays or loss, it is critical to determine the impact, if any, of hearing on observed speech and language problems.

When asking parents if their child's hearing has been tested, it is important to explore with them specifically what that process entailed. For example, the doctor may have looked in their child's ears with an otoscope to assess the condition of the ear canal and ear drum. Prior to any TPBA, parents should be asked specific questions about their child's ability to respond to environmental sounds and speech. In addition, throughout the assessment observers should note comments about a child's responses to various environmental sounds, both novel and familiar, and speech.

There are many aspects of a child's ability to listen and respond to sound that can be observed during the TPBA session. The Observation Guidelines for hearing are a screening tool to determine if a child needs further, more comprehensive audiological assessment or if a child is benefiting from amplification. Auditory Observation Guidelines should be seen as just one aspect of the larger "communication umbrella" (see Chapter 5). In Chapter 3, there is a section on Observation Guidelines for vision that also have an important role in communication. Both of these aspects of communication are important to document for children who have any kind of hearing loss.

If the parents have concerns about their child's hearing, or if a child arrives at the assessment with an identified hearing loss, then care should be taken to document responses to auditory stimuli with or without hearing aids. If the child wears hearing aids, request that the parents bring the aids to the assessment; do not assume that they will do this without encouragement. An audiologist, teacher of the deaf, or a speech-language pathologist who is trained in this area should check the hearing aids prior to beginning to make sure they are in working order.

The following Observation Guidelines for assessing hearing can be used with all children who participate in TPBA. Some children already may have been identified as having a hearing loss and others may not. If a child has a hearing aid, it is essential that the aid be worn during the session. During the assessment process, use a variety of noisemaking toys to observe the child's responses to loud and soft (decibel level) sounds, high and low (frequency) sounds and localization, which is turning toward the sound source. The facilitator should speak to the child in varying volumes—soft to loud—to determine the response for each level. For an infant or toddler, the facilitator can assess informally the child's ability to orient to sounds depending on the child's motor coordination as noted in Table 6.1.

The Observation Guidelines for hearing screening are not designed to take the place of a formally administered audiological assessment or to be used for diagnosis or intervention planning. Rather, they should serve to refer children who may be in need of further hearing evaluation. Any concerns or indications of a hearing loss, such as a lack of response to sounds or voices, should be examined further by a pediatric audiologist, who is an individual with a degree, license, and certification in audiology. Audiological information should be included as part of the full assessment prior to the development of the child's program plan.

Each of the questions that follow is judged as a pass or fail item on the Observation Guidelines for auditory skills (see p. 311).

▰▰▰ I. A. What behaviors indicate that the child hears voices and sounds?

The team should observe the child's response to sounds and speech throughout the play session. Observers should note the intensity (loudness) of the sounds to which the child responds.

For example, does the child respond if the source of the sound is soft, such as a tap on a table or a whisper; if it is moderate, such as the scraping of a chair on the floor or a word spoken in conversational tone; or only if the sound is very loud, such as a slamming door or a shout? Varying pitch and loudness should be tried, because the child may respond to some sounds but not to others. For instance, a child might smile at a high-pitched sound, such as the "motherese" used by mothers of infants, but may not respond to the lower pitch of the father's voice. Loudness of the sound may also have an impact. A light ring of a bell or rattle may go unheeded, but a loud ring, such as that from a xylophone, might cause the child's head to turn. The facilitator may experiment by saying words at varying levels of intensity, going from soft to loud, in order to elicit a response when the child hears them. It is important to note that a lack of response does not necessarily indicate that the child did not hear the sound. These are gross indicators that, of course, should be documented more precisely with a formal hearing test. It is important to ensure that the play facilitator is not initially providing visual cues along with the sound. Addition of visual cues should occur only after the sound is presented alone.

I. B. Does the child look for or turn to the source of sound?

TPBA members should not present all sounds within the child's visual field. For instance, if a noise-making toy is introduced, rattle it behind and to the side of the child first. If the child sees a toy being activated, the observed response may be to the action of the toy rather than to the sound itself. Movement of the sound from one location to another should stimulate the child to search in another direction. Also observe the child's response to the various voices in the room. Does he or she turn to look when a parent is talking? When another team member speaks? Does the child shift attention from one speaker to another when different people are talking? Does the child appear to "search" for the sound if it is unfamiliar?

I. C. Does the child respond meaningfully to sounds or words?

Once the child is old enough to move and respond vocally to sounds, it is possible to observe the child's interpretation of the sounds he or she hears. For instance, when music is played, does the child start to move rhythmically to the sounds? If so, the interpretation is that the sounds are interpreted by the child as being music. Depending on the child's age, understanding the meaning of sounds should correlate with his or her developmental level. Responses to sounds may be seen in the child's actions, behaviors, vocalizations, verbalizations, signs, gestures, and emotional expression.

Accurate comprehension of sounds and words heard can be seen when the play facilitator uses sounds or words (without accompanying signs or gestures to give a cue) and the child responds appropriately. For example, the facilitator may say, "The cow says, 'Moo'!" If the child looks at the toy cow, or responds in some way with the cow, observers can infer that he or she understood the word "cow" or "moo." Some children, however, may hear the words said but fail to comprehend their meaning. These children may respond inappropriately to the facilitator's words. In the previous example, the child who has difficulty hearing or comprehending auditory information may look at the facilitator and then do something with another toy. The facilitator needs to keep sentences short and clear and provide subsequent follow-up comments or questions to ensure that the child's behavior reflects lack of comprehension rather than lack of interest or disregard of the facilitator.

The team needs to watch carefully to make sure that the child is responding to the sounds and words in the environment rather than to movements, gestures, or other visual stimuli. It is common for adults to pair verbal communication with gestures, so care should be taken to refrain from using gestures when hearing is in question. If the team does not originally have concerns about hearing, but questions arise during the play session, the team should cue the facilitator to not provide visual clues to the child. Young children may even use lip reading as a visual cue, so it is important to observe comprehension of speech when the child is not looking at the play facilitator's face. Observation of what the child understands with and without visual cues is essential, because the child may be using visual cues to compensate for lack of hearing.

I. D. How quickly does the child act in response to sounds or words?

In all of the interactions with the child throughout the play session, the play facilitator needs to allow time for the child to react to sounds in the environment and to verbal and other communication. As indicated earlier, most children respond immediately to what they hear and understand. Need for extended time, as indicated by delayed response time, may indicate hearing problems, processing problems, or intellectual deficits.

I. E. Does the child accurately imitate sounds?

The play facilitator needs to give the child opportunities to imitate sounds and words. Young children will typically imitate fun sounds, interesting new words, or sentences they like. During play interactions, the play facilitator can incorporate all of these as part of the play. Attempts should be made to see what the child's imitation is like when he or she is not looking at the facilitator and when his or her attention is focused on the facilitator's mouth. The child who is not looking is relying on accurate auditory input and mental representation for imitation. The child who looks and listens is combining the input of two sensory systems, auditory and visual, to help produce the imitation. As much as possible, eliciting imitations should be done as part of play. However, if imitation does not occur naturally, the facilitator may want to introduce an imitation game, in which each takes turns making noises for the other to imitate.

> *Alan, an 18-month-old boy, and the facilitator were playing with cars. Alan enjoyed pushing them on the floor and having them go up and down a ramp. He successfully followed simple commands when paired with a gesture (e.g., "Give me," "Come here," "Put in," "Get the ___," and "Give to Mommy"). He localized to the loud ambulance siren sound of one of the electronic toys. At one point during the assessment, his dad entered the room and called his name. Alan did not respond to the door opening and closing when his dad entered the room, or respond to his name but then he noticed his dad when he approached him. When observed in his child care center, Alan followed his peers by watching their movement as they transitioned from one activity to the next. According to his parents he likes to sit close to the television when he watches it. Alan communicated with eye contact, gestures, and vocalizations consisting primarily of a few vowel sounds (e.g., "ah, uh, eh").*
>
> *Alan was seen for TPBA because he was not talking and his parents reported that he was becoming frustrated and beginning to hit them. His parents reported that he had passed his newborn hearing test. Alan has had a significant history of ear infections from 6 to 16 months of age. His parents estimated that he had approximately five ear infections during this time period, with some episodes lasting up to 2 months in duration. His parents were not concerned about his hearing since he seemed to understand most of what they said to him; however, they stated that he did not always follow directions consistently but they felt it was more a behavior problem. TPBA showed that Alan relied on others' gestural and contextual cues paired with speech in order to respond successfully to others' communication.*

This vignette highlights the need for hearing testing to be completed before the TPBA in order to rule out any possible temporary or permanent hearing loss as a possible cause of a speech and language delay.

CENTRAL AUDITORY PROCESSING DISORDER (CAPD)

The American Speech-Language-Hearing Association (ASHA, 2005) defines *auditory processes* as the central nervous system mechanisms and processes responsible for the following behaviors: sound localization and lateralization; auditory discrimination; auditory pattern recognition; temporal processing of acoustic information; audition in the presence of competing signals; and auditory performance with degraded acoustic signals. Identification of central auditory processing disorder (CAPD) may be difficult, because hearing is not a unitary sensory-perceptual skill. Some neurocognitive mechanisms are strictly dedicated to auditory processing; others, such as attention, motivation, memory, and decision making, are not modality specific but must be actively deployed during auditory processing.

ASHA (1996) alerts practitioners to be "cautious in attributing spoken language comprehension difficulties to CAPD in any simple fashion." However, the team should explore the possibility of CAPD if the child is observed or reported by the parents to engage in many of the following behaviors:

- Ignores the speaker

- Habitually says "huh?" or "what?"

- Is overly sensitive to noises

- Has problems following directions in sentences; often leaves out a step

- Talks loudly in the absence of a hearing loss

- Misunderstands what is said, or thinks you said a different word

- Omits sounds from words

- Missequences sounds or syllables in words; for example, "aminal" for "animal"

- Gets frustrated listening when there is background noise or others are talking

ASHA (2005) states that a team approach constitutes best practice when identifying CAPD. The assessment team may consist of a speech-language pathologist with CAPD experience and other disciplines that collaborate with the audiologist. However, only the audiologist is qualified to diagnose CAPD. This assessment must include the following elements: a complete history; a nonstandardized but systematic observation of auditory behavior; speech and language measures to determine the child's ability and communicative function; and a thorough battery of behavioral and electrophysiological tests performed by an audiologist. The audiological component cannot be completed within the context of TPBA2, but the first three components may be. This will help the team to determine whether or not a referral for further CAPD testing is suggested. The ASHA requirements for CAPD assessment may be met, in part, in the TPBA in the following ways:

1. Historical information can be derived from the Child and Family History Questionnaire, along with any additional information from outside sources; the family can help with this process. Background information must include information about pregnancy and birth; health; speech and language behaviors and milestones; family history; psychological factors; cognitive skills; educational experience; social development; cultural and linguistic background; and auditory behavior.

2. The requirement for speech and language measures should be met by assessments and observations made in the TPBA communication domain. Particular attention should be given to the child's ability to follow directions, word discrimination er-

rors, sound omissions in speech, and syllable errors within spoken words or sequencing errors of words in sentences.

3. The systematic, nonstandardized observation of auditory behaviors can be recorded during play and expanded with questions to the parents. Observations should be made in the following areas:

- *Ability to localize and lateralize to sounds and speech* (see Hearing, above)

- *Auditory discrimination:* This is the ability to differentiate between two like sounds (e.g., *f/th*) or two like-sounding words (e.g., pig/big). If not elicited in play, the parents should be asked if the child often misunderstands words that sound alike.

- *Auditory pattern recognition:* This can be observed by having the child imitate clapped patterns and by making a game in which the child has to tell you if two clapped patterns are alike (must understand same/different).

- *Temporal processing:* The child must be old enough to identify the first sound in a word, or to remember the first word in a simple sentence or list of three words. This could be done in play with a baby doll, saying, "Baby wants (pause) peas, apples, and milk." What does baby want? (Must be able to answer "what" questions.)

- *Ability to listen in competing noises or with degraded signals:* This will require some preplanning, so that the child is set up to listen and respond when others are speaking nearby and when moderately loud environmental noises (e.g., a CD or tape, a fan, a noisy wind-up toy) are introduced. Team members should note whether or not the child becomes frustrated or less attentive, or shows difficulty understanding what is being said.

If the team suspects CAPD, the child should be referred for further formal audiological assessments. Efficacy research on interventions for children with CAPD-related language problems is limited, but ASHA indicates that best intervention practices include strategies that are interdisciplinary, intensive, and focus on direct skills remediation, compensatory strategies, and environmental modifications. The team may want to consider recommending the following strategies for a child with suspected CAPD, all of which are believed to increase the quality of linguistic input for the child:

- Speak more slowly to the child.

- Pause often between statements.

- Emphasize key words.

- Pair speech with visual information, such as gestures or pictures.

- Introduce new vocabulary words before they are used in activities, conversation, or group discussions.

Recommendations may also be made by the audiologist about ways to improve the acoustic signal quality for the child, such as preferential seating at school, reducing background noise, or using assistive devices to boost the speech signal.

Tommy's parents are concerned about his hearing, even though his pediatrician says it seems okay. He always speaks loudly and is often confused about words. He says that a coat hanger is a "hoat canger" and that his favorite vegetable is "cob-on-the-corn." Tommy almost always says, "huh?" when asked a question, but if it is repeated, he will answer it. When his parents tell him "Put away your toy and come to dinner," he just puts the toy away. They say this happens even more often when they are watching television or when the dishwasher is running. Tommy's parents aren't sure if he's not paying attention, misbehaving, or just can't hear well.

II. Visual Communication Skills

The TPBA team must consider both auditory and visual skills of children who are deaf or hard of hearing in the assessment process. Care should be taken not to ignore one set of behaviors because of possibly incorrect assumptions. For example, a child who is hard of hearing who has not been exposed to formal sign language either at home or in school should still be observed in a visual communication context as well as an auditory context. Both are important to the child's overall development. Although Observation Guidelines are offered in this chapter for special techniques or considerations when assessing a child who is deaf or hard of hearing, the assessment team should include members with specialized training in the area of deaf education.

The following skills act as a foundation for further acquisition of ASL or other visual languages, and are also important aspects of language learning for all children. Obviously, for a child to learn to communicate in sign language, visual attention on the part of the child is essential (Holzrichter & Meier, 2000). Infants begin by attending to the face and then later to coordinate gazing at the face of the person signing to them and then to the object of attention in the environment (Spencer, 2003). Children who are deaf must be able to visually monitor their surroundings in order to be connected to events and people in their environment. Finally, getting a person's attention in a visual environment is a fundamental skill when young children who are deaf are learning to communicate visually. Although the child who is deaf may use his or her voice to try to gain another person's attention, visual means such as waving or tapping the person are more effective.

II. A. Does the child coordinate visually to a communication partner (facilitator)?

Children who have hearing loss may be unusually attentive to a person's face as they attempt to lipread and understand facial expressions. Some children will not attend to a person's face but rather will focus on play objects because they have not yet developed strategies for communication. Children with a hearing loss may grab the facilitator's face and turn it toward them in order to try and either understand what the person is saying. Children who communicate in sign language will look at the person's face and not the hands when communicating. Visual attention is a prerequisite to visual communication.

II. B. Does the child coordinate visual attention with more than one focus?

A child with a hearing loss who uses the visual channel attends to objects and people in the environment in a sequential pattern (Mohay, 2000) coordinating his or her attention between the signer and an object in order to obtain linguistic information from the signer and information from the environment. Thus, it is important that the child be able to shift gaze from objects, to gestures, to a person's face.

II. C. Does the child use and respond to visual attention-getting behaviors?

A child with a hearing loss uses a variety of behaviors to elicit attention from others. Although children who are deaf or hard of hearing may use their voices to attract attention, they also use physical means to gain attention. Initially they may pull on a person's clothing, arm, or face to gain attention.

━━━ II. D. Does the child visually scan his or her surroundings?
Is the child aware of his or her environment?

Ability to scan the environment in order to locate objects and people within the environment is critical. If children cannot count on sound to help them locate a person's or object's location, they rely heavily on the use of sight and touch. Children need to be able to create mental maps of their environment, identify probable locations of objects and people, and draw relationships between people and objects. For example, the child who does not hear well may not be able to hear the parent turn on the washing machine, but if the adult is observed carrying the laundry basket out of the room, the child with understanding of the relationship between the clothes basket and the washing machine, and who has a mental map of the house, will know where to go to find the parent.

USING THE OBSERVATION GUIDELINES TO ASSESS VISUAL COMMUNICATION SKILLS

Children who have a hearing loss, whether or not they use sign language, have a visual orientation to their world (Meadow-Orlans, 2003). Therefore, the assessment process should pay particular attention to indicators that the child is using vision to support communication (both spoken and signed) and gain information about his or her world (Wood, Wood, Griffiths, & Howarth, 1986). The following are guidelines for assessing visual communication skills. These visual communication skills may be evident in children who have not yet learned sign language. In fact, studies indicate that children who are deaf who have not been exposed to a formal sign language invent sophisticated gesture systems that incorporate many of the elements of ASL (Goldin-Meadow, 2003; Goldin-Meadow & Feldman, 1975). Even children who are signing using a Manually Coded English system that uses ASL signs in an English word order will invent morphology that is similar to ASL grammar (Supalla, 1991).

━━━ II. A. Does the child coordinate visually to a communication partner (facilitator)?

The play facilitator should position him- or herself so that a child can easily attend to the toys at hand and to the facilitator. This is in contrast to positions the play facilitator may take when playing with a hearing child. For example, he or she may sit to the side and slightly behind the child as they talk while the child is playing. When playing with a child who has a hearing loss, the play facilitator should position him- or herself in a visually accessible way in order to encourage the child to look up to communicate. Moving the object of interest up to the face will encourage the child to engage for communication if the child does not automatically look at the facilitator's face during a play event.

━━━ II. B. Does the child coordinate visual attention with more than one focus?

Is the child able to attend to an activity or object, look up for information, and then return to activity or object? Does the child seem resistant to breaking his or her visual attention to the activity? Children with more developed visual attention skills will be able to "mark" both foci of attention in space and visually monitor the environment. The facilitator should follow the lead of the child and focus on what interests the child. When the child looks up to "communicate," the play facilitator can comment and then refocus his or her visual attention back on the object of interest to encourage the child to return to the topic of comment. Using eye gaze to "direct" a child's visual attention is an effective visual strategy (Mather, 1987). Care should be taken not to view a child's lack of eye-gaze coordination in a negative (deficit model) light but from a developmental perspective in which the child is seen as moving toward the ideal (Singleton & Morgan, 2004).

▓▓▓▓▓ II. C. Does the child use and respond to visual attention-getting behaviors?

If the child has been exposed to visual attention-getting behaviors that are a part of communicating in sign language, the child may wave his or her hand in the line of vision of the facilitator to attract attention, tap the facilitator, or stomp his or her foot or slap a table top to elicit sound and/or vibrations. The observers must note how the child responds to these attention-getting devices on the part of the facilitator as well. Does the child look up or indicate "wait a minute" in response to visual attention-getting behaviors?

▓▓▓▓▓ II. D. Does the child visually scan his or her surroundings?
     Is the child aware of his or her environment?

Does he or she "mark" locations of people or objects that he or she is interested in? How often does he or she look up to scan the room or check in with parents? Does he or she note when a new person enters the room? Deaf children will want to check the environment often to note changes. Observing team members should note in what context the child appears to scan the room for "new" information.

> *During the session, Sally would become interested in a toy, focus her attention on it, and then look up to comment or ask a question. Sometimes she would actually sign a question ("Where other car, where?"), and other times she would simply look at the play facilitator with a puzzled look on her face. When the play facilitator moved across the room and Sally wanted her attention, she stomped her foot, and when that got no response she waved her hand within the play facilitator's line of vision. When they were playing close to each other, Sally would tap the play facilitator's knee or shoulder to gain the facilitator's attention. Throughout the session, Sally visually monitored the environment, noting times when an observer moved to a different location in the room or when her mother got a drink of water.*

This vignette incorporates all of the previously mentioned visual communication skills. This typical scene illustrates the *visual framework* for communicating in either a spoken language or a signed language.

CONSIDERATIONS IN PLANNING FOR TPBA FOR CHILDREN WHO ARE DEAF OR HARD OF HEARING

All TPBA team members should have a basic understanding of issues that shape the lives of children who are deaf or hard of hearing. This is best accomplished by the process of transdisciplinary role release (see Chapter 2 in the *Administration Guide for TPBA2 & TPBI2*) with professionals who have expertise in working with children who are deaf or hard of hearing. Team in-service training could focus on a variety of topics. A section of the team's professional library should be devoted to materials related to the development of children who are deaf or hard of hearing (see the Recommended Reading section at the end of the chapter).

The assessment team should be flexible enough to respond to each family with a young child who is deaf or hard of hearing, regardless of the questions the parents raise.

This requires the assessment team to have extensive knowledge of a variety of topics, such as the impact of hearing loss on language and communication, the role of vision in language development, the nature of the Deaf community, the benefits and limitations of cochlear implants and other hearing technologies, strategies that support the development of literacy, accessing community services, and parenting strategies. Unfortunately, to date, the parents and majority of children and families who receive services in the early intervention system are served by professionals who do not have training in education of children who are deaf or hard of hearing (Stredler-Brown & Arehart, 2000). This practice must change for the benefit of children who are deaf or hard of hearing and their families and for the improvement of the field of early education. Assessment and intervention teams need professionals with training and knowledge regarding the cultural, linguistic, vocational, and educational practices in the lives of Deaf people in order to appropriately evaluate children who are deaf or hard of hearing and to provide information and recommendations to families regarding their child's educational future. Preparations for assessing children who are deaf or hard of hearing are provided in the paragraphs that follow.

Team Considerations: Specialized TPBA Team Members

The highly specialized knowledge base required to competently serve families with children who are deaf can be found in professionals who have training and experience with children and adults who are deaf or hard of hearing. The TPBA process enables the membership of the assessment team to change depending on the needs of the child and family. When a child who has been identified as deaf or hard of hearing is to be assessed, the team should include members who have had training and experience with children and adults who are deaf or hard of hearing. Depending on the child to be evaluated and the family's needs, the team should include some combination of the following: a certified Teacher of the Deaf, an ASL (American Sign Language) specialist, a Deaf adult, a sign language interpreter, a speech-language pathologist, and an audiologist.

Teacher of the Deaf

The Teacher of the Deaf should have either a BA or an MA in Deaf Education, plus certification (state or Council of Education of the Deaf) as a Teacher of the Deaf. Teachers of the Deaf, who may be deaf or hearing, have extensive knowledge of spoken language development and instruction, auditory training, hearing aid technology, language acquisition, Deaf culture, curriculum development, assessment, parent education, American Sign Language (ASL), and cochlear implants and other hearing technologies. Their specialized training provides both a broad and in-depth understanding of issues related to the social, emotional, and communicative development of children who are deaf or hard of hearing. In addition to their specialization in working with children who are deaf or hard of hearing, Teachers of the Deaf on the TPBA team should have certification and or training in early childhood education or early childhood special education. The Teacher of the Deaf will contribute the highly specialized knowledge regarding education of deaf children to the assessment process. The Teacher of the Deaf may serve in a variety of roles in the TPBA, including play facilitator, speech and language observer, or parent facilitator, for example.

ASL Specialist

The professional role of an ASL specialist is a relatively new addition to the field of Deaf Education. Often these specialists have a degree in Deaf Studies, ASL instruction, or linguistics. These professionals, who are deaf or hearing, have in-depth training and are fluent in ASL. They have training in both the assessment and instruction of sign language. Knowledge of Deaf culture and expertise in bringing Deaf and hearing communities together are important qualifications of this specialization. Professional attitude and skills important to this member of the TPBA team include assessing sign language skills, helping parents access the Deaf community, and providing guidance in designing a visually accessible environment.

Adults Who Are Deaf or Hard of Hearing

The adult who is Deaf (capitalization of the term *Deaf* is used to denote people who are deaf or hard of hearing who identify with the Deaf community and use sign language) may be an addition to the team of professionals brought together for the assessment or they may be functioning in one of the other roles (Teacher of the Deaf, ASL specialist, psychologist, social worker, family facilitator, or play facilitator). Adults who are Deaf, because of their life experience, approach the assessment process primarily from a visual perspective, providing insight on constructing a visually accessible environment, planning visually based interaction strategies for the play facilitator, and, most importantly, answering parents' questions at the postassessment meeting. The Deaf adult should also be able to provide practical information regarding the functional use of residual hearing and communication strategies including lip reading. Professional attitudes and skills important to the person functioning in this role are an acknowledgment of the importance of speech for many families and recognition of the potential for emerging technologies, such as cochlear implants, to greatly enhance the ability of some children to develop their hearing and speech potential. The participation of a Deaf adult in the assessment of a child who is deaf or hard of hearing and in the support and education of his or her parents ensures an authenticity to the assessment and intervention process (Hafer & Stredler-Brown, 2003). Parents who have a child who is deaf or hard of hearing should be provided, as a matter of policy, contact with Deaf adults at the initial stages of assessment and education. Increasingly, Deaf adults are viewed as valued team members who participate in the individualized family service plan (IFSP) and individualized education program (IEP) process (Andrews, Leigh, & Weiner, 2004).

Many programs provide parents with an opportunity to have a Deaf mentor if they choose to use sign language (Watkins, Pitman, & Walden, 1998), and results indicate that these parents communicate better with their children than parents who have not had the opportunity to interact with Deaf adults. Few programs introduce hearing parents to Deaf adults at the initial stage of assessment, yet this is a critical time for this contact (Andrews et al., 2004; Hafer & Stredler-Brown, 2003; Schlesinger & Meadow, 1972).

This initial consultation with a Deaf adult is crucial in order for the parents to receive the benefit of those who have life experience at developmental levels beyond early childhood (Schlesinger & Meadow, 1972). Many Deaf Americans are particularly concerned because parents are not told in the early stages of assessment and intervention about the benefits of sign language and Deaf culture (Andrews et al., 2004). Bodner-Johnson (2003) interviewed young, college-age Deaf adults whose poignant words describe how they want their parents to know what it means to be Deaf. A young man named David reflects:

> My parents don't know who I am. If they knew who I was they would know that I'm a very open person, that I'm a very fun person to be around . . . I think if I had the communication with my family, they would know who I am. Once that communication was there, if they could communicate with me like I am today, I think everything would have been fine. (p. 23)

This kind of information is routinely withheld, most often unintentionally, from parents by professionals who do not have a connection with the Deaf community. The inclusion of a Deaf adult on the TPBA team as parents begin to learn what their child needs will help ensure that parents have the opportunity to make fully informed decisions at the time of assessment. As with both the ASL specialist and the Teacher of the Deaf, the Deaf adult team member should have training and/or experience with young children.

Educational Interpreter

The Individuals with Disabilities Education Improvement Act (IDEA) of 2004 (PL 108-446) requires that interpreters be present during the assessment for parents who are speakers of languages other than English, if necessary. This service should be provided as well to parents who are deaf or hard of hearing who use sign language. Some adults who are deaf or hard of hearing can communicate through speaking and lip reading when they are interacting with only one person; in this case, an interpreter may not be necessary. However, when a larger group of people is involved, such as in TPBA, an interpreter should be provided to ensure that the parents are fully involved and have total access to the information discussed. An interpreter should also be provided for any team members who are deaf or hard of hearing. The sign language interpreter should meet with the team immediately before the assessment begins to determine the most effective communication strategies for the members involved. Educational interpreters support various forms of communication, including ASL, one of the manually coded English systems, cued speech, or other communication approaches. People who are deaf or hard of hearing who are present should discuss with the interpreter any specific needs that they may have. Professional attitudes important for an interpreter who serves on a TPBA team include recognition of the importance of maintaining a "family friendly" atmosphere during the assessment and postassessment meeting. The interpreter should be considered a valued and full member of the TPBA team. If possible, a small pool of interpreters could provide an orientation regarding their unique role on the TPBA team and information on key concepts regarding assessment of young children in general. Of course, interpreter services should be provided at no cost to the family.

Speech-Language Pathologist

A speech-language pathologist (SLP) should have special training in working with children who are deaf or hard of hearing. The effect of hearing loss on the acquisition of speech and language is a knowledge base that any SLP who works with young children who are deaf or hard of hearing should have. He or she should be able to troubleshoot hearings aids to ensure that they are in working order. He or she should also be able to structure communication to support the child in identifying and reproducing the sounds that are in the range of frequencies that a particular child may or may not hear, with or without hearing aids. SLPs should be skilled in an array of strategies and techniques that model and elicit spoken language and, to a lesser degree, a visual language such as ASL. SLPs who work with families who have children who are deaf or hard of hearing should have professional attitudes that reflect a respect for the Deaf community and an understanding that ASL is equivalent to any spoken language. Recognition of the role that vision plays in the communicative environment of people who are deaf or hard of hearing is important as well (Padden & Humphries, 1988). The SLP may serve as a language and communication specialist, observing the child during TPBA and providing suggestions for eliciting spoken language.

Audiologist

An audiologist on the TPBA team will be able to work with the SLP on structuring the assessment to elicit responses to auditory stimuli from the child. Audiologists should be skilled at providing the full range of auditory tests. The audiologist will be able to explain to the other team members and parents about the kinds of responses one might expect based on factors such as degree and type of hearing loss, length of time the child has been aided, consistency of hearing aid use by the child, and type and quality of support services the family has received. The audiologist on the TPBA team should be able to explain the issues regarding cochlear implants as well (Gatty, 2003). Skill in observing and interpreting a young child's auditory responses in natural environments should be evident. The audiologist should have an awareness of the Deaf community and experience in communicating with Deaf adults. Professional attitudes evident in audiologists working with families of young children who are deaf or hard of hearing include a respect for the Deaf community and the recognition of the equivalent status of ASL when compared with spoken languages. As with the other team members, the audiologist should have experience and/or training with young children who are deaf or hard of hearing.

Environmental Considerations: Orienting the Visual Environment in Preparation for TPBA

> . . . for they are first, last and all the time,
> the people of the eye.
> —George Veditz (1913)

When a child who is deaf or hard of hearing is assessed, the team must be aware of the primacy of vision in how the child learns about his or her world. No matter how much usable hearing a child may have, setting up an environment that supports learning and utilizes rules of visual communication is essential for optimal assessment (Padden & Humphries, 1988). Meadow-Orlans (2003) emphasizes that limited hearing requires a child to rely on vision to perceive and interact with the world. A child who is profoundly deaf will rely primarily on vision for communication, and one who is hard of hearing will learn to augment his or her residual auditory skills with visual information.

Setting up the Visual Environment

Because vision has such an important role in the lives of children who are deaf or hard of hearing, special attention must be given to designing the visual elements of the setting for TPBA when possible. Of course, the area should be well lighted. Adjust blinds to prevent glare. Arrange toys and materials so that they are available to the child with a visual scan of the room. If a child becomes visually distracted to the point that it interferes with the process, cover shelves with a sheet or remove some toys. Toys should also be arranged thematically in order to facilitate the linking of ideas and development of scripts during play. Dolls with hearing aids, TTYs (telecommunication devices for the deaf) for pretend play with a telephone, personal digital assistants (PDAs), or pagers are examples of culturally appropriate materials that are important to people who are deaf. Headsets and a microphone can be used to stimulate play around the theme of visiting the audiologist in addition to other "community helpers" thematic material. The child who is deaf should have a direct line of sight to the play facilitator during the session.

Place the family facilitator and family members in a visually accessible location in the room. Like other young children, children who are deaf or hard of hearing will "check in" with their parents or caregivers during the session, perhaps with only brief eye contact with the parent for reassurance. Hearing children can locate their parents talking in the background, but children with a hearing loss will depend on their sight to locate the parent. Be aware that items such as flags, mobiles, and streamers may be distracting when they move. Children may have to visually consider those items before moving to an activity. Think of these as distracters, as you would the auditory equivalent for hearing children.

The observation plan for the team must be flexible—the team members must be able to move in order to observe visual-gestural communication between the play facilitator and the child. Videotaping the sessions is an essential part of the accurate documentation of the child's visual communication skills.

Orienting the Auditory Environment for TPBA

Just as care should be taken in designing an environment that supports the visual needs of children who are deaf or hard of hearing, the environment should also provide optimal auditory support. Care must be taken to provide an environment that will elicit a child's auditory and speech skills in natural, functional situations.

The room should be acoustically treated to minimize ambient noise. Sound-absorbing carpet and wall treatments (such as cork) and acoustic tile on the ceilings will provide an environment that will support the auditory capabilities of children who are deaf or hard of hearing. An FM system should be available for those children whose auditory profile indicates its use. Regulation of noise in the area should be a consideration during the assessment. If a child has already been prescribed hearing aids, or has a cochlear implant, the device should be checked for problems prior to the assessment session and should be worn during the assessment.

Care should be taken to use a variety of toys that exhibit a range of sounds both in frequency and in loudness. The audiologist can assist in determining the decibel level (loudness) and frequency (range) of the toys' sounds.

Interaction Considerations: Facilitating Play

The team may decide to start the play session with the parent and child in order to see how the parent communicates with the child and then transition to the play facilitator once the team has a clear picture of the communication mode(s) used. The team should note "home signs" used by the parent and child, and the play facilitator should incorporate them into the play session. If a team is faced with assessing a child who is deaf or hard of hearing with deaf parents and does not have anyone on the team with the skills required to function as the play facilitator, it may be best to ask the parent to function as the play facilitator and have a sign language interpreter or other professional skilled in working with deaf children to interpret during the assessment. In some cases in which the team is assessing a child who uses sign language and the play facilitator is a skilled signer, it still may be necessary at times during the assessment to have the parent interpret the child's signs.

The play facilitator should systematically use, in combination and isolation, facial expressions, speech, gestures, signs, mime, and visual and auditory cues with objects to elicit a wide range of responses from the child. Responses from the child will dictate to what extent the play facilitator will use any and all of these techniques. Observers and the play facilitator should ask themselves questions regarding the child's responsiveness to various modes of communication. For example, if the play facilitator states that she "wants the doll," she may, at various times through the assessment, state it in sign language, orally, or by indicating with a gesture. Varying the kind of communication mode will help the observers see what seems to be effective and will indicate if further, more focused assessment is required. The play facilitator should employ the visual communication strategies mentioned in the following section.

The play facilitator's awareness of the importance of sequential visual attention is critical to the quality and effectiveness of his or her interactions with the child who is deaf or hard of hearing during the assessment process (Hafer & Stredler-Brown, 2003). Because a child with a hearing loss can only attend visually to one thing at a time, the play facilitator must allow time for the child to visually inspect an object before expecting the child to attend to the facilitator's face and hands as he or she communicates.

Effective Early Communication Strategies

It is often thought that children who are deaf have delayed language because they are deaf. The delay in language is a result of less than effective communication strategies between adults and the child, not of being deaf (Harris & Mohay, 1997). Most children who are deaf or hard of hearing have hearing parents who must learn effective visual communication strategies (with or without the use of sign language) in order to meet the communication needs of their child. The following strategies have been identified by observing how Deaf mothers communicate with their deaf babies (Koester, 1994; Mohay, Milton, Hindermarsh, & Ganley, 1998; Spencer, Bodner-Johnson, & Gutfrend, 1992; Swisher, 1984). Use of these strategies during TPBA with children who are deaf or hard of hearing may result in more effective facilitation. In addition, these strategies can be recommended to family members as intervention strategies:

- Nonverbal communication: Smiling, facial expressions, and gestures support the development of looking patterns essential to communicating in a visual mode.

- Gaining visual attention: Waving a hand, moving an object into the child's line of vision, or swaying back and forth will train the child to attend to an adult's face.

- Using touch to gain visual attention: Touching, patting, or stroking is an effective strategy used by Deaf parents to gain their child's attention. Deaf parents also use touch to provide positive feedback and reassure the child when parents are out of the child's visual field.

- Using pointing to direct attention while still permitting language input: Visual attention is sequential, not simultaneous. Deaf parents gain the child's attention, tell him or her what he or she will see, and then direct the child's attention to the topic. They also display their sign near the object under discussion so the child can see both the object and the sign.

- Reducing the frequency of communication so that it is recognized as important: Children who are deaf must switch attention between activities and the person with whom they are communicating. Deaf parents typically communicate less often and wait for their child to look at them in order to ensure that the child will see their communications as important.

- Using short utterances: Short utterances minimize disruptions of children's activities and the demands on memory as they shift visual attention from one focus to another.

- Positioning self and objects in the child's visual field: Deaf parents conserve the child's energy by placing themselves behind or next to their child, curving their body around so the child can see both them and the object of interest.

- Moving hands, face, or both into the child's visual field: Making signs on the child's body or displaying the sign in the child's field of vision helps reduce the need for the child to redirect attention from activities to their parents (when they are attending to something).

- Bracketing: Deaf parents name an object then point to the object and then sign the name for the object again, thereby clarifying the meaning of their language.

- Modifying signs: Deaf parents modify signs by repeating, enlarging, prolonging, and displacing them close to the object of attention. This promotes understanding by allowing the child a longer period of time to internalize the language.

Communication between Deaf mothers and their deaf babies naturally conforms to the requirements of communicating in a visual mode. When hearing parents incorporate these strategies into their everyday interaction with their child who is deaf or hard of hearing, "language is in sight" (Mohay, 2000).

PREPARING THE TEAM FOR CHILDREN WHO ARE DEAF OR HARD OF HEARING

All TPBA team members should have a basic understanding of issues that shape the lives of children who are deaf or hard of hearing. This is best accomplished by the process of transdisciplinary role release (see Chapter 2 in the *Administration Guide for TPBA2 & TPBI2*) with professionals who have expertise in working with children who are deaf or hard of hearing. Team inservice training could focus on a variety of topics mentioned earlier. A section of the team's professional library should be devoted to materials related to the development of children who are deaf or hard of hearing (see the Recommended Reading section at the end of this chapter).

Of course, there may be situations in which a child with an undiagnosed hearing loss will be referred for assessment. In this case, the specialized team members may not be present. For this reason, a strong professional education program in the development of children who are deaf or hard of hearing and behavioral indications of hearing loss will prepare the team to observe children who may have undiagnosed hearing loss.

Following is a summary of key concepts related to the development of young children who are deaf or hard of hearing of which all team members should be aware. Of course, when assessing a young child who is deaf or hard of hearing, at least one member of the team should have in-depth knowledge and training in working with young children who are deaf or hard of hearing and their families.

Basic Facts

It is estimated that there are 28 million people who are deaf or hard of hearing in the United States (Blanchfield, Feldman, Dunbar, & Gardner, 2001). Children who are deaf or hard of hearing are born at the rate of 1–4 in every thousand births (CDC, 2005; Culpepper, 2003). Of these, 90% are born to hearing parents who know little about what it means to be deaf or hard of hearing. More recently, Karchmer and Mitchell (2003) reported that 95% of all deaf children have hearing parents. The U.S. Department of Education (2000) reported approximately 70,000 school-age children who are deaf or hard of hearing for the school year 1998–1999. Holden-Pitt and Diaz (1998) reported that the percentage of school-age children who are deaf or hard of hearing with additional disabilities comprised 34% of the reported population.

There are many causes of hearing loss, some of which cause additional disabilities. The leading causes of deafness are *infections,* including rubella, cytomegalovirus (CMV), meningitis, herpes simplex virus, the human immunodeficiency virus (HIV), and congenital toxoplasmosis. Noninfectious causes of hearing loss include erythroblastosis fetalis (Rh factor), ototoxic drugs, prematurity, and a variety of genetic causes (Andrews et al., 2004). All of these nongenetic causes of hearing loss, and some of the genetic causes, also result in disabilities including language problems, developmental delays, vision impairments, seizures, cerebral palsy, and motor problems (Batshaw, 2007).

Two-thirds of genetic deafness results in hearing loss only, whereas the remaining one-third of this population have medical or physical characteristics that are perhaps disabling (Willems, 2000).

Understanding Parents

Once a formal evaluation is completed, these two groups of parents often react quite differently to the confirmation of hearing loss. Hearing parents likely will feel devastated, although they may feel a sense of relief that they finally know what is wrong. Deaf parents, however, may have a feeling of joy that their child is like them. Why do these two groups of parents, as a general rule, react so differently to their child being identified as deaf? The reasons are complex but understandable.

The thought of having a person who is deaf in the family likely never occurred to the hearing parents as they experienced the pregnancy. Hearing parents of children who are deaf or hard of hearing may never have met a Deaf person. They are unfamiliar with how being deaf affects communication and learning. Their mental image of a Deaf person may be that of an old man with a hearing aid, a signing Deaf actor on a TV drama, or, sadly, even a panhandler at the airport handing out communication cards for a donation.

Deaf parents, however, see parenting a child who is deaf as natural and easy (Erting, 2003; Lane, Hoffmeister, & Behan, 1996; Meadow, 1967). They have first-hand knowledge of what it means to be Deaf. They speak proudly of being a "third generation Deaf" family. In most cases, they know the adaptations and accommodations that are required to access the necessities and experience the joys of life. There is a well-established Deaf community that serves as a vital support for the family with members who are Deaf. Most importantly, Deaf parents of Deaf children can communicate effortlessly and effectively with their child. They have a sense of hope and confidence in a bright future for their Deaf child.

These two different family groups who are part of the heterogeneous group of young children with hearing loss have very dissimilar experiences and expectations and, thus, enter the assessment process with different questions to be answered, strengths and skills to be developed, and needs to be identified.

Technology and Sensory Aids

After a determination of the type, configuration, and degree of hearing loss is made, parents, working with the audiologist, determine whether the option of amplification is appropriate. In some cases parents may decide not to pursue amplification; however, most do. A variety of hearing aids, FM systems, vibrotactile aids, or a surgical procedure known as a *cochlear implant* are available. Hearing aids are personally selected for a child depending on his or her hearing loss. FM systems are used in the classroom. The teacher talks into a handheld microphone which then transmits his or her voice directly to the child's hearing aid. Vibrotactile aids are used by those children with little or no hearing and for whom a conventional hearing aid is not beneficial. It provides acoustic stimuli information to the child by transmitting sound from a microphone to a processor to a transducer that vibrates on the skin in response to the incoming sounds. A cochlear implant is a device that is surgically implanted; it stimulates the auditory nerve using electrical signals.

Matching the appropriate technology with the individual's hearing loss is a process that may require different decisions as the child grows. Further consultation with a variety of experts is needed to ensure appropriate selection of aids.

Communication Approaches for Children Who Are Deaf or Hard of Hearing

There are many communication choices for children who are deaf or hard of hearing. However, the most frequently used choices are oral, cued speech, sign language, total communication, and bilingual approaches. The goal of all approaches is to provide the child with a path for language and communication.

The *oral* approach supports the development of spoken language through the use of the child's residual hearing. Children need to receive adequate information from functioning hearing aids or other listening technologies in order to fully benefit from this approach. Depending on the philosophy of the program where the child is receiving services, lipreading/speechreading may or may not be emphasized. People who support this approach believe that speech is the medium for communication in the world and the path to literacy. Technology and an appropriate learning environment, proponents say, should provide any child who is deaf with success. Lack of success over a long period of time with children who are profoundly deaf is one of the main concerns with this approach. Although the approach is often successful with children who are hard of hearing, children who struggle with this approach and then start to use sign language may be far behind in critical language skills.

Cued speech is a system of eight handshapes in four locations of the handshapes (representing consonant sounds) and four locations near the face (representing vowel sounds) that are coordinated with natural speech. The system makes speech "visible." Supporters believe that this approach provides visible access to spoken language, which, in turn, leads to competency in reading and writing. A major concern with this approach is that the use of CS does not ensure that the child will develop expressive spoken language skills.

Research has shown that Deaf children exposed to *signed languages* (ASL and Québécoise Sign Language) from birth follow the same language acquisition timeline as children who use spoken languages, reaching all linguistic milestones (Newport & Meier, 1985; Pettito & Marentette, 1991). The ability to speak and hear are not necessary for the complete acquisition of a language (Pettito & Marentette, 1991). The use of sign language, regardless of the severity of the hearing loss, has been found to support the development of both spoken and written English for children who are deaf or hard of hearing (Marschark, Lang, & Albertini, 2002). In a study of 4-year-old deaf children enrolled in a program that used both signs and speech, the early reading achievement scores of these children exceeded those of hearing children (Notoya, Suzuki, & Furukawa, 1994).

Children who are hard of hearing are often thought to not need sign language because they can hear spoken language (often not clearly); however, a dual language approach for children who are hard of hearing, in which both ASL and spoken English were used, has yielded positive results (Rushmer, 2003). Signs may "bridge" meaning, sustaining the development of receptive language and then spoken English (Rushmer, 2003).

The *total communication* approach uses all modes of communication, though not equally, available to the child including, ASL, manually coded English (such as signed English, or Signing Essential English), spoken language, and so forth. Often the total communication approach is reduced to simultaneous communication or "simcom" as it is also known, where one simply signs in English or while one talks. Programs which use this approach believe they are providing the best of both worlds by emphasizing both signing and speech. Concerns with this approach recognize that if total communication is put into practice as "simcom" then both languages are compromised. Children may not develop a solid language base in either ASL or English (signed or spoken).

A *bilingual* approach uses American Sign Language (ASL) as the child's first language because it is vital to the child's linguistic, cognitive, social, and emotional growth. It is, proponents say, a pathway to communication skills, life success, and literacy development for children who are deaf or hard of hearing who learn easily and effectively through a visual medium. English as a second language is learned through reading and writing mediated through ASL. Auditory and speech skills can be addressed as the child is learning language visually. Concerns with this approach include that the environment required for fully implementing this approach (peers and role models who are Deaf, and teachers proficient in ASL) is not widely available in schools.

It is unfortunate that parents of young children who are deaf or hard of hearing often have to choose between one approach or another. Increasingly parents are "wanting it all" for their children and are demanding, for example, a bilingual program where their child (who has a cochlear implant) is receiving speech and auditory training and is also becoming fluent in ASL. Deaf teachers and other adult mentors are helping deaf children and their families to navigate both hearing and Deaf environments. English literacy is developed with visual strategies that include Visual Phonics. This is not to imply that a "one size fits all" approach to early education with children who are deaf should be used, but rather it is important to be flexible and responsive to parents' desires to explore every available resource. The TPBA team needs to be well-versed in the advantages, disadvantages, and research base for the various approaches, so families can make informed decisions regarding communication approaches for their child.

CONCLUSION

This chapter provides the reader with a basic introduction to the effects of hearing loss on the developing child. A primary emphasis of the chapter is to highlight the extraordinary role vision plays in how the child who is deaf or hard of hearing experiences his or her world. Both auditory and visual techniques that address the unique communication and language needs of children who experience hearing loss are provided. Guidance is provided for integrating both auditory and visual considerations when assessing a child who is deaf or hard of hearing. The reader is invited to view the developing child through the eyes of members of the Deaf community who know, in an authentic way, what it means to be deaf and how that valuable perspective can influence the assessment process. The importance of both Deaf adults and professionals trained to work with children who are deaf or hard of hearing is presented as an essential element in the overall composition of the transdisciplinary team.

CASE STUDY

The following case study serves as an example of typical adaptations required when conducting a TPBA with a child who is deaf. An example of a child who is learning ASL is provided because the literature most often describes assessments of children with hearing loss which present an auditory emphasis. The reader is invited to think about this case study and compare and contrast it to more familiar case studies. Finally, we invite the reader to find examples of the ideas presented in this chapter in Mia's story and consider how this experience influences their own professional understanding of the assessment of children who are deaf or hard of hearing.

MIA

History

Mia was born in Mexico. She and her parents immigrated to the Washington, D.C. metropolitan area soon after Mia was born. When Mia was 1 year old, she was diagnosed with a severe to profound hearing loss. Mia began speech and language therapy services and was fitted with a hearing aid. After 2 years, with little progress made in developing intelligible speech, her family was referred to a local program specializing in serving deaf children. Mia was enrolled in a bilingual (American Sign Language [ASL] and English) preschool class and began learning ASL, while her parents were offered an ASL class free of charge. Her parents attended the class when they could but found it difficult because a Spanish-language interpreter was not provided. Nonetheless, Mia's parents learned basic sign vocabulary that they used consistently with Mia, and they continued to speak to her in Spanish. When asked if they had any concerns regarding Mia's development, they mentioned that she seems to have a difficult time sharing with other children in the neighborhood.

Assessment Process

Mia was referred for assessment when she was 4 years, 10 months of age. The TPBA process began with a home visit with the play facilitator and the parent facilitator. The play facilitator was deaf, and the parent facilitator was hard of hearing and fluent in spoken Spanish. Background information was obtained, and the play facilitator had an opportunity to interact with Mia. It was decided that the assessment would take place in Mia's classroom on a Friday, and a transportation plan was made so Mia's mother and baby sister could attend the assessment. The TPBA team members included the play facilitator (deaf), the parent facilitator (hard of hearing), a speech-language pathologist (hearing), a school psychologist (deaf), Mia's teacher (hearing), the camera operator (hearing), and the coach (deaf). The team members were chosen because they valued native language skills (spoken Spanish, ASL) and the visual perspective of Deaf people. The coach coordinated visual communication among the team members. The parent facilitator functioned as the interpreter (ASL to spoken Spanish) when needed. The parent facilitator introduced the team to Mia's mother, Mrs. Suarez. She spoke in Spanish as team members either spoke in English or signed ASL. She signed ASL for everything Mrs. Suarez said.

Developmental Observations

When Mia first entered the room, she looked around and paused to observe each team member. She smiled and waved at two of the team members and signed, WHO? (Who are you?).

Initially Mia's activity level was high, jumping from one activity to another as she became used to the environment. Once the play facilitator engaged her in conversation, she seemed to calm. It appeared that Mia attended better to the structured activities during the assessment.

Mrs. Suarez encouraged Mia throughout the assessment when Mia became frustrated in play. This is one example of Mia's loving and positive relationship with her mother. Mia "checked in" visually with her mother throughout the session, and Mrs. Suarez responded with a smile or gesture of encouragement. When her mother left to feed her baby sister, Mia became anxious and asked in ASL, WHERE MOM? (Where's mom?). When her question was answered, she was reassured and resumed playing.

Because of her parents' concern regarding Mia's difficulty in playing with other children, the team decided to observe her later that week at school in the classroom and on the playground. She was observed to have some conflicts with peers and dealt with frustration with her friends by closing her eyes—making it impossible to communicate with her about her behavior and her feelings. One incident with Mia and her peers happened on the playground. Mia went off on her own to play a "Bus Activity." When another child tried to join her activity, she told him in ASL, NO DON'T-WANT (No, I don't want you to play with me). *She was aware of her friends playing nearby but decided against joining them. Shortly afterward, Mia did allow another child to join in her play, but only on her terms. When Mia wanted to play alone again she handed her book to the child and signed in ASL,* MY BOOK, READ YOU, SHARE (You can read my book; I want to share with you). *Mia appears to have some difficulty getting along with others her age. She does use language to direct children in play but was not observed to use language to repair social situations or resolve conflict.*

Mia's communication modalities include gestures and ASL. Mia is able to modify her gestures to ASL when given the ASL equivalent of the gesture. For example, she identified a horse animal cracker by gesturing, RIDING-HORSE. *When she was shown the ASL sign for* HORSE, *she signed the word correctly. Mia benefits from a competent ASL user for language modeling. Additionally, as Mia's fine motor skills continue to develop she will be able to imitate more complex signs, such as* NOISE, *and classifiers such as in the phrase,* CAR-MAKING-SEVERAL-TURNS.

Mia's language skills are in the locutionary stage, in which formal, symbolic communication—usually speech—develops along with the ability to communicate increasingly complex and abstract information. She also shows the ability in ASL to modify adjectives with intensity, such as the word HOT, *with appropriate facial expression. However, when she needs help with something such as putting a brick on top of the tower, she continues to use gestures or body language. Mia's language and communication skills indicate an inconsistency in complexity of expressive abilities.*

Mia signs for a variety of purposes, including asking questions (WHERE IS MOTHER?), *answering questions, requesting action, informing, and protesting. However, Mia was observed primarily to communicate for social means with her mother, her sister, the play facilitator, her peers, and her teacher.*

In ASL development, her sentence length consists of three to four signs/words that are simple in construction, with subjects and objects joined by verbs with appropriate agreement. She is ready for complex sentence structures that involve topicalization. In addition, raising of the eyebrows, an important grammatical feature in ASL, is still absent.

Mia responds to simple Wh- *questions. Mia showed comprehension of language by responding to simple questions; however, there were situations in which Mia did not respond to a question but it was unclear whether she did not understand the question or chose not to respond.*

Mia has emerging discourse skills. Because Mia is a visual learner, she has developed good eye-gaze skills. While reading a story to her mother, sister, and the play facilitator, and when maintaining a conversation, Mia shows appropriate use of her eye gaze. She follows signed conversation between two people by shifting eye gaze and looking toward an object or person present in the room when a signer makes reference to that object or person. She responds to and elicits appropriate attention-getting behaviors by shoulder tapping and hand waving.

Joan Smith, Mia's speech-language pathologist, reports that she works with Mia on suprasegmental aspects of speech; this is the basic stage of vocalization that is a typical beginning speech goal for deaf children. Mia did not use spontaneous speech but imitated basic simple vowels such as "ah" and "oh." She also imitated short and long vocalizations such as "Ahhhh" (long) and "Ba/Ba/Ba" (short). The goal for Mia is to develop receptive speechreading skills. She has just started to identify colors through speechreading. Mia does not wear her hearing aid consistently. Although she wore her hearing aid for the play session, she was not observed responding to a drum hit loudly behind her back.

Mia uses a variety of words, specifically nouns, verbs, adjectives, and some negatives. She is ready for expansion to include adverbs, prepositions, and conjunctions, which are rich in ASL modifiers (facial expressions). Mia demonstrates an understanding of the connection between the printed English word and fingerspelling. She could fin-

gerspell her name as well as the words cat, dog, ball, and cup *when shown a picture of the object. She recognizes letters in print by fingerspelling them.*

Postassessment Meeting

After the developmental observations of Mia had been completed, the team met with the parents to discuss their observations and learn more about Mr. and Mrs. Suarez's concerns and needs regarding Mia. For this meeting, a trilingual (English, Spanish, ASL) interpreter was used. Prior to the meeting, the team's initial report was translated into Spanish. The translator also attended so that she could make any final changes to the report quickly.

During the meeting, the Suarezes expressed frustration with trying to learn ASL. They felt that although the school provided a class for parents and also provided babysitting, they felt very uncomfortable and "stupid" in the spoken English/ASL environment. They requested that a Spanish interpreter be provided to them for the sign classes. The team agreed that that would help the parents learn ASL more easily and revised the recommendation to include the parents' request.

The team focused primarily on three areas of assessment in discussion with the parents: English and ASL development and social development. The assessment results indicated that Mia, although progressing in both English and ASL skills, is lagging behind her peers. Mr. and Mrs. Suarez expressed sadness and anger that Mia had wasted 2 years trying to learn how to talk when she could have been learning sign language. They wondered why they had not been told initially about Mia's present school where all the staff was fluent in sign language. The team explained that many professionals think that signing will prevent a child from developing speech and that it is often seen as a "last resort." However, despite the delay in receiving appropriate services, Mia is developing ASL skills that will provide her with a foundation for learning written English. It was pointed out by the team that Mia recognizes the alphabet and can fingerspell some words, including her name. She also loves to share books and has a clear understanding of sequencing in storytelling. Mr. and Mrs. Suarez were concerned that Mia would never talk despite continued speech therapy. The team acknowledged that Mia may not develop functional speech skills but that therapy would continue to be provided to her at the parents' request. Although Mia does not appear to respond to sound even with her hearing aid, the parents were encouraged to try to have her wear it as much as possible. The parents also expressed sadness that Mia was not learning Spanish. The team discussed how learning ASL could also be a bridge to spoken Spanish for Mia as it is with learning English skills.

The team described Mia's social skills with her classmates and asked the parents to comment on how she interacts with children at home. The parents agreed that Mia seems frustrated when she is playing with other children and either doesn't understand what is happening or doesn't get her way. The children in the neighborhood are hearing, and Mia has great difficulty in communicating with them beyond simple gestures. The team discussed how social skills and communication skills are interconnected. The team provided examples of how, even though Mia is communicating in ASL, she can become frustrated when she is playing with her classmates if she does not understand or is unable to express herself. The team reinforced the importance of strengthening Mia's exposure to ASL at home and at school. The team asked the parents if they would consider participating in the Shared Reading Project offered by the school, in which a Deaf adult visits the home and shows parents how to share books with their deaf child. Participation in this program would support Mia's ASL and English development and assist the parents in learning sign language. The school agreed to provide a Spanish interpreter for this activity. Mr. and Mrs. Suarez agreed that they would like to try the program with a Spanish translator. Strategies for facilitating communication with the neighborhood children were discussed. Teaching simple signs and reminding children that they should face Mia when talking to her and use gestures would be helpful. Expanding Mia's circle of play-mates to include her deaf classmates would provide her with more satisfying play experiences. Mr. and Mrs. Suarez and Mia's teacher were encouraged to explore how they could provide Mia with these play experiences and to determine the role of a Spanish language interpreter.

Mrs. Suarez lamented that there is so much she still does not understand about her daughter, sign language, the Deaf community, and hearing aids, to name a few topics. The team then revised the recommendations to include a biweekly home visit by a family–school liaison along with a Spanish interpreter from the school who could answer their questions and provide information regarding their concerns.

Recommendations

1. *Offer opportunities for Mia to solve problems independently (e.g., allow extra time, encourage Mia to ask for help by signing, provide toys/materials that are challenging).*

2. *Provide opportunities to sort, match, compare, and contrast objects in different ways to expand Mia's understanding and vocabulary.*

3. *Provide opportunities for Mia to be involved in activities that require a sequence of steps. The steps should be discussed, carried out, and reviewed with Mia (i.e., pop popcorn, plant seeds, make pudding).*

4. *Provide opportunities for Mia to identify numerals (1–10), basic words, and names (e.g., colors, family members' names, and students' names in her class).*

5. *Provide opportunities for Mia to copy letters, numerals, and shapes in a variety of ways using different media.*

6. *Provide opportunities for Mia to count objects in a group and match the printed numeral (1–15) along with the signs for the numbers.*

7. *Use language to provide support to Mia during a task.*

8. *When Mia begins exhibiting self-stimulating behaviors (e.g., jiggling leg, excessive facial and body movements), an adult should take care to ensure that Mia is understanding what is happening around her by communicating with her in ASL.*

9. *Allow more wait time for Mia to respond to questions before asking another or providing her with the answer.*

10. *Encourage Mia to ask for help with sign instead of using gestures or body language.*

11. *Provide opportunities for Mia to develop abstract skills to tell a story that would lead to development of role shifting, which involves body shifting, facial expression, and eye gaze.*

12. *Provide opportunities for Mia to be exposed to a natural ASL role model.*

13. *Encourage Mia to transition from pointing to using signs.*

14. *Follow up on Mia's understanding of questions through observation of her actions that demonstrate understanding and, if necessary, rephrase the question.*

15. *Add fingerspelling with sign whenever appropriate to expose Mia to English.*

16. *Provide role models to expand Mia's use of modifiers (e.g., big house).*

17. *Provide a Spanish interpreter for Mia's family for sign language instruction.*

18. *When situations arise, help Mia with conflict resolution skills. Encourage Mia to open her eyes so she can see (even if in her peripheral vision) to see language modeled that she might use to resolve conflicts.*

19. *When Mia refuses to express emotions, use dramatic play to help her act out how to appropriately handle her conflicts and emotions and provide adult role modeling of appropriate responses in ASL.*

20. *Provide a biweekly visit from a family–school liaison who can review these recommendations and provide further support to the parents in implementing them, answering their questions and providing additional information on topics of interest to the parents.*

RECOMMENDED READING

Bodner-Johnson, B., & Sass-Lehrer, M. (Eds.). (2003). *The young deaf or hard of hearing child: A family-centered approach to early education.* Baltimore: Paul H. Brookes Publishing Co.

Christiansen, K. (2000). *Deaf plus: A multicultural perspective.* San Diego: DawnSign Press.

Marschark, M. (1997). *Raising an educated deaf child.* New York: Oxford University Press.

Marschark, M., & Spencer, P. (Eds.). (2003). *Deaf studies, language and education.* New York: Oxford University Press.

Meadow-Orlans, K.P., Mertens, D.M., & Sass-Lehrer, M.A. (2003). *Parents and their deaf children: The early years.* Washington, DC: Gallaudet University Press.

Meadow-Orlans, K.P., Spencer, P.E., & Koester, L.S. (2004). *The world of deaf infants: A longitudinal study.* New York: Oxford University Press.

Ogden, P. (1996). *The silent garden: Raising your deaf child* (2nd ed.). Washington, DC: Gallaudet University Press.

Rousch, J., & Matkin, N.D. (Eds.). (1994). *Infants and toddlers with hearing loss: Family-centered assessment and intervention.* Baltimore: York Press.

Schick, B., Marschark, M., & Spencer, P.E. (2006). *Advances in the sign language development of deaf children.* New York: Oxford University Press.

Schwartz, S. (1996). *Choices in deafness: A parent's guide to communication options* (2nd ed.). Bethesda, MD: Woodbine House.

Spencer, P.E., Erting, C.J., & Marschark, M. (Eds.). (2000). *The deaf child in the family and at school: Essays in honor of Kathryn P. Meadow-Orlans.* Mahwah, NJ: Lawrence Erlbaum Associates.

RESOURCES

Alexander Graham Bell Association for the Deaf and Hard of Hearing
http://www.agbell.org

American Society for Deaf Children
http://deafchildren.org

Boys Town National Research Hospital
http://www.babyhearing.org

Deaf Education Web Site
http://www.deafed.net

Gallaudet University
http://www.gallaudet.edu

National Association of the Deaf
http://NAD.org

Raising Deaf Kids
http://www.raisingdeafkids.org

REFERENCES

American Speech-Language-Hearing Association. (2005). *Central auditory processing disorders: The role of the audiologist* [Position statement]. Available at http://www.asha.org/members/deskref-journals/deskref/default

American Speech-Language-Hearing Association Task Force on Central Auditory Processing Consensus Development. (1996, July). Central auditory processing: Current status of research and implications for clinical practice. *American Journal of Audiology, 5*(2), 41–54.

Andrews, J., Leigh, I., & Weiner, T. (2004). *Deaf people: Evolving perspectives from psychology, education, and sociology.* Boston: Pearson.

Batshaw, M.L. (2007). *Children with disabilities* (6th ed.). Baltimore: Paul H. Brookes Publishing Co.

Blanchfield, B., Feldman, J., Dunbar, J., & Gardner, E. (2001). The severely to profoundly hearing impaired population in the United States: Prevalence, estimates and demographics. *Journal of the American Academy of Audiology, 12,* 183–189.

Bodner-Johnson, B. (2003). The deaf child in the family. In B. Bodner-Johnson & M. Sass-Lehrer (Eds.), *The young deaf or hard of hearing child: A family-centered approach to early education* (pp. 3–33). Baltimore: Paul H. Brookes Publishing Co.

Cacace, A., & McFarland, D. (1998). Auditory processing disorder in children: A critical review. *Journal of Speech, Language, and Hearing Research, 41,* 355–373.

Calderone, R., & Greenberg, M. (1997). The effectiveness of early intervention of deaf children and children with hearing loss. In M.J. Guralnick (Ed.), *The effectiveness of early intervention* (pp. 455–482). Baltimore: Paul H. Brookes Publishing Co.

Centers for Disease Control and Prevention. (2005). *The Early Hearing Detection & Intervention (EHDI) program: Promoting communication from birth [Factsheet].* Retrieved December 1, 2006, from http://www.cdc.gov/ncbddd/ehdi

Culpepper, B. (2003). Identification of permanent childhood hearing loss through universal newborn hearing screening programs. In B. Bodner-Johnson & M. Sass-Lehrer (Eds.), *The young deaf or hard of hearing child: A family-centered approach to early education* (pp. 99–126). Baltimore: Paul H. Brookes Publishing Co.

Eliot, L. (1999). *What's going on in there? How the brain and mind develop in the first five years of life.* London: Penguin.

Erting, C. (2003). Language and literacy development. In B. Bodner-Johnson & M. Sass-Lehrer (Eds.), *The young deaf or hard of hearing child: A family-centered approach to early education* (pp. 373–403). Baltimore: Paul H. Brookes Publishing Co.

Flexer, C. (1999). *Facilitating hearing and listening in young children* (2nd ed.). San Diego: Singular.

Gatty, J.C. (2003). Technology: Its impact on education and the future. In B. Bodner-Johnson & M. Sass-Lehrer (Eds.), *The young deaf or hard of hearing child: A family-centered approach to early education* (pp. 403–424). Baltimore: Paul H. Brookes Publishing Co.

Goldin-Meadow, S. (2003). *The resilience of language: What gesture, creation in deaf children can tell use about how all children learn language.* New York: Psychology Press.

Goldin-Meadow, S., & Feldman, H. (1975). The creation of a communication system: A study of deaf children of hearing parents. *Sign Language Studies, 8,* 225–234.

Hafer, J.C. (1984). *The use of sign language as a multisensory approach to teaching sight word vocabulary to hearing, learning disabled children.* Unpublished doctoral dissertation, University of Maryland, College Park.

Hafer, J.C., & Stredler-Brown, A. (2003). Family-centered developmental assessment. In B. Bodner-Johnson & M. Sass-Lehrer (Eds.), *The young deaf or hard of hearing child: A family-centered approach to early education* (pp. 127–149). Baltimore: Paul H. Brookes Publishing Co.

Harris, M., & Mohay, H. (1997). Learning to look in the right place: A comparison of attentional behavior in deaf children with deaf and hearing mothers. *Journal of Deaf Studies and Deaf Education, 2,* 95–103.

Holden-Pitt, L., & Diaz, J.A. (1998). Thirty years of the annual survey of deaf and hard of hearing children and youth: A glance over the decades. *American Annals of the Deaf, 142,* 72–76.

Holzrichter, A.S., & Meier, R.P. (2000). Child-directed signing in American Sign Language. In C. Chamberlain, J.P. Morford, & R. Mayberry (Eds.), *The acquisition of linguistic representation by eye* (pp. 25–40). Mahwah, NJ: Lawrence Erlbaum Associates.

Individuals with Disabilities Education Improvement Act of 2004, PL 108-446, 20 U.S.C. §§ 1400 *et seq.*

Joint Committee on Infant Hearing. (2000). Year 2000 position statement: Principles and guidelines for early hearing detection and intervention programs. *American Journal of Audiology, 9,* 9–29.

Jones, T., & Jones, J. (2003). Young deaf children with multiple disabilities. In B. Bodner-

Johnson & M. Sass-Lehrer (Eds.), *The young deaf or hard of hearing child: A family centered approach to early education* (pp. 297–333). Baltimore: Paul H. Brookes Publishing Co.

Karchmer, M., & Mitchell, R. (2003). Demographic and achievement characteristics of deaf and hard of hearing students. In M. Marschark & P.E. Spencer (Eds.), *Deaf studies, language and education* (pp. 21–38). New York: Oxford University Press.

Koester, L.S. (1994). Early interactions and the socioemotional development of deaf infants. *Early Development and Parenting, 3,* 51–60.

Lane, H., Hoffmeister, R., & Behan, B. (1996). *A journey into the deaf world.* San Diego: DawnSign Press.

Marschark, M., Lang, H.G., & Albertini, J.A. (2002). *Educating deaf students: From research to practice.* New York: Oxford University Press.

Marschark, M., & Spencer, P. (2003). *Deaf studies, language, and education.* New York: Oxford University Press.

Martin, F.N., & Clark, J.G. (2000). *Introduction to audiology* (7th ed.). Boston: Allyn & Bacon.

Mather, S. (1987). Eye gaze and communication in a deaf classroom. *Sign Language Studies, 54,* 11–31.

Meadow, K. (1967). Early manual communication in relation to the deaf child's intellectual, social, and communicative functioning. *American Annals of the Deaf, 113,* 29–41.

Meadow-Orlans, K.P. (2003). Support for parents: Promoting visual attention and literacy in a changing world. In B. Bodner-Johnson & M. Sass-Lehrer (Eds.), *The young deaf or hard of hearing child: A family-centered approach to early education* (pp. 39–60). Baltimore: Paul H. Brookes Publishing Co.

Mertens, D.M., Sass-Lehrer, M., Scott-Olson, K. (2000). Sensitivity in the family-professional relationship: Parental experiences in families with young deaf and hard of hearing children. In Spencer, P.E., Erting, C.J., & Marschark, M. (Eds.), *The deaf child in the family and at school: Essays in honor of Kathryn P. Meadow-Orlans* (pp. 133–150). Mahwah, NJ: Lawrence Erlbaum Associates.

Moeller, M.P. (2000). Early intervention and language development in children who are deaf and hard of hearing. *Pediatrics, 106*(3), E43.

Mohay, H. (2000). Language in sight: Mothers' strategies for making language visually accessible to deaf children. In P.A. Spencer, C.J. Erting, & M. Marschark (Eds.), *The deaf child in the family and at school: Essays in honor of Kathryn P. Meadow-Orlans* (pp. 154–158). Mahwah, NJ: Lawrence Erlbaum Associates.

Mohay, H., Milton, L., Hindmarsh, G., & Ganley, K. (1998). Deaf mothers as language models for hearing families with deaf children. In A. Weisel (Ed.), *Issues unresolved: New perspectives in language and deafness* (pp. 76–87). Washington, DC: Gallaudet University Press.

Newport, E., & Meier, R. (1985). *Acquisition of American Sign Language: Volume I. The data* (pp. 881–938). Hillsdale, NJ: Lawrence Erlbaum Associates.

Northern, J.L., & Downs, M.P. (2002). *Hearing in children* (5th ed.). Baltimore: Lippincott Williams & Wilkins.

Notoya, M., Suzuki, S., & Furukawa, M. (1994). Effectiveness of early manual instruction of deaf children. *American Annals of the Deaf, 139*(3), 348–351.

Nussbaum, D. (2003). Support services handout # 4010 communication sheet: Communication choices with deaf and hard of hearing children. Retrieved October 30, 2006 from http://clerccenter.gallaudet.edu/SupportServices/series/4010.html

Padden, C., & Humphries, T. (1988). *Deaf in America: Voices from a culture.* Cambridge, MA. Harvard University Press.

Petitto, L., & Marentette, P. (1991). Babbling in the manual mode: Evidence from the ontogeny of language. *Science, 251,* 1493–1496.

Rushmer, N. (2003). The importance of appropriate programming. In B. Bodner-Johnson & M. Sass-Lehrer (Eds.), *The young deaf or hard of hearing child: A family-centered approach to early education* (pp. 223–251). Baltimore: Paul H. Brookes Publishing Co.

Schlesinger, H.S., & Meadow, K. (1972). *Sound and sign: Childhood deafness and mental health.* Berkeley: University of California Press.

Schuyler, V., & Rushmer, N. (1987). *Parent–infant habilitation: A comprehensive approach to working with hearing-impaired infants and toddlers and their families.* Portland, OR: Infant Hearing Resource.

Singleton, J.L., & Morgan, D.D. (2004, April). *Becoming deaf: Deaf teacher's engagement practices supporting deaf children's identity development.* Paper presented at the annual meeting of the American of Educational Research Association, San Diego.

Spencer, P. (2003). Parent–child interaction. In B. Bodner-Johnson & M. Sass-Lehrer (Eds.), *The young deaf or hard of hearing child: A family-centered approach to early education* (pp. 333–368). Baltimore: Paul H. Brookes Publishing Co.

Spencer, P., Bodner-Johnson, B.A., & Gutfrend, M.K. (1992). Interacting with infants with a hearing loss. What can we learn from mothers who are deaf? *Journal of Early Intervention, 16,* 64–78.

Stredler-Brown, A., & Arehart, K.H. (2000). Universal newborn hearing screening: Impact on intervention services [Monograph]. In C. Yoshinaga-Itano & A. Sedey (Eds.), Language, speech, and social-emotional development of children who are deaf or hard of hearing: The early years. *The Volta Review, 100*(5), 85–117.

Supalla, S. (1991). Manually coded English: The modality question in signed language development. In P. Siple & S. Fischer (Eds.), *Theoretical issues in sign language research. Vol 2: Acquisition* (pp. 85–109). Chicago: University of Chicago Press.

Swisher, M.V. (1984). Signed input of hearing mothers to deaf children. *Language Learning, 34,* 69–86.

U.S. Department of Education. (2000). *Twenty-second annual report to Congress on the implementation of the Individuals with Disabilities Education Act (IDEA).* Washington, DC: Author.

Watkins, S., Pittman., P., & Walden, B. (1998). The deaf mentor experimental project for young children who are deaf and their families. *American Annals of the Deaf, 143*(1), 29–34.

Widen, J.E., Bull, R.W., & Folsom, R.C. (2003, July/September). Newborn hearing screening: What it means for providers of early intervention services. *Infants and Young Children, 16*(3), 249–257.

Willems, P. (2000). Genetic cause of hearing loss. *The New England Journal of Medicine, 342*(15), 1101–1109.

Wood, D., Wood, H., Griffiths, A., & Howarth, I. (1986). *Teaching and talking with deaf children.* New York: John Wiley & Sons.

Yoshinaga-Itano, C., & Sedey, A. (Eds.). (2000). *Language, speech, and social-emotional development of children who are deaf or hard of hearing: The early years.* Washington, DC: Alexander Graham Bell Society.

Yoshinaga-Itano, C., Sedey, A.L., Coulter, D.K., & Mehl, A.L. (1998). The language of early- and later identified children with hearing loss. *Pediatrics, 102,* 1161–1171.

TPBA2 Observation Guidelines:
Auditory Skills

Child's name: _____ Age: _____ Birth date: _____

Parent(s): _____ Assessment date: _____

Person(s) completing the form: _____

If a child has a hearing aid, it should be worn during the screening unless otherwise advised by an audiologist.

♦ = failure of this item results in an automatic referral to an audiologist.

Scoring legend:

P = child successfully demonstrates behavior
F = child does not demonstrate behavior
✓ = further assessment is needed to quantify the score
NO = no opportunity to observe this behavior
NA = behavior is not developmentally appropriate for child

Questions	Strengths	Concerns	Pass/Fail
I. Hearing			
I. A. What behaviors indicate that the child hears voices and sounds?	Responds to a variety of sounds—loud/soft, high/low consistently by Startling Searching Localizing Responding (gestures, vocalizing, verbalizing, signing)	Responds inconsistently or not at all to voices and sounds in the environment	P F ♦
I. B. Does the child look for or turn to the source of sound?	Searches for and locates familiar sounds in the environment: Unilaterally Bilaterally	Responds inconsistently or does not locate voices and sounds in the environment: Unilaterally Bilaterally P F	♦
I. C. Does the child respond meaningfully to sounds or words?	Responds meaningfully with Eye gaze Gesture (e.g., pointing) Vocalization Verbalization Sign	Responds inconsistently or does not respond meaningfully Requires support: Visual Tactile Kinesthetic	P F ♦
I. D. How quickly does the child act in response to sounds or words?	Responds quickly and consistently to sounds and words	Responds inconsistently or slowly to sounds and words Requires support: Visual Tactile Kinesthetic	P F
I. E. Does the child accurately imitate sounds?	Imitates sounds and words consistently	Imitates sounds or words inconsistently	P F

Developed with Jan Christian Hafer.

(continued on next page)

Transdisciplinary Play-Based System (TPBA2/TPBI2)
by Toni Linder

Questions	Strengths	Concerns	"Ready for"
II. Visual communication skills			
II. A. Does the child coordinate visually to a communication partner (facilitator)?	Attends to communication partner's face when seeking information or communicating	Lacks attention to communication and does not look at communication partner's face and instead focuses on objects	Increase attention to communication opportunities to look at partner's face (move object near face)
II. B. Does the child coordinate visual attention with more than one focus?	Looks at communication partner and object of interest with ease	Has a difficult time dividing attention between object and communication partner	Increase opportunities to coordinate between one (then more) objects and communication partners
II. C. Does the child use and respond to visual attention-getting behaviors?	Uses a variety of attention-getting behaviors appropriate to the setting	Exhibits poor or inappropriate attention-getting behaviors such as waving, tapping, slapping table, or stomping foot	Increase opportunities for seeing and then demonstrating attention-getting behaviors
II. D. Does the child visually scan his or her surroundings? Is the child aware of his or her environment?	Monitors environment, notes new events, people, or objects. Visually "marks" location of people and or objects and continuously monitors	Is not able to monitor environment	Increase opportunities to attend to a variety of visual stimuli

Developed with Jan Christian Hafer.

7

Cognitive Development Domain

The development of cognition is intricately interwoven with development in the sensorimotor, language and communication, and emotional and social domains. A simplified definition of cognition suggests that primary aspects include: 1) basic processes, such as attention and memory; 2) strategies for problem solving; 3) metacognition, or understanding of one's own and others' thinking; and 4) content knowledge, or conceptual understanding (Siegler, 1998). Cognition can be examined through addressing neurophysiological aspects of brain functioning, psychological processes, or theoretical models. The primary focus of this chapter is to highlight psychological processes that can be inferred through observation of the child's behavior and to summarize what research tells us about the meaning of those behaviors in relation to development and learning. Neurophysiological aspects will be briefly highlighted in reference to this research. Transdisciplinary Play-Based Assessment (TPBA2) incorporates these critical cognitive processes into subcategories of the TPBA2 Observation Guidelines (see pp. 371–380) and Age Table (see pp. 383–396).

Assessment of cognition in young children is typically performed by examining skills or milestones that develop at different ages. For example, a common test item is that the child is able to stack three blocks at 17 months. This approach reveals something of what the child knows (things can be put on top of each other) and can do ("I can make this block sit up here"). What is not routinely explored on such test items, for example, is whether the child selected this task (selected focus), had done this task before (memory), how long it took him to do it (sustained attention), whether he used modeled or invented strategies (memory versus problem solving), whether he realized what was wrong when a block fell off (attentional shift and problem solving), and whether he stacked blocks because he understood that someone wanted him to (social cognition) or because he wanted to (goal setting). In addition, the demonstration of cognitive understanding can be influenced by gross and fine motor skills. Assessment

Note: Although literacy is included in the TPBA2 Observation Guidelines, Observation Notes, Age Tables for conceptual development, and Observation Summary Forms in Chapter 7, emerging literacy is addressed separately in Chapter 8.

of cognition needs to address not only the evident skills the child demonstrates, but also the motivation behind a child's behaviors, what the child understands of the meaning of specific concepts or actions, and the exercise of processes underlying an action or event. These aspects of cognitive assessment deserve attention if we are to adequately address how and why a child does or does not understand or complete a task or activity. Understanding what the child does, how he does it, and why, or why *not*, is critically important for effective intervention and thus should be elements of assessment as well.

The cognitive domain in TPBA2 examines what the child's play tells us about the level of the child's conceptual and procedural knowledge. Specific examination of the cognitive processes and strategies used during play can inform our understanding of the child's ability to learn about the physical, social, and preacademic world. The cognitive domain in TPBA2 therefore examines the subcategories of 1) attention, 2) memory, 3) problem solving, 4) social cognition, 5) complexity of play, 6) conceptual knowledge, and 7) emerging literacy skills. (See Table 7.1. for the definitions of these subcategories.)

EXECUTIVE FUNCTION

Although the global construct of executive function has received increasing attention in the literature, it is not addressed as a subcategory in the cognitive domain. A developmental perspective provides the rationale for why this construct has been broken down into separate subcategories.

The first four subcategories—attention, memory, problem solving, and social cognition—become increasingly interrelated as the child matures. The capacity to pay attention to important aspects of the environment, to retain and retrieve relevant information applicable to a given situation, and to select, use, monitor, and modify strategies as needed in each situation is fundamental to thinking and learning (Lyon, 1996). The ability to plan, carry out, and adapt actions is necessary for goal-directed behaviors. The child needs to be able to think about the result that is desired and envision the means for accomplishing the goal. In addition, the child needs to be able to maintain attention to the activity or problem, to remember what approaches have been successful or unsuccessful in the past, and to shift focus to relevant aspects as needed to solve problems as they arise. Although difficult to analyze, these pieces *can* be observed in the child's actions in play.

Table 7.1. Subcategories of cognitive domain

Subcategory	Description
Attention	Ability to select stimuli, focus on the stimuli, sustain concentration, shift focus, and ignore distractions
Memory	Ability to recognize, recall, or reconstruct routines, skills, concepts, and events after short-term and/or long-term delays
Problem solving	Ability to understand causal relationships and to independently organize and sequence thoughts and actions toward a goal in a timely process, to monitor progress, to make modifications as needed, and to generalize what is learned to new situations
Social cognition	Ability to infer social causes from consequences, to understand the thinking and intentions of others, and to differentiate intention from accident
Complexity of play	The predominant type, highest level, flexibility of and originality within various forms of play exhibited by the child in areas including: sensorimotor play, functional/relational play, construction, dramatic play, and games with rules
Conceptual knowledge	Ability to recognize or recall personal or conceptual information related to people, objects, events, categories, characteristics, and preacademic concepts
Literacy	Understanding and use of books, pictures and story comprehension, story reading behaviors, phonological awareness, phonemic awareness, letter recognition, word recognition, drawing, writing, and spelling

The study of *how* children solve problems and learn new concepts and procedures, such as how to operate a new toy, is increasingly becoming the focus of both neurological and psychological research. The construct of "executive function" (EF) is typically used to refer to these aspects of learning (Lyon, 1996; Zelazo & Muller, 2002). Although not clearly defined in the literature, executive function incorporates a variety of components, including self-regulation (see Chapter 4, Emotional and Social Development Domain), memory, sequencing of behavior, flexibility, and planning and organization of behaviors (Eslinger, 1996). These capacities are supported by the child's abilities to focus, initiate, inhibit, shift attention, concentrate, and strategize (Mirsky, 1996; Mirsky, Ingraham, & Kugelmass, 1995). EF is also seen as a problem-solving framework incorporating the ability to represent or identify a problem, to plan how to approach the problem, to execute the plan using rules to accomplish intended results, and then to evaluate the outcome and make modifications as needed (Zelazo, Carter, Reznick, & Frye, 1997). The development of efficient executive function skills appears to be critical to overall cognitive functioning.

Although EF emerges toward the end of the first year of life, many changes occur between the ages of 2 and 5. Because executive function has not been tested as a construct until after 4 years of age, however, TPBA2 examines the foundational skills (attention, memory, problem solving, and social cognition) that lead to the emergence of EF rather than the demonstration of EF itself. A quick overview of the early months and years of life reveals how many facets come together to shape executive functioning processes.

Within the first 4 months of life, the infant is learning to focus on various aspects of his or her environment. By 4 months of age, the infant can *anticipate* what will happen when objects move (Meltzoff & Moore, 1998). Between 8 and 12 months the infant develops means–ends, or *goal-directed,* behavior. The infant can plan how to achieve a simple goal through vocal or physical means. At around 12 months the child adds expressive or spoken *language* and early dramatic *representation* of actions to his or her symbolic thinking abilities. Language adds considerably to the child's ability to conceptualize problems and link past, present, and future, as others explain, discuss, and relate ideas. By 18 months, the child can anticipate the results of a sequence of actions, can represent thoughts in language and behavior, and can look for solutions to a problem. Between 18 and 30 months, the child's ability to exercise *self-control,* to start and stop activities when needed, develops. Being able to anticipate what will happen as a result of his or her own or others' actions is important for the development of *selective attention and planning* (Kopp, 1997, 2000). By age 4, the child can scan the environment, select a focus for attention, and plan how to achieve a goal rather than merely being drawn in by novelty (Halperin, 1996). Focused attention appears to be fully developed by age 7, while sustained attention continues to develop throughout adolescence (Halperin, 1996). The development of academic skills involves all of these dimensions, as well as representation abilities developed during play.

Social cognition involves attention to and understanding of social cues and understanding the consequences of different social actions and perspectives, and is, therefore, important to cognitive problem solving in the social arena. This area is directly related to the subcategory of social relations in the emotional and social domain, but addresses the *cognitive* aspects of how the child thinks about interactions and the thoughts of others.

Complexity of play examines how the child incorporates thinking skills such as originality, fluency, and flexibility into different types and levels of play activities. This subcategory looks at the child's ability to integrate cognitive, sensorimotor, communication, and social interactions into increasingly complicated play transactions. Understanding of procedural knowledge (how the world works) derives from experimentation in all types of play and interactions in the environment.

Conceptual knowledge (what something means) is derived from all of the above skills and leads to a framework of understanding of all of the various components that make up the world. Conceptual and procedural knowledge both develop in relation to understanding of mental states and human actions, comprehending physical concepts and technical procedures, conceptualizing biological processes, and learning numeracy and literacy concepts and processes. In order to develop this range of understanding, the young child builds on the foundation established through the development of the previously described cognitive processes. Each day of the early years sees knowledge become increasingly more complex and sophisticated.

The last subcategory, emerging literacy, integrates conceptual and procedural knowledge and includes the evolution of both reading and writing. Although emerging literacy could be included with conceptual development, it has been highlighted as a separate subcategory in order to address the importance of literacy for success in school. Assessment of emerging literacy skills is needed to ensure that professionals address literacy in a developmentally appropriate way for each child (see Chapter 8).

In the following sections, discussion of each of the subcategories is presented, with first the research and developmental information related to the subcategory, then observational strategies, followed by an example of observation of the subcategory in TPBA2. The questions, or guidelines, that provide direction for observation are found in the TPBA2 Observation Summary Form for the cognitive domain on p. 397 at the end of this chapter. Use of the Summary Form is described in Chapter 3 of the *Administration Guide* and in the directions with the form. The TPBA2 Age Table for when processes and skills develop across all cognitive domain subcategories is presented on pp. 383 at the end of this chapter. The TPBA2 Observation Guidelines for emerging literacy can be found on p. 378 and the conceptual development Age Table on p. 391.

I. Attention

Attention is critical to optimal development in all developmental domains. In order to learn, the child must attend to the most salient factors and features in the environment. Several aspects of attention are significant for learning. Selecting, focusing, sustaining concentration, switching attention, sharing attention, dividing attention, ignoring distractions, and modulating the intensity of attention are all important. Attention is necessary to build memory processes such as rehearsal, retrieval, and coding. Both attention, addressed in this section, and memory, discussed in the next section, are significant contributors to cognitive, social, language, and motor development and should be examined together.

I. A. How well can the child select, focus on, and maintain attention to a task?

In the subcategory of attention, the child's ability to *select* what he or she wants to attend to, to *focus* or concentrate attention on a specific object, and to *sustain* or prolong concentration on a specific task are the first elements of attention. Very early in infancy, the ability to *orient* to important sensory input develops. For the first 4 months of life, the infant is drawn to objects with greater light and dark contrast, those with a moderate number of edges, and those that move (Taylor, 1980). After this age, novelty becomes important and infants habituate, or lose interest, when the same stimuli are presented repeatedly (Bahrick, Hernandez-Reif, & Pickens, 1997). The ability to *select* the focus of attention is assisted as the child is able to respond as the caregiver directs attention to objects or events of interest (Moore, 1999; Posner, Rothbart, Thomas-Thrapp, & Gerardi, 1998). The parent will look at and point to an object of interest, a key aspect of a situation, or an action to be attended to, thus helping the child select aspects to which he or she should direct attention. This ability to share attention, which develops by 9–12 months of age, is critical to social, language, and cognitive development. Children with Down syndrome, autism spectrum disorders, or other disabilities may have difficulty with certain types of attention, particularly sharing joint attention with an adult (Conrood & Stone, 2004; Paparella & Kasari, 2004). Because joint attention is particularly salient to learning language and social skills, deficits in joint attention can have a profound impact.

The ability to *sustain* attention includes the ability to respond quickly and maintain focus on a desired object, action, or interaction. This requires prolonging interest in the object or event, which may require effort on the part of the child. Effortful control of attention begins to emerge toward the end of the first year (Ruff & Rothbart, 1996). Although attention varies by factors other than age, including interest and preference for a task, most 2-year-olds can sustain attention to a task (excluding television) for 3–5 minutes, 3-year-olds for 5–10 minutes, 4-year-olds for 10–12 minutes, and 5-year-olds for 15 minutes (Landy, 2002; Squires, Bricker, & Twombly, 2002).

I. B. How well can the child inhibit external stimuli?

The ability to *screen out* distractions and to *inhibit* reactions to external stimuli allows attention to be maintained. For example, it is important for the child in the preschool classroom to ignore noises from the hall to be able to listen to the teacher, solve a puzzle, or talk to a friend. Once the child is involved in an activity, he or she needs to inhibit his or her desire to divert attention to something else that is also appealing.

The ability to resist distractions develops slowly, until the child is able to avoid being distracted and stay on task at about the age of 4 years (Ruff & Capozzoli, 2003; Ruff & Rothbart, 1996). How interesting the competing stimuli are also plays a factor. As children become more independently goal-oriented, relying less on adults to help them stay focused, self-talk may help the child develop self-regulation of attention. Tomlin (2004) suggests that because of the slow development of attentional self-regulation, "discussion of 'short' attention span in children under 3 years of age should be undertaken with caution, if at all" (p. 32).

I. C. Can the child shift attention from one aspect of a stimulus or problem to another?

While attending to an activity or problem, the child not only has to maintain focus and ignore competing interests but also be able to attend to all of the relevant aspects of a situation. The ability to flexibly *shift* attention from one aspect of a problem to another is crucial for problem solving. Purposeful and perceptive attentional shifts are helpful, because rigid focus on one aspect of an activity may prevent the child from seeing connections and relationships that may help solve a problem or move to a next sequence of actions. For example, a child may pick up a puzzle piece and begin to try to force the piece into the first space he or she sees. In order to position the puzzle piece correctly in the appropriate space, the child needs to be able to shift attention to the color, shape, size, or features of the piece in order to solve the problem. In order to do this, the child attends and *retains* information in the memory long enough to represent and manipulate or perform mental operations in the mind (Mirsky, 1996).

Ability to shift attention from an object to an adult is also critical. As adults communicate with a child about an object or activity, the child often looks at the object, then up to the adult, then back to the object of focus. This ability to shift attention assists the child in learning language and concepts. Children with Down syndrome have difficulty with this attentional shift, as they may shift their attention to the adult and then not shift back to the toy (Harris, Kasari, & Sigman, 1996). This lack of attentional shift results in less manipulation of toys. Deaf mothers of deaf children have been found to help their children learn language by letting them focus on the object of play and waiting for them to shift their attention to the adult before a sign is made to comment on what was seen or done (Prendergast & McCollum, 1996). This wait time allows children to sequentially order their attention and thus more effectively use each attentional focus.

Different degrees of *effort* are also required for various tasks, with attention to some tasks being almost automatic, whereas other tasks require effortful attention (Ruff & Capozzoli, 2003). An infant may automatically attend to the bottle when she sees it, but she may need to "work" at looking at pictures for several seconds. The amount of effort required to attend involves both need, interest, and degree of challenge. The 4-year-old who needs to use the toilet may be able to focus on nothing else, whereas the 4-year-old being asked to write his name may find attention to this task difficult because of lack of interest and the degree of effort required.

Attention is also related to memory and comprehension. For example, when a child is looking for a dress to put on a doll, she needs to attend to (and remember) the various places she has seen in the room and then make a decision about which is the best place to look. Inability to remember or understand where the dress may be located may reduce efforts to attend.

Problems with these specific aspects of attention may be associated with various learning deficits or developmental disorders. A selective attention deficit would be seen in a child who is highly distractible and cannot choose the most salient features on which to focus. Selective attention problems are often seen in children with reading disabilities (Dykman, Ackerman, & Oglesby, 1979; Fletcher et al., 1994; Shaywitz et al., 1991; Torgesen, 1996). These children have difficulty determining what aspects of the reading process deserve their attention: the whole word, the letter sequence, or the individual letters. A sustained attention deficit, however, would be seen in a child who initially selects an appropriate focus for attention but then cannot sustain the necessary *level* of attention. Children with attention-deficit/hyperactivity disorder (ADHD) demonstrate problems with sustained attention (Seidel & Joschko, 1990; Van der Meere, van Baal, & Sargent, 1989). Attentional dysfunction has also been associated with children diagnosed with various types of neurological dysfunctions such as seizure disorders, various genetically linked disorders (such as fragile X syndrome), schizophrenia, extreme shyness and aggressiveness, and environmentally caused disabilities such as fetal alcohol syndrome (Dykens, Hodapp, & Finucane, 2000; Hodapp, DesJardin, & Ricci, 2003; Mirsky, 1996; Mirsky et al., 1995; Streissguth et al., 1994).

▬▬▬ USING THE OBSERVATION GUIDELINES TO ASSESS ATTENTION

In addition to providing information on attentional processes, attentional preferences can provide insight into what motivates the child. Observing the child for 1–1½ hours gives team members an opportunity to watch for fluctuations in attention span across stimuli, in different types of play, or during different parts of the session.

Following the child's attentional lead is a key facilitation strategy in TPBA. Careful attention should be paid to how the child attends at various times during the play session. While observing the play session and viewing the videotape after the session, team members can document the amount of time the child spends engaged in the various categories of play. Does the child spend more time in simple exploration or in one of the other categories of play? The team should especially notice the play activities that captivate the child for the longest periods of time because these are likely to be the ones that are most interesting, motivating, pleasurable, or an area of particular strength.

It is important to recognize that the attentional issues addressed in the cognitive domain overlap assessment targets in other domains. For example, the subcategories of emotional regulation, behavioral regulation, sense of self, and social relations in the emotional and social domain and the receptive and expressive subcategories in the communication and language domain are related to attention, memory, and problem solving. Motor skills are also essential to be able to demonstrate output associated with attention to tasks. The team should examine the interrelationships among these domains to identify potential patterns related to problems in thinking and problem solving. Children with problems with attention, memory, and executive function often demonstrate behavioral or emotional issues as well.

Observers need to keep in mind that issues related to attention and distractibility need to be interpreted carefully, so as not to overidentify attentional disorders in young children. Many young children appear to have a short attention span. It is important to discuss with parents their expectations, because their desires may not always match the reality of a young child's development. Discuss attentional issues with family members with regard to frequency, situational variables, and motivation to compare to the team's observations.

▬▬▬ I. A. How well can the child select, focus on, and maintain attention to a task?

The child's ability to sustain attention influences problem solving, especially when challenging tasks are encountered. For this reason, the team should examine how long the child can attend to difficult tasks. On the other hand, it should also be noted which types of activities engage the child for the least amount of time. Activities that hold the child's attention minimally may be uninteresting, unpleasant, or difficult.

The team should also be aware of whether the child is particularly attentive to certain characteristics of play objects or situations. Some children select objects that have strong visual features, such as bright colors, tiny pieces, or similar parts (e.g., wheels). Others attend for longer periods of time to objects that make noise or objects that have distinct tactile characteristics. All of this information may provide clues about the child's interests, strengths, and needs. Also of importance is the sequence of the child's attention. What the child chooses to do first or second and at various times during the session (beginning, middle, or end) may reveal interests that affect attention. The team also has an opportunity to observe the child interacting with the facilitator, family members, and a peer. The child's attention span may vary with different people, providing clues to social preferences.

With infants, the team can observe their ability to focus on people and objects, to anticipate actions, and to try to accomplish a goal. For example, the child may show interest and direct attention to a musical toy. Does the child try to make the adult activate the toy or does the child try to activate it independently?

▬▬▬ I. B. How well can the child inhibit external stimuli?

During the play session, the team observes the child's ability to sustain attention to an object or person without being easily distracted. The environment in a home or community setting may be particularly noisy or chaotic, particularly if other children are present. The team watches to see how the child handles distractions. He or she may be drawn away from play temporarily by sights or sounds but may be able to return quickly to the focus of play. However, some children are so distracted by other activities, sounds, smells, or visual distractions that they lose their focus and are lured from one stimulus to another. When this happens, the team observes how much support or encouragement the child needs to maintain attention. Can the child ignore distractions or redirect attention without adult assistance? Does auditory or visual redirection or physical assistance help the child sustain attention? Children with attention deficit disorder may demonstrate an inability to attend even to things in which they seem interested. They may not appear to have goals and may need extensive verbal or physical assistance to keep interested and thus focused on a particular activity. Examination of the parameters around attention and distractibility can help the team make useful intervention recommendations.

▨▨▨▨ I. C. Can the child shift attention from one
aspect of a stimulus or problem to another?

As the child plays, the team can observe the child's ability to solve problems by examining the situation and the characteristics of the problem. Some children with autism spectrum disorders or attentional problems may focus rigidly on one aspect of a problem and not look for alternative solutions. They may persist in repeating actions even though these actions are not successful. They appear unable to shift their focus from one aspect of a situation to another and to analyze the relationships between various aspects of the situation. Although they appear focused on the toy or situation, they are not able to demonstrate flexibility of attention within the activity.

Children with autism spectrum disorders, Down syndrome, deafness, and other disabilities may require prolonged wait time for appropriate shifts in attention, because they may require more time to process information (Paparella & Kasari, 2004). Use of sequential attention in play and communication (e.g., allowing the child to play and then visually shifting attention to the adult) may also allow the child to make more meaningful use of the adult's comments. The team can document whether and what type of cues (e.g., verbal, physical modeling, gestures) are beneficial and how much wait time is needed for the child to be able to successfully shift attention to pertinent aspects of play and interaction.

Eli is a 4-year-old child referred by his teacher for evaluation for behavior problems and hyperactivity in the preschool classroom. His teacher reports that Eli has difficulty attending and "flits" from one activity to another in the classroom. He is easily distracted and often gets in trouble with other children because he takes their toys. His parents state that Eli attends to his videos at home for long periods of time, but he does not like to play with puzzles, trucks, or books.

During TPBA, Eli was observed to enter the room and immediately run to the Marbleworks toy. He dropped a marble down the chute, watched it, looked up, spotted the kitchen area, and ran to it. He turned the faucet on and off and then saw the telephone, picked it up, and put it to his ear. He looked around, saw the puzzles on the table, dropped the phone, and went to the puzzles. After placing one piece he glanced around, saw his mother, and went to her. Without adult support, Eli continued to move from toy to toy, usually when he looked up and was visually distracted by a new object. His parents reported that this was typical for Eli. When the psychologist joined the play with Eli, she used pointing, exaggerated expressions of enthusiasm, and demonstration to help keep Eli on task. With visual redirection and verbal and gestural cues, Eli was able to complete a puzzle, look through a book, and play house. Eli was able to select a focus of attention but was unable to sustain attention without adult support. Eli also was unable to demonstrate divided attention. When his parents talked to him, he would look up and lose his concentration on the task at hand.

Eli demonstrated characteristics consistent with an attention deficit disorder. His lack of ability to sustain focus of attention was influencing his learning, and he showed cognitive delays as well as lack of attention. Eli focused longer on toys and materials that involved cause-and-effect, because they held his visual attention. Although he was easily distracted both visually and auditorily, these same modalities could also be used to keep him on task. His behavior problems seemed to stem largely from his visual distractibility, because he would head directly for any toy that caught his attention regardless of who else was playing with it. The team needed to help his family and teachers generate ways to increase Eli's concentration and problem-solving skills.

II. Memory ▬▬▬▬▬▬▬▬▬▬▬▬▬▬▬▬▬▬▬▬▬▬▬▬▬▬▬▬▬▬▬▬▬▬▬▬▬▬▬

Memory is a complex and controversial construct. Memory has been described in many ways, and although it seems a simple concept, it can quickly become confusing. For instance, multiple systems of memory have been described. *Declarative* or *explicit memory* involves recognition or recall of specific information, such as names of things, places, dates, and events. Declarative memory can be of two types, episodic and semantic. *Episodic memory* refers to the conscious recollection of personally experienced events, whereas *semantic memory* is the knowledge of language, rules, and concepts and comprises the vast, intricately organized knowledge system (Haith & Benson, 1998; Peterson & Rideout, 1998; Roediger & McDermott, 1993; Schneider, 2002). *Nondeclarative, procedural,* or *implicit memory* relates to nonconscious abilities such as the reproduction of habits and skills learned through experience (Bauer, 2002; Nelson & Collins, 1997; Zola-Morgan & Squire, 1993). *Visuospatial memory* involves two different types of information, including visualizing and remembering content, and spatially locating and remembering position (Schneider, 2002; Schumann-Hengsteler, 1996). *Working memory* is a term used to explain bringing information into the mind and operating on the information (Gaithercole, 1998; Pennington, 1997). Whether information to be remembered is of a general nature or is related to specific domains of knowledge, in which the person has prior knowledge of associated content, also influences the person's ability to remember (Hasselhorn, 1995; Schneider & Bjorkland, 1998). Memories can be expressed verbally or nonverbally. They can be retained for a short time (just a few seconds, hours, or days) or long term (weeks, months, or years) (Bauer, 2002; Bauer, Wenner, Dropik, & Wewerka, 2000; Carver & Bauer, 2000; Carver, Bauer, & Nelson, 2000). Memories can be recalled in great detail or in a vague "gist" (Reyna & Brainerd, 1995).

Memory is involved in every aspect of behavior and development; however, as can be seen from the previous brief description of the various elements of memory, it is not a simple construct. Even more complex and controversial are the theories of *how* memories are processed.

Information processing theory is built on the idea that the brain takes in information through the sensory system, *encodes* sensory information in the brain, stores and processes the information in the short-term, or working memory, and then stores knowledge in the long-term, or permanent memory for later retrieval and processing. The working memory is the conscious part of the mental system, where we actively work on a limited amount of information. At least two aspects of working memory are hypothesized to exist: one specialized for storage of speech-based information and one for storage of visual information (Torgesen, 1996). Another part of the working memory, the *central executive,* is conceptualized by Pennington (1997) as allocating attention to cognitive tasks: selecting, applying, and monitoring the effectiveness of the strategies used.

Long-term memory, on the other hand, is a complex system that contains our permanent knowledge base of different types of memories, including 1) semantic memory; 2) episodic memory, 3) procedural memory, and 4) memories for habits (Torgesen, 1996). Neural networks allow the child to take in information, relate ideas, formulate principles and classification systems, and generate new approaches to problems (Halford, 2002). (See Conceptual Knowledge, below.) Information is retrieved from the long-term memory as needed through recognition, recall, and reconstruction (i.e., reinterpreting complex information in terms of personal knowledge). The child then responds with some form of thought or action. In TPBA, the observers are looking for indications of the types of short- and long-term memory the child exhibits.

▮▮▮▮ II. A. What short- or long-term memory skills are evidenced
through the child's spontaneous actions and communications?

Several memory skills are integrated as the child simultaneously develops memory and problem-solving skills. Memory for sensory experiences such as touch, smell, and movement; memory for visual sights; memory for actions and events; memory for sequences and strategies; and memory for conceptual information are all critical to the development of cognitive skills. Within the first days and months of life, infants demonstrate behaviors that indicate the presence of memory for actions, sequences, and concepts. This has been studied using a research design that uses the infant's habituation to an event, during which infants are repeatedly exposed to a specific stimulus; after the infant's looking is greatly reduced, or habituated, the "familiar" and a novel stimulus are introduced. Differential attention to the novel stimulus is interpreted as evidence of recognitory memory (Bahrick & Pickens, 1995). The speed of habituation and "recovery" has been correlated with later IQ, possibly because attention, memory, response to novelty, and quick thinking are associated with intelligence (Sigman, Cohen, & Beckwith, 1997).

A second infant memory research paradigm involves attaching a ribbon from an infant's leg to a mobile. After accidentally kicking and activating the mobile numerous times, the infant learns the contingent response to kicking. Memory is tested through reattaching the ribbon some days later to see whether the child remembers and kicks to activate the mobile (Rovee-Collier & Gerhardstein, 1997).

These types of studies have revealed that newborns exhibit memory. Newborns recognize and prefer the smell of their own mother's amniotic fluid and breast milk, indicating the presence of an olfactory memory (Marleir, Schall, & Soussignan, 1998; Porter & Winberg, 1999). They even prefer a story passage read by the mother 2 weeks before delivery to a new story passage read after delivery, demonstrating auditory memory (DeCasper & Spence, 1986).

Newborns take 3–4 minutes to habituate to new stimuli, but by 4–5 months they require as little as 5–10 seconds. The exception to the increasing speed of recovery is seen in 2-month-olds who actually take longer to recover than newborns. It is hypothesized that dramatic visual perceptual changes at 2 months may temporarily promote longer looking on the part of infants (Slater, Brown, & Mattock, 1996). Two- to 3-month-olds remembered how to activate the mobile by kicking 1 week after training (Rovee-Collier, 1999). By the middle of the first year, infants can learn to press a button, lever, or switch to activate a toy and remember this for weeks after training. Memory within the first 6 months is highly context dependent, however. Babies need the same exact toys and situations to trigger the memory. After 12 months, when babies begin to move and explore different contexts, this dependency wanes (Hayne, Boniface, & Barr, 2000).

The ability to hold a mental representation of an object, action, or event in the mind is fundamental to learning. Mental representation ability is demonstrated in infants in several ways: 1) through deferred imitation, or ability to perform an action when the adult is no longer demonstrating the behavior; 2) through anticipation of events and reenacting behaviors previously experienced; and 3) through object permanence, or understanding that something continues to exist when it is no longer visible.

Deferred imitation skills also reveal something about the infant's memory, or ability to *recall* actions. Deferred imitation is important for expanding the infant's independent repertoire of actions on objects. Although imitation of adult facial expressions and head movements is first done at the same time as the adult, delayed imitation is seen in very young infants, revealing an ability to retain and process visual movement information (Butterworth, 1999). Studies have shown that deferred imitation of facial expressions is seen in 6-week-old infants (Melzoff, 2002) and by 6 months infants can recall and imitate the actions adults had demonstrated to activate a variety of toys (Collie & Hayne, 1999). Deferred imitation over a longer time frame (i.e., from 1 to 7 days) has also been shown in infants from 9 to 14 months (Hudson & Sheffield, 1998). The development of memory for action sequences, or ordered recall, appears to develop from 9 months of age, when infants can recall and reproduce two-step action sequences. The ability to remember and reproduce multistep action sequences increases during the second year (Bauer, 2002: Bauer et al., 2000). Between 12 and 18 months, babies will imitate not only adults but also other children and will retain imitative behaviors for several months (Hayne, Boniface, & Barr, 2000). Eighteen- to 20-month-olds can remember action sequences over delays of 2–8 weeks (Boyer, Barran, & Farrar, 1994).

Memory for actions or procedures, when combined with memory for the consequences of actions, leads children into goal-directed behaviors. Between 1 and 4 months, babies begin to anticipate actions based on a memory for previous occurrences. By 7–8 months infants are demonstrating clear goal-directed behaviors, and by 10–12 months infants will remember a strategy that was successful on one object and apply it to another (Chen, Sanchez, & Campbell, 1997; Willats, 1999). Between 18 months and 2 years, the child is able to mentally solve a problem *without* having to physically experiment, showing that he or she can remember strategies from various problems and apply them in new situations. By 2 years of age, the combination of mental representation demonstrated in deferred imitation of action sequences and the ability to remember and apply those sequences to new situations leads children into more sophisticated forms of play and problem solving in which children can imagine events they have not seen (Rast & Meltzoff, 1995).

Memory for concepts develops concurrently with memory for procedures as infants begin to store and compare information about the characteristics of things in their world. Between 1 and 4 months of age, infants *recognize* objects that are familiar based on motion or spatial orientation, and they can differentiate people from objects (Gelman & Opfer, 2002). They are beginning to obtain *object permanence,* or the knowledge that objects continue to exist when not in sight. By 4–8 months, babies are exploring objects using all of their senses and are recognizing objects and people based on shape, color, texture, and other sensory characteristics (Howe, 2000). As sensory, spatial, conceptual, and action memories develop in conjunction with increasing motor, verbal, and social skills, new abilities emerge. For example, children can remember where toys were left and go find them, they can categorize objects by function and behavior, and they also can remember and anticipate different social interactions with various caregivers.

Memory involves bringing previously experienced events or thoughts into the present. As early as 1½–2 years of age, children begin to talk about the past. They begin to act out previously seen or experienced events. Stories and dramatic sequences become more detailed and elaborate with age, demonstrating increased memory (Bauer, 1996). At first the imitated scheme sequences are short, increasing in length as the child's memory and representational abilities increase. The child of 4 and 5 years of age also can create new sequences and scripts made up of "pieces" of actions that were seen in different times and different places. The child now has a storehouse of memories of actions, roles, scenarios, and relationships from which to draw which can be structured creatively to help interpret experiences and achieve goals (Hudson, Sosa, & Shapiro, 1997). Cognitively, the child's imitative abilities are now limited only by his or her previous experiential base and capacity to draw on those experiences to formulate new ideas for play.

Preschoolers know that mental activity occurs, but they cannot talk about the processes or strategies they are using. A 3-year-old can accurately detail sequences of experiences verbally. By the age of 3 years, many children can verbally recall events that occurred up to 18 months in the past (Fivush, 1997; Rovee-Collier, 1999). What remains unclear is why by adulthood most people have no memory for what occurred prior to the age of 3. This phenomenon, known as infant amnesia, may to be related to the development of the frontal lobes of the cortex and other structures after the age of 3 (Diamond, Towle, & Boyer, 1994). After the age of 3, children expand their representational and dramatic play skills and can formulate scripts based on remembered routines and events in their lives. This ability may enhance the child's ability to remember and hold autobiographical events in his mind thereafter.

THE BRAIN AND MEMORY

Myelinization of the corpus callosum, a large bundle of fibers that connects the two hemispheres so they can communicate directly, does not begin until the end of the first year and undergoes major growth between 3 and 6 years of age (Giedd et al., 1999; Thompson et al., 2000). During this time many changes take place in the brain that support memory and problem solving. By 18 months most memory structures are in place (Liston & Kagan, 2002; Spencer, 2001). Between 2 and 3 years, children begin to use songs and finger plays, visual landmarks, and fingers to count, which appears to provide temporal or logical structure to aid memory (Gauvain, 2001; Spencer, 2001). Continued myelinization increases the communication between the hemispheres of the brain, integrating several aspects of thinking, including perception, attention, memory, language, and problem solving (Thompson et al., 2000).

▩▩▩▩ II. B. How long does it take for the child to process and recall concepts, action sequences, or events?

Processing time can vary depending on age, type of memory, and familiarity of subject matter. Memory for various types of material is dependent on brain maturation. Although research addresses how long various types of information are retained (Halperin, 1996), little research exists on the time it takes for children to process and express what they remember. Research suggests that speed of recall may reflect the efficiency of mental processes (Rypma & D'Esposito, 2000). The issue of processing time is particularly relevant for children with disabilities. For them, it may take longer to access information and respond.

▩▩▩▩ USING THE OBSERVATION GUIDELINES TO ASSESS MEMORY

Measurement of all the various aspects of memory described earlier cannot be done in a simple test. Certainly, TPBA2 is not a neurological evaluation and not all of these developmental aspects will be seen in TPBA, but many can be elicited and noted. In TPBA2, aspects of memory are addressed that can be observed in functional play interactions. Specifically, TPBA2 Observation Guidelines address 1) memory for concepts (related to concrete stimuli, pictures, or symbols) through both recognition and recall; 2) ability to imitate or recall concepts after short- or long-term time delays; 3) ability to remember procedures associated with routines or skills; 4) ability to reconstruct complex pictures, events, or stories in either general or detailed format; and 5) the time it takes for the child to remember concepts and actions. Additional aspects of memory are discussed in relation to other cognitive subcategories (e.g., problem solving and social cognition).

■■■■■■ II. A. What short- or long-term memory skills are evidenced
through the child's spontaneous actions and communications?

During TPBA, whether conducted in the home, community, school, or clinic setting, memory skills can be observed in the child's natural play interactions and through elicited play activities. When assessing infants, the team is looking at the child's ability to remember concepts through recognition (pointing, vocalizing, moving) or through recall using words or signs. Before 6 months of age it is important to use familiar materials, because the young infant's memory is very situation specific.

In addition, the team is watching to see what actions and routines the child generates spontaneously, indicating a long-term memory for how to produce these actions and procedural sequences. If the child is unable to produce specific actions, is the child able to imitate the actions or sequences, indicating processing in working memory?

Team members also observe the context in which the child's imitations take place. Developmentally, many infants will not imitate actions out of the context of the original action. However, some children with disabilities will imitate gestures, vocalizations, or sounds but not in the contexts for which they were intended. For example, the child may repeat words or phrases heard previously, but the context in which he or she uses them is inappropriate.

Observation of imitation of action sequences also is important. As the team observes the play, the family members can comment on the sequences they have seen at home and those that appear to be new. If new action sequences are observed, the play facilitator can test memory by returning to the activity after several minutes to see whether the child spontaneously demonstrates (or remembers) the demonstrated sequence. This is particularly important for children who are just beginning to combine actions. Children who are engaging in dramatic play often recreate familiar routines from home.

The team needs to determine whether the scenarios being enacted are those from memory or are new sequences composed of remembered actions coordinated in new and original ways. For instance, 3-year-old Brandy was observed to engage primarily in sensory play. However, one extended play sequence involved pouring "coffee," serving it, blowing on it, stirring it, and pretending to drink it. Discussion with her mother revealed that this was an activity they played together at home every day. It had, in fact, become a daily ritual. This demonstrated Brandy's ability to remember a practiced procedure that had become routine, but it was not representative of her memory skills for declarative information.

A variety of higher level memory skills can be elicited from the child who demonstrates many concepts and action sequences and is able to communicate verbally. As the play proceeds, the facilitator can help relate what the child is doing now to past experiences. For example, when a child makes a block construction, the facilitator might ask about what the child likes to build at home, where the child might have seen such a building, what the child knows about what happens in such a structure, and so on. This will enable the team to observe the child's recall of personal memories. Having the child develop a story, tell a story with action figures, or create a storyline in dramatic play provides another opportunity to observe memory. In addition, books or photo albums can be used to elicit discussions related to the child's past, present, or future activities.

The team should attempt to determine whether the child's ability to share verbal memories and information is at the same level as the child's ability to relate knowledge and experiences through physical representations. Some children with language disorders may demonstrate conceptual and procedural knowledge through their actions more than their words. Their memory, as demonstrated through actions, may thus give important clues to their cognitive level of ability.

Unusual memory abilities may be seen in some children. Children may demonstrate a memory for unusual details or content. For example, a 5-year-old with autism was able to recite all of his family's license plate numbers, phone numbers, addresses, shoe sizes, and anything relating to numbers. Another child related unusual details of his vacation, telling the facilitator about the hole in the fabric of the airplane seat and the hair style of the person sitting in front of him. Such memory for detail or specific information may point to an unusual ability or strength that may be channeled productively.

In addition, the team should observe for processes that appear to support the child's memory. The play facilitator can determine how much scaffolding (e.g., questioning, use of props) the child needs to prompt the recall of information. The type of sensory input, structure, demonstration, and feedback that assist the child can be documented for inclusion in intervention plans.

II. B. How long does it take for the child to process and recall concepts, action sequences, or events?

The length of time it takes to process information is important. As the facilitator is eliciting the types of information noted above, the team should observe the child's response time. The facilitator also needs to provide sufficient wait time for the child to think about and generate a response or action.

The child's ability to imitate is relevant to note, because this reflects processing of short-term memory. Some children may demonstrate a delayed response but they are still able to replicate the facilitator's actions. Several seconds, or even minutes, after the facilitator has demonstrated an action, the child may repeat the behavior. This delayed response may indicate that the child has difficulty processing the information. The team should note whether the stimuli presented are auditory, visual, kinesthetic, tactile or a combination of these, in order to better understand the type of processing problem the child is experiencing. It should be noted that repetition of actions or concepts later in the play session is not always an indicator of processing problems. In fact, delayed imitation can be an indicator of short- or long-term memory as well. The child who is able to imitate and recreate the concepts or actions later may be practicing this new skill. The difference is seen in the timing and the context of the imitation.

Another type of delayed imitation, deferred imitation, is not problematic. As described above, deferred imitation, or the ability to imitate behaviors and roles seen previously, is an important skill for the toddler and preschooler. Observation of deferred imitation will give the team insight into the experiential background of the child. Look for the types of actions the child performs and ask a caregiver if he or she has demonstrated the actions for the child previously. For example, in one play session, the 2-year-old being assessed was observed to pick up a toy hammer and pound it on the table. His mother indicated that his dad was a carpenter and he liked to "pound like his dad." In this instance, the child was exhibiting delayed imitation. If he had never seen a hammer or similar toy used before and performed this action, it might be interpreted as sensory exploration rather than deferred imitation. In deferred imitation, the child can reproduce experiences from memory at will. This differs from delayed imitation due to slowness of processing, in which the child cannot imitate immediately and needs time to organize. Discussion with caregivers can help to sort out what is an imitative behavior.

Seven-month-old Julio was referred for possible overall developmental delays. He was not yet turning over and was making no vocalizations. He was observed in his home with his mother, Wanda, and his brother, Juan. Sandy, the play facilitator, sat down on the couch next to Wanda, who was holding Julio. Julio looked at Sandy and then glanced up at his mother, and then he looked back at Sandy and stared at her. When Wanda put him down on a blanket on the floor, he quietly looked back and forth between them. When he heard Juan call from the kitchen, he smiled. Sandy commented that Julio seemed to recognize his brother's voice. Wanda laughed and said that Juan and his grandfather were Julio's favorite people. "He gets all wiggly when he hears the car honk. His abuelo always honks when he pulls in the driveway, and Julio know it's his abuelo." Sandy picked up the toy that his mother said he liked the best and gave it to Julio. He took the toy and began to mouth it. When Sandy held up an unfamiliar toy from her bag, Julio looked from one toy to the other for several seconds and then reached for the new toy.

This interaction with Julio and Wanda showed that Julio was able to differentiate between his mother and a stranger (visual recognition). He clearly recognized his brother's voice (auditory memory). He demonstrated memory for a sound followed by his grandfather's entrance (procedural memory). He showed memory for an action (nondeclarative memory or deferred imitation). He selected the novel toy over the familiar toy (preference for novelty). These memory skills show that even though Julio has a delay, he is able to recognize familiar people and objects, make contingent responses, and make choices. From these skills the family can begin to build more contingent responses and imitation skills.

III. Problem Solving

As mentioned previously, theoretical models are now incorporating problem solving into a larger construct of executive function (see p. 314) (Borkowski & Burke, 1996; Denkla, 1996; Lyon, 1996; Morris, 1996; Zelazo & Muller, 2002). Problem solving involves identifying the problem and representing it mentally in some manner, planning what needs to be done, executing a solution, evaluating the result, and making modifications if necessary (Zelazo & Muller, 2002). Problem solving integrates both conceptual knowledge (see below) and procedural knowledge. The young infant takes in information from the vestibular, proprioceptive, vision, hearing, tactile, taste, and olfactory sensory systems. The brain then organizes this information into perceptual and conceptual systems for understanding objects, people, events, relationships, and abstractions. Depending on how a problem is perceived and interpreted, the child's goals, individual processing strategies, and physical ability to implement the strategy, outcomes will vary. Attention, memory, and mental processes change as the child matures, and the problems he or she needs to solve and the strategies employed are different at various developmental levels.

Within the subcategory of problem solving, TPBA2 looks at the child's 1) ability to anticipate actions (which also reflects early memory skills); 2) understanding of causal relations (which also demonstrates a memory for previous consequences); 3) ability to organize sequences of actions (which also demonstrates memory and mental organization of thoughts and actions); 4) speed of response (which examines the time it takes for the child to remember and process information); 5) ability to observe and note success or failure in tasks (which addresses anticipation and monitoring of results of actions based on mental representations); 6) ability to correct mistakes (which examines mental restructuring of tasks or outcomes); and 7) ability to remember and apply solutions to new problems (which examines generalization skills). Attention, memory, and problem-solving skills are all intertwined, with problems in attention and memory having a direct impact on problem-solving skills. All three subcategories need to be examined closely for interrelationships.

RESEARCH RELATED TO
SUBCATEGORY OBSERVATION GUIDELINE QUESTIONS

In the following discussion, the TPBA2 Observation Guideline questions are not divided into separate research discussions, because research on problem solving involves many of these issues simultaneously. For this reason, all of the problem-solving guidelines are presented before the discussion of research. Discussion of how to observe each of these areas, however, is broken down.

III. A. What behaviors indicate understanding of causal reasoning skills or problem solving (executive function)?

III. B. How does the child identify and plan a solution to a problem?

III. C. How well is the child able to organize, monitor, and evaluate progress toward a goal and make corrections?

III. D. How quickly can the child analyze a problem situation and respond?

III. E. How well can the child generalize information from one situation to another?

Research using habituation techniques (capitalizing on the difference in the infant's attention when a change is introduced) has shown that in the first week of life, an infant can tell that an object at a close or far distance is the same object, and that the apparent difference in the size and shape of the objects presented to them stays the same (Slater & Johnson, 1999; Slater, Mattock, & Brown, 1990). This is a perceptual problem-solving task that is important for later understanding of the objects and problems infants will encounter as they begin to gain conceptual skills. Newborns also have been shown to use a form of procedural problem solving. They will suck to get interesting events to recur, such as producing sights (pictures) and sounds (music) (Floccia, Christophe, & Bertoncini, 1997).

By 2–4 months of age, infants are using motion and spatial arrangements to identify objects (Jusczyk, Johnson, Spelke, & Kennedy, 1999) and they are kicking, reaching, and grasping. This increase in their own ability to move, to explore objects, and to imitate leads to later problem solving. At this age, mouthing is the primary way of exploring objects. The infant of this age begins to associate people and objects with actions and to anticipate certain events (e.g., appearance of mother with a bottle means "I'm going to get fed!").

From 4 to 6 months, increases in the ability to sit, reach, and grasp affect problem solving. Children learn how to sit, freeing their arms and hands to play with objects. At the same time, they learn how (through proprioceptive input) to adjust their arms and hands to reach and manipulate objects (Thelan, Corbetta, & Spencer, 1996; Wentworth, Benson, & Haith, 2000). They now can transfer objects from hand to hand and hold an object with one hand while exploring it with the other. We know that searching for hidden objects (object permanence) also develops at this time, because infants from 5 to 8 months old will retrieve objects from behind a transparent screen (Shinskey, Bogartz, & Poirier, 2000). Infants of this age also can differentiate objects by shape, texture, and color (Cohen & Cashon, 2001). These skills are important as infants learn how to find, manipulate, and classify objects.

Between 6 and 8 months, neurological development in the frontal cortex increases potential for critical thinking and problem solving. At this time, children's goal-directed behaviors increase. They begin to be able to move their bodies to attain what they want, look at adults to involve them in problem solving, and actively explore objects. An increasing ability to understand depth cues enables children to use spatial awareness for problem solving. Around 7 or 8 months, children begin to be able to solve simple problems, such as pulling a cloth to uncover a toy (Willats, 1999). Increasing problem solving coincides with a growth in activity in the prefrontal cortex between 8 and 12 months. Increasing neurological organization helps establish the foundations for planning and rehearsing future actions and connects with the limbic system for emotional regulation. Also during this period, the development of finger and thumb opposition, or pincer grasp, allows more refined exploration.

From 9 to 12 months, problem solving becomes increasingly evident as infants are physically able to engage with a wider variety of toys and materials. At this age, children can solve problems by analogy, learning from one situation and applying it to another (Chen et al., 1997). Crawling and refined fine motor skills enable children to discover and compare objects, their effects, and their consequences. Ability to explore objects also contributes to understanding the functions of objects.

From ages 12 to 18 months, children are learning more about what makes things work. They know about objects, their parts, their mechanisms, their relationships to other objects, and how people can have an affect on objects. Trial-and-error problem solving increases, and children can search for a solution that may not be clearly visible. Ability to perform deferred imitation, indicating representational thinking, allows practice of previously seen problem-solving approaches (Barr & Hayne, 1999; Hayne et al., 2000).

From ages 18 to 24 months, children are learning to think about their actions. Combined with increasing fine motor skills and emerging language skills, children can explore with more precision and comprehend instruction from adults, allowing them to learn how to solve a problem through verbal explanation. Now children cannot only imitate actions they have observed; they can anticipate the goals and intentions of adults and dramatize their predicted actions (Meltzoff, 1995).

From ages 2 to 4 years, children's problem solving involves taking acquired knowledge and applying it to new situations. Thus, problem solving entails reasoning from situation to situation. By age 2½, children can categorize thoughts that happen in their heads, using terms such as *think, remember,* and *pretend,* versus events that happen in the real world. They are beginning to understand that problem solving is a mental activity. After the age of 3, children expand their representational and dramatic play skills and can formulate scripts based on remembered routines and events in their lives. Children of this age also show evidence of thinking ahead or reflecting about the problem at hand. Children may use visual scanning to search for a solution, physically try all alternatives, or use verbal mediation to think through the problem. For example, many children will verbalize their problem solving: "I don't think it fits here. Does it go this way? No. Does it go that way? I think I'll put it here."

By 4 years of age, children use real-life events to predict what will happen on similar occasions or to problem solve how to act in specific situations. For example, the child in the quiet doctor's waiting room may ask his parent, "Is this like church? Do I need to be quiet?" Children form these situations into categories from which they generate rules and principles for behavior. (See Representational Skills, below.)

From age 5, children's problem-solving ability relies less on perceptual problem solving and more on building an integrated understanding of the rules that govern how things work. By 5 years of age, children also become aware of their thinking processes and strategies that they are using to solve problems. They become cognizant of what helps them to remember things, such as repeating words to themselves. Cognitive self-regulation, or the ability to control and monitor progress toward a goal and make necessary adaptations, begins to expand between 5 and 6 years of age. Concept development, promoted through the child's increasing discrimination and classification skills, expands to enable literacy and numeracy skills to emerge. (See Concept Knowledge and Emerging Literacy Development, below.)

USING THE OBSERVATION GUIDELINES
TO ASSESS PROBLEM SOLVING

Problem-solving skills are important for all children. Limitations in this area can have a profound impact on overall development. Many children with disabilities have reduced problem-solving abilities. For example, children with fine and gross motor limitations may have the ability to mentally solve problems, but because of restricted movements they may be unable to execute the solutions. Children with cognitive delays may not be able to mentally generate a solution. Attentional problems can inhibit identification of the problem, resulting in attending to the wrong aspect of a problem or prohibiting a child from persisting on problem solving. Children with emotional or behavioral problems may not be able to inhibit impulsive responses, whereas children with autism spectrum disorders may focus exclusively on certain types of problems. The use of compensatory mechanisms may be required for children with visual or auditory impairments. Professionals need to observe carefully and consider all aspects of the child's problem solving, from identification of a problem through evaluation of the solution, to determine where support is needed.

III. A. What behaviors indicate understanding of causal reasoning skills or problem solving (executive function)?

The TPBA team should have available a variety of cause-and-effect toys and fine motor tasks that are unfamiliar to the child. For young infants, rattles, noise makers, or toys that create a visual, auditory, or tactile effect (e.g., vibration) are needed. For older infants and toddlers, toys are needed with switches, buttons, ramps, knobs, and other mechanisms that require the child to figure out how to activate the devices, anticipate the results of actions, and adapt actions if first efforts are not successful. With preschoolers, it is important to make available more complex toys or situations that require children to analyze the situation and understand what caused something to happen. Toys such as cash registers, key and lock boxes, and pop-up toys with different types of door-opening devices can be incorporated into the play time. A toy with ramps, spinners, chutes, and different size parts, for example, requires the child to figure out how to arrange the pieces to get a moving part to do what he or she wants it to do. The team can then observe the child's understanding of cause-and-effect.

III. B. How does the child identify and plan a solution to a problem?

Identification of solutions is related to causal understanding and can be observed in various situations. For example, how does the child find missing materials that are needed? During the play session, team members need to observe the means the child uses to accomplish goals, and how the child who is challenged by an activity, situation, or event attempts to attain the desired end. The team may observe problem-solving skills by arranging the environment so that the child encounters new toys and materials that are highly motivating yet challenging. Almost any materials or situation can be used to create a challenging situation for the child. For example, instead of opening the bottle of bubbles for the child, the facilitator can hand the bottle to the child to see how the child attempts to open it.

   The facilitator can set up situations that will require problem solving by having toys that do not work quite right or by creating a problem situation. The facilitator, while building with the child in the block area, might ask, "What can we use for a roof for our house?" and then, "I wonder what we can do to get the roof to stay on." The facilitator also can "sabotage" activities the child anticipates will be easy to do by adding a difficult element. For example, tape may be added to the cap of bubbles, the battery may be removed from an action toy, or a puzzle piece may be intentionally omitted to see how the child reacts. When building a block structure, odd-shaped blocks will require careful strategizing and balancing. The team can then observe the child's ability to monitor his or her progress and make adjustments as the structure is built.

III. C. How well is the child able to organize, monitor, and evaluate progress toward a goal and make corrections?

Problem solving requires the ability to organize and sequence thoughts. With young children, observation of how they sequence their actions tells us much about their ability to organize thoughts to solve a problem. When the child is using one object, the team observes the sequence of actions with that object to accomplish goals. For example, if the child is trying to write with a marker, does he or she try to make marks with the top on, then discover the cap, remove it, and proceed to write, demonstrating understanding of the problem and logical sequencing to solve it? Does the child give up and reach for another marker, demonstrating lack of understanding of the problem? Does the child hand it to the adult to "fix it," demonstrating understanding that someone else knows how to solve the problem?

When the child is playing with numerous objects, the team observes how the child organizes the materials to carry out a plan. For instance, when building a garage out of blocks, ramps, and miniature cars and people, how does the child approach the problem? How does he or she organize the materials, sequence actions, and use the adult?

The team observes the child's approach to each problem encountered to determine how the child generally organizes his or her thoughts and then puts thoughts into actions. Observation should include gross motor problem solving, as the child encounters unfamiliar gross motor toys or maneuvers through an obstacle course (see IV. Motor Planning in Chapter 2); fine motor manipulation of toys that require movement of small pieces; and social problem solving in which the child wants to get others to do something.

III. D. How quickly can the child analyze a problem situation and respond?

The facilitator should give the child enough time to allow for trial-and-error approaches. Some children may try the same tactic repeatedly, whereas others will alter strategies when they are ineffective. If the child is unable to attempt any solution, the facilitator can model for the child and see whether the child can implement or expand on the idea. The team observes how long the child takes to analyze, figure out, and solve a problem and whether the child can do this independently, with a model, or with more structured support. Some children will quickly see the situation and generate a solution. Others will come up with a solution if given time to try things out on their own. Still others will need suggestions to identify the problem or solution. Occasionally, children may be observed to give up on a problem, but then they come back to it later in the session and approach it again. It seems they need more time to process the information about the situation. It is important for the play facilitator to allow enough "wait time" before suggesting or modeling, so that the team has an opportunity to see what the child's processing time is and if the child will be successful if given more time to process information.

III. E. How well can the child generalize information from one situation to another?

Naturalistic observation of problem solving with unfamiliar materials during role play or while building with blocks reveals how well the child generalizes skills used in previous situations to new situations. For example, strategies the child uses to figure out how to open the oven door in the dollhouse, or what the child does when the pan won't fit in the refrigerator, will provide information about skill generalization and problem solving.

Skill generalization also can be seen in how the child uses materials in the environment as tools to solve problems encountered. For example, the child may be able get a chair to reach a toy that is too high, demonstrating application of a solution he or she has seen before. An older child may employ more complex types of tool use, such as figuring out how to use a lever or pliers in a novel situation.

The following example combines observations of the integration of attention, memory, and problem solving for Eli, the 4-year-old child discussed previously.

Four-year-old Eli demonstrated problems with memory and problem solving, partially related to the attentional issues addressed previously. However, even when the facilitator was able to get Eli to attend, he showed limited ability to organize and plan how to deal with various situations. When putting together a puzzle, Eli would repeatedly try to jam the puzzle piece in the puzzle without attending to the orientation or features of the specific piece. He had difficulty shifting his attention from one aspect of the task to another, and instead he would repeat the same unsuccessful attempt at problem solving until the facilitator provided a clue on the puzzle, such as "Look, here's the dog's head." Eli's understanding of basic concepts such as labels for objects, people, actions, and events was somewhat delayed and he often needed a visual cue to stimulate his recognition. For example, when the facilitator said, "I need a blue crayon," Eli handed her a brown one. However, Eli knew color concepts. When he pulled the blue crayon out of the box he said, "I like blue." Eli seemed to be focusing on one aspect, crayon, *when the facilitator made her request, rather than on two dimensions,* blue *and* crayon. *His problem solving was limited by his brief attention, but also by his narrow focus on limited elements of a problem. Eli showed difficulties with recall, planning, organizing, sequencing, and monitoring his actions. Reports from his teacher indicated that these same issues and lack of cognitive understanding of social consequences were also leading to social problems in the classroom.*

IV. Social Cognition

Children learn to reason not only about physical entities, but also about psychological or mental processes. Social cognition implies an understanding of the social world and the psychological thinking behind how and why people act the way they do under various circumstances. Social cognition, which is also referred to as *theory of mind,* is the development of an understanding about what goes on in the minds of the self and other people (Flavell, 2000; Wellman, 2002). The area of social cognition in the cognitive domain overlaps with several subcategories in the emotional and social domain. The emotional and social domain in TPBA2 addresses children's expression and understanding of emotions, their ability to regulate their emotions and behavior, and their sense of self and social relationships. These areas obviously have cognitive processes involved, but focus is more on the behaviors seen as a result of emotions and the development of social skills. Social cognition in the cognitive domain is concerned with how the child *reasons* about people's desires, motivations, and intentions, and how he or she infers the thinking behind the social actions and consequences encountered.

Comprehension of the thoughts, beliefs, and intentions of other people develops in concert with cognitive skills such as imitation (Meltzoff, 2002), understanding of cause-and-effect (Gergely, 2002), seeing relationships and developing classification systems, and comprehension of concepts related to *wanting, feeling, thinking, knowing,* and *believing* (deVilliers & deVilliers, 2000). The ability to inhibit inappropriate responses, attentional flexibility, and working memory are also important to social understanding (Carlson & Moses, 2001; Welsh, Pennington, & Grossier, 1991). In addition, social modeling and verbal exchanges about what people are thinking and feeling contribute to the development of social cognition. Social cognition includes the ability to understand the thoughts and motivations behind others' actions and is essential for the development of pretend play, joint planning and negotiation, and higher level thinking, including making moral judgments.

Social cognition is a complex area steeped in theoretical controversy. For the purposes of this discussion, emphasis will be on skills identified from research supporting theories that seem to be important for the development of social cognition and that may be observed in children's play interactions. In general, summaries of research reveal that social cognition 1) develops from infancy on in a rapid progression; 2) follows the same trajectory, although with different rates, worldwide; 3) appears to require the ability to attend to and imitate others and to form mental representations of a person's actions before, during, and after an event; and 4) may require an ability to take both first- and third-person perspectives and use one's experiences to consider what others may be thinking (Gergely, 2002; Lewis & Carpendale, 2002; Meltzoff, 2002; Wellman, 2002). It is unclear at this time whether social reasoning requires separate cognitive mechanisms, using different aspects of the brain than reasoning related to physical elements, or is a subset of thinking skills related to memory, problem solving, and abstract thinking (Wellman, 2002).

▪▪▪▪▪ IV. A. What foundational skills related to social cognition does the child demonstrate?

To understand social cognition, and how a child comes to understand the thoughts and intentions of another, we must examine the early months of infancy. Imitation is now thought to be foundational for later social cognition. Even infants a few days old are able to imitate the mouth and tongue movements of an adult. These early imitative actions are thought by some researchers to indicate an innate means of incorporating the actions of another, and that these and more sophisticated imitative abilities that develop later lead to the child understanding the intentions of others (Meltzoff, 2002). Imitation of complex actions and language requires the child to watch, mentally map, incorporate the other person's behaviors, and then plan how to execute them—a combination of social and physical problem solving.

Between birth and 8 months, infants not only imitate others, they begin to *anticipate* the actions of people and objects (Legerstee, Barna, & DiAdamo, 2000; Striano, 2001). An innate preference for faces and animate objects draws the child to attend more to people and thus notice changes in expression and actions. During this time infants become able to judge whether something or someone is or is not an agent (causing something to happen) and what the goal or basic intention of the agent is (Premack, 1990). They begin to develop object permanence, or the ability to know something continues to exist when it is not visible, which is a foundation for later representational thinking. At the same time, imitation abilities increase, both motorically and vocally, and increased memory allows deferred imitation, or the ability to imitate something when the model is not present, as noted previously in the subcategory of problem solving. This requires both memory and representational thinking. As children begin to play with objects, from age 6 to 9 months, they have an opportunity to observe and interact with adults and siblings who model use of objects and materials. They develop intentional behaviors and observe how others help them achieve their desired ends. These new skills allow children to begin to see how others achieve their goals.

Between 9 and 12 months, a "social-cognitive revolution" takes place (Gergely, 2002). Around 9 months of age, an infant begins to engage in joint referencing, or following the gaze of the adult, looking at what the adult is turning to. This ability is crucial to language development, as it focuses the child on the object the adult can then label. It also seems to be essential to social cognition, because the infant infers from the adult's shift in gaze an *intention* to look at something (Carpenter, Nagel, & Tomasello, 1998; Phillips, Wellman, & Spelke, 2002; Prizant, Wetherby, & Roberts, 2000). A second developmental shift at around 9 months involves social referencing, or looking at the parent in times of ambiguity to read the emotions on the parent's face (Prizant et al., 2000). The parent's reactions seem to guide the infant's subsequent actions. This can be interpreted as the infant, at some primitive level, understanding that people can share mental states, that the adult's emotions can be used as an emotional model. Also between 9 and 12 months, the infant's own actions become goal directed. Infants act on the environment with specific intentions in mind. They begin to use pointing and gestures to direct adults' attention to their goals (Wetherby, Prizant, & Schuler, 2000). Research with infants has also shown that by 9–12 months of age, infants perceive that movements of both animate and inanimate objects can have intended *goals* implied from their movements (Csibra, Gergely, Biro, Koos, & Brockbank, 1999; Gergely, Magyar, Csibra, & Biro, 1995; Woodward, 1999). Concurrently, infants are beginning to be able to take a solution from one problem and apply it to another, thus performing analogical thinking (Chen et al., 1997). (See III. Problem Solving, p. 327.) This ability to transfer ideas from one situation to another is important for the development of understanding of the thoughts and intentions of others. These early milestones appear to set the stage for the development of psychological understanding.

IV. B. How well does the child infer the thinking and actions of others?

From 12 to 18 months, motor and language skills increase dramatically, allowing the child to explore, experiment, and observe more people and their actions and the consequences of their actions. Consequently, children become more aware of the goals of adults' actions. Symbolic gestures increase, and language development enables the child to develop vocabulary to go with actions and emotions (Prizant et al., 2000; Wetherby et al., 2000). At the same time, children are becoming aware that various actions cause feelings not only in themselves but in others. They may now use social referencing to see how the adult is responding to their actions (e.g., "Am I in trouble?"). Deferred imitation also becomes more complex, and children begin to represent their lives through simple dramatic play.

From 18 to 24 months, children's thinking becomes more internalized, and they can think about what may be the social consequence of their behaviors (e.g., "If I throw this, Daddy will be mad"). At 18 months, children also can observe adults begin a task, understand what the adult intends to do, and complete the task for them (e.g., see the adult pretend to try and fail to pull a pop-bead apart, then pull the pop-beads apart as the adult watches) (Meltzoff, 2000). Children also begin to develop the ability to look and categorize things in more than one way, thus showing increasing flexibility in thinking. They are able to search for things they have not seen being hidden or put away, demonstrating ability to have a mental image of something they have not seen. This increase in representational thinking also is reflected in more complex and creative play sequences. New vocabulary allows children to express likes and dislikes, desires, and emotions (Bretherton & Beeghly, 1982); developing pragmatic skills enable children to differentiate meaning based on context and collaboration (Abbeduto & Short-Meyerson, 2002); and increasing conceptual skills help children understand that someone else may have different feelings and desires than they do (Gergely, 2002).

From 2 to 3 years of age, expanded language skills increasingly allow the child to deal with the past, present, and future without requiring actual referents to be present. Use of concepts such as *think, pretend,* and *know* demonstrates an awareness of mental activity (Bartsch & Wellman, 1995; Wellman, Hickling, & Schult, 2000). The term *know,* however, may be used to indicate they were successful rather than demonstrating understanding about the mind (e.g., "I know how to color," meaning "I can") (Lyon & Flavell, 1994). Children at this age think actions are guided by people's desires (e.g., "Mommy wants ice cream. We go to the store") (Bartsch & Wellman, 1995). Increasing understanding of various types of concepts allows children's dramatic play to go beyond everyday representations into imaginative dramatizations of things that may not be part of their experience (e.g., monsters) or their action repertoire (e.g., acting out nursery rhyme sequences). They begin to be able to use one object to symbolize another in their play, thus moving into a higher form of symbolic representation. As play becomes more symbolic, understanding the intentions of another becomes more complex. By 2½ years of age, children begin to incorporate others into their dramatic representations, although not always successfully. In terms of social cognition, this is relevant because each child in the dramatic play situation needs to understand what the other child is representing or intending. Early efforts at cooperative play often result in conflict, because children need to be able to see each others' goals and perspectives in order to develop a cooperative plan. The arguments that arise at this age actually are helpful to the development of social cognition, and adults can help children to share ideas, negotiate, and recognize others' feelings and intentions.

From age 3 to 4, children begin to understand more about mental processes versus physical actions, seeing desires and intentions as existing prior to and separate from the actions they perform (Gergely, 2002). They are aware that thinking is something that takes place inside one's head, and that they can think about things that are not present, but they are unaware that thinking is a continuous activity (Flavell, 2000). They also are able to use expressions such as "if x, then y" and "because z." Such causal reasoning is important to psychological reasoning; for example, "If I wear this dress Daddy will like it, because blue is his favorite color."

By age 4–5 years, children can understand a variety of roles at one time, can understand others' perspectives, can compare and negotiate ideas, and can cooperatively coordinate dramatic play of complex storylines (Dockett, 1999; Goncu, 1993; Goncu, Patt, & Kouba, 2002). Thinking is becoming multidimensional, because children are able to recognize that both desires and beliefs determine behavior. Research on "false beliefs," examining whether children can see that their beliefs may lead them to false conclusions, shows that between 3 and 5 years of age children begin to discover that their beliefs may not be accurate representations of reality (Bartsch & Wellman, 1995; Gopnik & Wellman, 1994). For example, in false belief experiments children are shown something, such as a box of chocolates, and asked what is inside. Then they are shown what is really inside (not candy) and asked to predict what another child will believe is in the box. Before the age of 4, children who do not yet understand how beliefs affect knowledge will predict that the next child will know what they now know, what is actually in the box. After this age, children can begin to incorporate into their thinking the knowledge that others may have different beliefs, causing them to become more sensitive to what causes others to act the way they do and, thus, to have better social skills.

School-age children become better at understanding false beliefs and understanding how others are interpreting situations (Gopnik & Astington, 2000). They therefore become better at using reasoning to change others' beliefs (or to justify their own). By 5 years of age, a child's understanding of others' thinking allows him or her to combine ideas in complex, coordinated play, including elaborate symbolic play. Make-believe and understanding others' thoughts appear to be mutually influential, with skills in one having a positive impact on the other. Children at this age also come to understand that the beliefs and actions of one person can affect the beliefs and actions of another. As a result of gaining a better understanding of what another person expects, feels, thinks, or believes, children also can become more adept at deception and manipulation (Wellman, Cross, & Watson, 2001).

One particular line of research is specifically significant with regard to the assessment of this subcategory of cognition. Children with autism spectrum disorders have been shown in numerous research studies to lack skills in social cognition. These children frequently display delays or deficits in many of the previously mentioned skills that contribute to social cognition. For example, children with autism may not demonstrate joint referencing, social referencing, or intentional pointing; distinguish mental from physical entities; recognize their own or others' emotions; express empathy; infer others' intentions or goals; and understand motivations and beliefs. Also, they may demonstrate difficulty with representational thinking, including gestures, language, and symbolic play (Baron-Cohen, Wheelwright, Lawson, Griffin, & Hill, 2002). Baron-Cohen (1995) describes autism spectrum conditions as having, among other characteristics, varying degrees of "mindblindness." In TPBA2, the emotional reaction to others' feelings included in social relations in the emotional and social domain, and the cognitive *understanding* of what others are thinking or "theory of mind" is included in the cognitive domain.

Children with disabilities such as deafness, blindness, Down syndrome, and significant language impairment, among others, also may demonstrate difficulties with social cognition, depending on their skills in the above areas and on their abilities in other developmental domains (Farmer, 2000; Garfield, Petersen, & Perry, 2001). Assessment of social cognition is an important aspect of the assessment of young children. Deficits in this area can have implications for diagnosis, as well as implications for early intervention, in order to prevent compounded deficits at a later age.

▓▓▓▓ USING THE OBSERVATION GUIDELINES TO ASSESS SOCIAL COGNITION

▓▓▓▓ IV. A. What foundational skills related
to social cognition does the child demonstrate?

IV. B. How well does the child infer the thinking and actions of others?

The TPBA team can analyze the child's social cognition at the same time they are observing other areas of cognitive and emotional and social development. For example, the first question in the Observation Guidelines relates to important foundational abilities that are observed in social interactions of children older than 1 year of age, such as noticing what an adult is looking at, referencing the adult for emotional clues as to how the child should respond, using symbolic forms such as gestures to make intentions known, and indicating an awareness of emotions of others. These behaviors are examined in the emotional and social domain in more depth. They are noted only if the child is *not* doing them at an age-appropriate level. Similarly, the foundational skills related to understanding social causality and ability to represent others' thoughts and actions through dramatic play are addressed in other subcategories. Their inclusion is important if these skills are absent. Absence of several of these abilities in combination may indicate problems in social cognition.

The team also watches for the child's attempts to perform actions in order to get a desired response from an adult. This may be as simple as repeating an action the parent laughed at or whining to get one's way. Both indicate that the child is aware of the consequences of previous behaviors and can consciously repeat or plan these behaviors in order to get a desired result. Opportunities to observe the child attempting to get what he or she wants usually occur spontaneously during TPBA.

Playing tricks on someone shows a higher level of understanding of others' responses. When a child plays a trick on someone, he or she knows what the adult expects to occur and then performs another action in order to surprise the person (a positive intention) or deceive the person (a negative intention). Parents may report the types of tricks the child likes to play at home. The facilitator also may elicit this behavior with a trick of his or her own.

The team can also look at the child's understanding of social inference when the facilitator uses varying forms of symbolic communication; for example, pointing (e.g., pointing to the hole where the shape goes), using an object to represent an action (e.g., holding the cracker box up to indicate it is time for a snack), gesture (raising the hand to show the child to throw the ball higher), or symbolic representation (pretending to drive a car with a paper plate). Even young infants know what the nipple or bottle infers. Interpretation of level of social inference can be made by observing the child's responses to objects, gestures, and actions throughout the session. Higher level understanding of the motivations behind gestures and actions does not emerge until after the age of 3.

Prediction of another's actions, desires, and beliefs is another important area of social cognition. Assessment of these aspects depends on the age of the child and may require some structuring on the part of the facilitator. For very young children, the team observes how the child responds to the facilitator's actions. It is important for the facilitator to use some actions and gestures without words, so that it can be determined whether the child understands and anticipates the facilitator's intentions. As children become able to answer higher level questions, the facilitator can integrate questions into the play that will elicit information from the child concerning his or her understanding of others' thinking and intentions and consequent actions.

> *Four-year-old Adrianne and the facilitator were playing with the baby dolls. The facilitator said, "My baby's crying. Why do you think she is crying?" Adrianne responded quickly, "She's wet. Let's change her." Her logical reasoning indicates understanding of motivations behind behaviors. Later Adrianne's play evolved into a birthday party. While she was making a cake for her daddy, the facilitator got out a variety of objects for presents for dad, including a baby doll, a dress-up necktie, a drum, and blocks. She said, "Let's go shopping over at that store and pick out a present for Daddy. Then we can wrap it for the party." Adrianne thought this was a great idea and ran over to the "store." She said, "My Daddy likes music. I'll get him the drum." This response indicated Adrianne's ability to think about others' desires and beliefs. The facilitator also set up a "false belief" situation to look at Adrianne's understanding of actions based on beliefs. The facilitator brought out a candy box with toy people in it (a false situation) and asked Adrianne, "I have something for the party, what do you think is in here?" Adrianne said, "Candy!" The facilitator replied, "Let's peek to make sure." After Adrianne peeked in the box and found out what was in it, her face registered surprise. The facilitator then said, "I wonder what your Daddy will think is in the box." Adrianne thought a minute and said, "Toys."*
>
> *The TPBA showed a developmentally appropriate level of understanding of how others think and act. Adrianne is beginning to think about another person's desires as being different from hers, but she is not yet able to put herself in the position of knowing what another person will perceive and therefore think. She bases her judgment on what she now knows. Adrianne is very observant and bright, and this skill will undoubtedly emerge soon.*

V. Complexity of Play

Children play in many ways with a variety of resources, including people, actions, objects, space, and language (Franklin, 2000). At each developmental level, children engage these different elements in distinctive ways and to varying degrees. For very young infants, even though they pleasurably kick, look at objects, are calmed or excited with alternative movements through space, and play with sounds, people are the primary objects of engagement. As children develop additional motor and cognitive skills, objects become more interesting. As social, motor, and cognitive skills continue to become more sophisticated in the toddler years, children explore and conquer large and small spaces. The development of language in combination with refined cognitive understanding adds another element that makes social play more pleasurable for children. By kindergarten, children enjoy a combination of all of these elements, with individual and cultural differences adding to the developmental "mix."

The subcategory of "complexity of play" within the cognitive domain examines the range of the child's play across all of these elements, looking at the highest level and predominant type of play in which the child engages, including face-to-face play, sensorimotor play, functional/relational play, construction, dramatic play, games with rules, and rough-and-tumble play. Although these types of play tend to be hierarchical and build on the base of the former, all types of play remain important to the child throughout childhood (and even adulthood). Each category of play has a period in childhood when it predominates, and each serves a role in promoting various aspects of cognitive, motor, language and communication, and social development. Although research shows conflicting evidence concerning the relationship between gender and play materials, themes, and types of play, this literature will not be addressed here. For the purposes of TPBA, gender differences are not significant enough to warrant differential discussion and age ranges.

In addition, this subcategory examines the patterns of the child's actions within each of these types of play. Whether the child uses repetitive actions or a variety of play actions and can make creative use of toys is also an important indicator of the complexity of the child's play. As with other areas, however, any extremes of behavior are worthy of note.

Humor is considered by some as another form of play (Bergen, 2003). The level of development indicated by the child's sense of humor is included in this section as well, because what the child finds humorous reveals his or her level of understanding of incongruities. For children with severe motor problems, who may not be able to demonstrate understanding through language and physical actions on objects, analysis of the child's responses to the actions and words of others can demonstrate his or her level of cognitive understanding. Sense of humor is also addressed in the social domain, because it relates to social relations, in addition to cognition.

■■■■■ V. A. What behaviors demonstrate the level and complexity of the child's play?

Many children with disabilities may exhibit both play and nonplay behaviors (e.g., passivity or disengagement, wandering, stereotypic, or destructive behaviors), even after they are developmentally capable of engaging toys in meaningful ways. For example, children with Down syndrome may have passive or unengaged behavior, whereas children with autism spectrum disorders may play with some toys in functional ways and others in a stereotypical or obsessive manner (Baron-Cohen & Wheelwright, 1999; Linn, Goodman, & Lender, 2000). Because cognitive, language, and social skills are all promoted through play, it is essential to look at the type of play and nonplay behaviors, the range of play behaviors, and the complexity of play the child exhibits.

Definitions of play in the literature are numerous and sometimes contradictory (Sutton-Smith, 1999). Within TPBA2, and also cited elsewhere, play is differentiated as including 1) face-to-face interpersonal play, 2) exploratory or sensorimotor, 3) functional/relational, 4) constructive, 5) dramatic, 6) games with rules, and 7) rough-and-tumble (Jennings, 1993; Piaget, 1962; Rubin, 1984; Rubin, Fein, & Vandenberg, 1983; Smilansky, 1968). Children may engage primarily in one type of play or they may exhibit various types of play, depending on their developmental level and their interests. Humor is considered a separate form of play, because it can overlap all seven types of play. Children's play behaviors become more complex and abstract as they get older (Harley, 1999; Van Hoorne, Nourot, Scales, & Alward, 1993), with the following types of play emerging approximately in sequence.

Interpersonal Play

Even from the first weeks of life babies enjoy pleasurable engagement with people. From birth through the first few months of life, play primarily revolves around looking, vocalizing, smiling, making sounds, and responding to sights and sounds in the environment. Solitary play may involve kicking and moving arms, vocalizing, and looking. Play with caregivers involves visual and vocal exchanges, simple imitation of facial expressions, and rhythmic body movements. Jennings (1995) includes this type of play in what he terms "embodiment play," or continual interaction and engagement through the body and the senses. Uzgiris and Raeff (1995) use the term *interpersonal play* to mean play involving face-to-face interactions, social games, or routines. Response to games such as Peekaboo or music games can be seen as early as 4 months (Rochat, 2001; Rochat, Querido, & Striano, 1999; Rock, Trainor, & Addison, 1999). These exchanges lay the foundation for later play interactions and become more complex as the child becomes able to smile, move voluntarily, gesture, and vocalize specific sounds. Infants are interested in looking at other infants as early as 2 months of age, and by 6–9 months they will try to get another infant's attention, smile, babble, and touch (Vandell & Mueller, 1995). Initiation, imitation, and turn-taking with both adults and peers is seen between 9 and 12 months. Increasing understanding of cause-and-effect also enables the child to indicate that he would like the adult to repeat an action (such as bouncing on the knee). These abilities combined with the child's increasing interest in objects after 6 months of age lead to independent exploration and sensorimotor play.

Exploratory/Sensorimotor Play

Exploratory/sensorimotor play is an activity that is done for the enjoyment of the sensory input it provides and is differentiated from exploration for discovery purposes, which usually involves manipulation or problem solving. Exploratory behaviors include mouthing, looking, touching, or repeating an activity in a repetitive fashion. Caregivers are typically less interactive and serve more as audience, commenter, and facilitator in object play (Uzgiris & Raeff, 1995). Young infants of 3–9 months may explore a toy by looking at it, touching it, or mouthing it—all sensory exploration. Examples of exploratory or sensorimotor play include repetitive motor movements, such as joyfully throwing the spoon off the table for mom to pick up and repeatedly knocking down blocks. As the infant gets older, pouring water in and out of containers, making noises with the mouth or objects, and repeatedly climbing up and down steps is pleasurable. An older child with disabilities may engage in similar behavior with a toy or may repeat an action, such as throwing blocks, just because he or she likes the sensations received from this action. An extended focus on this type of play may inhibit the child from moving into more functional play. Exploratory play is seen primarily between birth and age 2, but it remains important throughout childhood. In fact, even adults enjoy exploratory and sensorimotor play occasionally.

Functional-Relational Play

Functional-relational play is an expansion from simple manipulation and sensory exploration into the functional use of objects and combining objects in play. Functional play denotes the child's ability to use objects in play for the purposes for which they were intended (Fenson, Kagan, Kearsley, & Zelazo, 1976). This includes using simple objects correctly, such as a brush for the hair, and making objects do what they are made to do, such as pumping the handle on a top. Relational play also includes combining objects that go together, such as blocks in a shape box, or combining related objects, such as a truck and driver. Young children often will experiment with combining objects that are not meant to be combined, such as putting toys in the diaper pail. Caregivers play a role in the development of functional-relational play by modeling actions and reinforcing appropriate use of materials. The child from 9 months on may be seen playing with toys in functional or relational ways, using them as they were intended, seeing relations and combining toys that are functionally related (Belsky &

Most, 1981; Fenson et al., 1976). For example, the child may relate common objects that are functionally encountered every day, such as a bowl and a spoon. This ability to relate objects increases and is predominant from the first to the second year of life (Fenson et al., 1976; Snow & McGaha, 2003; Uzgiris & Raeff, 1995). It is a prerequisite for (and continues to be seen in) constructive and dramatic play. A child with disabilities may show developmentally prolonged relational play.

Constructive Play

"Manipulation of objects for the purpose of constructing or creating something" is how Rubin (1984, p. 4) defines constructive play. Constructive play requires that the child be able to meaningfully combine and relate objects. The difference between exploratory, relational, and constructive play is that in constructive play the child has an end goal in mind that requires the transformation of objects into a new configuration. Examples include building a fence with blocks, making a face from clay, drawing a picture, or putting together a puzzle. Although the child of 1 year can combine two blocks, true construction is not seen until the child creates a structure with the blocks. The 2-year-old may be seen stacking blocks and knocking them down, but constructive play is not predominant until the third year. The 3–3½-year-old will build enclosures. From 3½ years on, the child will build three-dimensional structures that represent buildings (Westby, 1980). It is important here to differentiate between simple relational play and constructive play. Stringing beads or combining pop-beads may be seen as relational play, because the child is relating like objects in a meaningful way; however, combining beads to make a necklace can be seen as constructive play. The latter is a higher level ability, requiring the child to combine objects into a new representation. "Patterning" with blocks is also seen after 3½ years of age, as children recognize and create patterns and solve problems of basic physics. "Children experiment with different patterns of blocks and make hypotheses regarding balance, symmetry, weight, and force" (Weiss, 1997, p. 37). Constructive play increases in frequency and complexity as children move from toddlerhood to preschool-age, becomes more cooperative as children learn to work together toward a goal, and provides a link to dramatic and symbolic play as children create a fantasy world (Johnson, Christie, & Yawkey, 1987; Owacki, 1999; Wilford, 1996).

Dramatic Play

Relational play leads the child into exploration of interrelationships among objects and events. As objects' purposes are discovered, they are used functionally (e.g., a comb is used to comb your hair). From this exploration evolves an understanding of spatial, causal, and categorical relations—all elements observed in dramatic play. Dramatic play (Rubin, 1984; Smilansky, 1968) involves the child pretending to do something or be someone. The child pretends with objects (drinks from an empty cup), pretends without objects (brushes his or her teeth with a finger), or pretends through other inanimate objects (has dolls pretend to feed the animals). In pretend play, children transform the meaning of objects, identities, situations, and time (Goncu et al., 2002). As a result of this mental transformation, Piaget (1962) referred to pretend actions as *symbolic play*. More recently, the definition of dramatic or symbolic play has been expanded to include personification of culturally relevant and emotionally significant experiences (Goncu et al., 2002; Sawyer, 1997). Thus, dramatic play has implications for both cognitive and emotional development. (See VI. Emotional Themes in Play, Chapter 4.)

The early dramatic play of toddlers is related to daily life experiences, whereas preschoolers become increasingly able to act out narratives from stories and make-believe situations. Dramatic play appears to occur in most cultures, but amount and type of dramatic play and the roles and scripts may vary from culture to culture (Goncu, Mistry, & Mosier, 2000; Haight, Wang, Fung, Williams, & Mintz, 1999; Roopnarine, Shin, Donovan, & Suppal, 2001). It is therefore important to know about the values of the family, the type of play encouraged or discouraged, and relevant experiences that might be reflected in the child's play. In families that value dramatic play as a learning opportunity, pretend play is encouraged and supported. In other families, in which time is needed for work purposes, pretend play may be viewed as a waste of valuable time. The family's level of schooling, level of income, and source of livelihood influence the value attached to pretend play (Goncu, Tuermer, Jain, & Johnson, 1999; Haight et al., 1999).

Early representational play, such as pretending to eat from a spoon, can be seen around 1 year of age, but dramatic play with sequences of pretend actions does not predominate until after 2 years of age (Belsky & Most, 1981; Howes & Matheson, 1992; McCune-Nicholich, 1981). One- to 2-year-olds spend about 5%–20% of their play time pretending (Haight et al., 1999), and 2-year-olds understand the pretend actions of others (Walker-Andrews & Kahana-Kalman, 1999). From 2 to 6 years of age, dramatic play becomes more elaborate, combining materials and events in increasingly more complex ways. As children learn to understand symbols, they can begin to substitute one object for another. For example, a 3-year-old may use a block as a banana and pretend to eat it. In dramatic play, more than in previous forms of play, the child becomes less controlled by the objects and materials at hand and better able to plan events and roles within dramatic play (Garvey, 1977).

Between 3 and 4 years of age, children begin to become more social in their dramatic play, particularly with support from parents or siblings, and sociodramatic play with peers emerges around age 4. The roles children play also expand between 3 and 4 years of age. In western societies, imagination takes children beyond simple familial role play into dramatization of imaginary characters or characters from television, books, and movies. Children from cultures that do not experience these media; where parents do not pass on myths, legends, or stories; or whose families do not value or have time for pretense, demonstrate simple play that imitates adult activities (Gaskins & Goncu, 1992; Haight et al., 1999). Children in these cultures may replicate actions of adults but may not create fantasy play. (See Table 7.2 for examples of cultural differences.) These cultural and familial differences in content, structure, and expression of dramatic play should be noted and taken into consideration when observing the child, interpreting observations, and discussing the child's play with the family.

Most preschool-age children find dramatic play a satisfying means by which to act on their knowledge of the world and also a safe way to express their inner emotions, both positive and negative (particularly fears and worries). Regardless of their culture, children's play reflects their cognitive and emotional understanding of their world and their place in that world (see VI. Emotional Themes in Play, Chapter 4).

Dramatic play also contributes to more formal symbolic understanding. Current research is finding a relationship between the child's ability to symbolically transform objects, actions, and situations in pretend play to the capacity to make symbolic trans-

Table 7.2. Examples of non-Western cultural variations in dramatic play

Culture	Dramatic play	Research
Taiwanese	Social routines and proper conduct	Haight et al., 1999
Mayan (Yucatan)	Adult work activities	Gaskins, 1999
Kpelle (Liberia)	Daily life	Lancy, 1996
Huli (Papua New Guinea)	Daily life, myths	Goldman, 1998
Aboriginal (Australia)	People, animals, symbols, play fighting	Johns, 1999

formations in reading and writing. Children often get to practice the roles of readers and writers in dramatic play and explore the purposes and processes of reading and writing (Neuman & Roskos, 1991; Rowe, 2000). Dramatic play has also been shown to be related to the child's ability to comprehend and recall stories (Rowe, 2000; Soundy & Genisio, 1994). In fact, Berg (1994) found "the degree of sophistication of a child's play was a better predictor of success in reading and writing in Grade 1 than either IQ or socioeconomic level" (p. 37). Furthermore, book-related dramatic play may be related to increased understanding of vocabulary and stories as a result of input and expression through multiple modalities (Rowe, 2000). (See Literacy Development, below.)

Games-with-Rules Play

Games with rules (Rubin, 1984; Smilansky, 1968) involve the child playing in an activity with accepted rules or limits. The game implies shared expectations and a willingness to conform to agreed-on procedures (Garvey, 1977). An element of competition may be suggested, either with another child or with the child him- or herself (Rubin, 1984). Parameters, routines, discipline, and responsibilities enable children to understand the purpose of rules and incorporate them into their play (Wilburn, 2000). From infancy on, the child is developing an increasing ability to regulate behaviors and internalize the expectations of others. Concurrently, cognitive abilities are developing to determine cause-and-effect variables, formulate predictive rules, apply rules to new situations, and maintain these rules under challenging circumstances (Siegler & Chen, 1998; Wilkening & Huber, 2002). These skills enable the child to understand and develop games with rules.

The game can be a preset standard game, such as the card game Go Fish, or it can be a game with rules that the child makes up. The child does not typically seek out games with rules until he or she has a social understanding of roles in games; a concept of competition, or winning and losing; and a grasp of the idea of rules or guidelines that remain the same from situation to situation (Piaget, 1962). Games with rules become important to the child over 5 years of age. Younger children may like to play games with rules as they learn to take turns, but they change the rules to meet their own needs; whereas older children negotiate and agree on the rules to be followed.

Physical Activity and Rough-and-Tumble Play

Physical activity play and rough-and-tumble play have received relatively little attention in the field of play. However, researchers believe that such play contributes to endurance, strength, and motor skill; to cognitive performance; as well as to social organization and social skills (Pellegrini & Smith, 1998). Physical activity play in the first year is characterized by Thelen (1980) as "rhythmical stereotypies," such as rocking or kicking. This type of play peaks around 6 months of age and gradually diminishes by the end of the first year. Interactions between the parents and the child often provide physical activity play. Parents will toss the child, bounce the child on the knee, and engage in other types of rough-and-tumble play (Roopnarine, Hooper, Ahmeduzzaman, & Pollack, 1993).

Exercise play, consisting of locomotor movements in play, begins at the end of the first year (Roopnarnine et al., 1993) and overlaps with rough-and-tumble play. This type of play appears to peak around 4–5 years of age but continues into early and middle childhood. Rough-and-tumble play increases during the preschool and primary years and declines in adolescence. Although there appear to be no gender differences in rhythmical stereotypies, exercise and rough-and-tumble play are more frequently observed in males than females, as a result of both hormonal and cultural influences (Maccoby, 1998; Pellegrini & Smith, 1998).

Boisterous and *physical* are two ways to describe rough-and-tumble play. But rough-and-tumble play (R&T) is more than just loud and active. There are characteristics that differentiate R&T from other forms of play and from aggression, which it resembles (Pellegrini, 2002). R&T play is composed of behaviors of running, chasing, fleeing, wrestling, and open-handed hitting. It is typically accompanied by smiles or a playful face. Aggression, on the other hand, is characterized by closed-hand hits, shoves, pushes, and kicks, usually accompanied by frowns or crying. Children usually stay together and play cooperatively after R&T but separate after aggression. An important characteristic of R&T is that children alternate roles, as the "chaser" and "chasee" or "victim" and "victimizer." The bigger player often lets the smaller or younger child gain the upper hand, while he or she becomes the "victim." In contrast, in aggressive actions no role exchange takes place. The victimizer stays in that role. R&T usually occurs in larger spaces, where running, falling, and roughhousing can take place, whereas aggression is not dependent on location.

Pellegrini (2002) theorizes that R&T serves an important role in development. It allows children to take perspective of each other in role exchange (Pellegrini, 1993) and provides a socially acceptable means for determining dominance structures within peer social structures (Pellegrini & Bartini, 2001). In the preschool and primary years, fantasy play is combined with R&T, especially for boys, with the characters the children dramatize providing the justification for R&T.

R&T does not co-occur or escalate to aggression except with socially rejected and aggressive boys (Pellegrini, 1988). Aggressive children may deliberately exploit R&T for their negative intentions, starting out with innocuous R&T and then moving to aggressive actions. Children who have difficulty with emotional regulation or are tactually defensive also may move into aggressive actions, not from malintent, as is the case with aggressive children, but because they misinterpret the intent of their peers as a result of neurological and physiological responses.

Knowing the child's primary mode of play is important to those who will work with the child. First, they will understand something about the child's developmental level in play. Second, they will be able to incorporate the child's preferences into intervention activities. Third, the staff will be better able to make recommendations to the parents about play activities at home and in the community. During the TPBA play session, the team has an opportunity to observe the child in various types of play activities, so patterns and preferences become apparent very quickly.

V. B. What approach typifies the complexity of the child's actions within the listed categories of play?

In addition to looking at the type of play that the child prefers and the highest level of play in which the child engages, it is also critical to look at the range of activities within a category and the type, variety, and style of play actions used at each level of play. For example, a child at the sensorimotor/exploratory level of play may enjoy all types of exploration. He or she may play with toys with lights, sounds, textures, movement, and find pleasure in discovering the characteristics of all of the toys and materials. Another child at this level may only be interested in toys that move or have big effects.

The same is true of higher level categories as well. For example, some children will enjoy dramatizing anything—a birthday party, driving to the store, or putting out a fire. Some children may only be interested in dramatic play with dinosaurs. Looking at the range of interest across categories can help identify motivators for choices but also may point to areas in need of further examination. For example, the child who is only interested in toys that move or have lights may have visual issues that are influencing his or her choice of toys. The child who only wants to play with dinosaurs may have rigid thinking patterns or have emotional issues that he or she is expressing through this medium. Some children only want to play with those things with which they are familiar and know they will experience success. It is important for the team to note any limited range of activity choices and relate this to other information learned about the child across other domains and subcategories of observation.

Besides looking at the range of activities in which the child is interested within each type of play, it is also relevant to look at the variety of actions the child does with objects. For example, the 9-month-old may mouth toys at the sensorimotor/exploratory level. That is appropriate, but if that is the *only* action the child does, the exploration is limited. Children at this level need to also be looking, handling, turning, shaking, banging, and discovering all the characteristics of objects in a variety of ways. As the child's fine and gross motor skills develop and cognitive skills become more sophisticated, taking the child into a higher level of play, the child's play actions need to reflect an increasing ability to sequence different action and thought sequences. Infants and toddlers will frequently repeat actions as they investigate, practice, watch, and learn about how the world works. They also begin to revise and modify their actions, add another different action, and experiment with action sequences. Even an infant will look at a rattle, recognize it, shake it, put it to his or her mouth, then take it out and shake it again or bang it.

When the team observes children who do not show a variety of actions with toys and materials, further investigation of what is happening cognitively is warranted. For example, a child who spins everything is clearly noted as having a limited repertoire of actions, even though he can figure out how to spin things that no one else can spin. In the same way, the child who repeats the same limited two-step sequence of actions with all toys (e.g., puts things in and takes them out) is also limited. Even if the child appears to be doing higher level play, this may be deceiving. For example, the child may be in the kitchen area and all play involves putting things in and out of the frying pan or in and out of the oven. This demonstrates a restricted range of action options for this child that may limit further learning.

V. C. What level of cognition is demonstrated in the child's sense of humor?

Humor is considered a form of play (Klein, 2003). Disagreement exists about the definition of humor and when, exactly, a sense of humor begins to be exhibited. Most believe that the playful component is present throughout life, that humor involves somewhat sophisticated cognitive processes, and that it frequently involves incongruities (Klein, 2003; Martin, 1998; McGhee, 1977; Roeckelein, 2002). Incongruity involves combining actions or ideas that are out of context or ordinarily do not belong together (Bergen, 1998; Kolb, 1990). Objects, actions, images or words are deliberately distorted to break underlying "rules" or conceptions of how things are or ought to be. Understanding these rules allows children to recognize the absurdities observed or experienced. Humor also allows children opportunities to solve problems (e.g., in jokes, riddles, cartoons), discover unique associations among ideas (divergent thinking), and learn the rules of "surprise" that cause delight in others (Klein, 2003). As a result the child's sense of humor can reveal much about his or her level of cognitive development (Bergen, 1998; Cicchetti & Sroufe, 1976; McGhee, 1977, 2002) and social awareness. Humor has been shown to enhance social interactions (making interactions easier and more pleasurable), popularity and friendship, socially acceptable expression of aggression, and make a dominant or assertive style of interaction more acceptable (McGhee, 1989). In fact, people view frequent originators of humor as leaders because they seem to be able to control social situations without triggering negative reactions. However, humor also can have negative social results (see Chapter 4).

Although true sense of humor begins after the first year of life, laughter begins by the third month of life. Usually in reaction to physical stimulation such as tickling, bouncing, or being tossed in the air, the child laughs exuberantly (Bergen, 1998). Later, the infant enjoys things that adults do to entertain him or her, such as making strange noises, making faces, and moving in unexpected ways. Still later, he or she can find objects amusing when they behave in expected or unexpected ways. As the child develops language, atypical words may become humorous, and the child may experiment with changing words and using words in nontraditional (or even culturally unacceptable) ways. The ability to make jokes or use words in new ways that are humorous to self and friends develops with increased language skills (Bergen, 1998; Clay, 1997; Garvey, 1977; Socha & Kelly, 1994). In addition, the child begins to be able to analyze situations and find incongruous situations humorous.

McGhee (1977, 1979, 1989) distinguished four stages of humor development that follow this initial phase. In the first stage (early in the second year) the child finds incongruous actions toward objects humorous. Laughter based on the inappropriateness of the action "reflects the pleasure derived from creating in fantasy play a set of conditions known to be at odds with reality" (McGhee, 1979, p. 67). A child in this first stage may laugh at the adult pretending to drink from a hat. In stage two (late in the second year) the child laughs at incongruous labeling of objects and events (calling a nose an ear). The third stage exhibits greater conceptual understanding, as the child of about age 3 gains a better understanding of characteristics of things. Humor at this stage relates to incongruous elements of a concept (a cow that barks) or distortions of familiar sights and sounds (rhyming words or nonsense words). The fourth stage, understanding multiple meanings of words, does not occur until about 7 years of age. The child needs to have acquired the cognitive correlates to understand humor at each of these stages. Humor, therefore, reveals both social and cognitive development (Bergen, 1998).

For children with physical disabilities who are unable to verbalize or act on their environment in the same ways that other children do, observation of humor can provide valuable information about cognitive and social understanding. The same is true of children with severe language impairments.

USING THE OBSERVATION GUIDELINES TO ASSESS COMPLEXITY OF PLAY

V. A. What behaviors demonstrate the level and complexity of the child's play?

TPBA allows the team to observe the range of play categories that the child spontaneously seeks out and those that can be elicited through scaffolding strategies. For example, the child being assessed may engage primarily in face-to-face interaction, exploratory or sensorimotor behaviors, examining objects and determining their characteristics. With an infant, the team can observe how the parents and infant engage each other. The facilitator can then join in the play to determine whether higher levels of play can be elicited. With an older child the team will be able to see what types of play the child chooses. The facilitator will want to try to expose the child to the full range of types of play (with the exception of face-to-face play, which is primarily appropriate for children who are developmentally between birth and 6 months of age), introducing simple objects and materials appropriate to each play category.

Regardless of the types of toys that are chosen, children will use the toys in a manner consistent with either preferences or abilities, or both. For example, older children, who are functioning at a developmentally younger stage, may choose a dramatic play prop such as a telephone but then begin to bang it against other toys to hear the noise it makes. This would be considered play at an exploratory or sensorimotor level. The facilitator could attempt to elicit a higher level of play by modeling putting the phone handle on its base. If the child imitates this behavior, the child could be credited with performing a functional/relational level play skill in imitation of the facilitator. The team would then watch to see if the child did any other functional relational play skills spontaneously. It is important for the team to observe both the highest level the child can perform, and the level of play the child chooses most frequently. The type of play chosen most frequently may indicate the child's primary skill level *or* the child's needs. For instance, a child who is capable of dramatic play, but who primarily chooses sensorimotor play, may be demonstrating a need for sensory input commensurate with a sensory integration dysfunction.

A variety of materials should be made available in each play category, because children's interests will vary depending on previous experiences. (See Chapter 7 in the *Administration Guide for TPBA2 & TPBI2* for a detailed list of types of materials that are useful.) For example, a variety of sensory materials that includes objects that are brightly colored, make different noises, have a variety of textures, and require different types of manipulation are needed. Functional everyday objects, such as combs, wash cloths, or spoons, are good. Objects that can be combined in a meaningful way, such as a spoon and bowl, blocks, and puzzles, are also important. For constructive play, a range of materials that can be used to create "something" is needed. It is particularly important to have materials that can be manipulated by children with motor problems, so that they are able to demonstrate what they can create. Dramatic play materials should also include both everyday, routine objects and more fantasy-type play items, such as hats, costumes, and props associated with different characters or people. Miniature action figures and small play scenes are good for children at higher levels of dramatic play, because they can then demonstrate their ability to act out several roles and have characters interact.

Play involving games with rules may be harder to observe in the TPBA play setting. The parent may be asked if the child initiates or likes to participate in games with rules, such as Duck-Duck-Goose. When observing an older child in the TPBA play session, it may be possible to entice the child into a favorite card game, such as UNO, various lotto or memory games, other simple card or board games, or a competitive ball game with rules that the child creates alone or with the facilitator. These games will give the facilitator an opportunity to look not only at the child's conceptual understanding, but also at turn-taking, organizational skills, memory skills, ability to understand the "story" a board game represents, and the idea of unchangeable rules. Observers can note how well the child understands and maintains the rules, how important winning is to the child, and how persistent the child is in this type of play.

Physical and rough-and-tumble (R&T) play is most easily observed in a group or classroom situation, where children are familiar with each other. If the observers have an opportunity to watch the child's class or talk to the child's classroom teacher, involvement in physical R&T play can be investigated. During the actual play session, the facilitator or parents may try to engage the child in fun physical or R&T activities (particularly if the parents report that this is something the child enjoys doing with them). Many children thoroughly enjoy this activity, but others are not at all interested and, in fact, may find even playful physical interaction to be unpleasant. For still other children, this type of play may provide a route to interaction not available in other forms of play.

In summary, exploration of all possible play categories enables the team to observe how the child's actions, reactions, and motivations vary with different forms of play. The facilitator needs to attempt to interest the child in various types of play and then scaffold the child's abilities to the highest level possible within each category. Also, experimentation with different toys and materials is important, because the child may demonstrate more interest, and therefore higher level skills, with motivating materials. Observation of different play categories will reveal developmental skill levels. In addition, observation of the predominant form of play in which the child engages can provide clues to other developmental issues. Such information is invaluable for program planning.

V. B. What approach typifies the complexity of the child's actions within the categories of play?

The TPBA team needs to observe the variety within the child's play: the variety of choices of toys and materials, the variety of actions on objects, the variety of action sequences, and the ability to vary sequences across types of activities. This requires looking for patterns and noting repetitions that exceed typical "practice" or mastery play. In practice play, children repeat actions and sequences for the pure pleasure of experiencing the activity again. In mastery play, the child repeats actions in order to succeed at a particular task or to reach a particular goal. Both of these types of play are seen in children of all ages. What the team may see in children with disabilities is repetition because the child cannot think of another action or has no interest in modifying his or her activity. This repetition is typically called *perseveration.* Children may appear to lack interest in other actions or may get started with an action and appear to be unable to stop. Other repetitive patterns are more subtle, because the child appears to have interest in many things but the action sequences are limited.

Observation of sequencing actions and seriation abilities (e.g., skill in placing the elements in a series in order) can be seen in the child's play with objects and in representational play. In TPBA observation, the team can distinguish whether the child's play demonstrates a logical sequence, a comprehension of beginning, middle, and end; whether the child demonstrates understanding of visual sequences; and whether the child understands abstract sequences such as the progression of time. These concepts will be reflected in the child's actions and conversation.

V. C. What level of cognition is demonstrated in the child's sense of humor?

The TPBA team examines the child's comprehension of others' humorous intentions and the expression of the child's own humorous intentions. When observing the play session, the team should note the times during which the child is seen smiling or laughing as an indicator that something seems funny. The facilitator may set up situations that might be perceived as funny, depending on the child's age (e.g., knocking down blocks, wearing a pan for a hat, putting a box of cereal in the oven, or telling a joke). In addition, when the child appears to be initiating a humorous event, the team should note the level of cognitive understanding and the social role of the child in the humorous event. It is important to try to differentiate a social smile or attention-getting laughter from actual humor. For some children with motor disabilities, a smile or even a grimace may indicate comprehension that something is funny. However, some children with disabilities may have learned that responding with a laugh always gets the adult to repeat the social interchange or pay attention. If this is the case, the team will probably observe that laughter is not always meaningful, but rather could be a contingent response.

> *Connor, a 4-year-old, was referred by his Head Start program for potential developmental delays. Connor entered the room and immediately ran to the cars and trucks. He began to race the cars around in a circle and then into each other, making car and crash noises. When the facilitator began to play with cars next to him, he ran into her car as well. Connor also drove the cars up and down a ramp and into the garage in imitation of the facilitator. He didn't comment during this play; he just made car noises. After a few minutes of imitating Connor's actions, the facilitator tried to see whether Connor could engage in interactive dramatic play. She drove a police car over and said, "I'm afraid I'm going to have to give you a ticket. You are driving too fast." She handed Connor a small piece of paper. He took the paper and then again raced his car around. The facilitator set the note paper and police car next to Connor, and began driving another car around. Connor then picked up the police car, drove it over to the facilitator's*

car, said, "Ticket," and handed her a piece of paper. After several more minutes of driving cars, and giving tickets, the facilitator drove her car over to the water table for a "car wash." Connor followed and washed his car. Throughout the play session, Connor used objects for their intended purposes, but in a repetitive fashion or in imitation of the adult.

Afterward, the team talked about Connor's play categories. The facilitator noted that at first she was unclear whether Connor was merely using the cars functionally and combining them with the other objects that were near, or whether he was interpreting his actions as dramatic play. His parents and teacher indicated that Connor frequently imitated his siblings and the other children's actions, but that most of his actions with dramatic play props were simple functional actions rather than a series of related, complex actions. Connor's parents discussed how the play of his older siblings often revolves around action figures and imaginative stories they make up. The team noted that this type of dramatic play is difficult for Connor to understand, so he imitates their actions instead. His ability to imitate allows him to perform actions in a dramatic play setting that make him appear to be doing more symbolic play. These imitative actions are strengths, because they allow Connor to maintain social interaction in play with peers and siblings who are functioning at a higher level. However, he is ready to learn to expand his spontaneous play sequences to two to three steps.

Two-and-a-half-year old Lucinda had cerebral palsy and was seated in a wheelchair with a tray. The play facilitator asked Lucinda if she could see the Big Bird she had gripped in her hand. Lucinda struggled to put the toy on the tray in front of her, and as she did so, her erratic movements accidentally knocked Big Bird on the floor. The toy began to roll across the room, and the play facilitator shouted, "Oh, no! He's running away! I'll catch him. Come back here Big Bird!" Lucinda squealed, her mouth open and twisted, her head back, as she made giggly noises. "She thinks you're pretty funny," her mother stated. When the facilitator captured Big Bird and brought him back she set him down on the tray, saying, "Here you go, Big Bird. I brought you back to your friend, Lucinda. You stay here now!" Lucinda, looked at Big Bird and then looked up at the facilitator as her mouth pulled back into a lopsided grin. Slowly she put her hand up by Big Bird, gave him an awkward swat, and burst out in another gasping peal of laughter as the toy went flying across the room.

Clearly, Lucinda was able to understand and initiate humor. She knew the first chase originated because of an accidental swipe, and she was able to anticipate what would happen if she purposefully swiped the bird again. This time she was playing a "trick" on the facilitator. This level of humor shows a high level of cognitive understanding. Lucinda's motor deficits prohibited her from using language to express her sense of humor, but she was able to use movement to create her joke. She not only comprehended the facilitator's funny actions, she was able to initiate an action to make someone else laugh.

VI. Conceptual Knowledge ▮▮▮▮▮▮▮▮▮▮▮▮▮▮▮▮▮▮▮▮▮▮▮▮▮▮▮▮▮▮▮

Imagine what it must be like to be a newborn entering the overwhelming world of sights, sounds, smells, tastes, textures, motion, pressure, temperature, and pain! How does the child begin to make sense of this flood of stimuli? How does perceptual information get structured to make the world meaningful for the child? The development of conceptual and categorical knowledge provides an important organizational framework for information.

Conceptual knowledge is the network of relationships between and among "pieces" of information (Hiebert & Lefevre, 1986). Categorization allows young children to compartmentalize all of the sensory information into manageable units, like file folders. These categories also make memory and retrieval of information easier, and provide a means for comparing and organizing new information. Conceptual and categorical knowledge is thus the means of organizing input to the brain so that it can be used (Quinn, 2002). The development of concepts related to physical knowledge and the cognitive processes involved in mentally manipulating these concepts leads to classification systems and higher level thinking related to psychology, biology, mathematics, and physics.

Controversy revolves around what aspects of cognitive development are innate, whether conceptual structures are general or domain specific, and how concepts develop (Gelman & Opfer, 2002). Although it is not the purpose of this section to address these issues, certainly intervention to increase conceptual knowledge is somewhat dependent on the answers to these questions. For this reason, research relating to these issues is touched on.

VI. A. What similarities and differences can the child recognize?

Human beings benefit greatly from being able to categorize experience, or organize information into meaningful groupings. Quinn (2002) identified three major benefits of categorization, as it enables 1) an infinite amount of detail to be reduced to a manageable amount of information; 2) organized storage of information in the memory, making retrieval more efficient; and 3) new stimuli to be quickly analyzed and assimilated into existing categories, reserving mental energy for other important cognitive tasks. For example, instead of having to remember over 7,000,000 potentially discrete colors, most languages have about a dozen major color categories.

Research on the development of conceptual knowledge has increased our understanding of how infants, toddlers, and preschoolers come to understand and relate to people, objects, and events in their world. Infants begin life being able to differentiate sights, sounds, tastes, textures, and smells and demonstrate a primitive ability to categorize their world. They not only can distinguish familiar from unfamiliar stimuli, but also expected from unexpected events. These early differentiation skills have allowed researchers to examine infants' early conceptual knowledge. Infants have been found to be able to perceptually discriminate most of the speech sounds in the human language, discriminate between small numbers of items (e.g., sets of two versus three objects), distinguish causal from noncausal event sequences, distinguish between animate and inanimate objects, and understand at a naïve level concepts such as space, size, number, object permanence, support, containment, and other physical characteristics and events (Baillargeon, 2002, 2004; Flavell, 2000).

Infants are aided in their growing appreciation of how the world works by a concomitant increase in the ability to differentiate characteristics of objects, people, and events. Several steps are involved in concept development: 1) recognizing the salient properties of objects, actions, or events; 2) noting similarities and differences; and 3) beginning to develop categories of concepts by identifying their common properties and grouping these into inclusive constructs. Thus attention, memory, and problem solving are necessary for conceptualization.

The brain of the young child is able to systematically relate various aspects of the world into categories of similarities. Characteristics that children attend to include both *featural* aspects (e.g., contours, face, texture, color) and *dynamic* aspects (i.e., how and why something moves). Dynamic aspects give the child clues about agency (who is doing something), intentionality (why someone is doing something), or goal-directedness (what is going to happen as a result) (Gelman & Opfer, 2002). In addition, featural and dynamic aspects help the child determine whether he or she is seeing the same person or object over different encounters (numerical identity) or whether this one is just like another but is a different object (qualitative or feature identity) (Meltzer, 2002). In other words, "This is the same ball I played with yesterday" (numerical identity) or "This just like the ball I played with, only it is red" (feature identity). For this reason, it is important to look at whether the child is able to differentiate features, identify dynamic aspects, and perceive similarities and differences across objects, people, and events. Children who have difficulty recognizing such characteristics will have problems with language development, social development, and other aspects of cognitive development such as problem solving.

VI. B. What evidence is seen of the child's conceptual or categorical knowledge?

As differential understanding of relations among people and objects develops, higher level classification systems evolve. *Discrimination*, or the ability to distinguish between sensations, is fundamental to the development and organization of concepts and can be seen very early. As noted earlier in the discussion on memory, as early as 3 days of age the young infant who is being breastfed can discriminate the smell of his or her mother's milk on breast pads, as well as her voice and face, from others (Stern, 1985). This demonstrates the concurrent development and relationship between memory and discrimination. Sensory discrimination becomes more finely tuned as the child matures.

From the ages of 2 to 6 months, the infant has a growing sense that he or she and the mother are quite separate, physically and emotionally, and that the mother is different from other humans; by 2 years of age, they perceive themselves as physically distinct beings (Pipp, Easterbrooks, & Brown, 1993; Stern, 1985). As noted previously, differential awareness of self and others is a critical link between cognitive and social development (Asendorpf, Warkentin, & Baudonniere, 1996; Fewell & Vadasy, 1983; Gergely, 2002). Social discrimination, or awareness of differences among people, allows the child to respond to and interact uniquely with each individual.

Social awareness and discrimination parallel the infant's developing awareness and discrimination of *object characteristics, use,* and *function*. In research studies, infants as young as 2 months can differentiate human from nonhuman entities (Legerstee, 1992). By 3–4 months, babies have been shown to discriminate different characteristics of categories in novelty-preference procedures. Three- to 4-month-olds, for example, have been shown to form separate categorical representations for cats and dogs (Eimas & Quinn, 1994). Studies have determined that young infants can discriminate orientation, color, and animal species (Bomba, 1984; Bornstein, 1981; Quinn, 2002; Quinn, Eimas, & Rosenkrantz, 1993). Infants between 7 and 12 months of age begin to structure objects into meaningful categories such as food, animals, vehicles, plants, and more (Mandler & McDonough, 1998). For instance, 7-month-olds believe people, but not inanimate objects, can move on their own (Poulin-Dubois, Lepage, & Ferland, 1996); whereas 9-month-olds differentiate animals and vehicles and basic-level animal categories (e.g., dogs and fish) and can separate birds from airplanes (Mandler & McDonough, 1993).

The mind appears to be able to distinguish continuities and discontinuities across different types of perceptions and then group these into categories. In addition to visual categorization, infants distinguish and categorize other types of sensory perceptions, including textures, sounds, movements, and so forth. As they begin to explore objects, infants discover that objects feel, sound, and move differently. First by looking and mouthing, then by manual exploration and experimentation, infants learn the characteristics of objects (Rakison & Butterworth, 1998). By 9 months of age, infants respond differently to unique objects.

From 9 to 12 months of age, children begin to see relationships between objects and to combine related objects, such as a shovel and a pail. Twelve-month-olds will touch objects that go together without grouping them (Gopnik & Meltzoff, 1997). By the end of the first year, children can not only group by *perceptual* categories, they are using *conceptual* categories—those based on function and behavior. An increasing amount of research is pointing to the development of global concepts (e.g., animals versus vehicles) before basic level concepts (e.g., horses from dogs versus cars from trucks). These discriminations are based first on perceptual differences and later build on conceptual understanding and differentiation of how things function and why.

Increased fine motor abilities, combined with greater perceptual discrimination and conceptual understanding of parts of objects, allow the child to experiment with putting things together (e.g., a top on a box) through nonsystematic trial and error. Improved problem-solving abilities enable the child to further refine discrimination and categorization skills as he or she learns what fits together, goes in, turns, pulls, goes on top of, and so forth. The child is beginning to discriminate functions, discovering which things roll, make noises, bounce—in other words, which things are alike in function (Morgan & Watson, 1989; Quinn, Johnson, Mareschal, Rakison, & Younger, 2000; Rakison & Butterworth, 1998).

Continual experimentation and comparison of objects lead to the ability to match by color, shape, and size. During the second year, the infant begins to recognize and sort by category (cars) or property (big ones). Children also become less perception-bound, and more abstract categories develop. By 2 years of age, the child can place a circle or square into a puzzle, and by 3 years of age the child can discriminate a triangle (Kusmierek, Cunningham, Fox-Gleason, Hanson, & Lorenzini, 1986). A 3-year-old can relate numerous ways objects are alike and different based on both perceptual and nonperceptual categories (Gelman, Spelke, & Meck, 1983). Also by 3 years of age, he or she has learned to discriminate size and is able to build three-dimensional block constructions (Cohen & Gross, 1979). Combining his or her increasing representational skills, spatial understanding, and problem-solving skills, a 4–5-year-old can put together complex puzzles and build elaborate symmetrical or asymmetrical block structures (Morgan & Watson, 1989).

Four-year-olds understand how numerous properties are important for a particular category. For example, they can understand that biological entities come in all sorts of forms and that they grow, eat, reproduce, get sick, and die (Gutheil, Vera, & Keil, 1998). Each of these defining concepts is not understood at a sophisticated level, and the relationships among them are not totally understood, but the child is looking at multifaceted concepts *within* a category. By 5 years old, such abstract concepts of speed, time, and gravity are understood at a simple causal level, with children learning to combine more than one dimension of thinking about the concept by the age of 6–7 years.

The skills described previously, which allow the child to engage in a rich repertoire of manipulative, constructive, and imaginative play, also set the foundation for the development of more complex conceptual systems related to academic skills.

■■■■ VI. C. What behaviors demonstrate that the child integrates concepts into a classification system?

Infants appear to naturally form mental categories to capture commonalities among objects, to which labels or *words* are then assigned in order to express them (Waxman, 2002). Conceptual development is thus the key link between cognitive and communicative development. Language development research across cultures has shown that infants pay more attention to those words and phrases that contain content words, thus helping them to map labels onto the objects in the world and fit them into categories (Jusczyk & Kemler Nelson, 1996). Adult–child language interactions are influential in conceptual development.

Certain aspects of language learning facilitate concept development. Gelman and Meck (1992) summarized three basic assumptions children make related to naming of objects. First, the object as a whole, rather than any of its parts or what surrounds it, is labeled (e.g., this is a chair) (Spelke, 1982). Second, once an object in a class has been assigned a label, that label applies to other members of the class (e.g., this big one is also a chair) (Waxman & Gelman, 1986). Finally, unique objects (e.g., dogs, fish, birds) have individual names, and different objects cannot be assigned the same name (Markman, 1984). As children assign labels to the entities in their environment, they then can begin to pay more attention to the characteristics of each of these entities to form larger conceptual categories.

Children begin to shape, recognize, and mentally represent particular concepts first at a *concrete* level, with three-dimensional representations ranging from real objects to objects with a form similar in configuration and shape to the real object or person (e.g., "This is my dog." "This cat is like my dog"). Children also learn to represent concepts at the *pictorial* level in the same sequence, first in actual pictures, and then in pictorial approximations, such as cartoons. As children begin to represent their understanding in drawings and dramatic play, concepts can be recognized and demonstrated in line drawings, gestures, pantomime, and dramatization. Abstract *representation* of concepts begins with language and extends into symbols, sign language, finger-spelling, and the written word (Goralick, 1975). The development of each of these types of representation of concepts commences in the first year of life and becomes more sophisticated as caregivers present new experiences and discuss and explain them (Nelson, 1995).

Numerous studies have shown that within the cognitive domain, specific subdomains of conceptual structures relating to various systems of knowledge may be formed independently of each other; specifically, knowledge related to at least four areas—*physics, mathematics, biology,* and *psychology* (Bjorkland & Sneider, 1996; Schneider, 2002; Wellman & Gellman, 1992). Others believe that an underlying central conceptual structure is responsible for learning and cognitive development (Case, 1996, 1998). It may be that both are true, and core structures support independent pathways for various types of knowledge. For young children, the foundation of each of these begins with physical knowledge.

VI. D. What understanding of measurement concepts in math and science does the child demonstrate?

Physical Knowledge

As indicated previously, infants appear to have innate tendencies to structure attention and information taken in through all of the various sensory systems, including input through muscles and joints (proprioceptive system) and through movement (vestibular system). Infants attend to the properties, actions, and outcomes of events in their environment. Their increasing neurological maturation and the mental activity resulting from studying, experimenting with, and comparing stimuli leads to increasingly sophisticated interpretation of the meaning of the physical world.

Through their experiences, infants acquire expectations about physical events and begin to formulate "rules" about what are likely outcomes of specific events. When these rules are violated, they appear surprised and stare longer at the event. Studies using this violation-of-expectation approach have discovered that infants have a primitive appreciation of a variety of concepts. Infants appear to have naïve knowledge of space, including depth, distance, size, and shape. For example, at 2½ months, infants recognize that objects continue to exist after they are occluded or no longer visible, in violation of expectation studies (Aguiar & Baillargeon, 1999). By 3 months old, infants expect an object in contact with a surface (any part of the surface) to be supported; by 6½ months, infants expect that a large part of the object must be in contact with a surface to be supported; and by 12½ months, the infant realizes that a larger proportion of the object must be on the surface rather than off the surface to be supported and not fall (Baillargeon, 2002). Ten-month-old infants recognize that heavier objects can both exert and resist greater forces than lighter objects (Wang, 2001). Infants' knowledge becomes more complex as they move from all-or-nothing determinations to determinations based on relative amounts or degrees. This process of increasing differentiation across relationships and outcomes continues throughout the early childhood period.

Infants and young children appear to learn about discrete types of physical knowledge independently, and only later do they combine the rules into overarching systems of physical principles. Although infants appear to have some innate concepts of physical knowledge that contribute to their growing comprehension, the process of learning concepts is influenced by experience with both expected and unexpected outcomes (Luo, 2001), as well as social influences or training (Baillargeon, 2001). Children learn to discriminate diverse characteristics, circumstances, and outcomes by building a repertoire of understanding relating to specific types of experiences and gradually combine these understandings into broader conceptual and procedural knowledge.

For example, children learn about space through exploration, and then shift to understanding space through mental representation. A child relies on his own body as a referent first, then his body and an external, but nearby referent, and only later use distal referents for orientation. A 2-year-old, for instance, will judge where the toy is in reference to her own body. Children with sensory deficits need to compensate (e.g., a deaf child will isolate an object through sounds in relation to his body). The 4-year-old will be able to picture familiar rooms in her mind and find the shoes she left by the bed. (The blind child will use memory of movement and direction.) Furthermore, mental representations of space move from thinking about local clusters, to linear relations, to configural relations (Liben, 2002). Thus, in order to organize play, the child will be able to first find the toys clustered close together, then will use a line of sight or movement to move to the next object, then will think about where everything that is needed is in relation to each other. This progression can be seen in other conceptual structures as well; for instance, in the development of the concept of number.

Sequencing, or the ordering of objects, concepts, and ideas, builds on concept development and one-to-one correspondence and is relevant to all of the cognitive domains. The child's early sequencing abilities are related to the linking of actions and differentiating sensory input. The child develops an ability to sequence events in the environment, beginning with actions and moving to sequences of ideas in conversation, stories, and dramatic play (Fein, Ardila-Rey, & Groth, 2000; Rowe, 2000). At the same time, the child detects differences between sounds, textures, tastes, degrees of light, sizes, and color (Fewell & Vadasy, 1983; Gelman & Opfer, 2002; Meltzer, 2002).

Eventually, the child is able to compare a series of elements and place them in order from one end of a continuum to another, beginning with two elements and increasing to a large number of comparisons in adulthood. It is this ability to compare and order units that enables the child to develop *seriation,* or the ability to arrange items along a quantitative dimension (e.g., sequencing blocks in order of size) (Case, 1998; Ginsburg & Opper, 1988; Piaget & Inhelder, 1969). The child must be able to see the relationship between the element that precedes and the element that follows any one element in the series, and understand the equivalence of units.

During the preschool years, children are developing more sophisticated reasoning abilities and moving from perceptual problem solving to logical problem solving. Particularly for preschool children, who are entering into the complex world of science, math, and literacy, a key aspect of Case's work (1998) is important. Across all of these cognitive areas of knowledge, a child works to relate and organize concepts in a way that allows systematic comparisons to be made using "units" of thought against a type of mental reference line. This will be illustrated below in the discussion of children's acquisition of number concepts.

Quantitative Knowledge

Although quantitative abilities are just one of the areas of conceptual development, the growing emphasis on preacademic skills for young children makes this a particularly relevant area for assessment. *Preacademic skills,* as defined by Wolery and Brookfield-Norman (1988), are "cognitive abilities that are necessary for later school learning" (p. 109). Reading, writing, and math abilities, considered fundamental to school success, are built on the development of discrimination skills, classification and conceptual skills, sequencing abilities, one-to-one correspondence, and drawing skills. The *integration* of these abilities is what contributes to the development of strong academic skills.

In the following section, the development of quantitative abilities will be summarized briefly, including recognition of amount, recognition of equivalence and ordinality, and ability to calculate. As with children's more global conceptual development discussed earlier, children make similarity matches before they make comparisons of other features such as equivalency. It appears that children first make judgments about "what" they are seeing and then "how much" they are seeing. Because children are drawn to the similarities in the items, they first recognize equivalence when both sets of items they are looking at are identical entities, or from the same category (Mix, 1999). It may be that the attention to "sameness" then allows the child to pay attention to amount as well. Infants initially determine quantity based on similarity in amounts and later develop the ability to think about differences in amounts and discrete number (Mix, Huttenlocher, & Levine, 2002).

Fuson (1992) notes that young children begin to understand and use number words in seven different kinds of contexts. Table 7.3 outlines these contexts.

Table 7.3. Contexts for understanding number concepts

1. Number is understood in a linked sequence context. Children count in a rote fashion, as if counting was one word. "Onetwothreefourfivesix." Sophian (1992) describes counting as a socially transmitted activity that differs across cultures. It is first performed in a rote way as a social routine with caregivers. Number is then counted with the words differentiated.

2. Number is understood in a cardinal context. The last number counted carries a special meaning and refers to the total amount counted. For example, after counting, the child labels the last word stated as the total amount, even without one-to-one correspondence (e.g., "One, two, four, five. There are five").

3. Number is understood in a counting context. Children use one-to-one correspondence, tagging each item counted with a number. Children count to find out "How many?" or "Which is more?" or to obtain a certain amount.

4. Number is understood in an ordinal context. Children understand that a number refers to one entity within an ordered set of entities and describes the relative position of that entity (e.g., 1st, 2nd). Children understand that "four" is one more than "three" and one less than "five."

5. Number is understood in a measurement context. A number word refers to a continuous quantity and describes the amount of units that cover or fill the quantity (e.g., temperature, mass).

6. Number is understood in a symbolic numerical context. Children use written numerals to express amount for a variety of purposes.

7. Number is understood as a non-numerical context. Children use numbers to identify something, but not in a sequential context (e.g., shoe size, phone number, address).

Source: Fuson (1992).

The understandings outlined in Table 7.3 develop approximately in sequence. Children seem to understand number procedurally before they understand it conceptually. Steffe (1992) described children's learning about quantity as first entailing a *perceptual* counting scheme, in which the child establishes an awareness of plurality, or which is greater in amount. Infants also are able to subitize (or determine an amount without counting) up to three items. A *figurative* counting scheme follows, in which the child can hold in mind an image of the object being counted as the child produces a sequence of number words. After this, the child is able to coordinate actions so that naming of numbers corresponds to the item to which the child has pointed. Some children begin to be able to use their finger patterns to substitute for objects as they perform counting operations. The child also needs to understand cardinality, or the ability to hold in mind all of the numbers previously counted together as one unit. Cardinality and counting may be dissociated at first and then become integrated. Once this happens, children can deal with adding and subtracting, conservation, transformation, and other more abstract abilities because they are able to internalize the objects and the quantifying process and to perform operations on the numbers in their mind.

In 1978, Gelman and Gallistel identified what have become five well-known principles that govern conceptual counting, or what Fuson (1988) refers to as necessary contexts for *conceptual, procedural, and utilization competence:*

> a) one-to-one correspondence—every item in a set must be assigned a unique tag; b) the stable order principle—the tags used must be drawn from a stably ordered list; c) the cardinal principle—the last tag used in a count has a special status; it represents the cardinal value of the set; d) the item-indifference (or irrelevance) principle—there are no restrictions on the collection of items that can be counted; and e) the order-indifference principle—the order in which items are tagged is irrelevant. (Gelman & Meck, 1986, p. 30)

These are important concepts to look for in the assessment of the child's quantitative understanding.

Three main changes take place in this development of quantitative understanding across the early childhood period: 1) the level of accuracy and precision improves, 2) the set size that can be handled increases, and 3) the range of abstraction increases (Mix et al., 2002). True understanding of number concepts does not occur until the child is 4–5 years old, but the precursors to number knowledge develop throughout infancy.

As the child learns to label and classify objects, he or she is laying the foundation for the development of one-to-one correspondence. Bailey and Wolery (1999) identify comparing, labeling, measuring, and using symbols related to quantity as pre-math skills. Comparing quantity involves knowledge of one-to-one correspondence, ability to sequence, and ability to make basic concept judgments such as one/many, more/less, and understanding relations between sets (Bryant & Nunes, 2002). Piaget (1952) believed that in order to grasp the meaning of number words, an understanding of cardinal properties (or absolute amounts) and ordinal properties (or understanding of relations between numbers) is necessary.

Measuring quantity is necessary for understanding quantification concepts such as weight, length, time, and money. The child also learns to identify written numerals with the correct verbal label (e.g., saying "eight" when looking at the numeral 8) (Bailey & Wolery, 1999). Infants between 14 and 16 months demonstrate an understanding that 3 is more than 2 and 2 is more than 1 (Starkey, 1992). Gelman and Gallistel (1978) found that children 2–3 years old understand many of the underlying principles of counting. They found that 2-year-olds are able to correctly use one-to-one correspondence to count two or three items, and 3-year-olds are able to count three to five items correctly. Even 3-year-olds who cannot assign the right number to the objects as they count show an ability to point to objects with one-to-one correspondence while counting (Geary, 1995). During the fourth year, the child counts up to 20 objects in a fixed order (Cohen & Gross, 1979). Between 4 and 5 years of age, children understand cardinality. They understand that the last number counted represents the total amount of items in a set (Bermejo, 1996). Also at this age, children begin to solve arithmetic problems by using their fingers to add on to the first number presented (Ginsberg, Klein, & Starkey, 1998).

Exactly how children acquire these mental processes is controversial. Case presented a theory as to how quantitative and other concepts, such as space, time, music, and narrative, develop. He believed that these concepts emerge as a result of central conceptual structures that provide a framework or sequence for the development of such domains of understanding. Between 4 and 6 years old, children move from a preliminary stage of thinking involving conceptualizing amounts as "a little" or "a lot" to being able to use counting actions to determine quantity. Case notes the importance of a "mental number line" or an ability to represent numbers on a line that allows the child to mentally manipulate the units in relation to each other (Case, 1998; Case et al., 1996). Between 6 and 10 years old, the child develops the ability to coordinate two and then multiple mental number lines to perform numerical operations.

What appears to be critical for higher level thinking across many areas of cognition is the mental reference line that serves as a point of demarcation enabling the child to draw relationships. This concept is particularly essential for intervention, because building the connections for this mental reference line is critical to later development. For many children with disabilities, connecting ideas and making relationships is particularly difficult. For this reason, examining the child's thinking processes in understanding of numerosity is important to assessment.

████ USING THE OBSERVATION GUIDELINES TO ASSESS CONCEPTUAL UNDERSTANDING

████ VI. A. What similarities and differences can the child recognize?

It is difficult to observe the early infant skills that are seen in the carefully orchestrated research procedures, because TPBA is play-based. However, the team can look for characteristics that will indicate the presence of early conceptual understanding. Unless the infant has been diagnosed at birth with a congenital disorder, most infants will not be seen until they are several months old. For example, one of the first things the infant will discriminate is familiar versus unfamiliar stimuli, including familiar smells, sounds, textures, and people who transport these. Consequently, one of the first things to look for is the infant's ability to differentiate his or her caregivers from others. This does not mean that the infant shows anxiety, unless the child is between 5 and 11 months of age. For the very young infant, this differentiation may entail looking at strangers for a longer period of time. When the facilitator and caregiver sit in close proximity to the child so that the child can look back and forth between the two faces, the infant may look longer at the facilitator. Be sure to let the parent know that this is "good" because it means the child is interested in new things—*not* that the infant likes the stranger better!

The facilitator also can look at the child's reaction to the expected and unexpected. Infants love to see interesting events recur, so it is possible to repeat an action or presentation several times to see how long the child attends at each presentation (see also Section II. Memory). Then the facilitator can substitute a different toy or action to see if the child's attention increases. This will show that the child does differentiate between items presented.

As the child becomes interested in objects and actions, it is important to watch the child's reactions to see if he or she is attending to the various characteristics of objects. Some children will remain more interested in people than in objects and need help focusing on the circumstances bringing about an outcome, or focusing on the outcome rather than the circumstances. For instance, a child may watch the facilitator or parent's face rather than look at the object being presented that makes something interesting occur. Alternatively, the child may focus on only one element rather than look at the effects that are produced by the situation. The facilitator may build a tower of blocks, for example, and knock it down, while the child continues to look at the blocks in the initial box. These situations indicate that the child may be having difficulty focusing on the elements that are relevant for him or her to form conceptualizations relating to characteristics, commonalities, and relationships.

VI. B. What evidence is seen of the child's conceptual or categorical knowledge?

VI. C. What behaviors demonstrate that the child integrates concepts into a classification system?

Because conceptualization involving categorical thinking and classification are closely related, these two observation questions are considered together. During the play session, the team will have many opportunities to observe how the child combines objects, matches objects, combines pieces into a whole, sorts, and nonverbally classifies objects. The verbal child is usually talking while playing, allowing the team to ascertain the labels, descriptions, and classifications that the child assigns to objects, actions, and events. As indicated earlier, words are an invitation to identify something in the real world with the label for that object, characteristic, or event. Children who have difficulty making these associations by looking, pointing, naming, or in some way acknowledging understanding may have problems forming conceptual categories.

The facilitator can elicit concepts and classification knowledge while playing with the child. For example, the facilitator might dump out a pile of varicolored beads of different sizes to make a necklace for a doll or the child. The child may automatically classify by color or size. If not, the facilitator might suggest, "Let's make one out of all the big beads," or at a higher level, "Let's make one out of small yellow beads." In the house area, the facilitator may inspire relational thinking by identifying a piece or part of a toy and then requesting the child's help in finding the parts that go with it. Sorting can be encouraged by putting out a basket of plastic food and other toys and suggesting that "we put away the groceries." The team will observe for indicators of a classification method that the child uses to solve the problem.

The team notes behaviors that demonstrate the child's ability to combine related objects; to combine objects in sets; to discriminate objects by color, shape, or size; and to classify by category, function, or association. More complex classification or matching may be observed in solving puzzles or creating block constructions as well. The team is also looking at the child's association of words with people, objects, and action.

The TPBA facilitator and caregivers will be presenting toys and situations throughout the TPBA that evoke interest and motivate the child to engage with the materials. Part of conceptualization is recognizing the salient properties of objects, action, or events. The team should observe the child's interactions with objects and materials in the environment to see whether he or she is selecting the most important and relevant aspects for play. Children who only attend to irrelevant aspects may have more difficulty with concept formation. For example, if toys need to be activated by buttons or switches, and the child ignores this feature, he or she may have difficulty forming categories related to mechanisms and causal relations. The child who cannot attend to color or shape features in puzzles may have difficulty forming part-to-whole concepts.

Noting similarities and differences is related to identification of salient properties. Again, the infant who is stacking rings or the toddler completing a puzzle needs to recognize size or shape similarities and differences. The preschooler who is engaging in dramatic play needs to recognize which size hat goes with which size doll. Ability to discriminate these differences aids problem solving and leads to the formulation of conceptualization about size, shape, space, direction, and other higher level concepts.

The TPBA team needs to provide a variety of similar items to be able to determine whether the child is able to sort or group items by various characteristics. Infants younger than 1 year of age may be observed to take all of the big balls and place them in the box before the little balls. Toddlers may begin to pick out the cars from the farm animals to drive on the "road." Preschoolers may pick out a variety of desserts from the "store." Having appropriate materials to enable the child to demonstrate sorting and classifying is important, but the facilitator also has to provide the opportunities if the child does not spontaneously demonstrate classification skills. For example, the facilitator could say, "Let's make a list of all the food we want at the store" (through drawing pictures or writing). Dramatic play also can display categorization. "I love desserts! Let's remember to get a bunch of desserts." It also is important to have similar toys available later, to see how the child responds in similar circumstances.

Understanding of higher level concepts can be explored through language. Pay attention to what the child says about people, objects, and events. What comments does the child make? How does the child explain events that occur? What questions does he or she ask? The facilitator can elicit information by "wondering" aloud about things (e.g., "I wonder why yours is taller than mine?") and asking open-ended questions (e.g., "My baby is sick, what should we do?"). The facilitator also can set up situations that require the child to do seriation (e.g., "We have five different dinosaurs. Let's find the right size food to feed each one. Here are some different sized blocks we can use for food").

The facilitator needs to ensure that all concepts addressed are incorporated into the child's interests. One common error made by many facilitators is that as soon as they begin trying to look at more complex concepts, they begin to "test." The facilitator should avoid saying things such as, "Show me the one that goes with this one" or "Which one is the same shape?" Children will feel as if they are being tested, and the relationship will change from a play partnership to an examination situation.

VI. D. What understanding of measurement concepts in math and science does the child demonstrate?

The TPBA team can assess the child's understanding of quantity and sequencing during the play session. Many opportunities will present themselves to see how the child understands and uses number. With infants, awareness of and attention to quantity and the ability to acquire simple concepts is assessed as described previously, by looking at the infant's attention to a change in amount or position. What is important is not whether the infant has a concept of number, but whether the infant is attending to the characteristics of objects and noticing differences relating to such things as size, placement, novelty, and so forth.

As the infant begins to play with objects, the facilitator can hold out two crackers in one hand and one cracker in the other to see whether the child discriminates "more." While looking at books, the child may point to all the ducks on the page one at a time. The 1-year-old child may respond to the question "How old are you?" by holding up one finger. This does not necessarily mean the child understands the concept of one, but that his parents have taught him to use his or her fingers to show a number. Children who are functioning around age 2 will begin to attempt to count "one, two" and may respond to the question, "How many do you have?" Even if the child has more than two objects, she may say the numbers she knows.

The facilitator needs to have in mind the type of skills to elicit and creative ways of stimulating the child's discussion of such concepts. The facilitator can arrange many opportunities for the child to count, to compare quantities, and to measure. In the block area of the playroom, cars, people, and blocks can be counted, and comparisons of sizes and number, measurements of light and heavy, and distinctions between short and long can be made. In the house area of the playroom, similar comparisons are possible.

Often, young children will count without prompting. Other times, the facilitator will need to elicit information about the child's understanding. For example, the facilitator might say, "I want the bowl with a lot of cherries," "You can take the napkin with the most cookies," "I need three more blocks," or "Let's see if yours is taller than mine. Let's count them." Observe whether the child uses one-to-one correspondence when counting, and when the child has finished, the facilitator should ask, "How many do you have?" Children who do not understand cardinality may begin to count all over again, not realizing that the last number they said is the total.

For children who are clearly counting with one-to-one correspondence and have cardinality, the facilitator will want to determine whether the child can understand ordinality, or the relationship of numbers to each other. To see if the child can understand that he or she can pick up a count from the previous total, the facilitator might say, "We've got five pieces of track, let's count as we finish the train track and see how many pieces it took to make the circle." Observe whether the child can pick up with the number five and continue to count as pieces are added. When drawing, the facilitator may say, "I have four markers. I'm going to borrow one of yours. Then I will have____?" or "You have seven markers? Well, here are a blue one and a red one for you. How many markers do you have now?" While playing with the train, the facilitator could say, "Let's put the giraffe in the last car." It is also important to see if older children can count an array of objects that are not arranged in a line. In other words, when all the food items are on the table, can the child count them accurately without counting each object more than once or omitting objects from the count? This requires that the child understand that each item must be counted only once. He or she therefore needs to have a strategy to make sure that happens. When assessing an older child, the facilitator also can explore the child's ability to do simple concrete calculation. For example, during snack the facilitator can ask, "Mom wants two crackers and you want two crackers. How many do I need to take out of the box?" Understanding of abstract representations of number through writing number symbols also can be done during play, while making signs or money for the "store" or while drawing or writing a list.

The facilitator needs to keep in mind not only what she is seeing in terms of concepts but also how to elicit a range of quantitative understandings. She needs to explore the level of precision in counting, the largest numbers the child can handle, and the level of abstraction the child can understand. Although the facilitator should foster conversation and turn-taking, using open-ended questions, and not "testing" the child, it may be necessary to ask some questions to find out how the child thinks. As much as possible, questioning should be in an informal conversational manner.

Two-year-old Tamara was seen in her home with her mother, Tyria, by the speech-language pathologist and the psychologist. Tamara previously had been enrolled in an early intervention program in another state and had just moved to the area. Information provided before the assessment revealed that Tamara was unable to talk or walk. She had extremely low tone and spent most of her day in a baby seat. Tamara looked intently at Lisa, the speech therapist, and then back to her mother, and clearly recognized that Lisa was different from her mother. Tyria gave Tamara her favorite toy, a rattle with nubby rubber bumps on the end, and she put it directly in her mouth. Lisa then brought out from her bag a clear plastic wand that had bright colors in liquid that fell and sparkled when it was tipped. She held the toy up and tipped it so that Tamara could watch the sparkles fall. Tamara dropped her rattle and reached for the new toy. After playing a few minutes with the wand, Tamara looked away. Her mother said to Tamara, "Look, there's Missy!" Tamara recognized the word Missy *and smiled in anticipation before she saw the cat. Tamara reached to touch the cat and smiled again.*

Although Tamara was functioning below her age level, she showed the ability to discriminate likenesses and differences; did not use each object in the same way, demonstrating the ability to classify objects; and revealed the ability to categorize objects by function when she petted the cat.

Meera was 5 years old and transitioning from an inclusive preschool to kindergarten. Meera's mother, Maya, and father, Sanjay, were from Pakistan and had been in this country for 1 year. They both spoke English to Meera in the home. With regard to Meera's understanding of number, they stated that she counts to 10 and gives them up to three items accurately.

The play assessment was conducted in Meera's preschool classroom and out on the playground. The TPBA team observed Meera interacting in her classroom at the various centers, observed her with peers on the playground for a few minutes, and then brought her back into the classroom to play with the facilitator while the rest of the class was still outside playing. During the classroom observation time, the team observed Meera in the math and science center where a group was comparing and measuring their feet and hands. Meera was able to say that her hands were "little" compared to Josh's and Carlo's. When the group at the table used small blocks to see how long their feet were, Meera watched her peers line up blocks by their feet. Meera randomly placed blocks by her feet.

Out on the playground, Annie, who was playing in the sandbox, called to Meera, "Hey, Meera, bring some shovels. I've got buckets." Meera went to the toy container, brought out two plastic shovels, and ran to Annie. Meera and Annie were burying plastic animals. The facilitator joined them with another shovel and began to play with them. "I'd like to dig too. I need an animal too, Meera." Meera smiled and handed her a cow. "Mr. Cow wants some friends to come over." Meera and Annie hastily found numerous animals to bring over and arranged them by the "house." "Oh my, look at all my friends! I wonder how many of my friends came over." Meera used her finger to point to each animal, but counted several animals twice and used two numbers on one animal, ending up with a total of 10.

Meera is able to rote count to 10 and understands the principle of identifying items, but she does not yet have accurate one-to-one correspondence. Nor does she understand that each item is counted only once. She is able to accurately identify global quantities, such as big *and* little, *but is not doing relational comparison using* bigger *or* smaller.

She was able to see that she needed to get two shovels for her friend and herself. Meera seemed to like to end her counting with "five" or "ten," perhaps because these are frequently end counts for fingers on a hand or in songs and finger plays.

REFERENCES

Abbeduto, L., & Short-Meyerson, K. (2002). Linguistic influences on social interaction. In S.F. Warren & M.E. Fey (Series Eds.) & H. Goldstein, L.A. Kaczmarek, & K.M. English (Vol. Eds.), *Communication and language intervention series: Vol. 10. Promoting social communication: Children with developmental disabilities from birth to adolescence* (pp. 27–54). Baltimore: Paul H. Brookes Publishing Co.

Aguiar, A., & Baillargeon, R. (1999). 2.5-month-old infants' reasoning about when objects should and should not be occluded. *Cognitive Psychology, 39,* 116–157.

Asendorpf, J.B., Warkentin, V., & Baudonniere, P. (1996). Self-awareness and other-awareness II: Mirror self-recognition, social contingency awareness, and synchronic imitation. *Developmental Psychology, 32,* 313–321.

Bahrick, L.E., Hernandez-Reif, M., & Pickens, J.N. (1997). The effect of retrieval cues on visual preferences and memory in infancy: Evidence for a four-phase attention function. *Journal of Experimental Psychology, 67,* 1–20.

Bahrick, L.E., & Pickens, J.N. (1995). Infant memory for object motion across a period of three months: Implications for a four-phase attention function. *Journal of Exceptional Child Psychology, 59*(3):343–371.

Bailey, D.B., & Wolery, M. (1999). *Teaching infants and preschoolers with disabilities.* Columbus, OH: Charles E. Merrill.

Baillargeon, R. (2001). Infants' physical knowledge: Of acquired expectations and core principles. In E. Dupoux (Ed.), *Language, brain, and cognitive development: Essays in honor of Jacques Mehler* (pp. 341–361). Cambridge, MA: The MIT Press.

Baillargeon, R. (2002). The acquisition of physical knowledge in infancy: A summary in eight lessons. In U. Goswami (Ed.), *Blackwell handbook of childhood cognitive development* (pp. 47–83). Malden, MA: Blackwell Publishing.

Baillargeon, R. (2004). Infants' reasoning about hidden objects: Evidence for event-general and event-specific expectations. *Developmental Science* 7(4), 391–414.

Baron-Cohen, S. (1995). *Mindblindness: An essay on autism and theory of mind.* Boston: The MIT Press/Bradford Books.

Baron-Cohen, S., & Wheelwright, S. (1999). Obsessions in children with autism or Asperger syndrome: A content analysis in terms of core domains of cognition. *British Journal of Psychiatry, 175,* 484–490.

Baron-Cohen, S., Wheelwright, S., Lawson, J., Griffin, R., & Hill, J. (2002). The exact mind: Empathizing and systemizing in autism spectrum conditions. In U. Goswami (Ed.), *Blackwell handbook of childhood cognitive development* (pp. 491–514). Malden, MA: Blackwell Publishing.

Barr, R., & Hayne, H. (1999). Developmental changes in imitation from television during infancy. *Child Development, 70,* 1067–1081.

Bartch, K., & Wellman, H.M. (1995). *Children talk about the mind.* New York: Oxford University Press.

Bauer, P.J. (1996). Development of memory in early childhood. In N. Cowan (Ed.), *The development of memory in childhood* (pp. 83–111). Hove, UK: Psychology Press.

Bauer, P.J. (2002). Early memory development. In U. Goswami (Ed.), *Blackwell handbook of childhood cognitive development* (pp. 127–146). Malden, MA: Blackwell Publishing.

Bauer, P.J., Wenner, J.A., Dropik, P.L., & Wewerka, S. (2000). Parameters of remembering and forgetting in the transition from infancy to early childhood. *Monographs of the Society for Research in Child Development, 65*(4, Serial No. 263).

Belsky, J., & Most, R. (1981). From exploration to play: A cross-sectional study of infant free play behavior. *Developmental Psychology, 17,* 630–639.

Berg, D.N. (1994). The role of play in literacy development. In P. Antonacci & C.N. Hedley (Eds.), *Natural approaches to reading and writing* (pp. 33–48). Norwood, NJ: Ablex Publishing.

Bergen, D. (1998). Development of the sense of humor. In W. Ruch (Ed.), *The sense of humor: Explorations of personality characteristics* (pp. 329–360). New York: Mouton de Gruyer.

Bergen, D. (2003). Humor, play, and child development. In A.J. Klein (Ed.), *Humor in children's lives: A guidebook for practitioners* (pp. 17–32). Westport, CT: Greenwood Publishing Group.

Bermejo, V. (1996). Cardinality development and counting. *Developmental Psychology, 32,* 263–268.

Bjorkland, D.F., & Sneider, W. (1996). The interaction of knowledge, aptitude, and strategies in children's memory performance. In H. Reese (Ed.), *Advances in child development and behavior* (Vol. 26, pp. 59–89). San Diego: Academic Press.

Bomba, P.C. (1984). The development of orientation categories between 2 and 4 months of age. *Journal of Experimental Psychology, 37,* 609–636.

Borkowski, J.G., & Burke, J.E. (1996). Theories, models, and measurements of executive functioning: An information processing perspective. In G.R. Lyon & N.A. Krasnegor (Eds.), *Attention, memory, and executive function* (pp. 235–262). Baltimore: Paul H. Brookes Publishing Co.

Bornstein, M.H. (1981). Psychological studies of color perception in human infants: Habituation, discrimination, and categorization, recognition and conceptualization. In L.P. Lipsitt (Ed.), *Advances in infancy research* (Vol. 1, pp. 1–40). Norwood, NJ: Ablex.

Bretherton, I., & Beeghly, M. (1982). Talking about internal states: The acquisition of an explicit theory of mind. *Developmental Psychology, 18,* 906–921.

Bryant, P., & Nunes, T. (2002). Children's understanding of mathematics. In U. Goswami (Ed.), *Blackwell handbook of childhood cognitive development* (pp. 512–539). Malden, MA: Blackwell Publishing.

Butterworth, G. (1999). Neonatal imitation: Existence, mechanisms and motives. In J. Nadel & G. Butterworth (Eds.), *Imitation in infancy* (pp. 63–88). Cambridge: Cambridge University Press.

Carlson, S.M., & Moses I.J. (2001). Individual differences in inhibitory control and children's theory of mind. *Child Development, 72,* 1032–1053.

Carpenter, M., Nagell, K., & Tomasello, M. (1998). Social cognition, joint attention, and communicative competence from 9 to 15 months of age. *Monographs of the Society for Research in Child Development, 63,*(4, Serial No. 255).

Carver, L.J., & Bauer, P.J. (2000). The dawning of a past: The emergence of long-term explicit memory in infancy. *Journal of Experimental Psychology: General, 130,* 726–745.

Carver, L.J., Bauer, P.J., & Nelson, C.A. (2000). Associations between infant brain activity and recall memory. *Developmental Science, 3,* 234–246.

Case, R. (1996). Introduction: Reconceptualizing the nature of children's conceptual structures and their development in middle childhood. In R. Case & Y. Okamoto (Eds.), The role of central conceptual structures in the development of children's thought. *Monographs of the Society for Research in Child Development, 61*(1-2, Serial No. 246), 1–26.

Case, R. (1998). The development of central conceptual structures. In D. Kuhn & R. Siegler (Eds.), *Handbook of child psychology: Vol. 2. Cognition, perception, and language* (5th ed., pp. 745–800). New York: John Wiley & Sons.

Case, R., Okamoto, Y., Griffin, S., McKeough, A., Bleiker, C., Henderson, B., & Stephenson, K.M. (1996). The role of central conceptual structures in the development of children's thought. *Monographs of the Society for Research in Child Development, 61* (1–2, Serial No. 246).

Chen, Z., Sanchez, R.P., & Campbell, T. (1997). From beyond to within their grasp: The rudiments of analogical problem-solving in 10–13-month-olds. *Developmental Psychology, 33,* 790–801.

Cicchetti, D., & Sroufe, L.A. (1976). The relationship between affective and cognitive development in Down's syndrome infants. *Child Development, 47*(4), 920–929.

Clay, R.A. (1997). Why are knock-knock jokes so funny to kids? *APA Monitor, 28*(9), 17.

Cohen, L.B., & Cashon, C.H. (2001). Infant object segregation implies information integration. *Journal of Experimental Child Psychology, 78,* 75–83.

Cohen, M.A., & Gross, P.J. (1979). *The developmental resource: Behavioral sequences for assessment and program planning.* New York: Basic Books.

Collie, R., & Hayne, H. (1999). Deferred imitation by 6- and 9-month-old infants: More evidence for declarative memory. *Developmental Psychology, 35,* 83–90.

Conrood, E.E., & Stone, W.L. (2004). Early concerns of parents of children with autistic and nonautistic disorders. *Infants and Young Children, 17*(3), 258–268.

Csibra, G., Gergely, G., Biro, S., Koos, O., & Brockbank, M. (1999). Goal-directed attribution without agency cues: The perception of "pure reason" in infancy. *Cognition, 72,* 237–267.

DeCasper, A.J., & Spence, M.J. (1986). Prenatal maternal speech influences newborns' perceptions of speech sounds. *Infant Behavior and Development, 9,* 133–150.

Denkla, M.B. (1996). A theory and model of executive function: A neuropsychological perspective. In G.R. Lyon & N.A. Krasnegor (Eds.), *Attention, memory, and executive function* (pp. 263–278). Baltimore: Paul H. Brookes Publishing Co.

deVilliers, J.G., & deVilliers, P.A. (2000). Linguistic determinism and the understanding of false beliefs. In P. Mitchel & K.J. Riggs (Eds.), *Children's reasoning and the mind* (pp. 87–99). Hove, England: Psychology Press.

Diamond, A., Towle, C., & Boyer, K. (1994). Young children's performance on a task sensitive to the memory functions of the medial temporal lobe in adults: The delayed nonmatching-to-sample task reveals problems that are due to non-memory-related task demands. *Behavioral Neuroscience, 108*(4), 659–680.

Dockett, S. (1999). Thinking about play, playing about thinking. In E. Dau (Ed.), *Child's play* (pp. 5–15). Baltimore: Paul H. Brookes Publishing Co.

Dykens, E.M., Hodapp, R.M., & Finucane, B.M. (2000). *Genetics and mental retardation syndromes: A new look at behavior and interventions.* Baltimore: Paul H. Brookes Publishing Co.

Dykman, R.A., Ackerman, P.T., & Oglesby, D.M. (1979). Selective and sustained attention in hyperactive, learning-disabled and normal boys. *Journal of Nervous and Mental Disease, 167,* 288–297.

Eimas, P.D., & Quinn, P.C. (1994). Studies on the formation of perceptually based basic-level categories in young infants. *Child Development, 65,* 903–917.

Eslinger, P.J. (1996). Conceptualizing, describing, and measuring components of executive function: A summary. In G.R. Lyon & N.A. Krasnegor (Eds.), *Attention, memory, and executive function* (pp. 367–395). Baltimore: Paul H. Brookes Publishing Co.

Farmer, M. (2000). Language and social cognition in children with specific language impairment. *Journal of Child Psychology and Psychiatry and Allied Disciplines, 41*(5), 627–638.

Fein, G.G., Ardila-Rey, A.E., & Groth, L.A. (2000). The narrative connection: Stories and literacy. In K.A. Roskos & J.F. Christie (Eds.), *Play and literacy in early childhood: Research from multiple perspectives* (pp. 27–44). Mahwah, NJ: Lawrence Erlbaum Associates.

Fenson, L., Kagan, J., Kearsley, R., & Zelazo, P. (1976). The devlopmental progression of manipulative play in the first two years. *Child Development, 47*, 232–236.

Fewell, R.R., & Vadasy, P.F (1983). *Learning through play.* Allen, TX: Developmental Learning Materials.

Fivush, R. (1997). Event memory in early childhood. In N. Cowan (Ed.), *The development of memory in childhood* (pp. 139–161). Hove, England: Psychology Press.

Flavell, J.H. (2000). Development of knowledge about the mental world. *International Journal of Psychology, 28*, 15–23.

Fletcher, J.M., Shaywitz, S.E., Shankweiler, D.P., Katz, L., Liberman, I.Y., Fowler, A., Francis, D.J., Stuebing, K.K., & Shaywitz, B.A. (1994). Cognitive profiles of reading disability: Comparisons of discrepancy and low achievement definitions. *Journal of Educational Psychology, 85*, 1–18.

Floccia, C., Christophe, A., & Bertoncini, J. (1997). High-amplitude sucking and newborns: The quest for underlying mechanisms. *Journal of Experimental Child Psychology, 64*, 175–198.

Franklin, M.B. (2000). Meanings of play in the developmental-interaction tradition. In N. Nager & E.K. Shapiro (Eds.), *Revisiting a progressive pedagogy: The developmental-interaction approach* (pp. 47– 72). Albany, NY: State University of New York Press.

Fuson, K.C. (1988). *Children's counting and conception of number.* New York: Springer-Verlag.

Fuson, K.C. (1992). Relationships between counting and cardinality from age 2 to age 8. In J. Bideaud, C. Maljac, & J. Fischer (Eds.), *Pathway to number: Children's developing numerical ability* (pp. 127–149). Mahwah, NJ: Lawrence Erlbaum Associates.

Gaithercole, S.E. (1998). The development of memory. *Journal of Child Psychology and Psychiatry and Allied Disciplines, 39*, 3–27.

Garfield, J.L., Petersen, C.C., & Perry, T. (2001). Social cognition, language acquisition and the development of the theory of mind. *Mind and Language, 16*(5), 494.

Garvey, C. (1977). *Play.* Cambridge, MA: Harvard University Press.

Gaskins, S., & Goncu, A. (1992). Cultural variation in play: A challenge to Piaget and Vygotsky. *The Quarterly Newsletter of the Laboratory of Comparative of Human Cognition, 14*(2), 31–35.

Gauvain, M. (2001). *The social context of cognitive development.* New York: Guilford Press.

Geary, D.C. (1995). *Children's mathematical development: Research and practical application.* Washington, DC: American Psychological Association.

Gelman, R., & Gallistel, C.R. (1978). *The child's understanding of number.* Cambridge, MA: Harvard University Press.

Gelman, R., & Meck, E. (1986). The notion of principle: the case of counting. In J. Hiebert (Ed.), *Conceptual and procedural knowledge: The case of mathematics* (pp. 29–57). Hillsdale, NJ: Lawrence Erlbaum Associates.

Gelman, S.A., & Opfer, J.E. (2002). Development of the animate-inanimate distinction. In U. Goswami (Ed.), *Blackwell handbook of childhood cognitive development* (pp. 151–166). Malden, MA: Blackwell Publishing.

Gelman, S.A., Spelke, E.S., & Meck, E. (1983). What preschoolers know about animate and inanimate objects. In D. Rogers & J.A. Sloboda (Eds.), *The acquisition of symbolic skills* (pp. 297–324). New York: Plenum.

Gergely, G. (2002). The development of understanding of self and agency. In U. Goswami (Ed.), *Blackwell handbook of childhood cognitive development* (pp. 26–46). Malden, MA: Blackwell Publishing.

Gergely, G., Magyar, Z., Csibra, G., & Biro, S. (1995). Taking the intentional stance at 12 months of age. *Cognition, 56*, 165–193.

Giedd, J.N., Blumenthal, J., Jeffries, N.O., Rajapakse, J.C., Vaituzis, C., & Liu, H. (1999).

Development of the human corpus callosum during childhood and adolescence: A longitudinal MRI study. *Progress in Neuropsychopharmacology & Biological Psychiatry, 23,* 571–588.

Ginsberg, H.P., Klein, A., & Starkey, P. (1998). The development of children's mathematical thinking: Connecting research with practice. In I.E. Sigel & K.A. Renninger (Eds.), *Handbook of child psychology: Vol. 4, Cognition, perception, and language* (5th ed., pp. 401–476). New York: John Wiley & Sons.

Ginsberg, H.P., & Opper, S. (1988). *Piaget's theory of intellectual development.* Englewood Cliffs, NJ: Prentice Hall.

Goncu, A. (1993). Development of intersubjectivity in the social-pretend play of preschool children. *Human Development, 36,* 185–198.

Goncu, A., Mistry, J., & Mosier, C. (2000). Cultural variations in the play of toddlers. *International Journal of Behavioral Development, 24,* 321–329.

Goncu, A., Patt, M., & Kouba, E. (2002). Understanding young children's pretend play. In P.K. Smith & C.H. Hart (Eds.), *Blackwell handbook of childhood social development* (pp. 418–437). Malden, MA: Blackwell Publishing.

Goncu, A., Tuermer, U., Jain, J., & Johnson, D. (1999). Childrens' play as cultural activity. In A. Goncu (Ed.), *Children's engagement in the world: Sociocultural perspectives* (pp. 148–170). New York: Cambridge University Press.

Gopnik, A., & Astington, J.W. (2000). Children's understanding of representational change and its relation to the understanding of false belief and the appearance of reality. In K. Lee (Ed.), *Childhood development: The essential readings* (pp. 177–200). Oxford: UK: Blackwell.

Gopnik, A., & Meltzoff, A.N. (1997). *Words, thoughts, and theories.* Cambridge, MA: The MIT Press.

Gopnik, A., & Wellman, H.M. (1994). The theory theory. In L.A. Hirschfeld & S.A. Gelman (Eds.), *Mapping the mind: Domain specificity in cognition and culture* (pp. 257–293). New York: Cambridge University Press.

Goralick, M. (1975, February 15). A classification of concept representation. In *Piagetian theory and its implications for the helping professions.* Proceedings of the fourth interdisciplinary seminar (p. 336). University of Southern California, Los Angeles. (ERIC Document Reproduction Service No. ED103125)

Gutheil, G., Vera, A., & Keil, F.C. (1998). Do houseflies think? Patterns of induction and biological beliefs in development. *Cognition, 66,* 33–49.

Haight, W.L., Wang, X-I., Fung, H., Williams, K., & Mintz, J. (1999). Universal, developmental, and variable aspects of young children's play: A cross-cultural comparison of pretending at home. *Child Development, 70,* 1477–1488.

Haith, M.M., & Benson, J.B. (1998). Infant cognition. In W. Damon [Series Ed.] and D. Kuhn & R. Siegler [Vol. Eds.], *Handbook of child psychology: Vol. 2. Cognition, perception, and language development* (5th ed., pp. 199–254). New York: John Wiley & Sons.

Halford, G.S. (2002). Information-processing models of cognitive development. In U. Goswami (Ed.), *Blackwell handbook of childhood cognitive development* (pp. 555–574). Malden, MA: Blackwell Publishing.

Halperin, J.M. (1996). Conceptualizing, describing, and measuring components of executive function: A summary. In G.R. Lyon and N.A. Krasnegor (Eds.), *Attention, memory, and executive function* (pp. 119–136). Baltimore: Paul H. Brookes Publishing Co.

Harley, E. (1999). Stop, look, and listen: Adopting an investigative stance when children play. In E. Dau (Ed.), *Child's play: Revisiting play in early childhood settings.* Baltimore: Paul H. Brookes Publishing Co.

Harris, S., Kasari, C., & Sigman, M. (1996). Joint attention and language gains in children with Down syndrome. *American Journal on Mental Retardation, 100*(6), 608–619.

Hasselhorn, M. (1995). Beyond production deficiency and utilization inefficiency: Mechanisms of the emergence of strategic categorization in episodic memory tasks. In F.E. Weinert & W. Schneider (Eds.), *Memory performance and competencies: Issues in growth and development* (pp. 141–159). Mahwah, NJ: Lawrence Erlbaum Associates.

Hayne, H., Boniface, J., & Barr, R. (2000). The development of declarative memory in human infants: Age-related changes in deferred imitation. *Behavioral Neuroscience, 114,* 77–83.

Hiebert, J., & Lefevre, P. (1986). Conceptual and procedural knowledge in mathematics: An introductory analysis. In J. Hiebert (Ed.), *Conceptual and procedural knowledge: The case of mathematics* (pp. 1–28). Mahwah, NJ: Lawrence Erlbaum Associates.

Hodapp, R.M., DesJardin, J.L., & Ricci, L.A. (2003). Genetic syndromes of mental retardation: Should they matter for the early interventions? *Infants and Young Children, 16*(2), 152–160.

Howe, M.L. (2000). *The fate of early memories: Developmental science and retention of childhood experiences.* Washington, DC: American Psychological Association.

Howes, C., & Matheson, C.C. (1992). Sequences in the development of competent play with peers: Social and pretend play. *Developmental Psychology, 28,* 961–974.

Hudson, J.A., & Sheffield, E.G. (1998). Déjà vu all over again: Effects of reenactment on toddlers event memory. *Child Development, 69*(1), 51–67.

Hudson, J.A., Sosa, B.B., & Shapiro, L.R. (1997). Scripts and plans: The development of preschool children's event knowledge and event planning. In S.L. Friedman & E.K. Scholnick (Eds.), *The developmental psychology of planning: Why, how and when do we plan?* (pp. 77–102). Mahwah, NJ: Lawrence Erlbaum Associates.

Jennings, S. (1995). Playing for real. *International Play Journal, 3,* 132–141.

Johnson, J., Christie, J., & Yawkey, T. (1987). *Play and early childhood development.* Glenview, IL: Scott Foresman.

Jusczyk, P.W., Johnson, S.P., Spelke, E.S., & Kennedy, L.J. (1999). Synchronous change and perception of object unity: Evidence from adults and infants. *Cognition, 71,* 257–288.

Jusczyk, P.W., & Kemler Nelson, D.G. (1996). Syntactic units, prosody, and psychological reality during infancy. In J. L. Morgan & K. Demuth (Eds.), *Signal to syntax: Bootstrapping from speech to grammar in early acquisition* (pp. 389–408). Mahwah, NJ: Lawrence Erlbaum Associates.

Klein, A.J. (2003). *Humor in children's lives: A guidebook for practitioners.* Westport, CT: Praeger.

Kolb, K. (1990). Humor is not a laughing matter. *Early Report, 18*(1), 1–2.

Kopp, C.B. (1997). Young children: Emotional management, instrumental control, and plans. In S.L. Friedman & E.K. Scholnick (Eds.), *The developmental psychology of planning: Why, how, and when do we plan?* (pp. 103–124). Mahwah, NJ: Lawrence Erlbaum Associates.

Kopp, C.B. (2000). Self regulation in children. In J.J. Smelser & P.B. Baltes (Eds.), *International encyclopedia of the social and behavioral sciences.* Oxford, England: Elsevier.

Kusmierek, A., Cunningham, K., Fox-Gleason, S., Hanson, M., & Lorenzini, D. (1986). *South metropolitan association birth to three transdisciplinary assessment guide.* Flossmoore, IL: South Metropolitan Association for Low-Incidence Handicapped.

Landy, S. (2002). *Pathways to competence: Encouraging healthy social and emotional development in young children.* Baltimore: Paul H. Brookes Publishing Co.

Legerstee, M. (1992). A review of the animate-inanimate distinction in infancy: Implications for models of social and cognitive knowing. *Early Development and Parenting, 1,* 59–67.

Legerstee, M., Barna, J., & DiAdamo, C. (2000). Precursors to the development of intention at 6 months: Understanding people and their actions. *Developmental Psychology, 36,* 261–273.

Lewis, C., & Carpendale, J. (2002). Social cognition. In P.K. Smith & C.H. Hart (Eds.), *Blackwell handbook of childhood social development* (pp. 375–393). Malden, MA: Blackwell Publishing.

Liben, L.S. (2002). Spatial development in childhood: Where are we now? In U. Goswami (Ed.), *Blackwell handbook of childhood cognitive development* (pp. 6–25). Malden, MA: Blackwell Publishing.

Linn, M.I., Goodman, J.F., & Lender, W.L. (2000). Played out? Passive behavior of young children with Down syndrome during unstructured play. *Journal of Early Intervention, 23*(4), 264–278.

Liston, C., & Kagan, J. (2002). Memory enhancement in early childhood. *Nature, 419,* 896.

Luo, Y. (2001, July). *Young infants' knowledge about occlusion events.* Paper presented at the Biennial International Conference on Infant Studies, Brighton, England.

Lyon, G.R. (1996). The need for conceptual and theoretical clarity in the study of attention, memory, and executive function. In G.R. Lyon & N.A. Krasnegor (Eds.), *Attention, memory, and executive function* (pp. 3–10). Baltimore: Paul H. Brookes Publishing Co.

Lyon, R. (2000, November 21). *Other factors that influence learning to read.* Available online at http://www.brainconnection.com

Lyon, T.D., & Flavell, J.H. (1994). Young children's understanding of "remember" and "forget." *Child Development, 65*(5), 1357–1371.

Maccoby, E.E. (1998). *The two sexes.* Cambridge, MA: Harvard University Press.

Mandler, J.M., & McDonough, L. (1993). Concept formation in infancy. *Cognitive Development, 8*(3), 291–318.

Mandler, J.M., & McDonough, L. (1998). On developing a knowledge base in infancy. *Developmental Psychology, 34,* 1274–1288.

Marlier, L., Schaal, B., & Soussignan, R. (1998). Neonatal responsiveness to the odor of amniotic and lacteal fluids: A test of perinatal chemosensory continuity. *Child Development, 69,* 611–623.

Martin, R.A. (1998). Approaches to the sense of humor: A historical review. In W. Ruch (Ed.), *The sense of humor: Explorations of a personality characteristic* (pp. 15–62). New York: Mouton de Gruyter.

McCune-Nicholich, L. (1981). Toward symbolic functioning: Structure of early pretend games and potential parallels with language. *Child Development, 52,* 785–797.

McGhee, P.E. (1977). A model of the origins and early development of incongruity-based humor. In A.J. Chapman & H.C. Foot (Eds.), *It's a funny thing, humor.* Oxford, England: Pergamon.

McGhee, P.E. (1979). *Humor: Its origin and development.* San Francisco: Freeman.

McGhee, P. (1989). *Humor and children's development: A guide to practical applications.* New York: Haworth Press.

McGhee, P. (2002). Understanding and promoting the development of children's humor. Dubuque, IA: Kendall/Hunt.

Meltzoff, A.N. (1995). Understanding the intentions of others: Re-enactment of intended acts by 18-month-old children. *Developmental Psychology, 31,* 838–850.

Meltzoff, A.N. (2000). Understanding the intentions of others: Re-enactment of intended acts by 18-month-old children. In K. Lee (Ed.), *Childhood development: The essential readings* (pp. 151–174). Oxford, England: Blackwell.

Meltzoff, A.N. (2002). Imitation as a mechanism of social cognition: Origins of empathy, theory of mind, and the representation of action. In U. Goswami (Ed.), *Blackwell handbook of childhood cognitive development* (pp. 6–25). Malden, MA: Blackwell Publishing.

Meltzoff, A.N., & Moore, M.K. (1998). Infant intersubjectivity: Broadening the dialogue to include imitation, identity, and intention. In S. Braten (Ed.), *Intersubjective communication and emotion in early ontogeny* (pp. 47–62). Paris: Cambridge University Press.

Mirsky, A.F. (1996). Disorders of attention: A neurological perspective. In G.R. Lyon & N.A. Krasnegor (Eds.), *Attention, memory, and executive function* (pp. 21–95). Baltimore: Paul H. Brookes Publishing Co.

Mirsky, A.F., Ingraham, L.J., & Kugelmass, S. (1995). Neuropsychological assessment of attention and its pathology in the Israeli cohort. *Schizophrenia Bulletin, 21,* 183–192.

Mix, K.S. (1999). Similarity and numerical equivalence: Appearances count. *Cognitive Development, 14,* 269–297.

Mix, K.S., Huttenlocher, J., & Levine, S.C. (2002). *Quantitative development in infancy and early childhood.* New York: Oxford University Press.

Moore, C. (1999). Gaze following and the control of attention. In P. Rochat (Ed.), *Early social cognition: Understanding others in the first months of life* (pp. 241–256). Mahwah, NJ: Lawrence Erlbaum Associates.

Morgan, E., & Watson, S. (1989). *Insight developmental checklist* (2nd ed.). Logan, UT: HOPE, Inc.

Morris, R.D. (1996). Relationships and distinctions among the concepts of attention, memory, and executive function. In G.R. Lyon & N.A. Krasnegor (Eds.), *Attention, memory, and executive function* (pp. 11–16). Baltimore: Paul H. Brookes Publishing Co.

Nelson, C.A. (1995). The ontogeny of human memory: A cognitive neuroscience perspective. *Developmental Psychology, 31,* 723–738.

Nelson, C.A., & Collins, P.F. (1997). The neurobiological basis of early memory development. In N. Cowan (Ed.), *The development of memory in childhood* (pp. 41–82). Hove, England: Psychology Press.

Neuman, S.B., & Roskos, K. (1991). The influence of literacy-enriched play centers on preschoolers' conceptions of the functions of print. In J. Christie (Ed.), *Play and early literacy development* (pp. 167–187). Albany, NY: State University of New York Press.

Owacki, G. (1999). *Literacy through play.* Portsmouth, NH: Heinemann.

Paparella, T., & Kasari, C. (2004). Joint attention skills and language development in special needs populations: Translating research to practice. *Infants and Young Children, 17*(3), 269–280.

Pellegrini, A.D. (1988). Elementary school children's rough-and-tumble play and social competence. *Developmental Psychology, 24,* 802–806.

Pellegrini, A.D. (1993). Boys' rough-and-tumble play, social competence and group composition. *British Journal of Developmental Psychology, 11,* 237–248.

Pellegrini, A.D. (2002). Rough-and-tumble play from childhood through adolescence: Development and possible functions. In P.K. Smith & C.H. Hart (Eds.), *Blackwell handbook of childhood social development* (pp. 438–454). Mauldin, MA: Blackwell Publishing.

Pellegrini, A.D., & Bartini, M. (2001). Dominance in early adolescent boys: Affiliative and aggressive dimensions and possible functions. *Merrill-Palmer Quarterly, 47,* 142–163.

Pellegrini A.D., & Smith P.K. (1998). Physical activity play: The nature and function of a neglected aspect of play. *Child Development, 69,* 577–598.

Pennington, B.F. (1997). Dimensions of executive functions in normal and abnormal development. In N.A. Krasnegor, G.R. Lyon, & P.S. Goldman-Rakic (Eds.), *Development of the prefrontal cortex: Evolution, neurobiology, and behavior* (pp. 265–281). Baltimore: Paul H. Brookes Publishing Co.

Peterson, C.C., & Rideout, R. (1998). Memory for medical emergencies experienced by 1- and 2-year-olds. *Developmental Psychology, 34,* 1059–1072.

Phillips, A.T., Wellman, H.M., & Spelke, E.S. (2002). Infants' ability to connect gaze and emotional expression to intentional action. *Cognition, 85*(1), 53–79.

Piaget, J. (1952). *Origins of intelligence in children.* New York: International Universities Press. [Original work published 1936].

Piaget, J. (1962). *Play, dreams, and imitation in childhood.* New York: Norton.

Piaget, J., & Inhelder, B. (1969). *The psychology of the child.* London: Routledge & Kegan Paul. (Original work published in 1967.)

Pipp, S., Easterbrooks, M.A., & Brown, S.R. (1993). Attachment status and complexity of infants' self- and other-knowledge when tested with mother and father. *Social Development, 2,* 1–14.

Porter, R.H., & Winberg, J. (1999). Unique salience of maternal breast odors for newborn infants. *Neuroscience and Biobehavioral Reviews, 23,* 439–449.

Posner, M.K., Rothbart, M.K., Thomas-Thrapp, L., & Gerardi, G. (1998). The development of orienting to locations and objects. In R.D. Wright (Ed.), *Visual attention: Vancouver studies in cognitive science* (Vol. 8, pp. 269–288). New York: Oxford University Press.

Poulin-Dubois, D., Lepage, A., & Ferland, D. (1996). Infants' concept of animacy. *Cognitive Development, 11,* 19–36.

Premack, D. (1990). The infants' theory of self-propelled objects. *Cognition, 36,* 1–16.

Prendergast, S.G., & McCollum, J.A. (1996). Let's talk: The effect of maternal hearing status on interaction with toddlers who are deaf. *American Annals of the Deaf, 141*(1), 11–18.

Prizant, B.M., Wetherby, A.M., & Roberts, J.E. (2000). Communication problems. In C.H. Zeanah, Jr. (Ed.), *Handbook of infant mental health* (2nd ed., pp. 282–297). New York: Guilford Press.

Quinn, P.C. (2002). Early categorization: A new synthesis. In U. Goswami (Ed.), *Blackwell handbook of childhood cognitive development* (pp. 84–101). Mauldin, MA: Blackwell Publishing.

Quinn, P.C., Eimas, P.D., & Rosenkrantz, S.L. (1993). Evidence for representation of perceptually similar natural categories by 3-month-old and 4-month-old infants. *Perception, 22*(4), 463–475.

Quinn, P.C., Johnson, M.H., Mareschal, D., Rakison, D.H., & Younger, B.A. (2000). Understanding early categorization: One process or two? *Infancy, 1*(1), 111–122.

Rakison, D.H., & Butterworth, G.E. (1998). Infants' use of object parts in early categorization. *Developmental Psychology, 34,* 49–62.

Rast, M., & Meltzoff, A.N. (1995). Memory and representation in young children with Down syndrome: Exploring deferred imitation and object permanence. *Developmental Psychopathology, 7,* 393–407.

Reyna, V.F., & Brainerd, C.J. (1995). Fuzzy-trace theory: An interim synthesis. *Learning and Individual Differences, 7,* 1–75.

Rochat, P. (2001). *The infant's world.* Cambridge, MA: Harvard University Press.

Rochat, P., Querido, J.G., & Striano, T. (1999). Emerging sensitivity to the timing and structure of protoconversation in early infancy. *Developmental Psychology, 35*(4), 950–957.

Rock, A., Trainor, L., & Addison, T. (1999). Distinctive messages in infant-directed lullabies and play songs. *Developmental Psychology, 35*(2), 527–534.

Roeckelein, J. (2002). *The psychology of humor: A reference guide and annotated bibliography.* Westport CT: Greenwood Press.

Roediger, H.L., & McDermott, K.B. (1993). Implicit memory in normal human subjects. In H. Spinnler & F. Boller (Eds.), *Handbook of neuropsychology* (Vol. 8, pp. 63–131). Amsterdam: Elsevier.

Roopnarine, J.L., Hooper, F., Ahmeduzzaman, A., & Pollack, B. (1993). Gentle play partners: Mother–child and father–child play in New Delhi, India. In K. MacDonald (Ed.), *Parent–child play* (pp. 287–304). Albany: State University of New York Press.

Roopnarine, J.L., Shin, M., Donovan, B., & Suppal, P. (2001). Sociocultural contexts of dramatic play: Implications for early education. In K.A. Roskos & J.F. Christie (Eds.), *Play and literacy in early childhood: Research from multiple perspectives* (pp. 205–220). Mahwah, NJ: Lawrence Erlbaum Associates.

Rovee-Collier, C. (1999). The development of infant memory. *Current Directions in Psychological Science, 8,* 80–85.

Rovee-Collier, C., & Gerhardstein, P. (1997). The development of infant memory. In N. Cowan (Ed.), *The development of memory in childhood* (pp. 5–39). Hove, England: Psychology Press.

Rowe, D.W. (2000). Bringing books to life: The role of book-related dramatic play in young children's literacy learning. In K.A. Roskos & J.F. Christie (Eds.), *Play and literacy in early childhood: Research from multiple perspectives* (pp. 3–26). Mahwah, NJ: Lawrence Erlbaum Associates.

Rubin, K.H. (1984). *The play observation scale.* Unpublished manuscript. University of Waterloo, Ontario, Canada.

Rubin, K.H., Fein, G.G., & Vandenberg, B. (1983). Play. In E.M. Hetherington (Ed.), *Handbook of child psychology: Socialization, personality, and social development* (pp. 693–774). New York: John Wiley & Sons.

Ruff, H.A., & Capozzoli, M.C. (2003). Development of attention and distractibility in the first 4 years of life. *Developmental Psycholpathology, 39,* 877–890

Ruff, H.A., & Rothbart, M.K. (1996). *Attention in early development: Themes and variations.* New York: Oxford University Press.

Rypma, B., & d'Esposito, M. (2000). Isolating the neural mechanisms of age-related changes in human working memory. *Nature-Neuroscience, 3,* 509–515.

Sawyer, R.K. (1997). *Pretend play as improvisation: Conversation in the preschool classroom.* Mahwah, NJ: Lawrence Erlbaum Associates.

Schneider, W. (2002). Memory development in childhood. In U. Goswami (Ed.), *Blackwell handbook of childhood cognitive development* (pp. 236–256). Mauldin, MA: Blackwell Publishing.

Schneider, W., & Bjorkland, D.F. (1998). Memory. In W. Damon (Series Ed.), D. Kuhn & R.S. Siegler (Vol. Eds.), *Handbook of child psychology: Vol. 2. Cognition, perception, and language* (5th ed., pp. 467–521). New York: John Wiley & Sons.

Schumann-Hengsteler, R. (1996). Children's and adults' visuo-spatial memory: The game Concentration. *Journal of Genetic Psychology, 157,* 77–92.

Seidel, W.T., & Joschko, M. (1990). Evidence of difficulties in sustained attention in children with ADHD. *Journal of Abnormal Psychology, 18,* 217–229.

Shaywitz, B.A., Shaywitz, S.E., Liberman, I.Y., Fletcher, J.M., Shankweiler, D.P., Duncan, J., et al. (1991). Neurolinguistic and biological mechanism in dyslexia. In D.D. Duane & D.B. Gray (Eds.), *The reading brain: The biological basis of dyslexia* (pp. 27–52). Parkton, MD: York Press.

Shinskey, J.L., Bogartz, R.S., & Poirier, C.R. (2000). The effects of graded occlusion on manual search and visual attention in 5–8-month-old infants. *Infancy, 1,* 323–346.

Siegler, R.S. (1998). *Children's thinking* (3rd ed.). Upper Saddle River, NJ: Prentice Hall.

Siegler, R.S., & Chen, Z. (1998). Developmental differences in rule learning: A microgenetic analysis. *Cognitive Psychology, 36*(3), 273–310.

Sigman, M., Cohen, S.E., & Beckwith, L. (1997). Why does infant attention predict adolescent intelligence? *Infant Behavior and Development, 20,* 135–140.

Slater, A., Brown, E., & Mattock, A. (1996). Continuity and change in habituation in the first 4 months from birth. *Journal of Reproductive and Infant Psychology, 14,* 187–194.

Slater, A., & Johnson, S.P. (1999). Visual sensory and perceptual abilities of the newborn: Beyond the blooming, buzzing confusion. In A. Slater & S.P. Johnson (Eds.), *The development of sensory, motor and cognitive capacities in early infancy* (pp. 121–141). Hove, England: Sussex Press.

Slater, A.M., Mattock, A., & Brown, E. (1990). Size constancy at birth: Newborns responses to retinal and real size. *Journal of Experimental Child Psychology, 49,* 314–322.

Smilansky, S. (1968). *The effects of sociodramatic play on disadvantaged preschool children.* New York: John Wiley & Sons.

Snow, C.W., & McGaha, C.G. (2003). *Infant development.* Upper Saddle River, NJ: Prentice Hall.

Socha, T.J., & Kelly, B. (1994). Children making "fun": Humorous communication, impression management, and moral development. *Child Study Journal, 24*(3), 237–253.

Soundy, C.S., & Genisio, M.H. (1994) Asking young children to tell the story. *Childhood Education, 72*(1), 20–23.

Spelke, E.S. (1982). Perceptual knowledge of objects in infancy. In J.J. Mechler, M. Garrett, & E. Walker (Eds.), *Perspectives on mental representations* (pp. 409–431). Mahwah, NJ: Lawrence Erlbaum Associates.

Spencer, J.P. (2001). Test of a dynamic systems account of the A-not-B error: The influence or prior experience on the spatial memory abilities of two-year-olds. *Child Development, 72,* 1327–1346.

Squires, J., Bricker, D., & Twombly, E., (2002). *Ages & Stages Questionnaires®: Social-Emotional (ASQ:SE).* Baltimore: Paul H. Brookes Publishing Co.

Starkey, P. (1992). The early development of numerical reasoning. *Cognition, 43,* 93–126.

Steffe, L.P. (1992). Learning stages in the construction of number sequence. In J. Bideaud, C. Maljac, & J. Fischer (Eds.), *Pathway to number: Children's developing numerical ability* (pp. 83–98). Mahwah, NJ: Lawrence Erlbaum Associates.

Stern, D. (1985). *The interpersonal world of the infant.* New York: Basic Books.

Streissguth, A.P., Sampson, P.D., Carmichael, O.H., Bookstein, F.L., Barr, H.M., Scott, M., Feldman, J., & Mirsky, A.F. (1994). Maternal drinking during pregnancy: Attention and short-term memory performance in 14-year-old offspring—A longitudinal prospective study. *Alcoholism: Clinical and Experimental Research, 18,* 202–218.

Striano, T. (2001). From social expectations to social cognition in early infancy. *Bulletin of the Menninger Clinic, 65*(3), 361–371.

Sutton-Smith, B. (1999). *The ambiguity of play.* Cambridge, MA: Harvard University Press.

Taylor, E. (1980). Development of attention. In M. Rutter (Ed.), *Scientific foundation of developmental psychiatry* (pp. 185–197). London: Heinemann Educational.

Thelen, E. (1980). Determinants of amounts of stereotyped behavior in normal human infants. *Ethology and Sociobiology, 1,* 141–150.

Thelen, E., Corbetta, D., & Spencer, J.P. (1996). Development of reaching during the first year: Role of movement speed. *Journal of Experimental Psychology: Human Perception and Performance, 22,* 1058–1098.

Thompson, P.M., Giedd, J.N., Woods, R.P., MacDonald, D., Evans, A.C., & Toga, A.W. (2000). Growth patterns in the developing brain detected by using continuum mechanical tensor maps. *Nature, 404,* 190–192.

Tomlin, A.M. (2004). Thinking about challenging behavior in toddlers: Temperament style or behavior disorder? *ZERO TO THREE, 24*(4), 29–36.

Torgesen, J.K. (1996). A model of memory from an information processing perspective: The special case of phonological memory. In G.R. Lyon & N.A. Krasnegor (Eds.), *Attention, memory, and executive function* (pp. 157–184). Baltimore: Paul H. Brookes Publishing Co.

Uzgiris, I., & Raeff, C. (1995). Play in parent–child interactions. In M. Bornstein (Ed.), *Handbook of parenting* (Vol. 4, pp. 353–376). Mahwah, NJ: Lawrence Erlbaum Associates.

Van der Meere, J., van Baal, M., & Sargent, J. (1989). The additive factor method: A differential diagnostic tool in hyperactivity and learning disability. *Journal of Abnormal Child Psychology, 17*(4), 409–422.

Vandell, D.L., & Mueller, E.C. (1995). Peer play and friendships during the first two years. In H.C. Foot, A.J. Chapman, & J.R. Smith (Eds.), *Friendship and social relations in children* (pp. 181–208). New York: John Wiley & Sons.

Van Hoorn, J., Nourot, P., Scales, B., & Alward, K. (1993). *Play at the center of the curriculum.* New York: MacMillan.

Walker-Andrews, A., & Kahana-Kalman, R. (1999). The understanding of pretense across the second year of life. *British Journal of Developmental Psychology, 17,* 523–536.

Wang, S. (2001, April). *Ten-month-old infants: Reasoning about weight in collision events*. Paper presented at the biennial meeting of the Society for Research in Child Development, Minneapolis.

Waxman, S. (2002). Early word-learning and conceptual development: Everything had a name, and each name gave birth to a new thought. In U. Goswami (Ed.), *Blackwell handbook of childhood cognitive development* (pp. 102–126). Malden, MA: Blackwell Publishing.

Waxman, S., & Gelman, R. (1986). Preschoolers' use of superordinate relations in classification. *Cognitive Development, 1*, 139–159.

Weiss, K. (1997). Let's build. *Early Childhood Today, 12*(2), 30–39.

Wellman, H.M. (2002). Understanding the psychological world: Developing a theory of mind. In U. Goswami (Ed.), *Blackwell handbook of childhood cognitive development* (pp. 167–187). Oxford, England: Blackwell.

Wellman, H.M., Cross, D., & Watson, J., (2001). A meta-analysis of false belief reasoning: The truth about false belief. *Child Development, 72*, 655–684.

Wellman, H.M., & Gellman, S.A. (1992). Cognitive development: Foundational theories of core domains. *Annual Review of Psychology, 43*, 337–375.

Wellman, H.M., Hickling, A.K., & Schult, C.A. (2000). Young children's psychological, physical, and biological explanations. In K. Lee (Ed.), *Childhood cognitive development: The essential readings* (pp. 267–288). Mauldin, MA: Blackwell Publishing.

Welsh, M.C., Pennington, B.F., & Grossier, D.B. (1991). A normative-developmental study of executive function: A window on prefrontal function in children. *Developmental Neuropsychology, 7*, 131–149.

Wentworth, N., Benson, J.B., & Haith, M.M. (2000). The development of infants' reaches for stationary and moving targets. *Child Development, 71*, 576–601.

Westby, C.E. (1980). Assessment of cognitive and language abilities through play. *Language, Speech, and Hearing Services in Schools, 11*, 154–168.

Wetherby, A.M., Prizant, B.M., & Schuler, A.L. (2000). Understanding the nature of communication and language impairments. In S.F. Warren & J. Reichle (Series Eds.) & A.M. Wetherby & B.M. Prizant (Vol. Eds.), *Communication and language intervention series: Vol. 9. Autism spectrum disorders: A transactional developmental perspective* (pp. 109–141). Baltimore: Paul H. Brookes Publishing Co.

Wilburn, R.E. (2000). *Understanding the preschooler.* (Rethinking childhood, Vol. 9). New York: Peter Lang.

Wilford, S. (1996). Outdoor play. *Early Childhood Today, 10*(7), 31–36.

Wilkening, R., & Huber, S. (2002). Children's intuitive physics. In U. Goswami (Ed.), *Blackwell handbook of childhood cognitive development* (pp. 349–370). Malden, MA: Blackwell Publishing.

Willats, P. (1999). Development of means–ends behavior in young infants: Pulling a support to retrieve a distant object. *Developmental Psychology, 35*, 651–667.

Wolery, M., & Brookfield-Norman, J. (1988). (Pre-) Academic skills for handicapped preschool children. In S.L. Odom & M.B. Karnes (Eds.), *Early intervention for infants and children with handicaps: An empirical base* (pp. 109–128). Baltimore: Paul H. Brookes Publishing Co.

Woodward, A.L. (1999). Infant's ability to distinguish between purposeful and non-purposeful behaviors. *Infant Behavior and Development, 22*, 145–160.

Zelazo, P.D., Carter, A., Reznick, J.S., & Frye, D. (1997). Early development of executive function: A problem-solving framework. *Review of General Psychology, 1*, 198–226.

Zelazo, P.D., & Muller, U. (2002). Executive function in typical and atypical development. In U. Goswami (Ed.), *Blackwell handbook of childhood cognitive development* (pp. 445–469). Malden, MA: Blackwell Publishing.

Zola-Morgan, S., & Squire, L.R. (1993). Neuroanatomy of memory. *Annual Review of Neuroscience, 16*, 547–563.

TPBA2 Observation Guidelines: Cognitive Development

Child's name: _____   Age: _____   Birth date: _____

Parent(s): _____   Assessment date: _____

Person(s) completing the form: _____

Directions: Record the child information (name, caregiver[s], birth date, age), assessment date, and person(s) completing this form. The Observation Guidelines provide common strengths, examples of behaviors of concern, and "ready for" next steps. As you observe the child, circle, highlight, or place a check mark next to the items listed under these three categories that correspond to the behavior(s) you observe. List any additional observations in the "Notes" column. Experienced TPBA users may opt to use only the TPBA2 Observation Notes as a method for collecting information during the assessment instead of the Observation Guidelines.

Questions	Strengths	Examples of behaviors of concern	"Ready for"	Notes
I. Attention				

I. A. How well can the child select, focus on, and maintain attention to a task?	Can select a focus
	Can focus briefly
	Can maintain focus until task is completed
	Good attention for
	  Sensory
	  Social play
	  Fine motor
	  Gross motor
	  Dramatic play
	  All of the above
		Difficulty
		  Selecting focus
		  Maintaining focus
		  Narrowing interest (focuses on only limited objects, actions, or events)
			Increase ability to maintain focus
			Expand attentional focus for
			  Sensory exploration
			  Social play
			  Fine motor activities
			  Gross motor play
			  Dramatic play
			  All of the above
			  Other:	

I. B. How well can the child inhibit external stimuli?	Can inhibit some types of external stimuli
	Can inhibit irrelevant external stimuli in order to attend
		Easily distracted by certain stimuli:
		  Auditory
		  Visual
		  Tactile
		  Other:
			Increase ability to inhibit stimuli:
			  Auditory
			  Visual
			  Tactile
			  Other:	

(continued on next page)

Transdisciplinary Play-Based System (TPBA2/TPBI2)
by Toni Linder.

(continued from previous page)

Observation Guidelines: Cognitive Development **TPBA** 2

Questions	Strengths	Examples of behaviors of concern	"Ready for"	Notes
I. Attention *(continued)*				
I. C. Can the child shift attention from one aspect of a stimulus or problem to another?	Can shift attention as needed to important aspects of a situation or problem From person to object From object to object From one aspect of an object to another aspect	Attention gets "stuck" on Person or object Specific aspect of object Specific aspect of problem	Increase ability to shift attention from one aspect of a situation to another as needed	
II. Memory				
II. A. What short- or long-term memory skills are evidenced through the child's spontaneous actions and communications? Short term = learned within an activity or the time span of the play session Long term = learned before the play session	Memory of concepts shown: Recognition of concepts by looking, pointing, or gesturing (Short/Long term) Generation of words, signs, symbols (S/L) Repetition of simple actions and routines (S/L) Repetition of *complex* actions and routines (S/L) Reconstruction of *simple* events or stories by verbal or dramatic means (S/L) Reconstruction of *complex* events or stories by verbal or dramatic means (S/L) All of the above (S/L)	Reduced short-term memory skills for: (list areas) Reduced long-term memory skills for: (list areas)	Increase memory related to Recognition of concepts Generation of words, signs, symbols Repetition of procedures and routines (simple/complex) Reconstruction of events or stories through verbal or dramatic means (simple/complex) Increase Short-term memory Long-term memory	

Transdisciplinary Play-Based System (TPBA2/TPBI2)
by Toni Linder.

(continued on next page)

Observation Guidelines: Cognitive Development **TPBA** 2

Questions	Strengths	Examples of behaviors of concern	"Ready for"	Notes
II. Memory (continued)				
II. B. How long does it take for the child to process and re-call concepts, action se-quences, or events?	Responds immediately to Requests for verbal informa-tion related to immediate situation Requests for verbal informa-tion related to time-distant situations Requests for action	Delayed processing time For verbal input For imitation of actions Needs verbal support to proc-ess visual or physical infor-mation Needs physical or visual model to process verbal information	Respond after several sec-onds wait time Respond after visual prompt Respond after verbal prompt	
III. Problem solving				
III. A. What behaviors indicate understanding of causal rea-soning skills or problem solving (executive function)?	Has causal understanding of and age-appropriate prob-lem-solving skills with Objects People Situations All of the above Emerging causal understand-ing of and problem-solving skills with Objects People Situations All of the above	Delayed problem-solving skills with Objects People Situations All of the above	Repeat movement to get something to recur Look at something and then at adult to get it Anticipate recurrence of events Use simple activators to make things "go" Use multiple steps to make things happen Combine causal actions with another person Determine cause of event Think of multiple possible causes for an event	
III. B. How does the child iden-tify and plan a solution to a problem?	Can identify age-appropriate solutions to problems Knows there is a problem but needs assistance to identify a plan	Reduced problem-solving skills	Increase exploration of ob-jects, people Anticipate results of actions Find parts of objects that pro-duce a result or relate Experiment to find a solution to a problem Solve a problem without con-crete manipulation	

Transdisciplinary Play-Based System (TPBA2/TPBI2)
by Toni Linder.

(continued on next page)

(continued from previous page)

Observation Guidelines: Cognitive Development **TPBA** 2

Questions	Strengths	Examples of behaviors of concern	"Ready for"	Notes
III. Problem solving *(continued)*				
III. C. How well is the child able to organize, monitor, and evaluate progress toward a goal and make corrections?	Can organize actions toward a goal Can monitor and correct self at an age-appropriate level Makes corrections with assistance	Reduced organization skills Reduced ability to monitor and alter plans	Try alternative actions Organize a series of actions Choose strategies based on situation Modify attempts based on results of actions	
III. D. How quickly can the child analyze a problem situation and respond?	Child analyzes the situation and responds immediately Child demonstrates a delayed response time, but not more than several seconds	Child needs 5–10 seconds or more before responding Child does not respond to the problem situation	Practice with problem-solving situations to increase attention and fluency	
III. E. How well can the child generalize information from one situation to another?	Can see similarities of problems and transfer strategies to new problems Sees similarities with support of adult	Cannot generalize solutions	Respond to suggestions Identify concrete similarities of problems See subtle or abstract similarities of situations	
IV. Social cognition				
IV. A. What foundational skills related to social cognition does the child demonstrate?	Has foundation skills: Interest in people Imitation of adults' actions Joint referencing Social referencing Gestures to indicate a desire Aware of own/others' emotions Understands social causes of consequences Symbolic play All of the above	Delayed social-communicative understanding	Develop Interest in people Imitation of adults' actions After 12 months: Joint referencing Social referencing Gestures to indicate a desire or goal After 18 months: Awareness of emotions Understanding of social causes of consequences Symbolic play	

(continued on next page)

Transdisciplinary Play-Based System (TPBA2/TPBI2)
by Toni Linder.

(continued from previous page)

Observation Guidelines: Cognitive Development **TPBA** 2

Questions	Strengths	Examples of behaviors of concern	"Ready for"	Notes
IV. Social cognition (continued)				

IV. B. How well does the child infer the thinking and actions of others?	Interest in actions of others
	Interest in thoughts of others
	Understands thinking and actions of others
	Understands consequences of own and others' actions
	Basic understanding of motivations of self and others
		Limited ability to understand the thoughts and feelings of others	Predict
			  Future actions based on contextual cues, gestures, or actions
			  Others' motivations based on actions
			  Others' actions/feelings based on the situation
			  Others' actions based on stated desires
			Understand
			  Others' desires are different from own
			  Others' beliefs are different from own
			  Difference between accident and intention	

V. Complexity of play			(See Age Table: Cognitive Development for detailed sequence)	
V. A. What behaviors demonstrate the level and complexity of the child's play?	Level of play demonstrated: Sensory Functional-relational Construction Dramatic play Games with rules Physical and rough-and-tumble play (Put an "h" by the highest level and a "p" by the predominant level.)	Delayed play skills within types and levels of play Focused on specific type of play	Increase Sensory exploration Combining, relating, and using objects functionally Construction: representational construction Dramatic play: action sequences, event sequences, story or script play Games with rules: ability to take turns and follow rules Physical play	

(continued on next page)

Transdisciplinary Play-Based System (TPBA2/TPBI2)
by Toni Linder.

Observation Guidelines: Cognitive Development **TPBA 2**

Questions	Strengths	Examples of behaviors of concern	"Ready for"	Notes
V. Complexity of play *(continued)*			(See Age Table: Conceptual Development for detailed sequence)	
V. B. What approach typifies the complexity of the child's actions within the listed categories of play?	Variety of actions Variety of sequences Variety of play interests Curiosity, experimentation, and creativity All of the above	Limited repertoire of actions Limited sequence of actions Limited interests	Increase variety of Actions Sequences Play interests Experimentation and curiosity All of the above	
V. C. What level of cognition is demonstrated in the child's sense of humor?	Smiles and/or laughs at Sensory input Funny actions/events Funny use of language Makes others smile/laugh at Sensory input Funny actions/events Funny use of language	Delayed understanding of causes of humor	Increase ability to understand incongruities of actions Increase ability to understand incongruities of language	
VI. Conceptual knowledge			(See Age Table: Conceptual Development for detailed sequence)	
VI. A. What similarities and differences can the child recognize?	Can differentiate People Animals Objects Parts of objects Actions Objects that are alike or go together Things that don't belong All of the above	Delayed ability to see likenesses and differences Delayed ability to classify	Increase ability to see similarities and differences in People Animals Objects Parts of objects Actions Events Functions Characteristics	

(continued on next page)

376

(continued from previous page)

Observation Guidelines: Cognitive Development **TPBA** 2

Questions	Strengths	Examples of behaviors of concern	"Ready for"	Notes
			(See Age Table: Conceptual Development for detailed sequence)	
VI. Conceptual knowledge (continued)				
VI. B. What evidence is seen of the child's conceptual or categorical knowledge?	Recognizes or relates concepts related to Objects People Animals Actions Places Events Functions Causality (e.g., *why and how*) All of the above	Delayed conceptual understanding of relationships	Increase conceptual knowledge related to Objects People Animals Actions Places Events Functions Causality Characteristics/properties, such as:	
VI. C. What behaviors demonstrate that the child integrates concepts into a classification system?	Understands One level (label) Two levels (e.g., ball is a toy) Multiple levels (e.g., apple is a fruit, fruit is a food) Interrelationships of concepts (e.g., fruit and vegetables are both food)	Limited classification of concepts	Increase ability to classify at Basic level Relationship level Multiple relationship level Interrelationship of concepts	
VI. D. What understanding of measurement concepts in math and science does the child demonstrate?	Understands measurement concepts at Global level (e.g., a little/a lot; heavy/light) Comparison level (e.g., more/less; tall/taller) Discrete amount level (tagging items with one-to-one correspondence)	Delayed comparative and sequential measurement skills	Increase understanding of measurement concepts: Global level Comparison level Discrete amount level Comparison of units Mental manipulation	

Transdisciplinary Play-Based System (TPBA2/TPBI2) by Toni Linder.

(continued on next page)

377

(continued from previous page)

Observation Guidelines: Cognitive Development **TPBA 2**

Questions	Strengths	Examples of behaviors of concern	"Ready for"	Notes
VI. Conceptual knowledge *(continued)*			(See Age Table: Conceptual Development for detailed sequence)	
VI. D. *(continued)*	Comparison of units on a mental number line (e.g., 5 is bigger than 4) Use of a mental number line to manipulate (add/subtract) units		(Underline concepts needed: numbers, size, time, speed, distance, force, weight, mass, temperature, money)	
VII. Literacy			(See Age Table: Conceptual Development for detailed sequence)	
VII. A. What listening skills does the child demonstrate?	Attends to or identifies environmental and speech sounds Listens to adults talking Listens to adult reading Listens and responds to songs, fingerplays, rhymes Attends to or identifies sounds in words Attends to or identifies sounds of letters	Reduced ability to Listen to auditory input Differentiate or identify sounds Listen to lengthy auditory information	Increase ability to Listen to and find source of sounds Identify sounds Categorize sounds (same, alike, different) Identify and reproduce rhymes Relate letter sounds with visual symbols (sound–symbol)	
VII. B. How does the child use books?	For sensory input (visual, tactile, taste) For picture identification For interaction with adult For the story in the book For the content in the book For letter identification For learning to read or reading	Delayed use of books and/or content of books	Increase Exploration of books Functional use of books Sharing picture books Sharing storybooks Sharing expository books Attention to technical aspects of reading (print, words, letter sounds)	

Observation Guidelines: Cognitive Development **TPBA 2**

Questions	Strengths	Examples of behaviors of concern	"Ready for"	Notes
			(See Age Table: Conceptual Development for detailed sequence)	
VII. Literacy (continued)				
VII. C. What does the child comprehend when looking at or sharing a book?	Comprehends pictures As interesting stimuli As representations of real objects/actions As representations of action sequences, a story, or information Understands Emotions in a book That sequences of pictures/words stay the same each time That words read are related to the print on the page Meaning of some print	Delayed comprehension of books	Increase comprehension of Pictures Vocabulary and concepts Picture/story sequence and relationship to life Relationship of emotions in stories to self/others Stability and predictability of words and story Relationship of print to words in the book Print (letters or words)	
VII. D. What does the child recall of words, phrases, story lines, and content from familiar stories?	Age-appropriate memory for literacy elements: Gets favorite books to read Relates details of pictures or story from memory Fills in omitted words Retells part or all of book Acts out part or all of story Creates pictures of a story or book Applies book concepts to life at home or school	Delayed memory for literacy elements	Increase Memory for vocabulary associated with pictures Memory for story words, phrases, or sentences Ability to tell, draw, or act out actions of a story Ability to apply concepts in books to new situations	
VII. E. What emerging literacy skills are evident in the child's attempts to read?	Uses "book babble" (i.e., jargon sounds like reading) Talks about pictures Reads symbols and logos Uses pictures to tell story Combines telling the story with "reading language" (i.e., using reading patterns and intonations)	Delayed expression of literacy elements	Increase Talking about pictures Recognition of symbols or logos Storytelling with picture books Print awareness	

(continued on next page)

Transdisciplinary Play-Based System (TPBA2/TPBI2)
by Toni Linder

Observation Guidelines: Cognitive Development **TPBA** 2

Questions	Strengths	Examples of behaviors of concern	"Ready for"	Notes
			(See Age Table: Conceptual Development for detailed sequence)	
VII. Literacy (continued)				
VII. E. (continued)	Recognizes some letters Recognizes some words Uses "sounding out" and blending of sounds Reads print with few errors		Use of symbols and print to "read" Knowledge of alphabet and letter sounds Literacy strategies in book reading	
VII. F. What does the child understand about writing?	Knows Writing is marks on paper Drawing represents something real Marks on paper can be read Print has special forms, containing lines and curves Lines and curves are shaped in ways to make letters Letters combine for words Words combine to share information in print	Delayed understanding of meaning of drawing and writing	Increase ability to Use marks to represent thoughts Relate marks to spoken words Relate marks to written words Form written letters Combine written letters in meaningful spatial groupings to form words	
VII. G. What characterizes the child's writing?	Draws or makes marks Draws pictures Attempts to write "words" with "mock" writing or letterlike forms Wants adult to write words Writes recognizable letters Writing marks are oriented appropriately on the page (top/bottom, left/right) Age-appropriate errors (reversals, rotations, orientation), sequencing, spacing, use of capital and small letters, punctuation	Lacks interest and motivation for drawing and/or writing Delayed writing and/or drawing skills	Increase Exploration of writing, drawing, and art materials Motivation to write Opportunities to draw or write in dramatic play Understanding of spatial orientation of writing Opportunities to practice meaningful writing with feedback and support from adult Technical aspects of writing	

Transdisciplinary Play-Based System (TPBA2/TPBI2)
by Toni Linder.

TPBA2 Observation Notes:
Cognitive Development

Child's name: _____ Parent(s): _____

Birth date: _____ Assessment date: _____ Age: _____

Person(s) completing the form: _____

Directions: Record the child information (name, caregiver[s], birth date, age), assessment date, and person(s) completing this form, and your observations about the child in the spaces below. You are encouraged to review the corresponding TPBA2 Observation Guidelines prior to recording your observations here, as the Guidelines list what to look for. Newer TPBA users may opt to use the TPBA2 Observation Guidelines as a method for collecting information during the assessment instead of the TPBA2 Observation Notes.

I. Attention (select, focus, inhibit stimuli, shift attention)

II. Memory (recognition, generation, repetition, reconstruction, simple, complex, short term, long term, processing time)

III. Problem solving (cause–effect, identify, plan, organize, monitor, adapt, analyze, processing time, generalization)

Transdisciplinary Play-Based System (TPBA2/TPBI2)
by Toni Linder.

(continued on next page)

(continued from previous page)

IV. Social cognition (foundations, inference of thinking, feelings of others, understanding social causes)

V. Complexity of play (developmental level, variety of actions, sequences, interests, curiosity, sense of humor)

VI. Conceptual knowledge (understanding similarities, differences, categories, classification level, measurement)

VII. Literacy (listening, book use, comprehension, recall, reading, comprehension of and use of writing and spelling)

TPBA2 Age Table: Cognitive Development

Child's name: _____ Age: _____ Birth date: _____

Parent(s): _____ Assessment date: _____

Person(s) completing the form: _____

Directions: Based on the observations recorded on the TPBA2 Observation Guidelines and/or TPBA2 Observation Notes, review the Age Table to determine the age level that most closely matches the child's performance. It may be helpful to circle items on the Age Table that the child can do. If items are circled across multiple age levels, find the child's age level by finding the mode (i.e., determine which age level has the most circled items). Age levels after 12 months/1 year represent ranges rather than individual months and are preceded by "By." If the most circled items appear in one of these age levels, consider the child's age level to be the month shown (e.g., if the most circled items appear in the "By 21 months" level, the child's age level for that subcategory is 21 months).

Note: The Conceptual Knowledge and Literacy subcategories are not included in this Age Table; rather, they are included in a separate Age Table, Conceptual Development.

Age level	Attention	Memory	Problem solving	Social cognition	Complexity of play
1 month	Stares at faces	Imitates tongue and mouth movements Remembers objects that reappear within 2.5 seconds Capable of remembering (recognizing) actions from one day to the next	Fixates and tracks objects and faces Nonvoluntary, reflexive responses to stimuli	Enjoys studying people and environment Focuses on mouth of adult	Smiles in response to high-pitched voice
2 months	Stares indefinitely at surroundings Attends to contours, contrasts Tracks objects horizontally	Retention of motor actions that result in interesting effects	Studies own hand movement Can scan objects for both contour and internal characteristics	Focuses on eyes of adults Seeks voices of familiar adults	Smiles in response to nodding face Repeats pleasurable physical activities directed toward self
3 months	Prefers people to objects Tracks in circles Definite listening to sounds Can remain focused for 2 or more minutes at a time	Becomes excited in anticipation of movement of objects Waits for expected events (e.g., feeding) Shows recognition of family members	Takes hands to mouth Reacts to disappearance of an object Shows excitement in anticipation of action Swats at objects, grasps objects voluntarily	Imitates facial movements (birth to 3 months) Smiles more at people than objects Quiets at sound of calming voice	Has physical enjoyment of kicking, arm waving (birth to 3 months) Explores environment with senses (birth to 3 months) Primarily mouths objects (birth to 3 months) Makes true social smile

(continued on next page)

Transdisciplinary Play-Based System (TPBA2/TPBI2)
by Toni Linder.

(continued from previous page)

Age Table: Cognitive Development **TPBA 2**

Age level	Attention	Memory	Problem solving	Social cognition	Complexity of play
4 months	Attends to individual fingers, not fist Turns head to find source of sounds Attends to internal aspects not just external contours	Responds with total body to recognized face Has memory span of 5–7 seconds Attempts imitation of sounds Anticipates actions based on previous occurrences Recognizes familiar objects based on movement or location	Uses kicking, reaching, and grasping to explore objects Mouthing is primary way to explore Repeats newly learned activities	Shows interest in others' facial expressions and sounds Begins to adjust responses to different people Picks up emotions from human speech	Displays laughter in social play, particularly with physical stimulation Enjoys repetition of actions, sounds Begins play with sound toys (e.g., rattles) Laughs
5 months	Object interest increases May prefer 1 or 2 toys Can focus at different distances Interest in different smells	Imitates sounds and movements deliberately Recognizes familiar objects	Searches for vanishing or moving objects Can reach, grasp, mouth to explore objects	Quiets to familiar voice Vocalizes to adult voice and expressions Can discriminate facial expressions in relation to emotions	Plays with sounds and patterns of sounds Plays with own hands, feet
6 months	Alert for almost 2 hours (5–6 months) Recognizes and shows interest in new environments Inspects objects for a long time Attends to new objects for up to 3 minutes	Remembers own actions in immediate past Can remember how to activate familiar toys Can remember and imitate actions performed by adults on toys Retrieves partially hidden object	Sits, uses hands to explore Uses fingers to explore and grasp Imitates mouth movements Becomes aware of effects of own actions versus others	Preferentially attends to faces rather than objects (birth to 6 months) Tries to imitate facial expressions Enjoys social play	Works to get toy Signals for repetition of actions Enjoys shaking and banging toys (5–6 months)
7 months	Shows attentional preferences Inspects objects for long time Concentrates on details	Remembers short sequence of actions if series involved his/her own actions Goal-directed behavior indicates memory	Explores with mouth and hands Grasps, manipulates toys Examines things from different perspectives Anticipates repetition of events Struggles to get objects out of reach	Distinguishes between friendly and angry voices Reacts to emotional displays of others Babbles to people	Bangs objects together Uses objects functionally Tries to get adult to laugh Responds enthusiastically to social games (4–7 months)
8 months	Follows what someone points to Shows objects to others Listens selectively to sounds and words	Recalls past events and actions on his/her own Anticipates events Recognizes objects and people based on sensory characteristics	Searches for objects seen hidden Combines different actions into new problem-solving attempts Looks to adults to solve problems Moves body to get what is wanted	Is able to share joint attention with someone else	Uses fingers in play to poke, pull, push

(continued on next page)

Transdisciplinary Play-Based System (TPBA2/TPBI2)
by Toni Linder

Age Table: Cognitive Development **TPBA 2**

Age level	Attention	Memory	Problem solving	Social cognition	Complexity of play
9 months	Interested in details of objects Grows bored with repetition of same stimuli Sustained interest (up to 1 minute) looking at pictures shown by adults	Responds with expectation to repetition of event or signal Remembers simple games Retrieves fully hidden object	Makes goal-directed actions Experiments with objects in different ways Can manipulate more than one object at a time Pincer grasp helps in activating toys Is persistent in search for desired toy	Produces peer-directed smiles and babbles Watches others to see how they accomplish their goals Understands gestures like "bye-bye" and games like Peekaboo Aware of others' reactions to his/her actions	Plays Peekaboo games (4–9 months) Combines objects in play Begins to show humor and teases Performs different actions with toys, depending on their characteristics (6–9 months)
10 months	Sustains interest in play (attends to both toy and adult) Deliberately chooses and attends to preferred toys Seeks social attention	Remembers and imitates actions performed by others, particularly with tools or objects	Dumps objects out of container Shows interest in fitting things together Searches for missing objects Experiments with trying things with both sides of body	Reacts to subtle emotional expression of others with behavioral response	Likes exploring cause-and-effect toys with actions and noises Begins to appreciate unexpected actions as funny Combines two objects functionally (e.g., putting things in) (7–10 months)
11 months	Attends to action toys	Remembers what words mean without object being present	Experiments with means–end (e.g., pushing chair as walker) Goes over or around obstacles to get to goal Imitates others' actions on toys	Seeks assistance of adult to activate toys	Imitates behaviors such as washing and feeding in play (11+ months) Pushes toys, cars, trucks Likes gross motor play Takes things off and out
12 months or 1 year	Shows intense attention to speech sounds Attention shifts from people to objects (7–12 months)	Can perform deferred imitation (imitation of actions without model present) Remembers a strategy that worked on one object and applies it to another	Finds hidden toys, searches for unseen objects Experiments with actions/reactions Experiments with heights, distances (e.g., dropping, throwing) Displays goal-oriented play Experiments with application of previously used solutions Explores all aspects of the environment with fine and gross motor skills Turns objects to find functional side Examines objects (6–12 months)	Joint referencing, follows gaze of adult (understanding gaze is directed toward something) (9–12 months) Social referencing, looks for emotions of others before acting (7–12 months) Uses preverbal pointing and gestures to communicate Knows one can share and change others' moods Knows movement of others implies actions toward a goal Imitates others' goal-oriented behaviors	Mouths, waves, bangs, shakes, drops, bats, throws objects Means–ends play; knows how to get objects to do what he or she wants (e.g., pulls string to get toy) Combines and matches several objects (e.g., stacks objects, fits piece in puzzle) Games of give-and-take, turn-taking Uses some toys appropriately/functionally (9–12 months) Enjoys games "so big," "catch me," Peekaboo (8–12 months) Tries to make adults laugh with antics

(continued on next page)

Transdisciplinary Play-Based System (TPBA2/TPBI2) by Toni Linder.

Age Table: Cognitive Development **TPBA 2**

Age level	Attention	Memory	Problem solving	Social cognition	Complexity of play
By 15 months	Sustains interest for 2–5 minutes while looking at named pictures or books Attends to specific physical characteristics of objects	Imitates peers Remembers previous actions of others for months (anticipates what will happen or recreates actions)	Makes plan to achieve goal Keeps searching for hidden objects Places things on top of each other Finds objects behind a barrier	Knows what adult wants and spontaneously offers object Watches adults' actions and anticipates result	Likes putting things in holes Enjoys water play Cares for doll, teddy (e.g., feeds, cuddles, covers) Likes to play near another child Imitates adults' actions with toys
By 18 months	Pays attention to distant objects	Recognizes and can identify pictures and objects by pointing Imitates sounds and words Recognizes familiar places (15–18 months)	Shows purposeful exploration of toys (13–17 months) Uses variety of actions in trial and error to operate toys (13–17 months) Uses adult to activate toy if unsuccessful (13–17 months) Looks for hidden objects with systematic search (12–18 months) Moves, shifts, rearranges, modifies things as desired (12–18 months) Adapts familiar actions to new situations (12–18 months)	Knows what to do to get reaction (e.g., happy, mad) (9–18 months) Can interpret the goal of an adult's simple action (9–15 months, by 18 months) Knows his/her actions cause feelings in self and others Looks to see how others are reacting to their actions Watches adult start a task and can complete the task (knows adult's goal)	Likes toys that activate or "do" something Knows what to do to make another laugh (9–18 months) Begins symbolic play with construction Enjoys stacking objects (up to six) (15–18 months) Autosymbolic play: child pretends to eat, sleep (17–19 months) Uses objects functionally in play (e.g., phone, comb) (17–19 months)
By 21 months	Can follow the attention lead of others (looks at what others look at and does what others do)	Attempts to tell about experience using words and jargon (autobiographical memory) Remembers action sequences for 2 months	Uses real objects functionally to solve problems (e.g., pushes a chair over to get item that is up high) (19–21 months)	Uses direction of speaker's gaze to infer the referent of a word Understands when someone is pretending to eat, drink, and so forth Shows genuine concern for another's distress (12–24 months)	Searches for objects to "go with" other toys (e.g., spoon for bowl, driver for car) Uses objects symbolically in play (18–21 months)

(continued on next page)

Transdisciplinary Play-Based System (TPBA2/TPBI2)
by Toni Linder.

(continued from previous page)

Age Table: Cognitive Development **TPBA** 2

Age level	Attention	Memory	Problem solving	Social cognition	Complexity of play
By 24 months or	**2 years** Needs help shifting attention from one thing to another Will attend to books for several minutes independently Highly variable attention span depending on stimuli; has preferences for play (18–24 months)	Long-term memory for events, talks about the recent past (gist of events within last 6 months) Remembers strategies seen or used previously (18–24 months) Can dramatize remembered events (18–24 months)	Balances objects on top of each other (18–24 months) Can solve simple problems mentally without trial and error (18–24 months) Can solve a problem with verbal instructions (18–24 months) Can use a tool (manipulative item) to solve a problem (21–24 months)	Knows others have different emotions, likes, dislikes Uses words relating to mental states for self and others (e.g., *happy, sad, want, like*) (18–24 months) Can differentiate own versus others' desires (18–24 months) Comforts another child (15–24 months) Still takes another child's toys without concern for feelings (12–24 months) Anticipates the consequences of actions if naughty	Begins sharing (12–24 months) Can direct dramatic play to self, doll, and adult (19–22 months) Combines 2 toys in dramatic play (e.g., stirs in bowls, pours from pitcher into cup) (19–22 months) Can dramatize simple 3-step sequence (e.g., feeding doll, putting to bed, saying "nite-nite") Loves chase games Shares humor with others (21–24 months)
By 30 months	Attends to more than one stimulus at a time (several pictures or toys)	Recognizes and labels covers of familiar books Recognizes familiar signs Fills in missing words or corrects adult with familiar rhymes, songs, or stories	Breaks things apart, unwraps, tears, and so forth, investigating (24–30 months) Experiments with putting together and taking apart (24–30 months) Understands that problem solving happens by "thinking"	Uses the word "pretend" Uses words "think" and "know" to refer to thoughts and beliefs Knows one can feel different in different situations Shows empathy Incorporates others into dramatic play and understands what other intends	Likes block play (e.g., stacking, knocking down, simple construction) (25–30 months) Likes filling, pouring, dumping (24–30 months) Begins fantasy and make-believe play (24–30 months) Dramatizes roles in familiar routines using realistic toys (24–30 months) Multistep sequences in dramatic play with others (25–30 months) Has dolls or action figures "perform" sequences and interact

(continued on next page)

Transdisciplinary Play-Based System (TPBA2/TPBI2)
by Toni Linder.

(continued from previous page)

Age Table: Cognitive Development **TPBA 2**

Age level	Attention	Memory	Problem solving	Social cognition	Complexity of play
36 months or 3 years	Attends to key aspects of an object or situation and compares to solve problem (e.g., in a puzzle) Attends to amount Looks for and attends to causal mechanisms to figure out how they work	Relates detailed sequences of experience from recent past and can remember events from up to 18 months in the past Remembers fingerplays Remembers visual landmarks Uses fingers to count to aid memory Formulates dramatic play scripts based on remembered routines and events Sings simple songs or rhymes (30–36 months)	Systematically takes objects apart (24–36 months) Understands questions about "why" and "how" things function (33–36 months) Understands position words (e.g., *in, on top of, on, under*) (33–36 months) Talks about how to solve a problem while working on it (verbal mediation) Uses visual searching to find solutions to problems Tries alternatives when first solutions don't work Can put together 4- to 5-piece interconnected puzzle (30–36 months)	Realizes others' needs may be different from own (24–36 months) May show signs of guilt if he/she hurts another child (24–36 months) Can distinguish happy emotions better than negative ones (24–36 months) Recognizes that he/she can cause emotional distress in others (24–36 months) Ascribes thoughts and feelings to play figures (31–36 months)	Likes to play with small items such as buttons, knobs, beads (31–36 months) Plays tag, hide-and-seek Enjoys making music and likes to dance (31–36 months) Plays through a sequence of events in common routines (e.g., feeding baby, washing, putting to bed) Dramatizes simple songs, scenes from books, movies Likes to dress up to role play (30–36 months) Plays more than one role (e.g., mother–baby, doctor–patient) (31–36 months) Acts out pretend play with others Ascribes thoughts and feelings to play figures Logically ties two or more complex thoughts and feelings together in play Finds humor in bathroom words Symbolic play with unrealistic substitutions for props

(continued on next page)

Transdisciplinary Play-Based System (TPBA2/TPBI2) by Toni Linder.

Age Table: Cognitive Development **TPBA** 2

Age level	Attention	Memory	Problem solving	Social cognition	Complexity of play
By 42 months	Attends to directionality (e.g., in arranging blocks, puzzle pieces) Attends to degree of difference (organizes by size, shape)	Remembers one of several objects shown and then hidden (36–42 months) Repeats 4 or more word-sentences containing adjectives (36–42 months)	Puts things together, shows imagination (36–42 months) Organizes toys, pictures by relationship to each other Knows what does *not* go together Uses diverse materials to create something Understands what to do in specific situations Self-initiates, plans, and organizes problem solving without assistance	Describes own feelings Is aware of people's wants, feelings, and perceptions	Builds, constructs primarily enclosures (36–42 months) Performs play rituals Likes puzzle play Uses miniatures in dramatic play (e.g., doll house, garage) Prefers play with peers to play with adults Develops a theme in dramatic play
48 months or 4 years	Sustains and controls attention on interesting activities Pays attention to specific visual, auditory, and tactile aspects of objects and situations	Creates dramatic play based on pieces of remembered events and stories from different times and different places Describes familiar objects without seeing them Recalls one to two elements of a story that was just read (42–48 months) Uses past experiences to decide how to act in specific situations	Asks about and identifies "why" and "how" (36–48 months) Puts complex puzzles together (8- to 12-piece interconnected) Sensitive to the effects of gravity in block and ramp play Categorizes by size, type, color, and shape in problem solving	Understands other people have feelings, attitudes, beliefs different from own and can discuss them Can differentiate others' point of view and own Can do "if–then" with regard to others (e.g., "If I do this, then Mommy will be happy, because . . .")	Begins coordinated dramatic play among several children with complex themes Builds 3-D block structures that are representational Plays simple card or board games with adult assistance Plays group games
54 months	Attends to more than one characteristic of an object or picture (e.g., shape and color, color and size)	Recalls 3–4 elements of a story without prompts (48–54 months) Sings songs or rhymes of at least 30 words (48–54 months) Determines what parts are missing in pictures, puzzles, toys Recognizes and names a familiar song when sung	Recreates complex patterns with blocks Creates a dramatic play area out of a variety of materials Describes how to do something Thinks up new uses for objects	Explains to others what will happen if they do something Asks questions to understand what another person thinks or feels	Creates representations with clay, sand, and so forth (48–54 months) Rhyming words (e.g., "teenie, weenie") (48–54 months) Laughs at funny words, word play Discusses and negotiates roles and actions in dramatic play Builds on other children's play (48–54 months)

(continued on next page)

Transdisciplinary Play-Based System (TPBA2/TPBI2) by Toni Linder.

(continued from previous page)

Age Table: Cognitive Development **TPBA** 2

Age level	Attention	Memory	Problem solving	Social cognition	Complexity of play
By 60 months or 5 years	Attends to the orientation of objects, letters, pictures Attends for long periods to difficult tasks Attends to long stories when read, especially with pictures	Gives detailed descriptions of past events Recites verses, short passages, songs Shares clear and explicit verbalizations of memories Creates elaborate dramatic play from remembered stories, movies, past history, and so forth Is aware of strategies to help remember things, such as repeating words aloud Retells the main elements of an unfamiliar story after it is read Remembers a sequence of four numbers or novel words	Uses "rules" and understanding rather than perceptions to figure out how to solve problems	Considers others' thoughts, imagination, knowledge (48–60 months) Makes inferences about the motivations of others Plans how to influence others' goals Understands that both beliefs and desires determine behavior Compares and negotiates ideas with others in play Understands multiple roles and coordinates complex story lines in dramatic play with peers Deceives or plays tricks on others	Plays board games, but may change the rules (48–60 months) Has play rituals with peers Creates elaborate socio-dramatic play Makes costumes up Likes chase games
By 72 months or 6 years	Maintains attention through complex problem solving Attends to stories read without pictures	Uses several strategies to aid memory (repeats to self, leaves a clue to remind, organizes needed objects) Uses rehearsal to remember facts Remembers rules of board games, physical games, and complex instructions Remembers a large number of songs, fingerplays, details of books and movies	Makes a plan to solve a problem, monitors progress toward a goal, changes approach as needed, and evaluates outcome Uses literacy materials to solve a problem Uses numerical reasoning to solve problems	Thinks about multiple characters; their actions, beliefs, and behaviors; and their influence on each other	Creates and acts out own stories Makes up characters and costumes Performs for others Likes card and board games Likes structured outdoor games and sports

Transdisciplinary Play-Based System (TPBA2/TPBI2)
by Toni Linder.

TPBA2 Age Table:
Conceptual Development

Directions: Based on the observations recorded on the TPBA2 Observation Guidelines and/or TPBA2 Observation Notes, review the Age Table to determine the age level that most closely matches the child's performance. It may be helpful to circle items on the Age Table that the child can do. If items are circled across multiple age levels, find the child's age level by finding the mode (i.e., determine which age level has the most circled items). Age levels after 12 months/1 year represent ranges rather than individual months and are preceded by "By." If the most circled items appear in one of these age levels, consider the child's age level to be the month shown (e.g., if the most circled items appear in the "By 21 months" level, the child's age level for that subcategory is 21 months).

Note: This Age Table is an extension of the Cognitive Development Age Table.

Age level	Conceptual knowledge: Math and science	Conceptual knowledge: Emerging literacy
1 month	Perceives patterns and categorizes familiar people and objects	Looks at contrasting patterns
2 months	Distinguishes animate (moving) from inanimate	Touches pictures
3 months	Clearly discriminates voices, people, tastes, proximity, and object size	Responds to a variety of sounds (0–3 months) Can locate the direction of a sound's origin (0–3 months)
4 months	Differentiates and responds to various sounds in the environment (e.g., mother's voice) Makes voluntary movements with intent	Intently looks at pictures for several minutes (2–4 months)
5 months	Recognizes familiar objects Uses shape, size, and color to tell the difference between objects	Listens to adult while attending to pictures
6 months	Can make things happen Likes to look at things upside-down Explores body parts with hands and mouth	Recognizes familiar objects and people (3–6 months) Starts to make verbal sounds such as "coo" (3–6 months) Can organize sounds into patterns and phrases (3–6 months)
7 months	May compare two objects Distinguishes near and far objects in space	Brings book to mouth to chew or suck (4–7 months)
8 months	Shows recognition of names of objects by looking at them when named	Holds book in both hands (6–8 months) Explores and manipulates books (e.g., opens, closes) (6–8 months) Helps adult turn pages by pressing pages to the left after adult has separated out each succeeding page (7–8 months) Offers book to adult to read
9 months	Is aware of vertical space; fears height	Begins to babble (6–9 months) Looks at pictures when named (8–9 months) "Mama/dada" used as nonspecific terms
10 months	Shows interest in combining objects Experimenting with causal actions on objects	Reaches for and grasps books (5–10 months) Shakes, crumbles, waves papers (5–10 months) Vocalizes while pointing to pictures (7–10 months) Gestures to request repeated reading of a book (8–10 months) Sits on adult's lap for extended periods of time to look at books (8–10 months)
11 months	Shows spatial understanding: puts things in/out, off/on (11+ months) Identification with the same sex (11+ months) Associates properties with objects (e.g., sounds of animals, location of objects)	Turns pages, but not necessarily one at a time Begins to label objects (11+ months) Moves to rhythms

Transdisciplinary Play-Based System (TPBA2/TPBI2)
by Toni Linder.

(continued on next page)

Age level	Conceptual knowledge: Math and science	Conceptual knowledge: Emerging literacy
12 months or 1 year	Learns characteristics of objects through observation and actions (7–12 months) Uses first meaningful word for an object (10–12 months)	Pulls books off shelf (6–12 months) Prefers pictures of faces (6–12 months) Pats pictures and vocalizes (6–12 months) Decreased physical manipulation of books decreases (8–12 months) Independently attends to books (8–12 months) Turns pages independently; may have difficulty separating pages but is persistent in trying (8–12 months) Laughs or smiles at a familiar picture, usually when an adult makes an interesting sound or reads in an interesting way (8–12 months) Points to individual pictures when named by adult (8–12 months) WRITING SKILLS Imitates scribble (8–12 months)
By 15 months	Attends to specific physical characteristics of objects Combines related objects (e.g., dress on doll) Shows categorization of function (e.g., pail and shovel) Places objects into categories (e.g., food, animals, plants) Can place round circle in puzzle (12–15 months)	Sustains interest for at least 2–5 minutes looking at named pictures Makes animal sounds when looking at pictures of animals in book (10–13 months) Relates an object or an action in a book to the real world (10–14 months) Shows a preference for a favorite page of a book by searching for it or holding the book open to that page repeatedly (11–14 months) Names objects pictured, points correctly to a familiar object when asked, "Where's the . . . ?" (11–14 months) Uses "book babble" (jargon that sounds like reading) (13–14 months) Selects books on the basis of content (10–15 months) Turns an inverted book right side up or tilts head (11–15 months) Helps reader turn pages of books (14–15 months) Turns pages in clumps when looking at books (14–15 months)
By 18 months	Knows functions of objects (12–18 months) Recognizes and points to body parts Uses spatial concepts, such as "up," "down" (12–18 months) Can place circle and square in puzzle	Carries books around while walking (12–18 months) Holds book open with help (12–18 months) Gives book to adult to read (12–18 months) Shows familiarity with the text on seeing illustration (says some of words in text) WRITING SKILLS Scribbles spontaneously (13–18 months)

By 21 months or 2 years	Understands and uses:
	  Agents (e.g., mama)
	  Actions (e.g., run)
	  Objects (e.g., cup)
	  Recurrence (e.g., more)
	  Cessation (e.g., stop)
	  Disappearance (e.g., all gone) (18–20 months)
	Matches familiar objects (e.g., picks out spoons from all silverware)
	Makes collections of things that are alike in some way (e.g., puts toys with wheels together)
	Knows location (e.g., "there") (18–20 months)
	Nests objects (relates sizes)
	Puts circle, square, triangle shapes in puzzle (18–24 months)
	Uses one-to-one correspondence with two objects
		READING SKILLS
		Points to a picture and asks, "What's that?" or indicates that a label is requested (13–20 months)
		Notices print rather than just pictures; may point to labels under pictures when pictures are named (15–20 months)
		Shows empathy for characters or situations depicted in books (16–20 months)
		Makes associations across books
		
		WRITING SKILLS
		Begins to draw vertical and horizontal lines
		Continues to scribble

Transdisciplinary Play-Based System (TPBA2/TPBI2)
by Toni Linder.

(continued on next page)

Age level	Conceptual knowledge: Math and science	Conceptual knowledge: Emerging literacy
By 24 months or 2 years	Points to and names body parts (13–24 months) Distinguishes living and nonliving things Has knowledge of basic-level categories, such as plants, animals, and people Knows "more" (18–24 months) Compares and matches form, size, color (18–24 months)	READING SKILLS Enjoys a variety of interactive books (12–24 months) Engages in reading behavior by verbalizing while looking at books (12–24 months) Performs an action shown or mentioned in a book (12–24 months) Sits for several minutes looking at a book (12–24 months) Takes books off shelf and replaces them (12–24 months) May accidentally tear pages; decrease in intentional tearing (12–24 months) May use book as transitional object (18–24 months) Recites parts of well-known stories, rhymes, songs (18–24 months) Distinguishes print from nonprint (18–24 months) Identifies objects in a photograph (18–24 months) Relates pictures in stories to own experiences (20–26 months) WRITING SKILLS Hand dominance may emerge (18–24 months) Explores making marks with pencil or crayon (18–24 months) Imitates vertical strokes (18–24 months) Imitates circular scribble (20–24 months) Draws zigzags, lines, and loops during scribbling
By 30 months	Counts first three count words (19–30 months) Counts two objects, knows "one more" (24–30 months) Knows "how many" up to two (24–30 months) Recognizes and points to functions of objects (e.g., rolls, jumps) (24–30 months) Recognizes size differences (e.g., pointing to *little*, *big*) (27–30 months) Names at least one color (27–30 months)	READING SKILLS "Reads" to dolls, stuffed animals, or self (17–25 months) Enjoys nursery rhymes, nonsense rhymes, finger-plays, poetry (18–30 months) Talks about characters and events in books in ways that show understanding of the story (20–26 months) Fills in a word in the text when the reader pauses, says the next word before the reader does, or reads along with the reader when a predictable/familiar book is read (15–28 months) Protests when adult misreads a word in a familiar story; typically offers correct word (25–28 months) Recites whole phrases from favorite stories if adult pauses at opportune times (24–30 months) Recognizes some familiar environmental signs or symbols WRITING SKILLS Makes crayon rubbing Imitates horizontal stroke (24–30 months)
36 months or 3 years	Understands most common descriptors (30–36 months) Understands gender (30–36 months) Gives both first and last name (30–36 months) Can do simple form puzzles (24–36 months) Asks "What," "Where," "Why," "When," "Who" (30–36 months) Makes spatial designs with blocks or shapes (18–36 months) Knows directional words (e.g., *up, down, out, in, over, under*) (24–36 months) Knows gender (30–36 months) Sorts basic shapes (30–36 months) Counts 1–10	READING SKILLS Searches for favorite pictures in books (24–36 months) May recite simple stories from familiar books (24–36 months) Coordinates text read (words) with pictures (24–36 months) Reads some environmental print (30–36 months) Moves finger or hand across a line of print in a favorite book and verbalizes text exactly or accurately paraphrased (32 months) Listens to longer stories (36+ months) Understands what print is (36+ months)

Transdisciplinary Play-Based System (TPBA2/TPBI2)
by Toni Linder.

(continued on next page)

Age level	Conceptual knowledge: Math and science	Conceptual knowledge: Emerging literacy
36 months or 3 years (continued)	Counts 1–4 items with one-to-one correspondence Subitizes, or instantly tells *how many* with groups of 1–3 items (24–36 months) Visually identifies the *same* or *more* by making a visual comparison (may be wrong) Understands concepts of *all, none* relating to number of objects Notices simple repeating patterns, such as *long-short, long-short* in block sets Matches shapes, first with same size and orientation, then with different sizes and orientation	WRITING SKILLS Imitates a cross (24–36 months) Engages in early scribble writing: makes organized marks (pictures/writing) (24–36 months) Can usually indicate which is a picture or writing in own products (24–36 months) Copies a circle (25–36 months) May label and talk about own drawings (30–36 months) Draws recognizable forms (30–36 months)
42 months	Counts to 3 meaningfully (not rote) (36–42 months) Knows several shapes, colors, sizes, textures Knows spatial relationships Knows what objects go together functionally and how they are used Understands functions of body parts	READING SKILLS Understands relationship among related pictures Names action when looking at a picture book Tells story when looking at a familiar picture book Recalls one or two elements from a story just read Matches uppercase letters Matches written numbers 0–9 (may mix up 6 and 9) WRITING SKILLS Holds pencil/crayon using 3-finger grasp (36–39 months) Draws circle independently Copies a cross (36–42 months) Draws person with head and at least one feature
By 48 months or 4 years	Compares textures (42–48 months) Identifies primary colors (36–48 months) Matches wide range of colors (30–48 months) Names examples of objects, animals, and so forth, in a class (e.g., fruit) Asks questions about bodily functions Counts 1–30 with emphasis on the counting pattern (e.g., "Twenty-*one*," with emphasis on parallel to 1, 2, 3) Counts 1–10 items, knowing the last number stated is the total number of items Subitizes groups of up to five items without having to count each item Recognizes and names variations of the circle, square, triangle, and rectangle Learns a simple route from a map placed in direct relation to the child's space Creates 2-D and 3-D constructions with symmetry Informally compares amount of items with clear discrepancies Copies simple repeating patterns	READING SKILLS Knows that alphabet letters are a category of visual graphics that can be individually named (36-48 months) Identifies about 10 alphabet letters, especially those in own name (36–48 months) Begins to identify rhymes and rhyming sounds in familiar words Begins to attend to the beginning sounds in familiar words Indicates enjoyment when hearing alliteration in stories (36–48 months) Begins to make letter–sound matches Dictates words, phrases, and sentences for others to write Identifies simple, high-frequency words Begins to break words into syllables Recognizes own name in print When read a story, connects details, information, and events to real-life experiences (36–48 months) Questions and comments demonstrate understanding of literal meaning of story (36–48 months) Recognizes print in the local environment (36–48 months) Knows that it is the print that is read in stories (36–48 months) Is interested in sequences of events in stories (36–48 months) Recalls 3–4 elements from a story Displays reading and writing attempts to others Begins to predict what will happen next in an unknown story WRITING SKILLS Copies diagonal lines (36–48 months) Traces a 6-inch line with no more than one deviation Draws person with head and at least four features (42–48 months) Makes visual representations of people, scenes, objects, animals, designs (recognizable but not precise) (42–48 months)

Transcdisciplinary Play-Based System (TPBA2/TPBI2)
by Toni Linder.

(continued on next page

Age level	Conceptual knowledge: Math and science	Conceptual knowledge: Emerging literacy
By 48 months or 4 years *(continued)*		Begins to realize that written symbols convey meaning and starts to produce own symbols (42–48 months) May intend that his/her scribbling is writing (36–48 months) Scribbling goes from left to right in lines across the page with repeated patterns and increased muscle control (36–48 months) Knows that different forms of text are used for different purposes (36–48 months) May use drawing to stand for writing in order to communicate a message (36–48 months) Reads drawings as if there were writing on them (36–48 months) Writes/scribbles messages as part of play activity (36–48 months) Holds marker with fingers in tripod position
54 months	Uses terms *longer, shorter* Recognizes *day* or *night* and relates to experience (48–54 months) Counts to 4 or more with one-to-one correspondence (48–54 months) Can do simple analogies (e.g., "the stove is hot," "the refrigerator is cold") Talks about past, present, and future time Understands "same number as" Can explain the similarities and differences between objects, people	READING SKILLS Begins obtaining phonemic awareness through rhymes, poems, songs (48–54 months) Makes rhymes to simple words WRITING SKILLS Differentiates between letters and numbers Draws simple pictures Copies a square Draws a person with head and at least six features
By 60 months or 5 years	Knows penny, nickel, dime (not their worth) (54–60 months) Compares weight (e.g., light, heavy) (54–60 months) Points to and names wide range of colors (48–60 months) Sorts wide variety of shapes (48–60 months) Uses relational words (e.g., *forward, then, when, first, next, backward, behind, in front of*) (48–60 months) Can identify the class when members of the class are named (e.g., apple, banana, pear are fruit) Counts with one-to-one correspondence up to 20 Counts to 100, with emphasis on the patterns (e.g., 20, 30, 40 plus the numbers 1, 2, 3, and to 13 to 19 add "teen") Subitizes up to six items visually Uses counting to compare amounts in different sets Solves simple word problems involving small numbers using fingers Creates or recreates a picture or pattern using shapes Creates a map using toy objects to recreate a space Compares lengths using another object Creates patterns with symmetry Meaningfully uses words *equal, more, less,* and *fewer* Discusses pattern of adding 1, gets the next number Uses hypothetical reasoning ("what would happen if . . . ?")	READING SKILLS Recognizes frequently occurring words and environmental print Dictates messages and stories Tells suitable ending to a simple story (57–60 months) Labels/names most uppercase letters (54–60 months) WRITING SKILLS Begins to write alphabet letters or close approximations in combination with scribble (48–60 months) Gradually, letterlike forms and actual letters replace scribbles in writing (48–60 months) Frequently reverses letters when writing (48–60 months) Imitates drawing triangle (48–60 months) Traces own name (48–60 months) Copies diagonal and zigzag lines (52–60 months) Draws a person with head and at least eight features Puts spaces between written words Independently writes capital and lowercase letters of the alphabet Writes messages left to right, top to bottom of page Begins to use punctuation in writing Traces outline of simple stencil SPELLING SKILLS Uses invented and conventional spellings using phonemic awareness and letter knowledge (48–60 months) Begins to build a repertoire of conventionally spelled words Copies a few words from the environment (48–60 months) Writes names of some friends and classmates May use a group of known letters (often consonants) to form a word (48–60 months) Writes labels for objects or locations and captions for illustrations

Transdisciplinary Play-Based System (TPBA2/TPBI2)
by Toni Linder.

(continued on next page)

Age level	Conceptual knowledge: Math and science	Conceptual knowledge: Emerging literacy
By 72 months or 6 years	Knows how old he or she is (meaningful, not rote) (60–66 months) Knows relationship of size, weight (e.g., thin, fat; light, heavy; narrow, wide) Discusses patterns in math, such as if you add 1, you get the next number Begins to ask math questions of adults Begins adding and subtracting simple numbers Knows morning versus afternoon (66–72 months) Knows right from left Sorts by size (60–72 months) Uses "in the middle" concept (60–72 months) Can count indefinitely, using tens, hundreds, thousands patterning	READING SKILLS Makes up and tells stories of real or imaginative content (plot, structure) (60–66 months) Knows the parts of a book and their functions (60–72 months) Uses picture cues to support reading and comprehension Tracks print when listening to a familiar story or when reading own writing Recognizes and names all upper- and lowercase letters Knows many, but not all, letter–sound correspondences Applies letter–sound correspondences to read words Demonstrates understanding that spoken words consist of sequences of phonemes Understands the alphabetic principle Able to switch from oral to written language styles Can name some book titles and authors Recognizes several types or genres of text (e.g., poems, newspaper, expository text, labels) Answers questions about stories read aloud Makes predictions based on illustrations or portions of text Identifies story problem and plot Produces rhyming words and distinguishes from nonrhyming words (5–6 years) Identifies, segments, and combines syllables in spoken words (5–6 years) Identifies first and final sounds in spoken words (5–6 years) Blends and segments one-syllable spoken words into phonemes (5–6 years) Scans letters of a word left to right (5–6 years) Matches identical words in a group of words presented visually (5–6 years) Reads simple three-letter words paired with pictures (66–72 months) Marks time by beating rhythm (66–72 months) (is important for matching syllables to sounds) Answers literal questions about stories (e.g., who, what, when, where) (4–6 years) Answers interpretive questions about a story (e.g., why, what if) (5–6 years) Reconstructs/retells stories (5–6 years) WRITING SKILLS Imitates drawing of diamond shape (52–64 months) Traces own hand (53–62 months) Draws recognizable face with eyes, nose, mouth (56–64 months) Writes own first and last name, copying model (62–70 months) Begins using symbols for representations as well as pictures (5–6 years) May begin printing or copying letters or numerals (5–6 years) Draws picture of three or more objects (5–6 years) Prints own first name without a model (5.2–6 years) Dictates messages and stories SPELLING SKILLS Prints name and simple words (60–66 months) Spells words phonetically Uses invented spellings Uses resources to find correct spelling Writes own first and last name

Transdisciplinary Play-Based System (TPBA2/TPBI2)
by Toni Linder.

(continued on next page)

TPBA2 Observation Summary Form: Cognitive Development

Child's name: _____   Age: _____   Birth date: _____

Parent(s): _____

Person(s) completing the form: _____   Assessment date: _____

Directions: For each of the subcategories below, shown in a 1–9-point Goal Attainment Scale, circle the number that indicates the child's developmental status, using findings from the TPBA2 Observation Guidelines or TPBA2 Observation Notes for this domain. Next, consider the child's performance in relation to same-age peers by comparing the child's performance with the TPBA2 Age Table. Use the Age Table to arrive at the child's age level for each subcategory (follow directions on the Age Table). Then, circle AA, T, W, or C by calculating percent delay:

If a child's age level < chronological age: $1 - (\text{age level/CA}) = $ _____ % delay

If child's age level > chronological age: $(\text{age level/CA}) - 1 = $ _____ % above

To calculate CA, subtract the child's birth date from the assessment date and round up or down as appropriate. When subtracting days, take into consideration the number of days in the month (i.e., 28, 30, 31).

TPBA2 Subcategory	\multicolumn{9}{c}{Level of the child's ability as observed in functional activities}	\multicolumn{5}{c}{Rating compared with other children of same age}

TPBA2 Subcategory	1	2	3	4	5	6	7	8	9	Above average (AA)	Typical (T)	Watch (W)	Concern (C)	Age level (mode)
Attention	Inattentive, unaware of surroundings, or distractible and unable to focus on one object or person for a sustained time.		Selective focus of attention. Has difficulty sharing a focus of attention with another person and pays attention only to specific interests. Alternatively, focus of attention shifts rapidly from one thing to another.		Attends to relevant people, objects, and events with prompts. Can share a focus of attention with someone, but needs verbal and physical support to maintain or shift attention.		Independently attends to relevant people, objects, and events. Needs occasional verbal or gestural suggestion to maintain attention.		Is able to select focus, maintain attention, and shift focus from objects to people, and person to person, appropriately.	AA	T	W	C	_____
										\multicolumn{5}{l}{Comments:}

Transdisciplinary Play-Based System (TPBA2/TPBI2) by Toni Linder.

(continued on next page)

Observation Summary Form: Cognitive Development **TPBA 2**

TPBA2 Subcategory	Level of the child's ability as observed in functional activities									Rating compared with other children of same age				
										Above average (AA)	Typical (T)	Watch (W)	Concern (C)	Age level (mode)
Memory	1	2	3	4	5	6	7	8	9	AA	T	W	C	___
	Shows memory by looking longer at novel items.		Anticipates what to do or how to react with familiar toys, people, or events. Imitates simple actions after demonstration.		Verbally or non-verbally shows recognition of names of simple objects, people, places, actions, and routines.		Demonstrates ability to accurately recognize, recall, and reconstruct routines, skills, concepts, and events after both short and long periods.		Relates complex classification and rule systems, conceptual processes, physical skill sequences, and multifaceted events in detail.	Comments:				
Problem solving	1	2	3	4	5	6	7	8	9	AA	T	W	C	___
	Recognizes changes in people, objects, or actions.		Is able to see the relationship between a simple action or event and what caused it to occur.		Is able to make a desired familiar event occur using another person or by him/herself.		Is able to perform a series of actions toward an unfamiliar goal and use trial-and-error manipulation to make corrections.		Is able to understand complex causal relationships, mentally organize sequences toward a goal, and make modifications as needed. Can then generalize results to new situations.	Comments:				
Social cognition	1	2	3	4	5	6	7	8	9	AA	T	W	C	___
	Does not attend to and/or attach meaning to others' facial expressions, gestures, or body language.		Is able to read and respond to others' facial expressions, gestures, body language, and movements.		Responds to emotions expressed by others by acting to sustain positive emotions and reduce negative emotions.		Anticipates and responds to others' needs, desires, and thinking based on own needs, desires, and logic, which may not match those of others.		Understands and responds to motivation, desires, and thoughts of others, even if they are different from own.	Comments:				

Transdisciplinary Play-Based System (TPBA2/TPBI2)
by Toni Linder.

(continued on next page)

(continued from previous page)

Observation Summary Form: Cognitive Development **TPBA** 2

TPBA2 Subcategory	Level of the child's ability as observed in functional activities									Rating compared with other children of same age				
	1	2	3	4	5	6	7	8	9	Above average (AA)	Typical (T)	Watch (W)	Concern (C)	Age level (mode)
Complexity of play	Enjoys people and investigating the environment with all the senses.		Enjoys sensory exploration, body movement, and exploring objects repetitively.		Enjoys putting things together, experimenting to make things happen, and recreating familiar actions and routines.		Combines various kinds of play to create actual and imagined structures, scenarios, and outcomes.		Demonstrates both logical and creative thinking in all forms of play (sensory, physical, functional, construction, dramatic, and games with rules). Creates own games with own rules.	AA Comments:	T	W	C	_____
Conceptual knowledge	Recognizes familiar sounds, smells, tastes, people, actions, and objects.		Notices salient properties, sees similarities and differences, and has simple labels for some animals, people, objects, actions, and events.		Recognizes, discusses, or uses concrete similarities and differences to categorize or group animals, people, objects, actions, and events into constructs, such as type, location, use, relationship, and causality.		Recognizes, describes, and organizes thoughts and actions by both concrete and abstract concepts and categories. Is forming a classification system into which new concepts and rules are structured and related.		Describes, compares, differentiates, and understands both featural and dynamic (e.g., who, where, when, why, how) aspects of concepts. Understands logical relations among mathematical, physical, biological, psychological, and literacy concepts, and can share ideas through symbolic representations.	AA Comments:	T	W	C	_____

Transdisciplinary Play-Based System (TPBA2/TPBI2)
by Toni Linder.

(continued from previous page)

Observation Summary Form: Cognitive Development **TPBA** 2

TPBA2 Subcategory	Level of the child's ability as observed in functional activities									Rating compared with other children of same age				
	1	2	3	4	5	6	7	8	9	Above average (AA)	Typical (T)	Watch (W)	Concern (C)	Age level (mode)
Literacy	Listens to sounds; recognizes familiar voices and like rhythms.		Likes to explore books, look at pictures, listen to the rhythms of someone reading, and make marks on paper.		Listens to a simple story, turns pages, labels pictures, repeats adult's words from a book and imitates intonation. Tries to represent objects or people on paper.		Listens to longer stories, pretends to read, talks about pictures, can retell a story, and makes letterlike forms on paper.		Understands stories, uses book-reading behaviors, has phonological awareness, has phonemic awareness, has letter knowledge, and some word recognition in meaningful contexts. Draws/writes letters or makes writing-like marks. Uses invented spelling. Composes written products (e.g., cards, notes, lists, stories).	AA	T	W	C	——
										Comments:				
Overall Needs:														

8

Emerging Literacy

Forrest Hancock

Note: Although the subcategory of literacy is included with conceptual development, it has been highlighted in this separate chapter in order to address the importance of literacy for success in school. In TPBA2, see Chapter 7 for the Observation Guidelines, Age Tables, Observation Notes, and Observation Summary Forms for cognitive development, which include literacy as a subcategory. In TPBI2, Chapter 8 addresses strategies for supporting emerging literacy in intervention.

Learning about reading and writing is an important outcome of early childhood development. Although literacy is included in the cognitive domain of this text, because it is typically thought of as an "academic" area, it is truly an area where all domains of development come together. It has become evident that development in language, communication, social abilities, cognition, and motor skills all influence the acquisition of literacy skills. Individuals who are engaged in observing, assessing, and supporting the growth of young children acknowledge that one cannot separate the individual developmental strands, but rather that development in one area influences development in other areas. The whole child must be embraced even as the specific strands of development are investigated.

Language and literacy are developmentally intertwined and grow from social interactions with others (Justice & Kaderavek, 2004; Reese, Cox, Harte, & McAnally, 2003; Snow, Burns, & Griffin, 1998; van Kleeck, 2004; Zevenbergen & Whitehurst, 2003; Zigler, Singer, & Bishop-Josef, 2004). Prelinguistic communication begins developing with the earliest communicative turn-taking experiences during infancy and supports the later development of linguistic skills which, in turn, supports the development of literacy (Wetherby et al., 2003). Children develop an interest in reading through interactions with others around books and environmental print, and their language development is enhanced as they listen to and participate in the vocabulary, rhymes, and rhythms of reading. Adults and more proficient siblings and peers provide scaffolding and encouragement as the toddler learns to associate words with people, objects, actions, events, and eventually pictures and symbols. Through ongoing social interactions, the child is supported in developing the foundational skills for literacy that include oral language, vocabulary, metalinguistic awareness, phonological awareness, the alphabetic principle, phonemic awareness, and semantic and syntactic understanding.

Play is another important strand in the braided development of language and literacy skills. During play children engage in experiences in which literacy can be naturally enfolded such as developing narrative for enacting stories during sociodramatic play, using symbolism to represent missing objects (e.g., when a block is used for a car), and using oral language skills during communication with play partners. Oral language ability is a key element for the foundation of literacy (Snow et al., 1998), and play offers a rich opportunity for children to use and enhance their oral language skills, thus creating a natural and powerful venue to support the growth of literacy (Bowman, 2004; Pellegrini & Galda, 1990, 2000; Roskos & Christie, 2004; Zigler et al., 2004). Blended together, these two avenues can create a superhighway for building and assessing emerging literacy skills.

The development of language and literacy is also supported by the child's growth in cognition and motor skills. Increasingly sophisticated cognitive skills related to attention, memory, problem solving, conceptual development and representational abilities (all discussed in Chapter 7) are significant contributors to the development of literacy. Developing motor skills contribute to the child's ability to obtain, hold, explore, and manipulate objects and written materials such as picture books, as well as to engage in drawing and writing experiences.

Recent research findings have enhanced our understanding of the development of literacy in young children and propelled initiatives focused on supporting literacy development from a very young age. The following section presents major research findings that guide our understanding and support for the development of emerging literacy for young children.

RESEARCH RELATED TO SUBCATEGORY OBSERVATION GUIDELINE QUESTIONS

In the past, authorities believed that literacy development began when children entered school at about 5 or 6 years of age and were introduced to formal reading instruction. However, it is now commonly accepted that learning to read and write actually begins in infancy in a literate society (Lyon, 2000; Miller, 2000; Morrow, 1989; Teale & Sulzby, 1986, 1989; Teale & Yokota, 2000; Whitehurst & Lonigan, 2002) and continues throughout life (Morrison & Morrow, 2002). Clay (1966) and Holdaway (1979) are often credited with initiating the theory of *emergent literacy,* which espouses the belief that the child's earliest linguistic achievements are integral to the development of literacy. This belief has been confirmed by results of a longitudinal study that revealed strong relationships between prelinguistic performance and later language development (Wetherby, Allen, Cleary, Kublin, & Goldstein, 2002) and even later formal reading abilities (Wetherby, 2002; Wetherby et al., 2003). Skills that were previously considered to belong only to the area of language development have been found to support the subsequent development of literacy skills.

In recent years the concept of literacy has broadened beyond merely ability to read and write to encompass the process of abstracting and conveying meaning using symbols in any situation in the environment (e.g., store logos, product labels, maps, signs, books, articles) (Whitehurst & Lonigan, 2002). Furthermore, literacy is viewed as a sociocultural construct in that it is the avenue for representing and transmitting a culture's identity, values, beliefs, norms, and experiences (Ferdman, 1990; Miller, 1990). Miller (1990, p. 3) stated that " . . . literacy is a phenomenon of cultural activity"; it is socially learned, socially transmitted, and socially meaningful. Shaywitz (2003, p. 3) describes reading as " . . . an extraordinary ability, peculiarly human and yet distinctively unnatural. It is acquired in childhood, forms an intrinsic part of our existence as civilized beings, and is taken for granted by most of us." The conventional forms of literacy (i.e., reading and writing of alphabetic texts) must be taught because they are not innate, yet they are only a small part of the realm of knowledge and behavior that is encompassed in literacy.

Emergent literacy is actually a developmental continuum of a child's increasing awareness of print and understanding of the components and functions of literacy. It is not a single skill but a complex system of skills that a child constructs over time through socially shared knowledge, experiences, behaviors, and attitudes (Sulzby, 1986; Teale & Sulzby, 1986; Whitehurst & Lonigan, 2002). For this reason the term "emergent literacy" increasingly is being substituted with the more descriptive term, *emerging literacy*, which reflects the ongoing nature of its development.

Through interactions with others, the child is supported in constructing her own understanding about literacy. Furthermore, as she observes and participates in naturally occurring, informal language and literacy activities, she gains specific knowledge and skills needed for later proficiency and independence in literacy. The child must develop knowledge and skills in the areas of language, print functions, and forms, as well as metalinguistic, phonological, alphabetic, and phonemic awareness in order to achieve competence, fluency, and independence in reading.

Even from an extraordinarily young age the roots of future literacy skills begin to develop. Wetherby et al. (2003) have identified several prelinguistic behaviors that predict later language abilities at 2, 3, and 4 years of age. These predictors included rate and function of preverbal communication, gestures, sounds, understanding of words, and use of objects in play (Wetherby et al., 2002; Wetherby, Cleary, & Allen, 2001). Additional findings from this longitudinal study indicated a significant, positive correlation between measures of language comprehension and play and later measures of language, phonological sensitivity, and print knowledge at 4 years of age (Wetherby et al., 2003). The results of these investigations indicate that "prelinguistic skills may be the earliest indicators of later reading achievement" and thus offer " . . . important implications for early identification of children at risk for future language and reading difficulties" (Wetherby et al., 2003, p. 1).

Several authorities in the field of early literacy have developed organizational frameworks for representing the foundational components of literacy development. Building on the work of Adams (1990) and Seidenberg and McClelland (1989), van Kleeck (1998, 2003) focused on the following four areas in which children must learn to process information in order to become literate: 1) context, 2) meaning, 3) phonological understanding, and 4) orthographic understanding (see Figure 8.1). As indicated by the absence of bidirectional arrows between the four "processors" in van Kleeck's model, the individual processors are loosely integrated for children who are emergently literate, whereas a diagram for fluent readers would have bidirectional arrows between all the processors indicating their interdependence and connectedness (van Kleeck, 2003). Each one of these processors is important, supports the development of the other processors, and can be examined through observation of the child's interactions with books and environmental print.

Whitehurst and Lonigan (1998, 2002) have developed a slightly different organizational framework for the components of literacy as reflected in their descriptions of "inside-out" and "outside-in" processes. The inside-out processes include alphabet knowledge, print concepts, and phonological awareness. The inside-out units supply information about the print that is embedded within the written message and help the reader decode the print. These units can be thought of as supports for "bottom-up" or part-to-whole, reductionist understanding. However, the outside-in processes that encompass context, semantics, and vocabulary supply information to the reader regarding meaning so the reader can understand the content and context of what he is reading. Outside-in units come from "outside" the words themselves and support "top-down" or holistic understanding (see Figure 8.2). The importance of models such

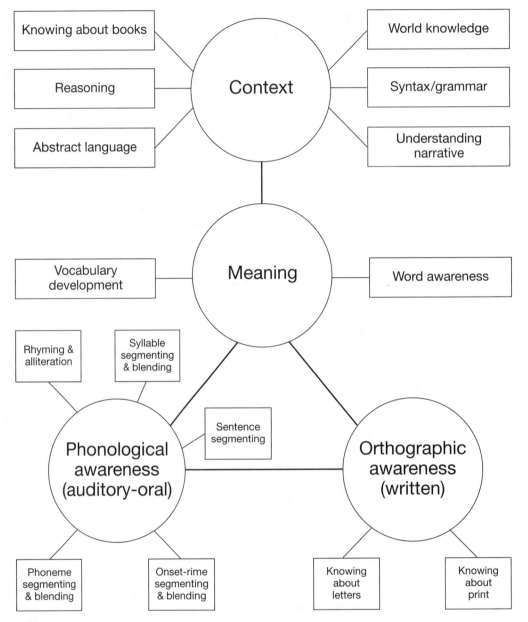

Figure 8.1. Model of components of emerging literacy. (Adapted from van Kleeck, A. [2003]. Research on book sharing: Another critical look. In A. van Kleeck, S.A. Stahl, & E.B. Bauer [Eds.], *On reading books to children: Parents and teachers* [pp. 271–320]. Mahwah, NJ: Lawrence Erlbaum Associates).

as the two just described is that they bridge the controversy that for many years divided the field of literacy development by recognizing the value and importance of each side's perspective, which is the interdependence of comprehension (top-down skills) and decoding (bottom-up skills).

The National Research Council (Burns, Griffin, & Snow, 1999, p. 8) delineated three main accomplishments in language and literacy that support successful readers: "(1) oral language skills and phonological awareness, (2) motivation to learn and appreciation for literate forms, and (3) print awareness and letter knowledge." Furthermore, the Council stressed that the best way for children to achieve these accomplishments is during activities that are integrated into all of the areas of development (i.e., cognitive, emotional-social, motor, and language). In accordance with this recommen-

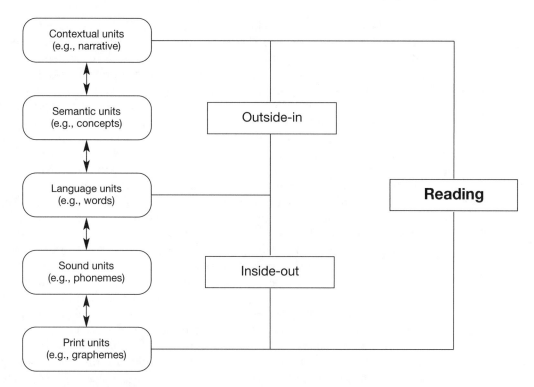

Figure 8.2. Skills and processes of literacy. (From Whitehurst, G.J., & Lonigan, C.J. [2002]. Emergent literacy: Development from prereaders to readers. In S.B. Neuman & D.K. Dickinson [Eds.], *Handbook of early literacy research* [pp. 11–29]. New York: Guilford Press. Reprinted by permission.)

dation, even though this particular subcategory of cognitive development focuses on emerging literacy skills, examination of the child's abilities in all of the developmental domains is essential to fully understand his or her literacy development. The following section of TPBA examines the child's listening skills during shared book reading, use of books, comprehension during shared book reading, recall from familiar stories, attempts to read, and understanding about writing and spelling.

Reading

VII. A. What listening skills does the child demonstrate?

Listening and comprehending the content of print as others read aloud provide a foundation for later independence in interpreting the meaning of print. The child's family and caregivers first introduce the contexts of symbols and print through such activities as pointing to pictures; naming objects, people, or actions in the pictures; explaining signs; shared book reading; talking about and using print in the environment, and so forth. Through interactions such as these, children learn about the context and importance of the elements of literacy in their world. Because shared book reading is such a rich venue for supporting the development of emerging literacy skills, it is examined in the following section.

The relationship between book sharing and literacy development has received research attention for three decades and, as in other areas of literacy, has experienced controversy (van Kleeck, 2003). Some authorities have questioned the belief that book sharing can contribute toward building skills that would later support literacy (see Kaderavek & Justice, 2002). However, results of research on book sharing have increasingly made it clear that this is an important element of family literacy practice that does in fact support the development of literacy skills (e.g., Justice & Kaderavek, 2002; Katims, 1991; van Kleeck, 1998; Whitehurst et al., 1988). Book sharing can occur in different forms such as joint attention to a picture book, quiet lap time with an adult, storybook reading by the adult, intentional teaching of reading skills, or creative exploration of a topic from a story (DeTemple, 2001). Storybook sharing also provides opportunities for the child to learn and practice new vocabulary, language, and discourse forms that the adult sensitively matches to the child's individual and unique zone of proximal development (see Vygotsky, 1978), even when the child has language delay (van Kleeck & Woude, 2003).

The predictable routines (verbal and behavioral) that occur during shared book reading enhance the child's language and literacy development by providing opportunities for communicative exchanges between the child and the adult. Also, the routines that develop during shared book reading allow the adult to capitalize on the child's interest and extend his language through discussions, explanations, questioning, recall, prediction, and inference (DeTemple, 2001; van Kleeck, 2004). DeTemple's research revealed that most mothers interact verbally with their children as they read to them by asking questions, eliciting conversation, and making comments. Additionally, the nurturing interactions involved in book-sharing experiences enhance the quality of the adult–child relationship and have been shown to be positively associated with acquisition of the alphabetic principle (Wasik & Hendrickson, 2004).

Most studies of book sharing with preschoolers have focused on storybooks (van Kleeck, 2003); however, the type of book can influence the interactions as well as the kinds of learning that occur. Results of research studies that have compared storybook, alphabet book, and expository book reading have revealed different types of interactions with each book type (van Kleeck, 1998, 2003). When adults and children share a storybook, they tend to focus on meaning rather than print concepts. For example, during storybook reading adults provide information about book conventions (author, illustrator), predictions, interpretation of story actions, and motivations of the characters. However, when adults share alphabet books with young children they tend to focus on the print even when the children treat them as picture books. As the children become older, the discussion during alphabet book reading increasingly focuses on print. Surprisingly, even when the child fails to understand, the adult often seems to be unaware of it. Van Kleeck (2003) has suggested that perhaps this phenomenon is evidence of the "gradual social transmission of knowledge" (see Vygotsky, 1978). Research investigating story reading practices by Japanese mothers (Kato-Otani, 2004) revealed that unlike U.S. mothers who took a "teacher role," Japanese mothers asked their children questions they knew they could answer and focused more on the social, relational aspects of shared book reading, thus preserving "interpersonal harmony." Kato-Otani felt that the differences between the U.S. and Japanese mothers reflected their cultural values.

When adults share expository texts (i.e., informational books) they tend to focus on vocabulary, concept-building, and questions posed in the text and the level of child participation tends to increase (van Kleeck, 2003). Also, children's participation increases when familiar books are re-read to them. As adults read familiar books they often increase their expectations of the child's contributions, challenge the child at higher levels of abstraction, or increase the cognitive demand regarding the content of the book (van Kleeck, 2003) (e.g., requesting recall or predictions). During interactions involving familiar books, the child often takes more responsibility during the reading of the book, such as supplying a word or pointing to pictures (van Kleeck, 2003). Because it is apparent that children at different ages learn different emerging literacy skills from different types of books, van Kleeck (2003) suggested that future studies are needed to provide a better understanding of this area of early literacy. One such study (i.e., Justice, Weber, Ezell, & Bakeman, 2002) focused on this research need by investigating preschoolers' responsiveness to parent prompts and comments during the reading of a rhyming book. Because parents typically refer to print less frequently as they read picture and rhyming books (van Kleeck, 1998), Justice et al. (2002) incorporated parent training into their research design. The results of the study indicated that the children did respond to their parents' print references and with greater frequency when the parents used prompts, as opposed to comments. Also, the children responded even when the literacy topic or skill was above their level of independent functioning, which illustrates how adult scaffolding can support a child's development at his next higher level (i.e., the zone of proximal development).

Van Kleeck (1998, 2003) has suggested that there are two stages in the development of emerging literacy, with the first being meaning-focused and the second being print-focused along with the expansion of meaning. In fact, Wetherby (2002) illustrated this in her adaptation of van Kleeck's model of Components of Emerging Literacy. Wetherby's model contains the following four categories of emergent literacy knowledge: book knowledge, word knowledge, print knowledge, and sound awareness. Based on van Kleeck's research findings, Wetherby divided the development of each category into two stages with stage one emphasizing print meaning and stage two emphasizing print form and early form–meaning correspondences (see Figure 8.3). Each category and stage contains a list of literacy behaviors that typically are attained at that level. The foundation for learning many of the behaviors that are listed can be attained as children are listening to and using books, which will be the focus of the next section.

VII. B. How does the child use books?

Very young children vary in the way they interact with books. Some children sit quietly and look at books, others look at them fleetingly, and still others vigorously handle books by waving, tearing, or chewing them. Sometimes the child's style of interaction with a book depends on the associated activity, if the child is alone or someone is reading to him or her, or the type of book being read. Despite the differences in the ways

Book knowledge	Word knowledge	Print knowledge	Sound awareness
Stage 1: Emphasizing print meaning			
Orients/opens books	Labels/comments	Recognizes pictures	Animal noises
Turns pages	Predicates	Words and letters on page	Sound effects
Looks at pictures	Makes up words	Letter names	Nursery rhymes
Books provide information	Asks for word definitions	Print goes left to right/ top to bottom	Segments words into syllables
Books tell stories	Segments sentences into words	Reads logos and predictable words	Rhymes/alliterates
Stage 2: Emphasizing print form and early form–meaning correspondences			
Books have	Defines words	Letter shapes	Sound awareness:
Titles, authors	Synonyms	Letter sounds	Word blending
Illustrations	Antonyms	Letter associations	Initial sounds
Books provide	Homonyms	Sight words	Segments sounds
Predictions	Nonliteral meanings	Sounds out words	
Explanations			
Factual knowledge			

Figure 8.3. Early literacy skills. (From Wetherby, A.M. [2002, June]. *Language, literacy, and reading in the early years. Do they make a difference?* Presentation at the 2002 NAEYC Institute, Albuquerque. Available online at http://firstwords.fsu .edu. Adapted from Van Kleeck, A. [1998]. Preliteracy domains and stages: Laying the foundations for beginning reading. *Journal of Children's Communication Development, 20*[1], 33–51.)

children interact with books, they build their knowledge of book use and context during these interactions.

Schickedanz (1999, pp. 30–34) synthesized her recorded observations of the behaviors of young children from 2 to 36 months old as they interacted with books. The behaviors included book-handling, looking at books, showing recognition and understanding of books, comprehending pictures and stories, and storybook reading. Many of these literacy behaviors have been included in the TPBA2 Age Tables for conceptual development (see Chapter 7, p. 391).

The use of books also can be thought of as an avenue to understanding books themselves: what they are for, how they entertain, how we can learn from them, and how we can recreate their stories in various visual forms. One of the four processors in van Kleeck's (1998, 2003) model of emerging literacy is the "context processor," which will be described more fully in a later section. Parents and caregivers are usually the first to introduce the various contexts of print to children. This can occur during naturally occurring daily routines, during shared book reading, and as adults teach children the meaning of print.

Understanding *context* is important in several ways. Symbols, print, and books have a cultural context within society, and children need to know how and why they are needed. This understanding grows from exposure to and use of symbolic materials. Books also have an internal context, so children need to understand language structure, grammar, and narrative development that comprise text. Additionally, the information or story itself has a context which needs to fit into the child's knowledge of the world. As all of these aspects of context become integrated, children are better able to comprehend written language, and they are being prepared to eventually progress from learning to read to reading to learn (Adams, 1990; van Kleeck, 1998).

VII. C. What does the child comprehend when looking at or sharing a book?

On a daily basis, family members not only demonstrate informal modeling of their own literacy practices, but also they often use direct and intentional activities to teach children about books; words; meaning; and letter names, shapes, and sounds (van Kleeck, 2004; Wasik & Hendrickson, 2004). The growing interest in the effectiveness of shared reading for supporting a child's literacy development has resulted in a surge of research investigations.

An extensive review of the literature indicates that shared book reading is related to the following critical components that support emerging literacy: language skills; vocabulary; oral language complexity; narrative skills; later language and literacy skills; reading comprehension skills in second grade; and reading, spelling, and IQ at age 13 (Zevenbergen & Whitehurst, 2003). They noted that the way in which children are read to influences the benefits they experience from the shared interactions. For example, when children are encouraged to be active participants in literacy experiences supported by the adult's questions, elicitations of responses, and guidance in telling the story along with the adult, children show greater gains than when they are simply passive listeners (Zevenberger & Whitehurst, 2003).

Several models have been developed for shared book reading. Justice and Kaderavek (2004; see also Kaderavek & Justice, 2004) developed the "Embedded-Explicit Emergent Literacy Intervention" model in which adults support the development of literacy during naturalistic, meaningful, contextualized (embedded) experiences as well as during explicit instruction. The *embedded* experiences are naturally occurring opportunities for social interactions involving oral and written language using shared storybook reading and scaffolded storytelling that occur in a print-rich environment and/or a literacy-enriched play setting. This portion of the model corresponds to the top-down, whole-language approach. The *explicit* instruction component of the model focuses on direct instruction in the bottom-up arena of phonological awareness, print concepts, alphabet knowledge and writing, and narrative and explicit language (Justice & Kaderavek, 2004; Kaderavek & Justice, 2004). This is a blended model that is built on the research findings from the two dichotomous fields that it spans (i.e., top-down and bottom-up approaches) (see Justice & Kaderavek, 2004).

Another strategy for shared book reading, called *dialogic reading,* was first described by Whitehurst et al. (1988). In this approach, the child gradually becomes the storyteller while the adult supports him or her using active listening, asking open-ended questions, prompting the child to elaborate by asking increasingly challenging questions, and expanding on the child's responses. Results of research studies focused on the use of dialogic reading with children from 2 to 5 years old indicate growth in oral language, vocabulary, and emerging literacy skills (Whitehurst & Lonigan, 1998, 2002).

In the seminal book, *Preventing Reading Difficulties in Young Children* (Snow et al., 1998), the National Research Council concluded that one of the avenues for helping prevent reading problems is through increasing children's oral language skills. Children with larger vocabularies progress in their development of phonological awareness skills with greater speed and facility and later are able to comprehend what they are reading more easily than children with smaller lexicons (Goswami, 2002; Whitehurst & Lonigan, 2002). Shared book reading appears to support early literacy development in these three important areas (i.e., oral language, vocabulary, and phonological awareness). In the next section we will focus on vocabulary, word awareness, and context.

VII. D. What does the child recall of words, phrases, story lines, and content from familiar stories?

Before a child can recall components of stories, he or she must be able to understand the story and have developed an adequate lexicon. Two processors in van Kleeck's model of the components of emerging literacy (see Figure 8.1) are related to comprehension and recall ability. These processors include the meaning and context processors.

Meaning Processor

Within the various contexts of literacy, the child needs to acquire knowledge in the domains of *semantics* and *word awareness* (Adams, 1990; van Kleeck, 1998). Semantics includes general vocabulary development as well as specific vocabulary about reading and books (e.g., *page, story, words, read,* and so forth). Word awareness includes the ability to break sentences into words, and to understand *word boundaries*; that is, words imply, but are separate from, their referents (e.g., the word *cat* refers to the real animal "cat"). Wishon, Crabtree, and Jones (1998) noted that understanding the concept of *wordness* (one spoken word to each written word) is a key component of learning to read.

The foundation for understanding the meaning of words (i.e., semantic understanding) begins in the first months of life during interactions between caregivers and infants. The child's vocabulary gradually grows from birth to 18 months, then it dramatically speeds up beginning around 19 months of age (Wetherby, 2002). As children continue to experience growth in their use and understanding of words, the stage is set for the emergence of phonological sensitivity, especially in their ability to make comparisons between similar-sounding words (Goswami, 2002). Whitehurst and Lonigan (2002) have found that shared reading and print exposure foster vocabulary development in preschool children. In older readers (e.g., fourth and fifth graders) the relationship between reading and language comprehension is direct and bidirectional (Whitehurst & Lonigan, 2002). In other words, children with more semantic knowledge are better able to comprehend what they are reading; they enjoy and engage in reading more which, in turn, supports even greater vocabulary growth. In summary, the meaning processor consists of the child's vocabulary and his or her understanding of individual words.

Context Processor

All of the elements of the *context processor* in van Kleeck's model contribute to the child's ability to understand written language. These elements include world knowledge (general knowledge about the child's world), syntax (grammatical structures), narrative skills (connecting and understanding text; e.g., story grammar), book conventions (how books are created and used), functions of print (understanding the uses of print, such as making a grocery list, sending a greeting card, writing a note, highway signs), and abstract language (decontextualized language that is removed from the here and now). This processor goes beyond understanding at just the word level to text-level comprehension. Both the meaning and the context processors function together to help the child attach meaning to written language at the word, sentence, and text levels.

> *Fifteen-month-old Maya pulled her favorite book,* ¿Dónde Está el Ombliguito? (Where Is Baby's Belly Button?) *(Katz, 2004), from the shelf containing her books. She took it to her grandmother, and as her grandmother opened the book to begin reading, Maya lifted her shirt, pointed to her stomach, and then looked expectantly at her grandmother who responded enthusiastically, "¡Si, mi amor, es tu ombliguito!" The storybook,* ¿Dónde Está el Ombliguito? *is a flap book about body parts (e.g., eyes, mouth, feet, hands, and, of course, bellybuttons). As Maya's grandmother read each page and lifted the flap to reveal the corresponding hidden body part, Maya pointed to that part on her own body. The last page of the book reads, "¿Dónde está mi bebé?" and is accompanied by a routine in which grandmother and Maya share a hug (abrazo). When her grandmother opens that page of the book, Maya shows her anticipation of the hug routine by holding her arms wide open to her grandmother.*

What do Maya's behaviors tell us about her emerging literacy skills? She knows that books are for reading, they can be shared, and it is fun to share them. She has recall of the topics in the story and of the routines that have been established for reading this particular book, as demonstrated by her anticipation of and participation in the routines. Maya not only can listen to the story, but also she can demonstrate understanding of the vocabulary related to body parts, as demonstrated by her ability to point to each body part that is named. She has associated the lifting of the flap in the book to reveal the body part named on that page with doing the same on her own body (e.g., lifting her shirt to point to her bellybutton), which also demonstrates her comprehension of the text.

▪▪▪▪▪ **VII. E. What emerging literacy skills are evident in the child's attempts to read?**

The importance of oral language skills, vocabulary, word meaning, and context in the development of literacy skills has been discussed. In this section, the focus will be on the following components of early literacy development: metalinguistic awareness, phonological awareness, phonemic awareness, and orthographic awareness, which includes alphabetic and print knowledge. The child's cognitive journey in learning to read is influenced and supported by skills in each of these critical areas of development.

Metalinguistic Awareness

When children are able to think about and use language to reflect on language, they are exhibiting *metalinguistic awareness* (Miller, 1990; Wallach & Miller, 1988). It is an awareness "that language can be manipulated, broken down, reassembled, and re-sequenced" (Miller, 1990, p. 15). This ability appears to be a universal phenomenon based on research conducted in several different languages (e.g., English, French, Spanish, Dutch, Finnish, Russian, Swedish) (Downing, 1986). Research with children who have visual impairments (Tompkins & McGee, 1986) and auditory impairments (Andrews & Mason, 1986) indicate that they too develop metalinguistic awareness skills, but at a slower rate than for children who have adequate vision and hearing.

Metalinguistic awareness begins to develop when the child interacts appropriately with books, distinguishes print from nonprint, and recognizes some printed symbols (e.g., brand names, signs, logos) (Miller, 1986, as cited in Wallach & Miller, 1988). It can be observed as children talk about language and in their understanding and use of language such as verbal humor (e.g., puns, "knock, knock" jokes, riddles), idioms (e.g., "cute as a bug's ear," "put on your thinking cap"), and figurative language such as similes (e.g., "he eats like a pig," "easy as pie") (Miller, 1990). Research studies have indicated a significant relationship between metalinguistic awareness and later progress and success in learning to read (Downing, 1986).

Metalinguistic ability is necessary for the development of phonological awareness as children begin to think about and understand components of language such as syllables, words, and speech sounds.

Phonological Awareness

When children have attained metalinguistic awareness, they can think about the structure of oral language separate from its meaning. When this happens they are equipped to hear, perceive, and manipulate the sounds of the words that make up their spoken language. This ability, called *phonological awareness,* is solely an oral-aural skill that includes 1) recognizing and producing rhymes and alliteration; 2) segmenting sentences into words; 3) orally segmenting and blending the sounds of words by syllables and by phonemes; and 4) identifying and manipulating the beginning, middle, and end sounds in words.

Experiences with listening to rhymes (e.g., nursery rhymes, stories with rhymes embedded in them, word play with rhyming words) as they are rhythmically read aloud or verbalized can support a child's awareness and enjoyment of words that rhyme and the sounds of language. Early exposure to rhymes will help the child to be able to generate rhyming words on his or her own later.

Onset-rime is a specific skill in the area of phonological awareness. *Onset* refers to the initial sound in a word, and *rime* refers to the last syllable in a word. In the word "book," for example, /b/ is the onset and "-ook" would be considered the rime; if the onset is changed to /l/ we would have the different (and rhyming) word "look."

The repeated use of a single initial consonant or vowel sound in successive words is called *alliteration*. An example of alliteration is "The big brown bear broke a branch when he bumped into the blackberry bush."

Learning how to separate words into syllables is another skill that develops from experiences with others who demonstrate or explicitly teach how words can be "pulled apart" into their spoken parts. Through these experiences, the child will gradually achieve independence in demonstrating syllabication. For example, phonological awareness of syllables is evident when a child can demonstrate or identify the syllables in her own name. When Shanikuwa was able to independently pair a hand clap with each spoken syllable of her name, her teacher knew that she had an understanding of syllabication.

Children's ability to recognize and manipulate the units of language progresses from large units (e.g., words, syllables) to small units (e.g., rhymes, onset-rimes, alliteration, phonemes) (Kaderavek & Justice, 2004). When a child can recognize that words begin with, contain, or end with the same sound and identify that specific sound, they have attained another skill in the area of phonological awareness that is called *phonemic awareness.*

Phonemic Awareness

In order to be able to decode written language, children must have attained *phonemic awareness,* which is the ability to recognize that language is composed of small speech sounds or phonemes that can be identified and manipulated. In English there are 26 letters of the alphabet and approximately 40 speech sounds that are represented in about 250 different spellings (Institute for the Development of Educational Achievement, 2002–2004).

The development of phonemic awareness has been a rich area of research investigation. Richgels's research on the development of phonemic ability led him to conclude that humans are born with the natural ability to perceive phonemes, and he reported that another research study revealed that infants as young as 4 weeks old can distinguish between phonemes (e.g., /g/ versus /k/) (Richgels, 2002, p. 143). During their first year, infants begin to practice producing the phonemes of their language and then distinguishing them in continuous speech of others (Adams, 1990). However, this is not truly "phonemic awareness" according to Richgels, because it is an *unconscious* perception of phonemes.

Typically, we do not consciously attend to the individual phonemes in spoken language; instead, we process them as part of the whole utterance and attend to their illocutionary force or meaning as described by Austin (1962). Richgels stated that this ability to process phonemes is "knowing-without-knowing-that-you-know" (p. 144); however, phonemic awareness is *conscious* attention to phonemes. It is the ability to think about and manipulate phonemes (not just distinguish them one from another in order to understand spoken language). For example, if a child responds correctly when an adult says, "What would happen if we changed the /f/ sound in 'fat' to the /h/ sound? What word would we have then?" the child would be indicating his or her phonemic awareness ability.

A child who has phonemic awareness understands that words are made up of sounds, and this child is able to manipulate the individual sounds in a word in order to separate and blend them. For example, the child would understand that the word "dog" has three sounds—/d/, /o/, and /g/—which can be pulled apart auditorally and blended to make the word that is typically heard when talking about this four-legged animal. Furthermore, a child who has achieved phonemic awareness is able to substitute the initial, medial, or final sounds in words to create "new" or different words. For example, the initial sound in "dog" can be substituted with /l/, which will make the word "log"; the medial sound in dog can be changed to /i/, which makes the word "dig"; and the final sound can be changed to /t/, making the word become "dot."

Phonemic awareness is a necessary and significant skill for early reading development and ongoing achievement during the elementary years. "Children who are not aware of phonemes are at serious risk of failing to learn to read" (Adams, Foorman, Lundberg, & Beeler, 1998, p. 2). Lyon (1995) stated that the best predictor of reading difficulty in kindergarten or first grade is the inability to segment words and syllables into their phonemic units. Internationally, among countries with alphabetic languages, measures of phonemic awareness of preschool-age children have been found to strongly predict their future success in learning to read (Adams, 1990; Adams et al., 1998).

Acquisition of phonemic awareness is the foundation for learning the alphabetic principle when the child applies his or her knowledge of the speech sounds to letters or groups of letters of the alphabet. Adams and colleagues (1998, p. 1) stated that "before children can make sense of the alphabetic principle, they must understand that those sounds that are paired with the letters are one and the same as the sounds of speech." The alphabetic principle is a construct in the area of orthographic understanding, which is discussed next.

Orthographic Understanding

Ability to understand, interpret, and generate language in a written form is based on *orthographic understanding*, which includes letter or alphabet knowledge and print knowledge.

Alphabetic Principle

Learning the names, sounds, and shapes of the letters of the alphabet is a critical skill for developing literacy. This skill supports the *alphabetic principle,* which is " . . . awareness that written words are composed of letters that are intentionally and conventionally related to phonemic segments of the words of oral language" (Burns et al., 1999, p. 147). Understanding of the alphabetic principal is one of the most important predictors of success in learning how to read and spell (Goswami, 2002; Shaywitz, 2003).

Most of the research in this area of literacy has focused on the use of the alphabetic system by English-speaking children (Whitehurst & Lonigan, 2002). Baker, Fernandez-Fein, Scher, and Williams (1998) (as cited in Whitehurst & Lonigan, 2002) found that letter knowledge in kindergarten was the second strongest predictor of word attack and word recognition skills in second graders. Interestingly, the strongest predictor was knowledge of nursery rhymes in kindergarten. Although the correlations between letter knowledge and later reading ability are strong, simply knowing the letters of the alphabet is not sufficient for learning to read. The child must also be able to associate phonemes with the letters. Furthermore, understanding and skills in all the components (or processors) of emerging literacy are needed in order to be a competent reader (van Kleeck, 2003).

Print Knowledge

As children gradually become aware of print in their environment, they gain understanding that print is worthy of interest; it carries meaning; it is organized in specific ways according to function; and the units of print can be differentiated, named, and combined to make other units (Justice & Ezell, 2004). As children acquire print knowledge and learn the functions and forms of writing, they also begin to talk about written language, which reveals the development of metalinguistic and metacognitive awareness of written language (Goodman, 1986). In other words, they learn how to think about communicating through writing.

Through their observations, interactions with others, and active involvement in producing written products, children learn about and experiment using writing as a vehicle for expressing themselves and conveying messages to others. For example, young children in a literate society learn the differences between the forms and functions of grocery lists, notes, letters, greeting cards such as birthday cards, and e-mail. These forms and their related functions are often recognizable as young children engage in writing during play.

Preschoolers from "high print" homes where there is an abundance of print such as newspapers, magazines, books, computers, writing paper and utensils, and so forth, are immersed in the presence, use, and value of print. These children naturally develop metalinguistic awareness and print awareness from the social and cultural experiences of sharing, talking about, and using print in their daily lives. Although research has not yet established the strength of the relationship between print awareness and later reading ability, it is generally accepted that print awareness is a necessary prerequisite for competence in reading (Justice, Skibbe, Canning, & Lankford, 2005).

Often the first words that children read are those that are meaningful in their everyday experiences such as their own names and environmental print or signs (e.g., food labels, restaurant logos, traffic signs). They recognize these words holistically and not by the individual alphabetical letters of the words (Moustafa, 2000). However, the recognition that such things can be read supports the development of *print knowledge*, which in turn supports the child in learning print conventions such as knowing the difference between pictures and printed words, punctuation, and directionality (Adams, 1990; van Kleeck, 1998, 2003). *Directionality* refers to the direction one should read (or write) print on a page and in a book; for example, in most western societies we read words from left to right, pages from top to bottom, and books from front to back.

Results of five research studies reported by Goodman (1986) indicated that at least 60% of the 3-year-old children in the studies were able to read environmental print when it was embedded in context, and an average of 80% of the 4- to 5-year-old children read environmental print in context. Interestingly, these children did not consider themselves as having the ability to "read." This informs educators and caregivers of the importance of acknowledging and supporting children as they interpret the print they encounter each day during naturally occurring activities.

It has already been noted that when preschool children and their parents engage in shared storybook reading, they typically focus on content rather than on print (van Kleeck, 1998; Justice et al., 2002). When parents read alphabet books, however, they often focus on the print (van Kleeck, 1998). In a study using eye-movement analysis to compare preschoolers' visual attention with print-salient versus picture-salient books, Justice et al. (2005) found that young children attended more to print in the print-salient book; however, their attention was very low and they preferred to look at illustrations even if they had well-developed early literacy skills. The authors suggested that perhaps it is the parents' perception of their role and their scaffolding ability that encouraged the child to attend to print, rather than the type of book being read.

Writing

▨▨▨▨ VII. F. What does the child understand about writing?

Authorities in the field of literacy consider reading and writing skills as interdependent and virtually one process. However, in this section we will tease the two apart and focus on the development of writing. This area of literacy is referred to as the "orthographic processor" in van Kleeck's model (1998, 2003) and was discussed in the previous section. Children demonstrate their understanding about writing as they observe, produce, manipulate, and talk about the marks, forms, or symbols they encounter in their daily lives.

Although research on the development of writing does not have as much depth as that of reading, its history is just as long. Early in the 20th century, Gesell and Ilg (1943) documented the development of children's writing behaviors, but not until much later—during the 1970s—did researchers begin to explore more deeply the forms and functions of the early writing of young children. Even though for some time during the 20th century there had been an interest in children's artwork, investigators initially failed to connect the significance of the writing embedded in children's drawings to the development of writing. They did not realize that children were actually inventing ways to write as they produced artwork (Goodman, 1990). Researchers studying children's artwork, scribbles, and written messages using alphabet letters have contributed to our understanding of the development of children's writing (e.g., Bissex, 1980; Clay, 1975; Schickedanz, 1990). We have learned, through documented observations and research studies, that during the process of inventing and reinventing different forms of writing, children appear to develop and refine their ability to write (Dyson, 1989; Graves, 1994; Miller, 2000).

Understanding the Forms and Functions of Writing

As they observe others in their environment using writing as a tool for communication, young children begin to imitate and experiment using writing behaviors by scribbling, drawing, making letter-like forms and then random letters, and subsequently using invented spelling (Morrow, 1989). Morrow (1997) called these early attempts at writing "proto-writing"; however, others (e.g., Koppenhaver & Erickson, 2000; Miller, 2000) believe that early writing should be referred to as authentic, valid ways to write instead of proto-writing or "pre-writing." Early writing leads to formal writing as children actively explore their literate environment (Goodman, 1986; Teale & Yokota, 2000) and desire to communicate information that is relevant to their lives (Vygotsky, 1978).

▬▬▬ VII. G. What characterizes the child's writing?

Scribbling

Children as young as 3 years of age can distinguish their drawing from their writing (Treiman & Bourassa, 2000), even though their writing may resemble scribbling. Goodman (1986) noted that children consider their scribbles or letter-strings meaningful written expressions and that "they are creating writing" (p. 7) when they engage in what some may consider meaningless scribbles. Clay (1975) reported that her research indicated that children's early writing attempts (i.e., scribbles) reflect the written language in their environment, and that scribbling differs among different cultures. This finding was supported by the investigations of Harste, Woodward, and Burke (1984; as reported in McLane & MacNamee, 1991, p. 5), who found that the "scribbling by children who speak Arabic or Hebrew looks quite different from the scribbling by English-speaking children." Just as infants' vocalizations gradually approximate the phonemes of their native language, so too with development their written marks or scribbles begin to approximate the letters or symbols of their native language. With increased exposure and experiences involving the forms of print, the features of conventional writing begin to appear, such as orientation, spacing, directionality (i.e., left to right, top to bottom), letter-like forms, letter-strings, and finally words.

Use of Written Symbols to Represent Objects and Events

Often, the first words that children are interested in writing are words that are familiar to them—for example, their own names or the names of significant people in their lives (Schickedanz, 1990; Schickedanz & Casbergue, 2004). When they begin to learn to write people's names, children seem to memorize "stable strings" of letters and often fail to recognize the similarities between names or that they may be making the same letters in different people's names. In other words, they see each person's name as a unique design or as a "sight word" (Ferriero & Teberosky, 1982, as cited in Schickedanz, 1990). Schickedanz called this the *visual design stage*. For example, at age 3 years 7 months, Adam (Schickedanz's son) was able to write *MAMA* and *ADAM,* which contain similar letters, but he treated each word as unique and not related to the other.

Treiman and Bourassa (2000) reported that young children frequently will produce words that represent nouns before words for verbs, and often a child's writing of nouns will contain features of those nouns. For example, a child may think that the word for daddy should be bigger than the word for baby because a daddy is bigger than a baby.

Ferreiro and Teberosky (1982) believe that developmentally children begin by graphically representing speech at the syllable level, and later they learn to attend to and represent the individual phonemes as they write words. According to Schickedanz (1990), several researchers including herself (e.g., Ferreiro & Teberosky, 1982; Harste, Burke, & Woodward, 1981, as cited in Schickedanz, 1990; Sulzby & Teale, 1985, as cited in Schickedanz, 1990) have observed that when children are experimenting with writing words they often make a mark or a letter for each syllable of the word. This is referred to as the *syllabic hypothesis*. For example, Schickedanz (1990, p. 96) reported that Harste, Burke, and Woodward (1981) observed a little girl named Lisa who had written a series of five numeral ones (i.e., 11111) and read it as "My name is Lisa." They surmised that each numeral stood for a syllable of the sentence she read.

Later, children begin to combine syllabic coding with the use of the first letters or sounds of the words as they write. For example, Harste, Burke and Woodward (1981, as reported by Schickedanz, 1990) noted the following example.

> A child wrote the letters *I L T P U MY TO* and read it as "I like to play with my toys." He then commented that it didn't look long enough, so he added an *A* and a *Q* to *TO*, making the word *TOAQ* (for the word *toys*).

A *visual-rule strategy* (Schickedanz, 1990) is another way children have been observed to write words and messages. Children who use this strategy seem to be aware of how words should look, and they use a variety of similar letters in different orders to make words. For example, a child may write *MOMA, OMMA,* and *AMOM* to represent the names of three different people. At times the child may write a string of letters and ask an adult what it says, becoming frustrated when the reader cannot comply.

As children gradually learn the alphabetic principle, they move from representing the syllables of words to pairing the sounds of the words they write with the alphabetic letters. This marks a major developmental step in the child's writing ability. At first, the most salient sounds of written words are more likely to be represented with an alphabetic letter. For example, when writing the word "her," a child at this level may write *HR*. Consonant clusters are frequently misspelled because the child represents only one speech sound instead of the two or three that make the cluster (e.g., writing *jee* for "tree"). In writing final consonant clusters, children often omit the first consonant of the cluster (Treiman & Bourassa, 2000). For example, a child may write *HEP* for "help." Interestingly, when young children write words with initial consonant clusters, they typically write the initial consonant and omit the following one(s) (e.g., a child may write *SUL* for the word *school*). Also, during the early stage of alphabetic awareness, children "begin to create very primitive phonemic spellings on their own" (Schickedanz & Casbergue, 2004, p. 37), and they may use single letters to represent words, such as *C* for *see, R* for *are,* and *U* for *you* (Schickedanz & Casbergue, 2004, p. 39). This will be discussed further in the section on spelling.

The Developmental Sequence of Writing

Based on her own research in addition to that of others (i.e., Gibson, 1975; McLane & McNamee, 1991; Morrow, 1989), Schickedanz (1999) developed the following six stages for the progression of writing for young children.

Stage 1: *Making marks* occurs around 18–24 months as the child explores with a pencil or crayon. This stage provides opportunities for learning the relationships between finger and hand movements that guide the writing tool and the resulting visual feedback.

Stage 2: *Early scribble writing* occurs between 18 months and 3 years as the child makes organized marks that look like pictures and/or writing; the child can usually indicate which is the picture and which is the writing. During this stage, the child is experimenting with organizational characteristics to create his or her own writing and is gaining increased mastery in the use of tools for drawing and writing. For example, by the end of 18 months scribbles begin to be produced in vertical or horizontal lines. This usually is followed by scribble spirals, loops, and rough circles. At age 3, the child typically still draws in scribbles, but the scribbles are made predominantly in one direction and less repetitively. By the age of 4 years, most children are able to make representative drawings.

Stage 3: *A few letters appear* in children's writing at about age 4 with continued development through age 5. The child begins to write alphabet letters or close approximations in combination with scribble. Often, the first letter of the child's name is the first letter (grapheme) he or she is able to make. During this stage the child is experimenting with writing, and recognition of letters increases.

Stage 4: *Mock letters* are made by children between the ages of 4 and 4½ years old when their writing contains fewer scribbles than in the previous stage and more letter-like forms blended with a few actual letters. During this stage, children's writing shows increases in letter approximations as they begin to show more characteristics of alphabet letters.

Stage 5: *Writing with and practicing letters* typically occurs when children are 4–5 years old. During this stage children write actual letter forms, although some may not be produced or oriented "correctly." Children seem to be practicing forming the letters to approximate the standard.

Stage 6: *Choosing from a writing repertoire* is a skill that appears when children are approximately 4½–5 years old. Even after a child produces letters correctly, he or she may revert to scribble or mock writing (e.g., creating a shopping list, letter, or note). In other words, children do not readily discard earlier forms when mature forms have developed and their repertoire has expanded. During this stage children may invent the spellings of words, copy letters or numbers from the environment, and begin to use punctuation in their writing.

Organizing Writing

Another area of writing development is that of organizing writing and incorporating space between words and sentences. Children learn early about the forms of different functions of writing, such as lists, greeting cards, and stories. This knowledge is often demonstrated in the dramatic play of 3- to 5-year-old children such as when they engage in role playing being a server and writing a list of food that is "ordered," being the daddy and taking a phone message, or making a card to send to a classmate who is ill.

Young children may exhibit difficulties writing the letters of the alphabet, particularly the letter *S* and letters with diagonal lines (e.g., *R* or *K*). According to Schickedanz and Casbergue (2004), the drawing of diagonal lines is a cognitive skill involving directionality and space, whereas other difficulties in producing letters may result from immature fine motor skills. Often, young children write uppercase letters before they write lowercase because uppercase letters require less fine motor dexterity (Schickedanz & Casbergue, 2004).

Directionality refers to the knowledge of the placement and order in which words should be read and written. For example, in our culture we write from left to right and top to bottom on a page. Children's early writing often indicates lack of understanding of the principle of directionality because it is not organized on the page in a fixed manner; that is, horizontal orientation is often mixed with vertical, and the direction of the print may be top to bottom, bottom to top, left to right, right to left, or scattered over the page in an unorganized fashion. Up to the age of 6 years, children frequently may reverse letters or whole words (Schickedanz, 1999; Schickedanz & Casbergue, 2004). Each letter may be reversed and the word written right to left so when held up to a mirror it appears to be a recognizable, standard form. This is called *mirror writing.* When children write in a line and run out of space on a page, they often solve this dilemma with creative strategies such as placing the remaining letters in reverse order under the first line of print or perhaps randomly on the paper. They may rotate the paper 180 degrees and continue writing the second line left to right, or they may turn the paper over and continue on the back of the page.

As children develop awareness that words are separate entities, they begin to experiment with strategies for separating them in their written messages. One way that children may do this is by using dots between words and syllables (e.g., *THIS.IS. MY.HOUS.* and *TAL.A.FON*). These two examples were produced by Bissex's son, Paul, when he was 5½ years old (Bissex, 1980, pp. 23 and 45). Other examples of ways that children separate words or syllables are by circling them, putting them in vertical arrangements, putting them in square boxes, and drawing lines or dashes between them (McGee & Richgels, 2004).

Schickedanz (1990, p. 115) stated that, "Children's errors often show us what they know about the conventions of writing, as well as what they have not yet learned." Observation of children's writing efforts offers clues to guide interpretations of their ability levels and can provide insights into ways to effectively support their learning.

Spelling

The Development of Spelling

After years of being the "stepchild" of literacy, spelling now is gaining serious attention and respect from researchers and authorities in the field. Spelling is no longer considered a visual-motor or visual-memory process (Kamhi & Hinton, 2000), nor is it considered a low-level literacy skill nor merely a school subject as it once was (Scott & Brown, 2001). This area of literacy is now regarded as a language-based skill supported by the same phonological and cognitive processes as reading (Kamhi & Hinton, 2000; Scott & Brown, 2001). In fact, reading ability is the best predictor of spelling ability (Kamhi & Hinton, 2000).

Two views about the relationship between reading and spelling have been proposed. One view is that they are two separate, disassociated processes; the other view is that spelling subsumes reading. Recent research findings have shown correlations between measures of reading and spelling, which would support the second view that spelling encompasses reading (Ehri, 2000; Kamhi & Hinton, 2000). Furthermore, researchers have found strong correlations between spelling ability and the child's phonologic, morphemic, phonemic (Kamhi & Hinton, 2000; Masterson & Apel, 2000), orthographic, semantic, syntactic (Kamhi & Hinton, 2000), and alphabetic knowledge (Cassar & Treiman, 2004).

The development of spelling ability corresponds with and is supported by the child's acquisition of both reading and writing skills. During reading and writing, the child repeatedly uses grapheme–phoneme relationships that help him or her learn to recognize and generate the spellings of words. Spelling ability involves not only the spelling of words but also recognizing when words are spelled correctly (Ehri, 2000; Kamhi & Hinton, 2000; Masterson & Apel, 2000). The spellings that are most easily generated and recognized are those that conform to the speller's prior knowledge of grapheme–phoneme relationships or the ones that follow spelling patterns of his or her language (Ehri, 2000).

Spelling is a "meta-phonological" task (Butler, 2000) in that the child must think about the sequence of sounds in a word in order to spell the word. It is also a "meta-orthographic" skill because the child must think about which letters and letter sequences are needed in order to symbolically represent the word with letters of the alphabet. Learning to spell evolves as the child learns the letters of the alphabet; acquires knowledge of grapheme–phoneme correspondences; understands the concept of "wordness"; differentiates beginning, medial, and ending sounds in words; and understands and applies the rules for spelling. Recent studies in this area of literacy have focused on using a constructivist model for spelling instruction in which the child is supported by adults or more competent peers in constructing and refining his or her understanding and knowledge about how to use the grapheme–phoneme relationships to spell (Butler, 2000; Cassar & Treiman, 2004; Ehri, 2000; Treiman & Bourassa, 2000).

Several different theories of the stages of spelling development have been suggested by authorities in the field (e.g., Bear, Invernizzi, Templeton, & Johnston, 2000; Ehri, 2000; Jones & Crabtree, 1999; McGee & Richgels, 2004). Although the terminology differs, the underlying tenets are similar. Stage theorists believe that initially children begin to learn about spelling as they apply their knowledge of letter names and the corresponding sounds to the spelling of words, and gradually they are able to use additional sources of information as they become cognitively available (Treiman & Bourassa, 2000). For example, a young child may spell the word *maybe* as *MA B* and later may spell the word as *mayB* before being able to spell it conventionally.

In her stage theory, Ehri (2000) called the earliest stage the "pre-alphabetic level," which is characterized by scribbling that may resemble cursive writing but with no apparent letter-like forms. Children in this stage do not yet understand the letter–sound correspondences, and any use of letters in their writing is purely coincidental and random. The next two stages (i.e., "partial-alphabetic" and "alphabetic") are typically evident in the spelling attempts of 5- to 7-year-old children. During the partial-alphabetic stage, children produce letter-name spellings using single letters to spell words (e.g., the letter *U* for the word *you*). When children are able to make connections between alphabet letters and the letter names and use this knowledge in spelling, they are demonstrating evidence of their developing understanding of grapheme–phoneme correspondences and their growing awareness that writing is connected to speech (Cassar & Treiman, 2004).

At the partial-alphabetic stage, children have not yet developed full understanding of the grapho-phonemic system. This is evident in the absence of vowels in their spellings and their difficulty in representing initial and final consonant clusters (Cassar & Treiman, 2004). For example, a child at this stage may write *TUK* for the word *truck* and *HEP* for *help*. The spelling of words at this stage suggests that the child understands that the alphabetic letters in written words correspond with the sounds in words but his attempts are often inaccurate because of limited phonological and alphabetic knowledge. However, at the next stage (i.e., full-alphabetic stage), the child's maturing knowledge and use of grapheme–phoneme correspondences becomes evident in his spelling ability. For example, by second grade, most children include vowels in their spellings of words (Treiman & Bourassa, 2000). Also, during this stage, morphological knowledge grows and supports spelling. For example, the child who initially spelled *kissed* as *KIST* will begin to use the morpheme *-ed* and then may go on to overgeneralize the used of *-ed* to such words as *slept* by spelling it as *SLEPED* (Cassar & Treiman, 2004, p. 629).

After children have become aware of the alphabetic principle, they frequently begin to ask others how to spell words (Bissex, 1980; Genishi & Dyson, 1984; Schickedanz, 1990). For example, when Schickedanz compared observations of her son, Adam, to those of Bissex (who observed her son, Paul) during this stage, she found similarities. Both boys requested spellings of words and speech sounds during the time they began to use phonemic spellings. A second episode of the children requesting spellings occurred after they had been using invented spelling for a period of time and began to realize that they needed help or verification for spelling parts of words or whole words. Both Bissex and Schickedanz reported that their sons became reluctant to spell after they began to read conventionally, and Schickedanz (1990) noted the same phenomenon with children she observed over a 5-year period in a nursery school at Boston University.

Invented Spelling

Ehri (2000) has proposed the following three processes for learning to spell words: 1) memory (recalling the spelling), 2) analogy (associating the spelling of words with already known words), and 3) invention (using phonemic skills and alphabetic knowledge to select phoneme–grapheme correspondences and create spellings). Because children who are beginning to learn to spell cannot yet use memory or analogy, they must rely on invention (Cassar & Treiman, 2004).

Invented spelling (also called "sound spelling") is seen throughout the process of learning to spell and is especially apparent in the spelling of 4–5-year-olds when they make hypotheses about how words are spelled (Ehri, 2000). Invented spellings provide us with a window into the child's understanding of the alphabetic principle and skill in pairing graphemes to phonemes. Young children often focus on the use of consonants in their invented spellings (e.g., *PHShAn* for *punishing*; *Vknl* for *volcano*) (McGee & Richgels, 2004, p. 105). A child's spelling may be influenced by the way he or she articulates words (e.g., *PUPO* for *purple*). Also, when children are not developmentally ready to attend to all the phonemes in words, their invented spellings may omit consonant clusters and short vowels, especially the schwa or "lax" vowel sound in words such as *about* and *circus*. Therefore, their representations of such words may contain a phoneme that is similar in articulation or phonemic characteristics to the one they are attempting to write, or the sound may not be represented in the word at all (e.g., *SRKS* for *circus*) (Schickedanz, 1999).

Ehri (2000) stated that experiences in inventing the spelling of words help young children learn more about the alphabetic system than being taught the conventional spellings of words. When a child uses invented spelling, he goes through a process of analyzing the word's phonemes and then selecting which letter of the alphabet to use to represent the phonemes. Through this process the child is constructing his own understanding of spelling.

All of the components of emerging literacy come together and mutually support each other as the child develops competence in the components of writing and spelling.

Bilingualism and Literacy

In stark contrast to the growing numbers of bilingual children in schools in the United States, there is a paucity of research surrounding the language and literacy development of bilingual children from 2 to 8 years of age (Barrera & Bauer, 2003).

Tabors (1997) distinguishes between simultaneous bilingualism and successive bilingualism by defining *simultaneous bilingualism* as exposure to two languages from an early age and *successive bilingualism* as learning a second language after the first has been fully or partially established. The emergence of "biliteracy" is the "simultaneous acquisition of reading and writing skills in two languages" (Zecker, 2004, p. 248). The development in one language influences the development in the other language. Children who are simultaneously bilingual should not be perceived as having one dominant language and limited ability in the other language. These children construct "parallel stores of language-specific literacy knowledge" (Zecker, 2004, p. 261). Their early literacy skills in each language develop side by side so there is no need for them to relearn skills they have already acquired.

Conversely, children who are successively bilingual and limited in their English proficiency are at risk for difficulties in their development of emerging literacy knowledge and skills (Snow et al., 1998). Downing (1986) found that children who are taught in a second language learn the concept of phoneme more slowly than children who are taught in their first or primary language. If a child has begun to develop metalinguistic awareness in her dominant language and then is expected to perform in literacy activities using her second language, she may suffer cognitive confusion in not being able to rely on her existing emerging literacy skills.

Schickedanz and Casbergue (2004) reported that children who speak other languages may display a different progression in their development of literacy than children who are native English speakers. For example, the early phonemic spellings of young children who are Spanish speakers often include vowels, as opposed to the predominant use of consonants by children who are English speakers. They surmised that this is probably because the vowels in Spanish are consistently pronounced the same way in a majority of the words and there is only one vowel sound per vowel, whereas in English there are multiple sounds for each vowel (e.g., long vowels, short vowels, diphthongs, schwas, r-controlled vowels).

Investigations of the writing skills of bilingual children have revealed that children need common linguistic knowledge for literacy development (Zecker, 2004). For example, all children need to have metalinguistic awareness no matter what language they speak. Zecker reported that studies of the development of graphophonemic knowledge (i.e., knowing which symbol or alphabetic letter to write to represent a speech sound) for children learning to write alphabetic languages indicated that the phonemic structure of the child's best-known language influences the child's reading and spelling abilities in the less dominant language. She stated that the children in her study did not revert to less mature forms when writing in their less dominant language but were able to apply their growing literacy knowledge in both languages. For example, Zecker (2004) found that English-dominant children who had command of phoneme–grapheme correspondences in Spanish were able to write words in Spanish fairly accurately, even though they did not know the meaning of the words they wrote.

In their review of the international literature regarding storybook reading with children who are bilingual, Barrera and Bauer (2003) found that typically the children in the U.S. studies were Spanish-speakers in the process of learning a second language (i.e., "successively bilingual") and the people who were reading the storybooks (usually parents or caregivers) were learning storybook reading (and often English, as well) as a new practice. The researchers noted that code-switching (using both languages interchangeably) was a natural aspect of the storybook interactions of the bilingual participants.

From their review of the existing research, Barrera and Bauer (2003) concluded that there is a limited understanding of the elements of storybook reading between people who are bilingual because the interactions have been viewed through a "monolingual lens." They stated that researchers should not apply knowledge about the elements of monolingual storybook reading to bilingual language users, but instead they should broaden their investigations to include the cultural and linguistic aspects that influence bilingual speakers. The studies Barrera and Bauer reviewed showed that during storybook reading, children who are bilingual are aware of and utilize the language(s) and information of their reading partners, but not how they make use of their bilingualism during the interactions. A suggested future focus is the exploration of the skills bilingual speakers bring to the storybook reading activity (e.g., the child's perceptions of storybook reading, how a child responds when people from different language backgrounds read storybooks) (Barrera & Bauer, 2003). According to Barrera and Bauer (p. 266) researchers should use a sociocultural perspective that invites "cross-cultural exploration of relationships among storytelling, story reading, and literacy" because "storybook reading is a socially created interactive practice" (p. 255) that is not universal across cultures.

Because literacy is a socially defined construct that is linked to cultural identity (Ferdman, 1990), it is important that teachers reflect on their own cultural beliefs and values as they prepare to teach children from other cultures. Additionally, Ferdman stressed that bilingualism should be valued and not viewed as a deficit.

The National Association for the Education of Young Children (NAEYC) recently developed a position statement titled, *"Screening and Assessment of Young English-Language Learners"* (NAEYC, 2005). The following are the recommended standards as stated in the position paper:

1. Screening and assessment should be implemented for appropriate purposes using linguistically and culturally appropriate instruments and strategies.

2. Culturally and linguistically appropriate assessments and translations should be used and reviewed by native speakers who are knowledgeable in the areas of assessment and translation that takes into account a child's language history, proficiency, dominance, and preference.

3. The primary purpose of assessment is to help programs support the child's learning and development. Assessments should:

   • Include systematic observations

   • Use multiple methods and measures

   • Be ongoing, repeated over time

   • Be age-appropriate

   • Involve two or more people

4. Use of standardized formal assessments is appropriate for program evaluation and accountability, and for identifying disabilities. However, those developing and conducting these assessments should be aware of cautions and concerns associated with using standardized assessments with young English-language learners.

5. Those conducting assessments should have cultural and linguistic competence; be bilingual and bicultural; and have knowledge of the child being assessed, language acquisition, second-language acquisition, assessment in general, and assessment of young English-language learners in particular.

6. The family should play a critical role in the assessment process. They are able to offer information and insight regarding the assessment of their child. Professionals conducting the assessment should seek information from the child's family regarding selecting, conducting, and interpreting assessments. Assessment personnel should refrain from asking family members to conduct the assessment, interpret during formal assessments, or draw assessment conclusions. Professionals should inform and update the family regarding the child's assessment results in a way that is meaningful to them.

7. Needs in the field:

- An expanded knowledge base about second-language learners
- More and better assessments
- Increase the number of bilingual and bicultural early childhood professionals
- Ongoing opportunites for professional development and support in assessment of young English-language learners

The processes and strategies used in TPBA can fulfill the first six of these NAEYC recommended standards.

▦▦▦ USING THE OBSERVATION GUIDELINES TO ASSESS LITERACY

TPBA provides a natural arena for observing the child's emerging literacy skills. During book sharing, art activities, in dramatic play, and other play interactions, the child's literacy skills are evident. The play facilitator needs to be aware of what props, materials, and environmental print can be used in play and be creative in eliciting the child's knowledge and skills pertaining to emerging literacy. Although many skills may be exhibited spontaneously, the facilitator needs to know how to extend actions, provide suggestions, or ask questions that will draw out the child's knowledge and skills—without making the play feel like a "test" (see Chapter 7).

During pretend play, children can assume different roles and activities of people who read and write. For example, during play a child might assume the role of teacher and engage in writing the names of children in the class on the chalkboard. During TPBA, the child can explore the use of a variety of writing implements and materials (e.g., paper, pencils, markers, crayons) and strategies (e.g., scribbling, drawing, writing). Literacy skills can also be observed in the child's responses to puzzles, directions for toys, environmental signs, and other symbolic and written materials in the play session. The TPBA2 Observation Guidelines and Age Table for emerging literacy are included with those on cognition in Chapter 7 (see pp. 378 and 391).

▦▦▦ VII. A. What listening skills does the child demonstrate?

Listening skills are critical to developing both language and literacy proficiency. As in the communication domain, the team observes what the child attends to, how he reacts to environmental sounds, and if he orients to sounds and/or names them or their source (e.g., pointing up and/or saying "airplane" when hearing the sound of an airplane). How the child imitates environmental and speech sounds is also indicative of what the child hears and how he processes what he hears. The play facilitator should present a variety of opportunities and materials for the child to attend to and make sounds.

Because the ability to rhyme words is important for phonological development and offers insight into the child's beginning development of phonemic awareness, the team can note the child's response if someone recites a familiar nursery rhyme or song that has rhyming words in it. Another skill that is important for literacy development is familiarity with the letters of the alphabet. Team members can listen for examples of alphabet knowledge as appropriate. For example, they will note if the child joins in singing the ABC song when hearing it sung by another child, adult, or in a recording. Another example of listening for alphabet knowledge would occur if the child shows interest in, points to, joins in reading, or names alphabet letters in an alphabet picture book or while writing on artwork or in dramatic play. For example, when making a shopping list, the child may say, "Cup Cakes, C P KAK." This not only demonstrates alphabet knowledge, but also demonstrates the child's phonemic and phonological awareness. Another indicator of the child's alphabetic knowledge can be observed when he sees his name in print and recognizes one or more of the letters.

As Dylan and Daryl (both 3¹/₂ years old) enter their preschool center, they both head for the cubby that has Dylan's name on it. As they argue about whose cubby it is, their teacher, Mr. Adams, approaches. He asks each boy why he thinks it is his cubby. Dylan points to the name above the cubby and says, "That says 'Dylan.' Dylan is me." When Mr. Adams turns toward Daryl and raises his eyebrows and hands in a questioning gesture, Daryl points to the "D" on the name tag and says, "It's my cubby." Mr. Adams retrieves the name tags for both boys from their cubbies, and placing them side by side says, "Well, I'll be! They DO start with the same letter. Both of your names start with 'D' (as he points to the "D" on each). How can we find out which one says 'Daryl' and which says 'Dylan'?" The boys decide to ask the director of the preschool, because obviously Mr. Adams doesn't know!

▬▬▬ VII. B. How does the child use books?

A variety of different types and levels of books should be available for the child. If the TPBA is done in the child's home, the books and materials in the home can be used, but a variety of novel books and writing materials should also be taken to the home. This will enable the team to observe what the child does with familiar books and literacy materials and how he or she responds to new pictures, stories, and so forth. During the play session the team can note the child's level of interest in books, how the child handles books, his or her response to familiar or unfamiliar books being read, and how the child attempts to share pictures, stories, or print with the adults. For example, the play facilitator may give the child choices of books to share. Does the child choose a picture book, counting book, storybook, or a familiar book? If the book is handed to the child upside-down or backward, does the child know how to reorient the book? Does the child turn the pages of the book from front to back? Does the child want to explore the book, look at the pictures independently, or share it with an adult? Does the child initiate interactions with a book or must the adult introduce books and lead the book sharing?

▬▬▬ VII. C. What does the child comprehend when looking at or sharing a book?

Observation of the child's interactions with books will reveal much about the child's comprehension of representational material. The team can observe whether the child is only interested in the book as an object of exploration, whether he understands that pictures in a book represent real objects, or that print represents words. The child's book handling skills will also provide information about what the child understands about *how* books are used. When stories are read, can the child identify the characters or objects in the book, the emotions of the characters, or the action sequences? Can he or she predict what might happen in a story? Can he or she reason about what is happening and why? As the play facilitator, parent, or caregiver looks at books with the child, the team observes what information the child provides without prompting and what the child can figure out if his or her attention is brought to a specific aspect of the book. For example, the adult might point to the print and say, "I wonder what this says?"

▬▬▬ VII. D. What does the child recall of words,
    phrases, story lines, content from familiar stories?

What the child remembers about favorite books provides clues to the child's growing understanding of the meaning of symbolic representations. The parent facilitator can ask family members about what the child recalls about the pictures, words, or stories in favorite books. For example, the play facilitator might pick up one of the child's familiar books and say, "I wonder what this book is about?" The facilitator should attempt to encourage the child to tell as much of the story as possible with minimal adult support. When the child pauses or says, "I don't know," the facilitator might comment. "Look at what this boy is doing. It looks like he is in trouble. What do you think happens?" When reading a familiar book, the adult can leave out key words or phrases and see if the child can fill in the missing words. Art activities and dramatic play that follow the reading of a story can also provide an insight into the child's comprehension of the story setting, characters, actions, and plot. An invitation to draw pictures of the story or act out a part of the story may motivate the child to demonstrate his or her understanding of the content of the book. Discussion about the book can also demonstrate the child's comprehension of the material in the book in relation to his or her own life. For instance, while reading a book about an airplane, one child expounded on a recent flight to visit his grandmother in another state. He stopped and looked at each picture and related how it was the same or different on "his" plane.

VII. E. What emerging literacy skills are evident in the child's attempts to read?

Observation of children's interactions with books reveals what they understand about the process of reading. Even during the first year, babies will vocalize to pictures in books and may even label some pictures. As they begin to recognize that books are associated with talking, they may be observed performing "book babble" (jargon using the intonation patterns similar to those used during book reading). The team can ask family members about the child's recognition of environmental symbols and print and his or her verbal interactions with books. They can also observe how the child shares a book with another adult or child. Does the child talk about the pictures; tell the story with a reading intonation; recognize a few words; point to and try sound out words? The child's actions with both familiar and unfamiliar books should be observed, because what is observed with familiar books may reflect memory as well as learned abilities. Strategies used with unfamiliar books, however, are indicative of how the child applies learned skills to new material. For example, the child may have memorized a familiar book and look as if she is actually reading the story. When given a novel storybook, however, she may use the pictures to figure out what the book is about. Discussion with caregivers; observation whenever pictures, symbols, or print are evident; and careful questioning as the child interacts with literacy materials should provide a functional picture of the child's emerging literacy abilities.

VII. F. What does the child understand about writing?

Even if the child is not able to write due to physical or developmental limitations, much can be learned about what the child understands about the process of writing. Instructions that he or she gives to the adult about writing during dictation can reveal what the child knows about where to start writing, what direction to write, where to put spaces or punctuation, and so forth. For example, one child told the facilitator to write her food order on a pad of paper by saying, "Start up here and write 'hamburger.'" The facilitator complied and said, "Anything else?" The child said, "Yes. French fries." When the facilitator started to write the words next to 'hamburger,' the child said, "No. You have to write it here" (indicating beneath the other word). This denotation of a list indicated that the child understood the various forms and functions of print, even though she was not yet able to generate the writing herself.

VII. G. What characterizes the child's writing?

It is important for the facilitator to provide opportunities for the child to have a reason to *want* to write various forms of print (e.g., lists, cards, labels, signs, or stories), whether the child produces these forms herself or dictates the messages to someone else. Making signs for a dramatic play area (e.g., Doctor's Office), making lists of things that are needed (e.g., presents for a party), or writing a story to go with a picture are just a few examples of how literacy can be incorporated. Having literacy tools and props available to stimulate the child to want to use them is important. As the play facilitator follows the child's lead in activities involving emerging writing skills, the team will observe how the child holds, manipulates, and uses painting, drawing, or writing tools, and if he attempts to make marks, draw, scribble, make mock letters, write his own name, or uses other conventional writing skills. The child who has emerging writing skills is often highly motivated to demonstrate these skills. The facilitator should make sure that an opportunity to write at least a sentence or two is provided, so that how the child structures words, phrases, and sentences can be observed. This usually can be done along with a piece of artwork that the child can take home. For example, the facilitator said to one child, "I think your teacher would love to see this. Let's write what you did down here." Other key factors that may be observed if the child engages in drawing, painting, or writing include the social aspects of sharing the written product with another and the interface between the child's reading and writing skills.

The TPBA2 Observation Guidelines for conceptual development (literacy) assist the assessment team in watching for the critical skills children need in order to develop competence in this area.

Disabilities in Reading and Writing

Although many of the children seen in TPBA are too young to exhibit reading and writing "disabilities," early indications of potential learning problems may be seen in young children. The preliminary indications of dyslexia and dysgraphia, discussed below, may be observed in young children's emerging literacy skills.

Dyslexia is probably the most commonly recognized disability in the area of literacy and results in reading, writing, and/or spelling difficulties. Dyslexia, as defined by the National Institute of Child Health and Human Development (NICHD), is a neurologically based disability, characterized by difficulties with accurate and/or fluent word recognition and by poor spelling and decoding abilities that result from a deficit in the phonological component of language. According to the International Dyslexia Association (2000), some of the characteristics of young children who have dyslexia may include

- Talking later than most children

- Difficulty pronouncing words (e.g., "busgetti" for spaghetti, "mawn lower" for lawn mower)

- Slowness in acquiring new vocabulary words

- Inability to recall the right word when talking

- Difficulty with rhyming

- Trouble learning the alphabet, numbers, days of the week, colors, shapes, how to spell and write his or her own name

- Difficulty telling and/or retelling a story in the correct sequence

- Difficulty separating sounds in words and blending sounds to make words

Many of the above-listed characteristics relate directly to the critical skills that researchers have found necessary for the development of literacy (e.g., Adams, 1990; Goswami, 2002; Hart & Risley, 1999; Morrison & Morrow, 2002; Shaywitz, 2003; Shaywitz & Shaywitz, 2004; Wetherby et al., 2003). Snow et al. (1998) reported that the majority of children who are identified as learning disabled have difficulties in learning to read, and they have stressed the importance of adequate instruction to meet the needs of these children in order to support them in developing literacy skills.

Dysgraphia is a neurologically based writing disability in which a person finds it hard to form letters, write within a defined space, or communicate using written language (International Dyslexia Association, 2000; National Institute of Neurological Disorders and Stroke, 2003). This disability may range from problems with fine motor coordination to a dysfunction in mentally transforming phonemes, words, and/or thoughts to graphemes or written symbols. Writing requires a complex interaction of cognitive structures that regulate motor, linguistic, visual, proprioceptive-kinesthetic, spatial, and memory skills. The dysfunction may result in illegible handwriting, extremely slow production of written language, or very small images. Handwriting for individuals with dysgraphia is physically, cognitively, and emotionally taxing.

Evidence of this disorder typically emerges when children are first formally introduced to writing. Despite adequate intelligence, experiences, and learning opportunities, children with dysgraphia may demonstrate

- Avoidance of writing and drawing

- Inappropriately sized and spaced letters

- Letter reversals and rotations

- Illegible messages

- Wrong or misspelled words

- Emotional reactions to requests or suggestions for written products.

Although typically developing children demonstrate many of these characteristics at some point in their development, young children with dysgraphia may demonstrate most of them in addition to extreme negative emotional reactions when asked to write or draw. During TPBA, the team will observe for indications of emotional overtones related to producing written products. Depending on the observations of the team, intervention to support the development of writing skills may be recommended.

At this time, most national organizations and state educational agencies do not consider *difficulties with spelling* to be a result of a learning disability (Kamhi & Hinton, 2000). Apparently the current research view of spelling being a language-based skill that is linked to literacy development has not yet had an impact on state and federal regulatory agencies and national organizations. Because reading and spelling are manifestations of the same underlying knowledge sources, if a child has problems in reading he or she will experience problems in spelling (Ehri, 2000). In fact, researchers have suggested that deficits in phonological skills underlie difficulties in spelling (Cassar & Treiman, 2004).

Children with dyslexia make more spelling errors than average readers and exhibit weak phonological skills that are slow to develop (Cassar & Treiman, 2004). Because spelling requires the ability to segment spoken words into syllables and phonemes, it is logical that poor phonological skills would result in poor spelling ability. Cassar and Treiman noted that the spelling errors made by children with dyslexia have a phonological base and are similar to those of typically developing children at a younger age. This is encouraging information for those who develop intervention plans because the developmental course is predictable.

When children younger than 5 years of age exhibit any of the above-mentioned language and learning disorders, a diagnosis of learning disabilities is not typically made. If this diagnosis is made, however, it is done so very cautiously. In either case, it is important to document the observed behaviors and develop intervention plans that address these foundational literacy skills. Parents should be informed of the connection between delays or deficits in early literacy skills to later reading, writing, and learning problems, and development should be monitored over time to ensure that appropriate supports are provided.

Four-year-old Marissa was referred for assessment by her Head Start teacher and her parents because they were concerned about her motor and language development. TPBA took place in Marissa's Head Start classroom. During TPBA, Marissa picked up a book (Brown Bear, Brown Bear, What Do You See?) (Martin, 1992) and held it close to her face and upside-down. She turned the pages right to left until she had turned most, but not all, of the pages. Then she opened the book in the middle and said, "Bow beh, bow beh, uh-da-ya see?" She looked at the play facilitator beside her expectantly, and the adult said, "I see a red bird looking at me." The play facilitator continued, "Red bird, red bird, what do you . . . ?" When she paused, Marissa said, "see." The facilitator then said, "I see a yellow duck . . . " (pause), and Marissa said, "ook ah me."

Initially Marissa resisted all adult-initiated enticements to draw; however, when she observed a peer painting, Marissa also painted at an easel. She held the paint brush in her left hand with the brush held across her palm with her thumb pointing toward the paper (see Chapter 2), a grasp typical of a 1-year-old child. Her brush strokes were in a vertical, up-and-down motion in the center of the paper.

During their discussion after the play observation, the TPBA team noted that Marissa was interested in and recognized verbal patterns in familiar books. Although she manipulated a familiar book, she did not rotate the book so it would be right-side-up, a skill most 11-month-old children perform; however, she did turn the pages correctly (i.e., right to left). They also noted that Marissa was able to correctly recite a phrase from a storybook (a skill shown by most 24- to 30-month-olds), although the phrases did not match the pictures on the page to which she had opened the book, and her articulation was difficult to understand. She also was able to fill in the next phrases in a familiar story when the reader hesitated (a skill typically performed by 24-month-olds).

Neither the parents nor the Head Start teachers had observed Marissa engaging in making marks, scribbling, or drawing, so observing her attempts to paint was encouraging. The team noted that Marissa engaged in painting and stirring ("making soup") using vertical motions and an immature grasp typical of a 1-year-old. Also, Marissa used her left hand for painting and her right hand for stirring. Her mother commented that Marissa uses both hands at home, as well.

The team agreed that delays in cognitive, language, and sensorimotor skills have influenced Marissa's acquisition of emerging reading and writing skills. In terms of recommendations, Marissa appeared to be ready for exposure to more oral activities using rhyme, such as chants, songs, and finger plays, and books with rhymes, beat, alliteration, and predictable text using repeated lines. Her teachers and parents were encouraged to continue reading to Marissa, to use picture books to help her orient books, and to draw her into looking at and naming the pictures and actions in the books. Based on the team's overall observations, Marissa was also referred for further assessment by an eye care specialist and a teacher of the visually impaired (see Chapter 3).

Motorically, Marissa engaged in manipulation of dramatic play props but did not show use of a dominant hand, had a primitive grasp, and avoided exploring use of utensils for drawing and writing. The team recommended that Marissa was ready for increased opportunities for exploring and manipulating small objects and increased opportunities for drawing and painting. They believed that peers may be important models and motivators to encourage this type of exploration; however, if she does not show progress the team will recommend an occupational therapy evaluation.

CONCLUSION

Language, literacy, cognitive, and motor development are integrally related. This chapter explores the research on the numerous aspects of emerging literacy, including book skills, such as listening, using books, comprehending books and recalling content of stories. In addition, knowledge and skills that support emerging literacy are examined, including metalinguistic, phonological, and phonemic awareness. Orthographic under-standing, including alphabet knowledge and print knowledge, is included as related to learning to read and write. The research on the development of understanding and producing symbols to represent thoughts is also traced developmentally, along with the child's developing organizational thinking to support spelling ability. Literacy is a cul-turally influenced process, and because society is becoming increasingly diverse, with children speaking more than one language, the issue of bilingualism and emerging lit-eracy is also addressed in this chapter. The process for assessing emerging literacy skills within TPBA is described, with an example of how listening, understanding, reading, and writing can be functionally and naturally assessed.

REFERENCES

Adams, M.J. (1990). *Beginning to read: Thinking and learning about print.* Cambridge, MA: The MIT Press.

Adams, M.J., Foorman, B.R., Lundberg, I., & Beeler, T. (1998). *Phonemic awareness in young chil-dren.* Baltimore: Paul H. Brookes Publishing Co.

Andrews, J.F., & Mason, J.M. (1986). Childhood deafness and the acquisition of print concepts. In D.B. Yaden & S. Templeton (Eds.), *Metalinguistic awareness and beginning literacy: Conceptualizing what it means to read and write* (pp. 277–290). Portsmouth, NH: Heinemann Educational Books.

Austin, J.L. (1962). *How to do things with words* (2nd ed.). Cambridge, MA: Harvard University Press.

Baker, L., Fernandez-Fein, S., Scher, D., & Williams, H. (1998). Home experiences related to the development of word recognition. In J.L. Metsala & L.C. Ehri (Eds.), *Word recognition in begin-ning literacy.* Mahwah, NJ: Lawrence Erlbaum Associates.

Barrera, R.B., & Bauer, E.B. (2003). Storybook reading and young bilingual children: A review of the literature. In A. van Kleeck, S.A. Stahl, & E.B. Bauer (Eds.), *On reading books to children: Parents and teachers* (pp. 253–267). Mahwah, NJ: Lawrence Erlbaum Associates.

Bear, D.R., Invernizzi, M., Templeton, S., & Johnston, F. (2000). *Words their way: Word study for phonics, vocabulary, and spelling instruction* (2nd ed.). Upper Saddle River, NJ: Prentice Hall.

Bissex, G. (1980). *Gnys at Wrk: A child learns to write and read.* Cambridge, MA: Harvard University Press.

Bowman, B. (2004). Play in the multicultural world of children: Implications for adults. In E.F. Zigler, D.G. Singer, & S.J. Bishop-Josef (Eds.), *Children's play: The roots of reading* (pp. 125–141). Washington, DC: Zero to Three Press.

Burns, M.S., Griffin, P., & Snow, C.E. (Eds.). (1999). *Starting out right: A guide to promoting chil-dren's reading success.* Washington, DC: National Academies Press.

Butler, K. (2000). From the editor. *Topics in Language Disorders, 20*(3), iv.

Cassar, M., & Treiman, R. (2004). Developmental variations in spelling: Comparing typical and poor spellers. In C.A. Stone, E.R. Silliman, B.J. Ehren, & K. Apel (Eds.), *Handbook of language and literacy: Development and disorders* (pp. 627–643). New York: Guilford Press.

Clay, M.M. (1966). *Emergent reading behavior.* Unpublished doctoral dissertation, University of Auckland, New Zealand.

Clay, M.M. (1975). *What did I write? Beginning reading behavior.* Auckland, NZ: Heinemann.

DeTemple, J.M. (2001). Parents and children reading books together. In D.K. Dickinson & P.O. Tabors (Eds.), *Beginning literacy with language* (pp. 31–51). Baltimore: Paul H. Brookes Publishing Co.

Downing, J. (1986). Cognitive clarity: A unifying and cross-cultural theory for language aware-ness phenomena in reading. In D.B. Yaden & S. Templeton (Eds.), *Metalinguistic awareness and beginning literacy: Conceptualizing what it means to read and write* (pp. 13–29). Portsmouth, NH: Heinemann Educational Books.

Dyson, A.H. (1989). *Multiple worlds of child writers: Friends learning to write.* New York: Teachers College Press.

Ehri, L.C. (2000). Learning to read and learning to spell: Two sides of a coin. *Topics in Language Disorders, 20*(3), 19–36.

Ferdman, B.M. (1990). Literacy and cultural identity. *Harvard Educational Review, 60*(2), 181–204. Reproduced in M. Minami & B.P. Kennedy (Eds.). (1991), *Language issues in literacy and bilin-gual/multicultural education* (pp. 347–371). Cambridge, MA: Harvard Educational Review.

Ferriero, E., & Teberosky, A. (1982). *Literacy before schooling.* London: Heinemann Educational.

Genishi, C., & Dyson, A.H. (1984). *Language assessment in the early years.* Norwood, NJ: Ablex.

Gesell, A., & Ilg, F.L. (1943). *Infant and child in the culture of today: The guidance of development in home and nursery school.* New York: Harper & Row.

Gibson, E.J. (1975). Theory-based research on reading and its implications for instruction. In J.B. Carroll & J.S. Chall (Eds.), *Toward a literate society.* New York: McGraw-Hill.

Goodman, Y.M. (1986). Children coming to know literacy. In W.H. Teale & E. Sulzby (Eds.), *Emergent literacy: Writing and reading* (pp. 1–14). Norwood, NJ: Ablex.

Goodman, Y.M. (1990). Discovering children's inventions of written language. In Y.M. Goodman (Ed.), *How children construct literacy: Piagetian perspectives* (pp. 1–11). Newark, DE: International Reading Association.

Goswami, U. (2002). Early phonological development and the acquisition of literacy. In S.B. Neuman & D.K. Dickinson (Eds.), *Handbook of early literacy research* (pp. 111–125). New York: Guilford Press.

Graves, D. (1994). *A fresh look at writing.* Toronto: Irwin Publishing.

Harste, J., Burke, C., & Woodward, V. (1981). *Children, their language and world: Initial encounters with print.* Washington, DC: U.S. Department of Education. (ERIC Document Reproduction Service No. ED 213041)

Harste, J.C., Burke, C., & Woodward, V.A. (1994). Children's language and world: Initial encounters with print. In R.B. Ruddell, M.R. Ruddell, & H. Singer (Eds.), *Theoretical models and processes of reading* (4th ed., pp. 48–69). Newark, DE: International Reading Association.

Harste, J.C., Woodward, V.A., & Burke, C.L. (1984). Language stories and literacy lessons. Portsmouth, NH: Heinemann.

Hart, B.H., & Risley, T.R. (1999). *The social world of children learning to talk.* Baltimore: Paul H. Brookes Publishing Co.

Holdaway, D. (1979). *The foundations of literacy.* Portsmouth, NH: Heinemann.

Institute for the Development of Educational Achievement. (2002–2004). *Big ideas in beginning reading.* Available online at http://reading.uoregon.edu/reading.php

International Dyslexia Association. (2000). *Just the facts.* Available online at http://www.interdys.org

Jones, M.E., & Crabtree, K. (1999). The emergence of literacy. In T. Linder (Ed.), *Read, Play, and Learn: Storybook activities for young children* (pp. 98–117). Baltimore: Paul H. Brookes Publishing Co.

Justice, L.M., & Ezell, H.K. (2004). Print referencing: An emergent literacy enhancement strategy and its clinical applications. *Language, Speech, and Hearing Services in Schools, 35,* 185–193.

Justice, L.M., & Kaderavek, J. (2002). Using storybook reading to promote emergent literacy. *Teaching Exceptional Children, 34*(4), 8–13.

Justice, L.M., & Kaderavek, J. (2004). Embedded-explicit emergent literacy intervention I: Background and description of approach. *Language, Speech, and Hearing Services in Schools, 35,* 201–211.

Justice, L.M., Skibbe, L., Canning, A., & Lankford, C. (2005). Preschoolers, print, and storybooks: An observational study using eye movement analysis. *Journal of Research in Reading, 28*(3), 229–243.

Justice, L.M., Weber, S.E., Ezell, H.K., & Bakeman, R. (2002). A sequential analysis of children's responsiveness to parental print references during shared book-reading interactions. *American Journal of Speech-Language Pathology, 11,* 30–40.

Kaderavek, J., & Justice, L.M. (2002). Shared storybook reading as an intervention context: Practices and potential pitfalls. *American Journal of Speech-Language Pathology, 11,* 395–406.

Kaderavek, J., & Justice, L.M. (2004). Embedded-explicit emergent literacy intervention II: Goal selection and implementation in the early childhood classroom. *Language, Speech, and Hearing Services in Schools, 35,* 212–228.

Kamhi, A.G., & Hinton, L.N. (2000). Explaining individual differences in spelling ability. *Topics in Language Disorders, 20*(3), 37–49.

Katims, D.S. (1991). Emergent literacy in early childhood special education: Curriculum and instruction. *Topics in Early Childhood Special Education, 11*(1), 69–84.

Kato-Otani, E. (2004, February). Story time: Mothers' reading practices in Japan and the U.S. *Harvard Family Research Project.* Available online at www.gse.harvard.edu/hfrp/projects/fine/resources/digest/reading.html

Katz, K. (2004). *¿Dónde está el ombliguito?* New York: Simon & Schuster.

Koppenhaver, D., & Erickson, K. (2000, February). *Technology supports for balanced literacy instruction: Guided reading.* [Television Broadcast] Houston, TX: Education Service Center, Region IV.

Lyon, G.R. (1995). Toward a definition of dyslexia. *Annals of Dyslexia, 45,* 3–27.

Lyon, G.R. (2000, November 21). *Other factors that influence learning to read.* Available online at http://www.brainconnection.com

Masterson, J.J., & Apel, K. (2000). Spelling assessment: Charting a path to optimal intervention. *Topics in Language Disorders, 20*(3), 50–65.

Martin, B. (1992). *Brown bear, brown bear, what do you see?* New York: Henry Holt & Co.

McGee, L.M., & Richgels, D.J. (2004). *Literacy's beginnings: Supporting young readers and writers* (4th ed.). Boston: Pearson.

McLane, J.B., & McNamee, G.D. (1991). The beginnings of literacy. *Zero to Three, 12*(1), 1–8.

Miller, L. (1986). *Language disabilities, organizational strategies, and classroom learning.* Workshop presented at the Language Learning Disabilities Institutes, Emerson College, San Diego.

Miller, L. (1990). The roles of language and learning in the development of literacy. *Topics in Language Disorders, 10*(2), 1–24.

Miller, W.H. (2000). *Strategies for developing emergent literacy.* Boston: McGraw-Hill.

Morrison, G., & Morrow, L.M. (2002). Early literacy and beginning to read: A position statement of the Southern Early Childhood Association. *Dimensions of Early Childhood, 30*(4), 28–31. Also available online at http://www.SouthernEarlyChildhood.org/position_earlyliteracy.html

Morrow, L.M. (1989). *Literacy development in the early years: Helping children read and write.* Englewood Cliffs, NJ: Prentice Hall.

Morrow, L.M. (1997). *Literacy development in the early years.* Boston: Allyn & Bacon.

Moustafa, M. (2000). Phonics instruction. In D.S. Strickland & L.M. Morrow (Eds.), *Literacy development in the early years* (pp. 121–133). Englewood Cliffs, NJ: Prentice Hall.

National Association for the Education of Young Children. (2005). Position statement on "Screening and assessment of young English-language learners": Supplement to the NAEYC Position Statement on Early Childhood Curriculum, Assessment, and Program Evaluation. Available online at www.naeyc.org/about/positions/pdf/ELL_Supplement.pdf

National Institute of Neurological Disorders and Stroke. (2003). NINDS dysgraphia information page. Available online at www.ninds.nih.gov/health_and_medical/disorders/dysgraphia.htm

Pellegrini, A.D., & Galda, L. (1990). Children's play, language, and early literacy. *Topics in Language Disorders, 10*(3), 76–88.

Pellegrini, A.D., & Galda, L. (2000). Children's pretend play and literacy. In D.S. Strickland & L.M. Morrow (Eds.), *Beginning reading and writing* (pp. 58–65). New York: Teachers College Press.

Reese, E., Cox, A., Harte, D., & McAnally, H. (2003). Diversity in adults' styles of reading books to children. In A. van Kleeck, S.A. Stahl, & E.B. Bauer (Eds.), *On reading books to children: Parents and teachers* (pp. 37–57). Mahwah, NJ: Lawrence Erlbaum Associates.

Richgels, D.J. (2002). Invented spelling, phonemic awareness, and reading and writing instruction. In S.B. Neuman & D.K. Dickinson (Eds.), *Handbook of early literacy research* (pp. 142–155). New York: Guilford Press.

Roskos, K., & Christie, J. (2004). Examining the play–literacy interface: A critical review and future directions. In E.F. Zigler, D.G. Singer, & S.J. Bishop-Josef (Eds.), *Children's play: The roots of reading* (pp. 95–123). Washington, DC: Zero to Three Press.

Schickedanz, J.A. (1990). *Adam's righting revolutions: One child's literacy development from infancy to grade one.* Portsmouth, NH: Heinemann.

Schickedanz, J.A. (1999). *Much more than the ABCs: The early stages of reading and writing.* Washington, DC: National Association for the Education of Young Children.

Schickedanz , J.A., & Casbergue, R.M. (2004). *Writing in preschool: Learning to orchestrate meaning and marks.* Newark, DE: International Reading Association.

Scott, C.M., & Brown, S.L. (2001). Spelling and the speech-language pathologist: There's more than meets the eye. *Seminars in Speech and Language, 22*(3), 197–207.

Seidenberg, M.S., & McClelland, J.L. (1989). A distributed, developmental model of word recognition and naming. *Psychological Review, 96*(4), 523–568.

Shaywitz, S. (2003). *Overcoming dyslexia: A new and complete science-based program for reading problems at any level.* New York: Knopf Publishing.

Shaywitz, B., & Shaywitz, S. (2004, March). *Overcoming dyslexia.* Lecture at The University of Texas, Austin.

Snow, C.E., Burns, S., & Griffin, P. (Eds.). (1998). *Preventing reading difficulties in young children.* Washington, DC: National Academies Press.

Sulzby, E. (1986). Writing and reading: Signs of oral and written language organization in the young child. In W. Teale & E. Sulzby (Eds.), *Emergent literacy: Writing and reading* (pp. 50–89). Norwood, NJ: Ablex.

Sulzby, E., & Teale, W. (1985). Writing development in early childhood. *Educational Horizons, 64*(1), 8–12.

Tabors, P. (1997). *One child, two languages: A guide for preschool educators of children learning English as a second language.* Baltimore: Paul H. Brookes Publishing Co.

Teale, W., & Sulzby, E. (1986). *Emergent literacy: Writing and reading.* Norwood, NJ: Ablex.

Teale, W., & Sulzby, E. (1989). Emergent literacy: New perspectives. In D.S. Strickland & L.M. Morrow (Eds.), *Emergent literacy: Young children learn to read and write* (pp. 1–15). Newark, NJ: International Reading Association.

Teale, W.H., & Yokota, J. (2000). Beginning reading and writing: Perspectives on instruction. In D.S. Strickland & L.M. Morrow (Eds.), *Beginning reading and writing* (pp. 3–21). New York: Teachers College Press.

Tompkins, G.E., & McGee, L.M. (1986). Visually impaired and sighted children's emerging concepts about written language. In D.B. Yaden & S. Templeton, (Eds.), *Metalinguistic awareness and beginning literacy: Conceptualizing what it means to read and write* (pp. 259–275). Portsmouth, NH: Heinemann Educational Books.

Treiman, R., & Bourassa, D.C. (2000). The development of spelling skill. *Topics in Language Disorders, 20*(3), 1–18.

van Kleeck, A. (1998). Preliteracy domains and stages: Laying the foundations for beginning reading. *Journal of Children's Communication Development, 20*(1), 33–51.

van Kleeck, A. (2003). Research on book sharing: Another critical look. In A. van Kleeck, S.A. Stahl, & E.B. Bauer (Eds.), *On reading books to children: Parents and teachers* (pp. 271–320). Mahwah, NJ: Lawrence Erlbaum Associates.

van Kleeck, A. (2004). Fostering preliteracy development via storybook-sharing interactions. In C.A. Stone, E.R. Silliman, B.J. Ehren, & K. Apel (Eds.), *Handbook of language and literacy: Development and disorders* (pp. 175–208). New York: Guilford Press.

van Kleeck, A., & Woude, J.V. (2003). Preschoolers with language delays. In A. van Kleeck, S.A. Stahl, & E.B. Bauer (Eds.), *On reading books to children: Parents and teachers* (pp. 58–92). Mahwah, NJ: Lawrence Erlbaum Associates.

Vygotsky, L.S. (1978). *Mind in society.* Cambridge, MA: Harvard University Press.

Wallach, G.P., & Miller, L. (1988). *Language intervention and academic success.* Boston: College-Hill Press.

Wasik, B.H., & Hendrickson, J.S. (2004). Family literacy practices. In C.A. Stone, E.R. Silliman, B.J. Ehren, & K. Apel (Eds.), *Handbook of language and literacy: Development and disorders* (pp. 154–174). New York: Guilford Press.

Wetherby, A.M. (2002, June). *Language, literacy, and reading in the early years: Do they make a difference?* Paper presented at the 2002 NAEYC Institute, Albuquerque. Also available online at http://firstwords.fsu.edu

Wetherby, A.M., Allen, L., Cleary, J., Kublin, K., & Goldstein, H. (2002). Validity and reliability of the Communication and Symbolic Behavior Scales Developmental Profile with very young children. *Journal of Speech, Language, and Hearing Research, 45*, 1202–1219.

Wetherby, A.M., Cleary, J., & Allen, L. (2001, November). *FIRST WORDS Project: Improving early identification of communication disorders.* Paper presented at the ASHA Convention, New Orleans. Also available online at http://firstwords.fsu.edu

Wetherby, A.M., Lonigan, C., Curran, T., Easterly, G., Trautman, L.S., & Ziolkowski, R. (2003, April). *FIRST WORDS Project: Improving early identification of young children at-risk for language and reading difficulties.* Paper presented at the 2003 biennial meeting of the Society for Research in Child Development, Tampa. Also available online at http://firstwords.fsu.edu

Whitehurst, G.J., Falco, F.L., Lonigan, C.J., Fischel, J.E., DeBaryshe, B.D., Valdez-Menchaca, M.C., & Caulfield, M. (1988). Accelerating language development through picture-book reading. *Developmental Psychology, 24*, 552–559.

Whitehurst, G.J., & Lonigan, C.J. (1998). Child development and emergent literacy. *Child Development, 69*, 848–872.

Whitehurst, G.J., & Lonigan, C.J. (2002). Emergent literacy: Development from prereaders to readers. In S.B. Neuman & D.K. Dickinson (Eds.), *Handbook of early literacy research* (pp. 11–29). New York: Guilford Press.

Wishon, P., Crabtree, K., & Jones, M.E. (1998). *Curriculum for the primary years: An integrative approach.* Columbus, OH: Merrill/Prentice Hall.

Zecker, L.B. (2004). Learning to read and write in two languages: The development of early biliteracy abilities. In C.A. Stone, E.R. Silliman, B.J. Ehren, & K. Apel (Eds.), *Handbook of language and literacy: Development and disorders* (pp. 248–265). New York: Guilford Press.

Zevenbergen, A.A., & Whitehurst, G.J. (2003). Dialogic reading: A shared picture book reading intervention for preschoolers. In A. van Kleeck, S.A. Stahl, & E.B. Bauer (Eds.), *On reading books to children: Parents and teachers* (pp. 177–200). Mahwah, NJ: Lawrence Erlbaum Associates.

Zigler, E.F., Singer, D.G., & Bishop-Josef, S.J. (2004). *Children's play: The roots of reading.* Washington, DC: Zero to Three Press.

Index

Page numbers followed by a *t* indicate a table. Those followed by an *f* indicate a figure on that page.